ANCIENT SYRIAC DOCUMENTS

RELATIVE TO

THE EARLIEST ESTABLISHMENT OF CHRISTIANITY

IN EDESSA AND THE NEIGHBOURING COUNTRIES,

FROM THE YEAR AFTER OUR LORD'S ASCENSION

TO THE BEGINNING OF THE FOURTH CENTURY;

DISCOVERED, EDITED, TRANSLATED, AND ANNOTATED

BY THE LATE

W. CURETON, D.D., F.R.S.,

CANON OF WESTMINSTER,

MEMBER OF THE IMPERIAL INSTITUTE OF FRANCE,

ETC. ETC.

WITH A PREFACE BY

W. WRIGHT, PH.D., LL.D.,

ASSISTANT IN THE DEPARTMENT OF MSS , BRITISH MUSEUM.

Wipf & Stock
PUBLISHERS
Eugene, Oregon

Wipf and Stock Publishers
199 W 8th Ave, Suite 3
Eugene, OR 97401

Ancient Syriac Documents
Relative to the earliest establishment of Christianity in
Edessa and the neighboring countries
By Cureton, W.
ISBN: 1-59244-826-7
Publication date 8/26/2004
Previously published by Williams and Norgate, 1864

PREFACE.

THE Syriac texts contained in this volume were discovered and transcribed by its lamented author so long ago as 1848; for in the preface to the *Festal Letters of Athanasius,* p. xxiii, note, he says: "I have found amongst the Syriac manuscripts in the British Museum a considerable portion of the original Aramaic document, which Eusebius cites as preserved in the archives of Edessa, and various passages from it, quoted by several authors, with other testimonies which seem to be sufficient to establish the fact of the early conversion of many of the inhabitants of that city, and among them, of the king himself, although his successors afterwards relapsed into Paganism. These, together with accounts of the martyrdom of some of the first bishops of that city, forming a most interesting accession to our knowledge of the early propagation of Christianity in the East down to about A.D. 300, I have already transcribed, and hope to publish, with a translation, and such illustrations as may appear necessary. I regret that the little leisure which I have for such labours will not allow me even to speculate upon the probable time when I may be able to fulfil this intention."

The printing of these documents was actually commenced about three years ago, but progressed at first very slowly, owing to the demands made upon Dr. Cureton's time by his parochial and other duties. Indeed, up to May 1863, when he met with the accident that ultimately caused his death, only, I believe, about forty pages had been printed. As soon, however, as he was again able to attend to business, he pushed forward the printing both of text and translation as rapidly as possible, availing himself to some extent of my assistance in correcting the proofs of the former; and happily his strength held out long enough to enable him to all but finish his task. When his health finally gave way, there remained only the preface to be written; but of that, although it was all arranged in his mind, he did not, it would seem, commit a single line to paper.

The main scope and object of this work—of which I can safely say that it is, with one exception, the most generally interesting of all Dr. Cureton's publications—is clearly enough stated in the passage from one of his own writings quoted above. He was himself firmly persuaded of the genuineness of the epistles attributed to Abgar, king of Edessa, and our Lord; an opinion which he shared with such illustrious scholars as Baronius,* Tillemont,† Cave,‡ R. Mountague, bishop of Norwich,§ and Grabe.|| Whether right in this particular point or not, his book indubitably proves the conversion of King Abgar Ukkāmā and a considerable number of the Edessenes at the hands of Addai or Thaddæus, one of the seventy Disciples; and presents us with authentic documents relative to the persecutions of the early Christians in that city, from the time of the first martyr Sharbīl, down to that of the last, Ḥabīb.

To those who, like myself, study the ancient Syriac literature principally from a linguistic interest, this volume offers several documents of high importance; in particular the two discourses on the martyrs of Edessa by Mār Jacob, bishop of Sĕrūg, one of the earliest and finest of Syrian writers, but of whose metrical homilies only one

* *Annales*, Lucca, 1738, tom. i. pp. 83, 84. † *Mémoires*, Paris, 1701, tome i. p. 362.

‡ *Hist. Literar.*, Oxford, 1740, vol. i. p. 2.

§ *Origines Ecclesiast.*, London, 1640, tom. i. pars poster., p. 61 foll.

|| *Spicilegium SS. Patrum*, Oxford, 1714, tom. i. p. 1 foll. and p. 314 foll.

other specimen has hitherto been published, I mean that on Simeon Stylites in the *Acta Martyrum* of S. E. Assemani (t. ii. p. 230.)

With regard to the share which I have taken in the production of this volume, only a very few words of explanation are necessary.

As mentioned above, I aided my departed friend in correcting the proof sheets of the Syriac text from p. ܠܐ to the end; and he made it his last request to me that I would undertake to usher the work into the world. To this I consented somewhat reluctantly, simply from a consciousness of my total incompetence to do it and him justice. As a mere linguist I am not his equal, nor is my historical knowledge to be compared with his. He had studied the questions connected with this volume for years and from every point of view; whereas I was new to them, having scarcely ventured at all into that particular field of history, nor having, for the present at least, the necessary leisure to do so. I have therefore confined myself entirely to a careful revision of the Syriac texts, which I have collated line for line with the original manuscripts. In this way I have been able, I hope, to note every error or misprint of any consequence; but I have not thought it necessary to swell the list of errata, and thereby uselessly augment the size of the volume, by pointing out every instance in which a mark of punctuation has been omitted or misplaced. Nor have I deemed it worth while to spend time in the revision of the translation and notes, being aware that the attentive reader can easily correct for himself the comparatively few and trifling misprints that occur in them.

I cannot conclude this preface without briefly tracing the literary career of my lamented friend; and in doing so, I shall avail myself of an article in the *Times* newspaper for Thursday, June 30, of the present year, the materials for which were contributed by myself and other friends.

William Cureton was born at Westbury in Shropshire, in the year 1808; received his earlier education at the Free Grammar School of Newport in the same county; and proceeded to Oxford with a Careswell exhibition at the age of eighteen. For private reasons, which reflected the highest credit on him, he entered Christ Church as a servitor, and graduated in 1830. In the following year he took holy orders, and was appointed Under-Librarian of the Bodleian Library in 1834. He continued in that post till 1837, when he was called to the British Museum as Assistant-Keeper of the MSS., having been selected for this office principally on account of his oriental scholarship.

The first duty assigned to him here was the preparation of a classified catalogue of the Arabic portion of the collection; and of this the first part, comprising the Christian writings and the divisions of Mohammedan theology, law and history, was published in 1846.

As early, however, as 1841 his Arabic studies had been interrupted by the acquisition by the Trustees of the famous Nitrian collection of Syriac manuscripts. This event furnished him with materials for researches, at once varied and profound, in a new field. On the arrival of the manuscripts—the first portion in 1841, the second in 1843—he threw himself heart and soul into the study of the Syriac language and literature. On him in the first instance devolved the task of classifying the volumes, of gathering together, collating, and arranging the numberless fragments and loose leaves of which the Nitrian collection consisted, and of drawing up a brief summary of their contents for the catalogue of additional manuscripts in the Museum.

One of the first results of these labours was an article in the *Quarterly Review*, No. cliii, Dec. 1845, giving an account of the way in which the manuscripts were procured, and a rough sketch of their contents; and in the same year appeared the first edition of the ancient Syriac version of the Epistles of St. Ignatius to St. Polycarp, the Ephesians, and the Romans. The views propounded by Dr. Cureton—that we have here the genuine epistles of St. Ignatius in their original form; that the previously known recensions of these three epistles are much altered and interpolated; and that all others ascribed to that Father are supposititious—views such as these were certain to excite much controversy in the theological world. Commenced by Wordsworth in the *English Review*, No. viii, July 1845, the strife was continued by S. Lee (*British Magazine*, vol. xxx), Bunsen, Baur, Hilgenfeld, Denzinger, Hefele, Jacobson, and others, of whom the first two supported Cureton, while the rest combated his views. Cureton himself took the field against Wordsworth in his *Vindiciæ Ignatianæ* (1846), a calm but crushing refutation of his opponent's allegation that the Syriac version was "a miserable epitome by an Eutychian heretic." The year 1849 saw the publication of the *Corpus Ignatianum*, an enlarged edition of the work of 1845, almost contemporaneously with which appeared Petermann's edition of the Ignatian epistles. Since then the discussion has been continued by Lipsius (1859) on the side of Cureton, and Merx (1861) on that of his opponents, and is not even yet brought to a final settlement. Cureton, however, remained stedfast to the views stated with such clearness and learning in the *Corpus Ignatianum*; and would, if his life had been spared, have once again stepped forward to sum up and conclude the controversy.

While the Ignatian controversy was at its height, Dr. Cureton edited the text of a portion of the Syriac version of the long-lost *Festal Letters of Athanasius*, of which he had been the fortunate discoverer. The preface to these letters contains an interesting account of the Nitrian collection, more especially of a third portion, which reached the Museum in 1847. These letters have been translated into English by Burgess (1854), and form one of the volumes of Pusey's Library of the Fathers. A German translation from the pen of the well-known Syriac scholar Larsow had already appeared in 1852.

In 1851 Cureton edited for the Trustees of the British Museum the palimpsest fragments of the *Iliad*, which are contained in the Nitrian manuscript now numbered Add. 17,210.

In 1853 there issued from the University Press of Oxford an important contribution to our historical knowledge—the third part of the *Ecclesiastical History of John, bishop of Ephesus*, edited by Cureton, from the Add. ms. 14,640. Of this he intended to publish a translation; but other labours prevented him, and his wishes were carried out by the Rev. R. Payne Smith, under-librarian of the Bodleian Library, whose version appeared in 1860. There is also a German translation by Schönfelder (1862).

Two years later this indefatigable scholar published his *Spicilegium Syriacum*, containing remains ascribed to Bardesanes, Melito of Sardes, and Ambrose, with an English translation and notes; and in 1858 he edited perhaps the most valuable of all his works, and one which has given rise to scarcely less controversy than the Ignatian Epistles. He discovered in the Add. ms. 14,451, which belongs to the latter half of the fifth century, the remains of an ancient recension of the Syriac Gospels, differing notably from the ordinary Pĕshīṭtā version. In his preface he dwelt on these divergences, more especially in the text of the Gospel of St. Matthew; summed up the evidence in favour of the Hebrew original of that Gospel; and endeavoured to prove that this particular manuscript represented the Hebrew far more faithfully than the Pĕshīṭtā does—at least in the shape in which it is generally known to European scholars. His views have been warmly espoused by that able critic Dr. Tregelles, and as warmly combated by other scholars, such as Hermansen (Copenhagen, 1859). It was Dr. Cureton's intention to have returned in after years to this subject, and to have made known additional evidence which he had collected upon these points.

Three years later Cureton brought out the last work that he was destined to finish—*the History of the Martyrs in Palestine* by Eusebius of Cæsarea, taken from the same venerable manuscript from which Dr. S. Lee edited the *Theophania* of that Father.

Dr. Cureton was an active promoter, if not the founder, of the Society for the publication of Oriental Texts, of which he was the honorary secretary until about the year 1850. For it he edited Esh-Shahrastānī's *Book of Religious and Philosophical Sects,* published in two parts in 1842 and 1846, and En-Nesefī's *Pillar of the Creed of the Sunnites,* published in 1843; having previously brought out in the same year Rabbī Tanchūm's *Commentary on the Book of Lamentations.* He was also an active member of the Committee of the Oriental Translation Fund, of which he became deputy-chairman in 1848, and chairman in 1863, on the death of Mr. Botfield. In 1859 he was appointed by the Queen Crown Trustee of the British Museum, a post of which he discharged the duties most zealously and efficiently. Of the estimation in which he was held on the Continent it is proof sufficient to mention that he was D.D. of the University of Halle, corresponding member of the German Oriental Society, and foreign associate of the Institute of France, besides being connected with many other learned bodies throughout Europe.

The eminence attained by Dr. Cureton was mainly founded on his Syriac publications, distinguished as they are by the intrinsic value of the works selected, by the accuracy of his texts, and the scholarship and honesty displayed in his translations and notes. In these qualities of judicious selection, accuracy, scholarship and freedom from prejudice, Cureton stands pre-eminent among all the Englishmen and foreigners who have followed him in the work of editing Syriac writings. I may add, too, that he was most liberal in communicating his knowledge of the contents of the Nitrian collection to all students who sought his assistance; and that not a few, nor the least important, of the publications from these manuscripts by other editors were undertaken at his suggestion and with his aid. Those who choose to refer to the *Nova Patrum Bibliotheca* of Cardinal Mai (tom. vi., p. x.), or to the *Spicilegium Solesmense* of Dom Pitra (tom. ii., p. xxxviii.), will find there well merited eulogies of his learning and liberality. I myself have received since his death several letters from foreign scholars, expressing the greatest grief for his loss, and I cannot deny myself the melancholy pleasure of quoting one of these, from the pen of that distinguished classic and orientalist the Rev. Antonio Ceriani, one of the Doctors of the Ambrosian Library. "La notizia della morte del Dr. Cureton mi tornò assai dolorosa; era ben lontano dall' aspettarmela. La letteratura Siriaca ha perduto in lui, io credo, *il migliore editore di testi*, che sapeva anche tradurre bene in modo che potessero approfittarne anche i profani, e accompagnare di buone note. E per i suoi lavori, e per la parte grande che ebbe all' acquisto di tanta parte dei MSS. Siriaci di Sceti, che altrimenti sarebbero forse andati smarriti, egli lascia sicuramente dietro di sè un bel nome. Pur troppo però deve essere dolorosa la sua perdita ai suoi amici, che ben difficilmente potevano averne uno più dotto e più amorevole. Quando io era a Londra, venni trattato da lui come un fratello; mi offerse anche copie di MSS. Siriaci da pubblicare, che io non accettai solo, perchè avendo già determinati i miei lavori, difficilmente avrei potuto soddisfare al suo voto; e volli perciò che potessero servire a qualche giovine di buona volontà."

Verily Cureton's life was one of unremitting and well directed labour, and the bread which he has cast upon the waters will doubtless be found after many days.

ܕܐܠܗܐ ܗܘ ܕܟܠܠ ܫܡܗ ܐܬܬܢܝܚ ܘܩܒܪ ܘܫܘܒܚܬܐ ܗܠܝܢ
ܪ̈ܘܚܢܝܬܐ. ܗܘ ܢܬܠ ܠܗ ܦܘܪܥܢܐ ܠܛܒܬܐ ܒܝܘܡ ܡܐܬܝܬܗ.
ܘܢܘܚܘܗܝ، ܕܢܫܡܥ ܩܠܐ ܕܒܪܬ ܩܠܐ ܗ̇ܝ، ܕܐܡܪܐ: ܕܬܘ
ܒܪ̈ܝܟܘܗܝ، ܕܐܒܝ ܐܪܬܘ ܡܠܟܘܬܐ ܕܡܛܝܒܐ ܗܘܬ ܠܟܘܢ ܡܢ
ܬܪܡܝܬܗ ܕܥܠܡܐ. ܐܡܝܢ ܀

W. WRIGHT.

London.

November, 1864.

ADDITIONS AND CORRECTIONS.

Page ܒ, line 5. After ܐܡܝܢ ܐܦ insert ܠܗܘܢ

.. ܓ, .. 4. For ܕܛܠܠ read ܢܛܠ

.. ܗ, .. 2. For ܕܡܫܘܪܬܗ read ܕܡܫܘܪܘܬܗ

.. .., .. 12. Read ܦܬܓܡ ܡܢ ܐܘܪܓܐ ܠܗܘܢܝܐ. ܒܪܒܝܢܗܘܢ

.. ܙ, .. 20. The word that has been effaced before ܠܗܘܢ is doubtless ܢܠܦ. Of ܢܟܣܢ in the next line only the last letter is distinctly legible.

.. .., .. 23. We should probably read ܠܬܪܥܝܬܗܘܢ

.. ܚ, .. 3. Read ܕܗܘ̣ܐ ܗܘ̣ܐ ܒܗ̇ܘ

.. .., .. 4. Read ܒܟܘܠܗ̇, and so also in line 5.

.. .., .. 10. Read ܒܟܝ̈ܢܐ ܘܒ̈ܙܘܟܐ

.. .., .. 12. Read ܘܪ̈ܕܝܢ

.. .., .. 23. Read ܠܟܐܢܬ

.. ܛ, .. 2. Read ܬ̈ܓܠܐ

.. .., .. 5. Read ܫ̈ܢܝܐ

.. .., .. 7. Read ܠܐܪ̈ܢܐ ܣܪ̈ܝܬܐ. The letters ܣܪ̈ܝ are conjectural.

.. .., .. 12. Read ܪ̈ܚܫܝܒܘܢ

.. .., .. 19—22. In this passage several words and parts of words are merely conjectural, the manuscript being a good deal damaged. In line 19, ܗܘܢܐ is doubtful. In line 20, read in both places ܗ̈ܘ. In line 21, I have very little doubt that we should substitute ܕܚܬ for ܕܗܟܢ (corresponding to ܣܥܝܢ in the next clause); the word is quite illegible in the manuscript.

Page ܘ, line 5. At the beginning, after ܠܐ, insert ܗܘ̣ܐ. The words printed ܫܘܪܒܐ and ܐܒܠ are very doubtful.

.. ܝܙ, .. 11. Read ܒܪ ܗܘܐ

.. .., .. 19. Read ܒܣܪ̈ܬܗ

.. .., .. 23. Read ܕܡ̈ܠܟܐ

.. .., .. 27. Read ܕܫ̈ܢܝ، ܗ̈ܘܝ،

.. ܝܚ, .. 8. Read ܕܒܠܝܗܘܢ

.. .., .. 21. Read ܠܗ̈ ܠܝܬܐ

.. ܝܛ, .. 2. Read ܘܒܫܪ̈ܝܗ

.. .., .. 14. Read ܒܠܗ

.. .., .. 19. After ܟܬܒ add ܗܘ̣ܐ

.. ܟ, .. 3. MS. ܘܩܡ ܕܗܘ̣ܐ

.. .., .. 13. The ܘ in ܘܬܫܒܫܬܐ seems to have been altered into ܕ.

.. ܟܐ, .. 20. Read ܐܫܝܪ̈ܐ

.. ܟܒ, .. 10. Read ܐܪ̈ܝܘ

.. ܟܓ, .. 3. Read ܦܩܘܗܝ،

.. .., .. 21. Read ܐܦ ܫܡ

.. ܟܗ, .. 24. In numbering the canons, *letters* have been substituted for the *arithmetical figures* of the manuscript.

.. ܟܘ, .. 4. Read ܦܠܡ ܗܘ̣ܐ

.. ܟܙ, .. 12. Read ܒܒܪܬܐ

.. .., .. 24. Read ܠܐ ܬܘܒ

.. .., .. 25. Delete ܗܘܐ after ܘܠܐ

.. ܟܚ .. 6. Delete ܕ before ܢܬܦܪܫ

.. ܟܛ .. 12. Read ܕܫܒܗܪܘܬܐ

.. .., .. 23. Delete ܗܘܘ after ܘܡܩܒܠܝܢ

.. ܠ .. 4. Read ܦܩܘ ܗܘܘ

.. .., .. 11. Read ܒܐܬܪܐ ܕܦܘܪܢܐ

.. .., .. 20. Read ܢܫܒܩܘܦ and ܪܫ.

.. .., .. 23. Read ܘܢܦܠܦ

.. .., .. 24. Read ܗܢܘܢ

Page ܟܐ line 2. Add ܗܘܘ after ܕܡܠܟܘ

.. .. , .. 7. Read ܕܬܘܕܘܢ

.. .. , .. 15. Read ܕܢ̈ܬܐ

.. .. , .. 19. Read ܗ̇ܘܢ

.. ܟܒ .. 3. Delete ܗܘܘ after ܘܐܬܚܙܘ

.. .. , .. 8. Read ܬܐܘܡܐ

.. .. , .. 11. Read ܚܕܬܐ ܘܒܬܫܒܚܬܐ

.. ܟܓ .. 9. Read ܘܬܬܦܪܣܘܢ

.. .. , .. 20. Instead of ܫܠܘ the manuscript has ܟܡ, which is certainly an error.

.. .. , .. 21. Read ܕܒܪܝܬܐ

.. ܟܕ .. 4. The manuscript has ܬܬܦܠܫܘܢ. ܐܒܝܠܐ ܗܘ̣

.. ܟܗ .. 2. Read ܗܡ ܒܪܘܣܐ

.. .. , .. 8. Read ܣܒܐܝܬ

.. .. , .. 12. Delete ܟܐܒܐ

.. .. , .. 16. Read ܒܪ̈ܬܐ

.. .. , .. 18. The manuscript has ܕܒܘܩ̈ܪܐ

.. .. , .. 25. In the manuscript there is a superfluous ܡܢܕܡ after ܡܬܘܪܐ

.. ܟܘ, .. 10. Read ܘܡܟܠܗ̇

.. ܟܙ, .. 21. Read ܕܐܠܐ ܗ̣ܘܐ

.. ܟܚ, .. 1. Read ܕܐܟܐ ܗܘܢ

.. .. , .. 10. Insert a point after ܕܡܒܝܢܐ

.. ܟܛ, .. 9. Read ܕܡܢܚܡܢ (for ܕܡܢܚܡ̈ܢ)

.. .. , .. 15. Insert a point after ܐܝܬ

.. ܠ, .. 14. Read ܡܢܗ ܣܘܓܐܐ

.. ܠܐ, .. 8. Read ܡܫܡܫܐ ܀

.. .. , .. 20. Read ܦ̈ܠܐ

.. ܠܒ, .. 2. Read ܕܡܬܬܢ ܀

.. .. , .. 18. The manuscript has ܒܥܡܪ̈ܐ, the points indicating the vocative.

.. ܠܓ, .. 10. Read ܕܢܦܫ ܗܘܐ

Page ܢܗ, line 18. ܨܡܚ has been altered in the manuscript into ܨܡ.

.. ܣ, .. 19. Read ܘܢܦܣ ܟܠ

.. ܣܐ, .. 14. Read ܘܢܐܬܪܘܢ

.. ܣܓ, .. 11. The manuscript has ܕܒܘܬܪܘܣ

.. ܣܕ, .. 6. The manuscript has ܘܐܢܫܡ, as on p. ܟܓ, line 11.

.. ܣܗ, .. 4. Read ܠܥܙܪܒܠ ܀

.. ܣܘ, .. 10. The manuscript has incorrectly ܘܐܬܦܠܓܣܘ

.. ܥܕ, .. 12. Read ܕܒܠܘܪܐ ܠܐܘܕ

.. .., .. 13. Read ܕܢܕܒܫܘܢ ܀

.. ܥܗ, .. 11. Insert a point after ܗܢܐ

.. ܥܙ, .. 20. The manuscript has ܘܗ̇ܝ, the ܘ being a later addition.

.. ܦܐ, .. 18. Read ܬܫܒܘܚܗ̇

.. ܦܕ, .. 20. The manuscript has ܚܠܦܬܐ, as if the scribe wished to alter the word into ܚܠܝܬܐ

. ܦܒ, .. 2. Read ܕܢܘܪܐ

.. .., .. 26. ܡܫܒܚܐ܂ Here, and in several other places, the point which marks the end of a verse has been placed *under*, instead of *after*, the letters ܐ, ܗ, ܘ, and ܝ.

.. ܦܛ, .. 11. Read ܡܛܠܠܬܗ, without ܘ

.. ܨܐ, .. 21. Read ܕܪܐ

.. ܨܒ .. 24. Delete the point after ܬܠܘܢܐ

.. ܨܓ .. 5. Read ܦܘܓܪܐ

.. .., .. 8. The manuscript has really ܢܘܠܟܘܗܝ, instead of ܢܠܟܘܗܝ

.. .., .. 26. Read ܕܓܠܛ.

.. ܨܕ, .. 9. Read ܕܢܒܐ, to distinguish the word from ܕܒܢܐ in line 12.

.. ܨܕ, .. 23. Read ܐܩܝܡܗ

.. , .. 25. Read ܗܘܘ.

. ܨܘ, .. 11. Read ܕܢܗܒ

.. ܨܙ, .. 3. Read ܕܫܪܝܪܬܐ

Page ܥܘ, .. 8. The word ܠܝܬ, before ܕܬܬܡܠܠ, ought to be deleted.

.. ..., .. 22. Read ܕܬܢ̈ܝܐ

.. ܦܥ, .. 24. Read ܘܐܬܒܠܒܠܘ

.. ܦܕ, .. 14. Read ܕܗܝܡܢܘܬܐ

.. ܦܗ, .. 13. The manuscript has really ܐܘܒܘܡܐ

.. .., .. 21—25. I fear that this passage is not quite correctly printed, owing to the leaf being slightly torn. In line 21, I believe ܗܘܐ should be inserted after ܥܠ. In line 23, read ܟܪ̈ܘܙܐ. In line 24, place the point after ܕܡܫܝܚܘܬܗ instead of ܘܡܫܒ̈ܚܢܐ. It is possible that a single word may be wanting after ܕܡܫܝܚܘܬܗ, and also after ܕܫܘܦ̈ܘܬܐ in line 25.

.. ܦܛ, .. 7—17. The following are the variants of Add. 17,193. Line 8, ܕܟܝܢ̈ܐ ܠܘܬܪܡܐ. Line 11, ܕܠܐ ܢܠܬܐ. Line 12, ܕܢܣܒܠܐ. Line 16, ܠܐ ܢܕܒܝ. ܕܕܠܐ

.. ܦܐ, .. 24. Read ܬܬܪܥܡܘܢ

Page 191, line 23. Like Dr. Cureton, I am ignorant of the meaning of the word ܠܬܠܡܘ in this passage. It is so written in both MSS. of the Sermons of Mār Jacob Persa (or Aphraates), and can hardly, therefore, be incorrect.

W. WRIGHT.

FROM THE HISTORY OF THE CHURCH.

[BY EUSEBIUS, OF CÆSAREA.]

[CHAPTER] THE THIRTEENTH.

CONCERNING THE KING OF EDESSA.

But the history which was about Thaddæus was in this fashion:—'When the divine nature of our Saviour and Lord Jesus Christ was published abroad among all men by reason of the wonderful mighty works which he wrought, and myriads, even from countries remote from the land of Judæa, who were afflicted with sicknesses and diseases of every kind, were coming to him in the hope of being healed, King Abgar also, who was renowned for his valour among the nations on the east side of the Euphrates, had his body afflicted with a severe disease, of such a kind as there is no cure for it among men: and when he heard and was informed of the name of Jesus, and about the mighty works that he did, which all men equally testified concerning Him, he sent to him a letter of request by the hand of a man of his own, and entreated him to come and heal him of his disease. Our Saviour, however, at the time that he called him, did not comply with his request: yet he deemed him worthy of a reply; for he promised him that he would send one of his disciples, and would heal his diseases, and give salvation to him and to all who were near to him. Nor was the fulfilment of his promise to him long deferred: but after he was risen from the dead, and was taken up into heaven, Thomas the Apostle, one of the Twelve, as by the instigation of God, sent Thaddæus, who also was numbered among the Seventy disciples of Christ, to Edessa, to be a preacher and Evangelist of the teaching of Christ, and through him the promise of Christ was fulfilled. You have in written documents the evidence of these things, which is taken from (ܒ) the Book of Records which is at Edessa; for at that time the kingdom was still standing. In the documents, therefore, that are there, in which is contained whatever had been done by those of old up to the time of Abgar, these things also are found preserved there up to the present hour. But there is nothing to hinder our hearing the very Letters themselves which are taken by us from the Archives, and have the following form of words which are translated out of the Aramaic into Greek.

Copy of the Letter which was written from King Abgar to Jesus, and sent to him by the hand of Hananias, the Tabularius, to Jerusalem.

"Abgar Uchama, Chief of the country, to Jesus, the good Deliverer, who has appeared in the country of Jerusalem, Peace. I have heard about thee, and about the cures which are wrought by thy hands, without medicines and herbs; for as it is reported, thou makest the blind to see, and the lame to walk; and thou cleansest the lepers, and thou castest out unclean spirits and devils, and thou healest those who are tormented with lingering diseases, and thou raisest the dead. And when I heard these things about thee, I settled in my mind one of two things: either that thou art God, who being come down from heaven, doest these things, or that thou art the Son of God, and doest these things. On this account, therefore, I have written to request of thee that thou wouldest trouble thyself to come to me, and cure this disease which I have: for I have also heard that the Jews murmur against thee, and wish to do thee harm. But I have a city, small and beautiful, which is enough for two."

Copy of those things which were written from Jesus by the hand of Hananias, the Tabularius, to Abgar, the Chief of the country.

"Blessed is he that hath believed in me, not having seen me. For "it is written concerning me; that those who see me will not believe "in me, and those who have not seen me, they will believe and be "saved. But touching what thou hast written to me, that I should "come to thee, it is meet (ܠ) that I should fulfil here every thing "for the sake of which I have been sent; and after I have ful-"filled *it*, then I shall be taken up to Him that sent me; and when "I have been taken up, I will send to thee one of my disciples, that "he may heal thy disease, and give salvation to thee and to those "who are with thee."

But to these same Letters these things also are appended in the Aramaic tongue: that after Jesus was ascended, Judas Thomas sent to him Thaddæus the Apostle, one of the Seventy: and when he was come, he lodged with Tobias, the son of Tobias. But when it was heard about him they made it known to Abgar, that the Apostle of Jesus is come here, according as he sent thee word. And Thaddæus began to heal every disease and sickness by the power of God, so that all men wondered. But when Abgar heard the great and marvellous cures which he wrought, he supposed that he was the person about whom Jesus sent him word, and said to him, "When I have been taken up, I will send to thee one of my disciples, that he may heal thy disease." Then he sent and called Tobias, with whom he was lodging, and said to him, I have heard that a mighty man is come, and is entered in, and lodges in thy house: bring him up therefore to me. And when Tobias came to Thaddæus he said to him, Abgar the King has sent and called me, and commanded me to take thee up to him, that thou mayest heal him. And Thaddæus said, I will go up, for it is for this purpose that I have been sent to him with power. Tobias therefore rose up early the next day, and took Thaddæus, and came to Abgar. But when they went up, his princes were assembled and standing there. And immediately as he entered in, a great vision appeared to Abgar on the countenance of Thaddæus the Apostle. And when Abgar saw it, he fell down before Thaddæus; and astonishment seized upon all who were standing there, for they had not seen that vision, which appeared to Abgar alone. And he asked Thaddæus, Art thou in truth the disciple of Jesus the Son of God, who said to me, I will send to thee one of my disciples, that he may heal thee (ܒ) and give thee salvation? And Thaddæus answered and said, Because thou hast nobly believed on Him that sent me, therefore have I been sent to thee; and again, if thou wilt believe on Him, thou shalt have the requests of thy heart. And Abgar said to him, thus I have believed on him, so that I have even desired to take an army and lay waste those Jews who crucified him, were it not that I was hindered on account of the dominion of the Romans. And Thaddæus said, Our Lord has fulfilled the will of his Father, and having fulfilled *it*, he has been taken up to his Father. Abgar said to him, I have believed both in Him and in his Father. And Thaddæus said, On this account I lay my hand upon thee in His name. And when he had done this, immediately he was healed of his sickness and of the disease which he had. And Abgar marvelled, because like as he had heard concerning Jesus, so he saw in deeds by the hand of his disciple Thaddæus, that without medicines and herbs he healed him; and not himself only, but also Abdu, son of Abdu, who had the gout; that he too went in, and fell at his feet, and when he prayed over him he was healed. And many other people of their city he healed, and did great works, and preached the word of God.

After these things, Abgar said to him, Thou, Thaddæus, doest these things by the power of God, and we are astonished at them. But in addition to all these things, I entreat thee to relate to me the history of the coming of Christ, and how it was; about his power also, and by what power he did those things which I have heard.

And Thaddæus said, For the present I will be silent; but because I have been sent to preach the word of God, assemble for me to-morrow all the people of thy city, and I will preach before them, and sow amongst them the word of life; also concerning the coming of Jesus, how it took place; and about his mission, for what purpose he was sent by his Father; and about (ܗܘ) his power and his deeds, and about the mysteries which he spake in the world, and by what power he did these things, and about his new preaching, and about his abasement and his humiliation, and how he humbled and stripped and abased himself, and was crucified, and descended into hell, and broke through the wall of partition which had never been broken through, and raised up the dead; and descended alone, and ascended with a great multitude to his Father.

Abgar then gave orders that in the morning all the people of his city should assemble, and hear the preaching of Thaddæus. And then he afterwards commanded gold and silver to be given to him; but he received it not, and said to him, If we have forsaken that which was our own, how can we accept that of others?

These things were done in the year three hundred and forty. But that these things might not have been translated in every word out of the Aramaic to no purpose, they are placed here in their order of time.

HERE ENDETH THE FIRST BOOK.

THE DOCTRINE OF ADDÆUS, THE APOSTLE.

* * * * * *

* Addæus [said] to him, Because thou hast so believed, I lay my hand upon thee in the name of Him on whom thou hast so believed; and at the same moment as he laid his hand upon him he was healed from the plague of the disease which he had had a long time. And Abgar was astonished, and wondered, because like as he had heard about Jesus himself, how he acted and healed, so Addæus also, without medicine of any kind, healed in the name of Jesus. And Abdu also, the son of Abdu, had the gout in his feet; and he too brought his feet near to him, and he laid his hand upon them, (ܘ) and healed him, and he had the gout no more. And in all the city also he wrought great cures, and shewed wonderful mighty works in it. Abgar said to him, Now that every man knoweth that thou doest these miracles by the power of Jesus Christ, and behold! we are wondering at thy deeds, I therefore entreat thee to relate to us the history about the coming of Christ, how it was, also about his glorious power, and about the miracles which we have heard that he did, which thou hast seen, together with thy fellow disciples. Addæus said to him, I will not be silent from declaring this, because I have been sent hither for this very purpose, that I might speak and teach every one who, like thee, is willing to believe. Assemble for me to-morrow all the city, and I will sow in it the word of life by the preaching which I will preach before you, about the coming of Christ, how it was, and about Him that sent him, why and how he sent him, and about his power and his marvellous deeds, and about the glorious mysteries of his coming which he spake in the world, and about the certitude of his preaching, and how and for what cause he abased himself, and humbled his exalted godhead by the manhood

which he assumed, and was crucified, and descended to the place of the dead, and broke through the wall of partition which had never been broken through, and gave life to the dead by being slain himself; and descended alone, and ascended with many to his glorious Father, with whom he was from all eternity in one exalted godhead.

And Abgar commanded that they should give to Addæus silver and gold. Addæus said to him, How can we receive any thing which is not our own? for, behold, that which was our own we have forsaken it, as we were commanded by our Lord; because without purses and without scrips, bearing the cross upon our shoulders, we were commanded to preach his Gospel in the whole creation, at whose (1) crucifixion for our sakes, for the deliverance of all men, the whole creation was affected and suffered.

And he related before Abgar the King, before his princes and his nobles, before Augustin, Abgar's mother, and before Shalmath, the daughter of Meherdath, Abgar's wife, the signs of our Lord and his wonders, and the glorious mighty works which he did, and his divine triumphs, and his ascension to his Father: and how they had received power and authority, and at the time when he ascended, by which same power he had healed Abgar and Abdu, the son of Abdu, the second *person* of his kingdom; and how he informed them that he would reveal himself at the end of the times, and at the consummation of all creatures; also the resuscitation and resurrection which is to be hereafter for all men, and the separation which will be between the sheep and the goats, and between the believers and the infidels.

And he said to them, "Because strait is the gate of life, and narrow is the way of truth, for this reason the believers of the truth are few; and through unbelief is Satan's pleasure. On this account there are many liars who lead astray those that behold. For were it not that there is a good end for men who believe, our Lord would not have

descended from heaven, and came to the birth, [and the suffering of death; but he is come, and us has he sent * *
* * * * * *

* of the faith which we preach, that God was crucified (for) all men. And if there be any who are not willing to be persuaded by these our words, let them draw near to us, and disclose to us what their mind is, that like as it were a disease, we may apply to their mind healing medicine (ܣܡ), for the recovery of their wounds. For although ye were not present at the time of Christ's passion, nevertheless, from the sun which was darkened, and ye saw *it*, learn ye and understand what great consternation there was at the time of the crucifixion of Him whose Gospel has been spread abroad throughout all the earth by the signs which his Disciples, my fellows, do in all the earth: and those who are Hebrews, and knew only the tongue of the Hebrews, in which they were born, behold, at this day they speak in all tongues, in order that those who are far off, as well as those who are near, may hear and believe that He is the same who confounded the tongues of the rebels, in this region, who were before us, and that it is He who at this day teaches through us the faith of truth and verity, by humble and uncultivated men, who are from Galilee of Palestine. For I myself also, whom ye see, am from Paneas, whence the river Jordan comes out, and I was chosen, together with my fellows, to be a preacher * * * * *

* For I, according as my Lord commanded me, behold, I preach and publish the Gospel; and behold I cast his money upon the table before you, and the seed of his word I sow in the ears of all men: and such as are willing to receive *it*, theirs will be the good reward of the confession; and they who will not believe, against them wipe I off the dust of my feet, as He commanded me. Repent therefore, my beloved, from evil ways and from abominable deeds, and

turn yourselves to him with a good and honest will, as he hath turned himself to you with the favour of his rich mercies; and be not like the generations of old that are passed away, which, because they hardened their heart against the fear of God, have received punishment openly, in order that they might be chastised thereby, and those who come after them may tremble and fear: for the whole object of our Lord's coming into the world was to teach us and to shew us, that at the consummation of the creation (\) there will be a resuscitation of all men; and at that time their acts of conduct will be represented in their own persons, and their bodies will be the volume for the writings of Justice, nor will any one be there who will not know how to read, because every man shall read the writings of his own book * * * * * *

* you that have eyes, inasmuch as ye perceive not, you also are become like those who see not and hear not, and in vain is it to exert your voice which has no effect upon the deaf ear. While they are without blame for not hearing, because they are by nature deaf and dumb, the blame which is justly incurred is yours, because ye are not willing to perceive, not even that which ye do see. For the thick cloud of error which overwhelms your minds suffers you not to obtain that heavenly light, which is the understanding of knowledge. Flee then from things made and created, as I said to you, which are called gods in name only, but are not gods in their nature, and draw near to this who in his own nature is God for ever, and from everlasting; and is not a thing made, like your idols, nor is he a creature and a device, like those images in which ye glory. Because even although he put on this body, still is he God with his Father: for the works of the creation, which trembled at his being slain, and were terrified at his suffering of death, they bear witness that he is God the Creator: for it was not on account of a man, who is of the earth, but on account of Him who

established the earth upon the waters: neither was it on account of a man that the sun became dark in the heavens, but on account of Him who made the great lights: nor was it by a man that the just and righteous were raised to life, but by Him who had granted (.) the power of death from the beginning: nor was it by a man that the vail of the temple of the Jews was rent from the top to the bottom, but by Him who said to them, "Lo, your house is left desolate." For, behold, unless they who crucified him had known that he was the Son of God, they would not have proclaimed the desolation of their city, nor would they have divulged the affliction of their soul in crying Woe! Nor, indeed, even had they been desirous of avoiding this confession, would the terrible commotions which took place at that time have suffered them *to do so*. For, behold, even some of the children of those who crucified *him* are become at this day preachers and evangelists, together with the Apostles, my companions, in all the land of Palestine, and among the Samaritans, and in all the country of the Philistines. The idols also of paganism are despised, and the cross of Christ is honoured, and the peoples and creatures confess God, who became man. If, therefore, while Jesus our Lord was upon earth ye would have believed in him, that he is the Son of God, and, before ye had heard the word of his preaching, would have confessed in him, that he is God, now that he is ascended to his Father, and ye have seen the signs and the wonders which are done in his name, and have heard with your own ears the word of his Gospel, let no man of you doubt in his heart how the promise of his blessing which he sent to you will be established with you— Blessed are ye that have believed in me, not having seen me; and because ye have so believed in me, the city in which ye dwell shall be blessed, and the enemy shall not prevail against it for ever. Turn not aside, therefore, from his faith, for, behold, ye have heard and seen what things bear witness to his faith, that he is the adorable Son and is the glorious God, and he is the invincible King, and he is the power omnipotent; and through faith in him a man is able to acquire the eyes of a true mind, and to perceive that whosoever worshippeth creatures, the wrath of justice will overtake him.

"For every thing which we speak (ܗܐ) before you, as we have received of the gift of our Lord, we speak, and we teach, and we shew, in order that ye may obtain your salvation, and not destroy your spirits through the error of heathenism; because the heavenly Light is arisen over the creation, and He it is that chose the patriarchs of old, and the righteous men, and the prophets, and spake with them by the revelation of the Spirit of Holiness. For He is the God of the Jews who crucified him; the erring heathen also worship Him, even while they know it not, because there is no other God in heaven and in earth; and behold, confession ascendeth up to him from the four quarters of the creation. Behold, therefore, your ears have heard that which was not heard by you *before*, and behold again, your eyes have seen that which was never seen by you *before*. Do no violence, therefore, to that which ye have seen and heard. Put away from you the rebellious heart of your fathers, and free yourselves from the yoke of sin which hath dominion over you in libations and in sacrifices before graven images, and be careful for yourselves about your lives, which are perishable, and the stay of your head, which is frail, and get you a new mind which worships the Maker, and not the things made, in which is represented the image of verity and of truth, of the Father, and of the Son, and of the Spirit of Holiness, while ye believe and are baptized in the triple and glorious names. For this is our doctrine and our preaching. Because it is not in many things that the belief of the truth of Christ consists. And such of you as are willing to be obedient to Christ, ye know that I have many times repeated my words before you, in order that ye might learn and understand what ye hear. And we shall rejoice in this, like the husbandman who rejoiceth in his field which is blessed; God also will be glorified by your repentance towards him. While ye obtain salvation through this, we also, who give you this counsel, shall not be defrauded of the blessed reward of this. And because I am confident that you are a land blessed according to the will of the Lord Christ (ܒܗ), for this reason, instead of the dust of our feet, which it was commanded us that we should wipe off against the city which receiveth not our words, behold I have wiped off to-day at the door of your ears the words of my lips, in which are represented both the coming of Christ which has been, and that which is still to be; and the resurrection also, and the resuscitation of all men, and the separation which is to take place between the believers and the infidels, and the sad punishment which is reserved for those who know not God; and the blessed promise of future joy which they shall receive who have believed in Christ, and worshipped him and his Father most high, and have confessed him and the Spirit of his Godhead. And now it is meet that I conclude my discourse for the present: let those, therefore, who have accepted the word of Christ, and those also who are willing to join with us in prayer, remain with us, and then let them go to their own homes."

And Addæus the Apostle himself rejoiced at this, because he saw that many of the people of the city remained with him, and they were but few who did not remain at that time, while even those few, after not many days, accepted his words, and believed in the Gospel of the preaching of Christ.

And when Addæus the Apostle had spoken these things before the city of Edessa, and King Abgar had seen that all the city rejoiced in his doctrine, men and women equally, and were saying to him, True and faithful is Christ who sent thee to us, he himself also greatly rejoiced at this and praised God; because, like as he had heard from Hanan, his Tabularius, respecting Christ, so he had seen the wonderful mighty works which Addæus the Apostle did in the name of Christ. And Abgar the King also said to him, Like as I sent word to Christ in my letter to him, and like as he sent word to me, and I have received from thee thyself this day, so will I believe all the days of my life, and in the same things will I continue and exult, because I also know that there is no other (ܠܐ) power, in whose name these signs and wonders are done, but by the power of Christ, whom thou preachest in verity and truth. Henceforth, therefore, I will worship him, I and my son Maanu, and Augustin, and Shalmath the Queen. And now, wheresoever thou desirest, build a church, a place of assembly for those who have believed and shall believe thy words: and according as it has been charged thee by thy Lord, so minister thou at *all* times with confidence. Moreover, those who shall be teachers of this Gospel with thee, I am prepared to give to them large gifts, in order that they may have no other work besides the ministry. Whatsoever, also, is required by thee for the expenses of the building, I will give to thee without taking account, and thy word shall be of authority, and prevail in all this city; further, be thou authorized, without any other, to come and enter into my presence, in my royal palace of honor.

And when Abgar went down to his royal palace, he rejoiced, he and his princes with him, Abdu, son of Abdu, and Garmai, and Shemashgram, and Abubai, and Meherdath, together with the rest of their companions, at all that their eyes had seen and their ears had also heard; and in the gladness of their heart they also praised God for having turned their mind to him, and they renounced the paganism in which they stood, and confessed the Gospel of Christ. And when Addæus had built a church, they offered in it vows and oblations, they and the people of the city, and there they offered praises all the days of their life.

And Avida and Barcalba, who were chiefs and rulers, and wore the royal headband, drew near to Addæus, and asked him about the matter of Christ, that he would tell them, how He, being God, had appeared to them like a man: And, How indeed were ye able to look upon him? And he satisfied them all about this, about all that their eyes (ܥܝܢ̈) had seen, and about every thing which their ears had heard from him. And all that the prophets had spoken concerning him he repeated before them, and they received his words gladly and faithfully, and there was not a man that stood against him, for the glorious acts which he did suffered not any man to withstand him.

But Shavida and Ebednebu, chiefs of the priests of this city, together with Piroz and Diku, their companions, when they had seen the signs which he did, ràn and threw down the altars on which they sacrificed before Nebu and Bel, their gods, except the great altar in the midst of the city, and they cried out and said, Truly this is the disciple of that distinguished and glorious Master, of whom we have heard all that he did in the country of Palestine. And Addæus received all those who believed in Christ, and baptized them in the name of the Father, and of the Son, and of the Spirit of Holiness. And those who used to worship stones and stocks sat at his feet, and were recovered from the plague of the foolishness of paganism. Even Jews skilled in the law and the prophets, who traded in silks, they too were convinced, and became disciples, and confessed Christ, that He is the Son of the living God.

But neither did King Abgar nor the Apostle Addæus compel any man by force to believe in Christ, because, without the force of man, the force of the signs constrained many to believe in him. And they received his doctrine with love, all this country of Mesopotamia, and all the regions round about it.

But Aggæus, who made the chains and headbands of the King, and

Palut, and Barshelama, and Barsamya, together with the rest of their companions, clave to Addæus the Apostle, and he received them, and associated them with him in the ministry, while they read in the Old Testament and the New, and the Prophets, (ܗܘ) and the Acts of the Apostles, meditating upon them every day: and he charged them cautiously, to let their bodies be pure and their persons holy, as it is becoming in men who stand before the altar of God, "Be ye indeed also far removed from false swearing, and from wicked murder, and from false witness, which is mixed up with adultery, and from magic arts, which are without mercy, and from soothsaying, and divination, and fortune-tellers; and from fate and nativities, in which the erring Chaldæans boast; and from planets and signs of the Zodiac, on which the foolish trust. And put away from you evil hypocrisy, and bribes, and gifts, by which the innocent are condemned. And besides this ministry to which ye have been called have no other service; for the Lord himself is the service of your ministry all the days of your life. Be also diligent to give the seal of baptism, and love not the superfluities of this world. Listen ye to judgment with justice and with truth, and be not a stumblingblock to the blind, lest through you should be blasphemed the name of Him who opened the eyes of the blind, as we have seen: all therefore who see you will perceive that whatsoever ye preach and teach *to others* you perform yourselves."

And they ministered with him in the church which Addæus had built, at the order and command of King Abgar, and they were furnished from what belonged to the King and to his nobles with some things for the house of God, and others for the supply of the poor. But a large multitude of people assembled day by day, and came to the prayers of the service, and to *the reading of* the Old Testament and the New of Ditonron. They also believed in the revival of the dead, and they buried their departed in the hope of the resurrection. They kept also the festivals of the Church at their proper seasons, and continued every day in the vigils of the Church. And they made visits of almsgiving (ܩܝ) to the sick and to those that were whole, according to the instruction of Addæus to them. Moreover, in the places round about the city, churches were built, and many received from him the Hand of Priesthood: so that the people of the East also, in the guise of merchants, passed over into the country belonging to the Romans, in order that they might see the signs which Addæus did. And those who became disciples received from him the Hand of Priesthood, and in their own country of the Assyrians they taught the sons of their own people, and built houses of prayer there secretly, through danger of the fire-worshippers and the adorers of water.

And Narses, the King of the Assyrians, when he heard of the things which the Apostle Addæus did, sent a message to the same King Abgar: Either send to me the man who doeth these signs before thee, that I may see him and hear his words, or send me word of all that thou hast seen him do in thine own city. And Abgar wrote to Narses, and informed him of all the history of the matter of Addæus from the beginning to the end, and he left nothing which he did not write to him. But when Narses heard those things which were written to him, he was astonished and marvelled.

But Abgar the King, because he was not able to pass over into the country belonging to the Romans, and go to Palestine, and slay the Jews, because they had crucified Christ, wrote a letter and sent it to Tiberius Cæsar, writing in it thus:

"King Abgar to our Lord Tiberius Cæsar: Knowing that nothing is concealed from your Majesty, I write and inform your great and dread Sovereignty that the Jews who are under your hand, and dwell in the country of Palestine, have assembled themselves together, and crucified the Christ, without any fault worthy of death, after he had done before them signs and wonders, and had shewn them great and mighty works, so that he even raised the dead to life for them; and at the time that they crucified him the sun became darkened, and the earth also shook, (ܒ) and all creatures trembled and quaked; and, as if of their accord, at this deed the whole creation quailed, and the inhabiters of the creation. And now your Majesty knoweth what order it is meet for you to give respecting the people of the Jews who have done these things."

And Tiberius Cæsar wrote and sent to King Abgar, and he wrote to him thus:

"The letter of thy Fidelity towards me I have received, and it has been read before me. Touching what the Jews have had the audacity to do with the cross, the Governor Pilate also has written and made known to my Proconsul, Aulbinus, respecting these same things which thou hast written to me. But because the war of the people of Spain, who have rebelled against me, is on foot at this time, for this reason I have not been able to avenge this matter; but I am prepared, when I have leisure, to bring a charge legally against the Jews, who act not according to the law. And on this account Pilate also, who was appointed by me Governor there, I have sent another in his stead, and dismissed him in disgrace, because he exceeded the law, and did the will of the Jews, and, for the gratification of the Jews, crucified Christ who, according to what I hear about him, instead of the cross of death, deserved to be honoured and adored by them, and the more so, because they saw with their own eyes every thing that he did. But thou, according to thy Fidelity towards me, and thine own true compact, and that of thy fathers, hast done well in thus writing to me."

And Abgar the King received Aristides, who had been sent to him by Tiberius Cæsar. And he replied, and sent him back with presents of honor which were suitable for him who sent him to him. And he went from Edessa to Thicuntha, where Claudius, the second from the Emperor, was; and from thence, in the next place, he went to Artica, where (ܬܡܢ) Tiberius Cæsar was. But Caius was watching the regions round about Cæsar. And Aristides himself also related before Tiberius the history of the mighty works which Addæus had done before King Abgar. And when he had leisure from the war, he sent and put to death some of the chiefs of the Jews who were in Palestine. And when King Abgar heard, he was very glad of this, that the Jews had received punishment as it was right.

And some years after the Apostle Addæus had built the church in Edessa, and had furnished it with every thing that was requisite for it, and had converted many of the people of the city, he also built churches in other villages which were far off and near, and completed and ornamented them, and established in them deacons and presbyters, and he taught persons to read the Scriptures in them, and he taught the Ordinances and the Ministry without and within. After all these things, he was seized with that disease of which he departed from this world. And he called for Aggæus before the whole assembly of the Church, and brought him near, and made him Guide and Ruler in his own place. And Palut, who was a deacon, he made him presbyter; and Abshelama, who was a scribe, he made him deacon. And while the Nobles and Chiefs were assembled, and stood near him, Bar Calba, the son of Zati, and Maryhab, the son of Barshemash, and Senac, son of Avida, and Piroz, son of Patric, together with the rest of their companions, the Apostle Addæus said to them, "Ye know and can testify, all of you who hear me, that whatsoever I have preached to you and have taught you, and ye have heard from me, so have I conducted myself among you, and ye have seen it also in practice; because our Lord thus charged us, that whatsoever we preach in words before the people, we should also practise it in deeds before all men. And according to the

Ordinances and Laws which were appointed by the Disciples in Jerusalem, and even the Apostles, my fellows, were guided by them (ܠ), so likewise you, turn ye not aside from them, nor diminish aught from them: in the same manner as I myself also am guided by them amongst you, and have not turned aside from them to the right or to the left, in order that I might not become a stranger to the promised salvation which is reserved for such as are guided by them. Give heed, therefore, to this ministry which ye hold, and continue in it with fear and trembling, and minister every day. Minister not in it with neglectful habits, but with the discretion of faith: neither let the praises of Christ cease out of your mouth, nor let weariness in the prayer of *stated* times approach you. Give heed to the verity which ye hold, and to the teaching of the truth which ye have received, and to the inheritance of salvation which I commit to you, because before the judgment-seat of Christ will it be required of you, when He maketh reckoning with the pastors and superiors, and when He taketh his money from the traders, with the increase of the profits. For He is the King's Son, and goeth to receive a kingdom, and return; and He will come and make a resurrection of all men, and then He will sit upon the throne of his righteousness, and judge the dead and the living, according as he has told us. Let not the secret eye of your minds from above be blinded, that your offences may not abound in the way which has no offences in it, but error is abominable in its paths. Seek those that are lost, and direct those that err, and rejoice in those that are found; bind up the bruised, and watch over the fatlings; because at your hands will the sheep of Christ be required. Look ye not to honour which passeth away; for the shepherd that looketh to receive honour from his flock, badly, badly stands his flock with respect to him. Let your care over the young lambs be great, because their angels behold the face of the Father which is invisible. Neither be ye stones of offence before the blind, but clearers of the way and of the paths (ܢ) in a difficult country, among the Jews, who crucified Him, and the Pagans who are in error; for with these two sides ye have war, in order that ye might shew the truth of the faith which ye hold: even while ye are quiet, your modest and honourable appearance will fight for you against those who hate the truth and love falsehood. Smite not the poor in the presence of the rich; for their poverty is an infliction bad enough for them. Suffer not yourselves to be beguiled by the abominable deliberations of Satan, lest ye be stripped naked of that faith which ye have put on." * * * *

* * * * * * * *

* * * * * * * *

"Nor will we mingle ourselves with the Jews, who crucified him; nor will we let go this inheritance which we have received from thee, but with it will we depart out of this world; and on the day of our Lord, before the tribunal of his righteous judgment, there will He restore to us this inheritance, according as thou hast told us."

And when these things had been spoken, Abgar the King rose up, he and his Princes, and his Nobles, and he went to his own palace, while they all of them grieved over him because he was dying. And he sent to him honourable and noble apparel, that he might be buried in it. But when Addæus the Apostle saw it, he sent word to him, During my life I have taken nothing from thee, neither will I now at my death take any thing from thee, nor will I belie in myself the word of Christ, which he spake to us, "Accept not any thing from any man, and possess not any thing in this world."

And three days more after these things had been spoken by the Apostle Addæus, and he had heard and received the testimony of the doctrine of their preaching from those belonging to his ministry in the presence of all the Nobles, he departed out of this world; and that day was the fifth of the week, and the fourteenth of the month Iyar. And the whole city was in great mourning and bitter suffering on account of him. Nor was it the Christians (ܥܡܐ) only that grieved over him, but the Jews also, and the Pagans who were in this same city. But Abgar the King grieved over him more than all, he and the Princes of his kingdom. And in the sorrow of his heart he despised and abandoned the honour of his kingdom on that day; and with tears and sighs he wept over him with all men. And all the people of the city that saw him marvelled how greatly he was afflicted on his account. And with great and exceeding honour he conveyed and buried him like one of the Princes when he dies, and he placed him in a large sepulchre of sculpture by the fingers, in which those of the house of Ariu, the ancestors of Abgar the King, were laid: there he laid him compassionately, with sorrow and great grief. And all the people of the Church went from time to time, and offered prayers there diligently; and they celebrated the commemoration his death from year to year, according to the ordinance and instruction which had been committed to them by the Apostle Addæus himself, and according to the word of Aggæus, who himself became Guide and Ruler, and the successor of his chair after him, by the Hand of Priesthood, which he had received from him in the presence of all men.

He, too, by the same Hand that he had received from him, made Priests and Guides in the whole of this country of Mesopotamia. For they also, like the Apostle Addæus, thus held fast his word, and listened and received, as good and faithful heirs of the Apostle of the adorable Christ. But silver and gold accepted he from no man, nor did the gifts of the Princes approach him: for instead of gold and silver, he enriched the Church of Christ with the souls of believers. But the whole state of the men and the women were modest and decorous, and they were holy and pure; because they dwelt in union and modesty without spot, in watchfulness of the ministry decorously, in their carefulness towards the poor, and in their (ܒܩ) visitations to the sick: for their ways were full of praise from those who beheld, and their conduct was invested with commendation from strangers, so that even the priests belonging to Nebu and Bel divided the honour with them at all times, by their honourable aspect, by the truth of their words, by the plain speaking which was in their freedom, that was neither subservient to greediness, nor in bondage under blame. For there was no one who saw them that did not run to meet them, that he might greet them honorably, because the very sight of them diffused peace upon the beholders; for their words of peace were spread like a net over the rebellious, while they were entering within the fold of truth and verity. For there was no man who saw them and had any ground to be ashamed of them, because they did any thing which was not just and not becoming: and by these means, their countenances were open, in the preaching of their doctrine towards all men; for whatsoever they said to others and exhorted them *to do*, they themselves exhibited the same in deeds in their own persons, and the hearers, who saw that their actions and words went together, became their disciples without much persuasion, and confessed Christ the King, while they praised God for having turned them to him.

And some years after the death of King Abgar, there arose one of his rebellious sons, who was not obedient to peace, and he sent word to Aggæus, as he was sitting in the Church, Make me a headband of gold, such as thou usest formerly to make for my fathers. Aggæus replied to him, I will not leave the ministry of Christ, which has been committed to me by Christ's disciple, and make the headbands of the evil one. And when he saw that he did not obey him, he sent and brake his legs as he was sitting in the church and expounding. And as he was dying he adjured (ܡܐ) Palut and Abshelama, Lay me and bury me in this house, for whose truth's sake, behold, I am dying.

And as he had adjured *them*, so they laid him within the centre door of the church, between the men and the women. And there was great and bitter mourning in all the Church, and in all the city, beyond the suffering and mourning which there had been in its interior, like the mourning had been when the Apostle Addæus himself died.

And because he died suddenly and quickly, at the breaking of his legs, he was not able to lay his hand upon Palut, and Palut himself went to Antioch, and received the Hand of Priesthood from Serapion, Bishop of Antioch, which Hand Serapion himself also received from Zephyrinus, Bishop of the city of Rome, from the succession of the Hand of Priesthood of Simon Cephas, who had received it from our Lord, and was bishop there in Rome twenty and five years in the days of that Cæsar who reigned there thirteen years.

And as is the custom in the kingdom of King Abgar, and in all kingdoms, that whatsoever the king orders, and whatsoever is spoken in his presence is committed to writing, and laid up among the records, so also Labubna, son of Senac, son of Ebedshaddai, the king's scribe, wrote these things of Addæus the Apostle from the beginning to the end; while Hanan the Tabularius, the kings' Sharir, set to the hand of witness, and placed it among the records of the kings, where the ordinances and the laws are laid up, and there *the contracts* of the buyers and sellers are kept with care, without any negligence whatever.

Here endeth the Doctrine of the Apostle Addæus, which he preached in Edessa, the faithful city of Abgar, the faithful King.

THE DOCTRINE OF THE APOSTLES.

(ܟܕ) When Christ ascended to his Father: and how the Apostles received the gift of the Spirit; and the Ordinances and Laws of the Church, and whither each one of the same Apostles went: and from whence the countries belonging to the Romans received the Hand of Priesthood.

In the three hundred and thirty-ninth year of the kingdom of the Greeks, in the month Heziran, on the fourth day of the same, which is the first day of the week, and the completion of Pentecost, on this same day the Disciples came from Nazareth of Galilee, from the place where the conception of our Lord was announced, to the mountain which is called Baith Zaithe, our Lord being with them, but not being visible to them. And at the time of the great morning our Lord lifted up his hands, and laid them upon the heads of the Eleven Disciples, and gave to them the gift of the Priesthood; and suddenly a bright cloud received him, and they beheld him as he went up to heaven. And he sat down on the right hand of his Father. And they were praising God because they saw his ascension as he had told them; and they were rejoicing, because they had received the Right Hand of Priesthood of the house of Moses and Aaron. And from thence they went up and proceeded to the upper room, that in which our Lord had celebrated the Passover with them, and in the place where the inquiries had been: Who is it that betrayeth our Lord to the crucifiers? There also were the inquiries, How they should preach his Gospel in the world. And as within that upper room the mystery of His body and blood began, that it might prevail in the world, so also from thence did the teaching of his preaching begin to have authority in the world. And when (ܗ) the Disciples were thrown into this difficulty, How they should preach his Gospel to strange tongues which they knew not, and they were speaking one to the other after this manner: Although we be confident that Christ will perform by our hands mighty works, and miracles before strange peoples whose tongues we know not, neither are they acquainted with our tongue, who shall teach them and inform them, that it is by the name of Christ, who was crucified, that these mighty works and miracles are done? And while the Disciples were in these deliberations, Simon Cephas rose up and said to them: My brethren, This is not our business, how we shall preach his Gospel, but it is our Lord's; for He knoweth how it is possible for us to preach his Gospel in the world; but we rely upon his care for us, which he promised to us and said: "When I am ascended to my Father I will send to you the Spirit, the Paraclete, that he may teach you every thing which it is meet for you to know, and to make known." And when Simon Cephas had spoken these things to his fellow Apostles, and reminded them, a voice of mystery was heard by them, and a sweet odour, which is strange to the world, was diffused on them, and tongues of fire, between the voice and the odour, came down to them from heaven, and alighted and sat upon every one of them; and according to the tongue which each one of them had received, so he prepared himself to go to the country in which that tongue was spoken and understood. And by the same gift of the Spirit which was given to them on that day, they also appointed Ordinances and Laws which were agreeable with the Gospel of their preaching, and with the true and faithful teaching of their doctrine:

I. The Apostles therefore appointed: Pray ye towards the East, "because as the lightning which lighteneth from the east, and is seen even to the west, so shall the coming of the Son of Man be": that by this we may know and understand that He will appear from the East suddenly.

(ܟܘ) II. Again the Apostles appointed, That on the first day of the week there should be service and reading of the Holy Scriptures, and an Oblation. Because on the first day of the week our Lord rose from the place of the dead, and on the first day of the week he manifested himself in the world, and on the first day of the week he ascended up to heaven, and on the first day of the week he will appear in the end with the Angels of heaven.

III. Again the Apostles appointed, That on the fourth day of the week there should be service, because upon it our Lord disclosed to them about his trial and his suffering, and his crucifixion, and his death, and his resurrection. And the Disciples were in this sorrow.

IV. Again the Apostles appointed, That on the sixth day of the week, at the ninth hour, there should be service, because that which had been spoken on the fourth day of the week about the suffering of our Saviour was accomplished on the sixth day of the week, while the worlds and the creatures trembled, and the lights in the heavens were darkened.

V. Again the Apostles appointed, That there should be Presbyters and Deacons like the Levites, and Subdeacons like those who carried the vessels of the hall of the Sanctuary of the Lord, and an Overseer, the same is the Guide of all the people, like Aaron the chief and master of all the priests and Levites of the whole city.

VI. Again the Apostles appointed: Celebrate the day of the Epiphany of our Saviour, which is the chief of the festivals of the Church, on the sixth day of the latter Canun, in the long number of the Greeks.

VII Again the Apostles appointed: Forty days before the day of the Passion of our Saviour fast ye, and then celebrate the day of the Passion, and the day of the Resurrection, because our Lord himself also, the lord of the festival, fasted forty days, and Moses and Elias, who were invested (ܚܐ) with this mystery, they also fasted forty days each, and then they were glorified.

VIII. Again the Apostles appointed, That at the conclusion of all the scriptures, the Gospel should be read, as being the seal of all the scriptures: and the people should listen to it standing up on their feet, because it is the glad tidings of Salvation of all men.

IX. Again the Apostles appointed: At the completion of fifty days after his resurrection, make the commemoration of his ascension to his glorious Father.

X. The Apostles appointed, That, except the Old Testament and the Prophets and the Gospel, and the Acts of their own Triumphs, let not any thing be read on the pulpit of the Church.

XI. Again the Apostles appointed, That whosoever is not acquainted with the Faith of the Church, and the Ordinances and Laws which are appointed in it, should not be a Guide and Ruler; and whosoever is acquainted with them and has transgressed them, should not minister any more, because, not being confirmed in his ministry, he acts falsely.

XII. Again the Apostles appointed, That whosoever sweareth, or lieth, or beareth false witness, or goeth amongst sorcerers and soothsayers, and Chaldæans, and putteth faith in fate and nativities, which they hold who know not God, should also, as being a man that knoweth not God, be dismissed from the ministry, and not minister.

XIII. Again the Apostles appointed, If there be any man that doubteth touching the ministry, and it is not confirmed to him, this man should not minister again, because the Lord of the ministry is not confirmed to him, and he deceiveth man, and not God, "before whom no artifices avail."

XIV. Again the Apostles appointed, Whoso lendeth and taketh (ܚܒܠ) usury, and is occupied with merchandise and greediness, he should not minister again, nor continue in the ministry.

XV. Again the Apostles appointed, That he who loveth the Jews like Iscariot, who loved them, or the Pagans, who worship creatures instead of the Creator, should not enter in amongst them and minister: but if he be already amongst them they should not suffer him, but he should be separated from amongst them, and not minister with them again.

XVI. Again the Apostles appointed, If any one from the Jews or Pagans come and join himself with them, and if, after he has joined himself with them, he turn and go back to the side on which he had stood, if afterwards he return and come to them a second time, he should not be received again, but, like the side on which he had been before, so let those who know him look upon him.

XVII. Again the Apostles appointed, That it is not lawful for the Guide to do the things which pertain to the Church apart from those who minister with him; but with the counsel of them all let him order, and that be done which all of them assent to and object not.

XVIII. Again the Apostles appointed, That all those who depart out of this world with the good testimony of the faith of Christ, and with affliction for his name's sake, make ye a commemoration of them on the day on which they were put to death.

XIX. Again the Apostles appointed, In the service of the Church repeat, day by day, David's songs of praise, on account of this: "I will bless the Lord always," and "His praises are always in my mouth," and "In the day and in the night will I meditate and speak, and cause my voice to be heard before thee."

XX. Again the Apostles appointed, Such as divest (ܚܠܨ) themselves of mammon, and run not after the gain of money, let them be chosen and advanced to the ministry of the altar.

XXI. Again the Apostles appointed, The Priest who accidentally bindeth improperly, let him receive the punishment which is just; but let him that has been bound receive the bond as if he had been properly bound.

XXII. Again the Apostles appointed, Those who are accustomed to hear trials, if it appear that they have respect of persons, and condemn the innocent and acquit the guilty, let them not hear another trial, receiving again the rebuke of their hypocrisy as it is fit.

XXIII. Again the Apostles appointed, Such as are high-minded and puffed up with the pride of boasting, let them not be promoted to the ministry, "because that which is exalted among men is abominated before God"; and against them it is said, "I will return the recompense upon those that are proud."

XXIV. Again the Apostles appointed, That there should be a Ruler over the Presbyters who are in the villages, and that he should be acknowledged the chief of them all, at whose hand they should all be required; for Samuel thus went to visit from place to place and ruled.

XXV. Again the Apostles appointed, Those kings who shall hereafter believe in Christ, it shall be lawful for them to go up and stand before the altar together with the Guides of the Church, because David also, and those who were like him, went up and stood before the altar.

XXVI. Again the Apostles appointed, That no man should dare to do any thing by the authority of the Priesthood unjustly and improperly, but with justice, and without the blame of hypocrisy.

(ܠ) XXVII. Again the Apostles appointed, That the bread of the Oblation should be placed upon the altar on the day that it is baked, and not some days after, which is not lawful.

But all these things, it was not for themselves that the Apostles appointed them, but for those who should come after them, for they feared that wolves were about to put on sheeps' clothing: because for themselves, the Spirit, the Paraclete which was in them, was sufficient to conduct them lawfully, according to these Laws which he had appointed by their hands. For they who had received from our Lord power and authority needed not that laws should be appointed for them by others; for Paul also, and Timothy, while they were going about in the country of Syria and Cilicia, committed these same Regulations and Laws of the Apostles and Elders to those who were under the hand of the Apostles, for the churches of the countries in which they were preaching and publishing the Gospel; but the Disciples, after these Ordinances and Laws which they had appointed, ceased not from the preaching of the Gospel, or from wonderful mighty works which our Lord did by their hands. For much people was collected near them every day, who believed on Christ, and they came to them from other cities and hearkened to their words and received them. But Nicodemus and Gamaliel, chiefs of the Synagogue of the Jews, came to the Apostles secretly, consenting to their doctrine. But Judas, and Levi, and Peri, and Joseph, and Justus, the sons of Hananias, and

Caiphas and Alexander the priests, they also came to the Apostles by night, confessing Christ, that he is the Son of God; but they were afraid of disclosing their minds towards the Disciples on account of the sons of their own people. And the Apostles received them with love, saying to them: Destroy not, through the shame and fear of (ܠ) men, your lives before God, and have the blood of Christ required of you, as well as of your fathers who took it upon themselves: for it cannot be accepted before God, that while ye be with those who worship him, ye should go and mingle yourselves with those who slew his adorable son. How do ye expect that your faith should be accepted with those who are true, so long as ye are with those that are false? but it is right that you, as men who believe in Christ, should confess openly this faith which we preach. And when they heard these things from the Disciples, those sons of the priests cried out, all of them equally, before the whole people of the Apostles, We confess and believe in Christ who was crucified, and we confess that he is the Son of God from everlasting; and we renounce those who dared to crucify him; for even the priests of the people confess Christ secretly, but on account of the headship of the people which they love, they are not willing to confess openly, and they have forgotten that which is written that "He is the Lord of knowledge, and artifices avail not before him." But when their fathers had heard these things of their sons, they threatened them greatly, not, indeed, because they had believed on Christ, but because they had declared and spoken openly of the mind of their fathers before the sons of their people. But those who believed clave to the Disciples, and turned not from them, because they saw that whatsoever they taught to the multitudes, they fulfilled the same themselves in deeds before all men. And whenever affliction and persecution arose against the Disciples, they rejoiced in being afflicted with them, and they received stripes and imprisonment with gladness, in the confession of their faith in Christ; and all the days of their life they preached Christ before the Jews and the Samaritans. And after the death of the Apostles there were Guides and Rulers in the churches, and whatsoever (ܠܟ) the Apostles had committed to them, and they had received from them, they taught to the multitudes all the time of their lives. They again, at their deaths also committed and delivered to their disciples after them every thing which they had received from the Apostles; also what James had written from Jerusalem, and Simon from the city of Rome, and John from Ephesus, and Mark from the great Alexandria, and Andrew from Phrygia, and Luke from Macedonia, and Judas Thomas from India; that the epistles of an Apostle might be received and read in the Churches, in every place, like those Triumphs of their Acts, which Luke wrote, are read, that by this the Apostles might be known, and the Prophets, and the Old Testament and the New; that one truth was preached by them all, that one Spirit spake in them all from one God, whom they had all worshipped and had all preached. And the countries received their doctrine. Every thing, therefore, which had been spoken of our Lord by the hand of the Apostles, and the Apostles had delivered to their disciples, was believed and received in every country, by the intimation of our Lord, who said to them, "I am with you, even till the world ends:" while the Guides were disputing with the Jews from the books of the Prophets, and contending against the erring Pagans with the terrible mighty works which they did in the name of Christ: for all the peoples, even those who dwelt in other countries, were quiet and silent at the Gospel of Christ; and those who confessed cried out under the persecution, "This persecution of us to-day shall be an advocate for us because we were formerly persecutors." For there were some of them against whom death by the sword was decreed, and some of them from whom they took away whatsoever they possessed and dismissed them; and as often as affliction arose against them, their congregations became enriched and increased (ܠܒ), and with gladness of their heart they received death of every kind. And by the Hand of Priesthood, which the Apostles themselves had received from our Lord, their Gospel was spread abroad in the four quarters of the world rapidly. And while they visited one another, they ministered to each other.

Jerusalem received the Hand of Priesthood, and all the country of Palestine, and the parts of the Samaritans and the Philistines, and the country of the Arabians, and of Phœnicia, and the people of Cæsarea, from James, who was Ruler and Guide in the Church of the Apostles, which had been built in Sion.

The great Alexandria and Thebais, and the whole of Inner Egypt, and all the country of Pelusium, and even to the borders of the Indians, received the Apostles' Hand of Priesthood from Mark, the Evangelist, who was Ruler and Guide there in the church which he had built there, and ministered.

India, and all its own countries, and those bordering on it, even to the farthest sea, received the Apostles' Hand of Priesthood from Judas Thomas, who was Guide and Ruler in the church which he built there, and ministered there.

Antioch, and Syria, and Cilicia, and Galatia, even to Pontus, received the Apostles' Hand of Priesthood from Simon Cephas, who himself laid the foundation of the church there, and was Priest, and ministered there up to the time when he went up from thence to Rome, on account of Simon the Sorcerer, who was deceiving the people of Rome by his sorceries.

(ܠܓ) The city of Rome, and all Italy, and Spain, and Britain, and Gaul, together with the other remaining countries which bordered on them, received the Apostles' Hand of Priesthood from Simon Cephas, who went up from Antioch, and became Ruler and Guide there in the Church which he built there and in its environs.

Ephesus, and Thessalonica, and all Asia, and all the country of the Corinthians, and of all Achaia and its environs, received the Apostles' Hand of Priesthood from John the Evangelist, who had leaned upon the bosom of our Lord, who built a Church there, and ministered there in his office of Guide there.

Nicæa, and Nicomedia, and all the country of Bithynia, and of Gothia, and of the regions round about it, received the Apostles' Hand of Priesthood from Andrew, the brother of Simon Cephas, who was Guide and Ruler in the Church which he built there, and was Priest and ministered there.

Byzantium, and all the country of Thrace, and its environs, even to the great river, the border which separates between the Barbarians, received the Apostles' Hand of Priesthood from Luke the Apostle, who built a Church there, and ministered there in his office of Ruler and Guide there.

Edessa, and all its environs which were on all sides of it, and Soba, and Arabia, and all the North, and the regions round about it, and the South, and all the places of the borders of Mesopotamia, received the Apostles' Hand of Priesthood from Addæus, the Apostle, one of the Seventy two Apostles, who taught there, and built a Church there, and was Priest and ministered there in his office of Guide there.

The whole of Persia of the Assyrians and Armenians and Medians, and of the countries round about Babylon, the Huzites and the Gelæ, even to the borders of the Indians, and even to the country (ܠܗ) of Gog and Magog, and again all the countries from all sides, received the Apostles' Hand of Priesthood from Aggæus, a maker of *golden* chains, the disciple of Addæus the Apostle.

But the rest of the other fellows of the Apostles went to the distant countries of the Barbarians, and taught from place to place, and passed on, and there they ministered with their preaching; there also was their departure out of this world, while their disciples after them continued to go on up to the present day. And there was no change or addition made by them to what they preached.

But Luke the Evangelist had this diligence, and wrote the Triumphs of the Acts of the Apostles, and the Ordinances and Laws of the ministry of their Priesthood, and whither each one of them went. By his diligence, therefore, Luke wrote these things, and more than these, and he placed them in the hand of Priscus and Acquilas, his disciples; and they accompanied him even up to the day of his death: like as Timothy and Erastus, of Lystra and Menaus, the first disciples of the Apostles, accompanied Paul until he went up to the city of Rome, because he had withstood the orator Tertullus. And Nero the Emperor slew him with the sword, and Simon Cephas, in the city of Rome.

DOCTRINE OF SIMON CEPHAS, IN THE CITY OF ROME.

In the third year of Claudius Cæsar, Simon Cephas departed from Antioch to go to Rome. And as he passed on he preached in the countries the word of our Lord. And when he drew nigh to enter in there, many had heard and they went out to meet him, and the whole Church received him with great joy. And some of the princes of the city who (ܠܗ) wore the headbands of kings came out to him that they might see him and hear his word; and when the whole city was gathered together near him, he stood up to speak with them, and to shew them the preaching of his teaching how it was; and he began to speak to them thus: Men, sons of Rome, saints of all Italy, hearken to what I say to you. To-day I preach and proclaim Jesus the Son of God, who came down from heaven, and was made man, and was amongst us like ourselves, and wrought marvellous mighty works and signs and wonders before us, and before all the Jews who are in the land of Palestine. And you also have heard of those things which he did, because they came to him also from other countries on account of the fame of his healing, and on the report of his marvellous helps. And every one that came near to him was healed by his word. And because he was God, at the same time as he healed he also forgave sins: for his healing which was manifest bare witness to his secret forgiveness, that it is true and to be believed. For this Jesus the prophets preached in their mysteries, while they waited to see him, and to hear his words: that he who was with his Father for ever and from everlasting, is God, who was hidden in the height, and is appeared in the depth, the glorious Son, who is of his Father, and is glorified together with his Father and with the Spirit of his Godhead, and the terrible power of his majesty. He also was crucified of his own will by the hands of sinners, and was taken up to his Father, while I and my companions beheld, and he will come again in his own glory and that of all his holy angels, as we have heard him say to us. For we are not able to speak any thing which has not been heard by us from him, nor do we write in the book of his Gospel any thing which he has not spoken to us, because (ܠ) this word is spoken that the mouth of the liars may be stopped, on the day that the sons of men shall give an account of their idle words at the place of Judgment. But because we were catchers of fish, and not skilled in books, on this account he said to us, 'I will send you the Spirit, the Paraclete, that he may teach you what ye do not know;' for by his gift we speak these things which ye hear. And further by it we bring aid to the sick and healing to the deceased; that by the hearing of his word, and by the aid of his power, ye may believe in Christ, that he is

God, the Son of God, may be delivered from the service of bondage and may worship him and his Father, and glorify the Spirit of of his Godhead. For when we glorify the Father we also glorify his Son with him, and when we worship the Son we also worship the Father with him; and when we confess the Spirit we also confess the Father and the Son, because in the name of the Father, and the Son, and the Spirit, were we commanded to baptize those who believe, that they might live for ever."

"Flee therefore from the words of the wisdom of this world, in which there is no profit, and draw near to those which are true and faithful, and accepted before God; and their reward is reserved, and their recompense abideth. And now that the light is arisen upon the creation, the world also has obtained the eyes of the mind, that every man might see and understand that it is not right that creatures should be worshipped instead of the Creator, neither together with the Creator, because every thing which is creature ought to be a worshipper of its maker, and is not to be worshipped like its creator. But this one who came to us is God, the Son of God, in his own nature, although he mingled his godhead with our manhood, in order that he might renew our manhood by the aid of his godhead. And on this account it is just that we should worship him, because he is to be worshipped together with his Father, and that we should not worship creatures, which were created for the worship of the Creator. For he is the God of Truth (ܫܪܪܐ) and of Verity: it is he who was before the worlds and things created: he is the Son of Truth, and the glorious fruit who is of the Father most high. But ye see the wonderful deeds which accompany and follow these words: one would hardly believe the short time since he ascended to his Father, and see how his Gospel is spread abroad through the whole creation, that by this it may be known and believed that he is the creator of the creatures, and by his assent the creatures subsist. And inasmuch as ye saw the sun become darkened at his death, ye yourselves also are witnesses. But the earth shook when he was slain, and the vail was rent at his death: and touching these things the Governor Pilate also was witness, for he sent and made them known to Cæsar, and these things, and more than these, were read before him and before the princes of your city. And on this account Cæsar was angry against Pilate, because he had unjustly been persuaded by the Jews, and for this reason he sent and took away from him the authority which he had given to him. And this same thing was published abroad and made known in all the dominion of the Romans. What, therefore, Pilate saw and made known to Cæsar and to your honourable Senate, the same I preach and declare, and my fellow-Apostles. And ye know that Pilate could not have written to the Government any thing which did not take place and he saw with his own eyes: but that which did take place and was done in reality, the same he wrote and made known. And those who watched the sepulchre were witnesses also of those things which took place there; they became like dead men: and when those watchers were questioned by Pilate, they confessed before him how large a bribe the chief priests of the Jews had given to them, in order that they might say that we, his disciples, stole away the body of Christ. Behold, therefore, ye have heard many things, but if ye be not willing to be convinced by those things which ye have heard, nevertheless be convinced by the mighty works that ye see, (ܠܕ) which are done in his name. Let not Simon the Sorcerer deceive you, by semblances that are not real which he exhibits to you; like as to men without understanding, who know not how to discern what they see and hear. Send, therefore, and bring him where your whole city is assembled together, and choose for you some sign for us to do before you, and the one whom ye see perform that same sign, your part will be to believe in him."

And in the same hour they sent and fetched Simon the Sorcerer, and the men who were of his opinions said to him : As a man, in whom we are confident that there is power in thee to perform any thing, perform thou some sign before us all, and this Simon the Galilæan, who preacheth Christ, shall see. And as they were thus speaking to him a dead man happened to be passing by, the son of one of the chiefs, and well known and illustrious among them. And all of them being assembled together said to him : The one of you that shall restore to life this dead man, he is true, and to be believed and accepted, and we will all follow him in every thing that he saith to us. And they said to Simon the Sorcerer, Because thou hast been here before Simon the Galilæan, and we have known thee before him, exhibit thou first the power which accompanieth thee. But Simon hesitatingly drew near to the dead man, and they set down the bier before him ; and he looked to the right hand and to the left, and gazed up to heaven, saying many words : some of them he spake aloud, and some of them secretly and not aloud. And he waited a long while and nothing took place, and nothing was done, and the dead man was lying upon his bier. And in the same hour Simon Cephas drew near to him that was dead with confidence, and cried aloud before all the assembly which was standing there : In the name of Jesus Christ, whom the Jews crucified at Jerusalem, and whom we preach, rise up from thence ; (ܡܐ) and immediately, as the word of Simon was spoken, he that was dead revived and rose up from the bier. And all the people saw and marvelled. And they said to Simon : Christ, whom thou preachest, is true : and many cried out and said, Let Simon the Sorcerer and deceiver of us all be stoned. But Simon, by reason that every one was running to see the dead man who was come to life again, escaped from them from one street to another, and from house to house, and fell not into their hands on that day.

But the whole city took Simon Cephas and they received him gladly, and with love: and he ceased not to perform signs and wonders in the name of Christ, and many believed in him. But Cuprinus, the father of him who was restored to life conducted Simon Cephas with him to his house, and received him in a proper manner, while he and all his household believed in Christ, that he is the son of the living God. And many of the Jews and of the Pagans became disciples there. And when there was great rejoicing at his doctrine, he built a church there in Rome and in the neighbouring cities, and in all the villages of the people of Italy; and he ministered there in the office of Guide and Ruler twenty-five years.

And after these years Nero Cæsar seized him, and bound him in prison: and he knew that he would crucify him, so he called Ansus, [*Linus*] the Deacon, and made him Bishop in his own stead in Rome. And these things Simon himself spake, and the other remaining things also which he had, he commanded Ansus [*Linus*] to teach before the people, saying to him, Besides the New Testament and the Old, let there not be read any thing else before the people, which is not right. When therefore Cæsar had given orders that Simon should be crucified with his head downwards, as he had himself requested of Cæsar, and that Paul's head (ܪܫܐ) should be taken off, there was great trouble among the people, and bitter grief in all the Church, because they had been deprived of the sight of the Apostles. And Isus [*Linus*] the Guide arose and took up their bodies by night and buried them with great honour, and a house of assembly for many was made there. And at that time, as if by the judgment of righteousness, Nero abandoned his empire and fled, and there was a short cessation from the persecution which Nero Cæsar had raised against them. And many years after the great crowning of the Apostles who had departed out of the world, while the Hand of Priesthood was proceeding in all Rome and in all Italy, it happened then that there was a great famine in the city of Rome.

HERE ENDETH THE DOCTRINE OF SIMON CEPHAS.

THE ACTS OF SHARBIL, WHO HAD BEEN THE HIGH PRIEST OF IDOLS, AND WAS CONVERTED TO THE CONFESSION OF THE CHRISTIAN RELIGION IN CHRIST.

In the fifteenth year of the Autocrat Trajan Cæsar, and in the third year of the reign of King Abgar the seventh, which is the year four hundred and sixteen of the kingdom of Alexander, King of the Greeks, and during the high-priesthood of Sharbil and of Barsamya, Trajan Cæsar gave command to the Governors of the countries of his dominions, that sacrifices and libations should be increased in all the cities of their administration, and that those who did not sacrifice should be arrested and be delivered over to stripes and lacerations, and to bitter inflictions of all kinds of tortures, and should afterwards receive the sentence of death by the sword. And when this edict arrived at the city of Edessa of the Parthians, it was the great (ܡܒܝ) festival on the eighth of Nisan, on the third day of the week. The whole city was assembled together near the great altar which is in the middle of the city opposite the office of records, all the gods having been brought together, and been decorated, and set up in honor, both Nebu and Bel together with their companions. And all the high-priests were offering sweet incense and libations, and the odour of the sacrifices was diffusing itself, and sheep and oxen were being slaughtered, and the voice of the harp and the tabor was heard in the whole of the city. But Sharbil was the chief and ruler of all the priests, and he was greatly honoured above all his fellows, and he was clad in splendid and magnificent vestments, and a headband which was embossed with figures of gold was set upon his head, and at the intimation of his word every thing that he ordered was done. And Abgar the king, son of the gods, was standing at the head of the people; and they were obedient to Sharbil, because he drew nearer to all the gods than any of his fellows, as being also the one who returned an answer to every man according to what he heard from the gods. And while these things were being done by the command of the king, Barsamya, the Bishop of the Christians, went up to Sharbil, he and Tiridath the presbyter and Shalula the deacon, and he said to Sharbil, the great high-priest: Christ the King, to whom belong heaven and earth, will require at thy hands all these souls against which thou sinnest and leadest them astray, and turnest them away from the God of verity and truth, to idols which are made and deceitful, that are not able to do any thing with their hands. Neither dost thou spare thine own soul which is perishing from the true life of God; and thou declarest to this same people that the dumb idols talk with thee, and thou approachest thine ear to them one after another, as if thou heardest something from them, and sayest to this (ܗܢܐ) people: The God Nebu commanded me to say to you, 'On account of your sacrifices and your oblations I cause peace in this your country.' And Bel saith, 'I cause great plenty in your land,' and those who listen to thee do not discern that thou art deceiving them greatly, because "they have a mouth and they speak not, and eyes have they and they see not with them," which same you support, and it is not they which support you, as ye suppose; you also set tables before them, and it is not they which supply you. Now therefore be persuaded by me as to what I say to thee and advise thee. If thou be willing to hear me, abandon idols which are made, and worship God the Maker *of all things*, and his Son Jesus Christ. Let it not be that thou be ashamed of him, and worship him not, because he took upon him flesh, was made man, and was stretched out upon the cross of death: for all these things which he endured, it was for the sake of the salvation of men, and for the sake of their deliverance. For he who put on flesh is God, the Son of God, Son of the essence of his Father, and Son of the nature of him who begat him; for he is the adorable brightness of his Godhead and the glorious manifestation of his majesty, he also has existed with his Father from eternity and for ever, his arm, and his right hand, and his power, and his wisdom, and his might, and the living Spirit, which is from him, the propitiator and sanctifier of all who worship him. Which things Palut taught us, whom thy reverence is acquainted with, and thou knowest that Palut was the disciple of Addæus the Apostle. King Abgar also, who was older than this Abgar, who worshippeth idols as well as thou, he too believed in Christ the King, the Son of him whom thou callest Lord of all the gods. For it is commanded to Christians that they should not worship any thing that is made and is a creature and in its nature is not God: like as ye worship idols made by men, who themselves (ܡܟܝ) also are made and are creatures. Be persuaded, therefore, by these things which I have said to thee, because they are the faith of the Church; for I know that all this people looketh up to thee, and I am certain that if thou be persuaded, many also will be persuaded with thee.

Sharbil said to him, Very acceptable unto me are these words of thine which thou hast spoken before me, and they are greatly accepted by me. But I know that I am lost from all these things, and there is no longer for me any remedy; and now that hope is cut off from me, why weariest thou thyself about an obscure dead man, for whose death there is no hope of resurrection: for I have been slain by paganism and am become a dead corpse of the evil one: in sacrifices and libations of deceit have I consumed all the days of my life.

And when Barsamya the Bishop heard these things, he fell down at his feet and said to him, There is hope for the penitent, and healing for those that are wounded. I will be surety to thee for the abundant mercies of the Son Christ, that he will forgive thee all that thou hast sinned against him, in that thou hast worshipped and honoured his creatures instead of himself; for that gracious one who extended himself upon the cross of death, will not withhold his grace from souls which are convinced and flee for succour to his favour which is over us: like as he did towards the thief, he is able to do towards thee, and also towards those who are like thee. Sharbil said, Thou, like a skilful physician, who suffers pain himself at the pain of the afflicted, hast done well in being careful about me. But now, because it is the festival to day of this people—of every one—I am not able to go down with thee to day to the church; depart, go thou down with honour, and to morrow at night I will come down to thee. Henceforth I have renounced for myself the gods which are made, and I will confess the Lord Christ, the maker of all men.

And the day after, Sharbil arose and went down (ܢܚܬ) to Barsamya by night, he and his sister Babai, and he was received by the whole Church: and he said to them, Offer prayers and supplications for me, that Christ may forgive me all that I have sinned against him, during all this long period of years. And because they were afraid of the persecutors, they gave him the seal of salvation, as he made his confession of belief in the Father, and in the Son, and in the Spirit of holiness.

And when the whole city had heard that he was gone down to the church, there began to be a commotion among the multitude, and they arose and went down to him, and saw him clad in the fashion of the Christians. And he said to them, May the Son Christ forgive me all the sins that I have sinned against you, and all which I have declared to you that the gods spake to me, when they did not speak: and inasmuch I have been to you an abominable cause, may I be to you now a good cause;

instead of the idols made *with hands* which ye once did worship, may ye henceforth worship God the maker *of all things*. And when they had heard these things, there remained with him a great multitude of men and of women, and Labu also, and Hafsai, and Barcalba, and Avida, chief persons of the city, they said to Sharbil all of them, Henceforth we also renounce whatsoever thou hast renounced, and we confess Christ the King, whom thou hast confessed.

But Lysanias, the judge of the country, when he had heard that Sharbil had done this, sent by night, and took him away from the Church, and many Christians went up with him: and he sat down to hear him and to judge him, before the altar which is in the middle of the city, where he was sacrificing to the gods; and he said to him, Wherefore hast thou renounced the gods whom thou formerly didst worship and offer sacrifice to them, and hadst been made high priest to them, and behold, to-day thou confessest Christ, whom thou didst deny of old. For see how those Christians, to whom (ܠܘܬ) thou art gone, renounce not any thing in which they stand, like as thou hast renounced that in which wast born. If thou believe the gods to be true, why hast thou renounced them to-day? but if thou believe them not, as thou declarest respecting them, why didst thou sacrifice to them and worship them? Sharbil said, When I was blind in my mind, I worshipped that which I knew not; but to-day, because I have obtained the clear eyes of the mind, there is no ground for me henceforth to stumble at carved stones, or that I should any longer be the cause of stumbling to others. For to him whose eyes be open, it is a great disgrace to go and fall into the pit of destruction. The judge said, Because thou hast been high priest of the gods who ought to be honoured, and hast been partaker of the mystery of those, whom the mighty emperors worship, I will have patience with thee, in order that thou mayest be persuaded by me not to turn away from the service of the gods; but if thou wilt not be persuaded by me, I swear by the same gods whom thou hast renounced, that I will punish thee in the same manner as a man guilty of murder, and will take vengeance on thee for the violence done to the gods, against whom thou hast rebelled and renounced them, as well as for the insult with which thou hast insulted them, nor will I omit to inflict upon thee every kind of torture; and like as thy honour formerly was great, so also will I make thy disgrace great this day.

Sharbil said, Neither shall I be content for thee to look upon me as of old, when I worshipped gods made *with hands.* But look thou upon me to-day, and interrogate me as a Christian man, who renounceth idols, and confesseth Christ the King. The judge said, How is it that thou art not afraid of the emperors, nor ashamed of saying before those who are listening to thy trial, 'I am a Christian?' But confess that thou wilt sacrifice to the gods according to thy former custom, so that thy honour may be great (ܪܒܐ) like it formerly was: lest I make all those, who have believed like thyself, to tremble at thee. Sharbil said, I fear the King of kings, but of any king of earth I am not afraid, nor of thy threats regarding me, which lo! thou denouncest against the worshippers of Christ, in whom I made my confession yesterday, and lo, to-day for his sake I am tried, like as he also was brought to judgment for the sake of sinners who resemble me. The judge said, Even although thou wilt not spare thyself, still I spare thee, by refraining from cutting off those hands of thine, with which thou hast placed incense before the gods, and from stopping with thy blood those ears of thine with which thou hast heard their mysteries, and that tongue of thine which has declared and explained to us their secret things. Behold I fear them and spare thee; but if thou continue thus, may those gods be witness against me, that I will not spare thee.

Sharbil said, Thou, as a man who fearest the emperors and art afraid of idols, spare thou me not. For I know not what thou sayest: on this account also my mind is not moved nor troubled by these things which thou sayest, for through thy judgments shall all those, who will not worship any thing which is not god in its own nature, escape the judgment to come. The judge said, Let him be scourged with thongs, because he has had the daring to answer me thus, and has withstood the edict of the emperors, nor has he regarded the honour with which the gods honoured him, because, lo, he has renounced them. And he was scourged of ten, who seized him according to the command of the judge.

Sharbil said, Thou art not aware of the torment of the justice of the world to come: for thou must cease, and thy judgments also will pass away, but justice will not pass away, nor will its vengeance end. The judge said, Thou art so drunken with this same Christianity, that thou dost not even know before whom thou art being judged, and by whom thou art scourged,—by those who formerly honoured thee, and paid adoration to thy office of high-priest (ܟܘܡܪܐ) to the gods. Why dost thou hate honour and love this disgrace? For although thou speakest unlawfully, nevertheless I am not able to turn aside from the emperor's laws. Sharbil said, As thou lookest that thou mayest not transgress the laws of the emperors, and if indeed thou do transgress, thou knowest what order they will give against thee, so I also look that I may not turn aside from the law of Him who said, 'Thou shalt not worship any image, nor any similitude,' and on this account I will not sacrifice to made idols. For sufficient is the period that I sacrificed to them when I was in ignorance. The judge said, Bring not upon thyself judgment in addition to that judgment in which thou already standest: it is sufficient for thee that thou hast said, 'I will not sacrifice.' Be not audacious and insult the gods by calling them made idols, whom even the emperors honour. Sharbil said, If, on behalf of the emperors who are far away, and are not near, nor aware of those who slight their commands, thou biddest me to sacrifice; why biddest thou me to sacrifice on behalf of idols who are present and are seen, but themselves see not? And by this thou hast declared before all thy Officials, that because 'they have mouths and they speak not,' thou art become an advocate on their behalf, which 'they who made them will be like to them; and every one who trusteth upon them,' like thee. The judge said, It was not for this purpose that thou wast called before me, that instead of the honour which is due, thou shouldest insult the emperors; yet draw near to the gods and sacrifice, and spare thyself, oh self-reviler.

Sharbil said, Why is it requisite that thou shouldest ask me many questions after that which I have said to thee—'I will not sacrifice,' and thou hast called me a self-reviler? Would indeed that from my childhood I had had this mind, and had thus reviled my own soul which was perishing. The judge said, (ܬܠܘ) Hang him up and tear his sides with combs. And when he was thus torn, he cried out and said, For Christ's sake, who has caused his light to shine secretly into the darkness of my mind.—And after he had thus spoken, the judge again commanded him to be torn with the combs, on his face.

Sharbil said, It is better that thou shouldest torture me *here* because I will not sacrifice, than that I should be condemned there for having sacrificed to the work of men's hands. The judge said, Let his body be bent backwards, and let straps be bound upon his hands and his feet, and when he has been bent backwards, let him be scourged upon his belly. And they scourged him in this manner according to the command of the judge. Then he ordered him to be taken up to the prison and cast into a dark pit. And the executioners and the Christians who came up with him from the church, carried him, because he was not able to walk upon his feet, on account of his being bent backwards; and he was in the prison many days.

But on the second of Ilul, on the third day of the week, the judge arose and went down to his judgment-hall by night, and all his Officials were with him, and he commanded the keeper of the prison, and they brought him before him, and the judge said to him, Thou hast been in the prison this length of time, what is thy determination touching those things about which thou hast been interrogated before me? art thou persuaded to minister to the gods according to thy former custom, agreeably to the edict of the emperors? Sharbil said, This has been my determination in the prison, that what I had begun before thee, the same will I complete even to the end: nor will I belie my word, for I will never again confess the idols, which I have renounced, nor will I renounce Christ the King, whom I have confessed. The judge said, Hang him up by his right hand, because he has withdrawn it from the gods, that he may not again offer incense with it, until (ܓ) his hand with which he ministered to the gods be disjointed, because he persists in that one saying of his. And while he was hanging by his hand they questioned him and said to him Wilt thou comply and sacrifice to the gods? But he was not able to return them an answer, on account of the dislocation of his arm Then the judge gave orders, and they loosed him and took him down. But he was not able to bring his arm up to his side until the executioners had pressed it and brought it up to his side.

The judge said, Put on incense, and go whither thou desirest, and no one shall compel thee to become high-priest again. But if thou wilt not *do so*, I will shew thee bitterer tortures than these. Sharbil said, Gods, which made not the heaven and earth, may they perish from under these heavens. But thou, menace not with words of threatening, but, instead of words, shew upon me the deeds of threats, so that I may not hear thee again make mention of the name of gods accursed. The judge said, Let him be burnt with the cautery of bitter fire between his eyes and upon his cheeks. And the executioners did so until the stench of the cautery rose in smoke in the midst of the judgment hall, but he would not sacrifice.

Sharbil said, Thou hast thyself heard from me what I said to thee; that thou art not aware of the smoke of the tribulation of the fire which is prepared for those who, like thee, confess idols made *by hands*, and deny the living God, after thy fashion. The judge said, Who taught thee to say all these things before me in this manner—a man who wast once a friend of the gods and an enemy of Christ? for lo, now thou art become his advocate. Sharbil said, Christ in whom I have confessed, he it is that taught me to speak thus, for he needeth not that I should be his advocate, because his mercies are eloquent advocates for guilty men such as I am, they also are availing to plead on my behalf, at that day on which the eternal sentences will be passed. The judge said, Let him be hanged up (ܬܠܐ), and let him be torn with combs upon his former wounds; let also salt and vinegar be rubbed into the wounds upon his sides. Then he said to him, Renounce not the gods in whom thou once confessedst. Sharbil said, Spare me again from saying that there be gods, and powers, and fates, and nativities: but I confess one God who made the heaven and earth, and the seas, and every thing that therein is; and the Son, who of him is Christ the King. The judge said, It is not about this thou art interrogated before me, as to what is the belief of the Christians, in which thou hast confessed, but about that which I spake to thee, that thou shouldest not renounce those gods to whom thou wast made high-priest.

Sharbil said, Where is thy wisdom, and that of the emperors in whom thou pridest thyself? because ye worship the work of the hands of artificers and confess them, but the artificers themselves, who made these idols, ye insult by the burdens and the imposts which ye lay upon them. The artificer standeth up in thy presence to do honour to thee, and thou standest up before the artificer's work and doest honour to it, and bowest down to it. The judge said, Thou art not the person to inquire into these things, but art thyself to be strictly inquired into, as to the cause why thou hast renounced the gods, and refusest to offer incense to them like thy fellow high-priests. Sharbil said, Death on account of this is true life, for those who confess Christ the King; them also will he confess before his glorious Father. The judge said, Let candles of fire be brought, and let them be passed round about his face and the sides of his wounds: and they did so a great while.

Sharbil said, It is well that thou burnest me with this fire, in order that I may escape "from that fire which is not quenched, and the worm that dieth not," which is denounced against those [who worship things made instead of the Maker; for it is commanded to the Christians not to honour and worship any thing except Him who, in his own nature, is God most high (ܪܒ); for whatsoever is made and created ought to worship its maker, and is not to be worshipped together with its creator as thou supposest. The governor said, This is not what the emperors commanded me to inquire at thy hands, whether there be judgment and vengeance after the death of men; nor do I care about this, whether that which is made is to be honoured or not to be honoured: as for myself, what the emperors commanded me is this: that whosoever will not sacrifice to the gods, and offer incense to them, I should employ against him stripes, and combs, and keen edged swords.

Sharbil said, The kings of this world have perception of this world only, but the King of all kings, he hath revealed and shewn to us that there is another world, and a future judgment, in which a recompense will be made between those who have served God, and those who have not served him nor confessed him: for this reason I cry aloud, that I will not sacrifice to idols again, and I will not offer oblations to devils, and I will not honour evil spirits. The judge said, Let nails of iron be driven in between the eyes of the rebel, and let him go to that world which he is looking for, like one that dealeth in fables. And the executioners did so to him while the sound of the knocking of the nails was heard which were driven into him sharply.

Sharbil said, Thou hast driven in nails between my eyes, in the same manner as nails were driven into the hands of that glorious architect of the creation, and on account of this all natures of the creation trembled and quaked at that time. For these tortures, which, lo! thou art inflicting upon me are nothing with respect to that future judgment: for "they whose ways are always loose, because they have not the judgment of God before their eyes," on this account do not even confess that there is a God, neither will he confess them. The judge said, Thou sayest in words, (ܠܐ) that there is a judgment but I will shew to thee in deeds, that instead of that judgment which is to come, thou mayest tremble and be afraid of this which is before thine eyes, in which, behold, thou now standest, and mayest not multiply thy speech before me. Sharbil said, He who desireth to set God before his eyes in secret, God himself is at his right hand, I, also, am not afraid of thy threats of torture with which thou menacest me and triest to terrify me. The judge said, Let Christ, whom thou hast confessed, deliver thee from all the tortures which I have inflicted upon thee, and am about still to inflict on thee, and let him shew his deliverance towards thee openly, and save thee out of my hands. Sharbil said, The true deliverance of Christ towards me is this,—the secret power which he has bestowed upon me to endure whatsoever tortures thou hast inflicted upon me, and whatsoever thou hast settled in thy mind to inflict upon me further; and although thou hast well seen this, thou hast not been willing to believe my word. The judge said, Take him away from my presence, and let him be hanged upon a tree, turned with his head downwards, and let him be beaten with whips while he is hanging; and the executioners did so at the door of the judgment hall.

Then the governor commanded, and they brought him up before him and he said to him, Offer sacrifice to the gods, and perform the will of the emperors, thou high-priest, that hatest honour and lovest disgrace instead. Sharbil said, Why dost thou repeat thy words again, and command me to sacrifice, after having oftentimes heard from me that I will never sacrifice again? For it was not any force of the Christians that withheld me from sacrifices, but their truth; this has delivered me from the error of paganism. The judge said, Let him be thrown into a chest of iron like a murderer, and let him be scourged with thongs like a malefactor; and the executioners did so, until there remained not a sound place on him.

Sharbil said, These tortures, which thou supposest to be bitter, out of the midst of their bitterness (ܢܒܥ) spring up for me fountains of deliverance and mercies on the day of the eternal sentences. The governor said, Let small and round pieces of wood be placed between the fingers of his hands, and let them squeeze upon them bitterly; and they did so to him, until the blood came out [from under the nails] of his fingers.

Sharbil said, If thine eye be not yet satisfied with the tortures of my body, add still to its tortures whatsoever thou desirest The judge said, Let the fingers of his hands be loosed, and make him sit upon the ground, and bind his hands upon his knees, and place a piece of wood under his knees, and let it pass over the bands of his hands, and hang him up by his feet, when bent, with his head downwards; and let him be scourged with thongs; and they did so to him.

Sharbil said, Those who fight against God cannot be victorious, neither can they be condemned whose confidence is God; and for this

P

reason I say that "neither fire, nor sword, nor death, nor life, nor height, nor depth, are able to separate my heart from the love of God which is in our Lord Jesus Christ." The judge said, Make hot a ball of lead and brass, and place it under his armpits; and they did so, even till the top of his ribs became visible.

Sharbil said, These tortures of thine against me are too little for thy rage against me, unless thy rage were little and thy tortures were great. The judge said, Thou wilt not hurry me by these things which thou sayest, for I have room in my mind [to have patience with thee, and to see every evil, and hateful, and bitter thing that I shall exhibit in the torture of thy body, because thou wilt not comply and sacrifice to the gods whom thou once didst worship. Sharbil said, Those things which I have said and repeated before thee thou knowest not in thine unbelief, how] to hearken to them, how then supposest thou that thou knowest what things are in my mind? The judge said, The changes of words (ܫܘܚ) which thou utterest will not help thee, but will rather increase the afflictions upon thee manifold. Sharbil said, If one of the stories of one of thy gods be believed by thee, it is a shame to say how it is; for one had intercourse with boys, which is not right, and another fell in love with a virgin who took refuge in a tree, as your shameful stories tell. The judge said, This fellow, who formerly honoured the gods, but now is turned and has reviled them, and has not been afraid, who likewise has despised the edict of the emperors and not trembled, set him to stand upon a gridiron heated with fire; and the executioners did so, until the under part of his feet was burnt.

Sharbil said, If thy rage is excited at the mention of the abominable and indecent stories of thy gods, how much more oughtest thou to be ashamed of their acts? For, behold, were a man to do what one of thy gods doeth, and they were to bring him before thee, thou wouldest pass sentence of death upon him. The judge said, I will take vengeance upon thee to-day for thy blasphemy against the gods, and thine audacity in insulting even the emperors, nor will I leave thee alone until thou [offer incense to them, according to thy former custom.

Sharbil said, Stand therefore by thy threats and belie not thyself, but shew towards me in deeds that power which the emperors have given to thee, nor disgrace the emperors by thine own falsehood, and be also despised thyself] in the eyes of thine own Officials. The judge said, Thy blasphemy against the gods, and thine insolence towards the Emperors, have brought upon thee these tortures in which thou now standest; and if thou add further to thine insolence, afflictions which are bitterer than these shall be further added upon thee. Sharbil said, Thou hast the authority as judge: do whatsoever thou wishest, and spare not. The judge said, He that hath not spared his own body from enduring these tortures, how can he be afraid or be ashamed (ܒܗܬ) of obeying the command of the emperors? Sharbil said, Thou hast well said that I am not ashamed, because near at hand is he that justifieth me, and my whole mind is caught up in rapture towards him. For because I formerly offended him by the sacrifices of idols, I am trying to appease him to-day by the afflictions of my own person; for my mind is carried away captive to God who became man. The judge said, It is a captive, then, that I am interrogating, and a madman without sense, and, lo, I am talking with a dead man who is burnt already. Sharbil said, If thou believe that I am mad, question me no further, for it is a madman that is interrogated, for, rather, I am a dead man who is burnt, as thou hast said. The judge said, How can I count thee a dead man, for lo! thou hast just cried aloud, I will not offer sacrifice. Sharbil said, Even I know not how to return an answer to thee who hast called me a dead man, and comest back and interrogatest me like one that is alive. The judge said, Rightly I have called thee a dead man, because thy feet are burnt and thou carest not for it; and thy face is scorched and thou holdest thy peace; and nails are knocked in between thine eyes and thou takest no account of it; thy ribs also are seen between the wounds and thou revilest the emperors; and thy whole body is torn to pieces and wounded with stripes, and still thou blasphemest the gods; and because thou hatest thy body, lo! thou sayest whatsoever pleaseth thee. Sharbil said, If thou call me audacious because I have endured these things, for thyself who hast inflicted them upon me, it is right that thou shouldest be called a murderer in thy acts and a blasphemer in thy words. The judge said, Behold, thou hast insulted the emperors and the gods as well, and, lo! now thou insultest me too, in order that I may doom thee to death speedily; but instead of this which thou lookest for, I am ready to inflict upon thee yet bitter and severe tortures. Sharbil said, Thou knowest that which I have said to thee many times; Instead of denunciations and threats, exhibit upon me the act of the threat (ܠܗ) in order that thou mayest be known to do the will of the emperors. The judge said, Let him be torn with the combs upon his legs and the sides of his thighs; and the executioners did so until his blood ran down and fell upon the ground.

Sharbil said, Well is it that thou treatest me thus, because I have heard that one of the Doctors of the Church has said, "The scars, indeed, of my body—that I may come to the resurrection from the dead:" and I, who was an obscure dead man, lo! thy tortures raise me up again. The judge said, Let him be torn on his face; because he is not ashamed of the nails which are driven in between his eyes, and they tare him upon his cheeks, and between the nails which were driven into them.

Sharbil said, I will not obey the emperors, who command that to be worshipped and honoured which is not of its own nature, God; neither is God in its nature, but is the work of him that made it. The judge said, Like as the emperors worship, so also worship thou; and as the judges honour, so also honour thou.

Sharbil said, Even although I insult that which, being the work of men, has no sense or perception of any thing, yet insult not thou God, the maker of all things, and worship together with him that which is not of him, and is foreign to his nature. The judge said, Does your doctrine teach you thus, that you shall insult even the luminaries which give light to all sides of the earth? Sharbil said, Although it be not written for us that we shall insult them, still it is written for us that we should not worship them nor honour them, because they are things made: for this were a bitter evil that any thing made should be worshipped together with its maker; it is also an insult to the Maker that his creatures should be honoured together with himself. The judge said, Christ, whom thou confessest, was hanged on a tree; upon a tree also I will hang thee like thy master. And they hanged him upon a tree a long while.

Sharbil said, Christ, whom, lo! thou mockest, see (ܚܙܝ) how thy many gods stood not before him: for behold! they are despised and neglected and are made a laughing-stock and a jest to those who formerly bowed down to them. The judge said, How is it that thou renouncest the gods and confessest Christ, who was hanged on a tree? Sharbil said, The great glory of Christians is the cross of Christ; because through it was effected deliverance of salvation for all those who worship him, and through it they have acquired that clear sight, which keeps them from worshipping creatures together with the Creator. The governor said, Let thy glorying in the cross be kept within thy heart, and by thy hands let incense be offered to the gods. Sharbil said, Those who have obtained deliverance through the cross cannot any more worship the idols of error which are made *with hands;* for creature cannot worship creature, because it also ought to worship him who made it, and it is an insult to its maker that it should be worshipped together with its maker, as I have said before. The Governor said, Let thy books alone which have taught thee this, and do thou the commandment of the emperors, that thou die not by the emperors' law. Sharbil said, Is this the righteousness of the emperors in whom thou pridest thyself, that we should abandon the law of God and keep their laws? The governor said, The citation of the books in which thou believest, and from which thou hast quoted, these have placed thee in these afflictions; for if thou hadst offered incense to the gods, great would have been thine honour, like it formerly was, as being high-priest of the gods. Sharbil said, To thine infidel heart these things seem as if they were afflictions, but to the true heart affliction begetteth patience, and from the same is experience, and from experience is the hope of confession. The Governor said, Hang him up and tear him with combs upon his former wounds. And through the fury of the judge towards the executioners, his bowels ([illegible]) were near being seen; and in order that he might not die under the combs, and escape from still further tortures, he gave orders, and they took him down.

And when the judge saw that he was become silent, and was not able to return him any further answer, he refrained from him a little, until his soul returned unto him again. Sharbil said, Why hast thou spared me even this little time, and deprived me of the gain of martyrdom? The governor said, I have not spared thee at all, but I have refrained a little because thy silence made me cease awhile; and if I were able to exceed the laws of the emperors, I should be pleased to torture thee, in order that I may further take vengeance upon thee for thine insult towards the gods; for in despising me thou hast despised the gods, and I also have endured thee and tortured thee thus, like a man who so deserves it.

And the judge gave orders, and the curtain fell suddenly before him for a short time, and he made ready and settled the sentence which he was to give against him publicly. And suddenly the curtain was opened again, and the judge cried aloud and said, This Sharbil, who was formerly high-priest of the gods, but has turned, and this day renounced the gods, and cried aloud, I am a Christian, and has not been afraid of the gods, but has insulted them, and further, has had no fear of the emperors' edict, whom I commanded to offer sacrifice to the gods according to his former practice, and he has not offered sacrifice, but also *has greatly* insulted them: I have looked and seen that a man who doeth these things, it is right that no mercy should be shewed towards him, even were he to sacrifice: and it is not right that he should any longer behold his lords' sun, because he has slighted their laws; I have order that, according to the law of the emperors, a strap be cast into the mouth of this insulter, as if it were the mouth of a murderer, and that he should be taken outside the city of the Emperors with haste, like one who has insulted the lords of the city and the gods who preside over it: I give sentence that he be sawn with a saw of wood, and when (ܣ) he is near to die, then his head be taken off by the sword of the slayers.

And at the same moment the strap was suddenly thrust into his mouth, and the executioners seized him, made him run quickly upon his feet which had been burnt, and they took him outside the city, while the people were running after him. They also had stood and looked on at his trial all day, and wondered how he had had no suffering under his afflictions: for his countenance, which was cheerful, testified to the joy of his heart. And when the executioners arrived at the place where he was to receive the punishment of death, the people of the city also were with them to see if they did according as the judge had ordered, and to hear what Sharbil might say at that time, in order that they might inform the judge of the country.

And they gave him wine to drink, as is the custom for the murderers to drink, and he said to them, I will not drink, because I desire to feel the saw with which ye saw me, as well as the sword which ye pass over my neck; but instead of this wine which will not help me, grant me a little time to pray while ye stand. And he stood up and looked towards the east, and lifted up his voice and said, Forgive me, O Christ, all that I have sinned against thee, all by which I have made thee angry in the polluted sacrifices of dead idols; spare also all my life, and deliver me from the judgment to come, and be merciful to me as thou wast merciful to the thief, receive me also like those penitents who repent and are turned to thee, and thou art turned to them: and because I entered into thy vineyard at the eleventh hour, instead of judgment, deliver me from justice: let thy death for the sake of sinners, raise up my dead body on the day of thy coming.

And when the Sharirs of the city heard these things, they were angry against the executioners for having given him leave to pray. And while the nails were standing which had been driven in between his eyes, and his ribs were to be seen between the wounds of the combs; and from his burnt sides and (ܟܦܐ) the soles of his feet which were scorched and burnt, as well as from the wounds of his face, and his sides, and his thighs, and his legs, the blood was running and dropping down on the ground; they brought the carpenter's instruments, and thrust him into a wooden vice, and pressed it upon him until the bones of his joints creaked from the pressure: then they put upon him a saw of iron and began to saw him asunder: and when he was at the point to die, because the saw had nearly reached his mouth, they smote him with the sword and took off his head while he was still squeezed down in the vice.

And his sister Babai drew near and spread out her skirts and caught his blood, and she said to him, May my spirit be united with thy spirit near Christ whom thou hast known and believed. And the Sharirs of the city ran and went up and made known to the judge what things Sharbil had uttered in his prayer, and how his sister had caught his blood; and the judge commanded them to return and tell the executioners, that in the same place in which she had caught the blood of her brother, she also should receive the punishment of death. And the executioners laid hold upon her, and every one of them on his own part tortured her; and while she was carrying her brother's blood, her soul took its flight from her, and they mingled her blood with his. And when the executioners were entered into the city, the brethren and some young men ran and stole away the dead bodies of them both, and they laid them in the sepulchre of the father of Abshelama the bishop, on the fifth of Ilul, and on the sixth day of the week.

I wrote these acts on paper, I, Marinus, and Anatolus, the notaries; and we placed them in the archives of the city, where the charters of the kings are placed.

But this Barsamya, the bishop, converted Sharbil the high-priest. But he lived in the days of Binus, [Fabianus] bishop of Rome, in whose days the whole (ܣܒܝ) people of Rome assembled themselves together and cried out to the Prætor of their city, and said to him, There are too many strangers in this our city, and they cause the famine and the dearer price of every thing: we therefore intreat thee to order them to depart out of the city. And when he had given the order for them to depart out of the city, these strangers assembled themselves together and said to the Prætor, We beseech thee, my lord, command also that the bones of our dead may also go out with us; and he commanded them to take the bones of their dead, and to depart; and all the strangers assembled themselves together to take the bones of Simon Cephas and of Paul, the Apostles; and the people of Rome said to them, We will not give you the bones of the Apostles: and the strangers said to them, Learn and see that Simon, who is called Cephas, is of Bethsaida of Galilee, and Paul, the Apostle, is of Tarsus, a city of Cilicia. And when the people of Rome knew that the matter was so, then they let them alone. And when they took them up and were removing them from their places, at the same moment there was a great earthquake, and the walls of the city were near falling down, and the city near to be overthrown; and when the people of Rome beheld it, they turned and intreated the strangers to remain in their city, and that the bones might be laid in their places again. And when the bones of the Apostles were returned to their places, there was a calm, and the earthquakes ceased, and the winds became quiet, and the air became bright, and the whole city was cheerful. And when the Jews and Pagans saw, they ran and fell at the feet of Fabianus, the bishop of their city, while the Jews cried out, We confess Christ whom we crucified: He is the son of the living God, of whom the prophets spoke in their mysteries. And the Pagans also cried out and said to him, Wc renounce idols and graven images, because there is no use in them, (ܦܠ) and we believe in Jesus the King, the Son of God, who is come and is about to come again; and if there were any other doctrines in Rome and in the whole of Italy, they also renounced their doctrines, like as the Pagans had renounced, and confessed the Gospel of the Apostles, which was preached in the Church.

HERE END THE ACTS OF SHARBIL THE CONFESSOR.

MARTYRDOM OF BARSAMYA, THE BISHOP OF THE BLESSED CITY EDESSA.

In the year four hundred and sixteen of the kingdom of the Greeks, which is the fifteenth year of the reign of the Autocrat, our lord, Trajan Cæsar, in the consulship of Commodus and Cyrillus, in the month Ilul, on the fifth day of the same, the day after Lysinas, the judge of the country, had heard Sharbil the high-priest; while the judge was sitting at his seat of judgment, the Sharirs of the city entered into his presence, and said to him, We give information before your lordship respecting Barsamya, the Guide of the Christians, that he went up to Sharbil, the high-priest, as he was standing and ministering before the gods, who are to be honoured, and sent and called him to him secretly: and he spake to him out of the books which he reads in the church of their place of assembly, and he repeated to him the faith of the Christians, and said to him, It is not right for thee to worship many gods, but rather one (ܚܕ) God only, and his son Jesus Christ: until he converted, and made him renounce the gods which he had formerly worshipped; and by the means of Sharbil himself many also have been converted, and are gone down to the church, and lo! this day they confess Christ; Avida also, and Nebo, and Barcalba, and Hafsai, honourable and chief persons of the city, have yielded to Sharbil in this; we, therefore, as being the Sharirs of the city, make this known before your lordship, in order that we may not subject ourselves to punishment, as offenders, because we had not made known before your lordship what things had been spoken in secret to Sharbil by Barsamya the Guide of the Church. Now, therefore, your lordship knoweth what is right to command respecting this same thing.

And in the same hour as the judge heard these things, he sent the Sharirs of the city and some of the Officials with them, to go down to the church and bring up Barsamya from the church. And they took him and brought him up to the judgment-hall of the judge; and many Christians went up with him, saying, We also will die together with Barsamya, because we also agree with him in the discipleship to which he has also converted Sharbil, and in whatever he has spoken to him, and in whatever he received from him and was persuaded by him, and was ready to die for the sake of what he heard from him. And the Sharirs of the city went in and told the judge:—Barsamya, as thy lordship gave orders, lo! he standeth at the door of the judgment-hall of thy authority; and honourable chief persons of the city, who have been converted as well as Sharbil, behold! they are standing by Barsamya and crying out, We all will die with Barsamya, who is our instructor and our guide!

And when the judge heard these things which the Sharirs of the city said to him, he commanded them to go out and write down (ܣܣ) the names of the men who were crying out, We will die with Barsamya. And when they went out to write down these men, they who so cried out were too many for them, and they were not able to write down their names, because they were too many for them; because the cry came to them from all sides, that they would die with Barsamya for Christ's sake. And when the tumult of the people became great, the Sharirs of the city turned back and went in to the judge, and said to him, We are not able to write down the names of the men who are crying aloud outside, because they are very many, and cannot be numbered. And the judge commanded that Barsamya should be taken up to the prison, in order that the people might be dispersed which was collected together about him, lest through the tumult of many people, there might be some trouble in the city. And when he went up to the prison those remained with him who had become disciples together with Sharbil.

And when many days were passed, the judge rose up in the morning and went down to his court of justice, in order that he might try Barsamya; and the judge gave orders, and they brought him from the prison; and he went up and stood before him; and the staff said, Behold, he standeth before your lordship. The judge said, Art thou Barsamya who hast been made Ruler and Guide of the people of the Christians, and hast converted Sharbil, who was great high-priest of the gods and worshipped them? Barsamya said, It is I who have done this, and I do not deny it: I am also ready to die for the sake of the truth of this. The judge said, How wast thou not afraid of the emperors' edict, that when the emperors give command that every one should offer sacrifice thou hast made Sharbil the high-priest, while he was standing and sacrificing to the gods, and offering them incense, to renounce that which he confessed, and to confess Christ whom he denied? (ܣܘ) Barsamya said, Inasmuch as I am become entirely a pastor of men, it was not for the sake of those only who are found, but also for the sake of those who have strayed from the fold of truth, who are made a prey for the wolves of paganism: and had I not instructed Sharbil, his blood would have been required at mine own hands, and had he not listened to me I should have been innocent of his blood. The judge said, But now that thou hast confessed that it was thou who madest Sharbil a disciple, at thine own hands will I require his death; and on this account it is right that thou shouldest be condemned before me rather than he, because through means of thee he has been put to death by the sad deaths of severe tortures, for having left the edict of the emperors and having obeyed thy words. Barsamya said, Not to my words was Sharbil converted, but to the word of God which he spake: "Thou shalt not bow down to images and the similitudes of men." And not I alone am content to die the death of Sharbil for his confession in Christ, but also all the Christians, children of the Church, likewise desire this, because they know that by this they will find their salvation before God. The judge said, Answer me not in this manner, like thy disciple Sharbil, lest thine own tortures be even worse than his: but promise that thou wilt sacrifice before the gods on his behalf. Barsamya said, Sharbil, who knew not God, I taught him to know him, but me, who know God from my youth, biddest thou me renounce God? God forbid that I should do this thing. The judge said, You have converted the whole creation to this teaching of Christ, and lo, they renounce the many gods whom the many worshipped. Pass on from this mind, lest I make those who are near to tremble while they look on at thee to-day, and those that are far off, who shall hear of the tortures of thy trials. Barsamya said, If God be the help (ܣܐ) of those who call upon him who is able to oppress them? or what is the power that can prevail against them? or thine own threats, what can they do to those who, before thou give order against them that they should die, have set their death before their eyes, and are expecting it every day. The judge said, Bring not the matter of Christ before my judgment-seat; but instead of this, obey the edict of the emperors, who command to offer sacrifice to the gods. Barsamya said, Even when we do not bring the matter of Christ before thee, Christ's passion is pourtrayed and fixed in those who worship Christ; and more than thou hearkenest to the commands of the emperors: we Christians hearken to Christ the King of kings. The judge said, Lo thou hast obeyed Christ and worshipped him up to-day; henceforth obey the emperors themselves, and worship the gods which the emperors worship. Barsamya said, How biddest thou me to renounce that in which I was born, when, lo, thou didst require it at the hand of Sharbil, and saidest to him, Why hast thou renounced the paganism in which thou wast born and confessed the Christian religion to which thou wast a stranger; for, behold, even before I came into thy presence thou hast given testimony beforehand, and said to Sharbil, The Christians, to whom thou art gone, renounce not that in which they were born, and in which they stand: abide, therefore, by thy word which thou hast spoken. The judge said, Let Barsamya be scourged, because he has rebelled against the edict of the emperors, and has caused also to rebel with him those who were obedient to the emperors.

And when he had been scourged of five he said to him, Reject not the emperors' edict, nor insult the gods of the emperors. Barsamya said, Thy mind is greatly blinded, oh Judge! and also that of the emperors who gave thee authority; neither are the things which are false perceived by you: nor do ye understand that the whole creation, (ܗܐ) behold, it has worshipped Christ; and to me, sayest thou to me, Worship him not, as if I alone worshipped him whom the angels above worship in the height. The judge said, And if ye have taught men to worship Christ, who is it that has persuaded those above that they should worship Christ? Barsamya said, Those above themselves have declared and taught those who are below about the living worship of Christ the King, which they pay to him and to his Father together with the Spirit of his godhead. The judge said, Let alone these things which are written for you, and which ye also teach to others, and comply with those things which the emperors have commanded, and reject not their laws, lest ye be rejected by means of the sword from the light of this honoured sun. Barsamya said, The light, which passeth away and abideth not, it is not that true light, but it is the similitude of that true light, whose rays darkness approacheth not, which is reserved and standeth fast for the true worshippers of Christ. The judge said, Speak not in my presence of any thing else, but of that about which I have asked thee, lest I cast thee out from life to death, because thou hast renounced this light which is seen, and confessest that which is not seen. Barsamya said, I have not the power to neglect that about which thou askest me, and to speak about what thou dost not question me. It is thou that spakest to me about the light of the sun, and I said before thee that there is a light in the height which is superior in its light to this of the sun which thou worshippest and honourest; for it will be required of thee touching this, why thou hast worshipped thy fellow-creature instead of God thy creator. The judge said, Insult not even the sun, the light of the creation, nor slight the emperors' commandment, and stand in contention against the lords of the country, who have the authority over it. Barsamya said, What help does the light (ܡܠܐ) of the sun afford to a blind man who cannot see it, for without the eyes of the body it is not possible for its rays to be seen; so that by this thou mayest know that it is the work of God, because it is not able to shew its light to the blind.

The judge said, After I have tortured thee, as thou deservest, then I will write against thee to the government what insult thou hast done to the gods, in that thou hast converted Sharbil the high-priest who honoured the gods, and that ye despise the laws of the emperors, and that ye make no account of the judges of the country, and ye are living in the dominions of the Romans like barbarians. Barsamya said, Thou dost not terrify me by these things which thou sayest. Although I be not near to the emperors to-day, still, behold, I am now standing before the authority which the emperors have given to thee, and am being tried, because I have said, I will renounce not God, to whom belong heaven and earth, nor his son Jesus Christ, the King of all the earth. The judge said, If thou be sure of this, that thou art standing before the authority of the Emperors and being tried, obey their commands, and rebel not against their laws, lest thou receive the punishment of death like rebels. Barsamya said, Even if those who rebel against the Emperors, when they righteously rebel, are condemned to death, as thou sayest; such as rebel against God, the King of kings, even the punishment of death by the sword is too little for them. The judge said, It was not that thou shouldest expound in my judgment-hall that thou camest in before me, because the trial in which thou standest is far removed from expounding and near to the punishment of death, for such as insult the Emperors and comply not with their laws. Barsamya said, Because God is not before your eyes, neither are ye willing to listen to the word of God: but carved images that have no sense, "which have a mouth and speak not," (ܚ) are reckoned by you as though they spake, because your intellect is blinded by the darkness of heathenism in which ye stand. The judge said, Let alone these things of which thou speakest, because they will not help thee at all; and worship the gods, before bitter combs and severe tortures come upon thee. Barsamya said, Do thou let alone these many questions with which, behold, thou interrogatest me, and give orders for the stripes and the combs with which thou threatenest me, for thy words will not help thee so much as thy inflictions help me. The judge said, Let Barsamya be hanged up and be torn with combs.

And at that moment letters came to him from Alusis [*Lusius*] the chief Proconsul, father of Emperors. And he gave command, and they took down Barsamya, and he was not torn with combs, and they took him outside the judgment hall. And the judge commanded that the nobles, and the chief persons, and the princes, and the honourable persons of the city, should come into his presence in order that he might hear what was the order which was issued by the Emperors, through the Proconsuls, who were the rulers of the countries of the dominion of the Romans. And it was found that the Emperors had written by the hand of the Proconsuls to the judges of the countries,—Since our Majesty gave orders that there should be a persecution against the people of the Christians, we have heard and learned from our Sharirs, which we have in the countries of the dominion of our Majesty, that the people of the Christians are men who avoid murder, and sorcery, and adultery, and theft, and bribery, and fraud, and those things for which even the laws of our Majesty require punishment from such as do them: we therefore, by the justice of our Rectitude, have given command, that on account of these things the persecution of the sword should cease from them, and that there shall be rest and quietness in all our dominions, they continuing to minister according to their custom, and that no man should hinder them. But it is not that we shew affection towards them, but towards their laws, which agree with the laws (ܕܒܐ) of our Majesty; and if any man hinder them after this our decree, that sword which is ordered by us to pass upon those who neglect our decree, the same have we ordered to pass upon those who slight this decree of our Clemency.

And when this decree of the Emperors' Clemency was read, the whole city rejoiced that there was quietness and rest for every man. And the judge gave orders, and they released Barsamya, that he might go down to his church. And the Christians went up in great numbers to the judgment hall, and a vast multitude of the people of the city, and they received Barsamya with great and exceeding honour, repeating psalms before him, according to their custom, with the women of the chiefs of the wise men, and they thronged upon him and saluted him, and they called him Persecuted Confessor, friend of Sharbil the

Martyr. And he said to them, Persecuted I am like yourselves, but from the tortures of Sharbil and his fellows I am far removed. And they said to him, We have heard from thee that a doctor of the church has said, "The will, according to what it is, so is it accepted." And when he was entered into the Church, he and all the people that were with him, he stood up and prayed, and blessed them and dismissed them to go to their own houses, rejoicing and praising God for the deliverance which he had wrought for them and for the church. And the day after Lysinas the judge of the country had set his hand to these Acts, he was dismissed from his authority.

But I, Zenophilus and Patrophilus, are the notaries who wrote these things, Diodorus and Euterpes, Sharirs of the city, bearing witness with us by setting to their hand, as the antient laws of the antient kings prescribe.

But this Barsamya, the Bishop of Edessa, who converted Sharbil, the highpriest of the same city, lived in the days of Fabianus, the Bishop (ܦܦܐ) of the city of Rome. And the hand of priesthood was received by this same Barsamya, from Abshelama, who was Bishop in Edessa; and Abshelama, the hand was received by him from Palut the former; and Palut, the hand was received by him from Serapion, Bishop of Antioch; and Serapion, the hand was received by him from Zephyrinus, Bishop of Rome; and Zephyrinus of Rome received the hand from Victor, of the same place of Rome; and Victor received the hand from Eleutherius; and Eleutherius received from Soter; and Soter received from Anicetus; and Anicetus received it from Dapius [*Pius*]; and Dapius received from Telesphorus; and Telesphorus received from Xystus; and Xystus received from Alexander; and Alexander received from Erastus; and Erastus received from Cletus; and Cletus received from Anus [*Linus*]; and Anus received from Simon Cephasi; and Simon Cephas received from our Lord, together with his fellow Apostles, on the first day of the week of the ascension of our Lord to his glorious Father, which is the fourth day of Heziran, which is the nineteenth year of the reign of Tiberius Cæsar, in the consulate of Rufus and Rubelinus, which year is the year three hundred and forty one: for in the year three hundred and nine was the manifestation of our Saviour in the world, according to the testimony which we have found in a correct volume of the Archives, which errs not at all in whatever it declares.

HERE ENDETH THE MARTYRDOM OF BARSAMYA, BISHOP OF EDESSA.

MARTYRDOM OF HABIB THE DEACON.

(ܥܛ) In the month Ab, of the year six hundred and twenty of the kingdom of Alexander of Macedon, in the consulate of Licinius and Constantine, which is the year in which he was born, in the rule of Julius and Barak, in the days of Cona, Bishop of Edessa, Licinius made a persecution against the church and all the people of the Christians, after that first persecution which the Emperor Diocletian had made. And the Emperor Licinius gave orders that there should be sacrifices and libations, and that the altars should be repaired in every place, that they should burn perfumes and frankincense before Jupiter. And when many were being persecuted they cried out of their own free will, We are Christians, and they were not afraid of the perseuction, because those who were persecuted were more numerous than those who persecuted them. But Habib, who was of the village Telzcha, and had been made a deacon, both went about to the churches in the villages secretly, and read the scriptures, and encouraged and strengthened many by his words, and admonished them to stand fast in the truth of their faith, and not to be afraid of the persecutors, and he gave them instructions. And when many were confirmed by his words, and received what he said affectionately, being cautioned not to renounce that position in which they stood, and when the Sharirs of the city, who had been appointed for this same purpose, had heard, they went in and made known to Lysanias the governor, that was in the city of Edessa, and said to him, That Habib, who is a deacon in the village Telzeha, goeth about, and ministers (ܡܫܡܫ) secretly in every place, and he withstandeth the Emperor's command, and is not afraid. When, therefore, the governor heard these things, he was filled with rage against Habib; and he made a report, and sent and made known to Licinius the Emperor all that Habib had done, both that he might learn and see what command would be given respecting him and those who would not sacrifice: for although an edict had been promulgated that every man should sacrifice, still it had not been ordered what was to be done to those who would not sacrifice; because they had heard that Constantine, in Gaul and Spain, was become Christian, and did not sacrifice. And Licinius the Emperor gave orders to Lysanias the governor, Whosoever thus dares to transgress our command, our Majesty has decreed, that he should be put to death by fire: and that the rest who do not comply and sacrifice, should be put to death by the sword.

And when this command came to the city of Edessa, Habib, the same on whose account the report had been made, was gone over to the country of the people of Zeugma, in order that he might also minister there secretly. And when the governor sent and inquired for him in his own village, and in all the surrounding country, and he could not be found, he commanded that all his family should be arrested, and the inhabitants of his village, and they arrested them and put them into irons, his mother and the rest of his family, and also some of the people of his village and they brought them to the city, and bound them in prison. And when Habib heard of this which had taken place, he considered in his mind, and meditated in his thoughts, It is expedient for me that I go and appear before the judge of the country, rather than that I should remain in secret, and others go up and be crowned on my account, and I should find myself in great shame. For what benefit will the name of Christian confer upon him who fleeth from the confession of Christianity. (ܗܐ) Behold, if he escape this, the death of nature is before him whithersoever he goeth, and he is not able to flee from it, because this is decreed against all the children of Adam.

Then Habib arose and went to Edessa secretly, having prepared his back for the stripes, and his sides for the tearing of the combs, and his body for the burning of fire. And he went alone to Theotecna, a veteran, who was the chief of the governor's band, and he said to him, I am Habib of Telzeha, whom ye are seeking. And Theotecna said to him, If it be that no man saw thee when thou camest to me, obey what I say to thee, and depart and go to the place where thou wast before, and be there at this time, and let no man know or be aware of this, that thou camest to me and spakest with me, and that I gave thee this advice; neither be thou at all anxious about thy family and the inhabitants of thy village, for no man will hurt them in any thing, but they will remain a few days in prison, and the governor will then dismiss them, because the Emperors have not ordered any thing bad or dreadful touching them: if, therefore, thou wilt not obey me in these things which I have said to thee, I am free of thy blood, because if it be that thou appear before the judge of the country, thou wilt not escape from death by fire, according to the command of the Emperors, which they have given respecting thee.

Habib said to Theotecna, I am not anxious about my family and the inhabitants of my village, but about my own salvation, lest it should be lost. Also I am much grieved about this, that I did not happen to be in my village on the day that the governor inquired for me, and behold many are thrown into irons on my account, and I have been suspected by him as a fugitive. Wherefore, if thou wilt not comply and take me up before the governor, I will go alone and make my appearance before him. And when Theotecna heard him speak thus to him, he laid hold upon him firmly, (ܒܗ) and delivered him up to his domestics, and they conducted him with him to the judgment hall of the governor. And Theotecna went in and made it known to the governor, and said to him, Habib of Telzeha, whom thy lordship was searching after, is come. And the governor said, Who is it that has brought him? and where did they find him? and what was he doing where he was? Theotecna said to him, He came hither of his own free will, and without the constraint of any one, for no one was aware of him.

And when the governor had heard this, he was embittered against him greatly, and spake thus. This fellow, who has so acted, has shewn great contempt towards me and has despised me, and has accounted me as no judge; even because he has so done, it is not right that any mercy be shewed towards him, neither that I should be in a hurry to pass sentence of death against him, according to the command issued against him by the Emperors; but it is right for me to have patience with him, in order that his tortures and bitter judgments may be the more increased, and through him I may terrify many from daring again to flee. And when many people were collected together and standing by him at the door of the judgment hall, some of them being his own Officials and others being the people of the city, there were some of them that said, Thou hast done badly in coming and shewing thyself to those who were searching for thee, without being compelled by the judge: and there were others again who said to him, Thou hast done well in coming and making thy appearance of thine own free will, rather than that the compulsion of the judge should bring thee: for now is thy confession in Christ known to be of thine own will, and not by the compulsion of men.

But these things, which the Sharirs of the city had heard from those who were speaking to him, while they were standing at the door of the judgment hall, and that also, which had been told to the Sharirs of the city, that he had gone secretly to Theotecna, and that he had not wished (ܨܒܐ) to denounce him, they made known to the judge, every thing that they had heard. And the judge was angry against those who had been saying to Habib, Wherefore didst thou come and shew thyself to the judge, without being compelled by the judge himself? And he said to Theotecna, It was not right for a man, who has been made the chief of his fellows, to act so deceitfully towards his own ruler, and frustrate the Emperors' edict, which they denounced against the rebel Habib, that he should be burned with fire. Theotecna said, I have not acted deceitfully towards my fellows, neither have I looked to frustrate the edict which the Emperors promulgated; for what am I before thy lordship, that I should have dared to do this thing? I strictly questioned him as to that which thy lordship also inquired at my hands, in order that I might know and see if it was of his own free will that he came hither, or whether the compulsion of thy lordship had brought him by the hand of others; and when I had heard from him that he came of his own will, I carefully brought him to the honourable door of the judgment hall of thy rectitude.

And the governor gave orders on a sudden, and they brought Habib into his presence. The band said, Behold he standeth before thy lordship. And he began to interrogate him thus, and said to him, How is thy name? and whence art thou? and what art thou? He said to him, My name is Habib, and I am from the village Telzeha, and I have been made a deacon. The governor said, Wherefore hast thou transgressed the edict of the Emperors, and dost minister in thine office, which is forbidden to thee by the Emperors, and art not willing to sacrifice to Jupiter, whom the Emperors worship? Habib said, We are Christians. We do not worship the works of men, who are nothing, neither are their works any thing; but we worship God who made (ܥܒܕ) the men themselves. The governor said, Stand not with that bold heart with which thou art come before me, and insult not Jupiter the great glory of the Emperors. Habib said, But Jupiter is this idol, the work of men: thou hast said well, that I insult him. But if the carving of him out of wood and fixing of him with nails proclaim aloud respecting him that he is a thing made, how sayest thou to me that I insult him, for lo, his insult is from himself and against himself. The governor said, By this very thing that thou art not willing to worship him, thou insultest him. Habib said, If, because I do not worship him, I insult him, how great an insult then has the carpenter inflicted on him, who carved him out with an axe of iron, and the smith, who struck him and fixed him up with nails. And when the governor heard that he spake thus, he commanded him to be scourged unsparingly. And when he had been scourged of five, he said to him, Wilt thou now obey the Emperors? but if thou wilt not obey, I will tear thee severely with combs, and I will torture thee with all kinds of torture, and then at last I will give orders against thee, that thou be burnt with fire.

Habib said, These threats, which, lo, thou art now threatening me with, are much less and smaller than those which I had already made up my mind to endure; therefore I came and made my appearance before thee. The judge said, Cast him into the iron cage of murderers, and let him be scourged as he deserves: and when he had been scourged they said to him, Offer sacrifice to the gods; and he cried aloud and said, Accursed are your idols, and so are they who, with you, worship them like you. And the governor gave orders, and they took him up to the prison, but they did not give him permission to speak with his own family, nor with the inhabitants of his village, according to the command of the judge. But that day was the Emperors' festival.

And on the second (ܒܠ) of Ilul, the governor gave orders, and they brought him from the prison, and he said to him, Renounce that in which thou standest, and obey the edict which the Emperors have promulgated. But if thou wilt not obey, I will make thee obey them by bitter tearings of combs. Habib said, I have not obeyed them, and I am also determined in my mind that I will not obey them, not even if thou condemn me with judgments which are also worse than those which the Emperors have decreed. The governor said, By the gods I swear, that unless thou offer sacrifice, I will not omit any severe and bitter torture that I will not inflict upon thee: and we shall see if Christ, whom thou worshippest, will deliver thee. Habib said, All those who worship Christ, are delivered by Christ, because they have not worshipped creatures together with the Creator of the creatures. The governor said, Let him be stretched out and be scourged with whips, until there remain not a place in his body, on which he has not been scourged. Habib said, These inflictions, which thou supposest to be bitter in their scourgings, of them are platted crowns of victory for those who endure them. The governor said, How can ye call afflictions ease, and account the tortures of your bodies a crown of victory? Habib said, It pertaineth not to thee to ask me concerning these things, because thine unbelief is not worthy to hear the persuasion of these things. That I will not sacrifice, I have already said, and still say. The governor said, Because thou deservest these judgments, thou art set in them. I will put out those eyes of thine, which look upon this Jupiter, and are not afraid of him; and I will stop thine ears, which hear the laws of the Emperors, and are not terrified. Habib said, God, whom thou deniest here, hath another world (ܦ), but there thou wilt confess him with scourgings, after thou hast further denied him. The governor said, Let that world alone about which thou hast spoken, and attend now to this trial in which, behold, thou standest, for there is no one who is able to deliver thee from it, unless the gods deliver thee if thou sacrifice to them. Habib said, Those who die for the sake of Christ's name, and worship not things made and creatures, will find their lives in the presence of God: and those who love the life of this present time more than that, their torment will be for ever.

And the governor gave order, and they hanged him up and tare him with combs, and as they were tearing him with the combs they pushed him about: and he was hanging a long time, until the shoulder-blades of his arms creaked. The governor said to him, Wilt thou comply even now, and place incense before this Jupiter. Habib said, Before these sufferings I would not comply with thee, and now that I have suffered, how thinkest thou that I should comply with thee, and lose thereby that which I have gained by them. The governor said, By judgments fiercer and bitterer than these I am prepared to make thee obey, according to the Emperor's edict, until thou do their pleasure. Habib said, Thou art judging me for not having obeyed the decree of the Emperors, when, behold, even thou, whom the Emperors have elevated and made thee a judge, hast transgressed their decree, in that thou hast not done to me, what the Emperors commanded thee. The governor said, Thou sayest thus, like a man who prefers an accusation, because I have had patience with thee. Habib said, If thou hadst not scourged me, and bound me, and torn me with combs, and put my feet into the stocks, it might have been supposed that thou hadst had patience with me: but if these things have intervened, where is thy patience towards me of which thou hast spoken? The governor said, These things which thou hast said will not help thee, because (ܦܟܐ) they are all of them against thee, and they will bring upon thee afflictions which are even bitterer than those which the Emperors have decreed against thee. Habib said, If I had not been aware that they will help me, I should not have spoken a word about them before thee. The Governor said, I will silence these words of thine, and at the same time appease the gods by thee for thy not having worshipped them, and I will satisfy the Emperors on account of thee, because thou hast rebelled against their decrees. Habib said, I am not afraid of the death with which thou threatenest me, for had I been afraid of it, I should not have gone about from house to house, and ministered: for its sake it was that I did so minister.

The governor said, How is it that thou worshippest and adorest a man, but art not willing to worship and adore this Jupiter? Habib said, A man I worship not, because it is written for me, "Cursed is every one that putteth his trust in man;" but God, who took upon him flesh and became man, I worship and glorify. The governor said, Do thou what the Emperors have commanded; and as to what is in thy mind, if thou be willing to let it alone, *well*, but if thou be not willing, then let it not alone. Habib said, Both these things cannot be, because falsehood is contrary to truth, nor is it possible for that to be taken away from my thoughts which is firmly fixed in my mind. The governor said, By bitterer and severer tortures, I will make thee put away from thy thoughts, that of which thou saidest, It is firmly fixed in my mind. Habib said, These inflictions respecting which thou supposest that by them it will be rooted up from my mind, by these it is that it groweth in the midst of my heart like a tree which beareth fruit. The governor saith, What help can stripes and tearing of combs give to this tree of thine? and more especially at the time that I order fire against it, to burn it unsparingly. Habib said, (ܦܕ) It is not to those things which thou lookest to, that I look, because I contemplate the things which are not seen, and on this account I do the will of God the maker *of all things*, and not that of a made idol, which cannot even perceive any thing whatever. The governor said, Because he thus denies the gods whom the Emperors worship, let additional tearing of combs be laid upon his former wounds; for in the multitude of questions which I have had the patience with him to ask him, he has forgotten his former tearings of combs. And while they were tearing him he cried aloud, and said, "The sufferings of this time are not equal to that glory which is about to be revealed in those who love Christ."

And when the governor saw that even under these afflictions he would not sacrifice, he said to him, Does your doctrine teach you thus, that you should hate your own bodies? Habib said, It is not that we hate our bodies, but in the scriptures it is written for us: "Whosoever will lose his life shall find it;" and another thing also is written for us, "that we should not give that which is holy to dogs, and that we should not cast pearls before swine." The governor said, I know that all which thou thus speakest is in order that my rage and the anger of my mind may be excited, and that I should give sentence of death against thee speedily. I will not therefore be hurried on to that which thou desirest, but I will have patience; not, indeed, for thy ease, but in order that the infliction of thy tortures may be increased, and that thou mayest see thy flesh falling off before thee from the combs which are passing over thy sides. Habib said, I also am looking to this, that thou shouldest multiply thy tortures upon me as thou hast said. The governor said, Comply with the desire of the Emperors, because they have power to do whatsoever they will. Habib said, It does not belong to men to do whatsoever they will, but to God, who has the power in heaven, and over all the inhabitants of the earth; (ܘܠܐ) nor is there any one that can rebuke him and say, What doest thou?

The governor said, Death by the sword is too little for this insolence of thine: I am therefore prepared to pass against thee a sentence of death, which is bitterer than that of the sword. Habib said, But I look for a death more lingering than that of the sword, which thou wilt decree against me at the time that thou wishest.

And afterwards the governor began to give the sentence of death against him; and he called out aloud before his Officials, while they were listening, and the nobles of the city also, This Habib, who has denied the gods, as ye also have heard from him, and has likewise insulted the Emperors, it is right that life also should be denied to him from under this honoured sun, and that he should no longer behold this luminary, the associate of gods; and were it not that it has been decreed by former Emperors that the corpses of murderers should be buried, it would be right that the body of this fellow should not be buried, because he has been so insolent. I give sentence therefore, that a strap be cast into his mouth as into the mouth of a murderer, and that he be burned by a slow lingering fire, in order that the torture of his death may be increased.

And he went out from the presence of the governor with the strap thrust into his mouth, and a multitude of the people of the city ran after him. And the Christians were rejoicing because he had not turned aside nor abandoned his position, and the Pagans were threatening him because he would not sacrifice. And they took him out by the western door of the arches over against the cemetery, which was built for Abshelama, Abgar's son.

But his mother was clad in white, and she went out with him. And when he was arrived at the place where they were going to burn him, he stood up and prayed, and all those who came with him, and he said, Oh King Christ, for thine is this world and thine is the world (ܕܐܬܐ) to come, behold, and see, that while I might have been able to flee from these afflictions, I did not flee, in order that I might not fall into the hands of thy justice: let therefore this fire, in which I am to be burned, be to me for a recompense before thee, so that I may be delivered from that fire which is not quenched. And receive thou my spirit into thy presence, through the spirit of thy Godhead, oh glorious Son of the adorable Father. And when he had prayed, he turned and blessed them, and they gave him the salutation as they wept, men and women, and they said to him, Pray for us in the presence of thy Lord, that he would cause peace for his people, and the renewal of his churches which are cast down.

And while Habib was standing they dug a place, and took him and set him in the midst of it, and they fixed up by him a stake. And they came to bind him to the stake, and he said to them, I will not stir from this place in which ye are going to burn me. And they brought faggots and set them in order, and placed them on all sides of him: and when the fire burnt up and the flames ascended fiercely they called out to him, Open thy mouth. And the moment he opened his mouth his soul mounted up; and they cried out, both men and women, with the voice of weeping. And they drew him and took him up out of the fire, and they threw over him fine linen and choice unguents and spices, and they seized upon some of the faggots for burning him, and the brethren carried him and some laics. And they wound him up and buried him by Guria and Shamuna the martyrs, in the same grave in which they were placed, on the hill which is called Baith Allah Cucla, repeating over him psalms and hymns: and they conducted his body, which was burnt, in an affectionate and honourable manner.

And even some Jews and Pagans took part with the Christian brethren in winding up and burying his body. And at the time when he was burned, and also at the time when they buried him, there was one spectacle of grief spread over those within and those without, and tears were running down (ܡܠܐ) from all eyes, while every one gave glory to God, because he had given his body the burning of fire for his name's sake.

But the day on which he was buried was the sixth day of the week, the second of the month Ilul; on the day that it was heard how Constantine the Great had begun to depart from the interior of Spain, in order to proceed to Rome, the city of Italy, that he might carry on the war against Licinius, who at this day has the dominion over the Eastern parts which pertain to the Romans; and, lo, the countries are in commotion on all sides, because no man knoweth which of them will be victorious and continue in the power of the empire. But the Notaries wrote down every thing that they had heard from the judge: and the Sharirs of the city wrote the rest of the things which were spoken outside the door of the judgment hall, and, as is the custom, they make known to the judge all that they heard and saw, and their sentences are recorded in their Acts.

But I, Theophilus, who had renounced the evil inheritance of my fathers, and made my confession in Christ, gave diligence and wrote a copy of these Acts of Habib, as I had also formerly written of Shamuna and Guria, his fellow martyrs; and inasmuch as he had felicitated them upon their death by the sword, he resembled them himself also in his being crowned by the burning of fire. Moreover I have written the year, and the month, and the day of their being crowned as martyrs, not indeed for the sake of those who saw the deed as I did, but in order that they who come after us might learn what was the time of these Martyrs, and what kind of men they were; and also from the Acts of the former Martyrs, who *lived* in the days of the Emperor Domitianus, and of the rest of the Emperors who also raised a persecution against the church, and likewise put many to death, by stripes and lacerations, and by bitter inflictions (ܩܘ), and by keen edged swords, and by burning fire, and by the terrible sea, and in the merciless mines. Both all these things, and things like them, they *suffered*, for the hope of the future reward.

Now the afflictions of these Martyrs, and of those whom I had heard of, opened the eyes of me, Theophilus, and enlightened my mind, and I confessed Christ, that he is the Son of God, and that he is God. And may the dust of these Martyrs' feet, which I received as I ran after them at the time of their departure and reception of their crown, procure me pardon for having denied Him, and may He confess me before those who worship him, because I have now confessed him.

And after the twenty-seven interrogatories, which the judge put to Habib, he gave against him sentence of death to be burned with fire.

HERE ENDETH THE MARTYRDOM OF HABIB THE DEACON.

ORATION ON HABIB THE MARTYR, COMPOSED BY MAR JACOB.

Habib the Martyr, clad in flames, hath called to me out of the fire, that also for him I should form an image of beauties among the glorious. Companion of the victorious, lo, he beckoneth to me out of the burning, that for his Lord's glory I should sing of him. In the midst of glowing coals stands the man, and, lo, he calleth to me to form his image, but the flame permits me not. His love is fervent, also warm his faith, his fire too burneth; and who is able to recount his love? But with that love which placed the martyr in fire, no man is able to describe his godly beauties (ܦܐܝ). For who could dare approach and see in the flame, whom he resembleth, and how he is to be represented with the glorious? Shall I form his image by the side of the Children of the Furnace? With Hananiah, shall I reckon Habib? I know not. Lo, they were not burned there; how then does he resemble them, for he was burned and the Children not? Which then more comely, Habib the martyr, or Azariah? The image is difficult for me: how to view it I know not. Lo, Mishael was not burned by the flame; but Habib was burned: then which more comely to him that looketh on? Who would dare to say this less lovely is than that, or not so comely this as that, to him who seeth him? Three in the fire, and the flame toucheth them not. But the one was burned. And how am I able to tell what is the Fourth's, who went down into the midst of the furnace, to form an image for Habib there, together with the Three? He gave to him a place in the fire, to him who was burned, that he might be instead of him the fourth with the victorious. If then, the beauties of the Three be glorious although they were not burned, how shall not this, who was burned, be mingled with the glorious? If a man have the power either to be burned or not be burned, he that was burned, more exalted is his beauty than that of the Three. But because the disposal is of the Lord, glorified is He to be where he rescues and where he delivers up. But the will also of the Three who were not burned, and of him who was burned, was one and the same, here and there. And had the Lord of the fire commanded it to burn them, burned had been the Three, so far as pertained to them; if, too, to it he had intimated not to burn that one, burned had he not been; nor was it of himself that he was rescued. It was of their own will to go into the fire when they went in; but that they were not burned, the Lord of the fire willed and ordered it. Therefore one equal beauty is that of him who was burned, and of him who was not burned, because the will was also equal.

Beloved martyr, exalted is thy beauty; high is thy degree; becoming too thy crown (ܟܠܝܠܐ); and thy story associated with that of the glorious! Choice gold art thou, the fire, too, hath tried thee, and thy beauty shineth bright. And, lo, into the King's crown art thou wrought, together with the victorious! Good labourer, who, in the doctrine of the Son of God, runneth his course like a prosperous man, on account of the beauty of his faith! Habib the martyr was a doctor of the truth; a preacher, too, whose mouth was filled with faith. Watchful he was and prompt, and with his doctrine encouraged by his faith the household of the house of God. Full of light he was, and contended against the darkness which covered the country from the paganism which had obscured it. The Gospel of the Son filled his mouth in the congregations; and as a leader he became to the villages at that time when he arrived. Zealous he was because he was anxious about the doctrine divine, that he might establish the party of the faith. At the time when blew the winds of the heathen he was a lamp, and blazed forth when they blew upon him; and was not quenched. Ardent was he, and full of his Lord's love, and careful for his sake, that he might speak of him without dismay.

The thorns of error sprang up in the place from paganism, and so far as he could he rooted them up by his diligence. He taught, admonished, and confirmed in faith the Christians who by persecutors were oppressed. Against the sword and fire contended he, with love hot as the flame, nor did he fear. Like a two-edged scimetar, keen was his faith, and against error did he contend. He became leaven in this country, which was sunken through the love of vanity's idols, that error had introduced. Like salt was he in savoury doctrine to this clime, which was become insipid through unbelief. A deacon was he, and filled the chief-priest's place, by preaching and by teaching of the truth. He was a good shepherd to the flock while he was superintendant; and his life he laid down for the flock while he tended it (ܦܠ). He drove away the wolf, and thrust back from it beasts of prey. The fissures he stopped up, and carried the lambs into their folds. He went out secretly and encouraged the congregations: he strengthened and admonished them, and made them to lie down. Armour of faith he forged, and put on them, that they might not be despised by paganism, which was rife. The flocks of the fold of the Son of God were being laid waste by persecutors, and he encouraged the lambs and ewes.

He was an advocate for the children of the house of faith. Them, too, he taught not to be alarmed by persecutors; them he taught to run to meet death, without being afraid either of sword or fire. In the doctrine of the Son of God he prospered, so that faith ran without being terrified. Then Error grew envious, furious, and maddened on account of him. Out after him she went to shed on the earth innocent blood. The Calumniator, who hates the race of man, laid snares for him, to rid the place of his society. The Hater of truth went out after him to put him to death, that his voice might cease from the teaching of the house of God. Error strove that Habib might die, because she hated him; and pain stimulated her, and she sought him to draw out his soul. His story, too, was agitated before the country's pagan judge; and the report of him reached the king: incited by great rage, and because the diadem was interwoven with paganism, he decreed death on Habib's account, because he was full of faith. And when the edict reached the judge, he armed himself with rage and fury; so with a mind thirsting for blood, and, like hunters, which throw nets for the young stag, they went out after Habib to hunt. But this man was a preacher of the faith, who, in the highway of the cross, had prospered. And by his doctrine his people's children to help, his labour had embraced the countries round. But when after him Error went out, she found him not;—not that he was fled, but was gone out to preach. And because the pagans' fury transgressed (ܟ) all right, his kindred and his mother they seized on his account.

Blessed art thou, oh woman, because thou art the martyr's mother; on his account they seized and bound thee wickedly. What seek they of thee, oh thou full of beauty? why did they search for thee? Behold, they seek thee, that thou mayest bring the martyr to be a sacrifice. Bring, bring to the place of offering thy sweet fruit, whose savour fragrant is, that it may incense be to the Deity. Graceful shoot, thy cluster bring whence it is, that its wine may become libation of sweet taste.

The lamb heard that they were seeking him to be a sacrifice, and walked and came rejoicing to the sacrificers. That others on his account oppressed were he heard, and his own pain in many's stead came to bear. The lot fell on him to be alone a sacrifice; and the fire that was to offer him up beheld at him as he came. Of many who were imprisoned on his account, not even one was seized to die, except himself alone. Worthy was he; and martyrdom was reserved for him; nor is man able to snatch the martyr's place. Therefore, of his own free-will, he came to be arrested by the judge and die for Jesus' sake. He heard that they were seeking him; and came to be arrested, while they sought for him. And he went in before the judge, with open countenance. Himself he hid not, nor wished to escape the judge; for he was full of light, and from the darkness fled not. No thief was he, nor murderer, nor robber, nor child of night, for in the day was all his race. To whom from his fold should the good shepherd flee, and leave his flock to be devoured by thieves? To whom the physician flee, who goes out wounds to heal, and cure souls by the blood of the Son of God? Openness of countenance and a large heart the man possessed; and to meet death marched on, rejoicing for Jesus' sake. He went in, and stood before the judge, and said to him, I am Habib, (ܚܒܝܒ) whom ye did seek: lo! here I stand. And the pagan shook, and wonder seized him, and he marvelled at him—at the man who neither feared sword nor fire. When he supposed that fleeing he would flee, he entered in and laughed at him. And the judge shook, because he him beheld courageous against death. A disciple was he of that Son of God, who said, Rise, come, let us go, for lo, he that betrayeth me is at hand. And to the crucifiers again he said, Whom seek ye? They say, Jesus. And he said to them, I am he. The Son of God, of his own free will, approached the cross; and to Him the martyr looked, and offered himself before the judge. On him the pagan looked, and was disturbed, and was embittered, and his rage arose, and in his fury questions he began to moot; and, as if he were a man who had shed on the ground blood of the slain, that holy man he questioned, nor was ashamed, threatening, and terrifying, and frightening him, and telling over sufferings which he had prepared on his account. But Habib, when questioned, feared not; ashamed he was not, nor was he frightened by his threats. Lifting up his voice, he confessed Jesus God's Son, that he his servant was, and was his priest, and minister. While the pagans' fury roared at him like a lion, he was not shaken to withhold his confession of the Son of God. Scourged he was, and greatly dear to him the scourges were, because a little of God's Son's stripes he bare. He put on bonds, and looked up to his Lord, whom also they had bound: his heart rejoiced, too, that he had now begun to go along the path of his sufferings. He was raised on the tree, and they tare him, but his soul was bright, because he was worthy that on him should come the agony of crucifixion's pains. He set his face to walk along the way of death; and what desired he to find in it but sufferings? The fire of sacrifice was betrothed to him, and to her he looked; but she to him sent combs and stripes and wounds that he might taste. While she was coming, sufferings to him she sent, that by their means he might prepared be (ܡܝܒ); so that she might not trouble him when they met. Sufferings purged him, so that when the flame proved him, no dross in his choice gold might then be found. And he endured all pains that fell upon him, that he might be experienced, and in the fire stand like one excellent. And he received with joy the sufferings he endured, because he knew that at the end of them he should find death. Neither of death was he afraid nor sufferings, because with crucifixion's wine his heart was drunk. His body, while dragged by persecutors, he disregarded; his limbs, too, while they bitterly were torn. Stripes on his loins, combs on his sides, upon his feet the stocks, fire, too, before him, still was he brave and faithful.

They mocked him, Lo, thou worshippest a man. But he replied, A man I worship not, but God, who took upon him flesh and became man, him worship I, because, together with his Father, he is God. The martyr Habib's faith was full of light, and by it was enlightened Edessa full of faith. The daughter of Abgar, whom Addæus to the cross betrothed, her light is in him, in him her truth, her faith also: of it her king is, her martyrs of it, her truth of it, the teachers of her faith are of it also. Abgar believed that Thou art God, the Son of God; and received a blessing for his faith's excellence. Sharbil the martyr, son of the Edessæans, likewise said, My heart is captive with God who became man. Habib the martyr, also at Edessa crowned, confessed the same, that He took upon him flesh and became man; that He is the Son of God, and God, and became man. Edessa learned from teachers of the truth: her king taught her the faith, her martyrs taught her, but to others, teachers of error, she would not obey. Habib the martyr, out of the midst of fire, in Edessa's ear thus cried, Man I worship not; for God, (ܗܘ) who took a body and became man, him I worship, confessed the martyr, with uplifted voice. From confessors, lacerated, burnt, uplifted, slain, and from a righteous king, Edessa learned the faith, and knows our Lord, that He is even God, the Son of God: she also learned and believed that He took flesh and became man. Nor learned she from common scribes the faith: her king taught her, her martyrs taught her, and she believed them: and if she ever be accused of worshipping man, she shews her martyrs who died to prove, That He is God. Man, indeed, I worship not, Habib said, for it is written, "Cursed is he that putteth his trust in man." Because He is God I worship him, and honour him, nor on his account will I renounce his faith. This truth Edessa from her youth maintained, nor, daughter of the poor, in her old age, changed she it. Her righteous king to her became a scribe, and of him she learned about our Lrod, that He is the son of God, and God. Addæus, who brought the bridegroom's ring and placed it on her hand, betrothed her thus to the Son of God, his only Son. Sharbil, the priest, who tried and proved all gods, died, as he said, for God's sake, who became man. Shamuna and Guria, for the sake of the only Son, stretched out their necks and died for him, because he is God; Habib the martyr, the congregations' teacher, preached of him, that He took upon him flesh and became man. For a man's sake the martyr would not have been burned in fire, but burned he was for God's sake, who became man. And witness Edessa is that, in the fire, he thus confessed; and from the confession of a martyr that was burned who will flee? All hearts faith puts to silence and convicts, being full of light: nor stoopeth down to shades: him it condemneth who maligns the Son, by saying, He is not God; him also that saith, He took not on him flesh, and became man. Faithful in truth upon the fire he stood, (ܓܕ) and became incense, whose perfume appeased the Son of God. In all afflictions, tortures, and sufferings, thus did he confess, and thus also the blessed *city* taught. And this truth Edessa held touching our Lord; both that He is God, and of Mary was made man. And him who denies his Godhead the bride hates, and condemns and despiseth him who speaks against his manhood; but Him in Godhead and in manhood she knows as one, the only Son, whose body is not separated from him. And thus to believe the daughter of the Parthians learned, thus she affirmed, and thus she teaches all who listen to her.

The heathen judge then issued his command that the martyr

should be taken out and burned in the fire which was reserved for him. Forthwith a strap was thrust into hi mouth, as though he were a murderer, while in his heart was kept his confession with God: and him they seized, and from the judgment hall he went out with joy, because the hour was near that his faith's crown should come. And crowds of men with him went out, to bear him company; nor looked they on him carried forth as a dead man, but as a man who went to be a bridegroom through fire; and to receive the crown for him reserved of righteousness. They looked upon him as one who went to battle, and spears, and lances, and swords, surrounded him, but them he vanquished. Him they beheld go up, like a champion from the contest; and chaplets for his victory were brought to him by those who beheld. Him they beheld conquer dominions and powers which all made war on him: them he put to shame. In him rejoiced the whole Christian crowd, because he raised up the side of faith by sufferings which he endured. The Church with him went out, like a bride full of light; and her face was beaming at the beloved martyr joined to her.

His mother, then, for it was her son's marriage feast, in garments nobler than her wont, adorned herself; since sordid raiment suits not the banquet hall, all tastefully she clad herself in white. Here to the battle love came down to fight, within the mother's soul, the love of nature and the love of God (ܣܠ). She saw her son dragged to be thrown in flames; yet, having in her the Lord's love, she grieved not. The mother's yearning womb cried out on its fruit's behalf, but faith put it to silence, so that its tumult ceased. Nature yelled aloud over her severed limb, but the Lord's love made the soul drunken, so that it perceived it not. Nature loved, but in the strife the Lord's love prevailed within the mother's soul, so that she murmured not for her beloved. Instead of pain, her heart was all full of joy; and instead of mourning, she went out in gay array. When he went to be burned she followed him, and was elate, because the Lord's love nature's vanquished. And in white garments, as for a bridegroom, she made a feast, and the martyr's mother was cheerful on his behalf. Shamuni the second may we this blessed woman call; because, had seven been burned instead of one, she would have been content. One only had she, and gave him up to be the fire's food; and like that one, had she had seven she would have given them. Into the fire he was cast, and the flame surrounded him. His mother looked on, and grieved not at his being burned. There is another eye that looketh to the things not seen. Dear to her soul was he, therefore rejoiced she when he was burned. She looked for jewels of light, which are in martyrs' crowns; and glory reserved for them after their pains; and promised blessings which they inherit there through their afflictions; and the Son of God, who doth invest their limbs in robes of light; and to the varied beauties of that kingdom which will not perish; and that great door which is open for them to enter in to God. To these the martyr's mother looked while he was burned, so she rejoiced, exulted, and accompanied him in white. She looked upon him while the fire consumed his body; and grieved not because his crown was very great. Into the fire, upon the coals, the sweet root fell, and became incense, and cleansed the air from filth. With sacrifice's smoke the air was foul become, (ܥܘ) but, by this martyr's burning, it was purified. The sky was fetid from altar's sacrifices, but the martyr's sweet perfume mounted up, and it grew sweet. Then ceased the sacrifices, and in the congregations there was peace. The sword was sheathed, nor Christians any more laid waste. With Sharbil it began, with Habib ended in our land. From that time, and until now, not one has it slain: since he was burned, Constantine, the chief of victors, reigns;

and now the Cross the emperor's diadem surmounts, and is set upon his head. Idolatry's lofty horn is crushed, and since the martyr's burning, and until now, it has not pierced one. His smoke arose, and incense to the Deity became; and the air was purified, which paganism had infected. By his burning, too, the country was entirely cleansed. Blessed be he that gave to him a crown and glory, and a good name.

HERE ENDETH THE ORATION ON HABIB, COMPOSED BY MAR JACOB.

AN ORATION ON SHAMUNA AND GURIA, COMPOSED BY MAR JACOB.

SHAMUNA and Guria, martyrs who triumphed in their afflictions, have asked me, in love, to tell of their exploits. To faith's combatants the doctrine calleth me, to go and see their contests and their crowns. Children of the right hand, who with the left have battle done, to-day have called me to recount the wonder of their struggles: simple old men, who entered (ܐܟ) the battle like the mighty, and in the war of blood became richly victorious. These were their country's salt, and it was glad of it, for it restored its flavour, which was grown tasteless through unbelief. Lamps of gold, full of crucifixion's oil, were they, from which was lighted up all our quarter, then grown dark. Two lamps, whose lights were not put out when all the winds of every error blew. Good labourers, who laboured from the dawn of day in the blessed vineyard of God's house righteously. Walls of our country, which became for us a shelter from all robbers, in all the surrounding wars. Havens of peace, homes of refuge, too, for all who are distressed; and place to lay the head for every one in need of help. Two precious pearls, which were the ornament of my lord Abgar's bride, Aramæan's son. Doctors they were, who practised their doctrine in their blood; whose faith by their own sufferings was known. On their own bodies, in frequent wounds and stripes, the story of the Son of God they wrote. Their love they shewed not only by words of mouth, but by tortures, and the dislocations of their limbs. For love of God's Son's sake, their bodies they gave up, because the lover it behoves for his love himself to give. Fire and sword had proved their love, how firm and true it was. And more than silver tried in earth, their necks were beautiful. They looked to God, and because they saw his beauties high above, therefore their sufferings for his sake were able to despise. The Sun of righteousness above was risen within their hearts: by which they were enlightened, and with light the darkness chased. Vanity's idols, by error brought, they mocked at in the faith of the blessed Son of God, which is full of light. As a fire within their hearts the Lord's love became, nor could the thorns of unbelief at all withstand its force. Captive with God was bound their love, which will not ever change (ܫܢܐ): therefore they could despise the sword which was athirst for blood. With harmlessness and wisdom at the judgment-seat they stood, as they commandment had received from him who taught the truth. When they despised and gave up kindred and family, harmless they were, for possessions and wealth were lightly esteemed by them: yet prudent in the judgment-hall, with serpents' wisdom wise, cautiously they watched o'er the faith of God's house. When seized a serpent is and struck, his head he always guards; but yielding, giveth up his body to those who seize upon him. So long as guarded is his head, his life abideth in him; but if his head be smitten, then his life to destruction goes. The soul's head is the faith of men: if this then be preserved, in it also their salvation is kept unhurt: be the whole body bruised with strokes, so long as faith be kept, the soul still lives. But should the faith by unbelief be smitten and struck down, lost is the soul, and perisheth the salvation of men. Shamuna and Guria guarded the faith as men, that it might not be beaten down by persecutors, for well they knew if faith preserved be, safe from destruction soul and body are. Therefore they were careful of their faith, that it might not be smitten, for in it was their salvation hidden. Their bodies they gave up to blows and dislocation, and every torture, that their faith might not be smitten. Like as the serpent also hides his head from blows, so they their faith concealed in the centre of their hearts. Smitten was the body, endured stripes, and sufferings sustained, but yet within their hearts the faith was not smitten down. By speaking, the mouth to death gives up the soul, and like a sword, makes slaughter with the tongue; from which spring up both life and death for men. He that denieth dies; confesseth lives, possessing the power: denial is death, but in confession of the soul is life. Over both, the mouth hath power too, even like a judge. The word of mouth (ܡܠܐ) opens the door for death to enter in: it also bids salvation rise upon the sons of man. The Thief, too, by one word of faith, the kingdom of heaven gained, and Paradise inherited, of every blessing full. The wicked judges required the martyrs, sons of the right-hand, only by word of mouth to utter blasphemy; but like true men holding fast the faith, no word they gave which might serve unbelief.

Shamuna, beauty of our faith, who can suffice for thee? because too weak and feeble is my mouth to tell thy praise: thy truth thy beauty is, thy crown thy sufferings, thy wealth thy stripes: and by thy blows illustrious the glory of thy combat. Proud of thee our country is, as of a treasure full of gold; for thou to us art riches, and an envied treasure not to be stolen.

Guria, martyr, mighty champion of our faith, who, to recount thy godly beauties is sufficient? Lo, tortures on thy body are like beryl set, and on thy neck the sword, like a chain of choice gold. Thy blood upon thy body a glorious splendid robe, and thy loins' scourging like raiment the sun cannot compare with. Adorned thou art and beautified by these, thy many sufferings; and glorious are thy beauties, from the wounds severe upon thee.

Shamuna, our riches, thou art richer than the wealthy, for lo, at thy door the wealthy stand that thou mayest make them sit. Small is thy village, thy country poor, yet who has granted thee, that lords of villages and towns should try to do thee pleasure? Lo, judges in their robes and garbs take from thy threshold dust, as if it were the medicine that would ensure them life. Rich is the cross, and addeth wealth to those who fall before it, but still its poverty rejects all the riches of the world.

Shamuna and Guria, sons of the poor, lo, at your doors bow down the rich, to gather up from you their own necessities. The Son of God in poverty and need shewed to the world that all its riches nothing be (ܦ). All fishermen, all poor, all weak, all those of little note, became victorious by his faith. One fisherman, whose village, was Baithsaida, him chief made He and steward of the twelve. One tentmaker, who before had been a persecutor, him took He and caused to become a chosen vessel of faith.

Shamuna and Guria, arose from villages not wealthy, and lo, in a mighty city became lords, at whose doors chiefs and judges stand, and from them ask compassion their need to satisfy. By confession of faith in God's Son, these blessed men uncounted wealth obtained. Poor He became, and made rich the poor; and lo, the whole creation, through his poverty, grows rich. Chosen martyrs! against error they waged war, and by confession of God's Son as brave men they stood. In went they, and before the judge they confessed Him, with open face, that he might them, as they had him, confess, before his Father. The war of pagans assailed them like a storm, but their pilot was the cross, and onward steered them. Required they were to sacrifice to idols without life, yet ceased they not from their confession of the Son of God. Blasts of idolatry blew full against their face, but firm were they as rocks against the raging storm. Like a swift whirlwind, error snatched at them; but because they were protected, it could not injure them. The wicked one set on his dogs to bark and bite at them, but having for a staff the cross, they drave them all to flight. And who sufficient is to tell their struggles, their sufferings, or their dislocated limbs? or who is able to pourtray their crowns, how they returned victorious from the fight? To judgment they went up, but of the judge thought not, nor careful were when questioned what to speak. The threatening judge spake much in threats, and of all tortures told, and (ܡܐ) suffering; that he might frighten them: His words he magnified in menaces and threats; that he by terror might compel them to offer sacrifice. His threats the combatants despised, his menaces, and doom, and all corporeal deaths. For insults they prepared themselves, for stripes and provocation, for blows, and to be dragged and burned, and for imprisonment; for bonds and every evil thing, for torture and all pains, being full of joy. They were not terrified, nor frightened, nor disturbed, nor did the tortures' violence bend them to sacrifice. Their body they despised, and counted as earth's dung, because they knew the more it suffered, its beauty would greater be. The more the judge, to frighten them, increased his menaces, him so much the more did they despise, nor fear his threats. To them told he how many tortures he had prepared for them, to him they told about Gehenna, which was reserved for him. By what he spake he tried to make them sacrifice; to him spake they of that dread judgment there. Truth is much wiser than the words of wisdom; but very odious, however adorned, a lie. Shamuna and Guria persisted in speaking truth, and still the judge made use of lying words. Therefore his threatening they feared not, for all his menaces failed against the truth. The world's life they contemned, despised, abandoned, and neglected it; nor did they wish to enter it again. From the tribunal they set their face to go to the promised place of life in the new world. They thought not of possessions, nor of houses, nor of the superfluities of this world full of evil. In the world of light with God was their heart bound, and to that same place set they their face to go. To the sword they looked, to come and be a bridge, to pass them over to God, in whom they hoped. This world they counted as a (ܡܛܠ) tabernacle, but that world yonder a city full of beauties. They hastened to depart hence by the sword to the place full of light and of blessings for the worthy. The judge commanded to hang them by their arms, and without mercy they bitterly stretched them out. A demon's fury breathed rage in the judge's heart, and embittered him to crush those faithful ones. Between the height and depth he stretched them out, that he might torture them. And they became a wonder to both sides, how much they suffered. Heaven was astonished and earth at these old men's frame, how great suffering it endured, nor begged for help from pain. Their feeble bodies were hung and dragged by their arms, yet there was silence deep, nor cry for help nor murmur. All those who saw their contests marvelled how their extended bodies the pains endured. Astonished, too, was Satan at their chaste frames, what weight of grief they bare without a groan. The angels, too, rejoiced at their patience, how it endured that fearful contest then. But combatants who waited for their crown, into their hearts entered no weariness. The judge, however, weary grew, and wondered; but these brave men by afflictions were not wearied. Them asked he, were they willing to sacrifice: the mouth from pain no utterance could give. And, so, their persecutors increased their pains until they left the word no place to speak. Silent was the mouth, under their limbs' afflictions, but like a hero, the will was vigorous with its own. Alas for persecutors! how are they cut off from righteousness; but children of light, how are they clad in faith? Speech they required when there was no place to speak, for the mouth's utterance was cut off by pain. Fast bound the body was and silent the mouth, nor could it give the word when questioned wickedly (ܡܠܐ). And what could the martyr do who had no strength to say, when asked, he would not sacrifice. Quite silent were these old men full of faith, nor were they able to speak out from pain; yet they were questioned: how then, if one speak not when questioned, does he assent to what is said? That these old men be not thought to assent, they show, by beckoning, the word too hard to speak: they moved their heads, and by a nod for speech disclosed the will of the new man within. Their heads hung down while in their pains they beckoned that they would not sacrifice, and all men knew their minds. While there was place for speech in them, they confessed with speech, but when this was taken away by pain, they spake by a nod. Faith with and without the voice they spake, so that both speaking and when silent they were true. Who would not wonder how narrow life's path is; how strait, likewise, to such as walk therein? Who will not marvel how to the watchful will and prompt, it is very broad and full of light for such as go therein? Around the way are ditches; it is also full of pits: and if one turn aside a little from it a pit receiveth him. Between the right and left there is but a nod: on Yes and No stands sin and righteousness. By a nod only these blessed men refused to sacrifice, and by a nod only the way led them to Eden. But had this same nod inclined and turned a little towards the depth, their way had been down to hell. Upwards they nodded, prepared upwards to go: and by that nod they rose and mixed with the heavenly ones. Between nod and nod was Paradise and hell: they beckoned dissent to sacrifice, and the kingdom's heirs became. Even silent for God's Son advocates they were, for faith consisteth not in many words. (ܡܙ) Confession full of voice their patience was, as though with open mouth, they beckoned faith's assent; and all knew what they said when silent. And the faith of God's house grew rich, increased; and error was ashamed, because two old men, that, while they even spake not, vanquished her: silent they were, and their own faith stood fast. And when troubled voices from the judge were heard, and the emperor's edicts dreadful were and fierce, and paganism had its face uncovered, its mouth, too, open, and its voice was high, yet the old men were quiet under pain; then was the edict null, and the judge's voice grew cold, and the martyrs' voiceless sign bare off the palm. Voices and tumult and sound of stripes on the left, but on the right great calm and suffering stood. And by one nod, which these old men upwards raised, faith's head was elevated, and error put to shame. Condemned were they who spake, and the silent had victory, for without voice they beckoned the word of faith.

When they by silence triumphed, they took them down, and bound them, threatening still to vanquish them. Prison for the martyrs, and a pit void of light; and yet by them esteemed as light interminable. No bread, no water, no light, yet them it pleased for the love's sake of the Son of God. The judge commanded to hang them by their legs with downward heads, by a sentence far from just. Hanged, with head downward, Shamuna was, and prayed; prayer innocent and strained clear from pain. Sweet fruit hung on the tree in that judgment hall; whose taste and fragrance made even the angels marvel. Oppressed his body was, but his faith was sound. Bound was his body, but his prayer was loose over his work: for even nothing can prayer impede, nor either sword or fire hinder it. His body was subverted, but his prayer abounds; and straight his way (ܪܗܛ) up thither to the angels' place. The more affliction on this choice martyr grew, the more confession from his lips was heard. For the keen sword the martyrs dearly longed: they sought it like a treasure full of wealth. A new work in the world God's Son has wrought, that dreadful death by many should be beloved. Never was it heard that men ran to meet the sword, excepting those whom Jesus enlisted by his cross. That death is bitter all men know, lo, from eternity. To martyrs alone, when slain, it is not bitter. At the keen sword they laughed when they saw it, and in it rejoiced, for it gained them their crowns. They let the body be smitten as something hated: nor, had they loved it, would have held it back from pain. The sword they looked for, and the sword out went and crowned them. Because for it they looked, it met them as they desired. By his crucifixion the Son of God slew death; and because death was slain the martyrs it distressed not. With a crushed serpent one playeth without fear; a coward, too, will drag at a dead lion. Our Lord crushed the great serpent by his cross, and by his passion the dread lion God's Son slew. Death bound He, and cast him down and trode upon him at hell's door; and all who wish may now draw near and mock him because he is slain. Shamuna and Guria, old men, mocked at death; especially at that lion by God's Son slain. That great serpent, which slew Adam among the trees, who that has not drunk of the cross's blood could seize? By his cross the Son of God the dragon crushed; and, lo, that bruised serpent now boys and old men mock at. Pierced is that lion by the lance of God's Son's side, and every one that wishes now tramples, despises, mocks him. The cause of all (ܟܠ) good things is the Son of God himself; Him, therefore, ought all mouths duly to celebrate. With blood which ran down from his wounds he did espouse the bride: and from the necks' of his bridegroom friends the spear demanded blood. The Lord of the feast hung nakedly on the cross, and cast his blood on every one who came to be a guest. Shamuna and Guria for his sake gave up their bodies to sufferings, and to torture, and to every kind of woe. Him they looked to while mocked at by wicked men, and so endured without murmur the mockery of themselves. By your deaths, oh ye blessed men, Edessa waxed rich, for well ye ornamented her with your crown and suffering. Ye are her beauty, her bulwark ye, her salt ye are likewise; her wealth, her store, her boast, and all her treasury. Ye are the stewards of her faith; for by your suffering the bride ye did array with beauty. Parthians' daughter, spouse of the cross, she boasts herself of you, for, lo, she was enlightened by your teaching. Her advocates are ye, teachers, who by silence conquered error, which lifted up on high its voice in unbelief. The old men of the Hebrews' daughter were sons of the evil one; lying witnesses who killed Naboth, being mad. Her Edessa surpassed by two excellent old men, who became witnesses of the Son of God, and like Naboth died. Two aged men were there, and here also two, and these and those were both alike called witnesses. Now, let us see which of these were witnesses of God's choice, which city also is beloved for its good old men's sake. Lo, the sons of the evil one, who did Naboth slay, are witnesses: and here again are witnesses Shamuna and Guria. Now let us see which witnesses, which old men, which city have open countenance with God. That harlot's witnesses were sons of the evil one, and lo! in their very names their shame is all pourtrayed. Edessa's aged witnesses righteous were and just, and resemble Naboth, who was slain for righteousness, (ܨܪ). They were not two false liars, like the sons of the evil one: nor does Edessa resemble Sion, which nailed Him on the cross. Her old men, lying like herself, dared wickedly to shed on the ground innocent blood. By the witnesses of this place, behold, the truth was told. Blessed be He who gave to us the treasure of their crowns.

HERE ENDETH THE ORATION ON GURIA AND SHAMUNA.

CANTICLE OF MAR JACOB THE DOCTOR, UPON EDESSA, WHEN SHE SENT TO OUR LORD TO COME TO HER.

EDESSA sent to Christ, by an epistle, to come to her and enlighten her. For all Gentiles she to Him made intercession that he would quit Sion which hated him, and come to the Gentiles who loved him.

She sent to him and besought him that he would enter into friendship with her. By her righteous king she made intercession to him, that he would leave the People and towards the Gentiles direct his burden.

From among all kings, one wise king the daughter of the Gentiles found: him she made ambassador, by him to her Lord she sent.—Come to me; in thee will I forget idols and all graven images.—

The harlot that was standing in the market-place heard of his fame from afar, as she was erring with idols, playing the girl with graven images. She loved, she desired him while he was far away, and begged him to admit her into his chamber.

Let the beloved bridegroom kiss me; with the kisses of his mouth shall I be blessed. I have heard of him from afar; may I see him from near; and may I place my lips upon his, and delight mine eyes with the sight of him.

Thy teats are better to me than wine, for the scent of thy sweetness is eternal life. I will nourish myself with thy milk; with thy scent will I make myself sweet from the smoke of idols, which, with its fetid odour, did make me stink.

Draw me after thee into thy fold (ܕܝܪܐ); because I am a sheep gone astray in the world. After thee I run, and thy voice do I seek, that the number a hundred by me may be made complete, by a lost one which is found.

Let Gabriel rejoice and be glad with all the angels' host in thee, the good shepherd, who the wounded sheep didst carry on thy shoulders, that the number a hundred might be preserved.

Thy love is better than wine, and thy affection than the countenance of the upright. In wine let us remember thee, how by the cup of thy blood thou hast obtained for us new life; and the upright praised thy love.

I am a church of the Gentiles, and I have loved the only Son, who has been sent. Because his betrothed hated him I have loved him; and through Abgar the Black have I entreated him to come and visit me.

I am black and comely: ye daughters of Sion, pure is your envy, because the son of the glorious one has espoused me to make me enter into his chamber. When I was odious he loved me, because he is able to make me clearer than water.

Black was I in sins, and comely am I become, because I have turned and repented: I have cast away in baptism all that odious colour, because the Saviour of all creatures has washed me clean in his pure blood.

HERE END THE EXTRACTS FROM THE CANTICLE ON EDESSA.

EXTRACTS FROM VARIOUS BOOKS, RELATING TO ABGAR THE KING AND ADDÆUS THE APOSTLE.

I.

Of the Blessed Addæus the Apostle. From his Doctrine which he delivered in Edessa before Abgar the King and the assembly of the city.

And when he entered the sepulchre, he rose again and came out of the sepulchre together with many; and those who were watching the sepulchre saw not how he came out of the sepulchre: and the Watchers from on high, they were the proclaimers and announcers of his resurrection. For, had he not willed he had not died, because he is the Lord of death, the exit; nor (ܐܦ) had it not pleased him, would he have put on the body, inasmuch as he is himself the creator of the body: for that will which caused him to stoop to the birth from the virgin, the same again humbled him to the suffering of death. *And after a few words*, For although his appearance was that of men, nevertheless his power, and his knowledge, and his authority, was that of God.

II.

From the Doctrine of Addæus the Apostle, which was spoken in the city Edessa.

Ye know that I said to you, that all the souls which go out of the bodies of men are not under death, but live and subsist; and there are for them mansions and abodes of rest. For the thought of the soul does not cease, nor the knowledge, because it is the image of the immortal God. For it is not devoid of perception like the body, which has no perception of its corruption which hath dominion over it. But recompense and reward it will not receive apart from its body, because the passion is not of itself alone, but of the body also in which it dwelt for a time. But those who believe not, because they knew not God, are without advantage, then they repent.

III

From the Epistle of Addæus the Apostle, which he spake in the city of Edessa.

Give heed, therefore, to this ministry which ye hold, and continue in it with fear and trembling, and minister every day. Minister ye not in it with neglectful habits, but with the discretion of faith; neither let the praises of Christ cease from your mouths, nor let weariness in the time of prayers approach you. Give heed to the verity which ye hold, and to the teaching (ܦܪ) of the truth which ye have received, and to the teaching of salvation which I commit to you. Because before the judgment seat of Christ will it be required of you, when he maketh reckoning with the pastors and superintendants, and when he taketh his money from the traders with the increase of the doctrines. For he is the King's Son, and goeth to receive a kingdom, and he will return, and come and make a resurrection of all men.

IV.

Addæus preached at Edessa and in Mesopotamia, but he was from Paneus, in the days of Abgar the king. And when he was among the Zophenians, Severus, the son of Abgar, sent and slew him at Agel Hasna, and a young man his disciple.

V.

71. And Narcissus. For they did not suffer the selection of the

Seventy-two to fail, as neither that of the Twelve. But he was of the Seventy-two: perhaps he was a disciple of Addæus the Apostle.

VI

From the exit of my Lady Mary from the world, and the birth and childhood of our Lord Jesus Christ.

Book the Second.

In the year three hundred and forty-five, in the month Tishrin the latter, my Lady Mary went out from her house, and went to the sepulchre of Christ, because she used to go every day and weep there. But the Jews, immediately after the death of Christ, seized the sepulchre and heaped great stones at the door of it. And they set men to watch over the sepulchre and Golgotha, and charged them, that if any one should go and pray by the sepulchre or by Golgotha, he should forthwith be put to death. And the Jews took away the cross of our Lord and those two other crosses, and that spear with which our Saviour was struck, and those nails which they had fixed in his hands (ܦܣܐ) and his feet, and those robes of mockery in which he had been clad, and they hid them, because they were afraid lest any one of the kings or the chief persons should come and inquire about the death of Christ.

And those that kept watch went in and told to the priests that Mary cometh evening and morning, and prayeth there. And there was a tumult in Jerusalem on account of my Lady Mary. And the priests went to the judge, and said to him, My lord, send and command Mary that she go not and pray at the sepulchre and at Golgotha. And while they were considering, lo, letters came from Abgar, the king of the city Edessa, to Sabina, the governor, who had been appointed by the Emperor Tiberius, and even as far as to the river Euphrates the governor Sabina had authority. And because the Apostle Addæus, one of the Seventy-two Apostles, was gone down and had built a church at Edessa, and had cured the disease which king Abgar had; for king Abgar loved Jesus Christ, and was always inquiring about him; and when Christ was put to death, and Abgar the king heard that the Jews had slain him on the cross, he was greatly grieved. And Abgar arose and rode until he came to the river Euphrates, because he desired to go up against Jerusalem and lay it waste. And when Abgar came and was arrived at the river Euphrates, he considered in his mind, that if I pass over, there will be enmity between me and the Emperor Tiberius. So Abgar wrote letters and sent to Sabina the governor, and Sabina sent them to Tiberius the Emperor. For after this manner wrote Abgar to the Emperor Tiberius.

From Abgar the king of the city Edessa. Much peace to thy Majesty, our Lord Tiberius. In order that thy Majesty might not be offended at me, I have not crossed the river Euphrates, for I wished to go up to Jerusalem and lay her waste, because she had slain Christ, a wise physician. But thou, inasmuch as thou art a great king, and hast authority over all the earth and over us, send and do me judgment upon the people of Jerusalem. For let thy majesty know that I desire that thou do me judgment upon those crucifiers.

And Sabina received the letters, and sent them to the Emperor Tiberius. And when he read them, the Emperor Tiberius was greatly incensed, and he desired to destroy and slay all the Jews. And the people of Jerusalem heard and were troubled. And the priests went to the governor, and said to him, My lord, send and command Mary that she go not and pray near the sepulchre and Golgotha. The judge said to the priests, Go ye, charge and caution her what ye desire.

VII.

From the Oration composed by my Lord Jacob, the Doctor, on the fall of Idols.

He turned to Edessa and found in it a great work, that the king was become a labourer for the church, and was building it. The Apostle Addæus stood in it like a builder, and king Abgar laid aside his diadem and builded with him. An Apostle and a king, when they agree the one with the other, what idol must not fall before them? Satan fled from the disciples to the land of Babylon: and the story of the crucifixion had gone before him to the Chaldæans. He saw, when they were laughing at the signs of the Zodiac, that he was nothing.

VIII.

From the Oration about the city of Antioch.

To Simon Rome, and to John fell Ephesus; to Thomas India, and to Addæus the country of the Assyrians. And when they were sent each one to the country which fell to him, they set their faces to convert the countries.

MARTYRIUM SANCTORUM CONFESSORUM SAMONÆ, GURIÆ ET ABIBI, EX SIMEONE METAPHRASTE.

AGEBATUR quidem sexcentesimus annus ab imperio Alexandri Macedonis: novem autem annos jam transegerat Diocletianus, sceptra tenens Romanorum: et sextum jam consultatum obtinebat Maximianus: Augarus autem Zoaræ filius, his temporibus erat Prætor, et Cognatus erat Episcopus Edessenorum, et magna excitabatur persecutio adversus ecclesias omnibus, qui erant sub ditione Romanorum. Et nomen quidem Christianorum, tanquam nefarium, probris appetebatur et exagitabatur: sacerdotes autem et monachi, propter firmam fidem et inexpugnabilem, miserabilibus tradebantur suppliciis, desiderioque et metu distrahebantur pii. Nam cum libere eloqui veritatem propter Christi vellent desiderium, refugiebant rursus metu suppliciorum. Nam ii quidem, qui se armabant adversus pietatem, studebant ut Christiani Christianismum abjurarent, Saturnoque et Rheæ se adjungerent: contra autem fideles, ut nihil esse ostenderent ea, quæ ab illis colebantur.

Illo ergo tempore Gurias et Samonas apud Judicem accusantur, quorum ille quidem ex Sarcigitua, hic autem ex vico Ganade erat ortus, ambo educati Edessæ, quam vocant Mesopotamiam, quod sit media inter Euphratem et Tigridem, et antea quidem ejus fama ad paucos pervaserat: post martyrum autem certamina erat omnium sermone celebrata. Atque sancti quidem nequaquam versabantur in civitate: sed procul ab ea remoti, ut qui vellent procul abesse ab ejus tumultibus, studebant esse Deo soli manifesti. Et Guriæ quidem continentia et charitas, erat bona et honesta possessio, et ex illius studio cognomen est ei impositum, adeo ut ex nomine eum non cognoveris, nisi prius dixeris continentem. Samonæ autem erat in Deum corpus et animus juvenilis et alacris, et cum Guria virtute contendebat. Ii ergo accusantur ad Judicem, quod non solum omnem finitimam Edessæ regionem sua doctrina confirmarent, et ut suæ adhærerent fidei, animum adderent: sed etiam efficerent, ut despicerent persecutores, et ut illorum impietatem omnino nihil facerent, docerent, convenienter ei, quod scriptum est: Nolite confidere in principibus, in filiis hominum, in quibus non est salus. Quibus Judex ad magnam accensus insaniam, jubet omnes, qui habent in honore religionem Christianam, sequentes doctrinam Guriæ et Samonæ, simul cum iis, qui eos ad id inducebant, comprehensos, in tuta includi custodia. Jussus autem ad effectum est deductus, et capta occasione, cum aliis quidem ex his plagas imposuisset, alios autem aliis tormentis subjecisset, et ut Imperatoris decreto parerent, suasisset: tanquam qui benigne et clementer se gereret, alios quidem sinit domum abire: sanctos autem ut primos, et qui pietatem aliis impertiissent, jussit adhuc affligi in carcere, qui ipsi quoque martyrii gaudebant societate. Audiebant enim in aliis provinciis multos idem, quod ipsi, certamen suscepisse: ex quibus crat Epiphanius et Petrus, et sacrosanctus Pamphilus cum multis aliis in Cæsarea Palestinæ, Timotheus Gazæ, in magna Alexandria Timotheus, Agapetus Thessalonicæ, Hesychius Nicomediæ, Philippus Adrianopoli, Melitinæ Petrus, Hermes, et ejus socii in confiniis Martyropolis: qui fuerunt etiam redimiti corona martyrii a Duce Heracliano cum aliis confessoribus, quorum est major numerus, quam ut possit ad nostram venire cognitionem. Sed redeundum est ad ea, de quibus prius dicebamus.

Antonius ergo Præses Edessæ, cum concessisset aliis, ut domum reverterentur, ei in altum erecto tribunali, jubet ad se adduci martyres: et cum fecissent, quod jussi fuerant apparitores, sanctis dicit Præses: Divinissimus noster Imperator hæc jubet, ut et a Christianismo deficiatis, quem sequimini, et imagini Jovis cultum divinum tribuatis, thus in ara sacrificantes. Ad hæc Samonas: Absit, inquit, ut vera fide relicta, propter quam speramus fore, ut vitam assequamur immortalem, manuum opus et figmentum colamus: Præses autem: Imperatoris, inquit, jussa omnino sunt implenda. Respondit Gurias: Puram et divinam nostram fidem nunquam inficiabimur, sequentes voluntatem hominum, in quos cadit interitus. Habemus enim patrem in cælis, cujus sequimur voluntatem, qui dicit: Qui me confessus fuerit coram hominibus, ego quoque eum confitebor coram patre meo, qui est in cælis. Qui me autem negaverit coram hominibus, ego quoque eum negabo coram patre meo, et Angelis ejus. Judex autem: Non vultis ergo, inquit, parere voluntati Imperatoris? Quomodo vero non fuerit absurdum, ea quidem, quæ visa fuerint hominibus, iisque qui non multum et quantum vos, possunt, reipsa ad effectum deduci: eorum autem, qui rerum potiuntur, jussa fieri irrita? Qui Regis regum, inquiunt sancti, faciunt voluntatem, carnis voluntatem respuunt ac rejiciunt. Deinde cum Præses minatus esset mortem, nisi parerent: Samonas, Non moriemur, inquit, ô Tyranne, si creatoris sequamur voluntatem: imo vero vivemus potius. Sed si ea secuti fuerimus, quæ jubet vester Imperator, scias, quod etiamsi tu nos interemeris, nos tamen male peribimus.

Postquam hæc audivit Præses, jubet Anovito commentariensi eos in tutissimam conjicere custodiam. Veritatem enim ægre fert animus, qui sua sponte est ad malum propensus: ut, qui ægrotant oculi, splendorem solis. Postquam autem ille fecit, quod ei fuerat imperatum, et martyres fuerunt in carcere, in quo etiam multi alii sancti prius inclusi fuerant a militibus, Imperator quidem Diocletianus, accersito Musonio Præside Antiochiæ, jubet eum venire Edessam, et Christianos, qui in ea erant inclusi, sive erant communis, sive sacrati ordinis, de sua interrogare religione, et eis finem dare convenientem. Cum is ergo venisset Edessam, et Samonam et Guriam primos curâsset sistendos ad tribunal judiciale, dicit eis: Domini hic est orbis terræ, hic est jussus, ut vos aræ Jovis vinum libetis, et thus imponatis. Sin minus, ego vos variis consumam suppliciis. Corpus enim flagris lacerabo, donec perveniam usque ad ipsa viscera: plumbum autem fervens non prius cessabo vestris axillis infundere, quam id pervaserit usque ad intestina. Deinde nunc quidem manibus, nunc vero pedibus suspendam, et efficiam, ut solvantur compages articulorum: novaque et inaudita excogitabo supplicia, quæ nec omnino quidem ferre poteritis.

Respondit autem Samonas: Vermem, cujus minæ sunt intentatæ iis, qui negant Dominum, et ignem, qui non extinguitur, magis, quam ea, quæ tu enumerâsti, tormenta formidamus. Ipse enim, cui cultum offerimus rationalem, primum quidem nos corroboratos adversus varia hæc tormenta, eripiet a tuis manibus. Deinde etiam in tuto collocabit, ubi est habitaculum omnium lætantium. Alioqui autem omnino adversus solum corpus armaris: Quid enim animam potueris lædere? Quæ quandiu quidem habitat in corpore, tormentis evadit præclarior: ea autem recedente, nullus est omnino sensus corpori. Quo magis enim homo noster externus corrumpitur, eo magis internus renovatur in dies: per patientiam enim hoc propositum certamen peragimus. Præses autem rursus veluti protestans, ut, si non parerent, puniret justius: Discedite ab errore, inquit, vobis consulo, et cedite jussui Imperatoris. Non poteritis enim ferre tormenta. Cui sanctus Gurias, Neque errori, ut tu dicis, servimus, respondit: nec Imperatoris jussui unquam paruerimus: absit ut tam pusilli animi simus, et tam amentes. Sumus enim illius discipuli, qui animam suam pro nobis posuit, divitias benignitatis et suam in nos ostendens charitatem. Resistemus ergo peccato usque ad mortem, neque quicquid acciderit, supplantabimur a machinis adversarii, quibus primus homo captus, decerpsit mortem per ligni inobedientiam: et Cain persuasus, fratris quidem sanguine manus polluit: gemere autem et tremere, invenit præmia peccati. Sed nos

Christi verbis mentem adhibentes, non timebimus eos, qui occidun corpus, animam autem non possunt occidere: illum potius timebimus, qui nostram animam et corpus potest perdere. Tyrannus autem, Non ut, inquit, vestras percurrentes scripturas, possitis refellere, quæ a nobis objiciuntur, ideo ira non moveor, et me præbeo patientem: sed ut jussum Imperatoris exequentes, cum pace domum revertamini.

Hæc oratio nihil flexit martyres, sed propius accedentes: Quid nostra, aiunt, refert, si irasceris, et es ad iram propensus, et tanquam nives pluis tormenta? Tunc enim nobis magis benefacies, clariorem reddens nostram probationem patientiæ, et concilians majores remunerationes. Hæc est enim summa nostræ spei, hunc incolatum, qui est ad tempus, relinquere, et migrare ad æternum. Habemus enim tabernaculum non manu factum in cælis, quod etiam sinum Abrahæ scriptura, propterea quod is esset familiaritate Deo conjunctus, solet vocare. Cum itaque vidisset Præses immutabilem eorum constantiam, statim mittens dicere, processit ad castigandum, et jubet Anuino Commentariensi utrunque una manu suspendi, et eis toto pondere corporis divulsis, adhuc eorum pedibus gravem suspendere lapidem, ad sensum acrioris doloris. Atque hoc quidem ita se habebat, et ab hora tertia usque ad octavam tale tormentum forti animo tolerabant, non vocem emittentes, non gemitum, non aliquid aliud ostendentes, quod esset pusilli et abjecti animi. Dixisses eos pati in alieno corpore, aut aliis patientibus, ipsos solum esse spectatores eorum, quæ fiebant.

Interim autem, dum ii penderent manibus, occupatus erat Præses in aliis audiendis. Deinde cum ab eis quievisset, jubet Commentariensem interrogare sanctos, an jussui, Imperatoris vellent parere, ut liberarentur a tormento: et cum ille quidem interrogaret, hi vero non possent, aut non vellent respondere, jubet eos includi in interiore custodia, in lacu tenebroso et nomine et re ipsa, et pedes usque ad diem sequentem affixos esse ligno. Die autem jam apparente, a ligni quidem vinculis pedes sunt relaxati: carceris autem aditus fuit obstructus, ut nec solaris quidem radius posset subire: edictum autem fuit custodibus, non frustum panis, nec parvam quidem guttam aquæ tres totos dies eis præbere. Quamobrem decætero tenebrosus carcer et longa inedia erat condemnatio martyribus. Cum autem adesset tertius dies circa principium mensis Augusti, apertus quidem fuit aditus carceris: illi autem in eo retenti sunt usque ad decimum Novembris. Deinde Judex eos curat sistendos pro suo tribunali. Et nec tantum, inquit, tempus vobis præbuit, ut mutati aliquod salutare caperetis consilium? Illi autem respondent: Quod nobis videtur, tibi jam sæpius ostendimus: tu autem fac ea, quæ tibi fuerunt imperata. Præses autem statim jubet Samonam altero pede in genu inclinari, et ferreum vinculum injici ejus genui. Quod cum factum esset, eum quidem suspendit præcipitem a pede, quem inclinaverat, alterum deorsum trahens pondere ferri, quod verbis non potest explicari: et sic athletam moliens discerpere. Quo quidem tempore cum coxæ acetabulum per vim sedem suam reliquisset, effectum est, ut Samonas claudicaret: Guriam autem, quod esset imbecillus et subpallidus, sinebat impunitum, non quod eum benignis adspexisset oculis, non quod esset misertus ejus imbecillitatis: sed ut qui, quod cum punire cuperet, potius pepercisset. Ne forte, aiebat, nobis imprudentibus consumeretur ante cruciatus.

Et jam erant quidem duæ horæ diei, ex quo suspensus erat Samonas: hora autem quinta jam aderat, et is adhuc pendebat sublime: et qui circumsistebant milites, movebantur misericordia, et hortabantur ut Imperatoris pareret imperio. Sed peccatorum misericordia caput sancti non pinguefecit. Ille enim etsi acerbe premeretur a tormento, ipsos ne ullo quidem dignabatur responso, sinens eos lugere, et se potius, non illum dignum censere misericordia. In cælum autem tollens oculos, precabatur Deum ex profundo cordis, et ei revocabat in memoriam miracula, quæ a seculo facta sunt: Domine Deus, dicens, sine quo nec passerculus quidem cadet in laqueum: qui Davidi dilatâsti cor in afflictionibus: Qui Prophetæ Danieli vim dedisti etiam contra leones: Qui pueros Abramiæos et Tiranni et flammæ victores effecisti: tu quoque nunc Domine adspice ad bellum, quod contra nos geritur, qui nostræ naturæ nôsti imbecillitatem. Conatur enim inimicus figmentum tuæ dexteræ avertere ab ea, quæ est apud te, gloria. Sed tu benignis tuis nos intuens oculis, conserva in nobis, qui extingui non potest, lucernam tuorum mandatorum: tua autem luce dirige nostras semitas, et dignare nos frui ea, quæ est in te, beatitudine: Quoniam es benedictus in sæcula sæculorum. Atque ille quidem Agonothetæ emittebat hanc gratiarum actionem: quidam autem scriba, qui aderat, literis mandavit quæ dicta sunt.

Jussit autem Præses Commentariensi eum solvere a supplicio. Ille vero cum sic fecisset, et portâsset cum iis, qui aderant, jam doloribus defessum et confectum, in priorem ferentes custodiam, deponunt juxta sanctum Guriam. Cum autem esset Novembris decimusquintus, noctu circiter galli cantum surrexit Iudex: eum vero precedebant lampades et satellites: et cum ad basilicam venisset, quæ dicitur, ubi erat judicium, cum magno fastu sedet pro tribunali: et accersit athletas Guriam et Samonam. Et hic quidem venit ambulans in medio duorum, et fultus utriusque manibus. Nam et premebat inedia, et gravabat senectus, bona spe solummodo eum refrigerante. Gurias autem ipse quoque portatus ducitur, ut qui nec posset omnino ingredi, utpote quod pes ei fuisset graviter a vinculo sauciatus. Ad quos defensor impietatis: Cum data, inquit, fuerit vobis potestas, de eo, quod est vobis conducibile, simul deliberâstis. Dicite ergo, an novi aliquid sit a vobis consideratum: et an priorum vos aliqua subierit pœnitentia: et parete jussui divinissimi. Sic enim vestris opibus et possessionibus, quinetiam hac suavissima quoque luce fruemini. Ad hæc martyres: Nemo, inquiunt, qui sapit, magnifecerit parum manere in iis, quæ fluunt. Sufficit enim nobis tempus, quod præcessit, ad usus eorum et adspectum: nec eorum aliquid desideramus. Quam autem mortem nunc nobis intentas, ea nos ad immortalia transmittit tabernacula, et efficiet, ut simus participes ejus, quæ est illic, beatitudinis.

Præses autem: Quæ a vobis, inquit, dicta sunt, nostras aures magna affecerunt tristitia. Ego autem paucis exponam id, quod videtur. Nam si aræ quidem thus imponitis, et imagini Jovis sacrificatis, recte se habuerit: et unusquisque vestrûm domum abibit. Sin vero adhuc pergitis Imperatoris jussui non parere, amputabuntur vobis omnino capita, hoc enim vult et statuit magnus Imperator. Ad quæ respondens generosissimus Samonas: Si nos, inquit, tanto affeceris beneficio, ut liberemur quidem ab iis, quæ hic sunt, molestiis: transmittamur autem ad eam, quæ est illic, beatitudinem, quantum in nobis quidem situm est, tibi reddetur merces ab eo, qui nostra dispensat ad id, quod est utile. Ad hæc cum respondisset Præses, ut videbatur, benignius, et dixisset: Ego toleranter hucusque tuli, longas illas sustinens orationes, ut mora temporis mutati, traduceremini ad id quod est utile, et supplicium mortis non subiretis. Qui morti, quæ est ad tempus, inquit, se tradunt propter Christum, clarum est fore, ut ii liberentur ab æterna. Qui enim mundo moriuntur, vivunt in Christo. Nam Petrus quoque, qui resplendet in choro Apostolorum, cruce fuit condemnatus et morte: et filius tonitrui Jacobus, ab Herode Agrippa fuit interfectus gladio. Quinetiam Stephanus quoque fuit appetitus lapidibus, qui primus percurrit stadium martyrii. Quid autem dixeris de Johanne? an ne ejus quidem admittes egregiam illam constantiam, et loquendi libertatem, quod mori maluerit, quam cubilis tacere impudicitiam: adultera vero ejus caput acceperit præmium saltationis?

Rursus autem Præses: Non ut vestros, quos dicitis, sanctos enumeretis, vos fero toleranter: sed ut mutato consilio, jussis cedentes

Imperatoris, ab acerbissima morte liberemini. Si enim sitis nimium audaces et insolentes, quid aliud, quam vos majora excipient supplicia, quibus oppressi, vel inviti facietis id, quod nos exigimus: quo tempore nec omnino quidem poteritis refugium habere ad misericordiam? Nam quod sit per vim, ne potest quidem provocare ad commiserationem: quomodo contra quod sponte sit, est dignum misericordia. Christi autem confessores et martyres dixerunt: Non opus est multis verbis. Ecce enim nos sumus tibi præsto ad omnia subeunda supplicia. Quod ergo tibi fuit imperatum, ne differas exequi. Nos enim Christi veri Dei sumus adoratores, et rursus dicimus: Cujus regni non erit finis. Qui etiam potest solus vicissim glorificare eos, qui ejus nomen glorificant. Interim autem dum hæc dicerentur a sanctis, Præses tulit in eos sententiam, ut mortem subirent gladio. Illi vero lætitia, quæ verbis non potest explicari, affecti: Te vere decet gloria et laudatio, qui es Deus universorum, clamabant: quod tibi placuerit, ut susceptum certamen perageremus, ut a te quoque immortalem splendorem assequamur.

Cum ergo vidisset Præses immutabilem eorum constantiam, et quemadmodum in animæ exultatione extremam accepissent sententiam, sanctis quidem, Deus, inquit, eorum, quæ fiunt, sit inspector, quod non per me volebam vos vitæ finem accipere; sed inexorabilis jussus me ad id cogit Imperatoris. Spiculatori autem jubet accipere martyres, et in curru imponere, et procul a civitate abducere cum militibus, et eis illic finem afferre gladio. Ille autem cum per portam Romanensem sanctos noctu eduxisset, cum altus sopor teneret cives, ad septentrionalem partem civitatis abducit in montem Bethelabicla. Illi vero cum fuissent in eo loco, et in lætitia cordis et magna animi constantia e vehiculo descendissent, a spiculatore et iis, qui sub eo erant, tempus ad orationem petiêrunt, et acceperunt. Perinde enim, acsi non sufficerent tormenta et sanguis ad intercedendum pro eis, propter summam modestiam adhuc etiam opus habebant precatione. Cum itaque oculos in cælum sustulissent, et intense precati essent, Deus et pater Domini nostri Jesu Christi, suscipe in pace spiritus nostros, postremo dixerunt. Samonas autem conversus ad spiculatorem, Exequere, inquit, id quod est tibi imperatum: cumque genu simul inclinasset cum Guria, eis amputantur capita decimoquinto Novembris. Atque hoc modo quidem se habuerunt res martyrum.

Cum autem tertium quoque quæreret numerus, ut in his glorificaretur Trinitas, invenit (ô optimam providentiam) tempore quidem postea Abibum, qui autem idem cum iis, qui præcesserant, iter ingredi constituerat, et illo ipso martyrii die fuit consummatus. Magnus ergo inter martyres Abibus, ex eadem quidem, ex qua illi patria, nempe ex Thelsæa vico erat ortus: sacro autem diaconatûs fuerat honoratus chrismate. Cum vero Licinius teneret sceptra imperii Romanorum, et Lysanias creatus fuisset Præses Edessæ, excitata rursus erat persecutio adversus Christianos, et Abibo universum imminebat periculum. Is enim obibat civitatem, divinas cunctos docens scripturas, et magno animo confirmans ad pietatem. Cum autem hæc venissent ad aures Lysaniæ, ea Licinio Imperatori ab eo significantur. Studebat enim, ut ipse ei committeret quæstionem habendam de Christianis, et maxime de Abibo. Neque enim fuerat ei prius commissa. Ille vero literis datis, jubet ut morte Abibum afficiat. Literis ergo redditis Lysaniæ, quæritur ubique Abibus. Ipse autem degebat in quadam parte civitatis, propter statum Ecclesiasticum: mater vero et quidam ex iis, qui ad eum genere attinebant, cum eo versabantur. Ille autem cum rem rescivisset, ne daret pœnas,quod martyrii deseruisset ordines, cuidam, qui erat ex primis cohortis (is autem vocabatur Theotecnus) seipsum indicat: et tandem, Quem quæritis, inquit, Abibum? ipse sum, inquit. Ille vero benigne eum intuens: Nemo, inquit, adhuc novit te ad nos venisse, ô homo. Abi ergo, et servare: nec sis solicitus de matre, nec de iis, qui genere ad te attinent. Nullus enim eos potuerit omnino afficere molestia. Et hæc quidem Theotecnus.

Abibus autem, cum tempus vocaret ad martyrium, nolebat pusillo et abjecto animo suffurari salutem. Ei itaque dicit: Non propter charam matrem, nec propter cognatos me reddo manifestum: sed adsum propter Christi confessionem. Ecce enim vel te nolente apparebo coram Præside, et meum Christum prædicabo coram principibus et regibus. Theotecnus itaque veritus, ne sua sponte veniret ad Præsidem, et ea de causa ei afferretur periculum, ut qui eum non fecisset manifestum, assumit Abibum, et eum adducit ad Præsidem: Hic ille est, inquit, qui quæritur Abibus. Cum autem Lysanias audiisset Abibum sua sponte adiisse ad certamina, arbitratus eam rem esse contemptus et audaciæ, ut qui parvifecisset austeritatem tribunalis, eum statim curat ducendum in judicium: conditionemque ab eo petit, et nomen, et patriam. Cum vero respondisset se quidem esse ortum e vico Thelsæa, significasset autem, se esse Christi ministrum, statim martyrem est criminatus Præses, quod non obtemperâsset jussis Imperatoris. Hujus autem rei apertum esse dicebat indicium quod Iovi thus non sacrificaret. Ad hæc, se quidem Christianum esse, dicebat Abibus, et non posse verum Deum relinquere, sacrificare autem inanimis et nullo sensu præditis operibus manuum. Præses vero, eum brachia vinctum funibus, jussit in ligno sublimem extolli, et ferreis unguibus lacerari. Erat autem suspensio longe violentior, quam laceratio. Veniebat enim in periculum, ne discerperetur, cum violenta extensione ei divellerentur brachia.

Interim dum is penderet sublimis, conversus est Præses ad blanditias, et fingebat se esse patientem. Minabatur autem etiam graviora, si non mutaret propositum: Ille autem: Nemo, inquit, me abducet a fide: neque persuadebit, ut adorem dæmones, etiamsi plura tormenta inferat et majora. Cum autem vellet scire Præses, quamnam ei utilitatem tormenta conciliarent, quæ corpus solum consumunt, Christi martyr Abibus: Non ad præsens usque tempus, inquit, nostra consistunt: nec ea solum sequimur, quæ cernuntur. Quod si tu quoque volueris adspicere ad spem et promissam nobis remunerationem, forte etiam dices cum Paulo: Non sunt condignæ passiones hujus temporis ad gloriam, quæ est revelanda in nobis. Cum autem Præses ea, quæ dicebantur, damnaret stultitiæ: et nunc quidem blandiens et subiens personam patientiæ, nunc vero minans et acerbam ei mortem intentans, neutri eorum eum videret cedere: Non tibi repentinum et totum simul vitæ finem afferam, sententiam ei pronunciavit: sed te lento igne paulatim liquefactum, efficiam immitem et implacabilem animam deponere. Dixit, et cum versus septentrionem extra civitatem collecta fuisset materia, ducebatur ad rogam, sequente quidem matre, sequentibus autem iis quoque, qui aliâs cognatione ad eum attinebant. Ille vero postquam esset precatus, et bene dixisset omnibus, et eis osculum dedisset in Domino, accensa autem esset materia ab iis, qui ad id serviebant, in ignem injicitur: et cum aperto ore flammam accepisset, apud eum, qui dederat, spiritum deposuit. Deinde cum ignis esset sedatus, qui ad eum attinebant, precioso linteo eum circundederunt, et unguentis unxerunt: cumque psalmos et hymnos, ut par erat, cecinissent, prope Samonam et Guriam eum deposuerunt, ad gloriam Patris et Filii et Spiritûs Sancti, quæ est divina Trinitas, et in quam non cadit divisio. Quam decet honor et adoratio nunc et semper, et in sæcula sæculorum, Amen. Talem quidem vitæ finem invenit martyr Abibus tempore Licinii, et talem cum sanctis nactus fuit depositionem, et sic piis attulit requiem a persecutionibus. Nam deinceps quidem Licinio fuit diminuta potentia: Constantino autem floruit dominatio, et creverunt ei sceptra Romanorum: qui primus inter Imperatores libere professus est pietatem, et Christianis concessit vivere ut Christianos. —*From SURIUS: De Probatis Sanctorum Vitis,* 4 *vol. fol. Colon. Agrip.* 1618. *Nov.* 15*th, p.* 339.

MOÏSE DE KHORÈNE

HISTOIRE D'ARMÉNIE.

LIVRE SECOND. CHAPITRE XXVI.

Règne d'Abgar.—L'Arménie est entierèment soumise au tribut des Romains.—Guerre avec les Troupes d'Hérode.—Le Fils de son Frère, Joseph, est tué.

Abgar, fils d'Archam, monte sur le trône la vingtième année d'Archavir, roi des Perses. Cet Abgar était appelé Avak-aïr (grand homme), à cause de sa grande mansuétude et de sa sagesse, et de plus, à cause de sa taille. Ne pouvant bien prononcer, les Grecs et les Syriens l'appelèrent Abgar. La deuxième année de son règne, toutes les contrées de l'Arménie deviennent tributaires des Romains. Ordre est donné par l'empereur Auguste, comme il est dit dans l'Évangile de saint Luc, de faire un dénombrement en tous lieux: pour cela envoyés en Arménie, des commissaires romains y apportèrent la statue de l'empereur Auguste, et l'érigèrent dans tous les temples. En ce même temps, vient au monde notre sauveur Jésus-Christ, fils de Dieu.

A la même époque il y a trouble entre Abgar et Hérode; car Hérode voulait que sa statue fût érigée auprès de la statue de César, dans les temples de l'Arménie: Abgar se refuse à cette prétention. D'ailleurs, Hérode ne cherchait qu'un prétexte pour fondre sur Abgar; il envoie une armée de Thraces et de Germains faire incursion dans le pays des Perses, avec ordre de passer sur les terres d'Abgar.

Mais Abgar loin de consentir, s'y oppose, disant que l'ordre de l'empereur est de faire passer les troupes en Perse par le désert. Hérode, indigné, et ne pouvant pas agir par lui-même, accablé de douleurs, en punition de sa coupable conduite envers le Christ, comme le rapporte Joseph, envoie son neveu, à qui il avait donné sa fille, mariée d'abord à Phéror, son frère. Le lieutenant d'Hérode, à la tête d'une armée considérable, se hâte d'arriver en Mésopotamie, rencontre Abgar au camp de la province Pouknan, périt dans le combat, et ses troupes sont mises en fuite. Bientôt après, Hérode meurt: Archélaüs, son fils, est établi par Auguste ethnarque de la Judée.

XXVII.

Fondation de la Ville D'Édesse. — Notice abrégée sur la race de notre Illuminateur.

Peu te temps après, Auguste meurt, et Tibère en sa place est empereur des Romains. Germanicus, devenu César, trainant à sa suite les princes du royaume d'Archavir et d'Abgar envoyés à Rome, triomphe, au sujet de leur guerre, dans laquelle ces princes avaient tué le neveu d'Hérode. Abgar, indigné, médite des projets de révolte, et se prépare aux combats. Il bâtit une ville sur le terrain occupé par l'armée arménienne d'observation, là où précédemment on gardait l'Euphrate contre les entreprises de Cassius; cette nouvelle ville est appelé Édesse. Abgar y transporta sa cour, qui était à Medzpine, tous ses dieux, Naboc, Bel, Patnicagh et Tarata, les livres des écoles attachées aux temples, et même les archives royales.

Après quoi Archavir étant mort, Ardachès, son fils, règne sur les Perses. Quoique ce ne soit pas l'ordre de l'histoire quant aux temps, ni même l'ordre selon lequel nous avons entrepris ces annales, mais comme il s'agit des descendans du roi Archavir, du sang même d'Ardachès, son fils, nous allons, pour faire honneur à ces princes, les placer, par anticipation de temps, près d'Ardachès, afin que le lecteur sache qu'ils sont bien de la même race, de la race du brave Archag; puis nous signalerons le temps de l'arrivée de leurs pères en Arménie, les Garénian et les Sourénian de qui descendent saint Grégoire et les Gamsarian, lorsque, suivant l'ordre des événemens, nous arriverons au règne du roi sous lequel ils parurent.

Abgar ne réussit pas dans ses projets de révolte; car, des troubles étant survenus entre ses parens du royaume de Perse, il partit à la tête d'une armée pour apaiser et faire cesser la discorde.

XXVIII.

Abgar vient en orient, maintient Ardachès sur le Trône de Perse.— Concilie ses frères, de qui descendent notre Illuminateur et ses parens.

Abgar, étant allé en orient, trouve sur le trône de Perse Ardachès, fils d'Archavir, et les frères d'Ardachès en lutte avec lui; car ce prince pensait à régner sur eux dans sa postérité, et eux ne voulaient pas y consentir. C'est pourquoi Ardachès les cerne de toutes parts, suspend sur leur tête le glaive de la mort; les déchiremens, la discorde étaient entre leurs troupes et leurs autres parens et alliés; car le roi Archavir avait trois fils et une fille: le premier de ces fils était le roi Ardachès lui-même, le second Garène, le troisième Sourène; leur sœur nommée Gochm, était femme du général de tous les Arik, général choisi par leur père Archavir.

Abgar persuade aux fils d'Archavir de faire la paix; il en fixe entr'eux les conditions et stipulations: Ardachès règnera avec sa postérité comme il méditait, et ses frères seront appelés Bahlav, du nom de leur ville et de leur vaste et fertile pays, de manière que leurs satrapies soient les premières, plus élevées en rang que toutes les satrapies de Perse, comme vraiment race de rois. Des traités, des sermens stipulent que, en cas d'extinction d'enfans mâles d'Ardachès, ses frerès arriveront au trône ; après la race régnante d'Ardachès ses frères sont distingués en trois races ainsi dénommées: la race de Garène Bahlav, la race de Sourène Bahlav, et la race de leur sœur, la race Asbahabied Bahlav, race ainsi appelée du nom de la seigneurie de son mari.

On dit saint Grégoire issu de la race Sourène Bahlav, et les Gamsarian de la race Garène Bahlav. Nous rapporterons dans la suite les circonstances de l'arrivée de ces personnages, signalant seulement ici leurs noms auprès d'Ardachès, afin que tu saches que ces grandes races sont bien le sang de Vagharchag, c'est-à-dire la postérité du grand Archag, frère de Vagharchag.

Tout étant ainsi réglé, Abgar prend avec lui la lettre des traités, et retourne dans ses états, non en parfaite santé, mais en proie à de vives douleurs.

XXIX.

Abgar revient d'orient.—Il prête secours à Arète, en guerre contre Hérode Tétrarque.

Quand Abgar fut revenu d'orient, il apprit que les Romains le soupçonnaient d'y être allé pour lever des troupes ; en conséquence, il fait parvenir aux commissaires des Romains la connaissance des causes de son voyage en Perse, ainsi que le traité conclu entre Ardachès et ses frères, mais on n'ajouta aucune croyance à ses rapports ; car il était chargé par ses ennemis Pilate, Hérode le Tétrarque, Lysanias et Philippe. Abgar s'étant rendu dans sa ville d'Édesse, se ligua avec Arète, roi de Pétra, et lui donna des troupes auxiliaires, sous la conduite de Khosran Ardzrouni, pour faire la guerre à Hérode. Hérode avait d'abord épousé la fille d'Arète, puis l'avait répudiée, pris ensuite Hérodiade du vivant même de son mari, circonstance pour la quelle il avait fait périr Jean-Baptiste. Ainsi il y eut guerre entre Hérode et Arète en raison de l'injure faite à la fille d'Arète. Vivement attaquées, les troupes d'Hérode furent défaites, grâce au secours des braves Arméniens; comme si, par la Providence divine, vengeance était tirée de la mort de Jean-Baptiste.

XXX.

Abgar envoie des Princes à Marinus. — Ces députés voient notre Sauveur le Christ.—Commencement de la Conversion d'Abgar.

A cette époque, fut élevé par l'empereur au commandement de la Phénicie, de la Palestine, de la Syrie et de la Mésopotamie, Marinus, fils de Storoge. Abgar lui envoya deux de ses principaux officiers, Mar-Ihap prince d'Aghtznik et Chamchacram, chef de la maison des Abahouni, ainsi qu'Anan, son confident. Les envoyés se rendent dans la ville de Petkoupine pour faire connaître à Marinus les causes du voyage d'Abgar en orient, en lui montrant le traité conclu entre Ardachès et ses frères, et, en même temps, pour invoquer l'appui de Marinus. Les députés trouvèrent à Eleuthéropole le gouverneur romain; celui-ci les reçoit avec amitié et distinction, et fait cette réponse à Abgar: "Ne crains rien pour cela de la part de l'empereur, pourvu que tu aies bien soin d'acquitter entièrement le tribut."

A leur retour, les députés arméniens allèrent à Jérusalem voir notre Sauveur, le Christ, attirés par le bruit de ses miracles. Devenus eux-mêmes témoins oculaires de ces prodiges, ils les rapportèrent à Abgar. Ce prince, saisi d'admiration, crut véritablement que Jésus était bien le fils de Dieu, et dit: "Ces prodiges ne sont pas d'un homme, mais d'un Dieu. Non, il n'est personne d'entre les hommes qui puisse ressusciter les morts, Dieu seul a ce pouvoir." Abgar éprouvait dans tout son corps des douleurs aiguës qu'il avait gagnées en Perse, plus de sept années auparavant; des hommes il n'avait reçu aucun remède à ses maux; Abgar fit porter une lettre de supplication à Jésus, il le conjurait de venir le guérir de ses douleurs. Voici cette lettre.

XXXI.

Lettre d'Abgar au Sauveur Jésus-Christ.

"Abgar fils d'Archam, prince de la terre, à Jésus, sauveur et bienfaiteur des hommes, qui as apparu dans la contrée de Jérusalem, salut:

"J'ai ouï parler de toi et des cures opérées par tes mains, sans remèdes, sans plantes; car, comme il est dit, tu fais que les aveugles voient, que les boiteux marchent, que les lépreux sont guéris; tu chasses les esprits immondes, tu guéris les malheureux affligés de maladies longues et invétérées; tu ressuscites même les morts. Comme j'ai ouï parler de tous ces prodiges opérés par toi, j'en ai conclu ou que tu es Dieu, descendu du ciel pour faire de si grandes choses, ou que tu es fils de Dieu, toi qui produis ces miracles. En conséquence je t'ai donc écrit, te priant de daigner venir vers moi et de me guérir des maux qui m'affligent. J'ai ouï dire aussi que les Juifs murmurent contre toi et veulent te livrer aux tourmens: j'ai une ville, petite mais agréable, elle peut nous suffire à tous deux."

Les messagers, porteurs de cette lettre, rencontrèrent Jésus à Jérusalem, fait confirmé par ces paroles de l'Évangile: "Quelques uns d'entre les païens vinrent trouver Jésus; mais ceux qui les entendirent, n'osant rapporter à Jésus ce qu'ils ont entendu, le disent à Philippe et à André qui redisent tout à leur maître." Le Sauveur n'accepta pas alors l'invitation qui lui était faite, mais il voulut bien honorer Abgar d'une réponse ainsi conçue :

XXXII.

Réponse à la Lettre d'Abgar, réponse que l'Apôtre Thomas écrivit à ce prince par ordre du Sauveur.

" Heureux celui qui croit en moi sans m'avoir vu ! Car il est écrit de moi : " Ceux que me voient, ne croiront point en moi, et ceux qui ne me voient point, croiront et vivront." Quant à ce que tu m'as écrit, de venir près de toi ; il me faut accomplir ici tout ce pourquoi j'ai été envoyé, et lorsque j'aurai tout accompli, je monterai vers celui qui m'a envoyé ; et quand je m'en irai, j'enverrai un de mes disciples, qui guérira tes maux, te donnera la vie à toi et à tous ceux qui sont avec toi."

Anan, courrier d'Abgar, lui apporta cette lettre, ainsi que le portrait du Sauveur, image qui se trouve encore aujourd'hui dans la ville d'Édesse.

XXXIII.

Prédication à Édesse de l'Apôtre Thadée.—Copie de Cinq lettres.

Après l'ascension de notre Sauveur, l'apôtre Thomas, l'un des douze, envoie un d'entre les soixante-dix disciples, Thadée, dans la ville d'Édesse, pour guérir Abgar et évangéliser, selon la parole du Seigneur. Thadée vient dans la maison de Tobie, prince juif, qu'on dit être de la race des Pacradouni. Tobie, ayant quitté Archam, n'abjura point, avec ses autres parens le judaïsme, mais en suivit les lois jusqu'au moment où il crut au Christ. Bientôt le nom de Thadée se répand dans toute la ville. Abgar, en apprenant son arrivée, dit: " C'est bien celui au sujet duquel Jésus m'a écrit;" et aussitôt Abgar manda l'apôtre. Lorsque Thadée entra, une apparition merveilleuse se peignit aux yeux d'Abgar sur le visage de l'apôtre; le roi s'étant levé de son trône, tomba la face contre terre et se prosterna devant Thadée. Ce spectacle surprit fort tous les princes assistans, car ils ignoraient le fait de la vision. " Es-tu vraiment, dit Abgar à Thadée, es-tu disciple de Jésus à jamais béni? es-tu celui qu'il m'a promis de m'envoyer, et peux-tu guérir mes maux?"—" Oui," répondit Thadée, " si tu crois en Jésus-Christ, fils de Dieu, les vœux de ton cœur seront exaucés."— " J'ai cru en Jésus," dit Abgar, " j'ai cru en son père; c'est pourquoi je voulais aller à la tête de mes troupes exterminer les Juifs qui ont crucifié Jésus, si je n'avais été empêché à cause de la puissance des Romains."

Dès lors Thadée se mit à évangéliser le roi et sa ville; posant les mains sur Abgar, il le guérit; il guérit aussi un podagre, Abdiou, prince de la ville, très honoré dans toute la maison du roi. Il guérit encore tous les malades et les infirmes de la ville, et tous crurent en Jésus-Christ. Abgar fut baptisé et toute la ville avec lui, et les temples des faux dieux furent fermés, et toutes les statues des idoles placées sur les autels et les colonnes furent cachées, voilées avec des roseaux. Abgar n'obligeait personne par la force d'embrasser la foi, mais de jour en jour le nombre des croyans se multipliait.

L'apôtre Thadée baptise un fabricant de coiffures de soie, appelé Attée, le consacre, l'établit à Édesse et le laisse au roi en sa place. Thadée, après avoir reçu des lettres patentes d'Abgar, qui veut que tous écoutent l'Évangile du Christ, s'en va trouver Sanadroug, fils de la sœur d'Abgar, que ce prince avait établi sur le pays et sur l'armée. Abgar se plut à écrire à l'empereur Tibère une lettre ainsi conçue:

Lettre d'Abgar à Tibère.

"Abgar, roi d'Arménie, à mon seigneur Tibère, empereur des Romains, salut:

"Je sais, que rien n'est ignoré de ta majesté; mais comme ton ami, je te ferai encore mieux connaître les faits par écrit. Les Juifs, qui habitent dans les cantons de la Palestine, ont crucifié Jésus. Jésus sans péché, Jésus après tant de bienfaits, tant de prodiges et de miracles accomplis en leur faveur, jusqu'à ressusciter les mort. Sache bien que ce n'est pas là les effets de la puissance d'un simple mortel, mais de Dieu. Pendant le temps qu'ils l'ont crucifié, le soleil s'obscurcit, la terre fut agitée, ébranlée; Jésus lui-même, trois jours après, ressuscita d'entre les morts et apparut à plusieurs. Aujourd'hui, en tous lieux, son nom seul, invoqué par ses disciples, produit les plus grands miracles: ce qui m'est arrivé à moi-même en est la preuve la plus évidente. Ton auguste majesté sait désormais ce qu'elle doit ordonner à l'égard du peuple juif, qui a commis ce forfait; elle sait si elle doit faire publier par tout l'univers l'ordre d'adorer le Christ comme vrai Dieu. Salut et santé."

Réponse de Tibère à la Lettre d'Abgar.

"Tibère, empereur des Romains, à Abgar, roi des Arméniens, salut:

"On a lu devant moi ta gracieuse lettre, et je veux que remercîment t'en soit fait de ma part. Quoique nous eussions déjà de plusieurs ouï raconter ces faits, Pilate nous a informé officiellement des miracles de Jésus. Il nous a certifié qu'après sa résurrection d'entre les morts, il a été reconnu par plusieurs pour être Dieu. En conséquence j'ai voulu, moi aussi, faire ce que tu proposes; mais comme c'est la coutume des Romains, de ne pas admettre un dieu seulement d'après l'ordre du souverain, tant que l'admission n'a pas été discutée, examinée en plein sénat, j'ai donc dû proposer l'affaire au sénat, et lé sénat l'a rejetée avec mépris, sans doute, parce qu'elle n'avait pas été examinée d'abord par lui. Mais nous avons donnée ordre que tous ceux à qui Jésus conviendra, le reçoivent parmi les dieux. Nous avons menacé de mort quiconque parlerait mal des chrétiens. Quant au peuple juif, qui a osé crucifier Jésus, lequel, comme je l'entends dire, loin de mériter la croix et la mort, était digne d'honneur, digne de l'adoration des hommes; lorsque je serai débarrassé de la guerre contre l'Hispanie révoltée, j'examinerai l'affaire, et je traiterai les Juifs comme ils le méritent."

Abgar écrit encore une lettre à Tibère.

"Abgar roi des Arméniens, à mon seigneur Tibère empereur des Romains, salut:

"J'ai reçu la lettre écrite de la part de ton auguste majesté, et j'ai applaudi aux ordres émanés de ta sagesse. Si tu te ne fâches pas contre moi, je dirai que la conduite du sénat est extrêmement ridicule et absurde; car, pour les sénateurs, c'est d'après l'examen et par le suffrage des hommes que peut être donnée la divinité. Ainsi donc, si Dieu ne convient point à l'homme, il ne peut être Dieu, puisqu'il faut que Dieu soit jugé, justifié par l'homme. Il paraîtra sans doute juste à mon seigneur et maître, d'envoyer un autre gouverneur à Jérusalem en place de Pilate, qui doit être ignominieusement chassé du poste puissant où tu l'avais mis, car il a fait la volonté des Juifs, il a crucifié le Christ injustement, sans ton ordre. Porte toi bien, je le désire."

Abgar ayant écrit cette lettre, en déposa copie, ainsi que copie des autres lettres, dans ses archives. Il écrivit aussi au jeune Nerseh, roi d'Assyrie, à Babylone.

Lettre d'Abgar à Nerseh.

"Abgar, roi des Arméniens, à mon fils Nerseh, salut :

"J'ai reçu ta lettre et tes hommages ; j'ai déchargé Béroze de ses fers, et lui ai remis ses offenses ; si cela te fait plaisir, donne lui le gouvernement de Ninive. Mais quant à ce que tu m'écris de t'envoyer ce médecin qui fait des miracles et prêche un autre Dieu supérieur au feu et à l'eau, afin que tu puisses le voir et l'entendre, je te dirai : Ce n'était point un médecin selon l'art des hommes, c'était un disciple du fils de Dieu, créateur du feu et de l'eau ; il a été destiné, envoyé aux contrées de l'Arménie. Mais un de ses principaux compagnons, nommé Simon, est envoyé dans les contrées de la Perse. Cherche le et tu l'ententendras, toi, ainsi que ton père Ardachès. Il guérira tous vos maux et vous montrera le chemin de la vie."

Abgar écrit aussi à Ardachès, roi des Perses, la lettre qui suit :

Lettre d'Abgar à Ardachès.

"Abgar, roi des Arméniens, à Ardachès, mon frère, roi des Perses, salut :

"Je sais que tu as ouï parler de Jésus-Christ, fils de Dieu, que les Juifs ont crucifié, de Jésus qui est ressuscité d'entre les morts, et a envoyé ses disciples par tout l'univers pour instruire les hommes. L'un de ses principaux disciples, nommé Simon, se trouve dans les états de ta majesté. Cherche le, tu le trouveras et il vous guérira de toutes vos maladies, et il vous montrera le chemin de la vie, et tu croiras à ses paroles, toi, tes frères et tous ceux qui t'obéissent volontairement.

Il m'est bien doux de penser que mes parens, selon la chair, seront aussi mes parens, mes amis, selon l'esprit."

Abgar n'avait pas encore reçu réponse à ces lettres, lorsqu'il meurt, ayant régné trente-huit ans.

XXXIV.

Martyre de nos Apôtres.

Après la mort d'Abgar, le royaume d'Arménie est divisé en deux: Ananoun, fils d'Abgar, règne à Édesse, et le fils de sa sœur, Sanadroug, en Arménie. Ce qui se passa de leur temps, a été décrit par d'autres antérieurement: l'arrivée de l'apôtre en Arménie, et la conversion de Sanadroug, et son apostasie par crainte de satrapes arméniens, et le martyre de l'apôtre et de ses compagnons au canton Chavarchan, appelé aujourd'hui Ardaz, et le pierre s'entrouvrant pour recevoir le corps de l'apôtre, et, l'enlèvement de ce corps par ses disciples, son inhumation dans la plaine, et le martyre de la fille du roi, de Santoukhd près du chemin, et l'apparition des reliques des deux saints, et leur translation dans les rocailles; toutes circonstances rapportées par d'autres, comme nous l'avons dit, long-temps avant nous: nous n'avons pas cru important de les répéter ici. De même aussi ce qui se rapporte au martyre d'Attée, disciple de l'apôtre, à Édesse martyre ordonné par le fils d'Abgar, se trouve rapporté par d'autres avant nous.

Le prince qui régna après la mort de son père, ne fut pas l'héritier des vertus paternelles; il ouvrit les temples des idoles, embrassa le culte des païens. Il envoie dire à Attée: "Fais moi une coiffure en toile tissée d'or, comme celles que tu faisais autrefois pour mon père." Il reçut cette réponse d'Attée: "Mes mains ne feront point de coiffure pour un prince indigne, qui n'adore pas le Christ Dieu vivant." Aussitôt, le roi d'ordonner à un de ses gens d'armes de couper les pieds à Attée. Le soldat étant allé et ayant vu le saint personnage assis dans la chaire doctorale, avec son glaive lui coupa les jambes, et aussitôt le saint rendit l'esprit. Nous mentionnons ce fait sommairement, comme un fait rapporté par d'autres depuis longtemps.

Vint ensuite en Arménie l'apôtre Barthélemi qui fut martyrisé chez nous, en la ville d'Arépan. Quant à Simon, envoyé en Perse, je ne puis pas rapporter avec certitude ce qu'il fait, ni où il souffre le martyre. On raconte qu'un Simon apôtre est martyrisé à Vériospore. Le fait est-il vrai, ou pourquoi la venue du saint en ce lieu ? je ne sais ; j'ai seulement signalé cette circonstance afin que tu saches bien que je n'épargne aucun soin, pour te rapporter tout ce qui est nécessaire.

XXXV-

Règne de Sanadroug.—Meurtre des Enfans d'Abgar. —La Princesse Hélène.

Sanadroug étant sur le trône, lève des troupes avec le secours des braves Pacradouni et Ardzrouni, qui l'ont élevé, et va faire la guerre aux enfans d'Abgar, pour se rendre maître de tout le royaume. Pendant que Sanadroug était occupé de ces affaires, comme par un effet de la Providence divine, vengeance est tirée de la mort d'Attée ; car une colonne de marbre que le fils d'Abgar faisait élever à Édesse, sur le comble de son palais, comme il était dessous pour ordonner le travail, échappa des mains des ouvriers, tomba sur lui et lui écrasa les pieds.

Aussitôt de la part des habitans de la ville vint à Sanadroug un message, pour lui demander un traité par lequel il s'engageât à ne pas les troubler dans l'exercice du christianisme, moyennant quoi ils livreront la ville et les trésors du roi. Sanadroug promit, mais dans la suite viola son serment ; Sanadroug passa au fil de l'épée tous les enfans de la maison d'Abgar, à l'exception des filles, qu'il retira de la ville pour les établir au canton de Hachdiank. Quant à la première des femmes d'Abgar, appelée Hélène, il l'envoya dans sa ville à Kharan, et lui laissa la souveraineté de toute la Mésopotamie, en souvenir des bienfaits qu'il avait reçus d'Abgar par le moyen d'Hélène.

Hélène, pieuse comme son mari Abgar, ne voulut pas habiter au milieu des idolâtres; elle s'en alla à Jérusalem du temps de Claude, durant la famine qu'avait prédite Agabus; elle acheta en Égypte, avec tous ses trésors, une immense quantité de blé qu'elle distribua aux indigens, fait dont témoigne Joseph. Le tombeau d'Hélène, tombeau vraiment remarquable, se voit encore aujourd'hui devant la porte de Jérusalem.

XXXVI.

Restauration de la Ville de Medzpine. — Dénomination de Sanadroug. — Sa Mort.

De tous les faits et gestes de Sanadroug, nous ne jugeons digne de souvenir que la construction de la ville de Medzpine; car cette ville ayant été ébranlée par un tremblement de terre, Sanadroug la démolit, la reconstruisit plus magnifique, la ceignit de doubles murailles et de remparts. Sanadroug fit élever au milieu de la ville sa statue tenant à la maine une seule pièce de monnaie, ce qui signifie: "Tous mes trésors ont été employés à construire la ville, et ne m'est plus resté que cette seule pièce de monnaie."

Mais pourquoi ce prince fut-il appelé Sanadroug? nous dirons: C'est que, voyageant pendant l'hiver en Arménie, la sœur d'Abgar, Otéc, fut assaillie par un tourbillon de neige dans les monts Gortouk; la tourmente a dispersé tout le monde, au point que le compagnon ne sait pas où a éte poussé son compagnon. La nourrice du prince,

Sanod, sœur de Piourad Pacradouni, femme de Khosran Ardzrouni, ayant pris le royal enfant, car Sanadroug était encore au berceau, le mit sur son sein et resta avec lui sous la neige trois jours et trois nuits. La fable s'est emparée de ce fait; elle raconte qu'un animal, espèce nouvelle, merveilleux, d'une grande blancheur, envoyé par les dieux, gardait l'enfant. Mais, autant que nous en avons été informés, voici le fait: un chien blanc, qui se trouvait au milieu des hommes envoyés à la recherche, rencontra l'enfant et sa nourrice; le prince fut donc appelé Sanadroug, dénomination tirée du nom de sa nourrice, (et du mon arménien *dourk* don,) comme, pour signifier don de Sanod.

Sanadroug, monté sur le trône la douzième année d'Ardachès, roi des Perses, ayant vécu trente ans, mourut à la chasse d'un trait qui lui perça les entrailles, comme en punition des tourmens qu'il avait fait souffrir à sa sainte fille. Ghéroupna, fils de l'écrivain Apchatar, a recueilli tous ces faits, arrivés du temps d'Abgar et de Sanadroug, et les a déposés dans les archives d'Édesse.

The above extract is taken from the edition, in two vols, printed at Paris, of which the following is the title: MOÏSE DE KHORÈNE AUTEUR DU Ve SIECLE HISTOIRE D'ARMÉNIE TEXTE ARMÉNIEN ET TRADUCTION FRANÇAISE avec notes explicatives et précis historiques sur l'arménie par P. E. LE VAILLANT DE FLORIVAL.

NOTES.

PAGE 1.—The MS. from which this extract from Eusebius' Ecclesiastical History is taken is one of those found in the Nitrian Cloister and now in the British Museum, *Cod. Add.* 14,639, fol. 15 b. See a description of this MS. *Corpus Ignatianum,* p. 350. It is only the first volume: the second, I believe, is in the Imperial Library at St. Petersburgh.

Line 6.—*Abgar.* This seems to have been a title common to many of the Kings or Toparchs of Edessa. J. S. Assemani says that all bore it: "ܐܒܓܪ: Hoc prænomine omnes Toparchæ Edesseni appellabantur, non secus atque Imperatores Romani *Cæsares,* Reges Ægypti *Pharones* vel *Ptolemæi,* et Reges Syriæ *Antiochi. Abgar* autem Syriace *Claudum* sonat." See *Bibliotheca Orientalis Clementina-Vaticana,* Vol. I., p. 261. Spanheim and Valesius thought the word should be written *Acbar,* as if from the Arabic أكبر, signifying the *greatest.* See Assemani, *ibid;* Theop. Sigf. Bayer, *Historia Osrhoena,* p. 73; and Fabricius *Codex Apocryphus, N. T.,* p. 316. The more probable signification seems to be that given by Moses Chorenensis, Book II. c. xxvi. "Cet Abgar était appelé *Avak-aïr* (grand homme) à cause de sa grande mansuétude et de sa sagesse, et de plus, à cause de sa taille. Ne pouvant bien prononcer, les Grecs et les Syriens l'appelèrent *Abgar.*" See p. 125. Assemani gives a series of the Kings of Edessa from the *Chronicon Edessenum* and other sources: in *Bibl. Orient.* Vol. I. p. 387—423. See also Bayer's *Historia Osrhoena,* and T. Wise, *Historia de Nummo Abgari Regis,* p. 4. A list of those who bore the name of Abgar, as gathered from Greek and Latin authors, is given by J. E. Grabe in *Spicilegium SS. Patrum,* Vol. I., p. 314.

l. 8.—*A severe disease.* See respecting this disease which Abgar took in Persia, Moses Chor. B. II. c. 28, 30, p. above 128, 129. Procopius, *De bello Persico,* B. II. c. 12, says that Abgar suffered from gout, probably from confounding his disease with that of Abdu mentioned below: Cedrenus says it was the black leprosy: see Fabricius, *Cod. Apoc. N. T.* p. 318, and Grabe *Spicilegium,* Vol. I. p. 315.

l. 12.—*A man of his own.* Greek δι' επιστοληφορου. The rest of this passage is not very closely rendered in Syriac from the Greek.

l. 13.—*Our Saviour.* Not in the Greek.

l. 17.—*Who were near to him.* ܩܪ̈ܝܒܘܗܝ: those who were connected with him or belonged to him, Gr. των προσηκοντων.

l. 19.—*Thomas the Apostle.* His real name was Judas or Jude, see p. 3, line 14; the appellation *Thomas,* meaning a *Twin,* being added to distinguish him from others bearing the name Judas: see Preface to *Remains of a very antient Recension of the Four Gospels in Syriac,* p. L, and the authorities given there. Besides the Greek Acts of Thomas, published by Thilo, *Acta S. Thomæ Apostoli,* 8vo. Lips. 1832. There is also a copy of Acts in Syriac more extended than the Greek, which ought to be published, in the British Museum, Cod. Add. 14,645, fol. 1. In addition to the work of Thilo just spoken of, those who wish to know more of St. Thomas and his preaching in India may consult Fabricius, *Cod. Apoc. N. T.* p. 688; Assemani *Bibl. Orient.* Vol. III. Part II. pp. 25, 435; Buchanan, *Christian Researches in Asia,* 8vo. 1812; Swanston, *Memoir of the Primitive Church,* in the Journal of the Asiatic Society, Vol. I. p. 171, 1834, and Vol. II. p. 51, 1835; Ritter, *Erdkunde,* Vol. V. pp. 601, 945. There was a church dedicated to Thomas at Edessa, and his body is said to have been translated there, A. D. 394: see Assemani, *Bibl. Orient.* Vol. I. pp. 49, 399, and Vol. II. p. 387.

PAGE 2.—*l.* 1.—*Thaddæus:* so in this place translated from the Greek of Eusebius, but in the original Syriac treatises he is called *Addæus:* see *below,* passim.

l. 2.—*The Seventy.* In *Doctrine of the Apostles,* p. 34, he is said to be one of the *Seventy-Two Apostles.* Their names are given in Cod. Add. 14,601, fol. 164; and also by Assemani from the work called ܕܒܘܪܝܬܐ or *The Bee,* in *Bibl. Orient.* Vol. III. p. 319. Jerome supposed him to be the Apostle Jude. "Thaddæum Apostolum Ecclesiastica tradit Historia missum Edessam ad Abagarum Regem Chosdroenæ, qui ab Evangelista Luca Judas Jacobi dicitur, et alibi appellatur Lebæus, quod interpretatur corculum. Credendumque est eum fuisse trinomium, sicut Simon Petrus, et filii Zebedæi Boanerges ex firmitate et magnitudine fidei nominati sunt." See *Com. in Matt.* c. 10. His real name, like that of Thomas, seems to have been the very common one, Judas. *Edessa—fulfilled.* In the book ascribed to Abdias, *Historia Certaminis Apostolici,* this is mentioned in the Life of Thomas: — "Acceptoque Spiritus Sancti dono, Thaddæum unum ex septuaginta discipulis, ad Abgarum regem Edessenæ civitatis transmisit, ut eum ab infirmitate curaret, juxta verbum quod ei a Domino scriptum erat: see Fabricius, *Cod. Apoc.* N. T. p. 688.

l. 5.—*The Book of Records which is at Edessa.* These were kept in the archives of the kingdom, which were transferred by Abgar from Nisibis to Edessa when he made it the capital of his dominions. See Moses Chor. B. II. c. xxvii. p. 126, *above.* At a later period, under Vespasian and Titus, we read, "Les fonctionnaires de Romains, après avoir restauré magnifiquement la ville d'Édesse, y établissent des trésoreries destinées à recevoir les impôts perçus sur l'Arménie, la Mésopotamie, l'Assyrie. Ils rassemblent a Édesse toutes les Archives, organisent deux écoles, l' une pour la langue du pays, le syrien, et l'autre pour le grec; ils transportent à Édesse les Archives relatives au tributs et aux temples, Archives qui étaient à Sinope, ville du Pont:" B. II. c. xxxviii. The same writer also refers to ancient archives, B. I. c. 9, 19, 21. B. II. c. 10. See the extract from the *Chronicon Edessenum*, cited p. 143: see also p. 61, line 15. The archives appear to have been still kept at Edessa A. D. 550. See Assemani, *Bibl. Orient.* Vol. I., p. 387.

l. 6.—*For the kingdom was still standing.* Gr. τοτηνικαυτα βασιλευομενομενην πολιν, which Rufinus has rendered thus: "In qua tunc supradictus Abgar regnabat." These words appear to be an addition by Eusebius, and to confirm the conjecture of Grabe, that this extract from the Archives of Edessa was not made by Eusebius himself, but by Sextus Julius Africanus, and copied from his Chronographia into the Ecclesiastical History. See *Spicilegium,* Vol. I. p. 314. The kingdom of Edessa was brought to an end and entirely subjected to the Romans, A. D. 217 or 218. See Assemani, *Bibl. Orient.* Vol. I. p. 388; Bayer, *Hist. Osrh.* p. 177. This was precisely the time when Africanus was in these parts. See M. Routh, *Reliquiæ Sacræ,* Vol. II. p. 221, 2nd Edit.; Fabricius, *Bibl. Græc.* Vol. v. p. 270. A few years later, in the 9th year of Diocletian, we find Abgar no longer called *King,* but *Prætor.* See *Martyrium S. S. Confess. Samonæ.* p. 123. The fact of Eusebius having followed Africanus is also confirmed by Moses Chor., who writes thus, B. II. c. 10: "Nous commencerons à te faire le récit des événements d'après le cinquième livre d'Africanus le chronologiste, dont le témoignage est confirmé par Joseph, Hippolyte, et beaucoup d'autres grecs; car Africanus a extrait des cartularies et des Archives d'Édesse, est-à-dire Ourha, tout ce qui était de l' histoire de nos rois: ces livres avaient été apportés de Medzpine; Africanus se servit aussi des histoires des temples de Sinope du Pont; que personne n'en doute, car nous avons vu nous mêmes de nos propres yeux ces archives. En témoinage et garantie te vient encore l' histoire ecclésiastique d'Eusèbe de Césarée, que le bienheureux docteur Machdotz fit traduire en Arménien : cherche a Kégha-couni, au canton de Sunik, et tu trouveras, première rapsodie N°. treize, l'assurance que dans les archives d'Édesse est l'histoire de tous les faits et gestes de nos derniers rois jusqu'à Abgar, et après Abgar jusqu'à Érouant ; documents qui, je pense, se trouvent encore conservés dans cette ville." *Julius Africanus* is said not only to have translated Abdias into Latin, but also to have written *Narratio de iis quæ in Perside domino Jesu Christo nato acciderint.* This is published in *Beyträge zur Geschichte und Literatur.* 1804, Part IV. p. 49. This appears to be fabulous and worthless.

l. 10.—*Nothing to hinder :* Gr. ουδεν δε οἶον.

l. 13.—*King Abgar.* Gr. τοπαρχου. Rufinus *Rege Abgaro vel Toparcho.*

l. 14.—*Hananias.* This form seems to be taken from the Greek here. In the original Syriac document it is written *Hanan*, see p. 23; and so in Moses Choren., see p. 131. *Tabularius:* the Greek, has ταχυδρομου, and Rufinus *Cursorem.* This seems to have been an error. Galanus from the Armenian calls him *Tabellarius* : see *Concil. Ecc. Arm. cum. Rom.* Vol. I. p. 7. The post which Hananias filled must have been one of much more dignity and trust than that of *Cursor.* The office which Hananias held seems to have been that of a Secretary of State : see Moses Chor. B. II. c. 29 and 30; where, in the translation of L. Vaillant de Florival, he is called Abgar's *Confident*, which corresponds with *Sharir*, as he is styled in these Acts : see p. 23. The Sharirs had the custody of the archives, as we learn from the Chronicle of Edessa : ܡܪܝܗܒ ܕܝܢ ܒܪ ܫܡܫ ܘܩܝܘܡܐ ܒܪ ܡܓܪܛܛ ܣܦܪܐ ܕܐܘܪܗܝ، ܗܠܝܢ ܟܬܒܘܗܝ، ܠܡܘܟܪܢܐ ܗܢܐ ܘܠܦܘܩܕܢܐ ܕܐܒܓܪ ܡܠܟܐ. ܘܒܪܕܝܢ ܘܒܘܠܝܕ ܗܠܝܢ ܕܗܢܘܢ ܡܗܝܡܢܝܢ ܗܘܘ ܥܠ ܐܪܟܝܘܢ ܕܐܘܪܗܝ، ܗܢܘܢ ܩܒܠܘ ܗܘܘ ܘܣܡܘܗ ܠܗ ܒܣܝܡܗܘܢ ܐܝܟ ܫܪܝܪܐ ܕܡܗܝܡܢܘܬܐ. which Assemani translates thus : "Hæc Acta, Regisque Abgari Edictum conscripsere Mar-Jabus Bar Semes et Kajumas Bar-Magartat, Notarii Edesseni : eaque in Archivum Edessenum intulere Bardinus et Bulidus ejusdem Archivi Præfecti, utpote publicæ fidei testes (*Sharir*)." See *Bibl. Orient.* Vol. I. p. 393 ; see also p. 84. The Latin term *Tabularius* was well known in those parts certainly before this extract from the archives of Edessa was used by Eusebius. Julius Capitolinus tells us that Marcus Antoninus established *Tabularii* in all the provinces, in the chapter in which he is writing of these parts, c. 9; and Abdias, in the life of St. Simon and St. Jude, speaks of the *Tabularii fisci* in these countries: see Fabricius, *Cod. Apoc.* N. T. p. 616; and Eusebius, in *Hist. Ecc. Martt. Palest.* c. 9. The Latin term was *Notarius*: see Ammianus Marcellinus Vol. III., *Edit. Lips.* 1808. p. 464. Respecting the Tabularii, see Jacob Gothofridus *ad Cod. Theodos,* VIII. t. ii. Vol. II. p. 475., and Pancirolus *Notitia Dignitatum*, p. 126.

l. 16.—*Abgar Uchama.* Gr. Αβγαρος only, with the exception of one copy, which adds Ουχανιης υιος: see Burton's Edition. Rufinus, who followed the earliest editions of Eusebius, has also *Uchaniæ filius.* The Greek transcribers seem to have been ignorant of the meaning of *Uchama*, which signifies *dark*, and was an epithet peculiar to this king Abgar: see Assemani *Bibl. Orient.* Vol. I. p. 420. He was the 14th King: the 11th was called Abgar *Sumaca*, or the *red*: see Bayer, *Hist. Osrh.* p. 91. *Chief of the Country.* Gr. τοπαρχης: the later copies of the Greek add Εδεσσης, which is omitted in Rufinus.

l. 17.—*Peace.* The Gr. has χαιρειν. Rufinus *salutem.* *I have heard.* St. Matthew, iv. 24, tells us, "and his fame went throughout all Syria; and they brought unto him all sick people that were taken with divers diseases and torments, and those which were possessed with devils, and those which were lunatics, and those that had the palsy; and he healed them." Abgar therefore might easily have heard at Edessa of Christ, by common report. Another reason, however, for this account reaching Abgar is given by Moses Chor. see p. 129 *above*, and *note on that place below.*

l. 23.—*I settled in my mind.* See a conclusion similar to this of Abgar by the people of Lystra, &c., *Acts* xiv. 11, and the people of Melita, *ibid.* xxviii. 6. So also by the Centurion, *Mark* xv. 39; and by Nicodemus, *John* iii. 2.

l. 30.—At the end of this letter a passage is added in several Greek copies: "Thus wrote Abgarus, as then but little enlightened from above. It is also worth while to hear the answer of Jesus returned to him by the same courier. Short indeed it is, but it has much power and efficacy in it." *English Trans.* Valesius was convinced that these words were not written by Eusebius: see Fabricius, *Cod. Apoc.* p. 318. Burton omits them in his edition: see note on this place. Neither are they found in Rufinus.

Page 3. *l.* 1.—*Copy of those things which were written.* Gr. τα αντιγραφεντα. Rufinus, *Exemplum rescripti.*

l. 3.—*Blessed is he.* ܛܘܒܘܗܝ، ܠܐܢܫܐ: the other copy ܛܘܒܐ. The Gr. Editt. have μακαριος ει, though several MSS. have μακαριος ὁ: see

Burton's Edit. Valesius has the following note on this place: "In what part of the *Old Testament* these words occur I am yet to seek. Indeed, in the Gospel of St. John, c. xx. v. 29, it is written that our Lord said to Thomas after his resurrection, *Blessed are they that have not seen, and yet have believed.* But this Epistle of Christ to King Abgarus, if it be genuine, preceded that reprehension of the Apostle Thomas some years." *English Trans.* p. 14. There seems to be no ground whatever for this assertion of Valesius. The period of time intervening between the two events must have been short, as, indeed, Valesius himself shews in the Note cited by me on the next page. Fabricius compares these words, cited as being *written*, with Isai. vi. 9, Lii. 15, and observes, "Sane cum his Prophetæ locis sensui Epistolæ magis convenit quam cum loco quem plerique hic respici putant:" see *Cod. Apoc. N. T.* p. 318.

l. 26.—*A mighty man.* ܓܒܪܐ ܫܠܝܛܢܐ. Gr. ανηρ τις δυναστης. Rufinus, *vir quidam potens.*

l. 28.—*The king.* Gr. τοπαρχος. Rufinus *toparcha.*

PAGE 4, *l.* 7.—*There* ܬܡܢ. The other MS. has ܩܕܡܘܗܝ *before him.*

l. 12.—*Nobly.* ܪܘܪܒܐܝܬ. Gr. μεγαλως. Rufinus *magnifice.*

l. 15.—*So that—Romans.* Compare the letters of Abgar and Tiberius, p. 16 below; see also p. 111.

l. 18.—*Our Lord.* Some Gr. MSS. add Ιησους. Rufinus as here.

l. 25.—*Abdu, son of Abdu.* This same person is mentioned at p. 7, below, where he is called ܬܪܝܢܐ ܕܡܠܟܘܬܐ: which I have translated *the second person* of his kingdom. It probably means one of the second rank in the kingdom. Tacitus mentions a person of this name, who must have been cotemporary, if not the same—"Sed Parthis mittendis secretos nuntios validissimus auctor fuit Sinnaces, insigni familia, ac perinde opibus, et proximus huic Abdus, ademptæ virilitatis: non despectum id apud barbaros, ultroque potentiam habet. See *Annal.* vi. 31 and 32.

l. 26.—*He too went in and fell at his feet.* ܐܦ ܗܘ ܥܠ ܘܢܦܠ ܥܠ ܪ̈ܓܠܘܗܝ like the Gr. ος και αυτος προσελθων υπο τους ποδας αυτου επεσεν: ευχας τε δια χειρος λαβων εθεραπευθη; but the original Syriac at p. 6. ܘܐܦ ܗܘ ܩܪܒ ܗܘܐ ܠܗ ܪ̈ܓܠܘܗܝ ܘܣܡ ܗܘ ܐܝܕܐ ܥܠܝܗܘܢ ܘܐܣܝܗ ܗܘܐ: *He too brought his feet near to him, and he laid his hands upon them and healed him,* the variation, probably, having arisen from the translation into Greek and the re-translation into Syriac.

PAGE 5, *l.* 3.—*Christ.* Gr. Ιησου.

l. 5.—*For the present I will be silent.* ܗܫܐ ܫܬܩ ܐܢܐ. The original

Syriac at p. 6: ܡܢ ܗܕܐ ܠܐ ܫܬܩ ܐܢܐ: *I will not be silent from declaring this.*

l. 12.—*His new preaching.* ܟܪܘܙܘܬܗ ܚܕܬܐ. In the original Syriac, p. 6. ܚܬܝܬܘܬܐ ܕܟܪܘܙܘܬܗ: *the certitude of his preaching.* The Greek translator seems to have confounded ܚܬܝܬܘܬܐ, *diligentia, sedulitas, certitudo,* with ܚܕܬܐ: *nova,* an error which could hardly have happened in translating from Greek into Syriac.

l. 15.—*Hell.* ܠܫܝܘܠ. Greek ᾳδην. The original Syriac, p. 6 ܠܒܝܬ ܡܝ̈ܬܐ *the place of the dead*; and so we find it in the DOCTRINE OF THE APOSTLES, p. 26 below. *And brake through the wall of partition*: compare St. Paul *Ephes.* ii. 14, "and hath broken down the middle wall of partition."

l. 16.—*And descended alone and ascended with a great multitude to his Father.* In the longer Recension of the Ignatian Epistles, cix. of that to the Trallians, we read almost the same words. *και κατηλθεν εις ᾳδην μονος, ανηλθε δε μετα πληθους· και εσχισε τον απ' αιωνος φραγμον, και το μεσοτοιχον αυτου ελυσε.* The same thing is also referred to by Mar Jacob, the Persian, in his sermon on ܒ̈ܢܝ ܩܝܡܐ, Cod. 14,614, fol. 40. ܘܦܪܘܩܢ ܟܕ ܢܚܬ ܠܒܝܬ ܡܝ̈ܬܐ ܐܚܝ ܠܣܓܝ̈ܐܐ ܘܐܩܝܡ ܐܢܘܢ. *And our Saviour, when he descended to the place of the dead, gave life to many and raised them up.* Archbishop Usher in his Notes upon this passage of the Epistle to the Trallians cites words of Macarius of Jerusalem and of Cyril of Jerusalem to the same effect: see his Notes on Polycarp's and Ignatius' Epistles, p. 26. We read also, *Matt.* xxvii. 52, "And the graves were opened, and many bodies of the saints which slept arose, and came out of the graves after his resurrection, and went into the holy city, and appeared unto many."

l. 20.—*Silver.* The Gr. has *ασημον*, which this has imitated by using ܐܣܐܡܐ. The original Syriac at p. 7 has ܟܣܦܐ.

l. 23.—*The year three hundred and forty.* Valesius has the following note on this place: "This three hundredth and fortieth year, according to the account of the *Edessens*, falleth with the first year of the 202nd Olympiad. For the Edessens numbered their years from the 117th Olympiad, fixing their era upon the first year of Seleucus his reign in Asia (as Eusebius writes in his Chronicon), from which time to the beginning of the 202nd Olympiad there are just 340 years. Now the beginning of the 202nd Olympiad falleth with the 15th year of Tiberius, in which year as many of the Ancients believed our blessed Saviour suffered and ascended. So that this account falls right, placing Thaddæus his coming to Edessa and his curing King Abgarus on the same year in which our blessed Saviour suffered." *Eng. Trans.*, p. 15. In the *Doctrine of the Apostles,* our Lord's ascension is said to have been in the year 339 : see p. 24. Ebediesu says Christ was baptized in the 15th year of Tiberius, and the 341 of Alexander : see Mai, *Scriptt. Vett. Nov. Col.* Vol. X. p. 325. In the *Bee,* Ch. 52, Augustus is said to have reigned 57 years. In the 43rd year of his reign Christ was born. Tiberius reigned 23 years : in the 15th Christ was baptized, and in the 17th crucified. Orosius says Christ was crucified in the 17th year of Tiberius : see Lipomanus, *Sanct. Hist.*, Part I. p. 155. The Chronicon Edessenum places the birth of Christ in the year 309, and so does Barhebræus : see Assemani, *Bibl. Orient.* Vol. I. p. 389. According to these authorities, therefore, Abgar's conversion would have been in the 31st year from the birth of our Lord.

Page 6.—DOCTRINE OF ADDÆUS THE APOSTLE. The MS. from which the following fragment is taken is also from the Nitrian collection in the British Museum, No. 14,654, at fol. 33. It is contained on one leaf only, with the above inscription in red letters at the top of the page. The volume, as it is now bound, consists of several fragments of MS. of great antiquity, written in two columns, and contains chiefly Acts of Martyrs : its age appears to be certainly not later than the beginning of the fifth century. It is probably the same as that which Assemani saw at Scete, and describes as *pervetustus,* which contained the Acts of Addæus, Sharbil, &c. : see *Bibl. Orient.* Vol. III. p. 19. *Doctrine of Addæus.* At page 109, where I have given an extract from this, cited by another writer, it is called ܐܓܪܬܐ ܕܐܕܝ, *Epistle* or *Treatise* of Addæus.

l. 1.—*Because thou hast so believed.* The part comprised in this fragment corresponds with that given by Eusebius, from p. 4. line 20, to p. 5. line 22. It will be seen, that although the two are identical, this is the fuller. The extract in Eusebius seems to be abridged. There are also other slight variations, such as we may expect to find in the original language, and in a retranslation from the Greek into Syriac. Some of these have been already remarked upon, and I shall notice a few more. The other variations the reader will observe for himself.

l. 4.—*The plague of the disease.* ܡܢ ܢܓܥܐ ܕܟܐܒܐ : in the translation from Eusebius, p. 4 ܡܢ ܟܘܪܗܢܗ ܘܡܢ ܟܐܒܐ : *of his sickness and of the disease.* A variation which has evidently arisen from confounding ܕ and ܘ, which is not unfrequent. *A long time,* not in Eusebius. According to Moses Chor. he had been suffering for seven years from a disease which he caught in Persia : see B. II. c. xxx. p. 130.

l. 7.—*Abdu, son of Abdu.* Le Vaillant de Florival writes the name *Abdion*: see p. 132, where Moses Chor. calls him "Prince de la ville, très honoré dans toute la maison du roi." Compare what Tacitus says of him cited at p. 145 *above*. In the account of Constantine Porphyrogenitus, as given by Simeon Metaphrastes, he is said to have been the person who brought to Abgar information of Addæus' arrival at Edessa: "Quamobrem cum fama cito pervasisset, pervenit etiam ad Abgarum per quendam ex ejus proceribus, qui vocabatur Abdu, illic scilicet esse Christi Apostolum, &c.:" see Lipomanus, *Sanctorum Historia*, Part I. p. 189. The following also relates to him, but whether it refers to the fact just stated, or to his having been one of Abgar's envoys, who passed through Palestine (see p. 129 and the Notes on that paragraph), I know not: "Cum itaque multa prius effecerit miracula Domini Apostolus, et omnes curasset a morbis suis, inter quos is erat etiam, qui primus de eo famam retulit ad Barbarum (perhaps it should be read Abagarum) quem liberavit a podagra." *Ibid*, p. 190.

l. 8.—*Gout.* Here we have ܦܟܠܓܪܐ : but in the translation ܦܘܕܓܪܐ nearer to the Greek ποδαγρα.

l. 22.—*Him that sent him*, or *his sender.* ܫܠܘܚܗ : in the Greek της αποστολης αυτου; and therefore retranslated p. 5 ܫܠܝܚܘܬܗ.

PAGE 7. *l.* 11. — *The whole creation.* The same as *Mark* xvi. 15. παση τη κτισει. This is an Aramaism not unfrequently used by St. Paul, rendered in our English version, *Rom.* viii. 22, *the whole creation groaneth and travaileth in pain together until now.* It occurs several times in these pages. Compare Sharbil's words, p. 52.

l. 14.—*His princes and his nobles.* ܪ̈ܘܪܒܢܘܗܝ ܘܚܐܪ̈ܘܗܝ. It is difficult to know what is the exact political position of these two orders. The latter more literally would be *his free-men*, free citizens, in contradistinction to serfs and slaves.

l. 15.—*Shalmath.* I have no authority for the pronunciation of this word, there being no vowels. This observation will apply to almost all the proper names occurring in my translation. Any one, therefore, if he have better grounds, may supply other vowels, and a more accurate orthography. Referring, however, to Josephus, *Antiq. Jud.* B. XVIII. c. vii., I read the name of the wife of Phasaelus, Σαλαμψιω, which, if it be the same name as this, the name would be *Shalamtho* ܫܠܡܬܐ. *Daughter of Meherdath.* Who this Meherdath was does not appear. He may be the person mentioned at p. 13. He might also have been some connexion of Meherdates, the King of the Parthians, whom Tacitus mentions, *Annal.* B. xii. c. 12, and says that he was entertained at Edessa by Abgar, "qui juvenem ignarum, et summam fortunam in luxu ratum, multos per dies adtinuit apud oppidum Edessam:" see Assemani, *Bibl. Or.* Vol. I. p. 421. Moses Chor. B. II. c. xxxv. says that the first or chief wife of Abgar was *Helena*: see p. 138.

PAGE 8. *l.* 4. — *Of the faith.* The remaining part of the DOCTRINE OF ADDÆUS, from this place to the end, is taken from a MS. of the Nitrian collection now in the British Museum. Cod Add. 14,644. Dr. Land has given a description of this MS. in his *Anecdota Syriaca*, p. 19. I regret that the same want of knowledge or of attention, which characterizes all Dr. Land's publications,* which I have seen, should have rendered it necessary for me to furnish another description. The MS. is in 8vo., and consists at present of ninety-three leaves; two or three apparently are lost from the beginning, and a few others in the body of the volume. It was one of those MSS. procured in the year of the Greeks 1243, A.D 931, by the abbot Moses during his visit to Bagdad, who has written on the last leaf the same inscription as that given by me in the Preface to *Festal Letters of Athanasius*, p. xxv., which is also found in many of these volumes. It appears to be of the sixth century. The original contents of the volume are thus stated in red ink at the end of the volume, fol. 92 vers.

ܐܝܬ ܒܗ ܕܝܢ ܒܟܘܪܣܐ ܗܢܐ ܬܫܥܝܬܐ ܘܣܗܕܘܬܐ ܕܡܠܟܢ̈ܝܬܐ
ܫܡܘܢܐ. ܕܐܠܥܙܪ ܣܒܐ. ܘܡܠܦܢܘܬܐ ܕܐܕܝ ܫܠܝܚܐ. ܘܡܣܟܢܘܬܗ
ܕܐܠܝܫܒܥ. ܘܡܣܟܢܘܬܗ ܕܐܠܝܫܒܥ ܕܐܚܬܗܘܢ ܕܐܚ̈ܝܢ. ܘܣܗܕܘܬܗ
ܕܛܘܒܢܐ ܣܘܪܝܘܣ ܐܦܝܣܩܘܦܐ. ܘܡܠܦܢܘܬܗ ܕܡܫܒܚܢ
ܟܐܦܐ. ܘܡܠܦܢܘܬܐ ܕܩܠܝܡܐ. ܘܬܫܥܝܬܗ ܕܡܪܝ ܐܒܪܗܡ
ܚܣܝܐ. ܘܡܢܝܚܢܗ ܕܛܘܒܢܐ ܡܪܝ ܗܒܐ ܘܠܝܠܐ.
ܘܣܗܕܘܬܐ ܕܫܡܘܢܐ ܘܕܒ̈ܢܝܗ̇ ܬܠܬ ܦܘܠܘܣ ܘܡܠܘܣ
ܘܐܠܟܐ. ܘܣܗܕܘܬܗ ܕܫܡܥܘܢ ܟܐܦܐ. ܘܣܗܕܘܬܗ ܕܡܪܝ,

---

* It is with pain that I have to speak in such terms of the works of a gentleman who has shewn himself anxious to acquire distinction by pursuing these difficult and laborious studies; but when such an one, being a foreigner with no great knowledge of the English language, presumes to accuse the Version of the venerable Translators of our Authorized Translation of the Bible both of ignorance of the English tongue and of want of knowledge of the geography of the Holy Land, it shows a degree of hasty self-reliance which could not fail to lead him often into error, and to mislead others who have not the opportunity of bringing the accuracy of his writings to the test. See *Journal of Sacred Literature*, 1858.

ܫܪܒܝܠ. ܘܗܘܦܘܡܢܡܛܐ ܕܡܪܝ ܩܘܙܡܐ ܘܕܡܪܝ ܕܡܝܢܐ ܐܚܘܗܝ، ܐܣܘܬܐ ܫܪܝܪܐ. ܘܬܫܥܝܬܐ ܕܥܠ ܓܒܪܐ ܕܐܠܗܐ. ܕܗܘܝܢ ܒܡܢܝܢܐ ܐܪܒܥܣܪܐ "There are arranged, then, in this volume, Select Narratives and Martyrdoms. One of 'Abgar the King, (No. 1); and the Doctrine of Addæus the Apostle (2); and the Invention of the Cross (3); and the Invention of the Cross the second time (4); and the Martyrdom of the blessed Cyriacus, the Bishop (5); and the Doctrine of Simon Cephas (6); and the Doctrine of the Apostles (7); and the Narrative of Mari Abraham of Cheduna (8); and the Triumphs of Mari Saba Julianus (9); and the Martyrdom of Sophia and her three daughters, Pistis, Helpis, and Agape (10); and the Martyrdom of Jacob, who was cut to pieces (11); and the Martyrdom of Mari Sharbil (12); and the Hypomnemata of Mari Cosmas and Mari Damianus, his brother, true physicians (13); and the Narrative touching the Man of God (14); which are in number fourteen."

Of these fourteen, No. 1 is altogether lost. No. 2, printed in this volume, is imperfect, and is contained in the nine first folios. The order is then inverted. On folio 10 commences No. 7 to fol. 18. No. 3 begins on fol. 18, and comprises also No. 4, which is rather the Invention of the nails of the Cross, to fol. 23, vers. No. 5 follows. This Cyriacus was a Jew named Judas who found the Cross at the Empress Helena's instigation, and afterwards became converted to Christianity, and was ordained bishop by Sylvester, Bishop of Rome; from fol. 23 to fol. 27. The next is No. 8, fol. 28—43: it is imperfect at the end, about two lines wanted, as appears by comparison of Cod. Add. 12,160, fol. 116. No 11 comes next, imperfect at the beginning, two leaves supplied in a much later hand: it extends to fol. 53 vers., on which page is No. 9 to fol. 63, imperfect, several leaves missing. Next to this is No. 10, from fol. 63 vers. to fol. 72. Then comes No. 12, fol. 72 vers. to fol. 84 vers., printed in this volume. The next is No. 13, imperfect, wanting some leaves in the middle, fol. 84 vers.—fol. 87. And last, No. 14, from fol. 87 vers. to the end. Dr. Land did not observe the following rubric at the bottom of fol. 87 ܫܠܡܬ ܣܗܕܘܬܐ ܕܡܪܝ ܩܘܙܡܐ ܘܕܡܪܝ ܕܡܝܢܐ ܐܚܐ ܫܒܝܚܐ ܘܠܡܢܨܚܐ. "Here endeth the Martyrdom of Mari Cosmas and of Mari Damianus, glorious and triumphant brothers." He also overlooked the rubric on the other side of the leaf, at the top, ܬܫܥܝܬܐ ܕܥܠ ܓܒܪܐ ܕܐܠܗܐ ܕܗܘܐ ܡܢ ܪܗܘܡܐ. "The Narrative touching the man of God who was from Rome;" but seeing a blank leaf of vellum bound in between fol. 86 and 87, to show that something was missing, he has written "Inter fol. 86 et 87 initium Historiæ quatuordecim virorum Dei ex urbe Roma." The blunder, which, against sense and grammar, he has committed by confounding the number of works in the volume with the *Man of God from Rome*, and multiplying him by fourteen, has been already pointed out by Dr. W. Wright.

l. 10.—*The sun which was darkened.* See the same argument in *Doctrine of Simon Cephas*, p. 38.

l. 13. — *His disciples—knew only the Hebrew tongue.* See *Doctrine of the Apostles*, p. 25, and *Doctrine of Simon Cephas*, p. 36. Respecting the Apostles' ignorance of other tongues besides the *Syriac*, see Eusebius, *Theophania*, B. IV. c. 6, 8; B. V. c. 26; and Lee's Translation, pp. 217, 226, 309.

l. 18.—*The rebels in this region.* That is, "the whole of the country of Mesopotamia," as it is called *below*, p. 21; referring to the confusion of tongues at the Tower of Babel.

l. 21.—*From Paneas. Paneas,* otherwise *Cæsarea Philippi*: see Eusebius, *Hist. Ec.* B. VII. c. 17, and Valesuis' Note. Josephus, *Antiq. Jud.* B. XVIII. c. ii. 1. This is referred to in the Extract No. IV. p. 109.

l. 25.—*I cast his money upon the table.* Compare *Matt.* xxv. 27. Compare also the celebrated saying attributed to Christ, Γινεσθε τραπεζιται δοκιμοι. See Fabricius, *Cod. Apoc. N. T.*, p. 320. Grabe *Spicilegium*, p. 13. In the *Didascalia Apostolorum*, edited by Lagarde, in Syriac, this is given

ܗܘܘ ܡܦܪ̈ܫܢܐ ܒܚܝܪ̈ܐ ܡܬܒܥܐ ܠܗ ܗܟܝܠ ܠܐܦܝܣܩܘܦܐ

ܐܝܟ ܒܚܘܪܐ ܕܟܣܦܐ ܕܢܗܘܐ ܡܦܪܫܢܐ ܒܝ̈ܫܐ ܡܢ ܛܒ̈ܐ.

"Be expert discerners (or money-changers). It is requisite, therefore, that a Bishop, like a trier of silver, should be a discerner of the bad and the good," p. 42.

Page 9. *l.* 9.—*At that time—his own book.* See *Rev.* xx. 12. Compare also Mar Jacob, *On their own bodies*, &c., p. 97. A few lines are missing here in the MS.

l. 27.—*For the works of the Creation*, &c. Compare *Doctrine of the Apostles*, p. 26; *Doctrine of Simon Cephas*, p. 36; *Acts of Sharbil*, p. 52.

Page 10. *l.* 5.—See Josephus' account of the magnificence of the Vail of the Temple. *Wars of the Jews*, B. V. c. 5. sec. 4.

l. 7.—*For behold—in crying Woe.* This passage seems to accord with what is said in the antient Syriac Gospel of St. Luke, xxiii. 48: "And all those which were assembled there, and saw that which was done, were smiting upon their breast, and saying, Woe to us, what is this? Woe to us from our sins." See *Remains of a very antient Recension of the Four Gospels in Syriac*, p. 85. In our received text, instead of these last words, we have "Smote upon their breasts, and returned."

l. 26.—"*Blessed are ye that have believed in me, not having seen me; and because ye have so believed in me, the city in which ye dwell shall be blessed, and the enemy shall not prevail against it for ever.*" These words are not in the Epistle of our Lord to King Abgar, although the first part is similar to the beginning of that Epistle. They must, therefore, either have been a message brought by Addæus himself, as Ephraem Syrus seems to intimate in the passage quoted from his *Testament* below; or, what seems much more probable, they are a later amplification or interpolation, although anterior to the time of Ephraem. This is confirmed by Procopius:—*Φασι δε και τουτο αυτον επειπειν, ως ουδε η πολις ποτε βαρβαροις αλωσιμος εσται. Τουτο της επιστολης το ακροτελευτιον οι μεν εκεινου του χρονου την ιστοριαν ξυνγραψαντες, ουδαμη εγνωσαν· ου γαρ ουν ουδεπη αυτον εμνησθησαν. Εδεσηνοι δε αυτο ξυν επιστολῃ ευρεσθαι φασιν· ως τε αμελει και αναγραπτον ουτω την επιστολην αντ' αλλου του φυλακτηριου εν ταις της πολεως πεποιηνται πυλαις.* "Hoc enim subjunxisse aiunt, urbem semper inexpugnabilem fore Barbaris. Quod postremum epistolæ caput eos, qui historiam scripserunt illius temporis latuit: nusquam enim mentionem ejus fecerunt. Edesseni vero id literis annexum reperiri perhibent, adeo ut epistolam eo modo exscriptam in portis urbis pro quovis alio munimento posuerunt:" quoted by Grabe in his *Spicilegium*, Vol. I. p. 313. Respecting this, Evagrius writes in his Ecclesiastical History, Book IV. c. 27, "The same Procopius records what has been related by the antients concerning Edessa and Abgarus, and how Christ wrote to Abgarus. Further, also, how in another incursion Chosroes resolved upon a seige of the Edessens, supposing he should enervate what had been divulged to the faithful, to wit, that Edessa should never be subdued by an enemy. Which thing is not, indeed, extant in that letter sent from Christ our God to Abgarus, as may be gathered by the studious, from what has been related by Eusebius Pamphilus, who has inserted that letter word for word into his History. Nevertheless, it is both divulged and believed amongst the Faithful, and the event itself declared the truth, faith bringing the prediction to effect, &c." *English Trans.*, p. 488. In the Epistle of Christ to Abgar, edited by the Emperor Constantine Porphyrogenitus, the words *και ποιησει τῃ πολει σου το ικανον, προς το μηδενα των εχθρων κατισχισαι αυτῃ*: cited by Bayer,

Hist. Osrh. p. 107. This is translated by Lipomanus, "Et tuæ civitati cavebit ut nullus eam possit superare inimicus." Part I. p. 188. The first words of this are given by Cedrenus thus: και τῃ πολει σου γενησεται το ικανον: see Grabe *Ibid*, p. 8, and Fabricius, *Cod. Apoc. N. T.* p. 319. Constantine Porphyrogenitus' account of the conversion of Abgar, &c., is given by Simeon Metaphrastes, and printed in Greek by Combefis in his *Origg. Constantipoll. Manip.*, Paris, 1664. p. 75—101; and in Latin by Lipomanus, in *Sanctorum Hist.*, Part I., p. 187, *Constantini, cognomento Porphyrogeniti, Narratio collecta ex diversis historiis de non manu facta Christi Dei nostri imagine, missa ad Abagarum, et ex Edessa translata in hanc beatissimam urbium Reginam Constantinopolim.* (A. C. 944.) Also given by Surius, August 16th. See an account of this in Arabic, by Macarius of Antioch, *Cod. Add.* 9965, f. 33 vers.

In the Testament of Ephraem, as published by Vossius, we read, "Et benedicta vestra sit civitas, in qua habitatis. Ipsa enim sapientum est civitas, et mater, Edessa: quæ quidem etiam palam atque manifeste ex ore Christi Domini benedicta est per suos discipulos, nostros vero Apostolos. Nam quando Rex Abagarus, qui hanc civitatem extruxit, rogabat, exciperet eum qui peregrinus in terris apparuerat, Salvatorem inquam universorum, et Dominum Christum, dicebat: "Omnia audivi, quæ a te facta sunt, et quæcumque a reprobis et aspernantibus te Judæis passus es. Veni igitur huc, et nobiscum habita: habeo enim mihi civitatem hanc exiguam, quæ tibi et mihi sufficiet." Cujus etiam fidem admiratus Dominus, mittens ei per nuntios, perpetuò civitati illi benedixit, firmans ipsius fundamenta: benedictioque illa inhabitans in ea permanebit, donec Sanctus e cælo apparebit Jesus Christus Filius Dei, et Deus ex Deo:" see Ephraem Syrus, *Opera Omnia*, a Ger. Vossio, 3rd edit., p. 788. Assemani, upon comparing the original Syriac with both the Greek edition and the Latin, having observed that the Greek interpreter had added many things of his own, gives the original Syriac of the above passage, which he renders thus: "Benedicta civitas, in qua habitatis, Edessa sapientum mater, quæ ex vivo Filii ore benedictionem per ejus Discipulum accepit. Illa igitur benedictio in ea maneat donec Sanctus apparuerit." *Bibl. Orient.*, Vol. I. p. 141. This *Testament* is printed entire in Syriac with a Latin translation, with only three verbal variations from this cited here, in Ephraem Syrus, *Opera Omnia*, Rome, Vol. II. p. 395. Darius Comes, in Epist. ad Augustinum, also mentions this: "Affuit Deus Regi, et amplificato petitionis munere per Epistolam, non modo salutem ut supplici, sed etiam securitatem ut Regi transmisit. Jussit insuper et urbem ab hostibus in perpetuum esse ac semper immunem:" cited by Fabricius, *Cod. Apoc. N. T.*, p. 319.

This notion of the immunity of the City of Edessa is referred to by several Syriac writers. Thus Joshua Stylites cites the passage ܒܪܝܟܝ ܢܗܘܐ ܒܪܝܟܝ: ܘܒܥܠܕܒܒܐ ܠܐ ܢܫܬܠܛ ܒܗ ܠܥܠܡ. "And thy city shall be blessed, and the enemy shall not prevail against it for ever:" see Assemani, *Bibl. Orient.* Vol. I. p. 261. So Mar Jacob, in his Epistle to the Homerites: ܐܓܪܬܐ: ܕܫܕܪ ܡܪܝ, ܝܥܩܘܒ ܠܘܬ ܢܓܪ̈ܢܝ, writes ܘܬܘܒ ܡܠܟ ܐܬܘܗܝ, ܐܠܗܐ ܠܐܒܓܪ ܡܠܟܐ ܡܗܝܡܢܐ ܕܒܠ ܡܕܝܢܬܗ ܠܐ ܢܫܬܠܛ ܒܥܠܕܒܒܐ ܠܥܠܡ. "Moreover God promised to King Abgar the Faithful, that the enemy should not prevail against his city for ever:" see *Cod. Add.* 14,587, fol. 47 vers., see also fol. 48 rect.

Nor did the belief in the protecting power of this Letter of our Lord prevail in the East only, for we find, at a very early period also, that it obtained even in our own British Isles. In a very antient MS. in the British Museum, *Royal MS.*, 2 A. xx. f. 12, containing a Service Book of the Saxon times, we find this Epistle in the Latin version of Rufinus, immediately following the Lord's Prayer and the Apostle's Creed. "In nomine Patris et filii et Spiritus Sancti: *Incipit Epistola Salvatoris omnium Ihesu Christi ad Abagarum regem, quam Dominus manu scripsit et dixit.* "Beatus es qui me non vidisti et credidisti in me. Scriptum est enim de me, quia hi qui vident me, non credent in me: et qui me non vident, ipsi in me credent et vivent. De eo autem quod scripsisti mihi ut venirem ad te, oportet me omnia propter quæ missus sum hic explere; et postea quam complevero recipi me ad eum, a quo missus sum. Cum ergo fuero adsumptus, mittam tibi aliquem ex discipulis meis, ut curet egritudinem tuam, et vitam tibi, ac his qui tecum sunt præstet, et salvus eris, sicut scriptum, Qui credit in me salvus erit." *Sive in domu tua, sive in civitate tua, sive in omni loco nemo inimicorum tuorum dominabit. Et insidias diaboli ne timeas, et carmina inimicorum tuorum distruuntur* (sic), *et omnes inimici tui expellentur a te: sive a grandine, sive a tonitrua* (sic) *non noceberis, et ab omni periculo liberaberis: sive in mare, sive in terra, sive in die, sive in nocte, sive in locis obscuris. Si quis hanc epistolam secum habuerit, securus ambulet in pace,*" fol. 12. In this MS. p. 18 b, Thaddæus is called Tatheus, as in the first edition of Rufinus. Those who are curious may read the Story of Abgar in Anglo-Saxon, published by L. C. Müller, from a Cotton M.S., in *Collect. Anglo-*

Saxon, Havniæ, 1835; and "Abgarus Legenden paa Old-Engelsk," with an English translation by G. Stephens, Copenhagen, 1853.

The practice of keeping this letter as a phylactery prevailed in England till the last century, as I find from Jeremiah Jones. "The common people in England have had it in their houses in many places in a frame with a picture before it, and they generally, with much honesty and devotion, regard it as the word of God, and the genuine epistle of Christ." See his *New and Full Method*, Oxford, 1798, Vol. II. p. 6. I have a recollection of having seen the same thing in cottages in Shropshire.

PAGE 11, *l.* 2.—*The eyes of the true mind.* Compare p. 19, line 21: *The secret eye of your mind*; p. 37, line 13: *The eyes of the mind*; p. 45, line 23: *The clear eyes of the mind.* See also St. Paul *Ephes.* i. 18: τους οφθαλμους της διανοιας: and Clement. *Epist. ad Corinth*, 36; and *Epist. Smyrn. de Polycarpi Mart.* 2, τοις της καρδιας οφθαλμοις.

l. 23.—*The stay of your head.* ܡܪܝܡ ܪܫܟܘܢ This word is not in the dictionaries, but its derivative and form are known. Mar Jacob, p. 97, line 10, has ܘܡܪܝܡܟ ܪܫܐ ܕܟܠ ܡܢ ܕܗܝܡܢ ܠܫܪܪܐ. In *Cod. Add.* 14,484 fol. 63, rect. we read ܗܘ ܗܘܐ ܡܪܝܡ ܗܘܐ ܪܫܗ.

l. 27.—*Because it is not in many things that the belief of the truth of Christ consists.* This is alluded to by Mar Jacob—*For faith consisteth not in many words*, p. 103, line 9.

PAGE 12, *l.* 24. — *Accepted his words.* We might have expected here ܩܒܠܘ ܗܘܘ but the text has ܗܘܐ as the MS. reads it.

PAGE 13, *l.* 10.—*My son Maanu.* Abgar had two sons of the name. This is probably the elder, who succeeded his father at Edessa, and reigned seven years: see Assemani, *Bibl. Orient.* Vol. I. p. 421. Bayer makes him the 15th King of Edessa. "Maanu bar Abgar. Dionysius Telmariensis scribit, eum anno 2061. mortuo patri successisse et septem annos regnasse. Secundum nostras rationes regnare cœpit Edessæ A. Abrahæ 2060. Martis mense A. V. C. 798. a Christo nato 45. Moses Chorenensis Ananum vocat, quod non longe recedit a Syriaco nomine: *Hist. Osrh.* p. 125. Le Vaillant de Florival writes the name *Ananoun*: see p. 136. *Augustin*: she was Abgar's mother, as we have seen above, p. 7.

l. 23.—*Shemashgram.* I have written this name according to the vowels in the treatise of Bardesan. See, respecting this and the Greek forms of the word, Notes to my *Spicilegium Syriacum*, p. 77. Whiston, from the Armenian form, writes the name "*Samsagramum*, Apahuniæ gentis principem;"

and Le Vaillant de Florival, "*Chamchacram*, chef de la maison des Abahouni :" see B. II. c. 30. He was sent, together with Hanan and Maryhab, as envoy to Marinus : see *Ibid*, p. 129. *Meherdath* seems to be the person mentioned by Tacitus in connexion with Abdu : see note *above*, p. 145.

PAGE 14, *l.* 1.—*Avida.* The MS. reads distinctly here ܥܘܝܕܐ; but it is doubtless a mistake : Avida occurs several times in connexion with Barcalba : see pp. 18, 45, 63. The name Avida also occurs in Bardesan : see *Spicil. Syr.*, pp. 1, 77. *Barcalba*, he was the son of Zati, as we learn from p. 18.

l. 2.—*Royal headband.* ܠܒ̈ܫ ܣܘܕ̈ܪܐ ܕܡܠܟܐ: at line 30 we also read ܐܝܪ̈ܐ ܘܣܘܕ̈ܪܐ ܕܡܠܟܐ, but in the *Doctrine of Simon Cephas*, p. 36, line 1, ܠܒܝܫ ܣܘܪ̈ܐ ܕܡܠܟܐ, where I have translated it "headbands of the Kings," assuming that the true reading should be as here; but in the Peshito *Acts* x. 30, we have ܠܒܝܫ ܣܘܪ̈ܐ "indutus albis." Compare חורי *Is.* xix. 9 : ארגים חורי "weavers of white" (linen or silk). In either case the meaning would be to denote some mark of great distinction or nobility. Plutarch calls the "candida fascia" διαδημα βασιλικον : see Note on Suetonius, c. 79. p. 156, *edit. Varr.*, *Lond.* 1826.

l. 12.—*Piroz.* This may, perhaps, have been the same as the person mentioned by Abgar in his letter to Narses : see Moses Chor, p. 135. It is the same name as the Greek and Latin Berosus, and as the Persian فيروز of the present day.

l. 14.—*Nebu and Bel.* These were the chief gods of Edessa, of which the former represented the *Sun* and the latter the *Moon* : see Mar Jacob of Sarug in Assemani, *Bibl. Orient.* Vol. I. p. 327 ; Bayer, *Hist. Osrh.* p. 139.

l. 22.—*Jews—who traded in silk.* ܕܙܒܢܝܐ ܡܫܝܢ. These seem to have been Jews residing at Edessa for the purpose of carrying on traffic with the countries to the East. Batne, in the province of Osrhoene, about a day's journey from Edessa, which Ammianus Marcellinus calls, "Municipium Osdroenæ," B. XXIII. c. ii. 7, was the celebrated mart where the Indians and the Seres came to trade at a fair held at the beginning of September, "refertum mercatoribus opulentis: ubi annua sollemnitate, prope Septembris initium mensis, ad nundinas magna promiscuæ fortunæ convenit multitudo, ad commercanda, quæ Indi mittunt et Seres, aliaque plurima vehi terra marique consueta :" *Ibid*, B. XIV. c. iii. 3. See Huet, *Hist. du Commerce et de la Navigation des Anciens*, p. 370. These *Seres*, as Ammianus Marcellinus, as well as other writers, tells us, manufactured *Sericum*. "Nentesque subtemina, conficiunt sericum, ad usus antehac nobilium, nunc etiam infimorum sine ulla discretione proficiens," *Ibid.* B. XXIII, c. vi. 67. The reader will recollect Virgil's verse, Geor. ii. 121, "Velleraque ut foliis depectunt tenuia Seres." This seems to be the ܪ̈ܟܝܟܐ in which the Jews in this country traded. We find this word, which, as an epithet, means *mollis, tenuis, lenis,* used as a noun substantive, as it is here, in the *Ancient Recension of the Four Gospels in Syriac,* Matt. xi. 8. ܪ̈ܟܝܟܐ ܠܒܝܫ: and in the Greek Gospel of Matthew, following the original Hebrew, εν μαλακοις ημφιεσμενον; while St. Luke adds ιματιοις after μαλακοις. Yet both state that μαλακοις was the dress of the nobles, "they that wear soft *clothing* are in kings' houses;" identifying μαλακα with "Sericum ad usus antehac nobilium" of Ammianus Marcellinus. Although I have rendered it silk, it would appear, from the accounts given, to be cotton or muslin, *lana xylina,* not *bombycina*: see Plinius, *Hist. Nat.* vi. 20.

l. 30. — *Chains.* The word ܫܐ̈ܪܝܐ, which I have translated *chains,* upon the authority of Castel, (compare also Buxtorf. Lex. Chald. et Syr. ad שׁיר), would perhaps be more correctly rendered *silks* or *muslins.* Thus, in a passage cited by Assemani *Bibl. Orient.* Vol. I. p. 186, we find ܫܕܪ ܠܗ ܕܡܘܠܐ ܕܫܐ̈ܪܝܐ ܕܠܐ ܒܨܝܪ, "which he translates "non modicam quantitatem *fili serici* transmisit." In the *Doctrine of the Apostles,* at p. ܠܗ line 2, Aggæus is called ܥܒܕ ܫܐ̈ܪܝܐ, which I have there translated, "maker of *golden* chains," having reference to p. 22, line 23. Here C. reads ܫܝ̈ܪܝܐ, which Castel also renders "sericum." Moreover, in the account of Aggæus by Moses Choren., he is called "un fabricant de coiffures de soie," in the translation of Le Vaillant de Florival; and "quendam serici opificem," in that of Whiston: see B. II. c. xxxiii. p. 131. *Whiston's edit.* p. 137. *Headbands of the king,* or diadems. These seem to have been made of silk or muslin scarves, such as form the turbans of orientals at the present day, interwoven with gold, and with figures and devices upon them. Such, at any rate, was that worn by the high-priest of Bel and Nebu. See *Acts of Sharbil,* p. 41.

PAGE 15, *l.* 3.—*Old Testament and the New.* It is plain that these terms could only have been used here in the sense of the Law of Moses and the Gospel, and not in the full sense which we now give. If by the "Acts [or Visitations] of the Apostles," ܦܘܩ̈ܕܢܘܗܝ ܕܫܠܝ̈ܚܐ, we are to understand those written by St. Luke, this passage seems to shew that the compiler of these Acts of Addæus, wrote some years subsequently to the events which he relates, or that it has been added by an interpolator still later. For at the earlier period of Addæus' ministry, no other part of the New

Testament was written than the original Hebrew Gospel of St. Matthew, which, as giving an account of the new dispensation of Jesus Christ, might have been called the New Testament or Covenant. The Acts of the Apostles, in the Peshito, is ܟܬܒܐ ܕܦܪܟܣܝܣ ܗܢܘ ܕܝܢ ܬܫܥܝܬܗܘܢ ܕܫܠܝܚܐ ܛܘܒܢܐ "The Book of πραξεις, that is, Stories of the Blessed Apostles." Compare *Doctrine of the Apostles*, pp. 27, 32, where those by Luke are called "Triumphs of the Apostles," and *Doctrine of Simon Cephas*, p. 40.

l. 29. — *Ditornon.* The reading of the MS. here is not quite clear. I am disposed to consider that the word ought to be *Diatessaron*, which Tatian, the Syrian, compiled from the Four Gospels about the middle of the second century. This we know to have been in general use at Edessa up to the fourth century, and to have had a commentary written upon it by Ephraem Syrus. See Assemani *Bibl. Orient.* Vol. I. p. 517. Theodoretus states, *Hæret. Fab.* B. I. c. 20, that he found more than 200 copies of this work received in the churches in his own diocese, which he caused to be removed, and substituted copies of the Four Gospels in their stead. See Fabricius, *Cod. Apoc. N. T.* p. 377. Ebediesu writes thus of Tatian in the Preface to his Collection of Canons: "Tatianus quidam philosophus cum Evangelistarum loquentium sensum suo intellectu cepisset, et scopum scriptionis illorum divinæ in mente sua fixisset, unum ex quatuor illis admirabile collegit evangelium, quod et Diatessaron nominavit, in quo cum cautissime seriem rectam eorum, quæ a Salvatore dicta ac gesta fuere, servasset, ne unam quidem dictionem e suo addidit." See Card. Mai, *Scriptt. Vet. Nov. Coll.* Vol. X. p. 23. If this be so, there is here a later interpolation. It is stated by Bar Hebræus that some of the books of the Old Testament and the New were translated at Edessa in the time of Abgar and Addæus: see Assemani, *Bibl. Orient.* Vol. II. p. 279; Walton, *Proleg. ad Bibl. Polyglot*, p. 89. There is also a record preserved of a very antient copy of a Gospel written by the hand of Aggæus himself, the disciple and successor of Addæus, in the year of the Greeks 389, or A.D. 78: see Assemani *Bibl. Orient.* Vol. II. p. 486, and *Preface to Remains of a very antient Recension of the Four Gospels in Syriac*, p. lxxvii. This seems to derive some confirmation from the fact of Addæus having established deacons and presbyters in the churches, and taught persons to read the Scriptures in them: see p. 18.

Page 16, *l.* 11.—*Fire worshippers and adorers of water*: see Strabo *de Persis*, c. xv. διαφεροντως δε τῳ πυρι και τῳ υδατι θυουσι; see also Abdias *Hist. Cert. Apost.*, B. VI. c. 7, "Solem et lunam deorum numero applicantes, aquam simul deitatem habere docebant:" Fabricius, *Cod. Apoc. N. T.* p. 609, and his Notes there; see also Assemani, *Bibl. Orient.* Vol. I. p. 191, and Sim. A. Assemani, *Acta Martyr.* Vol. I. pp. 40, 113, 227. Mar Jacob of Sarug, in his sermon on the Fall of Idols, Cod. Add. 14,624, fol. 12, writes ܠܫܡܫܐ ܘܣܗܪܐ ܘܠܟܘܟܒܐ ܘܠܢܗܝܪ̈ܐ: ܠܢܘܪܐ ܘܡ̈ܝܐ ܘܠܢܦܫ̈ܬܐ ܐܣܓܕ: ܐܢܘܢ. "He made them worship the sun, and the moon, and the stars, and the lights, and fire, and water, and living creatures."

l. 17.—*And Abgar wrote to Narses.* This Letter is given by Moses Chor., see p. 135.

l. 22.—*Because he was not able to pass over into the country belonging to the Romans.* In consequence of the treaties by which the limits of the Roman Empire, fixed by Augustus, extended to the Euphrates: see Tillemont *Hist. des Empereurs,* Vol. I. p. 37.; see also Extr. vi. p. 111, Dio Cassius, liv. 8. ο Σεβαστος εστησεν ορια τῃ Ρωμαιων αρχῃ Τιγριν τε και Ευφρατην.

l. 24.—*Wrote a letter and sent it to Tiberius.* This letter, and the answer of Tiberius, are given by Moses Chor., with a few variations, which the reader will observe, p. 133. See, respecting this letter to Tiberius, Henke, Proleg. *De Pontii Pilati Actis in causa Domini Nostri ad Imp. Tiberium missis probabilia,* p. xxiii., Helmstad, 1784. Bar Hebræus mentions these Epistles, *Chron. Syriac.* text, p. 52.

Page 17, *l.* 13.—*Pilate also has written.* There can be no doubt that Pontius Pilate sent an account to the Roman Government of what took place with respect to Jesus, which it was his duty to do as governor of Judea. This is mentioned by Justin Martyr, Tertullian, Eusebius, Epiphanius, Chrysostom, &c., as well as in various Apocryphal writers. A full notice of all this has been given by Fabricius, *Cod. Apoc. N. T.* p. 24; Walchius, *Hist. Eccl.* p. 174; Baronius, *Annal.* A. 34. ccxxii.—viii. Tischendorf de antiquis Pilati Actis Cæsari distinctis, in *Proleg. ad Evangelia Apocrypha,* p. lxii. Bishop Pearson's Lectiones in Acta Apostolorum, in his *Opera Posthuma,* pp. 50, 63. To these I would add the early testimony given in the *Doctrine of Simon Cephas,* p. 38, already given.

l. 14.—*My proconsul Aulbinus.* There is evidently an error in this Syriac name, such as most frequently occurs in proper names in Syriac, both on account of their being foreign to the transcribers, and of the total omission of the vowels. The name may perhaps have been confounded with that of Albinus, who was made governor of Judea by Nero, A.D. 62: see Tillemont *Hist. des Empereurs,* Vol. I. p. 561; Eusebius, *Hist. Ecc.* B. II. c. 23: see Valesius' Note, p. 28, *English Trans.* In the Apocryphal work, p. 111, the name is also given "Sabinus, the governor who had been appointed by the Emperor Tiberius, and even as far as the River Euphrates the governor Sabinus had authority." Mention of this person is altogether omitted by Moses Chor. in his history, probably because he did not know how to give the name correctly: see p. 133. The person intended could be no other than Vitellius, who was then governor of Syria, and removed Pilate from the administration of Judea, sending Marcellus in his stead, and ordered him to appear before Tiberius at Rome. The Emperor died before he reached Rome: see Tillemont, *Hist. des Empereurs*, Vol. I. pp 129, 682; *Ibid*, p. 420. See Josephus, *Antiq. Jud.* B. XVIII. c. iv. 2.

l. 15.—*People of Spain.* The letter of Tiberius, as it is read in Moses Chor., differs a good deal from this, and the reference to Spain is found near the end: see p. 134. Whiston has the following Note on this place: "Tametsi bellum hoc Hispanicum nusquam forsan alibi disertè memoretur, tamen non desunt scriptorum testimonia, ex quibus conjectura in eam rem duci potest. Nam Tiberius Hispaniarum principes olim vexaverat, atque etiam hoc ipso tempore provinciam eam plane neglexit; adeò ut tum Hispanos ad rebellandum provocaverit, tum etiam ejus faciendi opportunitatem idoneam dederit: *Regressus in Insulam, Reipublicæ quidem curam usque adeò abjecit, ut postea non decurias equitum unquam supplêrit, non tribunos militum præfectosque, non provinciarum præsides ullos mutaverit: Hispaniam et Syriam per aliquot annos sine consularibus legatis habuerit.* Suet. in Tiberium, c. 41. *Præterea Galliarum et Hispaniarum, Syriæque et Græciæ principes confiscatos:—Plurimis etiam civitatibus et privatis veteres communitates et jus metallorum* (quod ad Hispaniam præcipuè spectabat) *ac vectigalium adempta,* Ibid. c. 49. Vide etiam Tacit. Annal. vi. 27. Cæterum non omnino præteriri debet Vellei Paterculi locus, qui, nisi in eo non vana mendi suspicio subesset, rem totam clarè confirmaret. *At Tiberius Cæsar, quum certam Hispanis parendi confessionem extorserat, parem Illyriis Dalmatisque extorsit,* L. ii. c. 39." We know, however, that about the very time at which this letter of Tiberius must have been written, Vitellius was mixed up with the wars of the Parthians and Hiberians: see Tillemont, *Hist. des Empereurs*, Vol. I. p. 131; and as Hiberi is a name common to Spaniards, as well as Hiberians, the difference might have arisen in translating Tiberius' Epistle out of Latin into Syriac: or, indeed, Tiberius, with his usual dissimulation, might have used this word to conceal some ulterior designs. See Amm. Marcell. "Itidem Hiberia ex Hibero, nunc Hispania," B. XXIII. c. 21.

l. 21.—*Because he exceeded the law.* Baronius says that there ought to have been a delay of ten days before the sentence was carried into execution, and that in this manner Pilate violated the law of the Roman Emperor by crucifying our Lord so soon after sentence had been passed: "recens quippe erat Senatusconsultum Tiberianum, sic dictum, quod Tiberio Imperatore, a quo ipse Præses in Judæam est missus, factum erat ante annos duodecim, ipso Tiberio quartum et Druso Coss., quo cautum fuerat, ut supplicia damnatorum in decimum usque diem differrentur, ut Suetonius, Dio et alii testantur:" see *Annal.* 34, sec. 92.

l. 24.—*Deserve to be honoured and adored.* Tiberius is said by Tertullian to have referred to the Senate the question of admitting Christ among the Gods. "Tiberius ergo, cujus tempore nomen Christianum in sæculum introivit, annunciata sibi ex Syria Palæstina, quæ illic veritatem istius divini revelârant, detulit ad Senatum cum prærogativa suffragii sui. Senatus quia non ipse in se probaverat, respuit. Cæsar in sententia mansit, comminatus periculum accusatoribus Christianorum." *Apol.* c. 5. Mentioned also by Eusebius, *Hist. Ecc.* B. II. c. ii.; Baronius, *Ibid.* sec. 222, &c.; Bishop Pearson, Lect. in Act. Apost. *Opera Posth.*, p. 63.: see Mosheim, *Diss. ad Hist. Ecc.*, Vol. I. p. 357; Steph. Le Moyne, *Varia Sacra*, Vol. II. p. 145. This has also been interpolated into the Epistle of Tiberius to Abgar as it is found in Moses Chor., see p. 135. There is also given by the same Moses another letter of Abgar to Tiberius, in reply to this: see *Ibid.*

l. 28—*Aristides.* There is no mention of this person in Moses. Chor.; nor of the presents with which he returned to Tiberius. He, however, gives an Epistle which Abgar is said to have written in reply, of which there is no indication here.

Page 18, *l.* 1. — *Thicuntha.* This word has been so much distorted and disfigured by the transcribers that I am not able to recognise what is the place intended. The same may be said of *Artica* in the next line. This, however, may, be pronounced *Ortyka*, and be intended for *Ortygia* near Syracuse, which was not very far distant from the Island Capreæ, where we know that Tiberius at this time resided, seldom leaving it to go further than to the neighbouring coast of Campania: see Tacitus, *Annal.* B. IV. c. 67; Suetonius, *Tib.* c. 40; Josephus, *Antiq.* B. XVIII. c. vi; Tillemont, *Hist. des Empereurs*, p. 93.

l. 19.—*Guide and Ruler.* It is plain from the context here, as well as wherever it occurs in these early Syriac documents, that this title is precisely the same as that of Bishop, although the Greek word Επισκοπος had not yet obtained in the East. The first mention which we find of the title *Bishop* is in the *Acts of Sharbil*, p. 65, about A.D. 105—112, where Barsamya is called the *Bishop of the Christians*, although more generally designated as here,

The occurrence of the word at p. 23 in these *Acts of Addæus* is in a passage evidently interpolated at a much later period: see Note p. 165 *below*. It is also found in the *Doctrine of Simon Cephas*, p. 40, which seems to have been written very early in the second century, or even at the end of the first.

l. 20.—*Palut.* If this word be not of Syriac origin, it may be an abbreviation from the Greek Φιλωτας, as Patric, four lines below, is from the Latin *Patricius*.

l. 23.—*Zati.* This is perhaps the same name as Izates: see Josephus, *Antiq. Jud.*, B. XX. c. ii. 1, 4; Tacitus *Ann.* B. XII. c. 14. See also Assemani, *Bibl. Orient.* Vol. I. p. 421. *Maryhab*, seems to be the same person that is spoken of by Moses. Chor. as having been sent by Abgar as one of the envoys to Marinus. "Mar-Ihap, prince d'Aghtznik:" see p. 129 *above.*

l. 24.—*Senac.* Tacitus writes this name Sinnaces: see Note on p. 145.

Page 19, *l.* 1.—*Ordinances and Laws which were appointed by the disciples at Jerusalem.* These are given in the *Doctrine of the Apostles*, see p. 25.

l. 7—19.—*Give heed—resurrection of all men.* This passage is cited in the extract given at p. 109.

Page 20, *l.* 10.—One leaf apparently is lost from the MS. in this place.

l. 25.—*Accept not any thing from any man, and possess not any thing in this world.* These words of our Lord are not found in this form in any of the Gospels; they are, however, tantamount to the instruction given by him to the Twelve when he sent them forth. *Matt.* x. 7—10.

Page 21, *l.* 2.—*Fourteenth of the month Iyar* (*May*). This date is not only confirmed by Amru, the historian cited by Assemani, *Bibl. Orient.*, Vol. II. p. 392, but also by a very antient Syriac Calendar. Bar Hebræus, therefore, is mistaken, not only in giving the day as the 30th of July, but also in saying that he was put to death: he has evidently confounded Addæus with his immediate successor Aggæus; like as Moses Chor. has mistaken the name, see p. 136. Bar Hebræus also confounds the places of their burial, saying that Addæus was buried in a church which he had built at Edessa: see Assemani, *Bibl. Orient.* Vol. II. p. 392. Addæus was buried by Abgar in the sepulchre of his ancestors, p. 21, and Aggæus in the church which he had built, p. 23. The death of Addæus took place before that of Abgar, which happened A.D. 45: see *Ibid*, Vol. I. p. 420; Bayer, *Hist. Osrh.*, p. 125. It would, therefore, appear that his ministry at Edessa was of about ten or eleven years duration.

l. 12.—*Those of the house of Ariu, the ancestors of Abgar the King.* See Moses Chor., B. II. c. xiv., and Abgar's descent from Arsaces: Bayer, *Hist. Osrh.* p. 97.

l. 17.—*The ordinance and instruction—by the Apostle Addæus.* Compare *Doctrine of the Apostles*, XVIII. p. 28.

l. 19.—*Aggæus who himself became Guide and Ruler and the successor of his Chair after him.* See *Doctrine of the Apostles*, pp. 32, 34 *below*; see Assemani, *Bibl. Orient.* Vol. II. p. 392; Vol. III. p. 611.

l. 28.—*The whole state* ܩܝܡܐ: this seems to apply to those who especially belonged to the ministry of the church; thus ܒ̈ܢܝ ܩܝܡܐ is used for "clerici," in contradistinction to ܒ̈ܢܝ ܥܠܡܐ "laici:" see Assemani, *Bibl. Orient.* Vol. I. p. 189, &c.

PAGE 22, *l.* 11.—*Like a net.* Alluding to our Lord's words, *Matt.* xix. 1, "I will make you fishers of men." Compare with this τῃ σαγηνῃ του ευαγγελιου ζωγρησαι, used by Nicephorus, as applied to this Addæus. *Hist. Eccl.* B. II. c. 40.

l. 14.—*One of his rebellious sons.* This would seem to be the second son of Abgar called Maanu, who succeeded his brother Maanu, and reigned fourteen years, that is, from A.D. 52 to A.D. 65, according to Dionysius, cited by Assemani, *Bibl. Orient.* Vol. I. p. 421; see also Bayer, *Hist. Osrh.* p. 130. Moses Chor., who evidently copied from this document, does not give the name of the king; unless, indeed, the words "Le prince, qui régna après la mort de son père" are to be referred to "Ananoun fils d'Abgar règne à Édesse" at the beginning of the chapter: see p. 136. Clem. Galanus also writes: "Secundus Rex post Abagarum fuit filius quidam ejus anonymus, qui Christianam Patris religionem aspernatus, fideles atrociter insectatus est; ac misere vitam complevit. Tertius fuit Sanatrughus, filius sororis Abgari, cujus imperio Sanctos Apostolos Bartholomæum et Thaddæum in regionibus illis interfectos fuisse narrant Armenii:" see *Conciliatio Ecc. Arm. cum Rom.* p. 9; see Assemani, *Ibid.* In the extract given at p. 109, *Severus*, son of Abgar, is stated to have slain Addæus. This is most probably a mistake in substituting Addæus for Aggæus, such as Moses Chor. has made: see Note p. 162, above. In the book called *The Bee*, by Solomon Bishop of Bassora, about A.D. 1222, (concerning which see Assemani *Bibl. Orient.* Vol.. III. p. 309), in the 49th chapter, Touching the Apostles, and the places of each one of them, and of their deaths, we find the following ܐܕܝ، ܡܢ ܦܢܝܐ ܐܬܪܘܬܗ، ܗܘܐ. ܘܐܟܪܙ ܒܐܘܪܗܝ، ܕܒܝܬ ܢܗܪܝܢ ܒܝܘܡܝ ܐܒܓܪ. ܘܩܛܠܗ ܒܪ ܗܘܪܕܘܣ ܒܪܗ ܕܐܒܓܪ ܠܘܬ ܚܣܢܐ ܕܐܓܝܠ. ܘܐܬܩܒܪ ܦܓܪܗ ܒܬܪܟܢ ܘܐܘܒܠܘܗ، ܠܪܗܘܡܐ. ܘܐܝܬ ܕܐܡܪܝܢ ܕܒܗ ܒܐܘܪܗܝ، ܐܬܬܢܝܚ. ܐܠܐ ܬܠܡܝܕܗ ܐܝܬܘܗܝ، ܗܘܐ ܠܗܘܕܪ ܒܒܕ

ܫܐܪ̈ܝܐ ܕܐܒܓܪ ܘܐܬܬܠܡܕ. ܘܒܬܪ ܡܘܬܗ ܕܐܒܓܪ ܐܡܠܟ
ܒܪܗ ܒܕܘܟܬܗ. ܘܬܒܥ ܡܢ ܐܓܝ ܕܢܙܩܘܪ ܠܗ ܫܐܪ̈ܝܐ. ܘܟܕ
ܠܐ ܐܬܛܦܝܣ ܟܕ ܐܡܪ ܕܠܐ ܡܨܐ ܐܢܐ ܕܐܫܒܘܩ ܬܘܠܡܕܐ
ܕܟܪܘܙܘܬܐ ܘܐܬܦܢܐ ܠܙܩܘܪܘܬܐ. ܚܒܛܗ܆ ܒܫܒܛܐ ܥܠ
ܫܩܘ̈ܗܝ ܘܬܒܪ ܐܢܝܢ. ܘܡܝܬ. ܬܕܝ܆ ܗܘܐ ܒܬܪܗ ܒܐܘܪܗܝ܆.
ܘܩܛܠܗ ܕܝܢ ܐܦ ܗܘ ܗܪܘܕܣ ܒܪܗ ܕܐܒܓܪ ܘܐܬܬܩܒܪ ܒܐܘܪܗܝ܆.

"Addæus was from Paneas, and he preached in Edessa of Mesopotamia in the days of Abgar. But Herodes, the son of Abgar, slew him at the Castle of Agel; and his body was afterwards taken up, and they brought it to Rome. There are some who have said that it was deposited at Edessa. *Aggæus*, his disciple, was formerly a maker of silks for Abgar, and he became converted. And after the death of Abgar, his son reigned in his stead, and he required of Aggæus to weave him silk. And when he did not comply, saying, I cannot give up the teaching of preaching and turn to weaving, he struck him upon the legs with a club and brake them, and he died. *Thaddæus* succeeded him in Edessa, but the same Herodes, the son of Abgar, slew him, and he was buried at Edessa." This is from a MS. in my possession. It is easy to see here that errors have arisen from the confusion of the name of *Addæus*, *Aggæus*, and *Thaddæus;* and that the *Herodes* here is the same as *Severus* in the extract at p. 109. Cedrenus, cited by Assemani *Bibl. Orient.* Vol. I. p. 421, writes: "Huic pio instituto obtemperatum est, quamdiu Abgarus, atque post hunc filius vixerunt. Nepos autem, quum in avi locum et regnum successisset, abjecta pietate, ad simulacrorum cultum descivit: statuitque, sublata Christi imagine, statuam dæmonis reponere." In the account of Constantine Porphyrogenitus, as given by Simeon Metaphrastes, we read, "Itaque conservatum est hoc hujus viri pietatis expressum monumentum et Deo dicatum donarium, donec in hoc vitæ incolatu mansit Abagarus, et ejus filius qui regni simul et pietatis paternæ fuit successor. Cæterum eorum filius et nepos fuit quidem successor paterni et aviti imperii, non fuit autem hæres etiam pietatis. Sed in pietatem calcibus, ut ita dicam, insultavit et ad dæmones et idola transfugit:" Lipomanus, *Sanct. Hist.* Par. I. p. 190. If, therefore, we assume that it was Abgar's grandson, Abgar, son of Maanu, as given by Dionysius, (whose reign of twenty years was extended from A.D. 65 to A.D. 86, see Bayer, *Hist. Osrh.* pp. 130, 147,) who caused Aggæus to be put to death, this would be perfectly consistent with the fact of a copy of the Gospels having been transcribed by Aggæus, A.D. 78, or eight years before the death of this king: see Note, page 158 *above.*

l. 27.—*And brake his legs.* This ignominious mode of execution, which put an end to the sufferings of the two Thieves on the cross, seems to have been of Roman rather than of oriental origin. Seneca *De ira*, B. III. c. 32, writes, "Magnam rem sine dubio fecerimus, si servulum infelicem in ergastulum miserimus. Quid properamus verberare statim, crura protinus frangere?" It was in use in the time of Plautus, "Crura hercle effringentur." Suetonius has "Thallo a manu, quod pro epistola prodita denarios quingentos accepisset, crura fregit." *Octavius*, c. 67. On which passage Casaubon has the following note: "Crurifragium olim servorum et ancillarum pœna erat, meminit iterum Suetonius, Lib. iii. c. 44. Fuit et publicum maleficorum hominum supplicium: ut delatorum sub Commodo. Eusebius Lib. v. δειλαιος παρα καιρον την δικην εισελθων, αυτικα καταγνυται τα σκελη. Vide etiam Agathiam L. iv. Sed exempla in Martyrologiis, et apud alios etiam scriptores passim." The object of the king in putting this early martyr to this kind of death seems to have been to degrade and disgrace him.

Page 23. *l.* 6—13. *And because he died—thirteen years.* This passage is a barefaced interpolation by some ignorant person much later, who evidently is also responsible for the interpolated passages in the Martyrdom of Sharbil, p. 61, and in that of Barsamya p. 72. For this Palut was made *Presbyter* by Addæus himself, when Aggæus was appointed *Bishop*, or *Guide and Ruler*, see p. 18. This took place before the death of Abgar himself, who died A.D. 45, as we have seen above. How then could he have been made Bishop by Serapion of Antioch, who did not succeed to that episcopal throne before the beginning of the third century, if, as is here stated, he was consecrated Bishop by Zephyrinus of Rome, who did not become Pope till A.D. 201? See H. Dodwell, *Diss. Sing. de Pontt. Rom. Primæva Successione*, p. 83.

l. 12.—*In the days of that Cæsar who reigned there thirteen years.* He seems to mean Claudius, although the twenty-five years of Peter's episcopate extended through his reign and that of Nero: the duration of each was about thirteen years: see *Ibid.* p. 77.

l. 17.—*Labubna.* Moses Chor. refers to this author, B. II. c. 36: "Ghéroupna, fils de l'écrivain Apchatar, a recueilli tous ces faits, arrivés du temps d'Abgar et de Sanadroug, et les a déposés dans les archives d'Édesse:" translation of Le Vaillant de Florival. Whiston writes the name "Lerubnas, Apsadari Scribæ filius:" Apsadar, of the one, and Apchatar of the other, are evidently corruptions in the Armenian from Abdshaddai or Ebedshaddai of the Syriac. The variation in the orthography of the names arises simply from the different way in which the first letter may be enunciated. On the interchange of the letter G, L, and R, see St. Martin, *Mémoires Historiques et Geographique sur l'Arménie*, Vol. I. p. 215. Guis. Cappellotti, in his Italian translation of Moses Choren. *Storico Armeno del quinto secolo*, Venez. 1841, writes the names "Lerubnase figlio de Afsadari." In a letter to me, dated St. Lazare, Venise, 23 Janvier 1863, the learned Dr. Alishan writes thus: "Vous vous rappelerez peutêtre, que notre historien Moïse de Khorène, traduit en plusieurs langues, fait mention d'un ecrivain nommé Ghérubna, qui vivait sous le règne d'Abgar, et qui ecrivit l'histoire de ce même roi ou les événements de cette époque. Or j'ai découvert dans un manuscrit probablement de XIIme. siècle une histoire d'Abgar et de Thaddé dont l'auteur, y est-il-dit, est un certain Ghérubnia, qui l'aura écrit avec l'aide d'Anané, confident du roi Abgar. Je suis porté a croire que c'est la traduction de l'original, que vous avez découvert en langue Syriaque. L'Arménien est complait: et bien que rédigé sous le roi Abgar, il y a eut beaucoup d'interpolations, selon moi, dans cet histoire, tout ou en partie, au commencement du siècle IIIme. Nous pensons aussi a publier cet histoire: en attendant nous serons heureux de vous voir, Monsieur, nous devancer. Il se trouve aussi dans nos Ménologues une biographie ou les Acts de Saints Barsémi et Sabylle, mais en abrégé. Je me réjouis avec vous de la découverte, que vous venez de faire, des ouvrages de St. Jaques de Nisibe, dont nous n'avons pas en Arménien d'exemplaires assez anciens."

Page 24.—Doctrine of the Apostles. This work is taken from the same MS. as the preceding, Cod. Add. 14,644, fol. 10, and is printed verbatim from it. It is also found in Cod. Add. 14,531, fol. 109. It has been already printed entire by A. P. de Lagarde in his *Reliquiæ Juris Ecclesiastici Antiquissimæ*, Vienna, 1856, p. ܠܐ It is there attributed to *Addæus*

ܬܘܒ ܡܢ ܡܟܬܒܢܘܬܐ ܕܡܠܦܢܘܬܐ ܕܐܕܝ ܫܠܝܚܐ: ܗܘ ܕܬܠܡܕ

ܘܐܠܦ ܠܐܘܪܗܝܐ ܘܠܟܠܗܘܢ ܗܢܘܢ ܕܒܐܬܪܐ ܕܒܝܬ ܢܗܪܝܢ

"Again from the Treatise of the *Doctrine of Addæus the Apostle*, who taught and instructed the people of Edessa, and all those who were in the region of Mesopotamia." And at the end of it is written, "Here endeth the Treatise of Addæus the Apostle." Dr. Land, in his *Anecdota Syriaca*, p. 19, in the imperfect description which he has given of the MS. 14,644, writes, "F. 10. r. sqq., Doctrina Apostolorum. Edidit de Lagarde e codice Sanctogermanensi 38 bibl. Imp. Paris. Lipsiæ anno 1854." It is plain that Dr. Land could never have compared the two. The book in which he says this treatise is published is altogether another work, was printed at a different place, with different type, and two years earlier: and its title is *Didascalia Apostolorum Syriace, Lipsiæ*, 1854.

It is well known that we owe the publication of the *Didascalia* to De Lagarde; although his name does not appear: indeed, the author in his preface gives the reason for withholding his name. This treatise had also been printed before, omitting the beginning, and commencing with the first Ordinance or Canon, in Syriac, in the 10th volume of the *Scriptorum Veterum Nova Collec.*, by the Cardinal Mai, with a Latin translation by A. Assemani, pp. 3—8; and Text, pp. 169—175. "Ebediesu Metropolitæ Sobæ et Armeniæ Collectio Canonum Synodicorum, ex Chaldaicis Bibliothecæ Vaticanæ codicibus sumpta, et in Linguam Latinam translata ab Aloysio Assemani. Præcedit Epitome Canonum Apostolicorum, auctore eodem Ebediesu." By Ebediesu this work is called ܩܢ̈ܘܢܐ ܕܛܘ̈ܟܣܐ ܘܢܡܘ̈ܣܐ ܕܣܡܘ ܫܠܝ̈ܚܐ: "Canones rituum et legum quos constituerunt Apostoli." And at the end ܫܠܡܬ ܣܘܢܗܕܘܣ ܩܕܡܝܬܐ ܕܫܠܝ̈ܚܐ "Explicit Synodus I. Apostolorum." It is cited by Bar Hebræus in his "Nomocanon," translated by J. A. Assemani, and printed by Cardinal Mai in the same Vol. X, Par. ii. p. 31, *Didascalia Adæi Apostoli unius e* 70. I also have found it quoted in Cod. Add. 14,173, fol. 37, as ܩܢ̈ܘܢܐ ܕܫܠܝ̈ܚܐ: "Canons of the Apostles." It was likewise known to Johannes Damascenus: see *Opera*, edit. Le Quien, Vol. I. p. 266. The text of the *Doctrine of the Apostles* I have printed exactly as I found it in 14,644. I have, however, carefully compared it with 14,531, and with that edited by De Lagarde, and made use of this collation in the English translation. Wherever I have had occasion to refer to these texts in the Notes, they are designated A. B. C. respectively.

l. 10.—*The three hundred and.* These words have been omitted in A. I have supplied them from B., which adds ܬܠܬܡܐܐ. C. reads ܫܡܒ or 342. Bar Hebræus, in his *Nomocanon*, has the following reference to this passage, "*Ex Didascalia Adœi Apostoli unius e* 70, Anno 339. Græcorum, die 4 Junii in complemento Pentecostes, cum glorificarent Apostoli Deum in cœnaculo, ubi fecerant Pascha, descendit super eos Spiritus Sanctus, et docuit eos ordines et leges, et ipsi imposuerunt eas illis, qui consenserunt prædicationi ipsorum." In a Note on this J. A. Assemani adds "In margine legitur 'Didascalia Adæi ad Edessanos et reliquos, anno Græcorum 342. die 14. mensis Junii." See Mai, *Scriptt. Vet. Nova Coll.* Vol. X. Par. ii. p. 31.

l. 11.—*Fourth day* ܐܪܒܥܬܐ: B. reads ܐܪܒܥܐ, but C. ܒܐܪܒܥܣܪ̈ܐ "fourteenth."

l. 12.—*Pentecost.* The Ascension of our Lord and the day of Pentecost seem to be confounded here.

l. 15.—*Baith Zaithe,* that is, the Mount of Olives. Luke in his Gospel, xxiv. 50, says that "he led them out as far as Bethany, and he lifted up his hands, and blessed them;" but says nothing about his conferring upon them the gift of the priesthood, as we find here. In the Acts, i. 12, he says after the Ascension, "then returned they unto Jerusalem from the mount called Olivet;" but omits there all mention of our Lord lifting up his hands and blessing them.

l. 24.—*Upper Room.* ὑπερῳον: see Bishop Pearson, *Lectiones in Acta Apostolorum*, pp. 30, 31, and Whiston's, *Essay on the Apostolic Constitutiones*, p. 20.

Page 25, *l.* 12.—*When I am ascended to my Father I will send to you the Spirit, the Paraclete, that he may teach you every thing which it is meet for you to know and to make known.* We find this promise, but not in the same words, in St. John xiv. 26, "But the Comforter (ὁ παρακλητος), *which is* the Holy Ghost, whom the Father will send in my name, he shall teach you all things, and bring all things to your remembrance, whatsoever I have said to you."

l. 17.—*A sweet odour, which is strange to the world.* There is no mention of this in the Acts. *Odour* ܪܐܝܚܐ; B. C. reads ܪܝܚܐ *Was diffused* ܦܚ, both B. and C. read ܦܐܚ, which seems to be more correct.

l. 19.—*From heaven.* ܡܢ ܫܡܝܐ: B. reads ܡܢ ܫܠܝܐ "suddenly."

l. 20.—*According to the tongue,* &c.: this leaves no doubt whatever as to the meaning which was from the first attached to the gift of tongues by the oriental Christians who used this.

l. 26.—*The Apostles.* Ebediesu adds *holy* all through.

l. 27.—*As the lightning, &c.* *Matt.* xxiv. 27.

l. 30.—*Suddenly.* ܡܢ ܫܠܝܐ. B. C. read ܠܚܪܬܐ "at the last." Ebediesu ܡܢ ܫܡܝܐ "de cœlo." This first Canon is cited by Bar Hebræus, in his *Nomocanon.* "*Adæi.* 1. Constituerunt itaque Apostoli—ad orientem orate—quia ab oriente apparebit Dominus in fine." Card. Mai, *Scriptt. Vet.* Vol X. Par. ii. p. 33; and by Johannes Damascenus. It is also found in Cod. Add. 17,193, fol. 37, with Nos. 2, 3, 4, and 14, where they are called ܩܢܘܢܐ ܕܫܠܝ̈ܚܐ "Canons of the Apostles." Respecting "praying towards the East:" compare *Apostolic Constitutions*, B. II. c. 57, VII. c. 44, and Tertullian, *Apol.* c. 16.

PAGE 26, *l.* 1.—II. Compare this Canon with *Apostolic Constitutions*, B. II. c. 59; compare also for this and the three following Canons, *Compendiaria Fidei Expositio*, cited by Grabe, *Spicilegium*, Vol. I. p. 53.

l. 7.—*Angels of heaven.* C. reads ܡܠܐܟ̈ܘܗܝ ܩܕܝ̈ܫܐ "His holy angels."

l. 9.—III. Compare *Apostolic Constitutions*, B. V. c. 13—15.

l. 11.—*His trial*, ܕܝܢܗ. B. reads ܕܢܚܗ "his manifestation."

l. 13.—*This sorrow.* C. has ܡܛܠ ܗܕܐ ܒܟܪܝܘܬܐ "on account of this in sorrow."

l. 20.—V. See *Apostolic Constitutions*, B. II. c. 25.

l. 23.—*Overseer, the same is the Guide*, ܕܘܩܐ. This does not correspond with the Greek επισκοπος, but with σκοπος, as we find upon comparing the Syriac Didascalia, edit. De Lagarde, p. 13, ܘܐܢܬ ܒܪܢܫܐ ܕܘܩܐ ܗܘ ܝܗܒܬܟ ܠܒܝܬ ܐܝܣܪܝܠ ܕܬܫܡܥ ܡܢ ܦܘܡܝ ܡܠܬܐ which corresponds with the Greek of the Constitutiones Apost., B. II. c. 6. sec. 2. Υιε ανθρωπου, σκοπον δεδωκα σε τῳ οικῳ Ισραηλ, και ακουσῃ εκ στοματος μου λογον: *Ezek.* xxxiii. 7; where in our English version, it is rendered *watchman*, "Lo thou, O son of man, I have set thee a watchman unto the house of Israel."

l. 24.—*The people.* ܥܡܐ. For this B. reads ܥܠܡܐ "world."

l. 25.—*City.* B. reads ܡܫܪܝܬܐ "camp."

l. 26.—*Celebrate.* Ebediesu adds here ܘܥܡܐ ܕܒܝܬ ܝܠܕܗ ܕܡܪܢ ܒܥܣܪܝܢ ܘܚܡܫܐ ܒܟܢܘܢ ܩܕܡܝܐ. : "Celebrate diem Nativitatis Domini nostri die 25. Decembris, quia hoc est caput omnium Festorum: et Festum Epiphaniæ die 6. Januarii in supputatione extensa Græcorum." This is evidently an interpolation by a much later hand: for we learn from Dionysius Bar Salibi, a writer of the 12th century, that in antient times these two festivals were kept on the same day, the 6th of January. Quoting Jacob of Edessa, he writes, "Sanctus Eusebius, anno, inquit, 312. Græcorum, qui est annus quadragesimus tertius Augusti, et 33. Herodis, quo tempore missus est in Syriam Cyrinus, Christus natus est. Jacobus Edessenus, quem nos sequimur: anno 309. Græcorum qui est annus 41. Augusti et 31. Herodis: ejusdem autem passio anno 21. Tiberii. . . . . S. Ephraem in quodam sermone scribit: 'Die decima (Martii) accidit ejus conceptio, et sexta (Januarii) ejus nativitas:' Jacobus vero Edessenus; Epist. ad Mosem Tur-Abdinensem: Nemo exactè novit diem nativitatis Domini: hoc dumtaxat indubitabile est, eum noctu natum fuisse, ex his quæ scribit Lucas. Et in provinciis quidem orientalibus, et quæ ad septentrionem vergunt, usque ad tempora Arcadii Imperatoris et S. Johannis, die 6. Januarii hoc festum agebant, illudque appellabant festum Nativitatis, hoc est, Epiphaniæ, quemadmodum in S. Theologi Oratione de Nativitate vocabatur." And an anonymous Syriac writer, also cited by Assemani, states: "Mense Januario natus est Dominus, eodem die quo Epiphaniam celebramus, quia veteres uno eodemque die festum Nativitatis et Epiphaniæ peragebant." *Bibl. Orient.* Vol. II. pp. 163, 164.

The following is also a Note of Assemani on this subject, *Ibid*, Vol. III. p. 87: "In Ægypto et reliquis Orientalibus Ecclesiis Festum Nativitatis et Epiphaniæ Domini usque ad tempora S. Johannis Chrysostomi simul celebratum fuit, ut idem Chrysostomus, Homil 72. tom. 5. quæ est *In Natalem Diem Salvatoris Nostri*, testatur, affirmans, quum illam recitasset Orationem, nondum decem elapsos fuisse annos, quum primum dies ille, Nativitatis nimirum, innotuisset Ecclesiæ Orientali."

l. 30.—VII. Compare *Apostolic Constitutions*, B. V. c. 13.

Page 27, *l.* 7.—VIII. This is No. X. in Ebediesu. It is cited by Bar Hebræus in his Nomocanon. "*Adæi Apostoli*, 8. In fine omnium librorum Evangelium legatur, tanquam coronis quædam, et populus stans illud audiat." Card. Mai, *Scrip. Vett.*, Vol. X. Par. II. p. 52. Compare *Apost. Constit.*, B. II. c. 57.

l. 12.—IX. This is No. VIII. in Ebediesu. *Fifty days.* C. reads ܐܪ̈ܒܥܝܢ "forty."

l. 15.—X. This is No. IX. in Ebediesu. It is cited on the margin of Cod. Add. 14,609, fol. 123. *Except the Old Testament, &c.* Compare *Doctrine of Simon Cephas*, p. 40; *Apost. Constit.*, B. II. c. 57. Philastrius, hæresi lxxxvii, quotes this with some additions, "Propter quod statutum est ab Apostolis et eorum successoribus, non aliud legi in Ecclesia debere Catholica, nisi Legem, et Prophetas, et Evangelia, et Actus Apostolorum, et Pauli tredecim Epistolas, et septem alias, Petri duas, Johannis tres, Judæ unam, et unam Jacobi, quæ septem Actibus Apostolorum conjunctæ sunt." Cited by Fabricius, *Cod. Apoc. N. T.*, p. 749.

l. 25.—*Or lieth.* ܐܘ ܡܬܟܪܟ. B. C. and Ebediesu read ܘܡܬܟܪܟ "and lieth."

Page 28, *l.* 5.—"*Before whom no artifices avail.*" 1 *Sam.* ii. 3, as in the Peshito: our English version has followed the קרי, substituting ולו for ולא, "and by him actions are weighed." The Septuagint has και θεος ετοιμαζων επιτηδευματα αυτου.

l. 28.—XVIII. This is cited by Gregory Bar Hebræus in his Nomocanon, translated by J. A. Assemani. "*Adœi.* Constituerunt Apostoli, ut illorum, qui exeunt ex hoc sæculo cum testimonio bono, et tribulationes passi sunt propter nomen Domini nostri, memoriam agatis, in die interfectionis eorum." See Mai, *Scrip. Vett. Nova Coll.* Vol. X. Par. II. p. 36. We find this carried out by the Church of Smyrna, as is testified by their letter respecting the Martyrdom of Polycarp, "The Lord grant we may with joy and gladness celebrate the birth-day of his martyrdom, both in memory of those who have hitherto undergone and been victorious in the glorious conflict, and also for the instruction and preparation of such as shall hereafter be exercised therein :" see Eusebius, *Hist. Eccl.* B. IV. c. 15. *English Trans.* p. 59.

Page 29, *l.* 13.—XXII. Compare this with *Doctrine of Addœus*, p. 15; *Apost. Constit.*, B. II. c. 45.

l. 29.—XXV. This is cited by Gregory Bar Hebræus in his Nomocanon. "Adaei. Reges, qui credituri sunt, poterunt ascendere ad altare una cum sacerdotibus, quoniam David quoque, et alii, qui instar ejus, ascendebant :" *Scrip. Vett.*, Vol. X., Part. II. p. 8.

Page 30, *l.* 8.—XXVII. This is also cited by Gregory Bar Hebræus, "*Adœi Apostoli*, 26. Panis oblationis in illa die, qua coquitur, ascendat ad altare, et non post aliquot dies, quod fieri non licet :" *Ibid*, p. 19. This is likewise quoted by Dionysius Bar Salibi in his *Expositio Missœ*, as given by Assemani, without the name of Addæus, but referring it to the Apostles, "Statuerunt Apostoli, sicut in Canone," &c., *Bibl. Orient.* Vol. I. page 183.

l. 19.—*For Paul also and Timothy*, &c. Compare *Acts* xv.

Page 31, *l.* 1.—*Caiphas.* There prevailed a common belief among the Jacobites that Caiphas, whose name was also Joseph (see Tillemont, *Mem. pour servir a l'Hist. Eccl.*, Vol. I. p. 14), was the same person as Josephus the historian, and that he was converted to Christianity: see Assemani, *Bibl. Orient.* Vol. II. p. 165. In the *Bee*, ch. 44, I read ܩܝܦܐ ܕܝܢ ܗ̇ܘ ܕܚܝܒ
ܠܡܪܢ ܗܘܝܘ ܝܘܣܦܘܣ ܫܡܗ ܕܝܢ ܕܒܪܐܒܐ ܝܫܘܥ ܡܬܩܪܐ
"But Caiphas, who condemned our Lord, the same is Josephus. And the name of Barabbas was called Jesus."

l. 27.—*Whatsoever they taught the multitudes, they fulfilled the same themselves in deeds before all men.* Compare *Doctrine of Addœus*, "Whatsoever they said to others and exhorted them to do, they themselves exhibited the same in deeds in their own persons," p. 22.

Page 32, *l.* 3.—*After the death of the Apostles there were Guides and Rulers in the church.* It would appear from this passage that this treatise must have been written anterior to the time when the title of Bishop, as especially appropriated to those who succeeded to the apostolic office, had generally obtained in the East.

l. 10.—*Andrew from Phrygia—Thomas from India.* From this it appears that there were Epistles, or other writings, both of Andrew and Thomas, acknowledged at this time in the church in the East. There still exists a writing, Πραξεις και μαρτυριον του αγιου αποστολου Ανδρεου, which was first published by Car. Christ. Woog, with the title "Presbyterorum et diaconorum Achaiæ de Martyrio S. Andreæ Apostoli epistola encyclica." *Lipsiæ*, 1749. This has been reprinted with emendations by Const. Tischendorf, in *Acta Apostolorum Apocrypha*, p. 106. It is also given in Latin by Surius, at Novemb. 30. Several learned men have held it to be genuine. See Tillemont, *Mem. p. s. a l'Hist. Ecc.*, Vol. I. p. 589. Tischendorf, *Prolegomena.* The Acts of St. Andrew are twice mentioned by Epiphanius, in connection with those of St. Thomas, *Hæres.* 42, 61 : see Fabricius, *Cod. Apoc. N. T.* p. 747. Respecting the Acts of St. Thomas, see p. 141 above. Although, perhaps, interpolated and changed, these Acts, which were then received and read in the Eastern churches, are, doubtless, very antient, and contain some germ of truth. There is no mention here of the Epistles of St. Paul. At this early period they might not have been collected together and become generally known in the East. The Epistle of Jude, likewise, is omitted here, but it was never received into the Syriac Canon : see De Wette, *Einleitung*, 6th edit. p. 342.

l. 14.—*Apostles—the Old Testament and the New.* It is plain that the Epistles were not at that time considered as a part of what was called the *New Testament*, nor the Prophets of the *Old*: see *Note*, p. 157.

Page 33, *l.* 14. — *Pelusium.* ܦܠܘܣܘܢ. B. ܦܠܘܣܝܡ. C. reads ܦܢܛܐܦܘܠܝܣ "Pentapolis." *Indians.* ܗܢܕܘܝܐ. B. reads ܗܢܕܘ. C. ܟܘܫܝܐ, "Ethiopians."

l. 24. — *The church there.* C. adds after this ܘܒܢܐ ܥܕܬܐ ܒܐܢܛܝܘܟܝܐ "and he built a church at Antioch."

l. 28.—*And Britain,* ܒܪܘܛܢܝܐ. B. reads ܒܪܝܛܢܝܐ, C ܒܪܛܢܝܐ. A. Assemani has wrongly rendered it "Bithynia :" see Card. Mai, *Scrip. Vett. Nova Coll.* Vol. X. p. 7.

Page 34, *l.* 9.—*Gothia.* C. reads ܓܠܛܝܐ ܓܘܝܬܐ "Inner Galatia."

l. 14.—*The great River.* C. reads ܕܢܘܒܝܣ : "the Danube."

l. 17.—*Soba.* This is the same as Nisibis : see Assemani, Diss. de Syris Nest. *Bibl. Orient.* Vol. III. Par. II. p. dcclxviii.

l. 22.—*The Seventy-two Apostles.* See Walchius, *Hist. Eccl.* p. 302, and Tillemont, Note sur les 72 Disciples, *Mem. Hist. Eccl.* Vol. I. p. 436 : "Le texte grec de St. Luc ne conte que 70 Disciples ; le latin en met 72. L'auteur des Recognitions, qui en met 72, aussibien que celui des Constitutions apostoliques, dit que J. C. les choisit en ce nombre a l'imitation de ceux de Moyse. D'autres anciens disent le mesme chose, ou d'autres equivalents. Baronius cite plusieurs anciens grecs et latins, qu'il dit avoir lu 72. . . . . Mr. Cotelier remarque fort judicieusement que l'usage aura plus aisément fait 70 de 72, que 72 de 70."

l. 24.—*Huzzites.* See, respecting these, Assemani, *Bibl. Orient.* Vol. III. Par. II. p. 419—421.

l. 25.—*Gog and Magog.* See Assemani, *Acta Martt.* Vol. I. p. 36.

l. 27.—*The chainmaker.* See Note, p. 157 *above.*

Page 35, *l.* 9.—*Priscus.* B. reads ܦܪܝܣܩܠܐ : "Priscilla." C. ܦܪܝܣܩܠܐܣ "Priscillas." In 2 *Tim.* iv. 19 the name is written Prisca ; but *Acts* xviii. 2, and *Rom.* xvi. 3, Priscilla. Correct here a misprint, and read Aquilas.

l. 11.—*Timothy and Erastus of Lystra.* We find from *Acts* xvi. 1, that Timothy was of Lystra, and at xix. 22 he and Erastus are mentioned together. *Meneas,* C. reads ܡܝܠܝܛܘܣ "Miletus ;" but the last three letters are in a more recent hand. It is probably the same as Manaen, whom, *Acts* xiii. 1, we find to be associated with Saul at Antioch. The name is there written in the Peshito *Manael.* Salomon of Bassora, in the *Bee,* mentions one of the Seventy of this name, ܡܢܐܘܣ, *Menaus* : see Assemani, *Bibl. Orient.* Vol. III. p. 319 ; and the same in a copy in my hands. In a list of the 72 given in Cod. Add. 14,601 fol. 164, the name is ܡܢܐ, *Mena* or Menas.

l. 14.—*The city of Rome.* After this C. adds ܟܕ ܙܩܦܗ ܥܠ ܨܠܝܒܐ "Crucifying him on the cross." C. also adds ܫܠܡ ܡܡܠܠܘܬܐ ܕܐܕܝ ܫܠܝܚܐ "Here endeth the Treatise of Addæus the Apostle."

l. 19.—Doctrine of Simon Cephas. This is found in the same MS. as the preceding, Cod. Add. 14,644, fol. 15, which I denote by A. There is also another copy of it, B., in Cod. Add. 14,609. This MS. B. is written in two columns quarto, and is imperfect, several leaves having been lost in the body of the volume. The Rubric on the first page is ܦܘܢܝܬܐ ܕܐܓܪ̈ܬܐ

2 Y

[illegible] ܕܟܠ : "Table of Treatises of all kinds." It contains an Epistle of John the Monk to Hesychius the Monk; Stories of the Triumphs of Mar Jacob the Bishop; of Mari Abraham, Bishop of Haran. This *Doctrine of Peter*, fol. 16 rect. to 19 rect.; Triumphs of St. Anthony, by Athanasius; Story of Brethren Monks in Egypt, which are separately enumerated, apparently by Palladius; a Letter of Herod to Pilate, and of Pilate to Herod; an Epistle of Cyril of Jerusalem; and the Story of Clement who followed Simon Cephas: which last work has been published by De Lagarde from Cod. Add. 12,150, collated with this, under the title "Clementis Romani Recognitiones Syriace, Lipsiæ, 1861."

l. 19.—*Simon Cephas.* B. reads ܦܛܪܘܣ ܫܠܝܚܐ, "the Apostle Peter."

l. 20.—*In the third year.* The MS. reads ܬܠܬܝܢ: evidently an error. Tillemont says that St. Peter went to Rome in the second year of Claudius: "Il y vint sous l'Empire de Claude, en la deuxieme année de son règne selon quelques anciens, qui est la 42ᵉ de J. C., lorsque ce prince mesme estoit Consul avec C. Cæcina Largus, et en la deuxieme aussi de la 205ᵉ Olympiade. C'estoit environ 25 ans avant sa mort, qui est le temps que l'Eglise Romaine donnait à son episcopat:" *Memm. Hist. Eccl.*, Vol. I. p. 162. Eusebius tells us that he went to Rome under Claudius: *Hist. Eccl.*, B. II. c. 14.

l. 23.—*There*: from this place to "that the light," Page 37, line 12, is lost in A., and the text supplied from B.

l. 25.—*Wore headbands of kings.* If the reading ܚܘܪܐ is to be retained, it should be rendered "were clad in white:" see Note, p. 156.

Page 36, *l.* 21.—*Nor do we write in the book of his Gospel.* No reference to any particular Gospel, perhaps, is intended by these words. St. Peter could hardly have referred to the Gospel of St. Mark, which is said to have been composed under his own direction; nor, indeed, to that of St. Matthew or St. Luke, which do not appear to have been written so early as the third year of Claudius, A.D. 42, still less to the Apocryphal Gospel attributed to him. See Grabe, *Spicilegium*, Vol. I. p. 56; Fabricius, *Cod. Add. N. T.* pp. 374, 375.

l. 26.—*I will send you the Paraclete, that he may teach you that which ye do not know.* These words are similar to *John* xiv. 26, "The Comforter (Paraclete), he shall teach you all things:" see Note on page 25, line 12.

l. 27.—*For it is by his gift, &c.* Compare Peter's speeches in *Acts* iii. and iv.

Page 37, *l.* 19.—*Mingled his godhead with our manhood.* ܚܠܛ. The word is much effaced in B., but it seems to be ܡܟܟ: "humbled" his God-head, ܡܛܠ ܐܢܫܘܬܢ "on account of our manhood," which would be, perhaps, a more appropriate reading. Respecting the word ܫܠܚ, which was supposed to countenance the Eutychian Heresy, see Assemani, *Bibl. Orient.* Vol. I. p. 81.

PAGE 38, *l.* 4.—*The Governor Pilate also was witness.* See Note, p. 159 above.

l. 10.—*Dominion.* ܐܘܚܕܢܐ. B. reads ܫܘܠܛܢܐ.

PAGE 39, *l.* 3.—*To perform any thing*: from this place to an "assembly," page 40 line 25, is lost in A.

l. 6.—*The son of one of the chiefs.* This story of Peter's raising a young man to life at Rome is also told by Abdias in his *Historia Apostolica*, de S. Petro, B. I. c. xvi., where he is called "adolescens nobilis, propinquus Cæsaris:" see Fabricius, *Cod. Apoc. N. T.* p. 431. In the Life of SS. Peter and Paul, attributed to Hegesippus, and printed by Lipomanus, he is also called "adolescens nobilis, propinquus Cæsaris:" see *Sanct. Hist.* Par. I. p. 295. The story of a contest between Simon Cephas and Simon the Sorcerer at Rome, after the former had driven away the latter from Cæsarea, is told, as by St. Peter himself, in the Apostolic Constitutions, but differently from this: see *Apost. Const.*, B. VI. c. 8. It is referred to in a very antient copy of Acts of Eleutherius, Codd. Add. 14,654, fol. 18, in the following terms:

ܘܫܪܝ ܠܡܐܡܪ ܓܒܪ̈ܐ ܪ̈ܗܘܡܝܐ ܪܒ ܗܘ ܐܠܗܐ ܗܘ ܕܠܗ
ܐܟܪܙܘ ܦܛܪܘܣ ܘܦܘܠܘܣ ܗܪܟܐ. ܕܒܫܡܗ ܥܒܕܘ ܗܘܘ ܗܪܟܐ
ܚܝ̈ܠܐ ܘܐܬ̈ܘܬܐ. ܕܠܗܘ ܪܫܐ ܕܫ̈ܐܕܐ ܫܡܥܘܢ ܚܪܫܐ.
ܗܘ ܕܦܠܚ ܗܘܐ ܠܗܠܝܢ ܛ̈ܠܢܝܬܐ. ܐܝܠܝܢ ܕܡܝܩܪ
ܗܕܪܝܢܘܣ ܝܘܡܢܐ. ܘܝܘܡܢܐ ܚܙܘ ܘܚܘܘ ܐܝܢܐ ܚܝܠܐ ܡܚܘܐ
ܐܠܗܐ ܒܐܝܠܝܢ ܕܪܚܡܝܢ ܠܗ "And he began to speak, Men of Rome, great is that God whom Peter and Paul preached here, in whose name they performed here those miracles and signs which put to shame that chief of devils, Simon the Sorcerer, who served these shadows which Hadrian honours this day. To-day, also, behold and see what power God shews forth in those that love him." These acts at the beginning state that what is there told took place in the 21st year of the reign of Hadrian, when he was returned from the East to Rome, ܗܕܪܝܢܘܣ ܡܠܟܐ ܒܫܢܬ ܥܣܪܝܢ ܘܚܕܐ ܕܡܠܟܘܬܗ. ܟܕ ܗܦܟ ܡܢ ܡܕܢܚܐ ܠܪܗܘܡܐ.

PAGE 40 *l.* 3.—*Cuprinus.* This should, perhaps, be Cyprianus, a name well known, and which I have seen written in Syriac exactly in the same manner as here, when there could be no doubt of Cyprianus being meant. I find no mention elsewhere of such a person being connected with St. Peter at Rome. Pudens is the name of the Roman, said also to have been a Senator, who is supposed to have received St. Peter in his house: see Baronius, *Annal.* 44, § 61; Tillemont, *Mem. Hist. Ecc.*, Vol. I. p. 163.

l. 11. — *Twenty-five years.* This is the time usually allotted to St. Peter's Episcopate at Rome; although it is certain that he did not constantly reside there during that period. We find him the year after at Jerusalem: see *Ibid*, p. 165.

l. 13.—*Ansus.* ܐܢܣܘܣ, at line 24 on the same page "Isus," ܐܝܣܘܣ, where B. has ܠܐܝܢܘܣ "*Lainus*;" and so likewise in an extract from this, found on the margin of Cod. Add. 14,609, fol. 123 rect. In the interpolated passage at the end of the Acts of Barsamya p. 71, line 29, we have "Anus," ܐܢܘܣ. The error can be chiefly traced to the scribe having mistaken ܠ for a prefix, instead of a part of the word. The person meant is undoubtedly *Linus.* In the *Bee* we find "Milus," which Assemani says is a mistake for "*Linus*:" see *Bibl. Orient.* Vol. III. pp. 3, 19. In the Apostolic Constitutions, B. VII. c. 46, we read "Of the church of Rome, Linus, the son of Claudia, was the first ordained by Paul, and after Linus' death, the second ordained by me, Peter." In Abdias, Peter is said to have ordained Clement shortly before his death. "Post hæc autem Petrus Romam veniens, in ipsis diebus sibi finem vitæ imminere præsensit. In conventu ergo fratrum positus, apprehensa Clementis manu, repente consurgens in auribus totius Ecclesiæ hæc protulit verba, Audite me fratres . . . . Clementem hunc episcopum vobis ordinabo, &c." De Petro, c. xv. This is, however, taken from the Epistle of Clement to James, as Fabricius observes, see *Cod. Apoc. N. T.*, p. 429; Tertullian also says that Clement was ordained by Peter, *De Præscript*, c. 22; see Bishop Pearson, *De Serie et Succes. Rom. Epis.* dis ii. c. 2, p. 154; and Dodwell, *Diss. Sing. de Rom. Pont.* p. 103. Linus is said, by Sigebertus Gemblacensis, and by an anonymous author of the Life of Nerius, given by Surius and Henschenius, in *Actt. Sanctt.*, to have written an account of the Martyrdom of Peter and Paul. This is consistent with the account given here in the *Doctrine of Peter*, which the Apostolic Constitutions, just cited, seem rather to contradict: see Fabricius, *Cod. Apoc. N. T.* page 775.

l. 17.—*Besides the New Testament and the Old, let there not be read before the people any thing else.* This agrees with the 10th Canon in the *Doctrine of the Apostles*, p. 27, see Note on that above. *Before the people.* In the Canon just referred to, it is said "in the pulpit of the church;" and in the Doctrine of Addæus it is stated "that a large multitude of the people assembled for the reading of the Old Testament and the New." It would seem, therefore, that this inhibition related only to public reading of other writings. The following from Philastrius, *Hæres.* 87. illustrates perhaps what is meant: "Hæresis est etiam quæ Apocrypha, id est secreta dicitur, quæ solum Prophetas et Apostolos accipit, non Scripturas Canonicas, id est, Legem et Prophetas, Vetus scilicet et Novum Testamentum. Et cum volunt solum illa Apocrypha legere studiose, contraria Scripturis Canonicis sentiunt, atque paulatim dogmatizant, contra eos dantes sententias, contra Legem et Prophetas, contraque dispositiones beatissimorum Apostolorum consulta ponentes. E quibus sunt maxime Manichæi, Gnostici, Nicolaitæ, Valentiniani, et alii quam plurimi, qui Apocrypha Prophetarum et Apostolorum, *i.e.* Actus separatos habentes, Canonicas legere Scripturas contemnunt. Propter quod statutum est ab Apostolis et eorum successoribus, non aliud legi in Ecclesia debere Catholica, nisi Legem et Prophetas, et Evangelia et Actus Apostolorum et Pauli tredecim Epistolas, et septem alias, Petri duas, Johannis tres, Judæ unam, et unam Jacobi, quæ septem Actibus Apostolorum conjunctæ sunt. Scripturæ autem absconditæ, id est Apocrypha, etsi legi debent morum causa a perfectis, non ab omnibus legi debent, quia non intelligentes multa addiderunt et tulerunt quæ voluerunt hæretici." *Cod. Apoc. N. T.* p. 749.

l. 29.—*The great crowning of the Apostles,* which would mean their martyrdom; but instead of ܟܠܠܗܘܢ, B. has ܕܥܡܠܗܘܢ "of their labour;" and on the margin of Cod. Add. 14,609, fol. 123 ܕܥܡܠܘ ܒܣܒܪܬܐ "that they had laboured in the Gospel."

Page 41, *l.* 1.—*It happened that there was a great famine in the city of Rome.* This abrupt termination seems to indicate that there was originally something more which followed. The famine referred to seems to be the same as that mentioned in the interpolated passage at the end of the Acts of Sharbil, p. 61, which doubtless is by the same hand as the interpolation in this place.

l. 6.—Acts of Sharbil.—There are two copies from which these *Acts of Sharbil* have been printed. The one which I have chiefly followed, is found in the same MS. as the preceding Cod. Add. 14,644, fol. 72 vers. The text of this has been printed exactly as it occurs, correcting one or two evident errors by the other MS., and also supplying from it the deficiencies. This is represented by A. in these Notes. The other copy, Cod. Add. 14,645, which also belongs to the collection from Nitria, is some three or four centuries later, and is a large thick quarto volume, written in two columns. It contains various Acts of Martyrdom, and is designated in these Notes as B. I have carefully collated it with A., but have not thought it necessary to notice all the variations. It contains several additional and enlarged passages, which seem to have been interpolated in the interval between the period of the transcription of the two copies. I may remark here, that I have almost invariably found in these Syriac MSS. that the older are the shorter, and that subsequent editors or transcribers felt themselves at liberty to add occasionally or paraphrase the earlier copies which they used. The *Acts of Sharbil* commence, fol. 221, rect. thus: ܥܠ ܣܒܪܐ ܕܐܠܗܐ ܫܪܝܢܢ ܕܢܟܬܘܒ ܣܗܕܘܬܐ ܓܒܝܬܐ. ܣܗܕܘܬܐ ܩܕܡܝܬܐ: ܕܫܪܒܝܠ ܟܘܡܪܐ ܪܒܐ ܘܕܒܒܝ ܚܬܗ ܕܣܗܕܘ ܒܐܘܪܗܝ ܡܕܝܢܬܐ ܡܒܪܟܬܐ: "In the hope of God we begin to transcribe Select Martyrdoms. Martyrdom the First, of Sharbil the High Priest, and of Babai, his sister, who suffered martyrdom in the blessed city of Edessa." In the *Martyrologium Romanum*, Januar 29. the following short notice is given: "Edessæ in Syria Sanctorum Martyrum Sarbelii et Barbeæ Sororis ejus, qui a Beato Barsimæo Episcopo baptizati, in persecutione Trajani sub Lysia Præside coronati sunt." And in the *Menologium Græcum*, on the 15th of September: "Sarbelius, idolorum sacerdos, unacum Sorore Barbæa conversus est ad fidem Christi per Barsimæum Edessæ Episcopum, et ambo tenti; post gravissima tormenta Sarbelius inter duo ligna sectus est; soror autem capite truncata." Assemani, *Bilb. Orient.* Vol. I. p. 331; see also the Bollandists at January 29.

Acts: the Greek word Υπομνηματα is retained here. From this and the occurrence of other Greek words it seems plain that these Acts were originally written in that language. The Greek Υπομνηματα corresponds with the Latin *Acta.* They were taken down by notaries called in Greek ταχυγραφοι: see Grabe, *Spicilegium*, Vol. I. p. 319, and in Latin *Exceptores.* They were then arranged in proper order by persons called Υπομνηματογραφοι, and by the Latins *Ab actis*, from notes taken down by the Exceptores, or Notarii: see below, p. 71. Valesius, in his notes to Eusebius, *Hist. Ecc.* B. I. c. 9. n. b. writes, "Acts were Books wherein the Scribes that belonged to the several places of judicature recorded the sentences pronounced by the Judges. See Calvin's Lex.

Jurid., the word Acta." And again, on B. VII. c. xi. n. d., "For the Greeks use Υπομνηματα in the same sense as the Latins use their word *Acta.* Those which wrote these, the Υπομνηματογραφοι, the Latins call *Ab actis.*" Bishop Pearson writes thus: "Ut enim actus Senatus et acta diurna Populi Romani conficiebantur; sic et in Provinciis Romanis idem a Presidibus et Cæsarum Procuratoribus factum est; qui ad Imperatores sæpissime de rebus alicujus momenti Epistolas scripserunt, ut passim observare est in historiis Romanis. *Lect. in Act. Apost.* p. 50. See the account of the writing of the Acts of Barsamya, p. 61, and of Habib, p. 84; and *Notes* thereon: see also Baronius, *ad Ann.* 238; Victor Le Clerc, *Des Journaux chez les Romains.* Thilo. *Cod. Apoc. N. T.* p. 489.

l. 9.—*The fifteenth year of the Emperor Trajan:* that is, A.D. 112. But A.G. commences 311, or 312 before Christ; and therefore A.G. 416 would answer to A.D. 405, There is, therefore, apparently some error in the dates.

l. 10.—*King Abgar the Seventh.* This should be the King who was reigning in the 15th year of Trajan, that is, Maanu Bar Ajazath, who was the seventh King of Edessa after Abgar Uchama: see Bayer, *Hist. Osrh.* p. 149, and Assemani, *Bibl. Orient.* Vol. I. p. 422.

l. 12.—*The high-priesthood of Sharbil and Barsamya.* Hence it would appear that Christianity and Paganism were both tolerated together in Edessa at this time, and equal honour attributed to the head of each religious party, agreeably to what is stated in the *Doctrine of Addæus*, p. 14, "Neither did King Abgar compel any man by force to believe in Christ."

l. 21.—*The great altar.* This we see was not overthrown when the other altars to Bel and Nebu were thrown down in Abgar's time: see *Ibid.*

l. 22.—*Office of records,* ܒܝܬ ܓܙܐ. This, perhaps, is the same as ܒܝܬ ܐܪܟܐ at p. 2.

l. 24.—*Their companions.* See, respecting these, Bayer, *Hist. Osrh.* p. 139, and *Note*, p. 156.

l. 25.—*And libations.* B. adds "before the god Jupiter:" ܩܕܡ ܙܘܣ ܐܠܗܐ.

l. 27.—*Sharbil.* The etymology of this word, as given by Dr. Land in his *Anecdota Syriaca*, p. 20, is unquestionably erroneous. He writes, "ܫܪܒܝܠ est 'progenies Dei;' contrahitur e ܫܪܒ (cæteroquin adhiberi solet forma fem. ܫܪܒܬܐ, sed vide Ewaldum in Gramm. Hebr. edit. VI. p. 326 init.) et ܐܝܠ, cum vocali copulente." The last syllable is ܒܝܠ, Bel, the same as we find used in Hebrew, in the compound of proper names, for Baal, whose

High Priest Sharbil was. The compounds in ܐܝܠ, Hebrew אֵל, refer to the God of the Israelites, the true God, and not to the Chaldæans, worshippers of Baal. The analogy, therefore, of ܐܒܝܠ and جبريل is not applicable. He might have found an analogy in ܒܐܒܝܠ : see Assemani, *Bibl. Orient.* Vol. II. page 222.

PAGE 42, *l.* 2.—*Abgar the King, son of the gods.* The Kings of Edessa, like other oriental sovereigns, seem to have arrogated to themselves this title. We find Sapor, King of Persia, in the Acts of Sapor and Isaac putting this question, ܠܐ ܝܕܥܝܬܘܢ ܕܡܢ ܙܪܥܐ ܐܢܐ ܕܐܠܗ̈ܐ : "Know ye not that I am of the seed of the gods?" see Assemani, *Act. Mart.* Vol. I. page 227.

l. 25.—*Which supply you.* B. adds here ܘܡܫܠܡ ܠܗܘܢ ܠܟܠܢܫ ܠܐܠܗܐ ܥܒܘܕܐ ܕܒ̈ܢܝܢܫܐ ܟܠܗܘܢ. ܘܡܛܠ ܢܓܝܪܘܬ ܪܘܚܗ ܗܐ ܡܫܬܥܠܝܬ ܥܠ ܡܪܚܡܢܘܬܗ. ܘܠܐ ܨܒܝܬ ܕܬܬܦܢܐ ܠܘܬܗ. ܐܝܟ ܕܢܬܦܢܐ ܗܘ ܠܘܬܟ. ܘܢܦܪܩܟ ܡܢ ܠܛܥܝܘܬܐ ܗܕܐ ܕܩܐܡ ܐܢܬ ܒܗ. "And in all these things thou hast forgotten God, the maker of all men, and because of his long-suffering hast exalted thyself against his mercy, and hast not been willing to turn to him, so that he might turn to thee and deliver thee from this error, in which thou standest."

l. 29.—*And was stretched out,* ܐܬܦܫܛ. B. ܘܐܬܦܫܛܬ.

PAGE 43, *l.* 11.—*King Abgar also, who was older than this Abgar, that worshippeth Idols as well as thou, he also believed in the King Christ, the Son of him whom thou callest the Lord of all Gods.* Instead of this, B. reads, ܐܒܓܪ ܡܠܟܐ: ܐܒܐ ܕܐܒܘܗܝ ܕܗܢܐ ܐܒܓܪ ܡܠܟܐ. ܕܗܢܐ ܦܠܚ ܥܕܟܝܢ ܘܡܣܓܕ ܠܦܬܟܪ̈ܐ ܡܝ̈ܬܐ. ܗܘ ܝܬܝܪܐܝܬ ܐܘܕܝ ܗܘܐ ܒܡܫܝܚܐ ܒܪܗ ܕܐܠܗܐ. ܗܿܘ ܕܩܪܝܬ ܠܗ ܡܪܐ ܕܐܠܗܘܢ ܐܠܗ̈ܐ. "King Abgar, father of the father of this King Abgar, who to this day worshippeth dead idols as well as thou, he abundantly confessed in Christ, the Son of that God whom thou callest the Lord of all Gods." In the Peshito of the New Testament, where the Greek has Ζευς, we find ܡܪܐ ܐܠܗܐ. *Acts,* xiv. 12.

l. 16.—*Idols made by men.* B has ܠܥܒܕ ܐܝ̈ܕܝܐ ܕܒܢ̈ܝܢܫܐ : "the work of men's hands."

l. 21.—*Persuaded with thee—remedy for me.* B. has this passage as follows: I omit the text, and give only the translation: "But if thou wilt not be persuaded by me, thy blood is upon thine own head, and I am clear of thy death. Sharbil answered and said to Barsamya, I did not know that the Christians teach according to what thou hast now spoken before me, because I am a High-Priest, the son of high priests, and I did not know that Jesus Christ, whom ye worship, is God and the Son of God, but I supposed that he was an ordinary man. Neither, again, did I know that he was crucified of his own free will, for I supposed that the Jews crucified him by force of themselves. But now having learned that he himself, of his own free will, gave himself up to be crucified for the salvation of man, although these words, which thou hast spoken to me, be very acceptable to me, still am I lost from all these things which I have heard from thee and for me there is no more any remedy."

l. 30.—*And when Barsamya, the Bishop, heard these things.* B. adds, "from Sharbil, his tears flowed and he wept."

PAGE 44, *l.* 22.—*The seal of salvation.* See Abdias, *Apost. Hist.*, de St. Thoma, where it is called "signum salutis," in Græco est σφραγις: see Fabricius, *Cod. Apoc. N. T.* pp. 537, 700, 701, 822. B. adds, "of baptism, baptizing him."

l. 26.—*Of the Christians.* B. adds here, "and he sat and listened to the Scriptures of the church, and the testimonies which are spoken in them, touching the birth, and the passion, and the resurrection, and the ascension of Christ, and when he saw those that came down to him."

PAGE 45, *l.* 8.—*Lysinias, the Judge of the country.* In B., in a passage added below, he is styled ܠܘܣܝܢܐ "Lysinas," and in the Martyrdom of Barsamya p. 63 ܠܘܣܝܢܘܣ: "Lysinus or Lusinus." In the Martyrologium Romanum he is called "Lysias præses:" see Assemani, *Bibl. Orient.* Vol. I. p. 331. Tillemont supposes him to be the same person as Lusius Quietus: "Nous aurons une preuve plus formelle que le persecution de Trajan a continué jusqu' à la fin du regne de ce Prince, si nous recevons, ce que on dit de la confession de S. Barsimée Evesque d'Edesse, honoré le 30. de Janvier, et de S. Sarbele honoré avec sainte Barbée ou Babée sa sœur le 29. du mesme mois. Car on met tout cela sous Trajan, et sous Lysias son Lieutenant. Ainsi ce ne peut estre qu'en l'an 116. auquel Lusius Quietus prit et brula la ville d'Edesse, un an avant la mort de Trajan." *Hist. des Emper.* Vol. II. p. 238. Bayer adopted the same view. 'Res igitur in Ægypto et Cypro gessit Lusius A. C. 117,

3 A

quo anno, decima die Augusti Trajanus decessit, et anno ante Edessa gravem sensit iracundiam victoris. Videtur autem Lusius is esse, quem Menologium Basilii Porphyrogennetæ vocavit Λυσιαν ηγεμονα, sub quo Barsimæus Episcopus Edessæ et Sarbelus, ejus quoque soror Babaea passi sunt martyrium:" see *Hist. Osrh.* p. 154. The time, however, does not agree. This martyrdom took place, at the latest, in the 15th year of Trajan, but the capture of Edessa under Lusius Quietus was four years later, in the 19th of Trajan. *Had heard.* B. adds here, "from the Sharirs of the city."

l. 9.—*Sharbil had done this.* B. adds here, "He wrote a letter and made known to the chief Præfect; and he sent to the city where the Emperor was staying, and informed him of the matter of Sharbil, the Chief Priest, who was become Christian; and inquired what he should do with him, for he feared to scourge and tear him, if he were to refuse to sacrifice according to his former custom, being in dread of this, because it had been ordered by the Emperors that the High Priests, who ministered to the gods should be duly honoured by the Judges of the countries. The Præfect then wrote to Lysinas, the Judge of the country, As it hath been ordered by the Emperors, so do to every one who will not sacrifice to the gods. And when Lysinas, the Judge of the country, received this command." *By night.* B. adds, "the Sharirs of the city."

PAGE 47, *l.* 5.—*With thongs.* The Syriac is ܒܓܠܘܪܝܣ, which is a foreign word. I suspect it to be the Latin *Loris*, which the Syriac translator, not understanding, or not knowing the exact equivalent, might have written ܒܠܘܪܝܣ, and a subsequent transcriber, have changed it into ܒܓܠܘܪܝܣ. It seems plain that the still later copyist to whom the text B. is due, did not know what it meant; and therefore omitted the word altogether, substituting "Sharbil" in its place.

l. 13.—*The Judge.* B. reads here ܗܓܡܘܢܐ "Governor," and so generally in the corresponding places below.

l. 14.—*Know.* B. ܬܦܪܘܫ: "discern."

PAGE 48, *l.* 4. — *Officials.* The Latin word retained. The Greek word was ταξις, used below, p. 77. These were the officers that attended upon the Presidents and chief Magistrates: "Officii nomine designantur publici ministri, qui Proconsulibus, Præsidibus et Magistratibus in publicis muniis inserviebant; hinc Officiales. De his quoque erudite disserit Baronius in notis ad diem 27 Mai": see Ruinart, *Acta Martyr.* p. 384.

l. 15.—*Hang him up and tear his sides with combs.* Compare Acta SS.

Saturnini et Dativi. "Statimque jubetur Officium eundem in equuleum sublevare, extensumque ungulis præcidi. Sed cum carnifices jussa crudelia atroci velocitate complerent, starentque sævientes in dictis, et denudatis ad vulnera martyris lateribus, erectis ungulis imminerent, &c." *Acta Martyr. Ibid.*

l. 26.—*The executioners.* ܩܘܣܛܘܢܪ̈ܐ : "Quæstionarii." See Ruinart, *Ibid*, p. 167, and Note p. 168 : "Quæstionarii dicti sunt carnifices, qui reos cruciabant ut veritatem ab eis extorquerent. Vide append. Cod. Theodos. Const. 3. Aliquando etiam isti a Græcis dicti sunt χουεστιοναριοι, ut notat eruditiss. Canguius in Glossar. Latino." At pp. 242, 244 *Ibid.* they are called δημιοι.

PAGE 49, *l.* 26. — *Gods which made not—under the heavens. Jer.* x. 11. We find the same words in the mouth of Charitne the Martyr, about A.D. 290, "Dii, qui cœlum et terram non fecerunt, pereant :" see Surius, *October* 5, p. 85.

PAGE 50, *l.* 2.—*The stench of the burning.* The same thing is told of the martyr Attalus in the Epistle of the Church of Lyons. Eusebius, Hist. Ecc. B. V. c. 1 : "But Attalus, when he was set in the iron chair and scorched all over, when the savour of his burnt flesh ascended from his body, said to the multitude in the Roman tongue." *English Trans.* p. 73. The *iron chair* mentioned here is the τηγανον.

PAGE 51, *l.* 12.—*Denounced against those.* The passage from this place tc "in the eyes," page 55, line 8, is lost in A. and supplied from B.

l. 15.—*Vinegar and Salt.* Sometimes vinegar and salt were put up th nostrils of the martyrs : see Martyrdom of Tarachus, Ruinart, *Acta Mart* page 429.

PAGE 52, *l.* 2.—*Like one that dealeth in fables.* I am by no means sur that this is the meaning of ܦܒܘܠܪ̈ܐ , which is a foreign word ; or tha "Fabularius" be the Latin word intended: it may be a Greek form, thoug apparently corrupted.

l. 7.—*The glorious architect of the creation.* We find a similar expressio to this in Mar Jacob's Sermon on the Fall of Idols.

PAGE 53, *l.* 17.—*Small and round pieces of wood.* These seem to be th Obelisci. The Martyr Minias, about A.D. 240, had the same torture inflicte on him, "sed deposito de eculeo, ligneisque verubus præacutis sub ungu ejus infixis, omnes digitos ejus præcepit pertundi :" see Surius, *Sanct Vit.*, October 25, p. 384.

PAGE 54, *l.* 9. — This passage inclosed in brackets thus [ ], has be torn out in A., and is supplied from B., and so likewise in the following passages.

l. 24. *Gridiron.* ܛܪܛܘܠܐ. This seems to be a corruption from the Latin *Craticula* ܩܪܛܘܠܐ : see Eusebius, B. V. c. 1, where the Greek is *τηγανον*. On this Valesius has the following note, "*τηγανον* is the Greek term; which Rufinus translates *craticulam*, *i.e.* a gridiron. It is the same, which before is called the *iron chair*, on the which the martyrs, being set, were broiled, as it were on a gridiron :" see *English Trans.* p. 73.

PAGE 58, *l.* 16.—*His bowels were near being seen.* Compare the Epistle of the Smyrnæans touching the Martyrdom of Polycarp, *οι μαστιξι μεν καταξανθεντες, ωστε μεχρι των εσω φλεβων και αρτηριων την της σαρκος οικονομιαν θεωρεισθαι υπεμειναν* : see *Patres Apost. Jacobson, Edit.* IV. p. 608.

l. 30.—*The curtain.* ܘܠܐ, Latin "velum" or "vela." We find this Latin word also retained in Greek, *βηλον*, in the Martyrdom of Euplus, published by J. B. Cotelerius in *Eccles. Græc. Monumenta*, Vol. I. p. 192, *εν σικριταριῳ προ βηλου.* The note of Cotelerius thereon, *Ibid.* p. 752, will illustrate the passage before us : "Assentior viris doctis, qui secretaria judicum interpretantur tribunalia, conclavia, loca in quibus jus reddebant, et reorum causas expendebant. . . . . Glossæ Nomicæ *Σεκρετον· δικαστηριον.* Rationem nominis reddit S. Augustinus libro de ovibus, cap. 3. *Ultimam* inquit *sententiam, quam dictaturus est judex, in tabella descripturus manu sua, ultra quam sententiam nihil jam judicaturus est, partes non audiunt. Illis foras exeuntibus scribitur : attonitæ sunt ambæ partes atque suspensæ, contra quam vel pro qua sententia illius procedat. Magnum secretum judicis ; unde secretarium nominatur.*" See also Ruinart, *Acta Martyr.* p. 407 : "Calvisianus intra velum interius ingrediens, sententiam dictavit. Et foras egressus afferens tabellam, legit : Euplium Christianum, edicta Principum contemnentem, deos blasphemantem, nec resipiscentem, gladio animadverti jubeo. Ducite eum." See more instances in Thilo, *Codex Apoc. N. T.* p. 576 : see also Note p. 268, *Ibid.* and Baronius, ad ann. 285, sec. 9.

PAGE 59, *l.* 1.—*The sentence.* ܐܦܘܦܣܣ, this is the Greek *αποφασις.* Compare Trajan's sentence on Ignatius in the Martyrdom of Ignatius, c. 2. *Patres Apost. Jacobson, edit.* IV. p. 580.

l. 14.—*A strap to be cast into the mouth.* Compare *χαλινον εμβαλειν*, in the Life of Euthymus in *Eccl. Græc. Monumenta*, Vol. II. p. 240, and Cotelerius' note thereon, *Ibid*, p. 623 : "Immittebantur in ora reorum et servorum cami, funes, frena. Morem firmabo aliquot testimoniis, &c." See also the sentence against Habib, p. 82.

Page 60, *l.* 1.—*They gave him wine to drink.* Compare the Acts of Fructuosus: "Cumque multi ex fraterna caritate eis offerent, uti conditi permixti poculum sumerent, ait, &c." Ruinart, *Acta Martyr.* p. 220.

l. 29.—*A saw of iron.* See Suetonius, *Calig.* c. 27, "serra dissecuit," and notes thereon, *Edit. Varior. Lond.* 1826, p. 1555.

Page 61, *l.* 11. — *Young men.* ܛܠܝ̈ܐ. B. reads ܥܠܡܝ̈ܐ "laics."

l. 16. —*Notaries.* ܐܟܣܦܛܘܪܣ. This is the Latin word "Exceptores." They were also called Notarii: thus we read in the Acts of Genesius the Martyr: "Accidit autem ut eodem ante tribunal Judicis *Exceptoris* munus implente, impia atque sacrilega mandatæ persecutionis jussa legerentur: quæ cum devotus Deo repudiaret auditus, et imprimere ceris manus sancta respuerat &c." see Ruinart, *Acta Martyr.* p. 539: and in the Acts of Pionius, "Post hæc Polemon, cum ceræ Notarius, quæ respondebantur, imprimeret, ait ad Pionium: Quis vocaris? &c." *Ibid.* page 144.

l. 17.—*Where the charters of the Kings are placed.* After this the following passage is found in B.: "And that which was spoken by the Judge, those who stood in the Judge's presence wrote down; but all the rest, which took place outside the tribunal, the Sharirs of the city wrote down, and they went in and made it known to the judge, and he, according as he heard from them, gave orders in the legal manner, agreeably to the custom of the ordinances and laws of old. Thus these Acts were written, and deposited in the chamber of antient records. But there are fifty-two questions which the Judge asked Sharbil; and then they gave against him the bitter sentence of death, which is widely apart from the laws of the Romans, and from the sentence of their edicts. But this transaction of the Confession of Sharbil took place in the first consulate of Commodus and Cerealis."

l. 18.—*But this Barsamya.* The passage commencing thus to the end is evidently an addition by a later person not well acquainted with chronology; for it is stated at the beginning of these Acts, that what is here recorded took place in the 15th year of the reign of Trajan or A.D. 112; but Fabianus was not made Bishop of Rome before the reign of Maximinus Thrax, about the year 236: see Dodwell, *Diss. Sing. de Rom. Pontif.* page. 84.

l. 19.—*Binus.* ܒܝܢܘܣ: B. ܦܒܝܢܘܣ, "Fabianus," and so at p. 62 line 14. The introduction of this passage probably arose from the fact of Fabianus having instituted Notaries for the express purpose of searching for and collecting the Acts of Martyrs, as we learn from a letter of his own cited by Bishop Pearson: "Denique septem similiter Subdiaconos ordinavimus, qui septem Notariis imminerent, et gesta Martyrum veraciter in integro colligerent, nobisque rimanda manifestarent:" see *De Succ. prim. Romæ Episc.* p. 20.

PAGE 63, *l.* 3. — MARTYRDOM OF BARSAMYA. This also is taken from the same MS. as that in which the later copy of the Acts of Sharbil is found, Cod. Add. 14,645, fol. 233, vers. It is called ܣܗܕܘܬܐ: "Martyrdom" on the title, but in the work itself, p. 71, it is called *υπομνηματα*. See *Martyrolog. Rom.* Jan. 25. There is also an Armenian version or extract from this still in existence: see Dr. Alishan's letter cited p. 166 *above.*

l. 8.—*In the consulship of Commodus and Cyrillus.* Cyrillus is evidently a mistake for Cerealis; and this must be the consulate of Commodus Verus and Tutilius Cerealis, which was in the 9th year of Trajan, A.D. 106: see Clinton, *Fasti Romani*, 92. This agrees nearly enough with the year of the Greeks 416, or A.D. 105, but does not correspond with the 15th year of Trajan, which falls A.D. 112: see Tillemont, *Hist. des Emp.*, Vol. II. pp. 193. 202; Clinton, *Ibid.* p. 96.

l. 9.—*Lysinas.* In the Acts of Sharbil, p. 45, called Lysanias: see Note, page 181, *above.*

l. 23.—*Nebo.* At page 45 this name is given Labu.

PAGE 67, *l.* 5.—*The Christians to whom thou art gone, &c.* See Acts of Sharbil, p. 45.

PAGE 69, *l.* 26.—*Alusis* [Lusius]. This seems to be Lusius Quietus, Trajan's general in the East at this time: see Tillemont, *Hist. des Emp.*, Vol. II. page 199.

PAGE 70, *l.* 6.—We have here probably the most authentic copy of the Edict of Trajan, respecting the stopping of the persecution of the Christians. Tertullian, in speaking of this persecution, refers to the letter of Pliny to Trajan, and to the Emperor's reply to him, but not to the edict itself: see *Apologeticum*, c. ii. It is to the same, also, that Eusebius refers, *Ecc. Hist.* B. III. c. 22. But in these Acts we have, as it would appear, the words of the Edict itself, as they were taken down by the notaries at the time. Those who wish to refer more fully to this matter may read Lardner's *Credibility*, and Tillemont, *Mem. pour servir a l'Hist. Ecc.* Vol. II. page 174 seq.

l. 8.—*Sharirs.* This word, which occurs many times in the course of this volume, does not seem always to represent officers discharging the same functions. It is not apparent what was the Latin title of these officers. Pliny, from whom Trajan received the information to which this edict refers, and whose words even are cited, was ηγουμενος της επαρχιας, according to Eusebius. The etymology of the word *Sharir* is nearest to the Latin *Corrector*, which title the governors of some countries had. Thus we find Calvisianus Consularis, in the Greek *Corrector*, was the governor or judge before whom the martyr Euplius was tried: see Ruinart, *Acta Mart.* Note II. p. 406.

PAGE 71, *l.* 11.—*Notaries.* ܐܟܣܦܛܘܪܣ : the Latin "Exceptores:" see Note p. 185, above.

l. 12.—*Euterpes.* ܐܘܛܪܦܝܣ. This may perhaps be "Eutropius."

l. 15.—*But this Barsamya.* From this place to the end is a much later addition, evidently made by the same ignorant person as that at p. 61 above: see *Note* thereon.

l. 26.—*Dapius* [Pius]. This blunder evidently arose from supposing the prefix ܕ to be a part of the name.

PAGE 72, *l.* 3.—*The nineteenth year of the reign of Tiberius Cæsar in the consulate of Rufus and Rubelinus.* There seems to be a mistake here in reading ܬܫܥܣܪܝܬܐ, "nineteenth," for ܫܬܬܥܣܪܝܬܐ, "sixteenth," which agrees with what is stated by Julius Africanus, who assigns the death of our Lord to the sixteenth year of Tiberius: see Routh, *Reliq. Sacr.* Vol. II. p. 187. It also accords with the year of the Consulate of Rubellius Geminus, and Fufius Geminus, and with the year 341 of the Greeks, A.D. 29 or 30: see Clinton, *Fasti Romani*, p. 10. *Rufus and Rubelinus.* These names are given by Tacitus, *Ann.* V. 1. "Rubellio et Fufio Consulibus, quorum utrique Geminus cognomen erat." Tertullian, *Adversus Judæos*, cap. 8, writes, "Passio perfecta est sub Tiberio Cæsare, consulibus Rubellio Gemino et Rufio Gemino (Junius and Rigaltius from the *Fasti Cons.* read "Fufio Gemino"), mense Martio, temporibus Paschæ, die viii. Calendarum Aprilium." Augustine, *De Civitate Dei*, XVIII. 58. "Mortuus est ergo Christus duobus Geminis Consulibus, octavo Cal. April." See further, respecting these Consuls, Thilo, *Cod. Apoc. N. T.* p. 497.

l. 7.—*Register.* ܐܠܛܪܝܢ: the Greek Ειληταριον: see Du Fresne, *Glossarium*.

l. 14.—MARTYRDOM OF HABIB THE DEACON. This is found in the same MS. as the preceding, Cod. Add. 14,645, fol. 238, vers. There is an account of the Acts of Habib, evidently taken from these, by Simeon Metaphrastes subjoined to the Acts of Shamuna and Guria, given in Latin by Surius at Nov. 15, p. 339, which I have reprinted in this volume, p. 113. Surius also gives another account, p. 345, "De Sanctis Christi Martyribus Samona, Guria, et Abibo, Arethæ Archiepiscopi Cæsariensis Oratio:" see also the Bollandists at Nov. 15.

l. 16.—*The consulate of Licinius and Constantine.* They were consuls together A.D. 312, 313, 315: see Clinton's *Fasti Romani*, pp. 360, 364, 368. Baronius puts the martyrdom of Habib in the year A.D. 316.

l. 18.—*In the rule of Julius and Barak.* ܒܐܣܛܪܛܓܘܬܐ, that is, while they were Στρατηγοι, *Magistrates;* or *Duumviri*, as Valesius renders it. "Στρατηγος is the word in the original, which the Latins called *Magistratus* or *Duumviri.* It is taken in this sense throughout the whole *Title Cod. Theodos de Decurionibus*, Et in *Optatus, Lib.* I. &c., in which places, and in many others, *Magistratus* and *Duumviri* are promiscuously used." See Valesius' Notes on Eusebius, *Hist. Eccl.* B. VIII. c. 11. *English Trans.*, p. 146. *Cona, Bishop of Edessa.* He is called Cognatus erroneously by Metaphrastes, see p. 113. This same Cona laid the foundation of the Church at Edessa, in the year of the Greeks, 624, or A.D. 313: see Chronicon Edess. in Assemani, *Bibl. Orient.* Vol. I. p. 394.

l. 9.—*Licinius made a persecution.* See, respecting this, Steph. Evod. Assemani, *Act. Mart.* Vol. II. p. 214.

l. 28. — *Telzeha.* This is called by Metaphrastes "Thelsæa." See page 122.

Page 74, *l.* 13.—*Theotecna*, or, in Latin, Theotecnus. There was a person of this name, Curator of Antioch, who urged on the persecution against the Christians: see Eusebius, *Hist. Eccl.* B. IX. c. 2, 3, 4, and Martyrdom of Theodotus in Ruinart, *Acta Mart.* p. 338. He was afterwards put to death by order of Licinius: see Eusebius, *Hist. Eccl.* B. IX. c. 11. The person here spoken of, although cotemporary, and of the same name, seems to have thought and acted very differently.

Page 77, *l.* 15.—*Ruler.* ܐܪܟܘܢ, Greek, *αρχων.*

l. 29.—*The band.* ܛܟܣܐ, Greek, *ταξις*, which is the same as the Latin word Officium: see Pancirolus, *Notitia Dignitatum.*

l. 30.—*And he began to interrogate him thus, and said to him, What is thy name.* This seems to have been generally the first question put by the judges to those accused of being Christians: see Martyrdom of Lucianus and Marcianus, A.D. 200. "Proconsul Sabinus dixit ad Lucianum: Quis diceris? Respondit: *Lucianus* . . . . Dixit ad Marcianum: Quis vocaris? Respondit:

Marcianus:" Ruinart, *Acta Mart.* p. 167. See also Acta Tarachi, Probi, et Andronici, circa A.D. 304: *Ibid*, p. 423, &c.

PAGE 83, *l.* 2. — *The cemetery which was built for Abshelama, Abgar's son.* Probably that in which Sharbil and Babai were buried: see p. 61 *above.* There was a church built at Edessa in honour of the martyrs Shamuna, Guria, and Habib in the 4th century: see Assemani, *Acta Mart.* Vol. I. p. 226.

PAGE 84, *l.* 3. — *The hill called Baith Allah Cucla.* In Simeon Metaphrastes this is written *Bethelabicla*, and is said to lie on the north side of the city: see p. 121. The copy which he followed would seem to have read ܒܘܠܐ for ܟܘܠܐ.

l. 19.—*The notaries.* ܐܟܣܩܦܛܘܪ̈ܐ: the Latin "Exceptores," called in Greek ταχυγραφοι: see Grabe, *Spicilegium*, Vol. I. p. 219; and *Note*, page 185.

l. 25.—*As I had also formerly written of Shamuna and Guria.* It seems probable that the account of these martyrs by this same Theophilus formed the basis of the history of their martrydom given by Simeon Metaphrastes, for the comparison of these Acts of Habib by Theophilus with the narrative of this martyr by Simeon Metaphrastes, shows that he made use of them: see p. 113.

PAGE 85, *l.* 6.—*Domitianus.* We might, perhaps, have suspected that the reading here should be *Diocletian.* We know, however, that Nero and Domitian were the first persecutors of the Christians, from Melito, in Routh's *Reliq. Sac.* Vol. I. pp. 111, 124, as well as from Tertullian, Lactantius, and Eusebius. See, respecting the persecution under Domitian, Tillemont, *Mem. Hist. Eccl.* Vol. II. p. 117.

PAGE 86, *l.* 1.—ORATION ON HABIB THE MARTYR, COMPOSED BY MAR JACOB. The MS. from which this is taken is Cod. Add. 17,158, fol. 30, vers. Mar Jacob, Bishop of Sarug, or Batnæ, was one of the most learned and celebrated among all the Syriac writers. He was born A.D. 452, made Bishop of Sarug A.D. 519, and died A.D. 521. He was the author of several Liturgical works, Epistles, and Sermons, and, amongst these, of numerous Metrical Homilies, of which the two printed here will serve as specimens. Assemani enumerates no less than 231 of such Homilies, and, amongst them, one on Habib, *Bibl. Orient.* Vol. I. p. 330, and that which follows on Shamuna and Guria, *Ibid.* p. 329. For a full account of Mar Jacob and his works the reader is referred to Assemani, *Ibid.* pp. 283—340. Ephraem Syrus also wrote a similar Homily on Habib, Shamuna, and Guria: see Assemani, *Ibid*, p. 50.

Page 90, *l.* 3.—Correct here a typographical error, and dele *at*.

l. 20.—*I am Habib.* Compare Martyrdom of Habib, p. 74.

Page 92, *l.* 4.—*A man I worship not.* Compare Martyrdom p. 80.

l. 7.—*The daughter of Abgar.* This seems to be a metonym for his city Edessa.

l. 12.—*My heart is captive with God who became man.* Compare Acts of Sharbil, p. 65.

Page 93, *l.* 27.—*Daughter of the Parthians.* Another metonym for Edessa.

Page 94, *l.* 2.—*A strap*: see p. 82, *l.* 24.

l. 21.—*She clad herself in white.* See p. 83.

Page 95, *l.* 5.—*Shamuni.* From the context this would appear to be the mother of the Maccabees.

l. 28.—*With Sharbil it began, with Habib ended in our Lord.* This passage is cited by Assemani, *Bibl. Orient.* Vol. I. p. 331, who, after quoting the passage from the Acts of Habib, by Simeon Metaphrastes, "Talem quidem vitæ finem" to the end, page 124, line 24, adds "Ubi manifeste alluditur ad relatam de Licinio victoriam anno Christo 324., de qua consule Pagium ad annum 317, sec. 5. Licinianam autem persecutionem ante annum Christi 319 inchoatam non fuisse, idem Pagius ostendit ad annum 316. sec. 6. Martyrio igitur defunctus est Abibus exeunte anno 323. quo persecutioni Licinianæ finis impositus fuit. Sarbelius vero, cujus a cæde initium duxisse persecutionem Sarugensis testatur, coronatus fuit sub Trajano Imperatore, de quo hæc in Martyrologio Romano die 29. Januarii. *Edessæ in Syria Sanctorum Martyrum Sarbelii et Barbææ sororis ejus, qui a Beato Barsimæo Episcopi baptizati, in persecutione Trajani sub Lysia Præside coronati sunt.* Et in Menologio Græcorum die 15 Septembris. *Sarbelius, idolorum Sacerdos, unacum Sorore Barbæa conversus est ad fidem Christi per Barsimæum Edessæ Episcopum, et ambo tenti; post gravissima tormenta Sarbelius inter duo ligna sectus est: soror autem capite truncata.*

Page 96, *l.* 12.—Oration on Shamuna and Guria, composed by Mar Jacob. This is also taken from the same MS. as the preceding, Cod. Add. 17,158, fol. 23, vers. The Acts of Guria and Shamuna from Simeon Metaphrastes are given by Surius, from whom they have been copied in this volume at page 113. Their day is celebrated, as we learn from these and also from the Roman Martyrology, on the 15th of November: see Assemani, *Bibl. Orient.* Vol. I. p. 329. This accords with what we find in Cod. Add. 14,504, fol. 140. ܩܢܘܢܐ ܕܥܠ ܡܘܕܝܢܐ ܩܕ̈ܝܫܐ ܠܓܘܪܝܐ ܘܫܡܘܢܐ ܘܚܒܝܒ ܕܗܘܐ ܕܘܟܪܢܗܘܢ ܒܚܡܫܥܣܪ ܒܬܫܪܝ. "Canon on the Holy Confessors, Guria, and Shamuna, and Habib, whose commemoration day is on the fifteenth of Tishri."

Page 97, *l.* 5.—*On their own bodies—wrote.* Compare *Doctrine of Addæus*, p. 9, line 14.

Page 103, *l.* 9.—*For faith consisteth not in many words.* Compare *Doctrine of Addæus*, p. 11.

Page 105, *l.* 7.—*And from the necks of his bridegroom friends the spear demanded blood.* This is wrongly translated in consequence of my having been ignorant of the meaning of ܪܘܡܝܢܐ, which is written in the MS. so that it seems like ܪܘܡܚܐ, "spear." I have since ascertained the true sense of ܪܘܡܝܢܐ, which is the same word as we find under the root, ܪܡܐ in Castel's Lexicon. "ܪܘܡܝܘܢܐ, strena nuptialis, *Off. Mar.* 474." Thus I have found in the Sermon of Mar Jacob Persa on ܫ̈ܠܝ ܡܫܝܚܐ Cod. Add. 14,619, fol. 36, vers. ܢܥܬܕ ܪܘܡܝܢܐ ܠܚܠܘܠܗ ܘܢܦܘܩ ܠܐܘܪܥܗ ܒܚܕܘܬܐ: "Let us prepare a nuptial gift for his marriage, and go out to meet him with joy;" and again, fol. 40, ܘܗܢܝܢ ܗܠܝܢ ܕܥܬܕ ܚܬܢܐ ܠܟ̈ܠܠܐ ܡܫܬܘܬܗ ܐܢܬ ܥܒܕ ܠܟܝ ܪܘܡܝܢܐ. ܘܥܬܕܝ ܠܡܦܩܢܟܝ ܠܐܘܪܥܗ: "And these same things which the bridegroom has prepared for the of his wedding feast, make thou for thyself a bridal gift, and prepare thyself to meet him." The word ܫܘܫܒܝܢܐ I find used in the marriage ceremony, given by Ebediesu in Card. Mai, *Script. Vett. Coll. Nova*, Vol. X. p. 211, ܘܢܬܪܫܡܘܢ ܫܘܫܒܝܢܐ ܘܫܘܫܒܝܢܬܐ ܒܨܠܝܒܐ: "And let the groomsmen and the bridesmaids be signed with the sign of the cross." The line will therefore be corrected thus: "And he demanded of his wedding friends their neck's blood as a bridal gift."

Page 106, *l.* 13.—Canticle of Mar Jacob the Doctor upon Edessa. This is taken from Cod. Add. 17,158, fol. 56.

Page 107, *l.* 20.—*Abgar the Black.* See Note p. 144 above.

l. 22.—*Your envy.* Correct here a misprint, and read ܚܣܡܟܘܢ for ܢܣܡܟܘܢ.

PAGE 108, *l.* 5.—Extract I. This is found in Cod. Add. 14,535, fol. 1. An octavo volume, imperfect at the beginning and the end, consisting at present of 115 folia. The contents are miscellaneous: see *Corpus Ignatianum*, p. 359.

l. 13.—*Watchers.* That is, the Angels.

l. 24.—Extract II. This is from Cod. Add. 12,155, fol. 53 vers. It is a large volume in quarto, written in two columns, and has the following title prefixed, ܦܢܩܝܬܐ ܕܬܚܘܝ̈ܬܐ ܕܐܒܗ̈ܬܐ ܩ̈ܕܝܫܐ ܠܘܩܒܠ ܗܪ̈ܣܝܣ "Table of the Demonstrations of the Holy Fathers against Heresies." See *Corpus Ignat.* p. 359. This Extract II., from Addæus, is taken from a chapter with the following heading, ܥܠ ܪܓܫܬܐ ܕܢܦܫܐ ܒܬܪ ܦܘܪܫܢܗ ܕܡܢ ܦܓܪܐ: "Touching the consciousness of the soul after its separation from the body." The part contained in this extract is wanting among some of the missing leaves of the manuscript from which the *Doctrine of Addæus* is printed. The same is also found in several other manuscripts in this Nitrian collection. It is written on the fly leaf of Cod. Add. 12,161, which is one of the books procured at Bagdad by the Abbot Moses, and presented to the Monastery of St. Mary at Nitria, being an antient copy of Chrysostom's Homilies on St. Matthew, containing Homilies 60—88. It is also quoted in Cod. Add. 14,532, fol. 139, which is a volume containing "Proofs from the Fathers against various heresies;" and in Cod. Add. 14,612, fol. 165, rect., a large quarto volume of miscellaneous contents, consisting of Homilies by Chrysostom and others. It is found, too, in Cod. Add. 17,193, fol. 37, vers., and in Cod. Add. 17,194, fol. 30, which is a small duodecimo volume bearing the title ܩ̈ܦܠܐ ܡܫ̈ܚܠܦܐ ܘܦܘܫ̈ܩܐ ܕܐܒܗ̈ܬܐ ܩ̈ܕܝܫܐ "Various chapters and explanations of the Holy Fathers."

PAGE 190, *l.* 7.—Extract III. is taken from Cod. Add. 17,193, fol. 36. It is a quarto volume, imperfect at the end, and at present consists of 99 folia. It bears the title ܦܢܩܝܬܐ ܕܬܚܘܝ̈ܬܐ ܘܕܟܢܘ̈ܫܝܐ ܘܕܡܐܡ̈ܪܐ: "A table of Proofs and of Collections and of Treatises." This Extract III. is found on fol. 36, vers., and is followed by Extract II. on the next page, with ܕܝܠܗ, "by the same," prefixed in red letters. According to this order it would appear that Extract III. preceded

Extract II. in the *Doctrine of Addæus*: this we find at page 19 above, line 7—16. The preceding Extract II. probably belongs to that part which has been lost from p. 20.

l. 26.—Extracts IV. and V. are taken from Cod. Add. 14,601, fol. 164. It is a large quarto volume in two columns, consisting at present of 182 folios, written apparently in the eighth century. Its contents are miscellaneous, containing Sermons by Basil, Gregory Theologus, John Chrysostom, Theodotus of Ancyra, Philoxenus, Severus of Antioch, &c. These extracts are found in a Chapter with the following heading, ܥܠ ܗܠܝܢ ܫܒܥܝܢ ܘܬܪܝܢ ܫܠܝ̈ܚܐ ܩܕ̈ܝܫܐ ܘܥܠ ܫܠܝ̈ܚܐ ܕܓ̈ܠܐ ܕܗܘܘ ܒܙܒܢܗܘܢ. "Touching those Seventy-two Holy Apostles, and touching the false Apostles who were in their time." Extract IV. is also in the *Bee*, and is found in the page cited in *Note*, p. 163 above.

Page 110, *l.* 4.—Extract VI. is taken from Cod. Add. 14,484, fol. 19. It is a very antient quarto volume, in two columns, of the fifth or sixth century; imperfect, a few leaves have been added in a more recent hand. It is an apochryphal work relative to the Blessed Virgin, in six Books, of which the title is that given at the heading of the Extract. There is also bound up in the same volume another Codex of still older date, containing the Acts of Simeon Stylites.

Page 112, *l.* 4.—Extract VII. is taken from Cod. Add. 14,624. A quarto volume, imperfect at the beginning, the end, and in the middle. It at present consists of 56 leaves, apparently written in the ninth century, and contains various Homilies, &c., of Jacob of Sarug, and others.

l. 18.—Extract VIII. is taken from Cod. Add. 14,590. Homilies of the same Mar Jacob, of the eighth or ninth century.

Page 113.—Martyrium Sanctorum Confessorum Samonæ, Guriæ et Abibi, ex Simeone Metaphraste. The account of the martyrdom of these three persons, collected by Simeon Metaphrastes, I have reprinted exactly as I found it in the well-known work of Surius, "De Probatis Sanctorum vitis, quas tam ex MSS. Codicibus, quam ex editis Auctoribus, R. P. Fr. Laurentius Surius, Carthusiæ Coloniensis Professus Primum edidit, et in duodecim menses distribuit. November. Hac postrema editione multis Sanctorum vitis auctus et notis marginalibus illustratus. Coloniæ Agrippinæ, Sumptibus Ioannis Kreps et Hermanni Mylii. Anno cIↃ.IↃc.xviii." I find no notice of the MS. whence this text was printed, nor of the author of the Latin translation. There are several obvious blunders in it, but

3 D

having no other copy to correct them by, and inasmuch as they are such as in no way affect the facts related, I have reprinted this text verbatim, without proposing any conjectural emendations of my own. The learned reader will do this for himself. There is subjoined, p. 345, "De Sanctis Christi Martyribus Samona, Guria et Abibo Arethæ Archiepiscopi Cæsareensis Oratio: viro docto interprete. Habetur 3 Tomo Aloysii." This I have not thought it worth while to reprint here, because it supplies no additional facts, but merely corroborates those related in the preceding Tract.

PAGE 125.—MOÏSE DE KHORÈNE HISTOIRE D'ARMÉNIE. I have thought it more convenient to give all that is told by Moses Chorenensis relative to Abgar and the establishment of Christianity at Edessa, in a continued narrative, rather than to break it up and cite it in isolated passages in the Notes. The first translation that appeared in any European language of this work of the Father of Armenian History was in Latin, by the two brothers Whiston. "MOSIS CHORENENSIS HISTORIÆ ARMENICÆ LIBRI III. Accedit ejusdem Scriptoris EPITOME GEOGRAPHIÆ. Præmittitur Præfatio, quæ de LITERATURA, ac VERSIONE SACRA ARMENICA agit; et subjicitur APPENDIX, quæ continet EPISTOLAS DUAS ARMENICAS; Primam CORINTHIORUM ad PAULUM Apostolum, Alteram PAULI Apostoli ad CORINTHOS; nunc primum e codice MS integre divulgatas. Armeniace ediderunt, Latine verterunt, notisque illustrârunt GULIELMUS ET GEORGIUS GUL. WHISTONI filii, Aulæ Clarensis in Academia Cantabrigiensi aliquamdiu Alumni. LONDONI: 1736." I have, however, thought it more desirable to give the French Translation by M. Le Vaillant de Florival, which was made at a more recent period, after the Armenian had been longer studied, and with more available sources at hand. "MOÏSE DE KHORÈNE, auteur de Ve Siecle, HISTOIRE D'ARMÉNIE, texte Arménien et traduction Française, avec notes explicatives et précis historiques sur l'Arménie: ouvrage dédié a S. M. Impériale NICOLAS I., Empereur de toutes les Russies, par P. E. LE VAILLANT DE FLORIVAL. Paris, 8vo." There is also a more recent translation in Italian, but that language is perhaps not so generally read as the French.

PAGE 129, *l.* 11.—*Marinus.* Whiston has the following Note on this, p. 132, "Per hæc tempora Syriam administrabat Ælius Lamia, cui tamen provinciam suam adire non fuit permissum, ut scribit Tacitus, l. vi. c. 27., qui etiam Julii cujusdam Marini meminit, c. 10. an vero is idem fuerit atque hic Marinus, id omnino incertum."

The account of Abgar having heard of the miracles of Jesus through his envoy Ananias, who met with him when in Palestine, is also given by Simeon Metaphrastes, but with some variations from this by Moses Chorenensis. "Cum Dominus et Deus et Salvator noster Jesus Christus ad genus nostrum erigendum apud nos versarctur, erat, ut dicit Propheta, Multitudo pacis in terra, et fuerat dissipatus multorum principatus et administratio, cum tamquam ab una zona Romano Imperio cinctus esset universus orbis terræ, et subjectus esset uni gubernatori. Ideo erat omnium cum omnibus secura congressio, neque sibi videbantur homines terram habitare divisam, sed ut quæ ab uno Domino possideretur, et esset tota unius opificis: et collum primo illi servo inclinantes, pacem inter se agitabant. Quamobrem qui tunc quoque erat Edessæ Toparcha Abagarus, erat Ægypti Præsidi notus, et amicus, et alterius ad alterum veniebant utrinque ministri. Quocirca illo quoque tempore, quo Dominus noster et Deus, paternam implens voluntatem, salutarem doctrinam proponebat hominibus, et per insignia miracula ad fidem in eum habendam convertebat homines: accidit ut quidam ex ministris Abagari, nomine Ananias, in Ægyptum vadens per Palestinam, in Christum incideret: et eum procul contemplaretur verbis ab errore attrahentem multitudinem, et quæ omnem superabant opinionem facientem miracula. Postquam ergo iter suum confecisset in Ægyptum, et iis quæ mandata fuerunt tractatis rediret, cum recordaretur dominum suum diuturno articulari morbo tyrannice vexari, et nigra lepra consumi, et duplicem calamitatem, vel multiplicem potius morbum sentire, quod et articulorum affligeretur doloribus, et lepræ malis cruciaretur (aderat quidem pudor quoque deformitatis, propter quam ab hominibus non erat aspectabilis: et neque solummodo erat fere semper in lecto, sed amicos etiam qui veniebant ad eum aspiciendum, præ pudore celabat) propterea hæc laboravit scire diligentius, ut posset certe renunciare domino suo, quo ille quoque forte per eum sanitatem consequeretur. Invenit ergo rursus Dominum in eisdem locis mortuos excitantem: cœcis visum donantem: claudos ad ingrediendum integros efficientem: sanosque et firmos reddentem omnes qui aliqua laborabant infirmitate.

Postquam ergo persuasum habuit, et aperte cognovit hæc fieri a Domino, ea Abagaro reversus significavit, et pluribus ea quæ viderat et audierat, edocuit. Quamobrem ut qui rem in transitu comparasset majorem quam quæ ei commissa fuerat, et ut qui bona afferet nuncia, benignissime fuit exceptus, et habitus fuit unus ex maxime benevolis. Et quoniam qui alicujus rei desiderio tenetur, tamquam rapinam existimat, si quod promissum fuerit differatur, re quæ narratur, et spe ipsa hominum excitante, vehementique studio incitatur ad venandum id quod significatum fuerat. Idcirco Abagarus est excitatus, ut literis eum accesseret, qui talia dicebatur posse curare. Et protinus scripsit ad Dominum eam, quæ ubique circumfertur, epistolam. See "Constantini cognomento Porphyrogeniti, in Christo Romanorum Imperatoris, narratio collecta ex diversis historiis de non manu facta Christi Dei nostri imagine, missa ad Abagarum, et ex Edessa translata in hanc beatissimam urbium Reginam Constantinopolim. *Per Simeonem Metaphrastem.*" In HISTORIA ALOYSII LIPOMANI EPISCOPI VERONENSIS DE VITIS SANCTORUM. Pars. I. p. 187.

ܘܠܒܝ. ܫܕܪ ܒܓܘ ܠܗ ܕܝܒܐ ܡܢ ܬܪ̈ܝ ܐܪ̈ܓܠܝ. ܬܗܘܐ ܟܕ ܢܒܚܐ ܡܠܒܘܫܬܝ ܕܕܝܒܐ ܢܟܝܐ ܐܝܟ ܕܐܬܒܥܝ ܠܗ ܡܢܗܘܢ ܕܩܘܦܐ. ܘܦܪܠ ܗܘܝܐ ܐܓܪܬܐ ܘܫܕܪ ܐܝܟ ܠܦܪܢܣ ܚܠܒܐ. ܘܟܕ ܦܢܐ ܐܝܟ ܐܬܥܕܪ ܥܠ ܦܪܢܣܘܗ ܚܠܒܐ. ܘܚܒܐ ܗܘܐ ܕܢܘܒܕ ܘܢܦܠ ܠܟܠܗܘܢ ܫܘ̈ܕܝܐ. ܘܢܦܩܘ ܬܪ̈ܝ ܐܪ̈ܓܠܝ ܘܐܬܦܪܕܘ. ܘܐܙܠܘ ܒܫ̈ܢܐ ܓܝܪ ܡܓܒܘܝܐ ܘܐܟܪܗ ܠܗ. ܟܕ، ܫܕܪ ܦܘܩܕܢ ܠܟܪܝܣ ܕܠܝܬ ܬܐܘܠ ܬܓܪܬܐ ܓܝܪ ܡܟܪܐ ܘܟܬܠܬܐ. ܐܡܪ ܠܗܘܢ ܕܝܢܐ ܠܒܫ̈ܢܐ. ܕܠܐ ܐܢܬܘܢ ܦܩܕܬ ܘܢܦܫܬ ܡܢܗ ܕܟܬܝܒ ܐܢܬܘܢ.

ܐ. ܡܢ ܡܐܡܪܐ ܕܣܝܡ ܠܦܪܢܣܐ ܡܪܝ، ܢܡܘܣ
ܡܠܟܐ ܕܥܠ ܡܫܘܠܡܘܬܐ ܕܬܫܒܘܚܬܐ

ܠܐܘܪܗ، ܥܒܕ ܘܐܥܒܕ ܗܘܐ ܟܕ ܒܡܠܟܐ ܪܒܐ. ܕܒܬܪ ܚܠܒܐ ܦܠܓܐ ܠܕܒܬܐ ܘܢܟܝܢܐ ܠܗ. ܥܠܝܗܐ ܐܕܝ، ܘܟܕ ܗܘܐ ܟܕ ܐܝܟ ܚܢܢܐ. ܘܚܠܒܐ ܐܓܪܐ ܗܒܬ ܠܗ ܬܓܪܐ ܘܚܢܢܐ ܒܟܪܗ. ܥܠܝܗܐ ܘܚܠܒܐ ܡܟܐ ܕܫܡܥ ܗܘܘ ܗܘ ܒܡ ܗܢܐ. ܐܝܢܐ ܦܬܓܡܐ ܠܐ ܢܦܠ ܗܘܐ ܡܢ ܦܘܡܗܘܢ. ܒܪܡ ܗܦܟܐ ܠܐܪܒܐ ܕܒܒܠ ܡܢ ܬܠܬܝܢܐ. ܘܡܢܗܘܢ ܥܪܒܐ ܕܪܡܫܘܬܐ ܠܒܝܬ ܩܠܝܢܐ. ܝܕܐ ܒܪ ܓܢܒܝܢ ܒܠ ܬܠܡܝܕܐ ܕܠܐ ܡܕܡ ܗܘ.

ܡܢ ܡܐܡܪܐ ܕܥܠ ܒܪܟܐ ܕܐܠܦܝܢ

ܠܫܡܥܘܢ ܪܗܘܡܝܐ ܘܠܝܘܚܢܢ ܡܠܟ ܐܦܣܘܣ. ܠܬܐܘܡܐ ܗܢܘ ܘܠܐܕܝ، ܒܝܬ ܐܬܪܘܬܐ. ܘܟܕ ܐܫܬܪܪܘ ܥܠܝܗ ܡܢܗܘܢ ܠܐܬܪܐ ܕܡܠܟܘܬ، ܗܟܢܐ ܐܦܢܝܘܢ ܠܡܬܠܡܕܘ ܠܐܬܪܘܬܐ.

ܘܒܟ̈ܠܗܘܢ܂ ܘܗܠܝܢ ܢܫ̈ܬܐ ܕܓܒܝܐ ܕܠܒܝܫ ܗܘܐ܂ ܘܐܬܦܢܝܘ
ܐܝܟ ܡܛܠ ܕܕܚܠܘ ܗܘܘ܂ ܕܕܠܡܐ ܠܡ ܐܢܫ ܡܢ ܡ̈ܠܟܐ ܐܘ
ܡܢ ܕ̈ܝܢܐ ܐ̈ܚܪܢܐ ܘܡܫܬܐܠܝܢ ܡܛܠ ܡܠܬܗ ܕܡܫܝܚܐ܂ ܘܥܠܘ
ܠܐܘܪܫܠܡ ܘܐܬܦܢܝܘ ܠܡܕܝܢܬܐ܂ ܕܐܬܬܐ ܡܢܝܢ ܒܪܡܫܐ ܘܒܢܝܗܐ
ܘܡܫܬܡܠܝܐ ܗܘܬ܂ ܘܗܘܐ ܫܠܡܘܬܐ ܒܐܘܪܫܠܡ ܡܛܠ ܡܢܗ܆
ܡܢܗ܂ ܘܐܬܠܗ ܒܥܘܕܢܐ ܕܝܢ ܕܢܗܘܐ ܘܐܬܬܚܝܡ ܠܗ܂ ܡܢ܆ ܒܝܕ
ܦܩܘܕܐ ܠܡܢܝܢ ܕܠܐ ܬܐܙܠ ܬܢܝܢܐ ܕܝܢ ܡܢܗ ܘܫܘܬܦܘܬܐ܂
ܘܟܕ ܣܠܩ ܡܬܦܫܩܝܢ܂ ܗܐ ܐܓܪ̈ܬܐ ܐܬܝ܆ ܡܢ ܐܒܓܪ
ܡܠܟܐ ܕܐܘܪܗܝ܆ ܡܫܬܕܪܬܐ ܠܣܒܝܢܐ ܐܦܛܪܘܦܐ ܕܒܝܬ ܗܘܐ
ܠܛܝܒܪܝܘܣ ܡܠܟܐ ܘܒܪܡܟܐ ܠܥܒܪ ܢܗܪܐ܂ ܐܝܬ ܗܘܐ ܠܗ ܫܘܠܛܢܐ
ܠܣܒܝܢܐ ܐܦܛܪܘܦܐ܂ ܘܡܛܠ ܕܫܡܝܥ ܗܘܐ ܐܕܝ ܫܠܝܚܐ܂ ܚܕ
ܡܢ ܥܒܕ̈ܘܗܝ ܘܬܪ̈ܝܢ ܫܠܝܚܝܢ ܘܥܒܕܐ ܒܕܘܟܬܐ ܒܐܘܪܗܝ܆ ܘܐܦ܆
ܟܬܒܐ ܕܐܝܬ ܗܘܐ ܠܗ ܠܐܒܓܪ ܡܠܟܐ܂ ܫܡܥ ܗܘܐ ܠܗ
ܓܝܪ ܐܒܓܪ ܡܠܟܐ ܠܫܘܒܚ ܡܫܝܚܐ܂ ܘܡܫܬܐܠ ܗܘܐ ܒܟܠ
ܐܦ ܡܛܠܬܗ܂ ܘܟܕ ܫܡܥ ܡܫܝܚܐ ܘܝܕܥ ܐܒܓܪ ܡܠܟܐ
ܕܒܝܫܬܐ ܡܛܠܬܗ܆ ܘܡܬܕܪܫܢ܂ ܟܬܒ ܠܗ ܠܩܣܪ܂ ܘܟܬܒ ܐܒܓܪ
ܘܐܡܪ ܘܐܟܬܒ ܒܐܓܪܬܐ ܠܡܪܢ ܩܣܪ܂ ܕܢܫܬܡܥ ܗܘܐ ܕܢܩܘܡ
ܥܠ ܐܘܪܫܠܡ ܘܢܚܪܒܗ܂ ܘܟܕ ܐܬܐ ܐܒܓܪ ܘܡܛܠܐ ܩܣܪܐ
ܦܪܘܫ ܐܬܦܢܝ ܗܘܐ ܒܐܝܕܝܗܘܢ ܕܐܝܟ ܒܒܪ ܐܢܫ ܗܘܐ ܠܗ
ܒܠܒܒܘܬܐ ܟܕ ܠܐ ܠܛܝܒܪܝܘܣ ܡܠܟܐ܂ ܘܟܬܒ ܐܒܓܪ ܐܓܪܬܐ
ܘܫܕܪ ܠܗ ܠܣܒܝܢܐ ܐܦܛܪܘܦܐ ܘܣܒܝܢܐ ܫܕܪ ܐܢܝܢ ܠܛܝܒܪܝܘܣ
ܡܠܟܐ܂ ܗܟܢܐ ܐܢܬ ܕܟܬܒ ܗܘܐ ܠܗ ܐܒܓܪ ܠܛܝܒܪܝܘܣ
ܡܠܟܐ܂ ܡܢ ܐܒܓܪ ܡܠܟܐ ܕܐܘܪܗܝ܆ ܒܪ ܡܢܘܬܐ܂ ܫܠܡܐ ܠܡܪܝ
ܠܡܠܟܘܬܟ ܡܪܝ ܛܝܒܪܝܘܣ܂ ܡܛܠ ܕܠܐ ܡܬܟܣܝܐ ܡܠܟܘܬܟ
ܡܕܡ ܠܐ ܡܟܣܝܬ ܡܢ ܦܪܘܫ܂ ܕܚܠܐ ܗܘܬ ܕܐܢܘܢ ܥܠ
ܐܘܪܫܠܡ ܘܐܣܪܩܘܗ ܥܠ ܕܡܛܠܬ ܠܡܫܝܚܐ ܐܝܟ ܐܢܫܐ ܣܓܝܐܐ܂
ܐܠܐ ܐܝܬܝܟ ܡܠܟܐ ܪܒܐ ܕܫܠܝܛ ܐܢܬ ܥܠ ܟܠܗܿ ܐܪܥܐ

ܕܡܫܝܚܘܬܐ ܕܩܒܠܘܗܝ. ܘܒܝܘܠܦܢܐ ܕܫܢܐ ܕܦܠܓܐ ܐܝܬ ܠܗܘܢ. ܡܛܠ ܕܗܘܐ ܒܐܡܬܐ ܕܡܫܝܚܐ ܡܬܬܒܥܝܢ ܐܢܘܢ ܠܗ. ܡܢܐ ܕܒܢܐ ܫܘܡܠܝܐ ܡܢ ܕܝܘܬܐ ܘܟܠܝܐ. ܘܡܢܐ ܕܢܦܩ ܒܣܘܦܗ ܡܢ ܬܪܬܐ ܒܪܝܬܐ ܕܫܠܝܚܐ. ܒܪ ܡܠܟܐ ܗܘ ܓܒܪ ܘܐܙܠ ܕܢܦܩ. ܫܠܡܘܬܐ ܘܢܨܚܢ ܘܢܝܬܐ. ܘܢܚܒܪ ܢܘܚܐ ܠܟܠܗܘܢ ܒܢܝܢܐ.

ܕ. ܐܕܝ ܐܒܓܪ ܒܐܘܪܗܝ ܘܒܝܬ ܢܗܪܝܢ. ܐܬܘܗܝ ܗܘܐ ܕܝܢ ܡܢ ܒܢܝܗ ܒܢܘܗܝ ܐܒܓܪ ܡܠܟܐ. ܘܒܪ ܐܬܘܗܝ ܒܝܬ ܢܗܪܝܢ. ܓܒܪ ܡܠܟܝ ܗܘܪܘܣ ܒܪ ܐܒܓܪ. ܠܘܬ ܐܕܝ ܫܠܝܚܐ ܘܬܠܡܝܕܐ ܬܠܡܝܕܘܗܝ.

ܗ. ܒܐ: ܘܢܪܣܝܣܘܣ. ܠܐ ܓܒܪ ܥܒܕܘ. ܕܐܝܬܘܗܝ ܓܒܪܐ ܗܘ ܕܥܒܕܝܢ ܘܬܪܝܢ: ܐܒܗܬܐ ܕܐܦܠܐ ܗܘ ܕܐܬܪܒܣܪ. ܗܘ ܕܝܢ ܕܥܒܕܝܢ ܘܬܪܝܢ. ܒܪ ܗܘ ܬܠܡܝܕܐ ܕܐܕܝ ܫܠܝܚܐ ܐܬܘܗܝ ܀

ܘ. ܡܢ ܡܟܣܝܢ ܕܡܪܬܗ ܡܪܝܡ ܕܡܢ ܒܠܒܐ. ܘܠܝܕܘܬܗ ܘܡܠܟܘܬܗ ܕܡܪܢ ܫܘܒ ܡܫܝܚܐ. ܣܦܪܐ ܕܬܪܝܢ.

ܒܝܬ ܬܠܬܡܐܐ ܘܐܪܒܥܝܢ ܘܫܬܐ ܫܢܝܢ ܒܐܝܕ ܬܫܪܝܢ ܐܚܪ ܢܚܬ ܡܪܢ ܡܪܝܡ ܡܢ ܒܬܘܠܬܐ. ܘܐܬܝܠܕ ܒܪ ܡܪܢ ܕܡܫܝܚܐ. ܡܛܠ ܕܒܠܝܡ ܒܝܘܡ ܐܪܒܥܐ ܗܘܬ ܘܟܝܢܐ ܬܡܢ. ܢܘܪܕܢܐ ܕܝܢ ܓܝܪܐ ܕܒܝܬ ܡܫܝܚܐ ܐܝܟܢܐ ܠܡܪܢܐ. ܘܓܒܗ ܠܐ ܦܪܚܘ ܒܟܢܘܫܐ ܙܘܓܬܐ. ܘܟܠ ܡܪܢܐ ܦܠܓܘܬܐ ܐܡܝܢܐ ܠܫܘܪܐ ܘܦܩܕܘ ܐܝܟ. ܕܐܝܟ ܐܝܟ ܐܙܠ ܘܡܠܟܐ ܓܝܪ ܡܪܢܐ ܟܘ ܓܝܪ ܓܢܘܢܝܬܐ. ܓܝܘܕܐ ܢܒܘܬ. ܘܥܒܠ ܢܗܘܪܐ ܓܠܝܢ ܕܡܪܢ. ܘܗܠܝܢ ܬܪܝܢ ܓܠܝܢ ܣܓܝܐ. ܘܗܘ ܠܗܝܢܬܐ ܕܟܠܝ ܒܗ ܦܪܘܩ. ܘܗܠܝܢ ܬܪܬܐ ܕܥܒܕܘ ܠܗ ܒܐܝܕܘܗܝ

ܦܓܪܐ ܠܒܪ ܗܘܐ ܟܕ ܕܗܘܐ ܒܓܘܫܡܗ ܕܦܓܪܐ. ܗܘ ܓܝܪ
ܓܒܠܗ ܕܐܦܪܝܡ ܠܠܒܢܐ ܕܡܢ ܒܬܘܠܬܐ. ܗܘ ܗܘܒ ܬܘܫܒܢܗ
ܠܒܢܐ ܕܐܦܘܬܐ ܀ ܘܡܢ ܒܬܪ ܒܠܝ. ܀ ܐܦ ܓܝܪ ܚܙܘܗ ܕܟܢܝܫܐ
ܗܘܬ. ܐܠܐ ܚܠܡ ܘܚܕܬܗ ܒܒܠܝܠܗ ܕܐܠܗܐ ܗܘܐ.

ܒ. ܡܢ ܡܠܟܘܬܐ ܕܐܝܟ ܚܣܝܐ. ܕܐܬܐܡܪܬ ܒܐܘܪܗ ܡܫܒܚܐ ܀

ܡܛܠ ܐܝܬܘܗܝ ܕܐܬܐܡܪܬ ܠܚܝ. ܕܟܠܗܝܢ ܢܒܝܘܬܐ ܕܢܦܩ ܡܢ ܦܓܪܐ ܕܒܣܝܡܐ. ܬܚܝܬ ܚܫܘܟܐ ܠܐ ܫܘܝܢ. ܐܠܐ ܚܝܝܢ ܘܩܝܡܝܢ. ܘܐܝܬ ܠܗܝܢ ܐܘܩܝܢܐ ܘܚܝܠ ܡܫܪܪܐ ܕܢܒܝܐ. ܠܐ ܓܝܪ ܦܠܠܐ ܡܫܡܥܬܐ ܕܢܒܝܐ ܕܠܐ ܡܚܬܐ. ܡܛܠ ܕܙܠܝܩܐ ܐܝܬܝܗ ܕܐܠܗܐ ܠܐ ܦܫܝܩܐ. ܠܝܬܝܗ ܓܝܪ ܕܠܐ ܙܠܝܩܐ ܒܡܫܬܐ ܕܓܘܫܡܐ: ܗܘ ܕܠܐ ܠܗ ܡܪܓܫܢܘܬܐ ܕܢܦܠܗ ܗܘ ܕܐܬܚܙܝ ܒܠܘܗܝ. ܦܘܪܫܐ ܕܝܢ ܘܐܓܪܐ ܠܐ ܡܦܩܠܐ ܒܠܒܕ ܡܢ ܓܘܫܡܗ: ܡܛܠ ܕܫܡܝܐ ܠܗ ܕܠܗ ܗܘ ܒܠܘܕܝܗ. ܐܠܝ ܘܓܘܫܡܢܝܐ ܗܘ ܕܝܚܝܕܬ ܒܗ ܒܟܝܢ. ܠܐ ܡܬܦܫܩܢܐ ܕܝܢ ܕܠܐܠܗܐ ܠܐ ܡܚܘ: ܕܠܐ ܡܬܒܪ ܡܕܡ ܡܬܬܘܡ ܀

ܓ. ܡܢ ܐܓܪܬܐ ܕܐܝܟ ܚܢܢܐ ܕܡܠܠ ܒܐܘܪܗ ܡܫܝܚܐ.

ܐܘܕܝܘ ܒܡܫܡܥܬܐ ܗܕܐ ܕܐܫܬܡܥ ܐܝܬܘܗܝ. ܘܡܫܝܚܬܐ ܘܡܐܬܝܬܐ ܗܘܝܬܘܗܝ ܦܢܝ ܒܗ. ܘܡܫܡܫܝܢ ܠܘܩܒܠܗ. ܠܐ ܗܘܝܬܘܗܝ ܡܫܡܫܝܢ ܐܝܬܘܗܝ ܒܗ ܒܟܝܢܐ ܒܫܝܢ. ܐܠܐ ܒܦܘܪܫܢܐ ܕܗܝܡܢܘܬܐ. ܘܒܫܘܬܦܘܬܗ ܕܡܫܝܚܐ ܡܢ ܦܘܪܫܢܗܘܢ ܠܐ ܢܦܠܠ. ܘܡܐܝܢܘܬܐ ܒܒܝܢܐ ܕܥܠܡܐ ܠܥܠܡܝܢ ܠܐ ܬܬܦܪܫ. ܐܘܕܝܘ ܒܟܪܙܐ ܗܢܐ ܕܐܫܬܡܥ ܐܝܬܘܗܝ: ܘܡܫܠܡܢܐ

ܐܝܟ ܓܢܒܬܐ ܒܠܠܝܐ. ܒܗܿܝ ܕܡܠܟܐ ܐܢܫܐ ܘܫܒܬܢ
ܒܒܝܐ ܐܢܐ. ܕܢܬܠܡ ܒܗ ܡܫܝܚܐ ܗ̇ܘ ܕܡܬܐܡܪ ܒܐܒܝܕܐ
ܕܐܬܬܟܝܠ ܃ ܫܪܝܐ ܘܝܗܒ ܒܪܢܫܐ ܒܗ ܒܢܝܐ ܕܫ̈ܠܐܟܐ
ܠܟܘܢ. ܒܗ ܙܒܢܐ ܓܒܪܐ ܕܠܒܪܟܐ ܬܒܝܪܐ. ܒܠ ܬ̈ܚܘܬܟ
ܘܫܬܩܘܗܝ ܕܡܫܝܚܐ ܗ̇ܘ ܕܡܬܐܡܪ ܢܛܦܪ ܃ ܓܒ ܗܘ ܫܘܒܚܟ ܡܢ
ܫܒܪܐ ܘܡܢ ܥ̈ܦܪܐ ܕܬܘܪܓܡܐ ܘܫܒܚܬܟ. ܒܫܒܪܐ ܢܛܪܬܟ
ܕܒܚܘܒܐ ܕܕܡܟ. ܫ̈ܢܐ ܫܬ̈ܝܬܐ ܐܘܫܝܬ ܘܬܘܪ̈ܓܡܐ ܥܒܝܕ
ܠܫܒܚܬܟ ܃ ܒܕܬܐ ܐܢܐ ܕܡܢ ܒܬ̈ܒܐ ܘܫܒܚܬܗ ܠܐܘܫܝܐ
ܕܐܬܟܠܝܢ. ܕܡܫܪܬܗ ܘܬܒܗ ܐܢܐ ܢܒܝܬܗ. ܘܒܐܝܕܝ ܐܟܣܢ
ܐܘܡܢܐ ܡܦܫܩܐ ܐܢܐ ܕܢܐܬܐ ܠܝ ܘܫܒܝܢ ܃ ܐܘܡܢܐ
ܐܢܐ ܘܡܠܐ ܐܢܐ ܒܝܬ ܓܘܫܡܐ ܕܒܢܝܐ ܗܘ ܢܫܘܩܝܢ.
ܕܡܒܪܢ ܒܪ ܓܒܪܐ ܕܒܠܝ ܠܓܘܫܡܐ. ܘܒܕ ܗܢܝܐ ܐܢܐ ܙܢܩ
ܠܝ ܕܡܫܒܚ ܗܘ ܕܡܢ ܩܢܝܐ ܢܦܪܢ ܃ ܐܘܡܢܘܬܐ ܐܢܐ ܒܬ̈ܓܡܐ
ܘܡܠܐ ܐܢܐ ܕܬܒܢܝ ܘܐܬܦܢܝ. ܥܠܝܗ ܒܒܒܕܐ ܠܗ̇ܘ ܓܘܢܐ
ܗܢܐ. ܕܬܪܘܨ ܒܕܡܗ ܕܢܝܐ ܦܪܘܩܐ ܕܒܬ̈ܬܐ ܥܠܡܝܢ ܃

ܫܠܡ ܦܘܫܩܐ ܡܢ ܗܘܓܝܬܐ ܕܥܠ ܐܘܪܗܝ.

ܦܘܫܩܐ ܕܡܢ ܟܬܒܐ ܡܫܝܚܝܐ

ܕܥܠ ܐܟܣܢܝ ܡܠܟܐ ܘܐܒܕ ܥܠܝܡܐ.

ܐ. ܕܓܘܒܝܐ ܐܒܕ ܥܠܝܡܐ. ܡܢ ܡܠܦܢܘܬܐ ܕܒܒܕ ܒܐܘܪܗܝ،
ܡܕܡ ܐܟܣܢ ܡܠܟܐ ܘܒܢܝܐ ܕܡܕܝܢܬܐ.

ܘܒܕ ܒܠ ܠܡܒܪܐ. ܐܬܝܫܡ ܗܘܐ ܘܢܦܩ ܡܢ ܡܒܪܐ ܒܡ
ܩܒܠܐ ܘܐܡܠܡ ܕܢܦܩܝܢ ܗܘܘ ܠܡܒܪܐ. ܠܐ ܫܘ ܐܡܒܝܐ ܢܦܩ
ܗܘܐ ܡܢ ܡܒܪܐ. ܘܒܝ̈ܢܐ ܕܘܡܒܝܐ. ܗܘܠܘ ܗܘܘ ܒܪܘܪܐ
ܘܡܫܒܝ̈ܢܐ. ܕܡܫܒܚܬܗ ܕܐܠܘ ܠܐ ܢܒܐ ܠܐ ܡܫܬܟܚܐ. ܡܛܠ
ܕܒܪܗ ܗܘ ܕܒܗܘܬܐ ܡܫܡܝܐ. ܘܐܠܘ ܠܐ ܕܡܦܪ ܠܗ: ܐܦ ܠܐ

ܫܠܡ ܒܐܢܘܬܐ. ܠܐ ܕܝܢ ܗܘܘ ܠܒܢܝ ܒܝܬܐ ܬܘܒ ܕܫܠܐ.
ܐܦ ܠܐ ܐܘܪܗܝ ܕܡܫܐ ܠܝܗܘܢ ܕܐܦ ܗܝ ܘܦܫܬ. ܗܝ
ܐܒܘܗ̇ ܗܘܝܢ ܗܘܘ ܐܦ ܡܝܬܝܢ. ܘܐܬܬܝܢ ܒܐܬܪܐ ܕܡܢܐ
ܘܡܬܐ ܒܥܠܬܗ. ܒܗܠܝܢ ܗܘܝܐ ܕܗܘܪܐ ܘܡܫܬܐ ܗܐ
ܡܬܡܠܠ. ܒܪܝܟ ܗܘ ܕܝܗܒ ܠܝ ܘܡܫܬܡܠܝܐ ܕܟܠܠܝܘܗܝ.
ܫܠܡ ܡܐܡܪܐ ܕܥܠ ܠܘܪܐ ܘܫܡܫܐ.

ܬܘܠܕܬܐ ܕܡܪܝ ܝܥܩܘܒ ܡܠܦܢܐ: ܥܠ ܐܦܪܝܡ
ܟܕ ܫܠܡܬ ܠܡܪܝ ܕܢܐܬܐ ܠܗ.

ܐܦܪܝܡ، ܫܠܡܬ ܠܡܫܝܚܐ ܒܐܓܪܬܐ ܕܢܐܬܐ ܠܗ ܘܢܚܙܝܗ.
ܫܠܡ ܥܠܝܟܘܢ ܒܡܫܝܚܐ ܦܝܫܐ ܒܟܕܘ ܠܗ ܕܢܦܩܐ ܠܝܗܘܢ
ܕܗܘܬܗ ܘܢܐܬܐ ܠܗ ܠܘܬ ܒܢܝܢܐ ܕܐܚܝܢܘܗܝ ܀ ܫܕܪܬ
ܓܐܪܘܗܝ، ܘܒܟܬܒܗ ܕܢܬܠܠ ܒܝܬܗ ܒܪܚܡܬܐ. ܟܕ ܡܠܟܐ
ܒܐܝܢ ܦܝܫܐ ܒܟܕܘ ܠܗ. ܕܢܦܩܐ ܠܗ ܡܢ ܒܝܬܐ ܘܓܕ.
ܒܝܬܝܐ ܢܬܪܘܢ ܗܘܐ ܡܬܟܠܡ ܀ ܡܢ ܟܠ ܡܠܟܝܢ ܚܕ
ܡܠܟܐ ܫܡܝܐ ܒܪܬ ܒܝܬܝܐ ܐܫܟܚܬ. ܐܢܓܕܐ ܒܟܕܘܬܗ
ܠܒܪܗ ܫܠܡܬ ܒܗ. ܗܐ ܠܝ ܓܐܕ، ܐܓܠܒܐ ܒܝ
ܠܗܬܒܪܐ ܘܠܓܠܝܢܐ ܒܠܝܘܢ ܀ ܫܟܒܬ ܓܒܗ ܡܢ ܪܘܚܢܐ
ܘܚܬܐ ܕܒܫܡܝܐ ܦܢܚܐ. ܓܒܢܬܐ ܒܬܓܠܒܐ ܫܒܪܬܐ
ܒܓܠܝܢܐ. ܪܫܡܬ ܪܓܬܗ ܟܕ ܪܚܡ ܘܟܐܠܬܗ ܕܠܓܢܘܢ
ܢܠܗ ܀ ܢܫܡܥ ܫܬܝܐ ܪܓܓܐ ܐܢܐ ܒܢܘܫܡܬܐ ܕܦܘܡܗ
ܡܒܪܟܐ. ܫܡܥܬܗ ܡܢ ܪܘܚܢܐ ܐܚܝܢܘܗܝ، ܡܢ ܦܘܪܩܐ.
ܘܐܗܘܐ ܩܦܘܬ، ܟܠ ܕܠܗ ܘܐܬܒܣܡ ܒܚܝܬܗ ܒܒܢܝ ܀
ܬܒܥܝܢ ܓܒܝܢ ܠܝ ܡܢ ܚܒܪܐ ܕܪܚܡ ܒܗܘܦܟܝܢ ܫܢܐ ܗܘ ܠܒܠܒܐ.
ܒܫܠܒܝܢ ܐܬܪܐ ܒܪܚܝܢ ܐܬܟܣܦ. ܡܢ ܬܢܝܢܐ ܕܬܬܒܪܐ
ܕܒܪܚܡܗ ܘܗܘܡܐ ܐܗܪܢ ܀ ܓܕܫ ܒܬܪܝܢ ܠܓܒܪܝܢ ܕܢܦܫܐ

ܦܬܬܐ. ܘܠܗ ܢܣܒ ܠܗܘܢ ܒܫܡܐ ܠܡܫܝܚܘ. ܗܘ ܡܪܢ
ܟܠܬܐ ܒܕܡܘܬܐ ܕܕܪܐ ܡܢ ܡܫܝܚܘܬܗ. ܘܠܫ̈ܡܫܝܢܘܗܝ ܬܒܥ
ܙܘܡܝܢܐ ܕܡܘܬܐ ܕܝܘܪܕܢܢ. ܡܢܐ ܫܠܘܡܐ ܬܠܬܐ ܒܪܘܚܐ
ܒܦܠܐܬܐ. ܘܥܠ ܡܢ ܕܐܬܝܐ ܕܢܦܫܐ ܫܘܠܛܢܐ ܕܡܢܗ ܐܢܫ
ܠܗ. ܫܡܘܥܐ ܦܘܪܫܐ ܢܣܒ ܦܬܓܡܘܗܝ ܡܦܠܬܗ. ܠܬܫܐ
ܘܩܕܫܐ ܘܠܫܘܒܚܐ ܕܥܠ ܐܘܠܝܢ. ܒܗ ܢܣܝܡ ܗܘܘ ܒܪ ܡܬܟܢܫ
ܡܢ ܒܩܠܐ. ܘܥܠ ܗܝ ܘܡܢܘ ܗܠܝܢ ܒܬܪܐ ܕܠܐ ܙܘܒܢܐ.
ܒܬܪܬ ܐܘܪܗܝ ܡܢ ܩܠܝܠܝܢ ܐܘ ܦܬܓܡܐ. ܕܢܬܬܘܣ
ܒܩܠܝܠܝܢ ܘܒܫܒܝܚܢ. ܫܘܦܪܗ ܐܝܬܘܗܝ ܫܘܦܪܗ ܐܝܬܘܗܝ
ܡܠܝܗ ܐܝܬܘܗܝ. ܒܬܪܗ ܘܡܬܬܗ ܐܦ ܫܘܒܚܗ ܘܒܩܠܗ
ܠܗ. ܐܝܬܘܗܝ ܐܝܟ ܗܢܐ ܕܡܬܝܕܥܢܘܬܐ. ܕܒܫܒܝܚܢ
ܐܠܗܘܬܗ ܠܟܠܬܐ ܫܘܦܪܐ. ܒܬܪ ܦܬܓܡܐ ܕܐܬܡܠܟ ܗܘܬ
ܠܡܫܡܫܘܬܐ. ܒܗܘܢ ܗܘ ܣܘܪܐ ܕܒܫܘܠܡܗܘܢ ܗܘܐ ܢܣܝܪܐ.
ܘܐܝܟܢܐ ܐܝܬܘܗܝ ܦܘܪܐ ܕܒܗ ܒܪ ܥܬܝܩ. ܠܟܠܗ ܦܬܓܡ
ܒܪ ܙܢ ܡܠܗ ܒܒܘܪܟܬܐ. ܗܠܝܢ ܗܟܢܐ ܕܒܪܬ ܒܒܪܬܐ
ܟܕ ܒܥܠܡܐ ܗܘܘ. ܗܫܐ ܕܫܘܪܝܐ ܕܦܬܓܡܐ ܠܢܦܫܬ ܒܪ
ܡܫܬܢܝܢ. ܘܒܬܪ ܐܘܪܗܝ ܒܬܪܝܢ ܗܟܢܐ ܟܠܗ ܫܘܦܪܐ. ܕܗܘ
ܗܫܐ ܠܒܪ ܐܠܗܐ ܘܡܫܝܚܐ ܐܝܟ ܢܦܫܬ. ܬܪܝܢ ܗܘܘ ܬܡܢ
ܘܬܪܝܢ ܗܘܐ ܐܝܟܢܐ ܗܟܢܐ. ܘܗܠܝܢ ܗܫܐ ܘܗܠܝܢ ܗܫܐ
ܡܬܐܡܪܝܢ ܗܘܘ. ܢܣܒܐ ܗܟܢܐ ܐܝܠܝܢ ܗܫܐ ܠܒܝܬ ܠܐܠܗܐ.
ܘܐܢܫܐ ܡܫܝܚܐ ܙܢܝܐ ܒܥܒܕܘܗܝ ܘܒܡܥܒܕܢܘܗܝ. ܗܐ ܟܕ
ܒܥܠܡܐ ܕܦܠܠ ܠܢܦܫܬ ܗܫܐ ܐܝܟ. ܘܗܪܟܐ ܫܡܘܥܐ
ܦܘܪܫܐ ܗܫܐ ܬܘܒ ܐܬܬܣܝܡ. ܢܣܒܐ ܗܟܢܐ ܐܝܠܝܢ
ܗܫܐ ܘܐܝܠܝܢ ܗܟܢܐ. ܘܐܢܫܐ ܡܫܝܚܐ ܬܠܝܢ ܒܢܦܫܗ ܡܢ
ܐܠܗܐ. ܟܕ ܒܥܠܡܐ ܗܘܘ ܗܠܝܢ ܗܫܐ ܕܡܢ ܢܣܒܬܐ. ܘܗܐ
ܒܗܬܬܗܘܢ ܓܒܪܐ ܟܠܗ ܒܦܘܪܫܢܗܘܢ. ܗܟܝܠ ܗܫܐ ܕܗܘܢ
ܕܐܘܪܗܝ ܒܬܪܝܢ ܐܦ ܕܕܝܢ. ܠܢܦܫܬ ܕܡܢ ܕܦܠܠ ܐܦ ܗܘ

ܐܘܪܚܗ ܠܪܘܡܐ ܠܟܝܬ ܡܠܟܘܬܐ. ܒܬܪ ܕܐܘܠܨܢܐ ܦܓܥܐ
ܗܘܐ ܠܗ ܠܥܘܕܪܐ ܓܒܝܐ. ܥܠ ܬܘܕܝܬܐ ܡܢ ܦܘܩܕܢܗ
ܡܫܬܡܥܢܐ ܗܘܬ. ܗܘܝܘ ܠܗ ܦܘܪܩܢܐ ܠܢܦܫܐ ܠܓܒܪܐ
ܫܒܝܚܐܝܬ. ܘܒܝܘܡ ܗܘܘ ܠܗ ܐܝܟ ܕܠܡܫܡܫܬܐ ܕܟܠܝܐ
ܒܘܬܪܐ. ܒܟܕܪܐ ܫܘܬܐ ܒܝܕ ܒܗ ܒܟܠܡܐ ܒܪ ܐܠܗܐ.
ܕܡܘܬܐ ܕܫܠܝܐ ܢܗܘܐ ܪܘܚܐ ܡܢ ܦܓܪܐ. ܐܝܟܐ
ܕܪܘܚܢ ܠܘܡܠ ܦܩܐ ܠܐ ܐܫܬܡܥܬ. ܐܠܐ ܗܠܝܢ
ܕܐܟܠܢ ܢܘܕ ܒܪܘܚܘܬܗ. ܕܡܪܝ ܡܘܬܐ ܥܠ ܐܝܟ ܢܕܒ
ܗܐ ܡܢ ܒܠܡ. ܠܦܘܪܐ ܒܠܝܢ ܠܐ ܡܪܝ ܗܘܐ ܒܪ ܡܬܘܬܠܝܢ.
ܒܫܡܝܢ ܗܘܘ ܠܗ ܠܥܘܦܐ ܠܢܦܫܐ ܡܢܐ ܕܢܐܘܗܝ. ܘܦܪܝܫܝܢ
ܒܗ ܕܝܘ ܗܘܐ ܒܠܬܐ ܠܬܠܝܬܝܘܢ. ܐܝܟ ܕܠܘܝܐ ܢܒܘܡ
ܗܘܘ ܠܗ ܠܦܘܢܩܢܐ ܢܟܠܒ. ܘܡܢ ܪܫܝܢ ܠܗ ܠܐ ܫܘܒܘܗܝ
ܗܘܘ ܡܢ ܐܘܠܨܢܐ. ܠܦܘܩܐ ܗܒܝܘ ܘܢܦܡ ܦܩܐ ܘܠܠܠ
ܐܝܟ. ܕܠܗ ܫܪܝܢ ܗܘܘ ܘܐܬܦܢܝ ܠܗܘܢ ܐܝܟ ܕܒܐܘܗܝ.
ܒܪ ܐܠܗܐ ܦܘܠܘܣ ܠܡܘܬܐ ܒܪܘܚܘܬܗ. ܘܥܠ ܕܦܘܠܘܣ ܗܘ
ܡܘܬܐ ܠܦܘܪܐ ܠܐ ܡܛܝ ܗܘܐ. ܒܝܘܡܐ ܕܦܢܝܢ ܡܫܬܒܚܐ
ܗܘ ܐܝܟ ܒܪ ܠܐ ܕܢܠ. ܠܐܘܪܚܐ ܕܦܘܠܘܣ ܓܒܪܐ ܗܘ ܠܗ ܐܦ
ܫܠܝܐ. ܠܝܘܡܐ ܪܒܐ ܡܪܢ ܦܓܪ ܒܪܘܚܘܬܗ. ܠܐܘܪܚܐ ܕܫܠܝܐ
ܒܪ ܐܠܗܐ ܒܫܡܗ ܦܘܠܘܣ. ܠܡܘܬܐ ܦܓܪܗ ܘܢܦܫܗ ܘܒܝܬܗ
ܒܬܪܒܐ ܕܫܘܠ. ܘܥܠ ܗܢ ܕܒܓܐ ܦܘܪܢ ܐܝܟ ܒܗ ܥܠ ܕܦܘܠܘܣ
ܗܘ. ܫܡܘܢܐ ܘܓܘܪܢܐ ܐܝܟܢܐ ܦܘܠܐ ܒܫܡܘܬܐ ܐܟܘܠ.
ܒܐܡܬܝ ܒܐܘܪܚܐ ܗܘ ܕܦܘܠܘܣ ܗܘܐ ܠܒܪ ܐܠܗܐ. ܠܓܒܪܐ ܪܒܐ
ܕܦܘܠܘܣ ܠܐܪܥ ܒܝܬ ܡܠܟܐ. ܡܢ ܠܒܪ ܗܘܐ ܒܪ ܠܐ ܫܘܬܐ
ܗܘܐ ܕܒܗ ܕܘܦܩܐ. ܒܪ ܐܠܗܐ ܪܝ ܬܫܢܐ ܒܪܘܚܘܬܗ.
ܘܗܘܐ ܡܚܠܝܢ ܒܗ ܦܠܓܐ ܘܦܬܓܡܐ ܒܫܘܠܐ ܕܦܘܠܘܣ. ܕܓܒܪ
ܗܘ ܐܪܥܐ ܒܪܘܡܝܐ ܕܕܦܘܠܘܣ ܕܒܪ ܐܠܗܐ. ܘܥܠ ܡܢ ܕܒܓܐ
ܕܒܗ ܘܫܠܡ ܐܦ ܐܘܠ ܒܗ. ܒܪ ܐܠܗܐ ܗܘܝܘ ܒܠܬܐ ܕܥܠ

ܫܘܡܠܝܗܘܢ ܬܘܕܝܬܐ ܗܘܐ ܕܡܠܟܐ ܗܠܐ. ܘܐܝܟ ܕܒܦܘܡܐ
ܦܬܝܚܐ ܙܟܘܗ̇ ܠܡܫܒܚܘܬܐ. ܘܕܒܪ ܟܠ ܐܢܫ ܡܢܗ ܡܡܠܠܝܢ
ܟܕ ܫܬܝܩܝܢ. ܘܟܬܪܬ ܢܟܬ ܗܝܡܢܘܬܐ ܕܟܢܫ ܐܠܗܐ. ܘܟܗܢܬܬ
ܠܘܩܒܠ ܕܟܬܪܝܢ ܘܩܝܡܝܢ ܕܟܕ ܠܐ ܡܠܠܘ. ܘܟܐܘܗ̇ ܘܫܬܩܘ
ܘܡܟܬ ܕܠܗܘܢ ܗܝܡܢܘܬܐ. ܘܟܕ ܡܫܬܡܥܝܢ ܩܠܐ ܠܐ ܫܦܝܪܐ
ܡܢ ܕܝܢܐ. ܘܟܕ ܦܘܩܕܢܐ ܕܡ̈ܠܟܐ ܕܫܠܝܛ ܐܦ ܒܝܫܝܢ. ܘܟܕ
ܣܦܘܬܐ ܟܠܝܢ ܫ̈ܦܝܪ ܘܦܬܝܚ ܦܘܡܗ. ܘܪܡܐ ܡܠܬܗ
ܘܥܠܝܢ ܩܠܐ ܡܢ ܐܘܠܝܢܐ. ܟܠܠ ܦܘܩܕܢܐ ܘܐܫܬܡܗ̇ ܗܘܐ
ܥܠ ܕܝܢܐ. ܘܕܠܐ ܡܠܬܐ ܙܟܝܐ ܕܗܘܕܐ ܥܒܠ ܚܝܠܐ.
ܡܡܠܠܐ ܘܪܘܚܐ ܘܡܠܐ ܕܢܓܕܐ ܡܢ ܗܡܠܐ. ܘܥܠܝܐ ܙܟܐ
ܘܥܒܕܐ ܕܩܐܡ ܡܢ ܡܫܝܚܐ. ܘܟܕ ܙܟܐ ܕܬܠܐ ܩܕܡ ܠܟܠ
ܕ̈ܝܢܘܗܝ. ܐܬܬܪܝܡ ܪܝܫܗ ܕܡܫܝܚܘܬܐ ܘܟܗܢܘܬܗ ܠܘܩܒܠ. ܫܒܘ
ܕܡܡܠܠܝܢ ܘܠܫܬܩܐ ܗܘܐ ܚܝܠܐ. ܕܕܠܐ ܡܠܐ ܘܟܪܘܙܘܬܗ
ܡܐܡܪܐ ܕܡܫܝܚܘܬܐ. ܘܐܚܝܕܘ ܐܢܘܢ ܡܛܠ ܕܗܘ ܒܙ ܫܬܝܩܝܢ.
ܘܫܒܩܘ ܐܢܘܢ ܒܕ ܠܒܝܬ ܗܘܘ ܢܦܩܘ ܐܢܘܢ. ܫܒܘܩܝܐ
ܠܡܘܕܝܐ ܘܠܓܘܢܐ ܕܠܒܝܫ ܡܢ ܢܗܝܪܐ. ܠܐ ܫܒܩ ܗܘܐ ܠܗܘܢ
ܐܠܐ ܢܗܘܪܐ ܕܠܐ ܡܫܬܘܝܢ. ܘܕܠܐ ܠܫܡܫܐ ܘܕܠܐ ܟܘܟܒܐ
ܘܕܠܐ ܢܗܘܪܐ. ܗܢ ܗܘܐ ܠܗܘܢ ܡܛܠ ܫܘܒܚܗ ܕܒܪ ܐܠܗܐ.
ܦܓܪ ܕܝܢܐ ܕܒܪܓܠܝܗܘܢ ܬܠܝܢ ܐܢܘܢ. ܒܬܪ ܙܒܢܘ
ܒܕܝܢܐ ܕܪܫܡ ܡܢ ܒܐܢܘܬܐ. ܬܠܝܐ ܗܘܐ ܫܡܘܢܐ ܒܬܪ
ܪܫܡܗ ܘܡܬܠܝܐ ܗܘܐ. ܠܘܬܐ ܕܒܝܬܐ ܘܡܬܠܠܬܐ ܡܢ ܐܘܠܝܢܐ.
ܦܐܪܐ ܚܠܝܐ ܬܠܝܐ ܗܘܐ ܒܢܫܐ ܒܗܘ ܒܬ ܕܝܢܐ. ܘܠܒܟܘܗ
ܪܚܝܡܘ ܐܬܬܪܝ ܐܢܘܢ ܠܩܛܝܠܐ. ܐܠܝܢ ܗܘܐ ܦܓܪܗ ܘܫܠܝܡܐ
ܗܘܬ ܡܫܒܚܘܬܗ. ܒܟܝܢ ܗܘܐ ܠܒܢܝܗ ܘܡܪܝܐ ܠܘܬܗ ܥܠ
ܗܘܒܕܝܗ. ܠܘܬܐ ܓܝܪ ܠܐ ܡܕܝܢܠ ܠܗ ܐܦ ܠܐ ܡܥܒܕ.
ܘܠܐ ܡܟܝܢ ܠܗ ܐܦ ܠܐ ܗܘܒܐ ܐܦ ܠܐ ܢܘܪܐ. ܠܒܢܝܢܐ
ܡܦܩܢ ܗܘܐ ܗܘ ܕܝܢ ܠܘܬܐ ܒܡܢܝܢܐ ܗܘܬ. ܘܬܪܝܨܐ ܗܘܬ

ܒܠܐܝܬ. ܘܡܢܝܢܐ ܕܒܒܐ ܗܘܕܐ ܕܠܐ ܡ̈ܢܝܢܐ ܕܢܦܠܠ ܗܘܐ.
ܡܢܐ ܕܡܫܬܐܠ ܕܠܐ ܢܓܕܐ ܗܘܐ ܠܡܕܒܪܘ. ܡܫܠܐ ܫܠܝܡ
ܗܘܘ ܗܦܟܐ ܡܠܝܬ ܡܫܒܘܚܘܬܐ. ܘܡܢ ܐܘܠܨܢܐ ܠܐ ܗܦܟܝܢ
ܗܘܘ ܠܡܫܠܠܘ. ܘܡܫܬܐܠܝܢ ܗܘܘ ܘܐܡܪܝܢ ܬܗܘܐ ܕܐ̱ܢܐ ܫܠܐ
ܐܢܐ. ܡܢܐ ܕܡܫܬܐܠ ܐܦ ܫܠܡ ܗܘ ܠܕܡܬܐܡܪ̈ܢ. ܘܕܠܐ
ܢܗܘܘܢ ܗܦܟܐ ܗܦܝܟܝܢ ܕܫܠܡܝܢ ܐܢܘܢ. ܡܢܗܪ ܪܚܡܘܗ̇
ܠܡܠܬܐ ܕܐܘܠܨܐ ܕܬܬܡܠܠ ܗܘܬ. ܪܫܡܘܢ ܐܢܫܘ ܘܫܠܦ ܡܠܬܐ
ܒܪܡܙܐ ܚܘܝܘ. ܗ̇ܘ ܢܓܒܢܐ ܕܗ̇ܘ ܒܪ ܐܢܫܐ ܫܪܝܬܐ ܕܠܟܘ. ܬܠܘ
ܪ̈ܫܡܘܢ ܒܪ ܪܚܡܝܢ ܗܘܘ ܒܐܘܠܨܢܗܘܢ. ܕܠܐ ܡܪܚܡܝܢ
ܗܘܘ ܘܠܒܟ ܒܠ ܐܢܫ ܪ̈ܚܝܡܘܢ. ܒܪ ܐܢܫ ܗܘܐ ܒܡܘܢ
ܐܬܪܐ ܠܡܠܬܐ ܒܡܠܬܐ ܕܐܘܪܒܘ. ܘܒܪ ܐܫܬܘܠܠ ܡܢ ܐܘܠܨܢܐ
ܒܪܡܙܐ ܡܠܠܘ. ܠܡܫܒܘܚܘܬܐ ܡܠܠܘܗ̇ ܒܡܠܐ ܘܕܠܐ ܡܠܐ.
ܕܡܢܐ ܕܡܡܠܠܝܢ ܐܦ ܡܢܐ ܕܫܠܡ ܫ̈ܪܪܐ ܗܘܘ. ܡܢ ܠܐ ܬܗܘܪ
ܒܐܘܪܚܐ ܕܫܢܐ ܒܡܢܐ ܘܦܢܝܐ. ܘܒܡܢܐ ܐܠܝܨܐ ܠܐܢܫܐ
ܕܢܓܕܐ ܕܢܗܠܟ ܒܗ̇. ܗ̇ܢ ܠܐ ܬܗܘܘܢ ܕܠܓܒܝܢܐ ܕܒܢܪ
ܘܡܠܝܢ. ܦ̣ܠܓ ܪܘܚܐ ܘܡܠܝܢܐ ܢܗܘܪܐ ܠܕܪ̈ܐ ܒܗ̇. ܫܪ̈ܪܗ̇
ܕܐܘܪܚܐ ܦܫܝܛܬܐ ܡܠܝܢܐ ܐܦ ܗܘ̈ܬܐ. ܘܡܠܠ ܡܢܗ̇ ܐ̱ܢ
ܡܗܦܟܐ ܐܢܫ ܘܡܠܗ ܦܫܬܐ. ܪ̈ܡܙܐ ܗܘ ܒܠܫܘܢ ܒܝܬ ܡܢܝܢܐ
ܘܠܗܡܠܐ. ܘܒܐܝܢ ܘܒܠܐ ܦܢܝܐ ܫܦܝܪܬܐ ܘܕܝܫܘܬܐ.
ܡܢܗܪ ܒܠܫܢ ܪ̈ܡܙܘ ܦܘܬܢܐ ܕܠܐ ܡܪܚܡܝܢ ܗܘܘ. ܘܡܢ ܫܪ
ܪܡܙܐ ܢܠܬ ܐܢܘܢ ܐܘܪܚܐ ܠܒܝܢ. ܘܗܘ ܗ̇ܘ ܪܡܙܐ ܐܠܘ
ܐܪܒܥ ܘܓܠܐ ܡܠܠ. ܠܬܪܝܢ ܒܗܡܘܢܐ ܐܘܪܚܐ ܕܦ̈ܢܝܐ
ܠܓܡܢܐ ܗܘܬ. ܠܒܠ ܪܚܡܝܢ ܗܘܘ ܕܠܒܠ ܢܗܘܘܢ ܐܬܦܢܝܘ
ܗܘܘ. ܘܡܢܗ ܕܪܡܙܐ ܗܠܡܘ ܘܐܫܬܠܦܘ ܒ̈ܪܡܙܝܢܐ. ܒܢܝܬ ܪܡܙܐ
ܠܪܡܙܐ ܓܢܝܬܐ ܐܦ ܓܗܢܐ. ܪ̈ܓܙ ܕܠܐ ܡܪܚܡܝܢ ܘܗܘܘ
ܬ̈ܬܐ ܒܢܝܬ ܡܠܒܘܬܐ. ܘܒܪ ܐܬܦܢܝ ܗܘܘ ܠܗ ܗܘܢ ܓܪ̈ܐ ܠܒܪ
ܐܠܗܐ. ܕܠܘ ܡܢ ܗܘܓܐܐ ܕܡ̈ܠܐ ܦܢܝܐ ܡܫܒܘܚܘܬܐ. ܗܘ

ܕܒܘܪܬܐ ܫܟܝܡܗ̇. ܘܠܗܘ ܕܠܥܠ ܐܝܟ ܠܡܕܝܢܬܐ ܕܡܠܟܐ ܫܡ̈ܝܐ. ܘܪܗܛܝܢ ܗܘܘ ܠܡܥܠܗ ܒܣܘܓܐ ܗܟܐ. ܠܐܬܪܐ ܕܢܘܗܪܐ ܕܡܠܟܐ ܦܬܓܡܐ ܠܕ̈ܝܢܘܗܝ ܠܗ. ܟܕ ܕܝܪܐ ܕܬܠܘ ܐܝܟ ܒܪ̈ܚܡܘܗܝ. ܘܕܠܐ ܙܘܥܐ ܡܬܠܝܘ ܗܘܘ ܐܝܟ ܡܢܪ̈ܬܐ. ܫܡܬܐ ܕܕܘܒܐ ܢܦܫܬ ܙܘܓܐ ܟܠܗ ܕܝܪܐ. ܘܡܢܗܪܬܗ ܗܘܬ ܟܠ ܥܘ̈ܢܝܐ ܕܢܚܫܘܢ ܐܝܟ. ܘܡܢܫܬ ܪܘܡܐ ܠܡܪܘܡܐ ܡܬܘܚ ܗܘܐ ܕܐܬܠܘܝ ܐܝܟ. ܘܗܘܘ ܬܗܪܐ ܠܬܪ̈ܝܢ ܓܒ̈ܝܢ ܕܕܝܪܐ ܘܒܕܝܪܐ. ܒܓܘܫܡܐ ܕܦܬ̈ܟܐ ܫܡܝܢܐ ܘܐܪ̈ܝܟܐ ܬܗܪܐ ܗܘܬ. ܗܟܐ ܦܬܝܚ ܫܟܝܚܐ ܘܠܐ ܡܬܟܠܐ ܗܘܐ ܡܢ ܐܘܠܨܢܐ. ܬܠܝܢ ܘܬܠܝܢ ܦܓܪ̈ܐ ܡܫܝܠܐ ܒܪ̈ܚܡܘܗܝ. ܘܪܒܐ ܥܠܝܐ ܘܠܝܬ ܕܡܠܟܝܢ ܐܘ ܕܡܪܢܐ. ܬܡܢܝܢ ܗܘܘ ܥܠ ܫܢ̈ܝܐ ܒܬ̈ܠܡܝܕܘܗܝ. ܕܠܡ̈ܫܡܫܢܐ ܡܬܝܢܐ ܒܡܫܐ ܘܡܢܪܘ ܗܘܘ ܥܠ ܐܘܠܨ̈ܢܝܢ. ܬܡܢܝܢ ܗܘܐ ܒܗܘܢ ܐܦ ܦܠܓܐ ܒܦܓ̈ܪܐ ܢܩܦܐ. ܕܒܡܐ ܢܡܘܪܐ ܦܓܪܗ ܒܐܘܠܨܢܐ ܕܠܐ ܙܘܒܢܐ. ܦܝܫܝܢ ܗܘܘ ܕܝܢ ܐܦ ܡܠܐ̈ܟܐ ܒܗܘ ܫܘܡܠܝܐ. ܕܒܡܐ ܐܟܙ ܗܘ ܐܓܘܢܐ ܕܫܠܐ ܕܡܘܬܐ. ܐܬܠܝܛܐ ܕܝܢ ܕܡܣܟܝܢ ܗܘܘ ܠܟܠܝܠܝܗܘܢ. ܠܐ ܟܠܬ ܗܘܬ ܡܟܐܒܘܬܐ ܠܓܒܝܗܘܢ. ܠܕܝܪܐ ܓܝܪ ܡܟܐܒܬ ܗܘܬ ܠܗ ܐܦ ܐܬܕܡܪ. ܘܠܬܪ̈ܝܨܐ ܠܐ ܡܟܐܒܬ ܗܘܬ ܒܐܘܠܨ̈ܢܝܗܘܢ. ܥܐܠ ܐܝܟ ܕܐܢ ܝܕܥܝܢ ܗܘܘ ܠܡܕܒܪܢܗ. ܘܠܐ ܡܫܟܚ ܗܘܐ ܦܘܡܐ ܢܟܠܠ ܡܢ ܐܘܠܨܢܐ. ܗܢܘܢ ܐܘܠܨܢܘ ܘܐܠܨܘ ܐܢܘܢ ܕܪ̈ܘܦܝܗܘܢ. ܒܕܡܐ ܕܠܐ ܢܦܩ ܐܬܪܐ ܠܡܠܬܐ ܕܬܬܡܠܠ ܗܘܬ. ܚܒܠܐ ܗܘܐ ܦܘܡܐ ܡܢ ܐܘܠܨܢܐ ܕܡܕ̈ܒܪܝܗܘܢ. ܝܚܝܕܐ ܕܝܢ ܐܝܟ ܚܒܝܒܐ ܒܕܠܗ ܥܠܡܐ. ܐܘ ܠܬܪܘܨܐ ܒܕܡܐ ܚܠܝܡ ܗܘܘ ܡܢ ܟܐܒܘܬܐ. ܘܟܠ ܢܗܘܪܐ ܒܕܡܐ ܠܚܝ̈ܝܢ ܗܘܘ ܡܫܒܚܘܬܐ. ܬܒܥܝܢ ܡܠܬܐ ܒܕ ܠܝܬ ܐܬܪܐ ܠܡܡܠܠܘ. ܕܡܡܠܠܐ ܗܘܬ ܡܠܬ ܦܘܡܐ ܡܢ ܐܘܠܨܢܐ. ܙܪܒ ܗܘܐ ܦܓܪܐ ܘܫܬܩ ܦܘܡܐ ܘܠܐ ܡܫܟܚ ܗܘܐ. ܕܢܬܠ ܡܠܬܐ ܒܕ ܡܫܬܐܠ

ܐܬܠܝܢ ܕܢܒܥ ܐܢܘܢ. ܘܪܒ ܬܠܡܘܗܝ ܕܩܕܘܫܐ ܘܒܢܘܬܐ.
ܐܦ ܟܢܘܫܝܐ ܢܛܪ ܐܢܘܢ ܠܡܢܝܢܗ. ܐܬܦܠܓܬ ܕܝܢ
ܐܦ ܠܓܘܫܐ ܠܬܪܬܝܢ. ܠܦܠܓ ܕܝܠܗ ܠܟܠ ܐܬܘܬܐ ܦܠܓܘܬܐ.
ܘܦܠܓܝܢ ܗܘܘ ܠܡܢܝܢܐ ܘܬܓܪܐ ܠܡܫܘܬܦܘܬܐ. ܘܠܦܘܪܢܣܐ
ܘܠܢܘܬܦܐ ܘܠܡܕܒܪܢܐ. ܐܦ ܠܫܘܕܥܢܐ ܐܦ ܠܐܘܪܚܐ
ܘܠܟܘܠ ܒܢܝܢ. ܘܠܟܠ ܡܬܒܥܝܢ ܘܠܟܠ ܫܐܠܝܢ ܗܘ ܝܗܒ ܗܘܐ.
ܠܐ ܐܫܬܪܝ ܘܠܐ ܐܬܩܪܒ ܘܠܐ ܐܬܥܕܪܘ. ܘܠܐ ܗܘ
ܐܢܘܢ ܗܘܝܢܐ ܕܡܢܝܢܐ ܠܡܢܝܢܗ. ܠܦܘܫܐ ܡܠܘܗܝ ܘܐܝܟ
ܕܠܟܠܐ ܕܐܪܥܐ ܡܩܡܗ. ܡܢ ܗܘܘ ܟܠ ܕܗܢܐ ܕܢܟܠ
ܥܒܕܘܗܝ ܗܘܐ. ܘܗܢܐ ܕܐܡܪ ܟܠܗ ܕܢܟܐ ܢܛܪ ܐܢܘܢ.
ܐܡܪܘ ܒܫܪܗ ܗܘ ܠܐ ܕܐܝܟ ܡܢ ܠܡܫܟܚܗ. ܬܢܐ ܗܘܐ
ܠܗܘܢ ܕܗܢܐ ܡܢܝܢܐ ܟܠ ܠܗܘܢ. ܘܬܢܝܢ ܗܘܘ ܠܗ
ܟܠ ܟܗܢܐ ܕܡܢܝܢܐ ܠܗ. ܒܗܠܝܢ ܕܬܢܝ ܡܪܝ ܗܘܐ ܠܗܘܢ
ܠܡܢܝܢܗ. ܘܩܢܘܢ ܐܡܪܝܢ ܡܛܠ ܕܝܢܐ ܕܢܝܠܐ ܕܠܗܠ.
ܥܕܪܐ ܢܦܫ ܟܠ ܡܢ ܬܠܬܐ ܢܦܫܬܗܐ. ܘܦܠܓ ܦܘܫܐ ܒܡܢܐ
ܕܬܠܬܐ ܕܟܠܗܬܐ. ܥܡܘܢܐ ܘܟܘܪܝܐ ܥܕܪܐ ܐܘܦܩܘ
ܠܡܚܠܠܘ. ܟܕ ܕܢܝܐ ܒܟܠܗܬܐ ܡܬܢܫܐ ܗܘܐ. ܘܡܛܠ ܗܢܐ
ܠܐ ܕܢܠܝ ܗܘܘ ܡܢ ܠܡܫܟܚ. ܕܗܟܠܐ ܫܢܝ ܗܘܐ ܒܠܗ
ܒܡܟܗ ܟܕ ܥܕܪܐ. ܠܟܡܪܗ ܕܟܠܗܐ ܢܦܫܗ ܒܫܪܗ
ܘܐܡܠܠ ܥܡܗܘܢ. ܘܕܝܠܗ ܠܗ ܠܐ ܟܕܝܢ ܗܘܘ ܐܘ ܢܟܠܘܢ
ܠܗ. ܡܢ ܒܝܬ ܕܢܒܐ ܦܘܡܗ ܬܫܒܘܚܬܐ ܠܡܫܝܚܐ. ܠܗܘ ܒܝܬ
ܘܟܕܐ ܕܟܠܗܘܢ ܫܢܐ ܕܟܠܗܐ ܣܕܪܬܐ. ܠܐ ܐܢܫ ܗܘܐ ܠܐ
ܒܩܘܫܐ ܘܠܐ ܒܟܬܒܐ. ܘܠܐ ܒܡܬܪܓܡܢܐ ܕܗܘܢܐ ܟܠܗܐ
ܡܠܐ ܒܫܠܘܬܐ. ܒܟܠܗ ܢܗܘܪܐ ܐܘܪܚ ܗܘܐ ܠܒܢܘܗܝ ܟܕ
ܐܠܗܐ. ܘܠܗ ܠܗܘ ܐܬܪܐ ܗܘ ܬܫܒܘܚܬܐ ܠܡܫܝܚܐ. ܘܚܙܝܢ
ܗܘܘ ܠܗ ܠܗܘܦܐ ܕܢܐܬܐ ܘܢܦܩܐ ܓܒܪܐ. ܘܢܕܒܪ ܐܢܘܢ
ܟܕ ܐܠܗܐ ܕܡܫܒܚܝܢ ܠܗ. ܠܗܢܐ ܟܠܗܐ ܐܝܟ ܠܡܦܠܠܬܐ

ܥܠ ܢ̈ܘܗܪܐ ܥܠ ܡܫ̈ܒܚܢܐ ܥܠ ܬܫ̈ܒܘܚܬܐ. ܥܠ ܕܡܢܗܪܝܢ ܗ̈ܘܘ
ܢ̈ܝܫܐ ܠܡܫܒܚܘܬܗ. ܠܡܢ ܢܘܗܪܐ ܕܐܦ ܗܘ ܡܢܗܪܗ ܒܗ
ܢܘܗܪܐ ܗ̇ܘ. ܒܒܪܗ ܪܒܐ ܠܬܪܥܝܬܗ ܐܦ ܪܒ ܒܢܬܐ. ܠܡܢ
ܠܦܠܛܪܐ ܕܒܝܬ ܕܝܢܐ ܪܘܡܝܐ ܗܘܐ. ܫܠܛܗ ܘܒܒܪܗ ܡܐܢܐ
ܓܒܝܐ ܠܡܫܒܚܘܬܐ. ܫܘܒܩܢܐ ܘܚܘܪܐ ܐܬܐ ܡܢ ܡܘܬ̈ܪܐ
ܕܠܐ ܒܨܝܪ. ܘܗܘܐ ܒܡܕܝܢܬܐ ܪܒܬܐ ܒܒܢܝܢ ܡܕ̈ܒܪܬܐ.
ܘܡܢܗܝܢ ܕ̈ܝܢܐ ܐܦ ܕܒܢܘܗ ܥܠ ܬ̈ܪܥܝܬܗܘܢ ܘܒܗܝܢ ܡܢܗܘܢ
ܪ̈ܚܡܐ ܢܬܠܘܢ ܫܘ̈ܒܩܢܗܘܢ. ܡܢ ܬܘܕܝܬܐ ܕܡܫܒܚܘܬܗ
ܕܒܪ ܐܠܗܐ. ܘܗܘ ܦܬܓܡܐ ܗܠܝܢ ܒܬܘ̈ܪܐ ܕܠܐ ܡܬܕܪܟܝܢ.
ܐܬܚܫܒ ܗܘ ܘܠܡܫܒܚܢܐ ܒܒܪ ܒܬܪܐ. ܘܗܘܐ ܒܬܪܐ ܬܘܪܐ ܒܗܠܝܢ
ܒܬܪܐ ܒܡܫܒܚܘܬܗ. ܫ̈ܪܝܐ ܓܒ̈ܝܐ ܕܝܪܐ ܒܒܪܗ ܗܘܘ ܠܗܘܒܠ
ܦܘܚܝܢ. ܘܒܬܘܕܝܬܗ ܕܒܪ ܐܠܗܐ ܘܒܗ ܐܝܟ ܦܪܘܩܐ. ܥܠܘ
ܐܘܕܝܘ ܒܗ ܡܕܡ ܕܝܢܐ ܓܠܝܘܬ ܐ̈ܦܐ. ܕܝܘܕܐ ܒܗܘܢ ܗܘ ܐܝܟ
ܕܐܘܕܝܘ ܒܗ ܡܕܡ ܢܠܘܗ. ܡܛܠ ܠܗܘܒܠܗܘܢ ܡܐܪܙܐ ܕܫܘܒܩܐ
ܐܝܟ ܡܫܒܠܢܐ. ܘܗܕܐ ܘܡܘܕܐ ܘܡܟܪܙܢܘܬܐ ܘܥܒܪ ܐܢܘܢ.
ܡܬܬܒܒܝܢ ܗܘܘ ܠܡܒܕܩܘ ܠܬܠܡܝܕܐ ܬܡܝܗܬܐ. ܘܠܐ ܢܦܩܝܢ
ܗܘܘ ܡܢ ܬܘܕܝܬܗ ܕܒܪ ܐܠܗܐ. ܢܣܒܬ ܪܘܚܐ ܕܟܬܒܘܬܐ
ܥܠ ܐܦܝܗܘܢ. ܘܗܘܘ ܡܝܬܝܢ ܫ̈ܘܒܚܐ ܠܦ̈ܠܚܝܐ ܡܕܡ
ܠܟܠܢܐ. ܐܝܟ ܕܢܟܠܬܐ ܪܡܝܬܐ ܠܦܓܪ ܫܠܛܬ ܐܢܘܢ.
ܘܥܠ ܕܐܬܬܪܬ ܒܡܫܒܚܘܬܐ ܠܐ ܢܦܠܬ ܐܢܘܢ. ܐܒܝܕ ܒܒܢܝܐ
ܠܟܘܢ ܠܥܡܗ، ܢܫܬܩܘܢ ܐܢܘܢ. ܘܥܠ ܕܐܡܪ ܗܘܐ ܠܗܘܢ
ܫܘܦܪܐ ܕܡܫܝܚܐ ܠܟܠܗܘܢ ܐܓܪܘܦܘ ܘܢܦܘܩ ܗܘܐ ܠܡܚܠܘ
ܐܦ̈ܩܢܘܗܝ. ܐܘ ܫ̈ܒܝܩܝܢ ܐܘ ܦܪܝܫܐ ܕܐܬܦ̈ܢܝܗܘܢ. ܐܘ
ܡܢ ܡܟܡܢ ܚܘܪ ܚܠܡܐ ܠܟܠܝܠܘܗܝ. ܕܐܝܟܢܐ ܦܠܓ ܡܢ
ܐܚܘܬܐ ܒܪ ܢܘܚܝܢ. ܠܕܝܢܐ ܥܠܘ ܗܘܘ ܘܠܕܝܢܐ ܠܐ ܫܟܚܘܗܝ
ܗܘܘ. ܘܠܐ ܢܦܩܝܢ ܗܘܘ ܕܡܟܢܐ ܠܐܬܪܘܗܝ ܒܪ ܐܬܬܐܠܘ.
ܓܝܪ ܕܢܝܢܐ ܘܐܦܟܐ ܡܠܠ ܒܪ ܡܬܠܝܡ. ܘܦܢܝܐ ܬܓܪܐ ܘܥܠ

ܘܕܢܚܝܢ ܠܒܢܝܐ ܩܪܝܐ ܗܝ܂ ܐܦ ܢܒܠ ܠܒܣܘܬܐ ܦܪܝܫܐ ܦܬܝܫܐ
ܟܠ ܒܪ ܐܢܫܐ܂ ܐܦ ܓܢܣܐ ܒܣܪܐ ܡܠܘܬܐ ܕܡܫܝܚܘܬܐ܂
ܥܡܠ ܡܠܟܘܬܐ ܘܢܘܪ ܓܢܬܐ ܕܡܠܝܐ ܦܘܪܩܢܐ܂ ܐܦ ܕܕܝܢܐ
ܕܚܝܠܐ ܠܣܘܕܐ ܒܢܝ ܡܫܝܚܐ܂ ܡܠܬ ܒܦܘܡܐ ܬܒܥܘ ܗܘܘ
ܒܠܫܢ ܠܡܓܪܦܘ܂ ܘܐܝܟ ܥܒܕܐ ܕܠܒܢܝܢ ܗܘܘ ܡܫܝܚܘܬܐ܂
ܠܐ ܢܣܒܘ ܡܠܬܐ ܕܬܫܥܝܬܐ ܒܗ ܒܒܘܪܘܬܐ܂ ܫܡܘܥܐ
ܫܘܦܪܐ ܕܡܫܝܚܘܬܟ ܡܢ ܡܘܦܐ ܠܝ܂ ܕܐܒܪ ܗܘ ܠܝ
ܦܘܡܝ ܘܟܝܪ ܗܘ ܠܝ ܕܐܬܬܡܠܠ ܒܗ܂ ܫܪܪܟ ܫܘܦܪܟ ܟܠܠܟ
ܣܥܪ ܒܡܬܪܟ ܠܟܪܝܟ܂ ܘܒܟܝܢܘܬܟ ܢܝܚ ܫܘܦܪܐ
ܕܐܬܠܒܫܬܟ܂ ܫܬܪ ܒܟ ܐܬܪ ܐܝܟ ܕܒܓܢܐ ܕܡܠܝܐ
ܕܡܢܐ܂ ܕܒܬܪܐ ܐܝܬ ܠܟ ܘܦܫܝܛܘܬܐ ܦܫܝܡܬܐ ܕܠܐ
ܡܬܓܠܝܐ܂ ܓܘܪܐ ܦܘܕܐ ܓܒܪ ܣܠܩܐ ܕܡܫܝܚܘܬܟ܂ ܡܢ
ܦܦܡ ܠܝ ܬܠܐ ܫܘܦܪܟ ܬܠܡܐ܂ ܗܐ ܬܫܒܘܚܐ ܒܓܙܪܟ
ܦܡܟܝܢ ܐܝܟ ܒܪܘܠܐ܂ ܘܦܘܬܐ ܒܝܘܪܟ ܐܝܟ ܡܫܝܚܐ
ܕܕܡܟܐ ܓܒܝܐ܂ ܕܟܝ ܟܠ ܓܘܫܡܟ ܐܘܦܠ ܫܘܟܢܐ
ܕܡܠܝܐ ܫܘܦܪܐ܂ ܘܓܙܪܐ ܕܢܝܟ ܠܓܘܫܐ ܕܫܡܫܐ ܠܐ ܦܢܘ
ܠܗ܂ ܗܕܪ ܐܝܬ ܘܦܬܐ ܒܥܠܡ ܥܝܢܐ ܕܓܠܝܬܐ ܠܝ܂ ܘܢܝܚ
ܫܘܦܪܟ ܡܠܘܠ ܒܥܝܢܐ ܕܒܣܝܡ ܒܟ܂ ܫܡܘܥܐ ܒܬܪܟ
ܕܬܪ ܐܝܬ ܗܘ ܡܢ ܒܬܪܐ܂ ܕܗܐ ܒܬܪܐ ܒܬܪܟ ܘܒܡܝܢ
ܬܡܡܟ ܐܢܘܢ܂ ܘܒܘܪܐ ܦܬܪܟ ܘܡܫܡܝܢ ܐܬܪܟ ܘܓܒܘ
ܢܣܒ ܠܝ܂ ܕܒܝܬ ܦܘܪܐ ܘܡܕܢܚܬܐ ܠܝ ܢܬܦܪܘܢ܂ ܗܐ
ܕܢܝܐ ܟܠܗܝܢܘܢ ܘܟܝܢܘܬܗܘܢ܂ ܒܦܪܐ ܫܘܠܝܡ ܡܢ
ܐܘܟܡܘܬܟ ܐܝܟ ܗܘ ܫܢܐ܂ ܘܡܦܐ ܒܬܪ ܘܠܘܓܕܘܗܝ
ܐܘܓܕ ܒܬܪܐ܂ ܘܡܘܟܝܘܬܗ ܠܟܠܗ ܒܬܪܗ ܕܟܠܡܐ ܒܦܪܬ܂
ܫܡܘܥܐ ܘܓܘܪܐ ܒܢܝ ܡܚܒܒܢܐ ܗܐ ܒܬܪܒܝܟܘܢ܂ ܕܒܝܢ ܒܬܪܐ
ܕܢܟܒܘܢ ܡܟܒܘܢ ܦܘܢܫܝܗܘܢ ܒܪ ܐܠܗܐ ܒܡܫܝܚܘܬܐ
ܘܒܦܫܝܛܘܬܐ܂ ܝܗܒ ܠܟܠܡܐ ܕܒܟܠܗ ܒܬܪܗ ܠܗ ܡܕܡ ܗܘ܂

ܗ̇ܝ ܐܘܟܝܬ ܥܠ ܦܘܪܫܐ ܕܝܗܝܒ ܠܒܢܝܐ. ܒܡܫܡܫܢܘܬܐ
ܘܒܪܫܝܢܘܬܐ ܡܛܠ ܒܗ̇ ܕܒܢܝܐ. ܐܝܟ ܕܐܬܦܩܕܘ ܡܢ ܡܠܦܢܐ
ܕܪܫܝܢܘܬܐ. ܟܕ ܢܦܠ ܘܐܪܥܐ ܠܒܘܫܐ ܘܦܘܡܐ ܡܬܚܫܒܐ
ܗܘܘ. ܘܕܠܐ ܢܫܒܩ ܗܘܐ ܠܗܘܢ ܡܫܝܚܐ ܘܠܐ ܢܬܪܥܐ. ܒܗ̇
ܕܒܢܝܐ ܐܝܟ ܒܪܫܝܢܘܬܐ ܕܫܘܘܬܐ. ܘܡܢܝܢ ܗܘܘ ܒܗ̇
ܒܡܫܝܚܘܬܐ ܕܒܗ̇ ܐܠܗܐ. ܐܝܟܢܐ ܕܡܬܬܢܝܚ ܗܘܐ ܘܟܠܗ
ܥܡܗ ܢܦܫ. ܘܡܛܠ ܫܡܐ ܕܠܗ ܦܓܪܗ ܡܢ ܐܫܬܕܘܗܝ. ܘܒܟܐ
ܕܢܦܫ ܥܡܗ ܢܦܫܗ ܒܗ ܡܫܝܚܐ. ܐܦ ܕܝܢ ܥܡܐ ܢܒܠ
ܢܪܥܬ ܢܦܫܐ ܠܐܒܕܢ. ܥܡܐ ܕܢܦܫܐ ܡܫܝܚܘܬܐ ܕܒܢܝ ܐܢܫܐ.
ܘܐܦ ܗ̇ܝ ܢܦܫܐ ܒܗ̇ ܡܬܢܦܫܢ ܐܦ ܫܡܫܘܗܝ. ܘܐܦ
ܡܬܒܣܒܣ ܒܗܘܢ ܦܓܪܐ ܡܢ ܡܫܘܬܐ. ܒܟܐ ܕܢܦܫܐ
ܡܫܝܚܘܬܐ ܢܦܫܐ ܫܢܐ ܗ̇ܝ. ܐܦ ܕܝܢ ܒܠܗܬ ܡܫܝܚܘܬܐ
ܒܒܣܪܘܬܐ. ܐܟܘܬ ܢܦܫܐ ܦܓܪܗܘ ܫܢܐ ܡܢ ܒܪܢܫܐ.
ܫܒܘܩܐ ܦܓܪܐ ܒܡܫܝܚܘܬܐ ܐܝܟ ܕܒܪ ܐܢܫܐ. ܘܡܢܝܢ
ܗܘܘ ܒܗ̇ ܕܠܐ ܬܒܠܥ ܗܘܬ ܡܢ ܕܪܘܫܐ. ܡܕܝܢ ܗܘܘ ܒܪ
ܕܐܝܟ ܡܬܢܦܫܐ ܡܫܝܚܘܬܐ. ܢܦܫܐ ܘܦܓܪܐ ܢܦܫܢ ܐܢܘܢ
ܡܢ ܐܒܕܢܐ. ܘܡܛܠ ܗܢܐ ܕܡܫܝܚܘܬܗܘܢ ܡܬܢܣܝܢ ܗܘܘ.
ܕܗܢ ܠܐ ܬܒܠܥ ܕܒܗ̇ ܗ̇ܘ ܒܗܝܢ ܗܘܘ ܐܦ ܫܡܫܘܗܝ. ܡܢܗ
ܦܓܪܗܘܢ ܘܠܢܦܫܬܗܘܢ ܘܠܡܫܝܚܐ. ܘܠܒܗܠ ܫ̈ܢܝܢ ܕܠܐ ܬܒܠܥ
ܗܘܬ ܡܫܝܚܘܬܐ. ܘܐܝܟ ܕܐܦ ܫܘܐ ܡܠܦܢܐ ܢܦܫܗ ܡܢ
ܡܫܘܬܐ. ܗܘ ܦܪܘܩܢ ܠܡܫܝܚܘܬܐ ܒܟܠ ܠܒܢܝܗܘܢ. ܘܟܠ
ܦܓܪܐ ܘܡܫܒܪ ܢܦܫܐ ܘܦܓܪܝܢ ܫܢܝܐ. ܘܠܐ ܐܬܬܡܣܪܬ
ܡܫܝܚܘܬܐ ܕܒܠܫܢܗܘܢ. ܒܡܟܐ ܡܟܠܝ ܢܦܫܐ ܠܡܘܬܐ
ܡܟܐ ܕܡܬܚܠܠ. ܘܒܠܫܢܐ ܐܝܟ ܕܒܡܟܐ ܡܠܠܐ ܒܟܕ. ܘܡܢܗ
ܢܒܥܝܢ ܫܢܐ ܘܡܘܬܐ ܠܟܠ ܐܢܫܐ. ܒܟܪ ܡܟܐܬ ܡܟܪܐ ܫܢܐ
ܘܫܠܝܛ ܗܘ ܠܗ. ܒܦܪܘܫܘܬܐ ܗܘ ܘܡܬܕܒܪܢܘܬܐ ܕܢܦܫܐ ܫܢܐ.
ܘܫܠܝܛ ܒܡܟܐ ܥܠ ܬܪܥܝܬܢ ܐܝܟ ܕܢܫܐ. ܡܠܬ ܒܡܟܐ

ܠܦܪܟܐ ܐܝܟ ܒܒܪ̈ܐ. ܘܐܬܦܢܝܬ ܐܬܚܙܝܘ ܒܗ ܒܡܐܪܘܬܐ
ܕܕܡܟܐ. ܫܠܝܡ ܕܗܘܘ ܡܠܟܐ ܠܐܬܪ̈ܝ ܘܐܬܟܢܫ ܒܗ. ܘܬܘܒ
ܓܒܪܗ ܕܟܒܫ ܗܘܐ ܠܗ ܒܟܘܪܣܘܬܐ. ܫܪ̈ܟܐ ܕܗܒܐ ܕܟܠܝܡ
ܡܫܝܚܐ ܕܐܘܟܣܘܬܐ. ܕܢܨܪܬ ܡܫܝܚܘ̈ܗܝ ܦܢܝܬ ܟܠܗ ܕܫܥܘܒܐ
ܗܘܬ. ܬܪ̈ܝܢ ܠܡܟܬܪ̈ܘ ܕܟܕ ܢܦܩ ܗ̄ܘ ܟܠܗܘܢ ܪ̈ܘܫܐ. ܕܟܠܗ
ܓܘܢܚܐ ܠܗ ܐܕܝܟ ܗ̄ܘ ܢܫܪ̈ܝܘܗܝ. ܦܪ̈ܝܐ ܬܓܪ̈ܐ ܕܡܢ
ܫܪܝܗ ܕܗܘܟܐ ܦܠܝܘ ܒܗ. ܒܟܪܟܐ ܕܪܟܐ ܕܒܝܬ ܐܠܗܐ
ܕܗܘܐ ܝܬ. ܫܘܪ̈ܗ ܕܐܬܪ̈ܝ ܕܕܒܝܫܝܢ ܠܝ ܐܝܟ ܗܬܪܐ. ܡܢ
ܟܠ ܓܢ̈ܣܝܢ ܕܟܠ ܕܪܐ ܕܒܪ̈ܝܢ ܠܝ. ܠܬܟܐܝܬܐ ܕܫܝܢܐ ܐܦ
ܒܝܬ ܓܘܒܐ ܕܟܠ ܕܫܝܫܝܢ. ܘܡܟܫܦܢܘܬ ܪܫܐ ܕܟܠ ܡܢ ܕܗܝܡ
ܟܠ ܒܘܕܝܢܐ. ܡܬܒܢܝܢܐ ܢܫܪ̈ܬܐ ܬܪ̈ܬܝܢ ܕܗ̄ܘ. ܓܒܬܐ
ܠܟܠܬܐ ܕܪܒ ܐܒܓܪ ܒܪ ܐܪ̈ܓܢܐ. ܬܠܦܢܐ ܗܘܘ ܕܠܝܠܘܬܗܘܢ
ܒܕܡܟܐ ܕܪܫܘ. ܘܡܫܡܠܝܘܬܗܘܢ ܡܢ ܫܪ̈ܒܗܘܢ ܡܬܡܕܟܐ ܗܘܬ.
ܟܠ ܦܓܪ̈ܝܗܘܢ ܒܬܟܒܘܗܝ ܫܪܟܗ ܕܒܪ ܐܠܗܐ. ܒܫܪ̈ܒܗܘܢ
ܘܒܦܓܪ̈ܝܗܘܢ ܕܗܒܝܫܝܢ ܗܘܘ. ܫܘܘ ܫܘܒܚܗܘܢ ܠܐ ܗܘܐ
ܒܬܠܬܐ ܕܦܘܡܐ ܒܠܫܢܐ. ܐܠܐ ܒܦܓܕܐ ܘܒܦܘܫܩܐ
ܕܗܕܒܝܗܘܢ. ܫܠܘ ܪܡܘܬܗ ܕܒܪ ܐܠܗܐ ܢܗܒܐ ܦܓܪ̈ܝܗܘܢ.
ܕܦܐܐ ܠܪܫܡܐ ܕܫܠܘ ܪܫܡܗ ܢܫܠܡ ܢܦܫܗ. ܢܘܪܐ ܘܗܘܦܐ
ܒܡܫܗ ܗܘܐ ܠܫܘܒܚܗܘܢ ܕܒܡܟܐ ܫܪܪ. ܘܓܒ ܡܢ ܗܐܡܟܐ
ܕܒܣܪ ܒܐܪܒܐ ܫܦܪܘ ܓܪ̈ܫܘܗܝ. ܫܪܘ ܒܐܠܗܐ ܘܡܓܒܠ
ܕܫܪܘ ܫܘܦܪ̈ܘܗܝ ܪ̈ܡܟܐ. ܒܠ ܗܢ ܐܡܫܪܘ ܟܠ ܫܪ̈ܒܗܘܢ
ܡܓܠܬܗ. ܕܢܝܚ ܗܘܐ ܫܡܫܐ ܕܕܢܦܩܬܐ ܒܪ̈ܝܫܝܗܘܢ.
ܘܢܗܪ ܡܢܗ ܘܠܫܘܒܚܐ ܒܢܗܝܪܐ ܪܕܘܗܝ. ܓܫܒܘ ܟܠ
ܬܠܡ̈ܝܕܐ ܕܗܝܡܢܘܬܐ ܕܐܟܠܘܗܝ ܓܘܦܢܐ. ܒܡܫܡܠܝܘܬܐ ܕܒܪ
ܐܠܗܐ ܕܡܠܟܐ ܢܗܝܪܐ. ܪܫܡܬ ܡܪܐ ܗܘܬ ܐܝܟ ܢܘܪܐ
ܒܪ̈ܝܫܝܗܘܢ. ܘܠܐ ܡܢ ܡܘܕܡܝܢ ܠܗ ܒܪܐ ܕܡܬܒܪܘܬܐ.
ܐܘܪ ܗܘܐ ܫܘܒܚܗܘܢ ܓܝܪ ܐܠܗܐ ܕܠܐ ܡܬܚܫܚ. ܘܟܠ

ܐܬܓܠܝܐ ܗܘܐ. ܘܡܢ ܡܕܝܢܬܗ ܕܗܢܐ ܣܗܕܐ ܐܬܕܒܪ ܗܘܐ.
ܣܪܐ ܗܘܐ ܢܦܩܐ ܡܢ ܕܒܝܬܐ ܕܟ̈ܠܘܬܐ. ܘܩܠܠ ܪܕܝܗ
ܥܠܝܐ ܕܣܗܕܐ ܘܐܬܟܢܫ ܒܗ. ܘܟܠܠ ܕܒܢ̈ܝܐ ܘܗܘܐ ܚܕܝܐ
ܒܒܢ̈ܝܬܐ. ܘܗܘܬ ܢܘܪܐ ܕܠܐ ܛܥܡ ܛܘܪܡ ܠܒ̈ܢܝܢܫܐ.
ܒܪܓܠ ܫܪܬ ܒܫܒܝܒ. ܫܠܗܬ ܒܐܬܪܐ ܕܠܝ. ܘܒܚܡ ܘܠܒܐ
ܠܐܢܫ ܠܐ ܦܠܠܬ ܡܢ ܕܐܬܚܙܝ ܗܘܐ. ܐܡܠܝܟ ܗܘܐ ܠܗ
ܘܡܣܬܦܠܓܝܢ ܥܠ ܐ̈ܚܝܗ. ܘܒܒܥܬܗ ܘܢܦܫܐ ܠܬܓܪܐ ܕܟܠܟܐ ܘܗܘ
ܥܠ ܪܒܗ. ܐܬܬܒܪܬ ܗܘܬ ܦܪܝܫܬ ܪܒܘܬܐ ܕܡܬܒܪܘܬܐ. ܘܡܢ
ܡܕܝܢܗ ܕܣܗܕܐ ܘܠܒܐ ܠܐܢܫ ܠܐ ܕܦܪܬ. ܩܠܠ ܬܘܒܗ ܘܗܘܐ
ܠܦܪܐ ܠܐܠܗܘܬܐ. ܘܐܫܬܦܩ ܒܗ ܐܐܪ ܕܕܠܝܫ ܡܢ ܚܫܘܒܬܐ.
ܘܒܡܕܝܢܗ ܐܬܕܒܪ ܗܘܐ ܐܬܪܐ ܠܟܠܗ. ܒܪܝܟ ܗܘ ܕܝܗܒ ܠܗ
ܟܠܝܠܐ ܘܫܘܒܚܐ ܘܫܒܚܐ ܠܥܠܡ.

ܫܠܡ ܡܐܡܪܐ ܕܥܠ ܚܒܝܒ ܣܗܕܐ

. ܘ . ܕܩܕܝܫ ܠܡܪܝ ܝܥܩܘܒ . ܘ .

ܡܐܡܪܐ ܕܥܠ ܓܘܪܝܐ ܘܫܡܘܢܐ

ܕܩܕܝܫ ܠܡܪܝ ܝܥܩܘܒ

ܫܡܘܢܐ ܘܓܘܪܝܐ ܣܗ̈ܕܐ ܕܐܠܝܨܘ ܒܐܘ̈ܠܨܢܝܗܘܢ.
ܒܫܘܒܐ ܬܒܥܘ ܠܡܫܠܡܘ ܢܦ̈ܫܬܗܘܢ. ܟܕ ܐܬܠܚܨܝܢ
ܕܡܫܝܚܘܬܐ ܡܪܢ ܡܠܘܟܐ. ܐܚܕܘ ܐܚܝܐ ܐܪ̈ܝܘܬܗܘܢ
ܘܟܠܝܠܝܗܘܢ. ܟܕ ܡܣܒܝܢ ܕܒܕܘ ܕܐܪܐ ܒܗ ܣܘܟܠܐ. ܡܪܐܘܢ
ܡܢ ܕܐܬܠܝܐ ܬܘܪܐ ܕܬܟ̈ܬܘܫܝܗܘܢ. ܣܟܐ ܒܬ̈ܪܝܐ ܕܟܠܗ

ܘܡܢ ܕܐܠܗܐ. ܚܙܐ ܒܒܪܗ ܕܒܗ ܢܬܬܘܣܩ ܥܠ ܓܘܠܬܐ.
ܘܥܠ ܕܐܝܬ ܗܘܐ ܒܗ ܪܘܚܬ ܡܪܝܐ ܠܐ ܚܫܐ ܗܘܬ. ܪ̈ܘܚܐ
ܕܒܪܘܗ ܕܐܠܗܐ ܓܒܝܢ ܡܛܠ ܦܐܪܗ. ܘܡܫܬܘܐ ܠܗܘܢ
ܡܫܒܚܘܬܐ ܕܠܐ ܢܬܓܒܘܢ. ܒܝܢܐ ܡܛܠܠ ܥܠ ܡܕܒܪܐ
ܕܦܪܫ ܡܢܗ. ܘܗܘܒܗ ܕܡܪܝܐ ܡܪܝܐ ܠܢܦܫܐ ܕܠܐ ܬܪܨ
ܒܗ. ܚܕ ܗܘܐ ܒܝܢܐ ܘܪܘܚܬ ܡܪܝܐ ܒܪܝܐ ܢܦܫܬ. ܒܢܦܫܗ
ܕܐܡܪܐ ܕܠܐ ܬܬܡܪܪ ܥܠ ܚܝܒܘܗ. ܘܠܐ ܚܫܐ ܡܠܐ
ܪܒܝܢ ܥܠ ܬܪܘܬܐ. ܘܠܐ ܐܟܠܐ ܒܝܫܬܐ ܠܚܡܐ ܢܦܫܐ
ܗܘܬ. ܘܡܠܘܐ ܠܗ ܕܢܐܪܠ ܠܐܦܪ ܘܫܬܪܐ ܗܘܬ. ܡܛܠ
ܕܒܬ ܪܘܚܬ ܡܪܝܐ ܠܡܪ ܕܒܝܢܐ. ܘܒܫܘܪܐ ܐܝܟ ܕܠܫܬܐ
ܫܠܠܐ ܒܒܪܬ. ܐܡܗ ܕܗܘܪܐ ܘܦܝܫܐ ܗܘܬ ܡܠܠܬܗ.
ܫܡܘܥ ܕܬܬܪܚܡ ܢܦܪܫ ܠܡܪܐ ܦܘܒܝܫܬܐ. ܕܐܠܘ ܐܦܪܘ
ܫܒܩܐ ܫܠܘ ܚܪ ܗܘܝ ܗܘܐ ܠܗ. ܚܪ ܐܝܬ ܗܘܐ ܠܗ ܘܗܒܬܗ
ܕܢܗܘܐ ܠܢܘܪܐ ܠܢܦܫܐ. ܘܐܝܟ ܕܠܗܘ ܚܪ ܐܠܘ ܐܝܬ ܗܘܐ
ܫܒܩܐ ܢܗܒܬ. ܢܦܠ ܥܠ ܢܘܪܐ ܘܚܪܬܗ ܗܘܬ ܫܠܗܒܝܬܐ.
ܘܚܙܪܐ ܐܡܗܐ ܘܠܐ ܫܐܒ ܠܗ ܥܠ ܢܦܪܫ. ܒܝܢܐ ܐܚܪܬܐ ܗ̇ܝ
ܕܡܕܢܚܐ ܥܠ ܒܦܘܬܐ. ܐܝܬ ܗܘܐ ܠܢܦܫܗ ܘܥܠ ܗ̇ܝ ܙܘܢܬ ܒܪ
ܢܦܪ ܗܘܐ. ܒܦܬܒܐ ܕܢܗܘܪܐ ܕܐܝܬ ܒܡܠܠܬܐ ܕܗܘ̈ܪܐ ܚܪܬ.
ܘܒܬܫܒܘܚܬܐ ܕܢܦܝܪܐ ܠܗܘܢ ܡܢ ܚܬ̈ܝܗܘܢ. ܘܦܬܓܡܐ
ܬ̈ܠܝܬܐ ܕܢܬܪܡ ܬܡܢ ܒܐܬܠܝܗܘܢ. ܘܒܪ ܐܠܗܐ ܕܡܠܒܫ
ܢܗܘܪܐ ܠܡܕܒܪܝܗܘܢ. ܘܫܘܦܪܐ ܡܦܬܒܐ ܕܗ̇ܝ ܡܠܠܘܬܐ
ܕܠܐ ܡܫܬܪܝܐ. ܘܬܪܒܐ ܪܒܐ ܕܦܬܚܝ ܢܒܠܗܘܢ ܝܘܡ ܐܠܗܐ.
ܒܡܠܝܢ ܚܪܬ ܐܡܗ ܕܗܘܪܐ ܒܪ ܢܦܪ ܗܘܐ. ܘܚܪܬ ܪ̈ܘܚܬ
ܘܒܫܘܪܐ ܒܒܡܗ ܢܦܫܬ. ܚܪܐ ܗܘܬ ܒܗ ܒܪ ܗܘܦܒܝܐ
ܦܠܚܒܡܗ ܢܦܪܐ. ܘܥܠ ܕܠܠܠܗ ܪܒ ܗܘܐ ܦܠܓ ܠܐ ܡܒܝܢܐ
ܗܘܬ. ܢܦܠ ܒܦܘܪܐ ܫܠܝܐ ܒܒܪܐ ܠܒܠ ܡܢ ܓܘܡܪܐ. ܘܗܘܐ
ܦܪܐ ܘܕܒ ܠܐܐܪ ܡܢ ܦܬܓܡܘܬܐ. ܡܢ ܬܠܝܐ ܕܕ̈ܒܝܐ ܐܐܪ

ܢܘܪܐ. ܘܗܘܐ ܟܦܪܐ ܘܪܟ ܒܪܚܡܗ ܠܒܪ ܐܠܗܐ. ܒܟܠ
ܫ̈ܘܠܓܝܢ ܘܒܟܠ ܫ̈ܢܕܝܢ ܘܒܟܠ ܫ̈ܢܩܝܢ. ܗܘ ܐܘܕܝ، ܘܗܘܐ ܐܠܦܗ̇
ܠܡܟܪܙܘܬܐ. ܘܗܘܢܐ ܙܪܥܐ ܠܒܟܬ ܐܘܪܚܗ، ܡܛܠ ܡܪܢ. ܐܦ
ܕܐܠܗܐ ܗܘ ܘܒܪܗ ܕܐܢܫܐ ܗܘܐ ܡܢ ܡܪܝܡ. ܘܫܢܝܐ ܥܠܬܐ
ܠܐܢܫܐ ܕܟܦܪ ܒܐܠܗܘܬܗ. ܘܒܣܪܐ ܘܫܒܩܐ ܠܐܢܫܐ ܕܢܛܠܡ
ܦܓܪܢܘܬܗ. ܘܝܕܥܐ ܠܗ ܚܕ ܒܐܠܗܘܬܗ ܘܒܐܢܫܘܬܗ.
ܐܣܝܪܐ ܕܦܓܪܗ ܡܟܝܢ ܠܐ ܡܬܦܪܫ. ܘܗܘܢ ܠܘܬ ܒܪܬ
ܦܪ̈ܘܫܐ ܠܡܫܝܚܝܐ. ܘܗܘܢ ܐܙܪܬ ܘܗܘܢ ܡܠܦܐ ܠܕܝܢܐ ܠܗ̇.
ܦܢܐ ܗܘܐ ܡܛܠ ܗܘ ܕܢܫܐ ܡܠܐ ܫܦܝܘܬܐ. ܕܢܦܘܩ ܢܐܡܪ.
ܫܗܕܐ ܒܢܘܪܐ ܕܢܦܪܐ ܠܗ. ܘܡܫܝܕܐ ܒܪܘܬܐ ܒܦܘܡܗ ܢܦܠܬ
ܐܝܟ ܡܦܠܠܐ. ܒܕ ܬܘܕܝܬܗ ܒܠܒܗ ܢܦܪܐ ܚܕ ܐܠܗܐ.
ܘܫܦܘܗܝ، ܘܢܦܩ ܡܢ ܒܝܬ ܕܢܫܐ ܒܕ ܫܪܐ ܗܘܐ. ܕܢܦܠܬ ܥܒܬܐ
ܕܐܢܬܐ ܥܠܝܠܐ ܠܡܫܝܚܘܬܗ. ܘܢܦܩ ܒܟܡܗ ܒܪ̈ܢܫܐ ܕܐܢܫܐ
ܕܢܠܘܫܝܗܝ، ܒܕ ܫܪܝܢ ܒܗ ܠܗ ܐܝܟ ܡܬܬܐ ܕܡܬܠܘܐ ܗܘܐ.
ܐܠܐ ܠܒܪܐ ܕܐܘܠ ܢܗܘܐ ܒܢܘܪܐ ܫܠܝܐ. ܘܐܢܬܐ ܥܠܝܠܐ
ܕܢܦܪ ܗܘܐ ܠܗ ܡܢ ܒܐܝܘܬܐ. ܫܪܝܢ ܗܘܘ ܒܗ ܐܝܟ ܕܠܒܪܐ
ܕܥܠ ܠܡܪܟܐ. ܘܫܪܘܗܝ، ܠܐܪܐ ܘܪ̈ܘܡܫܐ ܘܦ̈ܘܟܐ ܘܪܓܐ
ܐܢܘܢ. ܫܪܘܗܝ، ܕܢܦܠܘ ܐܝܟ ܐܬܠܝܛܐ ܡܢ ܐܓܘܢܐ
ܘܒܪܟܘܬܐ ܐܬܘ ܠܗ ܥ̈ܠܝܠܐ ܡܢ ܫ̈ܢܝܐ. ܫܪܝܢ ܗܘܘ ܒܗ ܕܢܓܕܐ
ܠܐܪ̈ܟܐ ܘܠܫ̈ܘܠܛܢܐ. ܕܒܪܕܘ ܕܪܐ ܒܪܡܗ ܥܠܗܘܢ ܘܐܬܡܗܬ
ܐܢܘܢ. ܙܦܪ ܗܘܐ ܒܗ ܥܠܗ ܒܢܫܐ ܕܡܫܝ̈ܚܝܐ. ܕܐܘܫܛ ܠܒܪܐ
ܕܡܫܝܚܘܬܐ ܒܢܫܐ ܕܟܒܠ. ܢܦܩܬ ܒܕܡܗ ܒܪܬܐ ܥܠܬܐ ܡܠܝܬ
ܢܗܘܪܐ. ܘܩܛܠܝܢ ܐܩܝܡܗ ܒܫܘܕܐ ܙܝܘܬܐ ܕܐܬܬܘܫܦ ܠܗ̇. ܡܕܡ
ܐܟܡܐ ܡܛܠ ܕܗܘܐ ܫܠܝܐ ܠܒܪܗ. ܢܬܬ ܢܦܫܗ ܒܫܘܬܐ
ܕܪܚܡ ܡܢ ܕܒܝܕܐ. ܕܠܐ ܫܒܩܝܢ ܗܘܘ ܩ̈ܫܝܐ ܓܪ̈ܐ ܠܒܝܬ
ܡܫܬܘܬܐ. ܥܠ ܢܘܪܐ ܓ̈ܐܝܐ ܠܒܝܬ ܦܓܪܢܘܬܐ. ܗܪܟܐ
ܠܪܐ ܢܣܒ ܙܡܪܬܐ ܠܡܬܬܒܘ. ܒܦܘܡܗ ܕܐܡܪܐ ܗ̇ܝ، ܕܢܣܒܐ

ܕܢܛܠ ܦܓܪܐ ܘܩܘܡܐ ܐܢܫܝܐ. ܠܗ ܦܠܓ ܐܢܫܐ ܐܡܪ، ܗܘܕܐ
ܒܡܠܐ ܙܒܢܐ. ܡܢ ܡܫܪܝܢܐ ܗܪܘܢܐ ܡܫܘܕܐ ܥܡܠܐ ܡܬܠܬܐ.
ܘܡܠܟܐ ܒܐܢܫܐ ܠܘܬ ܐܒܘܗܝ، ܡܫܝܚܘܬܐ. ܘܡܫܒܚܐ ܠܡܪܢ
ܕܐܦ ܐܠܗܐ ܗܘ ܒܪ ܐܠܗܐ. ܘܠܘܬ ܘܐܣܪܬ ܕܢܛܠ ܦܓܪܐ
ܘܩܘܡܐ ܐܢܫܝܐ. ܠܘ ܡܢ ܗܦܟܐ ܕܝܫܘܥܐ ܠܘܬ ܡܫܝܚܘܬܐ. ܡܠܟܘܬܗ
ܐܠܗܐ ܩܕܝܫܐ ܐܠܗܘܬܗ ܘܐܣܪܬ ܐܢܘܢ. ܘܐܦ ܡܬܦܠܓܐ
ܕܠܒܪ ܐܢܫܐ ܦܓܪܐ ܡܬܬܘܡܐ. ܠܩܕܝܫܘܬܗ ܒܫܘܡܐ ܕܡܬܠܬܝܢ
ܘܠܗܘܢ، ܒܠ ܕܐܠܗܐ ܗܘ. ܠܒܪ ܐܢܫܐ ܠܝ ܠܐ ܦܠܓ ܐܢܫܐ
ܐܡܪ ܚܕܝܢ. ܡܠܠ ܕܒܬܪ ܕܠܘܬ ܗܘ ܕܡܬܬܒܠ ܒܠ ܒܪ
ܐܢܫܐ. ܒܠ ܕܐܠܗܐ ܗܘ ܦܠܓ ܐܢܫܐ ܠܗ ܐܦ ܚܕ ܐܢܫܐ.
ܡܠܠܬܗ ܘܠܐ ܚܒܪ ܐܢܫܐ ܒܡܫܝܚܘܬܗ. ܗܢܐ ܕܝܪܐ ܠܒܝܬܐ
ܐܒܘܗܝ، ܡܢ ܠܠܦܬܗ. ܘܒܫܘܒܚܬܗ ܠܐ ܡܫܠܡܐ ܠܗ ܒܪܬ
ܡܫܒܚܢܐ. ܡܠܟܗ ܒܐܢܫܐ ܩܢܘܡܐ ܠܗ ܦܓܪܐ ܘܡܫܝܚ ܠܘܬ.
ܡܠܠ ܡܪܢ ܕܒܪ ܐܠܗܐ ܗܘ ܐܦ ܐܠܗܐ. ܐܝܟ ܕܐܡܪܬ،
ܒܝܘܡܐ ܕܝܠܕܐ ܘܥܡ ܠܗ ܒܐܒܘܗܝ. ܗܢܘܢ ܡܫܒܚܢܢ ܠܒܪ
ܐܠܗܐ ܕܡܫܝܚܐ ܗܘ. ܕܝܠܗ ܒܡܪܐ ܕܝܢ، ܘܒܗܘ ܠܟܠ
ܥ̈ܠܡܝܢ. ܫܠܡ ܐܠܗܐ ܕܩܘܡܐ ܐܢܫܝܐ ܡܢܗ ܐܝܟ ܕܐܡܪ.
ܕܡܘܫܐ ܘܦܓܪܐ ܡܠܠܬܗ ܕܡܫܝܚܐ. ܒܕܡܘ ܩܕܝܫܘܗܝ
ܘܫܠܡܘܗܝ، ܡܫܝܚ ܒܠ ܕܐܠܗܐ ܗܘ. ܘܫܒܚ ܗܘܕܐ ܡܠܟܢܐ
ܩܢܘܡܐ ܕܒܝܬܘܬܐ. ܘܕܢܛܠ ܦܓܪܐ ܘܩܘܡܐ ܐܢܫܝܐ ܡܒܪܝ
ܗܘܐ ܠܗ. ܫܠܡ ܒܪ ܐܢܫܐ ܗܘܕܐ ܒܡܘܬܐ ܠܐ ܢܦܩ ܗܘܐ.
ܐܠܐ ܐܝܟ ܫܠܡ ܐܠܗܐ ܕܩܘܡܐ ܐܢܫܐ. ܘܗܘܕܐ ܐܒܘܗܝ،
ܕܗܒ ܐܡܪ، ܒܗ ܢܦܩ ܗܘܐ. ܘܡܢ ܬܘܕܝܬܗ ܕܗܘܕܐ ܕܐܝܟ
ܡܢܗ ܢܒܘܥ. ܠܒܠ ܕܒܝܫ ܡܫܬܡܥܐ ܘܒܣܪܐ ܡܫܝܚܘܬܐ.
ܕܢܘܗܪܐ ܡܠܟܐ ܘܠܐ ܡܬܒܪܝܢܐ ܝܗܒ ܬܠܠܐ. ܒܣܪܐ ܠܐܢܫܐ
ܕܦܠܓ ܠܒܪܐ ܕܠܘ ܐܠܗܐ ܗܘ. ܘܠܐܢܫܝܐ ܕܐܡܪ ܕܠܐ ܢܛܠ
ܦܓܪܐ ܘܩܘܡܐ ܐܢܫܝܐ. ܒܡܫܝܚܘܬܐ ܕܡܠܟܐ ܢܝܪܐ ܡܢ ܒܠ

ܕܒܗܐ ܕܦܓܪܘܬ ܒܗ ܠܐ ܬܬܒܥܐ ܗܘܬ. ܢܦܫܗ، ܚܝ̈ܐ ܕܒܗܐ
ܕܒܝܬܐ ܠܗ ܫܠܡܘܬܐ. ܠܐ ܢܗܘܐ ܐܝܟ ܡܕܡ ܢܐܬܐ
ܒܗܘܢ ܠܒܠܐ. ܘܦܩܕ ܐܢܘܢ ܠܫܠܝܚܘ̈ܗܝ ܒܡ̈ܠܐ ܕܦܓܪܗ
ܗܘܘ ܒܗ. ܕܬܬܕܪܟ ܗܘܐ ܒܝܘܡܢܐ ܢܘܡܐ ܐܝܟ ܦܪܘܩܢ
ܘܡܫܡܠܝ ܗܘܐ ܒܕ ܚܕܐ ܗܘܐ ܠܚ̈ܝܐ ܕܦܓܪ. ܒܕ ܗܘܐ
ܒܪ ܕܒܫܠܡܘܬܗ ܒܗܘܬܐ ܡܚܝܐ. ܘܠܐ ܕܢܠ ܗܘܐ ܘܠܐ
ܡܢ ܒܗܘܬܐ ܘܠܐ ܡܢ ܚ̈ܝܐ. ܕܒܗܘ ܚܝ̈ܘܗܝ ܕܡܝܬܘܬܐ ܪܘܐ
ܗܘܐ ܠܒܗ. ܫܡܗ ܠܦܓܪܐ ܒܕ ܡܬܚܬܐ ܡܢ ܕ̈ܘܝܐ. ܘܠܗ̈ܕܡܘܗܝ
ܒܕ ܡܬܦܫܩ ܒܪܘܚܬܐ. ܚ̈ܕܪܐ ܒܚܝܠܗ ܗ̈ܘܢܐ ܒܦܓ̈ܪܘܗܝ
ܗܕܐ ܒܪ̈ܓܠܘܗܝ. ܘܢܘܪܐ ܠܡܘܒܠܗ ܘܠܒܝܬ ܘܟܠܐ ܡܫܝܚܘܬܐ.
ܒܚܫܕܗ ܗܠܝܢ ܕܠܒܪ ܐܢܫܐ ܗܘܐ ܦܓܪ ܐܢܬ. ܘܐܡ̈ܪܝܢ ܗܘܘ
ܗܘ ܕܠܒܪ ܐܢܫܐ ܠܐ ܦܓܪ ܐܢܐ. ܠܐܠܗܐ ܒܪ ܕܫܒܩ ܦܓܪܐ
ܘܦܓܐ ܐܢܫܐ. ܠܗ ܦܓܪ ܐܢܐ ܒܠ ܕܐܠܗܐ ܗܘ ܒܡ ܢܠܘܬܗ.
ܗܡܫܝܚܘܬܗ ܕܚܝܒܝ ܗܘܕܐ ܢܘܗܪܐ ܟܠܗ. ܘܒܗ ܢܘܗܪܐ
ܐܘܪܗ، ܟܠܝܬ ܡܫܝܚܘܬܐ. ܒܪܬܗ ܕܐܒܓܪ ܕܡ̈ܬܪ ܐܕ،
ܠܡܫܒܚܘܬܐ. ܒܗ ܗܘ ܢܘܗܪ̈ܗ ܒܗ ܗܘ ܙܪ̈ܥܗ ܘܡܫܝܚܘܬ̈ܗ.
ܟ̈ܠܒܗ ܒܢܗ ܗ̈ܘܕܢܗ ܒܢܗ ܙܪ̈ܥܗ ܒܢܗ. ܐܦ ܟ̈ܠܒܢܐ
ܕܡܫܝܚܘܬܐ ܒܢܗ ܐܢܘܢ. ܐܒܓܪ ܗܫܟܡ ܕܐܠܗܐ ܐܝܬ ܒܪ
ܐܠܗܐ. ܘܡܟܠ ܠܦܘܒܐ ܡܟܠܠ ܫܘܦܪܐ ܕܡܫܝܚܘܬܗ ܙܪܒܠ
ܗܘܕܐ ܒܪ ܐܘܪܗܝܐ ܬܘܒ ܐܡ̈ܪ ܗܘܐ. ܕܝܒܫܐ ܗܘ ܪܚܝܡ
ܝܫ. ܐܠܗܐ ܕܦܓܐ ܐܢܫܐ. ܘܫܝܒܬ ܗܘܕܐ ܕܐܦ ܗܘ
ܒܐܘܪܗ، ܐܬܟܠܠ ܗܘܐ ܡܠܝܡ ܐܘܕ، ܕܫܒܩ ܦܓܪܐ ܘܦܓܐ
ܐܢܫܐ. ܕܒܪ ܐܠܗܐ ܗܘ ܐܦ ܐܠܗܐ ܗܘ ܘܦܓܐ ܐܢܫܐ.
ܠܦܬ ܐܘܪܗ، ܡܢ ܟ̈ܠܒܢܐ. ܕܙܪ̈ܥܬܐ. ܡܟܠܗ ܐܠܦܗ ܗ̈ܘܕܝܗ
ܐܠܦܗ ܡܫܝܚܘܬܐ. ܘܠܟ̈ܠܒܢܐ ܐܚ̈ܪܢܐ ܕܐܬܦܐ ܠܗ
ܒܙܬܒܬܐ. ܫܒܝܩ ܗܘܕܐ ܒܐܕܝܗ ܕܐܘܪܗ، ܗܒܡ ܦܓܐ.
ܡܢ ܠܗ ܢܘܪܐ ܕܠܒܪ ܐܢܫܐ ܠܐ ܦܓܪ ܐܢܐ. ܠܐܠܗܐ ܒܪ

ܕܟܢܫܘܗܝ ܗܘܐ ܡܢܝܢ ܐܢܫܐ. ܘܐܬܬܥܝܪ ܫܠܝܚܐ ܘܐܣܝܗ
ܬܗܪܐ ܘܐܬܕܡܪ ܒܗ. ܒܚܙܘܐ ܕܠܐ ܕܝܠ ܐ̈ܢܫ ܗܟܢܐ
ܘܠܐ ܡܢ ܢܘܪܐ. ܟܕ ܦܬܪ ܗܘܐ ܕܡܚܪܡ ܒܪܝܫ ܟܠ ܟܝܢ ܒܗ.
ܘܐܦ ܕܢܠܐ ܕܢܘܚܝ، ܕܠܒܝܒ ܠܡܩܒܠ ܡܘܬܐ. ܬܠܡܝܕܗ ܗܘ
ܕܒܪ ܐܠܗܐ ܗ̇ܘ ܕܐܡܪ ܗܘܐ. ܕܡܩܒܠ ܬܘ ܢܐܙܠ ܕܗܘ
ܕܡܫܠܡ ܠܝ ܗܘܐ ܡܛܠ ܠܗ. ܘܠܩܘܒܠܐ ܬܘܒ ܐܡܪ ܗܘܐ ܠܗܝܢ
ܒܚܝܢ ܐܚܘܬܢ ܐܡܪܝܢ ܠܢܫܒܩ. ܘܐܡܪ ܗܘܐ ܠܗܘܢ ܕܐܢܐ
ܐܢܐ. ܒܪ ܐܠܗܐ ܗܘ ܒܚܝܢܗ ܐܬܐ ܠܥܠܡܐ. ܘܒܗ ܚܝ
ܣܗܕܐ ܘܐܢܬ، ܗܘ ܠܗ ܡܢܐ ܕܢܠܐ. ܘܚܝܘܗܝ، ܫܠܝܚܐ
ܘܐܬܕܠܚ ܗܘܐ ܘܐܬܬܡܪܡܪ ܗܘܐ. ܘܫܠܡ ܪܘܚܗ ܘܒܪ،
ܒܫܡܬܗ ܡܪܢ ܒܝܬ ܟܠܝܐ. ܘܐܝܟ ܕܠܚܒܪܐ ܕܐܙܠ ܒܐܪܒܥܐ
ܕܢܚܐ ܕܩܒܠܐ. ܡܫܐܠ ܗܘܐ ܠܗ ܠܚܒܪܐ ܫܦܝܐ ܘܠܐ
ܒܗܬ ܗܘܐ. ܟܕ ܚܙܐ ܠܗ ܘܡܕܢܚ ܠܗ ܘܡܫܘܕܥ ܠܗ. ܘܬܢܐ
ܦ̈ܬܟܐ ܕܡܠܒܫܝܢ ܠܗ ܡܢܐ̈ܢܘܗ̇. ܗܘ ܕܝܢ ܫܒܩ. ܟܕ ܡܫܬܐܠ
ܠܐ ܕܢܠ ܗܘܐ. ܠܐ ܒܗܬ ܗܘܐ ܘܠܐ ܡܫܬܪܐ ܡܢ ܠܘܬܗ̈ܘܢ
ܟܕ ܪܡ ܩܠܗ ܐܘܕܝ، ܒܫܡܥ ܒܪ ܐܠܗܐ ܕܐܝܬܘܗܝ، ܚܕ ܗ̣ܘ
ܘܐܝܬܘܗܝ، ܒܗܢܐ ܘܡܫܡܫܢܗ. ܒܫܡܬܐ ܕܫܡܥܐ ܟܕ ܢܗܘܐ
ܒܗ ܐܝܟ ܐܪܘܬܐ. ܠܐ ܐܦ ܢܦܠܐ ܡܢ ܬܘܕܝܬܗ ܕܒܪ ܐܠܗܐ.
ܡܬܢܨܚ ܗܘܐ ܘܫܒܪܐ ܦܬܚ ܫܒܝܚܝܢ ܠܗ. ܕܐܦܢ ܘܠܝܠ ܡܢ
ܡܫܒܚܬܗ ܕܒܪ ܐܠܗܐ. ܟܠ ܠܫܡܫܐ ܘܫܪ ܗܘܐ ܒܡܕܪܗ
ܕܐܦ ܠܗ ܫܒܩܘܗܝ. ܘܫܕ، ܠܗܘܢ ܕܒܐܘܪܚܐ ܕܫܡܘܗܝ، ܒܪ، ܝܕܐ.
ܗܠܝܢ ܗܘܐ ܠܡܫܐ ܘܦܪܣ ܗܘܘ ܠܗ ܘܢܗܘܬ ܢܦܫܗ. ܕܒܡܐ
ܕܢܦܠܘܗܝ، ܢܘܦܐ ܕܫܒܐ ܕܢܘܦܩܘܬܐ. ܒܐܘܪܚܐ ܕܡܘܬܐ ܗܘ
ܗܘܐ ܫ̈ܩܘܗܝ، ܠܡܗܠܟܘ. ܘܡܢ ܒܟܢܐ ܗܘܐ ܕܢܦܫܗ ܗܘܐ
ܒܗ̇ ܐܠܐ ܫ̈ܒܐ. ܢܘܪܐ ܕܕ̈ܒܫܐ ܡܚܝܪܐ ܗܘܬ ܠܗ ܘܠܗ̇
ܫܐܪ ܗܘܐ. ܘܗܘ، ܒܙܪܬ ܠܗ ܦܪܘܣܐ ܘܬܪ̈ܥܐ ܘܟܐ̈ܒܐ ܢܓܝܡ.
ܟܕ ܐܬܬܐ ܗܘܬ ܒܙܪܬ ܫ̈ܒܐ ܕܟܠܬܗܘܢ. ܢܗܘܐ ܡܓܝܒ

ܗܝ ܡܢ ܘܠܝܬܐ. ܠܒܢܝ ܓܢܣܗ ܘܠܐܚܘܗ ܠܒܟܘ ܗܘܘ ܡܛܠܬܗ.
ܠܒܢܝ ܐܢܫܘܬܐ ܐܡܗ ܕܣܗܕܐ ܡܢ ܗܝ ܕܐܬܝܠܕ. ܕܢܠܦ
ܡܢܗ ܠܒܢܝܢ ܚܒܫܘܗܝ ܒܗܠܝܢ. ܡܢܘ ܬܒܥܝܢ ܠܟ ܡܠܝܬ
ܫܘܦܪܐ ܡܢܐ ܬܒܥܘܢ. ܗܐ ܬܒܥܝܢ ܠܟ ܬܠܬܝܢ ܣܗܕܐ ܕܢܗܘܐ
ܕܟܢܫܐ. ܐܝܬ ܐܝܬ ܦܐܪܐ ܚܠܝܐ ܠܒܝܬ ܡܘܪܒܢܐ. ܕܒܣܝܡ
ܪܝܚܗ ܕܢܗܘܐ ܒܦܪܐ ܠܐܠܗܘܬܐ. ܣܬܐ ܦܐܝܬܐ ܫܦܝܠܐ
ܐܝܬ ܡܢ ܒܪ ܕܐܬܗܘܝ ܕܠܗܘܢܐ ܢܗܘܐ ܚܡܪܗ ܕܚܠܐ
ܠܒܒܢ ܥܒܕ ܗܘܐ ܐܡܪܐ ܕܒܒܝ ܗܘܘ ܠܗ ܢܗܘܐ ܕܟܫܢ
ܘܗܠܝܢ ܘܐܬܐ ܓܝܪ ܠܒܝܫܐ ܒܪ ܚܪܐ ܗܘܐ. ܥܒܕ ܕܐܫܪܝܐ
ܗܘ ܡܬܐܠܝܢ ܗܘܘ ܡܛܠܬܗ. ܘܐܬܐ ܢܦܩ ܚܫܐ ܕܠܗ ܚܠܦ
ܣܢܐܐ. ܦܝܬܐ ܡܛܬܗ ܕܗܘ ܒܠܒܘܕܗܘܢ ܢܗܘܐ ܕܟܫܐ.
ܘܢܦܪܐ ܕܕܟܫܐ ܠܗ ܚܙܪܐ ܗܘܬ ܒܪ ܐܬܬܐ ܗܘܐ. ܡܢ ܣܢܐܐ
ܕܚܟܡܝܢ ܗܘܘ ܡܛܠܬܗ. ܐܦ ܠܐ ܚܕ ܐܝܢ ܐܬܬܚܙܝ ܕܢܟܘܬ
ܐܠܐ ܐܢ ܗܘ. ܗܘ ܓܒܪܐ ܗܘܐ ܐܦ ܣܗܕܘܬܐ ܠܗ ܢܦܪܐ
ܗܘܬ. ܘܐܢܝ ܢܣܦܩ ܗܘܐ ܕܥܒܬ ܣܗܕܐ ܠܐ ܡܟܝܫ ܗܘܐ.
ܘܡܛܠ ܗܢܐ ܗܘ ܒܪܢܫܗ ܐܝܬ ܢܟܫܗ. ܓܝܪ ܕܢܗܐ ܕܬܬܚܫ
ܘܢܬܥܬ ܡܛܠ ܫܡܥܢ. ܒܚܕ ܕܒܟܐܘܗܝ ܘܐܬܐ ܕܬܬܚܫ ܐܝܟ
ܕܒܟܐܘܗܝ. ܘܐܚܠ ܗܘ ܠܗ ܡܕܡ ܕܢܬܠܐ ܘܬܠܝܢ ܐܩܦܘܗܝ. ܠܐ
ܐܬܦܠܥ ܘܠܐ ܓܒܐ ܕܒܪܘܢ ܡܢ ܕܢܬܠܐ. ܕܢܗܪܐ ܗܘܐ ܘܡܢ
ܫܡܥܐ ܠܐ ܚܙܘ ܗܘܐ. ܠܐ ܓܒܪܐ ܘܠܐ ܡܦܠܐ ܘܠܐ
ܓܒܪܐ. ܘܠܐ ܒܪ ܠܠܒܐ ܕܠܗ ܪܘܦܗ ܒܐܝܡܬܐ ܗܘܐ.
ܠܒܗ ܢܚܪܘܗ ܗܘܐ ܡܢ ܡܪܚܝܬܐ ܪܚܝܩܐ ܓܒܪܐ. ܘܢܪܦܐ
ܒܢܐ ܒܪ ܡܬܐܒܠܐ ܡܢ ܓܒܪܐ. ܠܒܗ ܒܪܘ ܗܘܐ ܐܣܐ
ܕܢܟܝܡ ܡܟܐܣܐ ܒܬܒܥܐ. ܘܠܦܨܬܐ ܓܝܪ ܒܕܡܗ ܕܒܪ
ܐܠܗܐ. ܓܠܝܬ ܐܦܩܐ ܡܢܐ ܗܘܐ ܓܒܪܐ ܘܠܒܐ ܪܒܐ.
ܘܠܗܡܠ ܡܬܐ ܪܗܛ ܒܪ ܚܪܐ ܡܛܠ ܫܡܥܢ. ܒܠ ܗܘܐ
ܡܢ ܠܗ ܡܕܡ ܕܢܬܠܐ ܒܪ ܐܚܪܢ ܠܗ. ܐܢܐ ܐܢܐ ܚܒܝܒ

ܐܝܟ ܕܐܒܝܐ ܘܟܬܪ ܟܠܗ̇ ܫܢܘܬ ܚܝܐ. ܘܗܝܟ ܠܡܬܚܪ̈ܬܐ
ܘܣܓܠ ܐܡ̈ܪܬܐ ܕܠܦܪ̈ܝܫܘܗܝ. ܢܦܩ ܒܫܐܠܬ ܠܒܒ ܫ̈ܢܝܢ
ܠܡܘܗ̈ܒܬܐ. ܬܠܬ ܫ̈ܢܝܢ ܘܐܪܒܥ، ܫ̈ܢܝܢ ܘܦܠܓܐ ܐܬܝ. ܘܣܓܠ ܗܢܐ
ܕܡܫܝܚܘܬܐ ܘܐܠܒܫ ܐܢܝ. ܕܠܐ ܢܬܟܣܪ̈ܘܢ ܡܢ ܚܣܝܘܬܐ
ܕܦܓܪܐ ܗܘܬ. ܓܪ̈ܪܐ ܕܒܝܬ ܕܒܪ ܐܠܗܐ ܡܬܚܪܟܝܢ ܗܘܘ.
ܡܢ ܕ̈ܘܟܐ ܘܠܒܒ ܠܐܡ̈ܪܐ ܘܠܩܘܬܐ. ܘܗܘܐ ܗܢܐ ܓܪܐ
ܠܒܝܬ ܒܝܬܐ ܕܡܫܝܚܘܬܐ. ܘܐܠܦ ܐܢܘܢ ܕܠܐ ܢܬܪܗܒܘܢ ܡܢ
ܕ̈ܘܟܐ. ܐܠܦ ܐܢܘܢ ܕܗܘܘ ܙܗܝܪܝܢ ܠܡܩܒܠ ܒܗܘܬܐ. ܒܕ
ܠܐ ܕܢܠܡ ܠܐ ܡܢ ܗܦܟܐ ܘܠܐ ܡܢ ܢܘܪܐ. ܒܡܠܦܢܘܬܗ ܕܒܪ
ܐܠܗܐ ܡܬܒܪ ܗܘܐ̇ ܕܗܘܬ ܙܗܝܪܐ ܡܫܝܚܘܬܗ ܕܠܐ ܗܘܪܕܐ.
ܘܫܘܟܬ ܓܘܝܢ ܒܦܪܬ ܘܒܢܝܬ ܘܡܓܠܠܬܗ. ܘܢܦܩܬ ܒܬܪܗ
ܬܐܒܘܕ ܒܐܪܒܥܐ ܕܒܢܐ ܪܒܢܐ. ܐܟܠ ܡܪܝܐ ܕܦܢܝܐ ܠܓܘܗܐ
ܕܒ̈ܢܝ ܐܢܫܐ. ܝܠܕܐ ܠܗ ܦܢܝܐ ܕܝܠܗܘܢ ܠܐܬܪܐ ܡܢ ܒܢܝܢܗ.
ܦܠܐ ܥܪܪܐ ܢܦܩ ܗܘܐ ܒܬܪܗ ܠܡܚܬܬܗ ܕܢܥܠܐ ܘܠܗ ܡܢ
ܘܠܦܢܝܐ ܕܒܢܬ ܐܠܗܐ̇ ܘܪܒܬ ܓܘܝܢ ܕܢܚܘܬ ܣܒܝܒ ܒܠ
ܕܗܢܬܗ̇ ܘܪܘܬܗ̇ ܒܐܒܗܐ ܘܒܒ̈ܢܝܐ ܗܘܬ ܠܗ ܕܢܦܩܗ ܬܐܒܘܦ.
ܘܐܬܬܪܝܒ ܥܪܒܗ ܘܡܩ ܕܢܠܐ ܚܠܦܐ ܕܐܬܪܐ. ܘܦܓܥܐ
ܠܢܦܠܐ ܓܒܗ ܙܚܡܐ ܒܪܦܓܐ ܪܒܐ. ܘܕܚܝܠܘܬܐ ܦܠܢ
ܗܘܐ ܬܓܢܐ ܦܓܪ ܗܘܐ ܡܗܘܬܐ̇ ܡܛܠ ܣܒܝܒ ܒܠ ܕܒܠܐ
ܗܘܐ ܡܫܝܚܘܬܐ. ܘܟܕ ܦܘܩܕܢܐ ܡܛܠܐ ܠܕܢܢܐ ܐܙܕܡ ܗܘܐ.
ܒܫܒܬܐ ܘܪܘܓܙܐ ܘܟܬܪܒܢܬܐ ܕܝܗܘܐ ܠܕܒܪ̈ܝ ܘܐܚܝܢ ܢܬ̈ܪܐ
ܕܠܐܒܠܐ ܒܠܒܒܐ ܢܩܒܐ ܙܚܡ. ܒܬܪ ܣܒܝܒ ܢܦܩܝܢ ܗܘܘ
ܠܡܝܢܕܘ. ܗܘ ܕܝܢ ܓܒܪܐ ܒܪܘܪܐ ܗܘܐ ܕܡܫܝܚܘܬܐ. ܕܒܐܘܪܚܗ̇
ܙܒܬܐ ܕܘܡܝܟܘܬܐ ܡܬܒܪ ܗܘܐ. ܘܕܢܚܬ ܗܘܐ ܒܡܠܦܢܘܬܗ
ܠܒܝܬ ܒܒܗ. ܠܚܝܝ ܗܘܐ ܒܒܪܗ ܒܐܬܪ̈ܘܬܐ ܕܡܕܝܢܝ ܠܗ.
ܘܟܕ ܢܦܩܬ ܗܘܬ ܒܬܪܗ ܓܘܝܢ ܠܐ ܐܫܟܚܬܗ. ܠܘ ܕܓܒܪܗ
ܗܘܐ ܐܠܐ ܕܢܦܩ ܠܡܦܩܢܘ. ܘܡܛܠ ܫܡܥܬܐ ܕܫܘܦܐ ܕܪܒܐ

ܘܠܝܬ ܕܢܦܩ ܒܪܢܫܐ. ܕܗܟܢܐ ܐܝܬ ܠܟܠܢܫ ܘܠܘܝܐ
ܒܡܬܝܢ ܘܐܡܪ ܕܦܩܢ. ܘܗܐ ܒܠܠܝܐ ܕܡܠܟܐ ܫܢܝܠ ܐܝܬ
ܠܗ ܪܒܐ. ܦܠܓܐ ܓܒܪܐ ܕܒܘܠܒܗ ܕܒܪ ܐܠܗܐ. ܪܗܛ
ܐܝܟ ܓܪܒܐ ܡܛܠ ܕܦܩܕܐ ܕܡܫܝܚܘܬܗ. ܢܒܝܒ ܗܘܕܐ
ܒܠܒܝܫܐ ܗܘܐ ܕܫܪܝܪܬܐ. ܐܦ ܒܪܘܚܐ ܕܡܠܟܐ ܦܘܩܗ
ܡܫܝܚܘܬܐ. ܒܪ ܗܘܐ ܘܒܬܪ ܘܡܠܒܒ ܗܘܐ ܒܡܠܟܘܬܗ.
ܠܒܢܝ ܒܝܬܐ ܕܒܝܬ ܐܠܗܐ ܒܡܫܝܚܘܬܗ. ܢܗܘܪܐ ܡܠܟܐ ܗܘܐ
ܘܡܬܒܬܒ ܗܘܐ ܒܢ ܫܘܒܚܐ. ܕܢܦܫܗ ܠܐܬܪܐ ܡܢ ܫܦܘܬܐ
ܕܐܫܬܒܬܗ ܗܘܬ. ܘܒܪܬܗ ܕܒܝܪܐ ܡܠܟܐ ܗܘܐ ܦܘܩܕܗ
ܒܬܘܕܝܬܐ. ܘܐܝܟ ܗܕܐ ܒܢܒܝ ܗܘܐ ܠܗܘܪܐ ܒܝܘܡܐ
ܕܒܠܝܗ. ܓܒܪܐ ܗܘܐ ܕܡܓܠܠ ܗܘܐ ܠܗ ܥܠ ܢܘܟܪܝܐ. ܐܠܗܐ
ܕܢܘܗܪ ܠܒܢܐ ܕܡܫܝܚܘܬܐ. ܒܝܬܐ ܕܢܒܝ ܪܘܚܐ ܕܫܘܒܚܐ ܗܘܐ
ܠܒܢܝܐܪܐ. ܘܡܬܓܘܠ ܗܘܐ ܒܪ ܢܩܦ ܒܗ ܘܠܐ ܕܪܘܝܢ ܗܘܐ.
ܓܒܪ ܗܘܐ ܘܡܠܟܐ ܙܒܢܬ ܒܪܗ ܘܡܓܠܠ ܗܘܐ ܠܗ. ܡܠܠܬܗ
ܕܒܡܠܠܗ ܗܘܐ ܕܠܐ ܕܗܘܕܐ. ܒܫܒܐ ܕܓܦܢܝܢ ܐܝܟ ܒܐܬܪܐ
ܡܢ ܫܦܘܬܐ. ܘܒܡܟܐ ܕܡܢܝܢ ܒܐܪ ܗܘܐ ܠܗܘܢ ܒܓܠܝܘܬܗ.
ܡܠܦ ܒܪܬܐ ܘܡܪܪ ܗܘܐ ܒܡܫܝܚܘܬܐ. ܠܡܥܢܝܢܐ
ܕܡܬܐܠܨܝܢ ܗܘܘ ܡܢ ܪܕܘܦܐ. ܠܗܘܢ ܗܦܟܐ ܘܠܗܘܢ ܢܘܪܐ
ܡܬܒܬܒ ܗܘܐ. ܒܗܘܦܟܐ ܕܢܦܫܗ ܐܝܟ ܓܒܝܠܬܐ ܘܠܐ
ܕܢܠ ܗܘܐ. ܐܝܟ ܗܘܦܪܐ ܕܬܪܝܢ ܦܘܪܫܢ ܚܪܦܐ ܗܘܬ.
ܡܫܝܚܘܬܗ ܘܠܗܘܢ ܓܒܪ ܡܬܒܬܒ ܗܘܐ. ܡܢܝܪܐ ܒܢܝ
ܗܘܐ ܒܗܘܢܐ ܐܬܪܐ ܕܓܦܪ ܗܘܐ ܠܗ. ܒܪܘܚܗ ܙܠܝܩܐ
ܕܪܘܡܘܬܐ ܕܐܠܗܐ ܓܒܪ. ܗܘܐ ܐܝܟ ܡܠܟܐ ܒܡܠܟܘܬܗ
ܓܒܝܢܘܬܐ. ܠܗܪܐ ܦܢܝܬܐ ܕܡܦܩܬ ܗܘܬ ܠܗ ܒܒܦܪܘܬܐ.
ܡܟܢܫܢܐ ܗܘܐ ܘܡܠܠ ܕܗܘܬ ܒܗܘܢܐ ܪܒܐ. ܒܪܘܪܘܬܐ
ܘܒܫܠܝܘܬܐ ܕܫܪܝܪܬܐ. ܗܘܐ ܠܗ ܠܒܢܐ ܪܒܐ ܓܒܪܐ ܒܪ
ܠܒܢܐ ܗܘ. ܘܒܬܪ ܗܢ ܗܘܐ ܫܠܝܡ ܕܒܢܐ ܒܪ ܢܦܪ ܠܗ.

ܫܒܝܒ̈ܘܗܝ ܫ̈ܠܡܘܬܐ. ܡܢ ܒܬܪ ܡܬܚܪܝܢ ܢܦܠ ܚܕܐ ܒܫܠܗܒܝܬܐ.
ܕܠܡܐ ܕܡܟܐ ܘܐܝܟܢ ܡܬܬܟܝܪ ܥܡ ܒܢܝ̈ܢܫܐ. ܐܝܟܘ ܡ̈ܠܟܘܗܝ ܛ̈ܒܐ
ܕܛ̈ܠܝܐ ܒܬܪ ܐܬܘܢܐ. ܟܕ ܚܙܝܐ ܐܝܟܢܐ ܚܒܝܒ ܠܐ ܢܒܝ
ܐܢܐ. ܗܐ ܠܐ ܐܡܘܨ ܗܘܐ ܬܘܒ ܘܐܝܟܢ ܕܟܪܐ. ܗܢܐ ܠܗܠܝܢ
ܕܒܕ ܗܢܐ ܘܢ̈ܒܝܐ ܠܗ. ܡܢ ܟܕ ܫܡܘܣ ܚܒܝܒ ܗܘܕܐ ܐܘ
ܒܪܐ. ܒܗܘܢ ܠܝ ܡܠܟܐ ܟܠ ܕܐܡܘܨ ܒܗ ܠܐ ܢܒܝ ܐܢܐ.
ܗܐ ܡܫܬܐܠ ܠܐ ܐܡܪ. ܗܘܐ ܡܢ ܒܬܠܬܐ. ܘܚܒܝܒ
ܐܡܪ ܘܐܢܝܐ ܫܡܘܣ ܠܒܪܐ ܒܗ. ܡܟܝܠ ܡܬܚܪܐ ܢܐܡܪ
ܕܗܢܐ ܗܢܐ ܐܘ ܗܘ. ܐܘ ܠܐ ܫܡܘܣ ܗܢܐ ܐܝܟ ܗܘ ܠܒܪܐ
ܠܗ. ܬܠܬܐ ܒܢܘܪܐ ܘܠܐ ܦܪܟܐ ܠܗܘܢ ܫܠܗܒܝܬܐ. ܚܙ ܕܝܢ
ܐܡܪ ܘܐܝܟܢ ܐܦܩ ܠܒܥܠܠܗ. ܕܪܒܝܢܝܐ ܗܝ، ܗܘ ܕܢܚܬ
ܗܘܐ ܠܟܠ ܐܬܘܢܐ. ܕܢܚܘܪ ܡܠܟܐ ܠܡܚܒܝܢ ܬܟܡ ܒܟ ܕܬܠܬܐ.
ܡܢ ܗܘ ܠܗ ܕܘܟܬܐ ܒܢܘܪܐ ܠܗܘ ܕܐܡܪ ܗܘܐ. ܕܪܒܝܢܝܐ
ܫܠܗܒ̈ܝܗ ܢܗܘܐ ܡܚܪ ܕܟܢܐ. ܘܐܦ ܕܬܠܬܐ ܢܚܫܚ ܫܘܦܪܐ ܒܪ
ܠܐ ܐܡܪܘ. ܗܢܐ ܕܐܡܪ ܐܝܟܢ ܠܐ ܫܠܝܛ ܥܡ ܒܢܝ̈ܢܫܐ.
ܐܠܐ ܥܠܝܟ ܐܢܐ ܐܘ ܢܐܡܪ ܐܘ ܠܐ ܢܐܡܪ. ܗܢܐ ܕܢܡܪ ܪܡ
ܗܘܐ ܫܘܦܪܗ ܡܢ ܕܬܠܬܐ. ܐܠܐ ܡܛܠ ܕܐܢܬܬܗ ܕܡܪܢܐ
ܡܕܒܪܢܘܬܐ. ܗܘ ܡܫܬܟܚ ܐܝܟܢܐ ܕܦܝܢ ܘܐܝܟܢܐ ܕܐܫܠܡ.
ܡܠܟܐ ܕܝܢ ܐܦ ܕܬܠܬܐ ܕܠܐ ܐܡܪܘ ܗܘܘ. ܘܕܗܘ ܕܐܡܪ ܚܙ
ܗܘ ܘܥܘܐ ܗܘ ܗܪܟܐ ܘܠܗܠ. ܘܐܠܘ ܦܩܕ ܠܗ ܡܪܢܗ ܠܢܘܪܐ
ܕܬܘܟܠ ܐܢܘܢ. ܠܬܠܬܝܗܘܢ ܡܢ ܡܐܢ̈ܝܗܘܢ ܢܦܩܝܢ ܗܘܘ.
ܘܐܠܘ ܪܡܙ ܠܗ ܕܐܦ ܠܗ ܠܗܘ ܚܙ ܠܐ ܬܘܟܠ ܗܘܬ. ܠܐ
ܢܦܩ ܗܘܐ ܘܠܘ ܕܠܡܗ ܗܘܬ ܢܬܦܝܐ ܗܘܐ. ܕܢܟܠܝܢ ܠܢܘܪܐ
ܕܡܟܝܠܘܢ ܗܘܬ ܟܕ ܟܐܠܝܢ ܠܗ. ܕܠܐ ܕܝܢ ܐܡܪܘ ܡܪܢܗ
ܕܢܘܪܐ ܡܬܚܐ ܘܦܩܕ ܠܗ. ܡܟܕܝܢ ܚܙ ܗܘ ܫܘܦܪܐ ܫܡܠܐ ܕܐܢܫܐ
ܕܐܝܬܝ. ܘܕܠܐ ܐܡܪ ܡܛܠ ܕܫܡܐ ܗܘ ܐܦ ܡܬܚܙܝܐ ܩܘܕܐ
ܪܚܡܬܐ. ܪܡ ܗܘ ܫܘܦܪܗ. ܪܡ ܗܘ ܪܒܘܬܗ. ܘܫܡܝܐ ܟܠܗܘܢ

ܘܬܫܘܥܬܐ ܚܬܝܬܐ: ܘܒܘܝܐܐ ܕܢܦܫܐ: ܘܡܗܝܡܢܐ ܕܚܝܠܐ
ܘܡܫܬܠܠܘܢ ܕܠܐ ܬܘܓܐ. ܘܗܠܝܢ ܟܠܗܝܢ ܘܐܝܠܝܢ ܕܕܡܝܢ ܠܗܝܢ.
ܥܠ ܗܕܐ ܕܡܘܪܒܐ ܕܒܬܘ. ܐܩܠܝܣܝܐ ܕܝܢ ܕܫܘܕܐ
ܗܠܝܢ. ܘܐܝܠܝܢ ܕܡܥܒܕܢ ܗܘܬ ܟܠܗܘܢ: ܦܛܘܪ ܚܢܘ ܕܝܠ
ܬܐܘܦܝܠܐ ܘܢܗܪܘ ܐܚܘܝ. ܘܐܘܕܝܬ ܒܡܥܡܘܕܝܬܐ. ܕܒܪܗ ܗܘ
ܕܐܠܗܐ ܘܐܠܗܐ ܐܬܘܗܝ. ܘܝܠܐ ܕܬܟܠܝܘܢ ܕܫܘܕܐ ܗܠܝܢ:
ܕܦܠܚܬ ܗܘܬ ܒܗ ܪܘܚܐ ܗܘܬ ܠܪܟܠܝܘܢ: ܒܒܕܢܐ ܕܢܦܫܝ
ܗܘܘ ܡܬܟܠܠܝܢ: ܢܥܒܘܕ ܠܝ ܕܢܦܪܘܬ ܗܘܬ ܒܗ. ܘܢܘܕܐ ܒܗ
ܡܢܝ ܩܪܝܒܘܗܝ ܕܐܘܕܝܬ ܒܗ ܡܟܝܠ ܀
ܒܫܘܐܠܐ ܕܝܢ ܕܒܥܬܝܢ ܘܡܟܒܐ: ܕܫܐܠܗ ܗܘܐ ܕܢܪܐ
ܠܚܢܢ. ܢܦܩ ܗܘܐ ܟܠܗܘܢ ܐܦܝܣܩܘܦܘܬܐ ܕܒܬܘܟܐ ܕܢܘܪܐ.

ܕܢܘܪܐ.

ܫܠܡܬ ܫܘܕܥܬܐ ܕܚܢܢܝ:

܀ ܡܟܬܒܢܐ ܀

ܬܘܒ ܡܐܡܪܐ ܕܥܠ ܚܢܢܝܫܘܥ. ܕܫܡܗ ܠܒܪ ܝܥܩܘܒ.

ܚܢܢܝܫܘܥ ܠܒܪ ܓܘܠܬܐ ܡܢܝ ܡܢ ܢܘܪܐ. ܕܐܦ ܠܗ
ܐܝܟ ܓܠܝܢܐ ܕܡܦܩܪܐ ܒܗܘ ܪܡܫܐ. ܫܪܝ ܕܒܝܐ ܗܘܐ ܪܥܝ
ܠܗ ܡܢܝܢܐ. ܕܐܝܟ ܕܠܡܘܒܠܐ ܕܒܪܗ ܐܘܪܝ ܡܠܬܗ. ܒܢܝܬ
ܓܘܡܪܐ ܘܐܡܪ ܓܒܪܐ ܗܘܐ ܦܩܪܐ ܠܗ. ܐܝܟ ܓܠܝܢܐ ܘܠܐ
ܢܣܒܐ ܠܗ ܥܠܡܒܝܬܐ. ܫܘܒܚܗ ܪܒܝܬ ܐܦ ܫܘܡܠܝܐ ܘܡܫܘܠܡܘܬܗ.
ܘܢܘܪܗ ܢܦܩܐ ܘܡܢ ܦܘܡ ܠܗ ܕܒܬܢܐ ܫܘܒܚܗ. ܐܠܐ ܒܫܘܒܐ
ܗܘ ܕܠܫܘܕܐ ܒܢܘܪܐ ܫܘܒܚܗ. ܠܐ ܐܝܟ ܡܫܡܫ ܒܬܢܐ

ܫܠܝܡܝ ܕܕܝܢ ܗܘܘ. ܟܕ ܫܘܒܚܐ ܟܠܗ ܡܢܗ ܗܘܐ ܠܐܠܗܐ:
ܕܟܠ ܫܒܚܗ ܡܢܗ. ܗܘܐ ܦܘܪܥܢܗ ܠܡܕܝܢܬܐ ܕܟܘܪܐ. ܀

ܐܬܘܗܝ ܗܘܐ ܕܝܢ ܢܘܗܪܐ ܕܝܗܒ ܗܘܐ ܒܗ ܒܥܘܒܕܬܐ ܟܬܝܒܬܐ ܒܐܨܒܥ ܐܠܗܐ. ܒܢܘܗܪܐ ܗܘ ܕܐܫܬܡܗ. ܗܘܐ ܒܗ. ܕܡܘܫܠܡܢܘܬܗ ܕܟܠܐ: ܦܪܝ، ܗܘܐ ܕܢܦܩ ܡܢ ܠܗ ܐܘܪܚܐ: ܕܐܬܚܙܝܬ ܗܘܐ ܠܢܘܗܪܐ ܡܕܡܝܢܬܐ ܕܐܬܓܠܝܐ. ܐܝܟ ܕܢܦܩ ܗܘܐ ܡܢ ܠܡܘܫܐ: ܗܢܐ ܕܡܬܓܠܐ ܒܡܕܒܪܐ ܒܐܦܐ ܡܟܪܝܫܬܐ ܒܗܬ ܕܡܘܫܐ. ܘܗܘܐ ܡܢ ܐܬܪܘܬܐ ܕܟܠ ܥܡܡ. ܕܠܐ ܐܝܬ ܗܘܐ ܐܢܫܐ ܡܢܗܘܢ ܕܚܙܐ. ܘܡܦܝܣܐ ܒܫܘܠܛܢܐ ܕܟܠܗܘܢ. ܘܒܗܢܐ ܡܠܟܐ ܦܩܕ ܥܠܝܗ ܕܢܘܦܩܐ ܡܢ ܡܕܝܢܬܐ. ܐܬܡܘܕܝܘ ܕܝܢ ܟܠܗܘܢ ܗܘܘ ܟܠ ܡܕܡ ܕܢܦܩܝܢ ܗܘܘ ܡܢ ܕܝܢܐ. ܘܫܪܝܪܐ ܕܡܕܝܢܬܐ ܟܠܗܘܢ ܗܘܘ. ܫܪܒܐ ܕܐܝܬܝܗܘܢ ܕܡܬܐܡܪܝܢ ܗܘ، ܠܒܪ ܡܢ ܬܪܥܐ ܕܒܝܬ ܕܝܢܐ. ܘܐܝܟ ܚܕܐ ܕܐܝܬ ܗܘܐ. ܟܠ ܕܫܡܥܝܢ ܗܘܘ ܘܟܠ ܕܚܙܝܢ ܗܘܘ. ܡܗܕܝܢ ܗܘܘ ܠܕܝܢܐ. ܘܡܬܕܡܪܝܢ ܗܘ، ܒܡܘܗܒܬܐ ܕܠܗܘܢ ܦܬܝ، ܕܝܗܒ ܀ ܐܢܐ ܬܘܒ ܐܠܗܐ ܕܟܦܪܬ ܗܘܝܬ ܒܫܪܝܪܘܬܐ ܒܫܒܬܐ ܕܐܬܓܠܝ. ܘܐܘܕܝܬ ܒܡܫܝܚܐ. ܐܬܟܠܠ ܠܝ ܘܟܬܒܬ ܦܘܫܩܐ ܕܡܘܫܐ ܕܦܩܕܢܘܬܐ ܗܠܝܢ ܕܐܒܘܢ. ܐܝܟ ܡܢܐ ܕܟܬܒܬ ܗܘܝܬ ܡܢ ܩܕܡ: ܕܒܪܐ ܘܫܡܥܘܢܐ ܫܗܕܐ ܚܕܝܘܗ، ܘܐܝܟ ܗܘܐ ܠܗܘܢ ܬܘܒܐ ܒܟܘܬܐ ܕܩܘܫܛܗܘܢ. ܐܬܕܟܪ ܗܘܐ ܠܗܘܢ ܐܦ ܗܘ ܒܢܘܪܐ ܕܡܫܝܚܐ ܕܟܠܠܗ. ܘܕܟܬܒܬ ܫܪܬܐ ܘܢܦܫܐ: ܘܡܘܬܐ ܕܟܠܠܗܘܢ ܕܫܗܕܐ ܗܠܝܢ: ܠܐ ܡܛܠ ܐܠܝܢ ܕܐܬܒܘܬ، ܚܝܘ ܒܟܢܫܐ. ܐܠܐ ܡܛܠ ܕܢܐܠܦܘܢ ܐܠܝܢ ܕܐܬܝܢ ܒܬܪܢ. ܐܝܟܢܐ ܗܘܐ ܐܝܟ ܗܢܘܢ ܕܫܗܕܐ ܗܠܝܢ: ܘܐܝܠܝܢ ܐܢܘܢ ܘܐܦ ܒܡܘܗܒܬܢܘܬܐ ܕܫܗܕܐ ܩܕܝܫܐ ܕܒܫܘܡܗ ܕܡܫܝܚܐ ܡܠܟܐ. ܘܕܫܪܟܐ ܕܩܛܠܐ ܐܚܪܢܐ. ܐܝܠܝܢ ܕܐܦ ܗܢܘܢ ܒܕܡܘ ܗܘܘ ܕܪܘܫܐ ܠܕܡܘܬܐ. ܘܡܫܠܡ ܗܘܘ ܘܐܦ ܠܩܛܝܠܐ: ܒܫܝܢܐ ܘܒܫܘܪܝܐ ܘܒܐܘܠܨܢܐ ܡܪܝܪܐ:

ܕܒܠܐܕ. ܢܡܪ ܘܚܝܘ. ܕܟܕ ܡܫܟܚ ܗܘܬ ܕܐܡܪܘܢ ܗܘܬ ܡܢ
ܐܦܠܝܓܐ ܗܠܝܢ: ܠܐ ܐܡܪܬ ܕܟܐܢܐ، ܒܟܐܢܘܬܟ. ܠܐ ܐܦܠ
ܗܘܝܬ. ܬܦܩܘܢ ܠܝ ܢܘܪܐ ܗܕܐ ܕܢܩܕ ܐܢܐ ܒܗ. ܠܦܘܪܥܢܐ
ܡܕܡܝܟ: ܐܝܟ ܕܐܬܦܠܓܐ ܡܢ ܢܘܪܐ ܗܘ، ܕܠܐ ܕܟܒܐ. ܘܩܒܠ
ܪܘܚ ܡܕܡܝܟ: ܒܪܘܚ ܐܠܗܘܬܟ ܒܪܐ ܫܒܝܚܐ ܕܐܒܐ
ܘܓܒܪܐ. ܘܟܕ ܢܦܠ ܗܘܐ. ܐܬܓܒܠ ܗܘܐ ܘܟܪܟܗ ܐܢܘܢ. ܘܗܟܢ
ܗܘܘ ܠܗ ܬܠܡܝܕܐ. ܟܕ ܩܡܝܢ: ܠܒܪܐ ܘܒܢ̈ܝܐ. ܘܐܡܪܝܢ ܠܗ.
ܟܕ ܒܠܝܢ ܘܕܡ ܡܪܢ: ܕܢܒܥܐ ܫܝܢܗ ܒܟܠܗܘܢ. ܘܫܘܕܥܬܐ
ܠܟܕܬܗ ܕܚܡܝܢ. ܘܟܕ ܡܐܡܪ ܗܘܐ ܫܒܝܚܐ: ܫܦܪܘ ܗܘܘ
ܕܒܟܬܐ ܫܕܝܐ. ܘܐܫܬܘ ܗܘܘ ܘܐܡܝܢܒܗܘܢ، ܗܘܘ ܒܟܠܗܘܢ.
ܘܡܒܟܝܢ ܗܘܘ ܒܟܠܗ ܡܠܘܐ ܫܢ. ܘܐܬܘ ܕܢܦܪܩܘܢ، ܒܗ ܒܡܐ
ܡܠܘܐ. ܘܐܡܪ ܠܗܘܢ. ܠܐ ܡܫܟܚܐ ܐܢܐ ܡܢ ܕܒܠܕܬܐ ܗܕܐ
ܕܐܬܗܕܡ ܐܢܬܘܢ ܠܝ ܒܗ. ܘܐܬܘܢ ܗܘܘ ܩܕܡܝ. ܘܦܢܝ ܗܘܘ
ܘܡܒܪܟ ܐܢܘܢ ܡܢ ܟܠ ܠܒܗܘܢ، ܘܟܕ ܐܬܟܢܫܬ ܗܘܬ ܢܘܪܐ.
ܘܦܠܓ ܗܘܐ ܕܠܡܗ ܢܦܫܐܝܬ. ܘܟܕ ܠܗ ܦܢܝ ܒܡܕܡܝܟ. ܘܒܗ
ܒܟܠܬܐ ܕܦܢܝ ܒܡܕܡܗ ܘܠܒܢܬ ܗܘܬ ܢܦܫܗ. ܘܠܒܘ ܗܘܘ
ܠܒܪܐ ܘܒܢܝܐ ܒܩܠܐ ܕܒܟܬܐ. ܘܠܒܘ ܗܘܘ ܘܐܦܝܘܗܝ، ܡܢ
ܢܘܪܐ. ܟܕ ܪܩܝܢ ܗܘܘ ܒܠܗܘܢ، ܟܬܒܐ ܠܒܢ̈ܐ. ܘܡܫܚܝܢܐ ܠܒܢܝ̈ܗ
ܘܒܩܕܡܐ. ܘܡܬܢܦܠܝܢ ܗܘܘ ܡܢ ܩܢܘܡܐ ܕܡܕܝܢܬܐ. ܘܫܠܡܘܗ، ܗܘܘ
ܐܢܫܐ ܘܐܝܬܝܐ ܒܠܒܝܗ. ܘܡܦܫܘ ܗܘܘ ܘܡܒܪܘܗ، ܠܘܬ
ܠܒܪܐ ܘܡܬܘܢܐ ܦܬܘܪܐ: ܒܡܕܝܪܐ ܗܘ ܕܦܢܝܬܝܢ ܗܘܘ ܒܗ.
ܒܪܬܐ ܕܡܠܟܘܬܐ ܕܒܝܬ ܐܠܗ ܗܘܝܐ. ܟܕ ܐܬܕܝܪ ܗܘܘ ܒܠܒܗ،
ܡܕܡܘܪܐ ܘܡܕܪܫܐ. ܘܡܬܦܬܝܢ ܗܘܘ ܩܕܡܝܗ ܕܡܕܝܢܬܐ ܫܒܝܚܐܝܬ
ܘܡܢܗܪܐܝܬ. ܘܐܦ ܡܢ ܬܘܕܝܬܐ ܘܫܘܒܚܐ. ܐܫܬܘܬܦܘ ܗܘܘ ܠܡܫܒܚܘ
ܘܠܡܘܕܝ ܦܬܘܪܗ ܒܡ ܐܢܫܐ ܒܪ̈ܩܠܝܐ. ܒܗܘ ܕܝܢ ܒܕܢܐ ܕܡܕܝܢܬܐ:
ܘܐܦ ܒܟܢܫܐ ܕܡܕܝܢ ܗܘܘ ܠܗ. ܫܕܐ ܫܠܝܬܐ ܕܡܫܝܚܘܬܐ
ܦܪܫܐ ܗܘܬ ܒܠ ܠܒܐ ܘܟܠ ܒܪܢܐ. ܕܒܟܝܐ ܕܝܢ ܡܢ ܟܠ

ܘܠܝܬ ܕܢܬܒܥ ܒܐܬܪܘܗܝ. ܘܐܡܪ ܠܗ ܗܝܢܐ ܚܒܝܒ. ܐܢܬ ܀ ܀

ܗܓܡܘܢܐ ܐܡܪ. ܠܗܕܐ ܡܪܘܬܟ ܕܥܒܪ ܗܘ ܦܘܩܕܢܐ ܕܡܠܟܐ. ܡܫܠܡ ܐܢܐ ܗܘ ܕܝܢ ܕܦܘܩܕܢܐ ܕܡܠܟܐ ܡܢ ܗܝܟܐ ܐܦܩܘܕ ܥܠܝܟ ܀ ܚܒܝܒ ܐܡܪ. ܐܢܐ ܕܝܢ ܠܗܘ ܦܘܩܕܢܐ ܕܡܠܟܐ ܡܬܚܫܒ ܡܢ ܕܦܘܩܕܐ ܚܣܝܪ ܐܢܐ: ܕܬܦܩܘܕ ܥܠ ܒܢܝܢܐ ܕܡܠܟܐ ܐܢܬ ܀ ܘܡܢ ܒܬܪ ܗܠܝܢ. ܦܩܕ ܗܘܐ ܗܓܡܘܢܐ ܕܢܬܠ ܗܘܐ ܠܗ ܐܦܣܦܣܐ ܕܡܘܬܐ. ܘܟܬܒܐ ܗܘܐ ܡܕܡ ܐܘܦܝܢ ܕܠܗ ܘܐܡܪ. ܟܕ ܫܡܥܝܢ ܗܘܘ ܠܗ. ܘܐܦ ܚܙܝܐ ܕܡܕܝܢܬܐ. ܚܒܝܒ ܗܢܐ ܕܒܓܘ ܒܩܠܝܬܐ: ܐܝܟ ܕܐܦ ܫܒܒܘܬܗ ܡܢܗ. ܘܢܦܩ ܬܘܒ ܠܩܠܝܬܝ. ܘܐܦ ܗܘ ܕܬܬܒܪܘܢ ܚܝܠܘܗܝ ܡܢ ܬܘܒ ܫܒܒܐ ܗܢܐ ܡܫܡܥ. ܘܠܐ ܢܚܘܐ ܢܗܘܪܐ ܗܢܐ ܚܕܪܐ ܕܐܠܦܐ. ܘܐܠܘ ܠܐ ܕܦܩܕ ܗܘܐ ܠܩܠܝܬܐ ܩܕܡܝܐ: ܕܬܬܦܩܕܘܢ ܩܠܝܬܗܘܢ ܕܩܘܠܣܐ. ܘܐܝܟܢܐ ܕܬܬܦܩܕ ܗܘܬ ܥܠܝܗ ܕܗܢܐ ܗܘ ܗܘܐ. ܡܠܠ ܕܡܒܝܢܐ ܐܡܪܝܢ ܗܘܐ. ܦܩܕܬ ܕܬܬܠ ܕܢܬܒܐ ܒܒܝܬܗ ܐܝܟ ܕܒܦܘܡ ܦܠܛܝܐ. ܘܐܡܪ ܒܗܘܢܐ ܕܒܝܬܝ. ܗܝ ܕܝܗܒ ܡܬܝܗܒ. ܕܢܦܩܐ ܫܒܝܩܐ ܕܡܢܬܗ. ܘܢܦܩ ܗܘܐ ܡܢ ܡܕܡ ܗܓܡܘܢܐ ܟܕ ܕܒܥܐ ܒܝܬܐ ܒܦܘܡܗ. ܘܫܠܚܐ ܕܐܒܝܫܘܬܐ ܕܡܕܝܢܬܐ ܕܢܦܠܐ ܗܘܬ ܠܬܚܬܗ. ܒܦܘܠܚܢܐ ܕܝܢ ܚܕܝܢ ܗܘܘ ܕܠܐ ܦܩܕ ܗܘܐ ܘܠܐ ܦܪܫ ܡܢ ܡܢܗܘܢ. ܘܫܒܩܐ ܠܚܝܒܝܢ ܗܘܘ ܠܗ. ܟܠ ܕܠܐ ܢܦܩ ܗܘܐ ܕܢܬܒܥ. ܘܒܪܥܘܬܗ ܡܢ ܬܪܥܐ ܡܕܝܢܬܐ ܕܩܕܡܝ. ܠܗܘܟܠ ܡܬܟܢܫܝܢ. ܗܝ ܕܒܝܬܐ ܗܘܬ ܠܒܝܠܬܐ ܒܝ ܐܟܪܙ. ܐܝܟܢ ܕܝܢ ܠܒܝܬܐ ܗܘܬ ܚܙܝܐ ܘܢܦܩܐ ܗܘܬ ܒܟܠܗ. ܘܟܕ ܢܦܠ ܗܘܐ ܕܝܢ ܠܡܕܝܢܬܐ ܗܝ ܕܒܗ ܡܬܟܢܫܝܢ ܗܘܘ ܠܗ. ܡܢ ܗܘܐ ܘܢܦܠ ܗܘܐ. ܘܟܠ ܐܢܫ ܕܢܦܩܝܢ ܗܘܘ ܒܟܠܗ. ܘܐܡܪ ܗܘܐ. ܡܠܟܐ ܡܫܝܚܐ: ܕܢܦܩ ܗܘ ܒܟܠܗ ܗܢܐ: ܘܢܦܩ ܗܘ ܒܟܠܗ

ܠܐ ܗܘܐ ܒܥܠܡ ܕܫܦܝܪ ܐܢܬ ܫܦܝܪ ܐܢܐ. ܡܛܠ ܕܒܥܠܡ
ܗܘ ܕܩܕܝܫ ܡܬܩܕܫܐ ܐܢܐ. ܘܡܛܠ ܗܢܐ ܫܒܩ ܐܢܐ ܠܒܝܫܐ
ܕܐܠܗܐ ܫܒܘܩܝ. ܘܠܐ ܕܬܬܒܪܐ ܒܒܝܫܐ. ܗܘ ܕܐܣܠܐ
ܒܒܝܫ ܢܐܫ ܀ ܡܠܦܢܐ ܐܡܪ. ܡܛܠ ܕܗܝܡܢܐ ܒܦܪ
ܒܐܠܗܐ ܕܗܘܝܢ ܠܗܘܢ ܩܠܝܒܝ. ܢܬܬܗܘܦܘܢ ܦܪܘܫܐ ܒܠ
ܦܪܘܫܘܗܝ ܩܕܝܫܐ. ܒܩܘܐܠܐ ܠܒܪ ܩܕܝܫܐ ܕܐܬܪܬ ܪܘܚ
ܒܒܗ ܘܫܐܠܬܗ. ܠܒܢܐ ܐܢܘܢ ܠܦܪܘܫܘܗܝ ܩܕܝܫܐ. ܘܟܕ
ܦܪܘܩ ܗܘܘ ܠܗ ܡܢܐ ܗܘܐ ܘܐܡܪ. ܕܠܐ ܫܘܩ ܚܕܘܗܝ ܕܒܝܫܐ
ܗܢܐ: ܠܡܫܝܚܘܬܐ ܐܢܫܐ ܕܒܬܪܝܐ ܕܬܬܓܠܐ ܒܥܠܡ
ܕܪܚܡܘܗܝ ܠܡܫܝܚܐ. ܘܟܕ ܚܙܐ ܗܘܐ ܡܠܦܢܐ ܕܐܣܠܐ
ܒܗܠܝܢ ܐܘܠܨܢܐ ܙܒܢܐ ܗܘܐ ܕܢܕܒܪ. ܐܡܪ ܠܗ ܗܝܡܢܐ ܟܠܗ
ܠܗܘܢ ܘܠܒܢܝܗܘܢ ܕܗܘܝܬܘܢ ܦܠܚ ܐܢܬܘܢ ܒܪܚܡܬܗܘܢ. ܀
ܚܒܝܒ ܐܡܪ ܠܐ ܗܘܐ ܦܠܓܝܢ ܗܘܝܢ. ܡܫܬܒܚ ܗܘ ܒܬܒܥ
ܗܘ ܠܝ: ܕܟܕ ܕܢܐܘܒܕ ܢܦܫ ܢܒܝܫܘ. ܐܠܐ ܐܦ ܐܪܝܬܐ
ܒܬܒܥܐ ܠܝ. ܕܠܐ ܢܛܠ ܡܘܕܝܐ ܠܠܩܕܝ. ܘܠܐ ܢܩܒܠ
ܡܬܓܝܚܬܐ ܡܢ ܫܒܩܐ ܀ ܀ ܀ ܡܠܦܢܐ ܐܡܪ. ܢܕܥ ܐܢܐ
ܕܠܗ ܕܐܡܪ ܐܢܬ ܗܝܡܢܐ. ܐܝܟ ܕܢܦܫ ܪܘܚܐ، ܘܡܫܒܚܬܐ
ܕܪܚܝܒ. ܘܡܦܩܘܕ ܒܠܝܢ ܩܘܡܬܐ ܡܠܠܐܝܬ. ܠܐ ܗܘܐ
ܩܕܡܬܘܗܝ ܐܢܐ ܒܠ ܗܕܐ ܕܪܚܝܒܬ. ܐܠܐ ܩܕܡ ܐܢܐ
ܪܘܚ: ܠܐ ܗܘܐ ܠܢܦܫܝ. ܐܠܐ ܐܝܟ ܕܡܫܒܚܐ ܐܘܠܨܢܐ
ܕܥܕܪܝܢ. ܘܬܒܪܐ ܒܦܪܘܩܝ ܒܕ ܢܛܪ ܡܕܡܝܢ: ܒܦܪܘܩܐ ܕܩܕܡܝܢ
ܒܠ ܚܛܗܝ ܀ ܚܒܝܒ ܐܡܪ. ܘܐܦ ܐܢܐ ܠܗܕܐ ܗܘ ܫܦܝܪ
ܐܢܐ. ܕܬܦܠܓܐ ܬܫܬܒܩ ܒܗ ܐܝܟ ܕܐܡܪܬ ܀ ܀

ܡܠܦܢܐ ܐܡܪ. ܐܬܚܫܒܘ ܠܩܠܝܒܐ ܕܐܝܬ ܠܗܘܢ
ܫܘܠܛܢܐ. ܕܒܠܒܕܘܡ ܕܢܒܥܘܢ ܩܕܡܝܢ ܀ ܚܒܝܒ ܐܡܪ. ܠܝܬ
ܡܢ ܒܢܝܫܐ: ܕܒܠܒܕܘܡ ܕܢܒܥܘܢ ܩܕܡܝܢ. ܐܠܐ ܐܢ ܐܠܗܐ
ܗܘ ܕܫܘܠܛܢܗ ܒܫܡܝܐ: ܘܒܠܗܘܢ ܒܒܪܝܬܗ ܕܐܪܥܐ.

ܕܟܠܗܘܢ ܕܠܡܘܕܠܝ ܐܢܘܢ. ܘܡܢܝܢ ܫܢܝܬܗܘܢ ܟܠܗܝ ܐܘ̈ܠܨܢܐ
ܕܡܣ̈ܝܒܪܢ: ܘܐܦ ܡܢ ܐܝܠܝܢ ܕܦܩܕܘ ܡ̈ܠܟܐ ܀ ܚܒܝܒ. ܐܡܪ.
ܐܠܐ ܠܐ ܕܐܬܪܓܫܬ ܒܗܝܢ ܕܡܨܥܪ̈ܢ ܠܝ: ܘܐܦ ܠܐ ܡܬܐܡܪ
ܐܡܪ ܗܘܝܬ ܒܗܝܢ ܘܡܚܝܢ ܀ ܗܓܡܘܢܐ ܐܡܪ. ܐܝܟܢܐ ܡܚܫܒܬ
ܐܝܢܐ ܠܗܘܢ ܠܩܠ̈ܝܟ. ܒܣܪ ܚܕܝܐ. ܘܩܪ̈ܒܐ ܐܝܢܐ ܒܝ
ܠܐ̈ܠܗܐ ܕܠܐ ܦܠܚܬ ܠܗܘܢ. ܘܡܚܝܫ ܐܝܢܐ ܒܝ ܡ̈ܠܟܐ.
ܕܦܩܕܬ ܥܠ ܦܘܠܚܢܗܘܢ ܀ ܚܒܝܒ. ܐܡܪ. ܠܐ ܕܝܠ ܐܝܢܐ
ܡܢ ܡ̈ܠܟܘܬܐ ܕܡܫܝܠ ܐܢܬ ܠܝ ܒܗ. ܐܠܐ ܒܪ ܕܝܠ ܗܘܝܬ
ܡܢܗ. ܠܐ ܗܘܐ ܒܝܬ ܡ̈ܠܟܐ ܡܬܒܥܝܢ ܗܘܝܬ ܘܡܫܬܡܫ ܗܘܝܬ:
ܗܘ ܕܡܠܟ ܗܘܝܢܐ ܡܫܡܫܢܐ ܗܘܝܬ ܀ ܗܓܡܘܢܐ ܐܡܪ. ܐܝܟܢܐ
ܠܒܪܢܫܐ ܦܓܪ ܐܝܬ ܘܡܚܣܪ ܐܢܬ. ܘܠܢܦܫ ܗܢܐ ܠܐ ܢ̈ܟܣܐ
ܐܝܬ ܕܬܬܦܨܐ ܠܗ ܘܬܥܡܪ ܀ ܚܒܝܒ. ܐܡܪ. ܠܒܪܢܫܐ ܠܐ
ܦܓܪ ܐܝܢܐ. ܡܛܠ ܕܒܬܘܒ. ܗܘ ܠܝ. ܕܠܒܫ ܗܘ ܥܠ ܟܠ ܢܦ
ܕܡܬܬܟܠ ܒܠ ܒܪܢܫܐ. ܠܐܠܗܐ ܕܝܢ ܕܒܫܠ ܦܓܪܐ ܘܗܘܐ
ܒܪܢܫܐ ܦܓܪ ܐܝܢܐ ܘܡܫܒܚ ܐܢܐ ܀ ܀ ܗܓܡܘܢܐ ܐܡܪ.
ܐܝܬ ܡܕܡ ܕܦܩܕܘ ܡ̈ܠܟܐ ܚܒܪ. ܘܗܝ ܕܐܡܬ ܒܪܚܡܝ ܕܠܝ
ܗܝ. ܐܦ ܢܦܫܐ ܐܝܬ ܕܬܦܨܝܗ. ܘܐܦ ܠܐ ܢܦܫܐ ܐܝܬ ܠܐ
ܬܫܒܘܗ ܀ ܚܒܝܒ. ܐܡܪ. ܠܐ ܡܫ̈ܬܒܚܝܢ ܕܢܗܘܘܢ ܬܫ̈ܒܘܚܬܗܘܢ ܡܛܠ
ܕܫܘܒܚܐ ܗܘ ܚܘܣܪܢܐ ܠܫܘܒܚܬܐ. ܘܕܐܫܬܟܠ ܡܢ ܬܫܒܘܚܬܐ
ܗܝ ܕܡܫܝܚܐ ܒܪܚܡܬܗ ܠܐ ܡܫܬܚܫܐ ܀ ܗܓܡܘܢܐ ܐܡܪ.
ܒܐܘ̈ܠܨܢܐ ܡܪ̈ܝܪܐ ܘܩܫ̈ܝܐ ܚܒܪ ܐܢܐ ܠܟ ܕܬܫܒܘܚܬܗ ܡܢ
ܬܫܒܘܚܬܟ: ܗܝ ܕܐܡܪܬ ܕܡܫܝܚܐ ܒܪܚܡܬܗ. ܚܒܝܒ. ܐܡܪ.
ܗܠܝܢ ܐܘ̈ܠܨܢܐ ܕܦܩܕܬ ܐܢܬ ܟܠܗܘܢ ܕܢܗܘܘܢ ܡܬܬܒܥܪܐ
ܡܢ ܬܫܒܘܚܬܝ. ܒܗܘܢ ܗܘ ܡܬܥܒܪܢܐ ܟܠܗ ܬܫܒܘܚܬܗ, ܐܝܟ
ܐܝܠܝܢ ܕܝܕܥܝܢ ܒܐܬܪܐ. ܀ ܗܓܡܘܢܐ ܐܡܪ. ܡܚܝܠܐ ܡܬܚܙܝܢ
ܚ̈ܪܫܐ ܘܗܕ̈ܡܐ ܠܗܘ ܐܠܗܟ. ܡܬܬܐܡܪ ܕܝܢ ܒܚܕܝܐ ܕܦܩܕ
ܐܢܐ ܟܠܗܘܢ, ܢܬܪܐ ܠܡܬܚܙܝܘ ܕܠܐ ܢܫܡܥܘܢ ܀ ܚܒܝܒ. ܐܡܪ.

ܗ̇ܘ ܕܟܦܪ ܐܢܬ ܒܗ ܡܪܟܒܐ. ܘܬܢܝ ܡܘܕܝܬ ܒܗ ܒܛܝܒܘܬܐ. ܒܪ
ܬܘܒ ܡܘܕܝܬ ܟܦܪ ܐܢܬ ܒܗ ܀ ܡܠܦܢܐ ܐܡܪ. ܫܡܥܘ ܗ̇ܘ
ܚܠܚܕܐ ܕܐܬܓܠܝܬ ܒܠܗܘܢ. ܘܐܦ ܗܕܐ ܕܗܢܐ ܕܝܠܗ ܕܗܘܐ
ܡܢܝܢ ܐܢܬ ܒܗ ܕܠܝܬ ܐܢܝ ܕܡܫܝܚ ܦܪܘ ܠܝ ܡܢܗ. ܐܠܐ
ܐܝܟܢܐ ܕܦܪܘܩܢ ܐܠܗܐ ܗ̱ܘ ܡܫܝܚ ܐܢܬ ܠܗܘܢ. ܀ ܣܒܝܐ
ܐܡܪ ܐܝܠܝܢ ܕܐܡܪܝܢ ܡܛܠ ܫܡܗ ܕܡܫܝܚܐ: ܘܠܐ ܦܠܓܝܢ
ܠܒܪܢܫܐ ܠܟܪܝܗܘܬܐ. ܫܪܝܘ ܡܫܚܝܢ ܡܢܗ ܐܠܗܐ. ܘܐܝܠܝܢ
ܕܐܡܪܝܢ ܫܪܝܐ ܕܘܟܝܐ ܢܠܒ ܡܢ ܗܕܐ. ܫܪܝܘ ܕܠܟܠܝܢ ܗ̇ܝ.
ܘܫܡܥ ܗܘܐ ܡܠܦܢܐ ܘܬܠܡܝܕܘܗܝ. ܗܘܘ ܘܦܪܘܩܘܗܝ. ܘܟܕ
ܦܪܝܫ ܗܘܘ ܠܗ ܡܢܗܘܢ ܗܘܘ ܠܗ. ܘܗܘܐ ܬܠܬܐ ܗܘܐ
ܠܦܘܪܐ ܦܢܝܬܐ: ܕܡܠܟܐ ܕܥܠܠܘ ܗܘܘ ܙܘܥܐ ܕܕܪܟܗܘܢ.
ܐܡܪ ܠܗ ܡܠܦܢܐ. ܡܬܦܠܫ ܐܢܬ ܐܦ ܗܫܐ: ܕܬܦܫ
ܒܡ̈ܠܐ ܡܢܡ ܘܗܘ ܡܠܝܐ. ܀ ܣܒܝܐ ܐܡܪ. ܡܢܡ ܫܟܐ ܗܘܝܬ
ܠܐ ܐܬܦܠܫܬ ܠܝ: ܗܫܐ ܕܗܘܐ ܫܟܬ ܐܢܐ: ܐܝܟܢܐ ܦܪܘܩ
ܐܢܬ ܕܡܬܦܠܫ ܐܢܐ ܠܝ: ܕܐܘܕܥ ܒܗܘܢ ܗ̇ܘ ܡܢܡ
ܕܐܫܬܟܚܬ ܒܗܘܢ ܀ ܀ ܡܠܦܢܐ ܐܡܪ. ܒܒܢܝܐ ܕܫܒܝܠ
ܘܡܬܢܝܢ ܡܢ ܗܠܝܢ ܡܬܢܐ ܐܢܐ ܕܐܫܬܥܝܟ: ܐܝܟ ܦܘܩܕܢܐ
ܕܬܠܡܝܕܐ. ܒܕܡܘܬܐ ܕܐܝܟܢܘܬܗܘܢ ܬܒܒ ܀ ܣܒܝܐ ܐܡܪ. ܐܢܬ
ܕܝܢ ܐܢܬ ܠܝ ܟܠ ܕܠܐ ܐܬܚܫܒܬ ܠܦܘܩܕܢܐ ܕܬܠܡܝܕܐ. ܕܗܘܐ
ܐܦ ܐܢܬ ܕܐܘܪܟܘܢ ܬܠܡܝܕܐ ܘܒܥܘܠܝܢ ܕܢܒܝܐ. ܒܒܪܬ ܟܠ
ܦܘܩܕܢܘܗܝ. ܒܗ̇ ܕܠܐ ܒܒܪܬ ܠܝ ܡܢܡ ܕܦܩܕ ܠܝ ܬܠܡܝܕܐ ܀
ܡܠܦܢܐ ܐܡܪ. ܟܠ ܕܐܬܒܪܬ ܙܘܥ ܒܒܝܬܝ ܐܢܒܪܬ ܡܒܠܢܐ.
ܐܝܟ ܒܒܪܐ ܡܦܠܓܢܐ ܀ ܣܒܝܐ ܐܡܪ. ܐܠܘ ܠܐ ܕܝܒܪܬܢ
ܘܫܒܩܬܢ ܘܦܪܘܬܢ ܘܐܢܒܝܬ ܬܠܬ ܒܫܢܐ. ܐܢܬ ܗܘܐ
ܠܡܫܟܚܘ ܕܐܢܒܪܬ ܙܘܥܝ ܒܒܫ. ܐܢ ܕܝܢ ܗܠܝܢ ܐܢܬ
ܒܡܫܒܚܬܐ. ܐܢܟܐ ܗܝ ܡܢܒܪܬ ܙܘܥܐ ܕܠܬܟ ܕܐܢܒܪܬ.
ܡܠܦܢܐ ܐܡܪ. ܠܐ ܡܒܪܟ ܠܝ ܗܠܝܢ ܕܐܢܒܪܬ: ܡܛܠ

ܕܝܢ ܒܐܝܠܘܠ܆ ܡܛܠ ܗܘܐ ܡܬܘܝܢܐ. ܘܐܬܬܚܝܠܘܗܝ ܗܘܘ ܡܢ
ܒܬ ܐܝܩܪܐ. ܘܐܡܪ ܗܘܐ ܠܗ. ܩܘܡ ܐܢܬ ܒܫܡ ܡܪܢ ܕܐܘܣܝܡ
ܐܢܬ ܒܗ܆ ܘܡܫܬܡܥ ܐܢܬ ܠܦܘܩܕܢܐ ܕܐܒܗ̈ܝܢ ܩܕܝܫ̈ܐ.
ܘܐܢ ܕܝܢ ܠܐ ܡܫܬܡܥ ܐܢܬ. ܒܣܘܦܐ ܡܪ̈ܝܪܐ ܚܒܪ ܐܠܐ
ܠܝ ܕܬܫܬܡܥ ܠܗܘܢ. ܀

ܣܒܐ ܐܡܪ. ܠܐ ܬܫܬܡܥܘܢ ܠܗܘܢ. ܘܐܦ ܠܐ ܕܬܫܬܡܥ
ܠܗܘܢ ܦܬܓܡܐ ܒܙܒܢ. ܘܐܦ ܠܐ ܐܢ ܗܘ ܕܕܐܢ ܐܢܬ
ܠ ܒܪ̈ܢܫܐ ܕܒܥܝܢ. ܐܦ ܡܢ ܐܝܠܝܢ ܕܡܫܘ ܩܕܝܫܐ ܀ ܡܬܘܝܢܐ
ܐܡܪ. ܒܫ̈ܠܡܐ ܢܗܘܐ ܐܠܝܐ. ܕܐܢ ܠܐ ܬܬܪܓܫ ܠܐ
ܐܫܟܘ ܡܢܝܢ ܕܦܓܪܐ ܘܡܢܘܪ ܕܠܐ ܬܫܬܘܫ ܒܟ. ܘܐܝܢܐ
ܐ ܦܪܘ ܠܝ ܡܥܝܢܐ ܗܘ ܕܦܠܓ ܐܢܬ ܠܗ ܀

ܣܒܐ ܐܡܪ. ܒܠܗܘܢ ܐܝܠܝܢ ܕܦܠܓܝܢ ܠܡܥܝܢܐ ܦܪ̈ܘܫܐ
ܐܢܘܢ ܕܡܥܝܢܝܢ. ܕܠܐ ܗܘܘ ܩܠܝܠܝܢ ܠܡܪ̈ܬܐ ܡܢ ܪ̈ܘܚܐ
ܕܒܪ̈ܝܬܐ ܀ ܡܬܘܝܢܐ ܐܡܪ. ܬܬܡܣ ܘܬܒܠܥ ܒܥܘܠܬܐ.
ܒܡܟܐ ܕܠܐ ܦܓܥ ܗܘܬ ܕܡܘܬܐ ܒܦܓܪܗ ܕܠܐ ܒܠܒ ܗܘܐ
ܒܗ ܀ ܣܒܐ ܐܡܪ. ܗܠܝܢ ܐܘܠܨܢܐ ܕܐܬܦܓܥܬ ܒܠܗܘܢ
ܕܡܪ̈ܝܪܝܢ ܒܦܓܪܗܘܢ. ܡܛܠܗܘܢ ܡܬܦܪܫܝܢ ܩܠܝܠܐ ܕܒܡܘܬܐ.
ܠܐܝܠܝܢ ܕܡܫܡܫܝܢ ܠܗܘܢ ܀ ܡܬܘܝܢܐ ܐܡܪ. ܐܝܟܢܐ
ܠܐܘܠܨܢܐ ܦܪܝܫ ܐܢܬܘܢ ܠܗܘܢ ܙܢܘܬܐ. ܘܠܬ̈ܫܘܒܚܬܐ
ܕܡܪ̈ܝܪܐ ܢܫܡܥܝܢ ܐܢܬܘܢ ܠܗܘܢ ܒܠܠܝܐ ܕܒܡܘܬܐ ܀

ܣܒܐ ܐܡܪ. ܠܘ ܕܝܠܝ ܗܝ ܗܕܐ ܕܐܫܬܐܠܬ ܥܠ ܗܠܝܢ.
ܡܛܠ ܕܠܐ ܫܘܝܐ ܒܒܘܪܘܬܝ ܕܐܫܡܥ ܦܢܘܢܝܐ ܕܗܠܝܢ. ܕܠܐ
ܡܕܝܢ ܐܢܐ. ܐܡܪܬ ܘܐܡܪ ܐܢܐ ܀ ܡܬܘܝܢܐ ܐܡܪ. ܐܢܬ
ܡܛܠ ܕܫܘܝܬ ܠܗܝܢ ܦܢܝܬ ܒܗܠܝܢ ܕܢܦܫ. ܐܢܐ ܡܚܘܪ ܐܢܐ
ܚܝ̈ܘܗܝ: ܗܠܝܢ ܕܚܕ̈ܝܢ ܒܗܘ ܗܢܐ: ܘܠܐ ܕܫ̈ܠܝܢ ܡܢܗ:
ܘܡܦܩܕ ܐܢܐ ܐܢ̈ܫܝܢ: ܕܫ̈ܡܥܝܢ ܢܦܫܗܘܢ ܕܡ̈ܠܟܐ ܘܠܐ
ܕܝܢ ܀ ܣܒܐ ܐܡܪ. ܐܢܬ ܗܘ ܒܠܚܘܕ ܐܢܫܐ ܠܐܠܗܐ.

ܠܬܫܥܝܬܐ. ܀ ܡܠܦܢܐ ܐܡܪ. ܠܐ ܬܗܘܐ ܒܪܝܫܐ ܡܪܝܫܐ:
ܗܘ ܐܝܢܐ ܕܐܬܩܢ ܒܗ ܨܒܝܢܗ. ܘܬܩܝܢ ܠܗܘܢ ܥܒܕ̈ܘܗܝ
ܝܒܐ ܕܬܠܡܝܕܐ ܀܀܀ ܚܒܝܒ ܐܡܪ. ܐܠܐ ܐܢܬܘܢ، ܘܗܘ ܗܢܐ
ܬܬܒܪܐ ܚܒܪܐ ܕܬܫܥܝܬܐ. ܫܦܝܪ ܐܡܪ ܐܢܬ ܕܬܫܐܠ ܐܢܐ
ܠܗ. ܐܝܟ ܕܡܢ ܟܠܗܘܢ ܕܡܘܫܐ ܘܡܛܠܬܗ ܕܒܬܪܝܗܐ: ܡܛܠ
ܟܠܗܘܢ ܕܒܢܝܢܗ ܗܘ: ܐܡܝܢܐ ܐܡܪ ܐܢܬ ܠܝ ܕܡܬܝܗܒ ܐܢܐ
ܠܗ: ܕܗܐ ܝܗܒܗ ܡܢܗ ܘܟܠܗܘܢ. ܀ ܡܠܦܢܐ ܐܡܪ. ܒܗ
ܒܗܕܐ ܕܠܐ ܢܦܫܐ ܐܢܬ ܕܬܫܬܡܥ ܠܗ ܡܬܝܗܒ ܐܢܬ ܠܗ ܀
ܚܒܝܒ ܐܡܪ. ܘܐܝܟ ܡܛܠ ܕܠܐ ܦܩܕ ܐܢܐ ܠܗ ܡܬܝܗܒ
ܐܢܐ ܠܗ. ܒܡܐ ܕܝܢ ܝܗܒܐ ܒܪ ܗܘܐ ܠܗ ܝܕܥܐ: ܕܟܠܗܘܢ
ܗܘܐ ܒܥܒܕܐ ܕܦܘܠܚܢܐ: ܘܡܫܝܚܐ ܕܡܫܝܚܘܗܝ، ܗܘܐ ܘܡܛܠܬܗ
ܗܘܐ ܒܬܪܝܗܐ ܀ ܘܟܕ ܥܒܕ ܗܘܐ ܡܠܦܢܐ ܕܗܒܢܐ ܐܡܪ
ܗܘܐ. ܟܕ ܗܘܐ ܕܢܬܒܥ ܕܠܐ ܚܘܒܐ. ܘܟܕ ܐܬܒܥ ܗܘܐ
ܡܢ ܫܡܥܐ ܐܡܪ ܠܗ. ܡܫܬܡܥ ܐܢܬ ܗܫܐ ܠܬܠܡܝܕܐ: ܘܐܝܟ
ܕܡܢ ܠܐ ܡܫܬܡܥ ܐܢܬ. ܡܛܘܠ ܦܘܩܕ ܐܢܐ ܠܟ. ܘܟܠ ܚܝܠܝܢ
ܡܫܬܡܥ ܐܢܐ ܠܟ: ܘܡܢ ܗܘ ܠܐܘܪܚܬܐ ܦܩܕ ܐܢܐ ܠܟܠܗܝܢ
ܕܟܠܢܫܐ ܬܐܡܪ. ܀܀

ܚܒܝܒ ܐܡܪ. ܗܠܝܢ ܠܘܩܒܠܐ ܕܗܐ ܡܬܦܢܠ ܐܢܬ ܠܝ
ܒܗܘܢ: ܐܬܐ ܙܒܢܝܢ ܘܡܝܬܪܝܢ: ܡܢ ܐܝܠܝܢ ܕܦܩܕܬ ܗܘܝܬ
ܦܩܕܬ ܒܪܝܫ ܕܐܬܡܠܟ. ܗ̇ܝ ܕܡܢ ܗܘ ܐܬܬܢܝܬ ܘܐܬܬܚܝܬ ܠܟ ܀܀
ܡܠܦܢܐ ܐܡܪ. ܐܪܡܐܗܘܢ، ܒܡܕܡܐ ܕܦܘܠܚܢܐ ܕܩܢܘܡܐ.
ܘܬܒܥܬ ܐܝܟ ܕܥܘܒܕ. ܘܟܕ ܡܬܒܥ ܗܘܐ ܐܡܪܝܢ ܠܗ. ܕܟܒܪ
ܠܩܠܗܘܢ. ܘܡܟܐ ܗܘܐ ܘܐܡܪ. ܕܫܡܥܐ ܐܢܘܢ ܦܬܓܡܘܗܝ.
ܘܡܢܗܘܢ ܕܫܟܪܝܢ ܠܗܘܢ ܒܡܟܟܘܢ ܐܒܘܬܟܘܢ. ܘܡܦܩ ܗܘܐ
ܡܠܦܢܐ: ܘܐܡܪܗܘܢ، ܗܘܘ ܠܒܝܬ ܐܒܗܬܐ. ܘܠܐ ܡܫܟܚ
ܗܘܐ ܠܗ ܕܢܟܠܠ ܒܡ ܐܢܫܘܬܗ ܘܟܕ ܩܪܝܬܗ. ܐܝܟ ܦܘܩܕܢܗ
ܕܕܝܢܐ. ܡܘܟܟܐ ܕܝܢ ܐܢܬܘܢ، ܗܘܐ ܐܢܕܐ ܕܬܠܡܝܕܐ ܀ ܒܬܪܐ

ܕܢܦܠܐ ܗܘܐ ܥܠܘܗܝ. ܐܫܬܟܚܬ ܗܘܬ ܠܗܘܢ ܠܥܒܪܝܐ ܕܡܕܝܢܬܐ: ܘܐܘܕܥܘܗܝ. ܠܕܝܢܐ ܥܠ ܡܕܡ ܕܚܙܘ ܗܘܘ. ܘܐܬܬܥܝܪܬ ܗܘܬ ܕܝܢܐ ܥܠ ܐܝܠܝܢ ܕܐܚܝܕܝܢ ܗܘܘ ܠܗ ܠܥܒܕܐ. ܕܥܠ ܡܢܐ ܐܬܝܬ ܘܐܬܒܝܫܬ ܠܕܝܢܐ: ܕܠܐ ܒܦܘܩܕܢܐ ܕܠܗ ܕܕܝܢܐ. ܘܠܐܬܦܠܘܢܐ ܐܡܪ ܗܘܐ ܠܗ. ܕܠܐ ܙܕܩ ܗܘܐ ܠܓܒܪܐ ܕܥܒܕ ܪܫܐ ܠܥܘܠܘܗܝ: ܕܗܟܢܐ ܢܬܟܠ ܗܘܐ ܥܠ ܐܝܕܗ ܕܠܗ: ܘܢܦܠ ܗܘܐ ܒܦܘܩܕܢܐ ܕܡܠܟܐ: ܕܢܦܩܘ ܥܠ ܚܝܒܐ ܡܢܘܕܐ ܕܒܠܘܥܐ ܢܐܡܪ ܀ ܬܐܦܠܘܢܐ ܐܡܪ ܠܐ ܗܘܐ ܥܠ ܚܒܪܝ ܐܬܢܟܠܬ. ܘܐܦ ܠܐ ܕܐܬܟܠ ܒܦܘܩܕܢܐ ܕܐܚܝܕܝܢ ܡܠܟܐ ܚܙܬ. ܐܝܟܐ ܓܝܪ ܡܕܝܢܐ ܐܢܬ، ܡܕܡ ܕܥܒܕܬܝ: ܕܗܕܐ ܡܩܪܒ ܗܘܝܬ ܕܐܥܒܕ. ܡܫܐܠܐ ܕܝܢ ܐܫܬܐܠܬܗ. ܐܢܬܬܐ ܕܐܦ ܥܒܕܬܝ ܬܟܝܠܬ ܗܘܝܬ ܒܐܝܕܝ: ܕܐܝܢܐ ܗܘܬ ܘܐܘܚܕܐ ܕܝܠܝ ܗܘ ܕܒܫܐܪܘܬܗ ܐܬܝܬ ܠܗܪܟܐ. ܐܘ ܕܠܡܢܐ ܩܛܠܬܐ ܕܥܒܕܬܝ ܐܝܬܝܗ ܗܘܐ ܒܗ ܐܚܪܢܐ. ܘܒܗ ܫܥܬܐ ܗܘܬ ܡܢܗ. ܕܗܘ ܒܣܒܝܠܗ ܐܬܐ ܗܘܐ. ܫܦܝܠܐܝܬ ܢܛܪܬܗ ܠܒܪܬܐ ܡܫܘܕܪܐ ܕܐܘܦܝܡܝܐ ܕܐܬܒܝܫܬܝ ܀

ܘܦܩܕ ܗܘܐ ܗܓܡܘܢܐ ܡܢ ܥܠܝܗ. ܘܐܚܠܦܗ ܗܘܘ ܠܥܒܕܐ ܡܢܗܘܢ ܀ ܦܠܓܘܬܐ ܐܡܪ ܗܘܐ ܩܛܘܠ ܡܕܡ ܕܥܒܕܬܝ. ܘܒܪ ܗܘܐ ܕܐܬܐܠܨܬ ܡܢܗ. ܘܐܡܪ ܠܗ. ܕܐܢܬܬܐ ܥܒܕܬܝ ܘܗܝ ܐܢܬܐ ܐܬܬܝ. ܘܗܝ ܐܬܬܝ. ܐܡܪ ܠܗ ܣܦܝܩ ܥܒܕܝ. ܘܐܢܬ، ܡܢ ܬܠܝܬܐ ܩܢܘܬܐ. ܘܥܒܕ ܐܝܟ ܡܫܒܚܢܐ ܀ ܀ ܀

ܗܓܡܘܢܐ ܐܡܪ. ܡܛܠ ܡܢܐ ܚܪܬ ܥܠ ܦܘܩܕܢܐ ܕܡܠܟܐ. ܘܡܫܡܫ ܐܢܬ ܒܥܒܕܬܝ. ܡܕܡ ܕܠܐ ܦܩܕ ܠܝ ܡܢ ܡܠܟܐ. ܘܠܐ ܢܦܫܐ ܐܢܬ ܠܡܪܕܘ ܠܗܘܢ ܕܡܢܚܡ ܠܗ ܡܠܟܐ ܀ ܣܦܝܩ ܐܡܪ. ܣܡ ܒܩܘܦܝܣܐ. ܠܐ ܗܘܐ ܠܡܪܕܐ ܕܩܝܣܐ ܘܡܢܚܡ ܣܒܪ. ܩܘܡܘ ܕܠܐ ܦܠܘܢ ܡܕܡ. ܘܐܦ ܠܐ ܠܡܪܕܘܢ ܡܕܡ. ܐܠܐ ܘܡܢܚܡ ܠܐܠܗܐ ܕܥܒܕ ܐܠܘ

ܘܐܫܬܡܥܗ ܗܘܐ ܠܟܠܗ ܒܝܬܗ. ܘܐܘܟܠܘܗܝ ܗܘܘ ܒܒܝܬܗ
ܠܐܘܣܦܪܝܢ ܕܡܠܟܘܬܐ. ܘܟܠ ܗܘܐ ܗܘ ܬܐܓܘܢܐ. ܘܐܘܕܥܗ
ܗܘܐ ܠܡܠܟܘܬܐ ܘܐܡܪ ܗܘܐ ܠܗ: ܕܐܬܐ ܫܠܝܚܐ ܕܡܢ
ܬܠܡܝܕܗ: ܐܝܟܐ ܕܒܥܝܐ ܗܘܬ ܠܗ ܪܒܘܬܟ. ܘܐܡܪ ܗܘܐ
ܡܠܟܘܬܐ: ܕܢܦܩ ܗܢܐ ܕܐܬܝܗ ܘܐܝܟܢܐ ܐܫܬܡܥܘܗܝ ܗܘܘ.
ܘܡܢܐ ܓܒܪ ܐܝܟܢܐ ܕܐܝܬܘܗܝ ܗܘܐ ܀ ܐܡܪ ܠܗ ܬܐܓܘܢܐ.
ܗܘܐ ܒܚܝܪܘܬܗ ܐܬܐ ܠܡܪܒܐ ܕܠܐ ܡܦܠܓܐ ܕܐܝܟ. ܒܪ
ܠܐ ܐܝܟ ܐܢܫ ܒܗ. ܘܟܕ ܫܡܥ ܗܘܐ ܡܠܟܘܬܐ:
ܐܬܟܪܝܪ ܗܘܐ ܠܒܗ ܣܓܝ. ܘܗܟܢܐ ܐܡܪ ܗܘܐ. ܕܗܢܐ
ܕܗܟܢܐ ܓܒܪ: ܡܣܬܪܘ ܒܣܦܪ ܟܠ ܡܕܡ. ܘܫܡܥܬ ܐܝܟ ܠܐ
ܕܝܢܐ. ܘܡܛܠ ܕܗܟܢܐ ܓܒܪ: ܠܐ ܙܕܩ ܕܢܗܘܘܢ ܒܠܒܗ
ܪ̈ܚܡܐ. ܘܐܦ ܠܐ ܕܐܬܦܪܣܘܢ ܘܢܦܩܘܢ ܒܠܒܗ ܚ̈ܫܒܬܐ
ܐܒܗܬܐ ܕܒܪܢܫ ܒܠܒܗ ܡܢ ܩܠܝܠܐ. ܘܠܐ ܙܕܩ ܗܘ ܠܝ ܕܐܢܐ
ܪܘܚܐ ܒܒܝܬܗ: ܐܝܟ ܕܬܬܪܐܝܬ ܢܦܠܘܢ ܚ̈ܘܫܒܘܗܝ ܘܪ̈ܚܡܘܗܝ
ܡ̈ܕܝܢܬܐ. ܘܐܡܪ ܒܗ ܥܠܝܡܐ: ܕܬܘܒ ܠܐ ܢܬܪܫܘܢ
ܠܡܕܝܢܬ ܀ ܘܟܕ ܥܠܝܡܐ ܒܠܚܘܕ ܗܘܘ ܘܦܩܕܝܢ ܒܠܒܗ ܒܠ
ܬܪܥܐ ܕܒܝܬ ܕܝܢܐ: ܡܢܗܘܢ ܕܝܢ ܡܢ ܟܠ ܐܘܦܣܝܢ. ܘܡܢܗܘܢ
ܡܢ ܟܠ ܡ̈ܕܝܢܬܐ. ܐܝܬ ܗܘܐ ܕܝܢ ܡܢܗܘܢ ܕܐܬܟܢܫܘ ܗܘܘ
ܠܗ. ܕܒܫܐܝܬ ܓܒܪܬ ܕܐܬܦܬ ܘܐܬܒܣܝܬ ܠܐܝܠܝܢ ܕܩܪܝܢ ܗܘܘ
ܠܝ ܕܠܐ ܡܦܠܓܐ ܕܕܝܢܐ. ܘܐܝܬ ܗܘܐ ܬܘܒ ܕܐܬܟܢܫܘ ܗܘܘ
ܠܗ. ܕܫܦܝܪ ܒܓܒܪܬ ܕܚܝܪܘܬܟ ܐܬܦܬ ܘܐܬܒܣܝܬ. ܘܬܘܒ ܡܢ
ܗܢ ܕܡܦܠܓܐ ܕܕܝܢܐ ܢܬܦܬܚܘܢ ܗܘܐ. ܗܫܐ ܗܘ ܓܒܪ ܡܬܕܒܪܐ
ܡܕܝܢܬܟ ܕܒܫܝܢܐ: ܕܐܦܪܝܫܘ ܗܝ. ܘܠܐ ܗܘܐ ܕܡܦܠܓܐ
ܕܒ̈ܝܫܬܐ ܀ ܀

ܩܕܝܡ ܕܝܢ ܕܫܡܥܘ ܗܘܘ ܫܪ̈ܝܪܐ ܕܡܕܝܢܬܐ ܡܢ ܐܝܠܝܢ ܕܐܬܩܪܝܢ
ܠܗ: ܟܕ ܦܩܕܝܢ ܗܘܘ ܥܠ ܬܪܥܐ ܕܒܝܬ ܕܝܢܐ. ܘܐܦ ܗܝ
ܗܕܐ ܕܐܬܐ ܗܘܐ ܒܫܠܝܐ ܓܒܪ ܬܐܓܘܢܐ: ܘܠܐ ܝܕܥܐ

ܗܐ ܐܢ ܢܒܘܣ ܡܢ ܗܕܐ. ܫܘܬܐ ܕܥܢܝܐ ܦܪܩ ܗܘ ܠܗ ܠܟܠ
ܐܢܫ ܕܐܬܐ: ܘܕܢܦܠ ܡܢܗ ܠܐ ܡܫܟܚ. ܡܛܠ ܕܝܘܡܐ ܗܘ،
ܗܕܐ ܟܠ ܟܠܗܘܢ ܝܠܕܘܗܝ ܕܐܕܡ ܀ ܘܗܟܢ ܗܘܐ ܝܘܚܢܢ
ܘܐܬܐ ܠܐܘܪܚܗ ܒܫܠܝܘܬ. ܟܕ ܡܠܦܢ ܗܘܐ ܝܬܝܪ ܠܬܠܡܝܕܐ
ܘܟܬܒܘܗܝ ܠܣܘܪܝܐ. ܘܡܫܡܫܢܘܬܗ ܠܡܣܟܢܐ ܕܒܥܐ. ܘܡܛܠ ܗܘܐ
ܠܗ ܫܪܪܐ. ܠܘܬ ܬܐܘܦܝܠܐ ܗܟܢܐ: ܐܝܟܢܐ ܕܪܚܡܐ ܗܘܐ
ܕܐܦܝܣܐ ܕܡܫܡܫܢܐ: ܘܐܡܪ ܗܘܐ. ܕܐܝܟܢܐ ܐܝܟܢܐ ܝܘܚܢܢ ܕܡܢ
ܬܠܡܝܕܐ ܕܡܪܢ ܐܠܗܘܢ ܠܝ. ܘܐܡܪ ܗܘܐ ܠܗ ܗܘ ܬܐܘܦܝܠܐ.
ܐܢ ܗܘ ܕܠܐ ܚܙܝܬ ܐܝܟ ܕܐܬܬܐ ܥܠܝ̈ܢ: ܐܬܒܥܐ ܠܝ
ܕܐܡܪ ܐܢܐ ܠܟ. ܘܗܝܕܝܢ ܐܦ ܠܐܢܫܐ ܕܐܬܬܐ ܗܘܬ. ܘܗܘܐ
ܬܡܢ ܒܟܢܫܐ ܗܢܐ ܘܗܕܐ ܕܐܬܬܐ ܥܠܝ̈ܢ ܘܡܛܠܬܐ ܒܗܝ.
ܘܡܠܬܟ ܗܢܐ: ܐܢ ܠܐ ܢܗܘܐ ܘܠܐ ܢܬܒ. ܘܕܐܬܡܢܬܟ
ܘܕܟܠܢ ܩܪܝܬܟ ܠܐ ܬܐܡܪ ܗܟܢ. ܠܐ ܓܝܪ ܐܢܐ ܚܙܝܬ ܠܗܘܢ
ܗܟܢ. ܘܡܛܠ ܗܘ ܩܘܪܒܐ ܫܘܝܢ ܒܟܠܗ ܚܘܫܒܝ. ܘܚܙܝܬ
ܠܗܘܢ ܡܫܡܫܢܐ. ܡܛܠ ܕܟܠܗܘܢ ܠܐ ܦܩܕܘ ܥܠܝܗܐ ܗܟܢ
ܕܟܠ ܡܣܟܢܐ. ܘܐܡܪ ܠܐ ܡܬܚܫܒ ܐܢܬ ܠܝ ܒܗܠܝܢ ܕܐܡܪܬ
ܠܝ: ܡܛܠ ܐܢܐ ܡܢ ܕܝܠܝ. ܡܛܠ ܕܐܦ ܗܘ ܕܐܬܬܚܙܝܬ
ܠܙܢܐ ܕܐܬܪܐ. ܡܢ ܫܘܬܐ ܕܥܢܝܐ ܠܐ ܦܠܛ ܐܢܬ. ܐܝܟ
ܕܡܣܟܢܐ ܕܟܠܗܘܢ ܕܥܒܕܘ ܟܠܝܢ ܀
ܐܡܪ ܠܗ ܝܘܚܢܢ ܠܬܐܘܦܝܠܐ. ܐܢܐ ܠܐ ܗܘܐ ܡܛܠ ܐܢܫܘܬ،
ܘܕܟܠ ܡܢܗ، ܐܬܒܛܠ ܠܝ: ܐܠܐ ܟܠ ܚܕ ܕܠܐ ܢܐܟܠܘܢ.
ܐܦ ܟܠ ܗܕܐ ܐܬܬܚܡܬ ܦܠܓ: ܕܠܐ ܐܫܬܟܚܬ ܗܘܬ
ܒܡܢܬ، ܒܗܘܢܐ ܕܟܠܢ ܗܘܐ ܡܫܡܫܢܐ. ܘܡܛܠܬ، ܗܐ ܕܝܢ
ܩܘܕܫܐ ܟܕ ܬܘܠܐ. ܘܐܫܬܒܪܬ ܠܗ ܐܝܟ ܒܪܘܫܐ. ܡܛܠ ܗܘܝܐ
ܐܢ ܗܘ ܕܠܐ ܡܬܚܫܒ ܐܢܬ ܠܝ ܕܐܬܟܠܝܬ ܡܢ ܡܫܡܫܢܐ:
ܐܢܐ ܟܠܝܘܡ، ܥܕܠ ܐܢܐ ܘܡܬܬܚܝܒܐ ܐܢܐ ܠܗ ܀ ܘܟܕ ܫܡܥ
ܗܘܐ ܬܐܘܦܝܠܐ ܕܗܟܢܐ ܐܡܪ ܗܘܐ ܠܗ. ܠܟܠܗ ܗܘܐ ܫܒܩܬ.

ܒܣܐܢܬ ܟܠ ܕܘܟ. ܘܦܣܩ ܠܗܘܢ ܦܘܣܩܢܐ ܕܡܠܟܐ ܘܠܐ ܕܚܠ. ܘܟܕ ܫܡܥ ܗܘܐ ܗܓܡܘܢܐ ܗܠܝܢ. ܐܬܡܠܝ ܚܡܬܐ ܥܠܘܗܝ ܕܚܒܝܒ. ܘܟܬܒ ܗܘܐ ܐܓܪܬܐ. ܘܫܕܪ ܗܘܐ ܘܐܘܕܥܗ ܗܘܐ ܠܠܝܣܢܝܘܣ ܡܠܟܐ ܥܠ ܐܝܠܝܢ ܕܥܒܕ ܗܘܐ ܚܒܝܒ. ܘܕܢܐܠܗ ܗܘܐ ܘܒܥܐ ܡܢܗ ܦܘܣܩܢܐ ܡܬܦܩܕ ܗܘܐ ܥܠܘܗܝ. ܘܥܠ ܐܝܠܝܢ ܕܠܐ ܨܒܝܢ ܕܢܕܒܚܘܢ. ܐܦ ܦܘܣܩܢܐ ܢܦܩ ܗܘܐ ܕܢܬܩܛܠ ܗܘܐ ܥܠܝܗ: ܐܠܐ ܠܐ ܢܦܩ ܗܘܐ. ܕܡܬܢܝܐ ܢܦܩ ܗܘܐ: ܠܐܝܠܝܢ ܕܠܐ ܡܬܛܫܝܢ ܗܘܘ. ܡܛܠ ܕܫܒܩܘ ܗܘܘ: ܕܩܘܣܛܢܛܝܢܘܣ ܐܝܛܠܝܐ: ܒܓܠܝܐ ܘܒܐܣܦܢܝܐ ܒܪܛܢܝܐ ܐܬܘܬܗ ܘܠܐ ܡܬܪܚܫ. ܘܦܩܕ ܗܘܐ ܠܝܣܢܝܘܣ ܡܠܟܐ ܠܠܘܣܢܝܘܣ ܗܓܡܘܢܐ. ܕܐܝܟܢܐ ܕܫܦܝܪܐ ܐܫܟܚܝܗ ܗܘܐ ܘܢܥܒܕ ܗܘܐ ܥܠ ܦܘܩܕܢܝ. ܦܩܕܬ ܡܠܟܘܬܗ ܕܒܢܘܪܐ ܢܐܩܕ. ܘܫܪܟܐ ܕܐܚܪ̈ܢܐ ܐܝܠܝܢ ܕܠܐ ܡܬܬܦܝܣܝܢ ܕܢܕܒܚܘܢ ܒܚܪܒܬܐ ܕܣܝܦܐ ܢܐܒܕܘܢ ∴ ∴

ܟܕ ܕܝܢ ܐܬܐ ܗܘܐ ܗܢܐ ܦܘܣܩܢܐ ܠܡܕܝܢܬܐ ܕܐܘܪܗܝ. ܚܒܝܒ ܐܝܢܐ ܕܡܛܠܬܗ ܗܘܬ ܗܘܬ ܐܓܪܬܐ. ܒܟܢ ܗܘܐ ܠܐܬܪܐ ܕܙܘܓܡܐ ܕܫܡܫ ܗܘܐ ܐܦ ܬܡܢ ܒܡܫܐܢܬ. ܘܟܕ ܫܡܥ ܗܘܐ ܗܓܡܘܢܐ ܒܫܡܗ ܒܦܢܝܬܗ: ܘܒܟܠܗ ܐܬܪܐ ܕܫܪ̈ܝܗ ܘܠܐ ܐܫܬܟܚ. ܦܩܕ ܗܘܐ ܕܢܬܬܠܒܟܘܢ ܗܘܬ ܐܢܫܘܬܗ ܘܟܠ ܩܪ̈ܝܒܘܗ. ܘܠܟܢ ܗܘܘ ܘܐܣܪܘܢ ܐܢܘܢ ܒܦܪܙܠܐ ܠܐܡܗ ܘܠܫܪܟܐ ܕܐܢܫܘܬܗ. ܘܐܦ ܡܢ ܒܢ̈ܝ ܩܪܝܬܗ. ܘܐܝܬܝܘ ܐܢܘܢ ܠܡܕܝܢܬܐ. ܘܚܒܫܘ ܐܢܘܢ ܒܒܝܬ ܐܣܝܪ̈ܐ. ܘܟܕ ܫܡܥ ܗܘܐ ܚܒܝܒ ܗܕܐ ܕܗܘܬ ܗܘܬ. ܡܬܥܝܩ ܗܘܐ ܒܪܘܚܗ ܘܪܢܐ ܗܘܐ ܒܬܪܥܝܬܗ. ܕܦܩܚ ܗܘ ܠܝ ܕܐܙܠ ܘܐܬܚܘܐ ܠܪܝܫܐ ܕܐܬܪܐ. ܡܛܠ ܡܢ ܗܕܐ ܕܐܦܘܗܝ ܒܟܣܝܐ: ܘܢܦܠܘܢ ܐܚܪ̈ܢܐ ܘܢܬܟܠܠܘܢ ܒܟܠܝܠܗ: ܘܐܫܬܟܚ ܠܝ ܒܟܣܝܐ ܙܟܐ. ܗܢܐ ܟܕ ܡܟܪ ܠܗ ܥܕܬܐ ܕܟܪܣܛܝܢܘܬܐ ܠܐܢܫܐ ܕܢܚܘܪ ܡܢ ܩܕܝܫܘܬܐ ܕܟܪܣܛܝܢܘܬܐ.

ܣܗܕܘܬܐ ܕܚܒܝܒ ܡܫܡܫܢܐ.

ܒܐܝܪܚ ܐܒ: ܕܫܢܬ ܫܬܡܐܐ ܘܥܣܪܝܢ ܕܡܠܟܘܬܗ ܕܐܠܟܣܢܕܪܘܣ ܡܩܕܘܢܝܐ: ܒܗܘܦܛܝܐ ܕܠܝܩܢܝܘܣ ܘܕܩܘܣܛܢܛܝܢܘܣ: ܕܐܝܬܝܗ̇ ܫܢܬܐ ܕܐܬܡܠܟ ܗܘܐ ܒܗ̇: ܒܐܝܦܪܟܘܬܐ ܕܐܘܠܝܣ ܘܕܟܪܝܢ: ܒܝܘܡܝ ܩܘܢܐ ܐܦܝܣܩܘܦܐ ܕܐܘܪܗܝ. ܓܙܪ ܗܘܐ ܗܘ ܠܝܩܢܝܘܣ ܪܕܘܦܝܐ ܠܥܕܬܐ: ܘܠܟܢܫܐ ܟܠܗ ܕܟܪܣܛܝܢܐ: ܒܬܪ ܪܕܘܦܝܐ ܗ̇ܘ ܩܕܡܝܐ: ܕܓܙܪ ܗܘܐ ܕܕܩܠܛܝܢܘܣ ܡܠܟܐ. ܘܓܙܪ ܗܘ ܠܝܩܢܝܘܣ ܡܠܟܐ. ܕܢܗܘܘܢ ܗܘܘ ܕܒܚܐ ܘܢܣܟܐ: ܘܫܠܡܬܐ ܒܟܠ ܕܘܟ ܢܬܩܪܒܢ ܗܘܝ. ܒܡܕܝܢܬܐ ܘܠܒܪܝܬܐ ܙܥܘܪ ܗܘ ܢܦܩܘܢ ܗܘܘ. ܘܟܕ ܡܬܦܪܣܝܢ ܗܘܘ ܦܘܩܕܢܐ. ܚܒܝܒ ܡܚܝܠ ܗܘܐ ܒܐܬܪܘܬܗܘܢ ܕܟܪܣܛܝܢܐ ܐܚܝܢ: ܘܠܐ ܕܚܝܠ ܗܘܐ ܡܢ ܪܕܘܦܝܐ. ܡܛܠ ܕܩܪܝܢܐ ܗܘܐ ܡܢܗܘܢ ܕܡܬܪܕܦܝܢ ܗܘܘ ܡܢ ܡܢܗܘܢ ܕܪܕܦܝܢ ܗܘܘ. ܚܒܝܒ ܕܝܢ ܐܝܟܢܐ ܕܐܝܬܘܗܝ ܗܘܐ ܡܢ ܬܠܝܗܐ ܩܪܝܬܐ: ܘܒܟܢܫܐ ܗܘܐ ܡܫܡܫܢܐ: ܘܩܪܐ ܗܘܐ ܠܟܬܒܐ ܕܩܘܕܫܐ ܒܥܐܕܘܬܐ. ܘܡܫܬܡܥ ܗܘܐ: ܘܦܪܐ ܗܘܐ ܒܬܒܐ: ܘܡܠܒܒ ܗܘܐ ܘܡܫܝܢ ܗܘܐ ܒܡܠܬܗ ܠܩܛܝܢܐ. ܘܢܬܗܪ ܗܘܐ ܠܗܘܢ. ܕܢܬܦܫܩܘܢ ܗܘܘ ܒܐܪܥܐ ܕܡܫܝܚܝܘܬܗܘܢ. ܘܕܠܐ ܢܕܚܠܘܢ ܗܘܘ ܡܢ ܪܕܘܦܝܐ. ܘܡܙܗܪ ܗܘܐ ܠܗܘܢ. ܘܟܕ ܩܛܝܢܐ ܡܬܚܙܝܢ ܗܘܘ ܒܡܠܘܗܝ, ܘܡܬܚܝܠܝܢ ܗܘܘ ܒܬܟܬܒܗ, ܫܡܝܥܬܐ: ܟܕ ܚܙܝܢ ܗܘܘ: ܕܠܐ ܢܕܚܠܘܢ ܗܘܘ ܒܡܪܕܘܬܐ ܕܣܒܪܝܢ ܗܘܘ ܒܗ. ܘܟܕ ܫܡܥܘ ܗܘܘ ܫܪܝܪܐ ܕܡܕܝܢܬܐ: ܐܝܠܝܢ ܕܗܢܘܢ ܦܩܝܕܝܢ ܗܘܘ ܡܛܠܬܗ ܕܗܝܡܢܘܬܐ ܗܕܐ. ܟܠܗ ܗܘܘ ܘܐܘܕܥܘܗ, ܠܠܘܣܢܝܘܣ ܗܓܡܘܢܐ ܕܐܬܪܐ ܗܘܐ ܒܡܕܝܢܬܐ ܕܐܘܪܗܝ. ܘܐܡܪܝܢ ܠܗ. ܕܚܒܝܒ ܐܝܢܐ ܕܐܝܬܘܗܝ, ܡܫܡܫܢܐ ܒܬܠܝܗܐ ܩܪܝܬܐ. ܡܬܚܪܐ ܘܡܫܬܥܐ

ܕܪ̈ܗܘܡܝܐ ܡܕܝܢܬܐ: ܘܡܩܒܠܐ ܗܘܬ ܐܝܕܐ ܕܟܗܢܘܬܐ
ܠܗ ܠܒܪܫܡܝܐ ܡܢ ܐܒܫܠܡܐ ܕܗܘܐ ܐܦܝܣܩܘܦܐ ܒܐܘܪܗܝ.
ܘܐܒܫܠܡܐ ܡܩܒܠܐ ܗܘܬ ܠܗ ܐܝܕܐ ܡܢ ܦܠܘܛ ܡܕܝܢܐ.
ܘܦܠܘܛ ܡܩܒܠܐ ܗܘܬ ܠܗ ܐܝܕܐ ܡܢ ܣܪܦܝܘܢ ܐܦܝܣܩܘܦܐ
ܕܐܢܛܝܘܟܝ. ܘܣܪܦܝܘܢ ܡܩܒܠܐ ܗܘܬ ܠܗ ܐܝܕܐ ܡܢ
ܙܦܝܪܝܢܘܣ ܐܦܝܣܩܘܦܐ ܕܪ̈ܗܘܡܝܐ. ܘܙܦܝܪܝܢܘܣ ܕܪ̈ܗܘܡܝܐ ܩܒܠ
ܗܘܐ ܐܝܕܐ ܡܢ ܒܝܩܛܘܪ ܕܬܡܢ ܕܪ̈ܗܘܡܝܐ. ܘܒܝܩܛܘܪ ܩܒܠ
ܗܘܐ ܐܝܕܐ ܡܢ ܐܠܘܬܪܝܣ. ܘܐܠܘܬܪܝܣ ܩܒܠ ܗܘܐ ܡܢ ܣܘܛܝܪ.
ܘܣܘܛܝܪ ܩܒܠ ܗܘܐ ܡܢ ܐܢܝܩܛܘܣ. ܘܐܢܝܩܛܘܣ ܩܒܠ ܗܘܐ
ܡܢ ܦܝܘܣ. ܘܦܝܘܣ ܩܒܠ ܗܘܐ ܡܢ ܛܠܝܣܦܘܪܘܣ. ܘܛܠܝܣܦܘܪܘܣ ܩܒܠ
ܗܘܐ ܡܢ ܣܝܣܛܘܣ. ܘܣܝܣܛܘܣ ܩܒܠ ܗܘܐ ܡܢ ܐܠܟܣܢܕܪܘܣ.
ܘܐܠܟܣܢܕܪܘܣ ܩܒܠ ܗܘܐ ܡܢ ܐܘܪܝܣܛܘܣ. ܘܐܘܪܝܣܛܘܣ ܩܒܠ ܗܘܐ
ܡܢ ܩܠܝܛܘܣ. ܘܩܠܝܛܘܣ ܩܒܠ ܗܘܐ ܡܢ ܐܢܘܣ. ܘܐܢܘܣ ܩܒܠ ܗܘܐ
ܡܢ ܫܡܥܘܢ ܟܐܦܐ ܘܫܡܥܘܢ ܟܐܦܐ ܩܒܠ ܗܘܐ ܡܢ ܡܪܢ
ܥܡ ܫ̈ܠܝܚܐ ܚܒܪ̈ܘܗܝ. ܒܝܘܡܐ ܕܚܡܫܝܢ ܕܣܘܠܩܗ ܕܡܪܢ
ܕܠܘܬ ܐܒܘܗܝ ܡܫܒܚܐ. ܕܐܝܬܘܗܝ ܗܘ ܐܘܚܕܢܐ ܒܚܝܪܢ:
ܕܐܝܬܘܗܝ ܥܡܗ ܬܫܒܘܚܬܐ ܕܡܠܟܘܬܗ ܕܠܒܪܝܬܗ ܡܢ ܩܕܡ
ܒܗܘܦܟܝܐ ܕܪܘܩܐ ܘܕܡܠܟܘܬܗ ܕܐܝܬܘܗܝ ܥܡܗ ܗܝ، ܥܡܗ
ܬܠܬܝܘܬܐ ܘܐܬܒܪܝ ܘܚܕܐ. ܒܥܠܡ ܬܠܬܝܘܬܐ ܠܥܠ ܘܐܡܝܢ.
ܗܘܐ ܕܢܚܘܐ ܕܦܪܘܩܢ ܒܟܠܗܝܢ ܐܝܟ ܗܘܕܥܬܐ ܕܐܒܗܝܢ ܣܡ
ܒܐܠܦܝܢ ܫܢܝܐ ܕܒܥܠ ܐܘܪܗܝ. ܕܠܐ ܦܓܥܐ ܡܕܡ ܕܟܠ
ܡܕܡ ܢܩܘܕܒ.

ܫܠܡܬ ܣܗܕܘܬܐ ܕܒܪܫܡܝܐ.

ܐܦܝܣܩܘܦܐ ܕܐܘܪܗܝ ⁘

ܕܫܠܡܘܬܗܘܢ܁ ܘܐܢ ܐܢܫ ܟܠܐ ܠܗܘܢ ܡܢ ܒܬܪ ܗܢܐ ܦܘܩܕܢ܆ ܗ̇ܘ
ܫܘܝܐ ܕܦܩܕ ܗܘܐ ܠܝ ܕܢܬܒܥ ܥܠ ܐܝܠܝܢ ܕܫܛܝܢ ܦܘܩܕܢܝ.
ܗ̣ܘ ܗ̇ܢ ܦܩܕܢ ܕܢܬܒܥ ܥܠ ܐܝܠܝܢ ܕܡܫܛܠܝܢ ܠܗܢܐ ܦܘܩܕܢܐ
ܕܟܪܣܛܝܢܘܬܢ ܀ ܘܟܕ ܐܬܦܪܣ ܗܘܐ ܗܢܐ ܦܘܩܕܢܐ
ܕܟܪܣܛܝܢܘܬܐ ܕܟܠܗܝܢ܆ ܢܦܩܬ ܟܠܗ̇ ܡܕܝܢܬܐ. ܕܗ̣ܘܐ ܗܘܐ
ܥܒܝܐ ܘܒܘܝܐ ܥܠ ܟܠܢ. ܘܦܬܚ ܗܘܐ ܕܢܚܐ ܘܢܗܪܐܘܗܝ ܗܘܘ
ܠܟܪܣܛܝܢܐ ܕܢܦܩܬ ܗܘܐ ܠܒܪܗ̇. ܘܫܠܡܘ ܗܘܘ ܒܪ̈ܘܦܠܛܝܢܐ
ܩ̈ܕܡܝܐ ܠܒܝܬ ܕܝܢܐ. ܘܗܘܠܟܐܗ̇ ܪܒܐ ܕܐܢܫܘܬܐ ܕܡܕܝܢܬܐ.
ܘܡܠܟܘܗܝ ܗܘܘ ܠܟܪܣܛܝܢܐ܆ ܒܐܘܪܚܐ ܙܟܐ ܘܡܫܝܢܬܐ. ܟܕ
ܐܬܟܢܫܝܢ ܗܘܘ ܡܙܡܪܝܢ، ܒܥ̈ܕܬܐ ܐܝܟ ܥܝܕܗܘܢ. ܘܒܥ̈ܐ ܕܙ̈ܒܢܐ.
ܕܫ̈ܒܚܐ. ܘܡܫܒܚܝܢ ܗܘܘ ܘܡܘܕܝܢ ܗܘܘ ܠܗ ܠܡܫܝܚܐ. ܘܦܬܚܝܢ
ܗܘܘ ܠܗ ܬܪ̈ܥܝܢܐ ܙ̈ܕܩܐ. ܣܒܪܝܢ ܕܐܢܝܟܠ ܫܡܗܐ. ܘܐܡܪ
ܗܘܐ ܠܗܘܢ. ܕܪܘܚܐ ܐܝܬܝ ܐܟܦܢܛܘܢ. ܡܢ ܩ̈ܕܡܐ ܕܡܢ
ܘܫܪܝܐ ܕܐܪܒܝܠ ܘܕܫܒ̈ܝܗܘܢ، ܙܕܩ ܐܢܐ. ܘܐܡܪܝܢ ܗܘܘ ܠܗ:
ܕܡܫܒܚ ܗܘ ܠܝ ܡܢܟ: ܕܐܡܪ ܡܠܦܢܐ ܕܥܕܬܐ. ܕܪܒܢܐ
ܐܝܟ ܡܢܐ ܕܐܬܬܘܣܦ ܡܢܝܢܐ ܗܘ ܡܬܬܩܒܠ ܀ ܘܟܕ ܥܠ ܗܘܐ
ܠܥܕܬܐ: ܗ̣ܘ ܘܟܠܗ ܥܡܐ ܕܐܬܐ ܗܘܐ ܥܡܗ. ܘܩܡ ܗܘܐ
ܘܨܠܝ. ܘܒܪܟ ܗܘܐ ܘܫܪܐ ܐܢܘܢ ܕܢܐܙܠܘܢ ܠܒ̈ܬܝܗܘܢ. ܟܕ
ܢܦܩܝܢ ܘܡܫܒܚܝܢ ܠܐܠܗܐ: ܒܦܘܪܩܢܐ ܕܥܒܕ ܗܘܐ ܠܗܘܢ
ܘܠܥܕܬܐ. ܘܡܢ ܒܬܪ ܙܒܢܐ ܕܐܡܪ ܗܘܐ ܐܒܓܪ: ܠܘܣܝܢܐ
ܕܢܝܐ ܕܐܬܐ ܒܗܘ̈ܦܡܢܡܛܐ ܗܠܝܢ: ܐܫܬܪܝ ܗܘܐ ܠܗ ܡܢ
ܥܠܝܗܘܢ. ܐܢܐ ܕܝܢ ܙܢܘܦܝܠܘܣ ܘܦܠܝܦܘܣ ܐܟܣܩܦܛܘܪ̈ܐ
ܕܟܬܒܢ ܗܘ̈ܦܡܢܡܛܐ ܗܠܝܢ: ܒܕ ܫܘܪܝܢ ܒܝܘܡ ܒܐܝܪܚ
ܐܒܝܒ. ܕܝܘܪܘ ܘܐܦܠܝܦܘܣ ܫܪ̈ܝܪܐ ܕܟܪܣܛܝܢܘܬܐ. ܐܝܟ ܕܦܩܝܕ
ܢܡ̈ܘܣܐ ܩ̈ܕܡܝܐ ܕܟ̈ܠܗܝܢ ܩ̈ܘܡܝܐ ܀ ܗܢܐ ܕܝܢ ܒܪ̈ܘܡܝܐ
ܐܦܝܣܩܘܦܐ ܕܐܘܪܗܝ: ܗ̇ܘ ܕܬܠܡܝܕܗ ܗܘܐ ܠܦܠܘܛ ܒܡܕܝܢܬܐ
ܕܠܗ ܕܡܫܝܚܐ: ܕܐܬܬܣܝܡܘܗܝ ܗܘܐ ܒܝ̈ܕܝ ܦܠܘܛ ܐܦܝܣܩܘܦܐ

ܗܘ ܕܡܫܡܠܠܝܢ ܫܒܚܝܢ ܠܟܘܢ. ܡܛܠ ܕܟܘܪ ܗܘ ܡܫܒܚܘܢ
ܒܫܘܒܚܐ ܕܫܘܒܚܬܐ ܕܡܫܒܚܝܢ ܐܢܬܘܢ ܒܗ ܀ ܕܢܒܝܐ ܐܡܪ.
ܥܒܘܕ ܐܝܠܝܢ ܕܐܬܦܢܝܬ ܕܠܐ ܡܒܕܪܢ ܠܟ ܡܪܝ. ܘܫܠܚܘ
ܠܫ̈ܠܝܚܐ: ܟܕ ܠܐ ܐܝܬܝܗܘܢ ܟܠܗܘܢ ܗܕ̈ܡܐ ܡܫ̈ܝܢܐ ܘܩ̈ܕܝܫܐ
ܩܕܝܫܐ ܀ ܒܪܘܚܐ ܐܡܪ. ܥܒܘܕ ܐܝܟ ܓܘܫܡܐ ܦܓܪܢܝܐ
ܕܗܘܐ ܡܫܬܐܠ ܐܝܬ ܠܗ. ܘܩܘܡ ܥܠ ܪ̈ܓܠܐ ܘܕܡܘܬܐ ܕܓܒܪ
ܐܝܬ ܒܗܘܢ ܟܠ. ܠܐ ܓܝܪ ܡܫܟܚܝܢ ܠܟ ܩ̈ܠܝܟ ܐܝܟ ܡܢܐ
ܕܡܫܒܚܝܢ ܠܗ ܐܠܗ̈ܝܟ ܀ ܕܢܒܝܐ ܐܡܪ. ܬܫܒܘܚܬܐ ܒܪܘܡܐ
ܘܫܝܢܐ. ܘܟܕ ܒܟܢܘܫܝܐ ܗܘ ܐܬ̈ܝ ܗܘܘ ܠܗ ܐܓܪ̈ܬܐ ܡܢ ܟܠ
ܐܠܗܘܬܗ ܗܘܦܟܐ ܪܒܐ ܐܝܟܐ ܕܫܠܝܚܐ ܀ ܘܟܕ ܗܘܐ
ܐܬܚܙܝܬ ܗܘܘ ܠܟܘܡܪ̈ܐ. ܘܠܐ ܐܫܬܪܝ ܗܘܐ. ܘܐܬܦܩܕܘ
ܗܘܘ ܠܒܪ ܡܢ ܟܠܗ ܕܝܢܐ. ܘܟܕ ܗܘܐ ܗܘ ܕܝܢܐ. ܕܢܦܠܘܢ
ܗܘܘ ܡܢܟܘܢ ܚܕ̈ܐ ܘܪ̈ܫܝܐ ܘܪܘܟܒܐ ܘܡܬܩܪܐ ܕܡܢܘܚܬܐ:
ܕܢܫܬܟܚ ܗܘܐ ܡܢܐ ܦܘܪܫܢܐ ܐܬܩܪܝ ܗܘܐ ܡܢ ܫܠܝܚܐ:
ܟܕ ܗܘܦܟܐ ܡܫܒܚܢܐ ܕܐܠܗܘܬܐ ܕܫܘܠܛܢܐ ܕܗܝܡܢܘܬܐ ܀
ܘܐܫܬܟܚܘ ܕܠܬܚܬ ܗܘܘ ܫܠܝܚܐ ܟܕ ܗܘܦܟܐ ܠܕܝܢܐ
ܕܐܠܗܘܬܐ: ܕܡܢ ܕܦܩܕܬ ܫܠܝܚܘܬܟ ܕܢܗܘܐ ܕܘܟܝܐ ܟܠ
ܒܢܝܐ ܕܐܘܪܬܢܝܐ: ܥܒܕܝܢ ܘܠܒܫ ܡܢ ܚ̈ܝܝܐ ܕܐܝܬ ܠܗ
ܒܐܠܗܘܬܐ ܕܐܘܚܕܢܗ ܕܫܠܝܚܘܬܟ: ܕܒܢܝܐ ܕܐܘܪܬܢܝܐ.
ܐܢܫܐ ܐܢܘܢ ܕܪܢܝܢ ܡܢ ܡܠܟܐ. ܘܡܢ ܚܝ̈ܠܐ. ܘܡܢ
ܟܘܪܐ. ܘܡܢ ܟܢܘܫܬܐ. ܘܡܢ ܥܘܕܪܢܐ ܘܢܦܠܐ.. ܘܐܝܠܝܢ
ܕܐܦ ܢܦܫܗܘܢ ܕܫܠܝܚܘܬܟ ܬܟܪܝܢ ܡܫܗܐ ܒܪܝܫܐ ܡܢ ܐܝܠܝܢ
ܕܦܪܝܢ ܠܗܘܢ. ܚܝ ܕܝܢ ܒܟܐܢܘܬܗ ܕܬܪܝܨܘܬܟ ܦܩܕܢ. ܕܡܛܠ
ܗܠܝܢ ܢܦܠܐ ܡܢܗܘܢ ܙܕܘܩܝܐ ܕܒܟܝܐ. ܘܢܦܫܐ ܢܦܫܐ
ܘܥܠܝܐ ܒܟܠܗ ܐܘܪܚܝ. ܟܕ ܗܘܝܢ ܡܬܟܬܒܝܢ ܒܟܬܒܗܘܢ ܘܠܐ
ܐܝܟ ܢܦܠܐ ܐܢܘܢ. ܠܐ ܗܘܐ ܕܝܢ ܒܠܒܗܘܢ ܟܒܝܪܝܢ
ܙ̈ܒܢܐ. ܐܠܐ ܟܠ ܢܦܫܗܘܢ ܐܝܠܝܢ ܕܥܠܝܢ ܠܢܦܫܗܘܢ

ܕܫܒܝܐ: ܠܡܣܟܢܐ ܕܠܐ ܡܫܟܚ ܚܙܐ ܠܗ. ܘܕܠܐ ܚ̈ܝܠܐ ܕܦܓܪܐ. ܠܐ ܡܫܟܚܝܢ ܕܢܬܚܝܒܘܢ ܠܢܩܘܫܗ̇. ܕܟܗܢܐ ܗ̇ܘ ܕܐܝܬ ܕܒܢܝܐ ܗ̇ܘ ܕܐܠܗܐ: ܕܠܐ ܡܫܟܚ ܕܢܫܬܐ ܢܩܘܡ ܠܬܘܕܝܐ ܀ ܕܢܝܚܐ ܐܡܪ. ܡܢܐ ܕܐܫܬܐܠܬ ܡܢ ܐܚܝܢܐ ܕܝܠܟ. ܡܢ ܗܘ ܗ̇ܘܬ ܐܢܐ ܥܠܝܟ ܠܩܠܝܬܐ ܐܝܢܐ ܨܒܐ ܓܒܪܬ ܠܫܠܡܐ. ܕܬܬܠܒܒ ܠܥܒܕܐ ܒܡܪܝܐ ܡܫܝܚܗܘܢ ܕܐܠܗ̈ܐ: ܘܕܬܫܬܠܡ ܐܝܟܘܢ ܢܚܘܘܢܝܗܘܢ ܕܩܠܝܬܐ: ܘܕܠܐ ܢܫܟܚܘܢ ܐܝܟܘܢ ܠܕܝܢܐ ܕܐܬܪܘܬܐ: ܘܐܝܟ ܒܙܒܢܐ ܒܚܪܝܢ ܐܝܬ ܒܫܠܝܐ ܕܬܘܕܝܬܐ ܀ ܀ ܒܬܘܕܝܬܐ ܐܡܪ. ܠܐ ܡܬܕܠ ܐܝܬ ܠܝ ܒܥܠܡ ܕܐܡܪ ܐܢܬ. ܐܦ ܠܩܠܝܬܐ ܠܐ ܩܪܒ ܐܢܐ ܘܡܩܒܠ. ܐܠܐ ܩܕܡ ܫܘܠܛܢܐ ܕܗܘܐ ܠܝ ܩܠܝܬܐ. ܗܐ ܦܐܡ ܐܢܐ ܗܢܐ ܘܡܬܬܕܡܐ ܐܢܐ. ܟܠ ܕܐܡܪܬ ܕܠܐ ܬܦܪ ܐܢܐ ܒܐܠܗܐ ܕܫܚܠܦ ܫܘܒܚܐ ܘܐܪܒܥܐ: ܘܡܛܪܗ ܥܘܒܕ ܡܫܝܚܐ ܩܠܝܬܐ ܕܟܠܗ̇ ܐܘܪܚܐ ܀ ܕܢܝܚܐ ܐܡܪ. ܐܢ ܗ̇ܘ ܕܫܪܝܐ ܠܟ ܗܪܐ: ܕܩܕܡ ܫܘܠܛܢܐ ܕܩܠܝܬܐ ܦܐܡ ܐܢܬ ܘܡܬܕܡܝܬ: ܐܫܬܡܥ ܠܦܘܩܕܢܝܗܘܢ ܘܠܐ ܬܥܒܪ ܥܠ ܢܡܘܣܝܗܘܢ. ܕܠܐ ܐܝܟ ܡܪܘܕܐ ܡܫܬܟܚ ܐܢܬ ܡܢ ܒܢܝܐ ܕܩܪܝܬܐ ܀ ܒܬܘܕܝܬܐ ܐܡܪ. ܘܐܢ ܐܝܠܝܢ ܕܡܢܗܘܢ ܥܠ ܩܠܝܬܐ: ܕܗ ܒܐܝܕܝܟ ܡܢܗܘܢ: ܩܘܬܐ ܫܢܝܢ ܐܝܟ ܕܐܡܪ ܐܢܬ: ܐܝܠܝܢ ܕܥܠ ܐܠܗܐ ܩܠܝܬܐ ܕܩܠܝܬܐ ܡܢܗܘܢ: ܘܗܢܐ ܗܘ ܠܗܘܢ. ܘܐܦ ܡܛܠ ܒܢܝܐ ܕܩܘܬܐ ܕܢܦܫܐ ܀ ܕܢܝܚܐ ܐܡܪ. ܠܐ ܗܘܐ ܕܬܬܪܥܡ ܒܕܝܘܩܢܝܢ ܕܠܐ ܟܠܗ ܘܕܟ. ܡܛܠ ܕܕܝܢܐ ܕܦܐܡ ܐܝܬ ܒܗ. ܙܢܝ ܗܘ ܡܢ ܬܘܪܥܡܐ: ܘܩܪܒ ܠܡܛܠ ܒܢܝܐ ܕܩܘܬܐ: ܠܐܝܠܝܢ ܕܡܢܨܒܝܢ ܠܩܠܝܬܐ ܘܠܐ ܡܬܦܠܓܝܢ ܠܢܡܘܣܝܗܘܢ ܀ ܀ ܒܬܘܕܝܬܐ ܐܡܪ. ܡܛܠ ܕܠܝܬ ܐܠܗܐ ܩܕܡ ܥܝܢܝܟ. ܘܐܦ ܠܐ ܡܠܬ ܐܠܗܐ ܢܨܝܢ ܐܝܟܘܢ ܠܡܫܬܡܥ. ܘܩܠܝܬܐ ܕܠܝܬ ܒܗܘܢ ܚܫܘܟ: ܕܟܘܟܒܐ ܐܝܬ ܠܗܘܢ ܘܠܐ ܡܬܠܠܝܢ: ܐܝܟ

ܒܪܬܐ ܗܝ ܗܘܬ ܠܗ ܠܡܫܝܚܐ: ܘܠܐ ܐܡܪܬ ܠܝ. ܕܠܐ ܬܗܘܐ ܠܗ. ܐܝܟ ܗܘ ܕܐܢܐ ܗܘ ܒܠܚܘܕ ܦܠܛ ܐܢܐ ܠܗ. ܠܗܘ ܕܒܝܬܐ ܟܠܝܐ ܦܓܪܗ ܠܗ ܒܪܘܡܝܐ ✥ ܕܢܝܐ ܐܡܪ. ܘܐܢ ܠܒ̈ܢܝܢܫܐ ܐܠܗܘܬܗ ܐܝܬ. ܕܗܘܐ ܦܓܪܗ ܠܗ ܠܡܫܝܚܐ. ܠܟܠܢܐ ܢܒܘ ܐܦܢܘ ܐܝܬ̈. ܕܗܘܐ ܦܓܪܗ ܠܗ ܠܡܫܝܚܐ ✥ ܒܪܘܡܝܐ ܐܡܪ. ܗܘܝܢ ܐܝܬ ܟܠܝܐ: ܦܓܪܘ ܘܐܠܗܐ ܐܝܬ ܠܬܪܬܝܗܝܢ: ܟܠ ܕܒܢܝܐ ܦܓܪܗ ܕܟܠܗܐ ܡܫܝܚܐ: ܕܦܓܪܗ ܠܗ ܘܠܐܠܗܘܬܐ، ܒܗ ܕܐܢܫܐ ܕܐܠܗܘܬܗ ✥ ܕܢܝܐ ܐܡܪ. ܫܒܘܩܘ ܗܠܝܢ ܕܡܬܒܝܢ ܠܟܘܢ: ܘܡܠܦܝܢ ܐܢܬܘܢ ܐܦ ܠܐܚܪ̈ܢܐ. ܘܐܬܚܦܛܘ ܠܐܝܠܝܢ ܕܟܦܪܘ ܒܟܠܗܝܢ. ܘܠܐ ܬܦܠܘܢ ܒܡܘܫܘܗܝ. ܕܠܐ ܬܫܬܠܘܢ ܒܪ ܗܢܐ ܡܢ ܢܘܗܪܗ ܕܡܫܝܚܐ ܗܢܐ ܡܢܗܪܐ ✥ ܒܪܘܡܝܐ ܐܡܪ. ܢܘܗܪܐ ܕܐܡܪ ܘܠܐ ܢܗܘܐ. ܠܐ ܗܘܐ ܢܘܗܪܐ ܗܘ ܫܪܪܐ. ܐܠܐ ܕܡܫܝܚܐ ܗܘ ܕܗܘ ܢܘܗܪܐ ܫܪܝܪܐ. ܕܠܐ ܦܪܫ ܫܡܫܐ ܠܗܬ ܠܢܘܗܪܗ: ܕܢܛܪ ܘܫܡܫ ܠܦܓܪܗ، ܫܪܝܪܐ ܕܡܫܝܚܐ ✥ ܕܢܝܐ ܐܡܪ. ܠܐ ܬܐܡܪ ܘܕܘܢ ܡܕܡ ܚܠܦ ܡܕܡ ܕܐܫܬܐܠܬ. ܕܠܐ ܡܢ ܫܡܐ ܠܢܘܗܪܐ ܡܫܪܪܐ ܐܢܐ ܠܟ: ܟܠ ܕܐܡܪܬ ܒܢܘܗܪܐ ܗܢܐ ܕܡܬܚܙܝܐ ܘܡܢܗܪܐ ܐܝܬ ܒܐܢܫܐ ܕܠܐ ܡܬܚܙܝܐ ✥ ܒܪܘܡܝܐ ܐܡܪ. ܠܐ ܡܫܟܚ ܐܢܐ ܕܐܬܦܢܐ ܗܘ ܡܕܡ ܕܡܫܐܠ ܐܢܬ ܠܝ. ܘܐܡܪ ܟܠ ܡܕܡ ܕܠܐ ܡܫܐܠ ܐܢܬ ܠܝ. ܐܢܬ ܗܘ ܐܡܪܬ ܠܝ ܡܛܠ ܢܘܗܪܗ ܕܫܡܫܐ. ܘܐܬܦܢܝܬ ܘܐܡܪܬ. ܕܐܢܬ ܗܘ ܢܘܗܪܐ ܒܪܘܡܝܐ ܕܡܛܠܬ ܒܢܘܗܪܗ ܡܢ ܗܢܐ ܕܫܡܫܐ ܕܦܓܪ ܐܢܬ ܘܡܫܪܪ ܐܢܬ ܠܗ. ܡܬܬܒܥܬ ܓܝܪ ܚܠܦ ܗܕܐ: ܕܦܓܪܗ ܠܟܢܗ ܚܠܦ ܐܠܗܐ ܒܪܘܗ ✥ ܕܢܝܐ ܐܡܪ. ܠܐ ܬܬܒܪ ܘܐܦ ܠܫܡܫܐ ܢܘܗܪܐ ܕܒܪܢܫܐ: ܘܬܬܟܠ ܒܡܘܕܝܐ ܕܟܠܗܐ: ܘܬܩܘܡ ܒܫܪܝܪܐ ܠܘܩܒܠ ܡܪܘܗܝ، ܕܐܬܪܐ: ܕܗܘܝܢ ܫܠܝܛܝܢ ܒܗ ✥ ܒܪܘܡܝܐ ܐܡܪ. ܡܢܐ ܡܕܝܢ ܢܘܗܪܗ

ܕܐܝܠܝܢ ܕܚܙܝܢ ܠܗ. ܢܚܒܘ ܡܫܡܫ ܢܚܝܢܐ ܠܗܘܢ: ܐܦ ܐܝܟܢܐ
ܢܛܠܐ ܕܡܫܡܫ ܢܦܫ ܠܗܘܢ. ܐܦ ܠܡܫ̈ܡܫܢܝܢ ܕܐܠܝܢ ܗܟܢܐ
ܟܬܒܝܢ ܠܗܘܢ. ܠܗܢܘܢ ܕܡܢ ܕܬܦܩܘܕ ܒܠܒܗܘܢ ܕܢܬܟܬܒܘܢ:
ܫܡܥ ܗܘ ܡܫܬܡܥܢܘܬܗܘܢ ܡܢ ܚ̈ܝܝܗܘܢ. ܘܠܗ ܗܘ ܡܫܬܡܥܝܢ
ܥܠܝܗܘܢ ∴ ܕܝܢܐ ܐܡܪ. ܠܐ ܬܬܢܐ ܫܪܒܗ ܕܡܫܝܚܐ ܡܕܡ
ܕܡܫܬܪܝܢ ܕܝܠܗ. ܐܠܐ ܫܠܘ ܗܕܐ. ܐܫܬܡܥ ܠܦܘܩܕܢܐ
ܕܡ̈ܠܟܐ: ܕܦܩܕܘ ܠܡܕܒܚܘ ܠܐ̈ܠܗܐ ∴ ܒܪܣܡܝܐ ܐܡܪ. ܐܦ
ܟܕ ܠܐ ܢܬܢܐ ܫܪܒܗ ܕܡܫܝܚܐ ܡܕܡ: ܫܡܗ ܕܡܫܝܚܐ ܓܒܪ
ܗܘ ܘܡܚܝܐ ܒܦܬܓܡܘܗܝ ܕܡܫܝܚܐ. ܘܐܬܪ ܡܢ ܗܪܟܐ ܕܫܡܥܬ
ܐܢܬ ܠܦܘܩܕܢܗܘܢ ܕܡ̈ܠܟܐ: ܫܡܥܬ ܒܝܘܠܦܢܐ ܠܡܫܝܚܐ
ܡܠܟܐ ܕܡ̈ܠܟܐ ∴ ∴ ܕܝܢܐ ܐܡܪ. ܗܐ ܐܫܬܡܥܬ ܠܗ
ܠܡܫܝܚܟ. ܘܫܡܥܬ ܠܗ ܒܗܕܐ ܠܝܘܡܢܐ. ܡܛܠ ܐܫܬܡܥ
ܠܗܘܢ ܠܡ̈ܠܟܐ. ܘܣܓܘܕ ܠܐ̈ܠܗܐ ܕܦܩܕܘ ܠܗܘܢ ܡ̈ܠܟܐ ∴
ܒܪܣܡܝܐ ܐܡܪ. ܐܡܝܢܐ ܐܫܬܡܥܬ ܠܗ ܕܐܡܠܟܢܝ ܒܡܠܟܘܬ ܕܝܠܗ
ܐܢܐ ܒܗ: ܕܗܘܐ ܠܫܪܒܝܠ ܬܠܡܝܕܐ ܒܟܝܢܗ ܘܐܫܬܡܥܬ ܠܗ:
ܕܟܠ ܡܠܟܐ ܕܒܪܐ ܒܡܠܟܘܬܐ ܕܝܠܗ ܐܢܬ ܒܗ: ܘܐܫܬܡܥܬ
ܒܬܫܡܫܬܐ ܕܝܠܗ ܗܘܝܬ ܠܗ. ܗܐ ܓܝܪ ܐܦ ܡܢ ܡܕܡ
ܕܐܡܠܟ ܡܕܡܟܝ. ܐܢܬ ܦܩܕܬ ܘܫܡܥܬ ܘܐܫܬܡܥܬ ܠܗ ܠܡܠܟܝ.
ܕܬܫܡܫܬܐ ܕܐܠܗܐ ܚܝܐ ܡܫܡܫܢܐ. ܠܐ ܓܝܪ ܒܗܘ ܡܕܡ
ܕܠܝܬ ܒܗ ܘܡܫܟܚ ܒܗ. ܦܘܩ ܗܟܝܠ ܓܝܪ ܡܠܬܐ ܕܐܡܪܬ
ܗܘܬ ∴ ∴ ∴ ܕܝܢܐ ܐܡܪ. ܢܬܒܛܠ ܫܪܒܟ. ܟܠ ܕܐܡܪܬ ܟܠ
ܦܘܩܕܢܐ ܕܡ̈ܠܟܐ: ܘܐܡܪܬ ܒܗܘ ܘܐܦ ܠܐ̈ܠܗܐ ܕܥܒܕܝܢ
ܗܘܘ ܠܗܘܢ ܠܡ̈ܠܟܐ. ܘܟܕ ܐܬܚܙܝ ܗܘܐ ܡܢ ܚܡܫܝܢ ܐܡܪ
ܠܗ. ܠܐ ܬܬܠܐ ܦܘܩܕܢܐ ܕܡ̈ܠܟܐ: ܘܬܬܒܪ ܠܐ̈ܠܗܝܗܘܢ
ܕܡ̈ܠܟܐ ∴ ܒܪܣܡܝܐ ܐܡܪ. ܗܢܐ ܒܥܐ ܡܢܟ ܕܝܢܐ:
ܘܐܦ ܕܡ̈ܠܟܐ ܕܗܘܝܘ ܠܟ ܫܘܠܛܢܐ. ܘܠܐ ܡܬܬܚܝܡ
ܠܟ ܐܝܟ ܕܟܬܝܒ: ܘܠܐ ܡܬܬܚܝܡ ܐܢܬܘܢ. ܕܗܠܝܢ

ܒܪܘܚܐ ܐܡܪ. ܟܠܗ ܕܒܟܢ ܐܢܐ ܪܓܫܐ ܕܡܢܝܢܐ.
ܠܐ ܗܘܐ ܡܛܠ ܐܝܠܝܢ ܕܚܫܝܢ ܒܠܚܘܕ: ܐܠܐ ܐܦ ܡܛܠ
ܐܝܠܝܢ ܕܙܟܝܢ ܡܢ ܙܠܝܠܐ ܕܦܘܫܩܐ. ܕܒܚܫܝܢ ܡܫܬܡܠܝܬܐ
ܠܐܪܙܐ ܕܢܒܝܘܬܐ. ܘܐܦ ܠܐ ܕܬܬܠܡܕ ܗܘܬ ܠܝܣܪܝܠ
ܒܐܝܕܘܗܝ ܗܘ ܕܠܐ ܡܬܬܒܥ ܗܘܐ ܕܡܢܗ. ܘܐܦ ܠܐ ܫܡܥܘ
ܗܘܐ. ܡܢܗ ܗܘܬ ܡܢ ܕܡܢܗ ∴ ܕܢܝܐܠ ܐܡܪ. ܗܫܐ ܕܝܢ
ܕܐܘܕܥܢ ܕܐܝܬ ܗܘ ܬܠܡܝܕܘܗܝ ܠܝܣܪܝܠ: ܒܐܝܕܝܗܘܢ ܗܘ ܕܠܗܘܢ
ܬܟܒ ܐܢܐ ܠܗ ܠܟܘܠܗܘܢ. ܘܡܛܠ ܗܢܐ ܙܕܩ ܗܘ ܕܬܬܪ ܡܢܗ
ܬܬܕܝܢ ܘܕܡܐ: ܕܡܢ ܐܝܕܝܗܘܢ ܡܢܗ ܗܘܐ ܫܘܬܐ ܟܪܝܗܐ ܕܫܪܪܐ
ܫܪܪܐ. ܕܫܡܥ ܗܘܐ ܦܘܩܕܢܐ ܕܫܠܝܚܐ: ܘܡܫܬܡܥ ܗܘܐ
ܠܟܠܗܘܢ ܕܠܗܘܢ ∴ ܒܪܘܚܐ ܐܡܪ. ܠܘ ܠܟܠ ܐܬܬܠܝܕ ܗܘܐ
ܝܫܪܐܝܠ. ܐܠܐ ܠܟܠܗܘܢ ܕܐܠܗܐ ܕܐܡܪ. ܕܠܐ ܬܬܟܠܘܢ
ܠܒܢܝܐ ܘܕܡܬܐ ܕܢܒܝܝܐ. ܘܠܐ ܗܘܐ ܐܢܐ ܒܠܚܘܕ
ܡܢܝܢ ܐܢܐ ܕܐܡܪܬ ܫܘܬܗ ܕܝܫܪܐܝܠ ܕܡܫܝܚܘܬܗ ܕܒܚܝܢܐ.
ܐܠܐ ܐܦ ܠܟܠܗܘܢ ܒܪܘܡܝܐ ܟܠ ܒܢܬܐ ܢܒܝܐ ܬܘܒ ܒܗܝܢܐ
ܕܡܢܝܢ ܕܫܠܝܚܐ ܡܫܝܚܝܢ ܡܢܢ ܐܠܗܐ ܒܗܕܐ ∴ ∴ ∴ ܕܢܝܐ
ܐܡܪ. ܠܐ ܬܦܢܐ ܠܝ ܦܬܓܡܐ ܗܟܢܐ ܐܝܟ ܝܫܪܐܝܠ
ܬܠܡܝܕܝ: ܕܠܐ ܗܘܘ ܟܢܝܢ ܫܘܥܝܐ ܕܠܝ ܡܛܪ ܡܢ ܕܠܗ.
ܐܠܐ ܐܫܬܘܕܝܐ ܕܡܚܝܕܝܢ ܐܝܬ ܦܘܩ ܐܠܗܐ ܫܠܡܗ ∴
ܒܪܘܚܐ ܐܡܪ. ܝܫܪܐܝܠ ܕܠܐ ܢܕܥ ܗܘܐ ܠܐܠܗܐ: ܐܠܗܘܗ
ܕܝܕܥ: ܐܢܐ ܕܠܐܠܗܐ ܢܕܥ ܡܢ ܛܠܝܘܬܗ: ܐܘܕܥܬ ܠܝ
ܕܐܬܦܘܪ ܒܐܠܗܐ. ܫܘ ܠܝ ܡܢ ܐܠܗܐ ܕܐܬܦܢܝ ܗܕܐ ∴
ܕܢܐ ܐܡܪ. ܐܢܫܝܢ ܬܠܡܝܕܘܗܝ ܠܟܠܗ ܒܪܝܬܐ ܠܝܫܠܝܡ
ܕܡܫܝܚܐ: ܘܗܘܐ ܦܪܝܫ ܒܐܠܗܐ ܦܘܠܚܢܐ. ܕܦܠܚܝܢ ܗܘܘ
ܠܗܘܢ ܦܘܠܚܢܐ. ܟܕ ܡܢ ܗܢܐ ܪܚܝܩ. ܕܠܐ ܐܘܪܚ ܒܗ
ܡܩܒܠܐ ܕܢܝܚ ܠܝ ܢܦܫܐ: ܘܪܘܚܐ ܕܡܫܝܚܐ ܢܘܗܪܐ
ܕܕܝܢܝ ∴ ܒܪܘܚܐ ܐܡܪ. ܟܠ ܐܠܗܐ ܒܟܘܪܗܢܐ ܗܘ

ܫ̈ܡܗܐ ܕܐܠܗ̈ܐ ܕܡܟܝܢ ܗܘܘ: ܕܡܢ ܪ̈ܗܘܡܝܐ ܡܢܨܚܝܢ. ܘܟܕ
ܢܦܩܘ ܗܘܘ ܕܢܣܓܕܘܢ ܐܢܘܢ ܠܐܠܗ̈ܐ ܗܠܝܢ: ܘܢܦܩܘ ܗܘܘ
ܠܗܘܢ ܐܝܠܝܢ ܕܡܟܝܢ ܗܘܘ ܡܚܕܐ: ܘܠܐ ܡܫܬܡܥܝܢ ܗܘܘ
ܠܡܣܓܕ ܐܢܘܢ ܠܫ̈ܡܗܝܗܘܢ. ܕܢܦܩܘ ܗܘܘ ܠܗܘܢ.
ܕܡܚܬܐ ܡܢ ܟܠ ܓܒ̈ܝܢ ܐܘܠܨܢܐ ܗܘܬ ܠܗܘܢ: ܕܡܬܪܕܝܢ ܗܘܘ
ܡܛܠ ܡܫܝܚܐ ܡܢ ܪ̈ܗܘܡܝܐ. ܘܟܕ ܫܡܥ ܗܘܐ ܠܗ ܪܘܒܐ
ܕܐܝܬܘܗܝ. ܦܩܕ ܗܘܘ ܥܒ̈ܕܐ ܕܡܕܝܢܬܐ. ܘܟܠܗ ܗܘܘ ܠܗܘܢ
ܠܘܬ ܕܝܢܐ ܘܐܡܪܝܢ ܠܗ. ܠܐ ܡܫܬܡܥܝܢ ܕܢܕܒܚܘܢ ܐܢܘܢ
ܠܫ̈ܡܗܐ ܕܐܠܗ̈ܐ ܕܡܟܝܢ ܠܒܪ. ܡܛܠ ܕܡܫ̈ܝܚܝܝܢ ܐܢܘܢ ܕܠܐ
ܡܫܝܚܐ ✣ ܘܟܕ ܗܘܐ ܕܝܢܐ ܕܢܦܩ ܗܘܐ ܪ̈ܗܘܡܝܐ ܠܟܠܗ
ܐܘܪ̈ܗܝ. ܐܝܟ ܕܐܬܬܟܪܝ ܗܘܬ ܐܢܫܘܬܐ ܕܡܫܝ̈ܚܝܐ ܗܘܬ
ܐܝܣܘܕܘܬܗ. ܕܕܠܡܐ ܪܘܒܐ ܕܩ̈ܛܠܐ ܬܗܘܐ ܗܘܬ ܒܡܬܐ
ܡܢ ܡܕܝܢܬܐ. ܘܟܕ ܫܠܡ ܗܘܐ ܠܟܠܗ ܫܘܠܛܢܗ. ܦܩܕ
ܗܘܘ ܠܗܘܢ ܐܝܠܝܢ ܕܒܟܠ ܐܬܬܠܒܕܘ ܗܘܘ. ܘܡܢ ܒܬܪ
ܕܗܘܐ ܗܘܐ ܫ̈ܒܝܬܐ ܩ̈ܕܝܫܐ: ܡܢ ܗܘܐ ܕܝܢܐ ܒܢܦܫܗ
ܘܢܦܩܬ ܠܐܢܬܘܦܛܘܣ ܕܠܗ. ܐܝܟ ܕܢܫܬܡܥ ܗܘܐ ܠܪ̈ܗܘܡܝܐ.
ܘܟܕ ܗܘܐ ܕܝܢܐ ܘܐܫܬܠܝܘܗܝ ܡܢ ܒܬܪ ܐܘܪ̈ܗܝ: ܘܟܠ ܗܘܐ
ܘܡܢ ܒܬܪ̈ܗܘܢ. ܦܒܝܢܘܣ ܐܡܪ. ܗܐ ܡܟܝܠ ܡܢ ܕܟܬܝܒ.
ܕܝܢܐ ܐܡܪ. ܐܝܬ ܗܘ ܒܪ̈ܗܘܡܝܐ ܕܟܬܝܒ ܐܝܬ ܦܘܩܕܢܐ
ܘܡܬܩܪܝܢܐ ܠܟܠܗ ܕܪ̈ܘܪܒܢܐ: ܘܬܠܡܝܕܘܗܝ, ܠܥܕܬܐ
ܒܡܕܝܢܬܐ ܪܒܬܐ ܕܐܠܗ̈ܐ ܕܣܓܝ ܗܘܐ ܠܗܘܢ: ✣ ✣ ܪ̈ܗܘܡܝܐ
ܐܡܪ. ܐܢܬܐ ܐܢܬܐ ܕܟܬܒܬ ܗܕܐ ܘܠܐ ܚܙܝ ܐܢܬܐ ܘܐܬܚܠܦ
ܐܢܐ ܕܐܡܪܬ ܥܠ ܐܦ̈ܝ ܫܪܪܗ ܕܗܕܐ ✣ ✣ ܕܝܢܐ ܐܡܪ. ܐܡܪܢܐ
ܠܐ ܕܫܠܛ ܡܢ ܦܘܩܕܢܐ ܕܡ̈ܠܟܐ: ܕܟܕ ܡ̈ܠܟܐ ܦܩܕܘ ܕܢܬܒܥ ܥܠܝܟ:
ܐܝܬ ܠܫܪܒܝܠ ܒܡܕܝܢܬܐ ܟܕ ܫܐܠ ܗܘܐ ܘܡܬܒܥ ܗܘܐ ܠܫ̈ܠܡܐ:
ܘܫܐܠ ܗܘܐ ܠܗܘܢ ܬ̈ܫܡܫܬܐ: ܒܟܕܬܗ, ܕܢܦܩܘܢ ܟܠܗ ܡܕܡ
ܕܥܒܕܐ ܗܘܐ ܒܗ: ܘܐܢܘܕܐ ܒܡܫܝܚܐ ܕܟܦܪ ܗܘܐ ܒܗ ✣ ✣

ܠܘܬ ܐܠܗܐ̈ ܘܠܒܪܗ ܝܫܘܥ ܡܫܝܚܐ: ܒܙܒܢܐ ܕܬܠܡܝܕܘܬܗ
ܗܘܐ: ܘܒܥܒܕܗ ܗܘܐ ܕܢܦܘܩ ܒܫ̈ܠܡܐ ܕܡ̇ܠܟ ܗܘܐ ܠܗܘܢ
ܡܢ ܩܕܝܡ. ܘܒܟܠܗܝܢ ܕܠܗ ܕܒܪܢܫ ܐܦ ܦ̈ܠܚܐ ܐܬܬܠܡܕܘ
ܗܘܘ ܘܢܣܒܘ ܠܥܕܬܐ. ܘܗܐ ܡܗܝܡܢܐ ܩܥܕܝܢ ܒܡܫܝܚܐ. ܘܐܦ
ܒܥܕܬܐ ܘܥܠܘ ܘܟܪ ܒܠܒܐ ܘܢܦܩܘ: ܡܫܝ̈ܚܐ ܘܪ̈ܫܝܢܐ
ܕܡܕܝܢܬܐ: ܫܠܚܘ ܗܘܘ ܠܗ ܠܪܒܘܠܐ ܒܥܕܬܐ. ܘܡܢ ܐܝܟ
ܐܢ̈ܫܐ ܫܪ̈ܝܪܐ ܕܡܕܝܢܬܐ. ܡܬܕܟܪܝܢ ܗܘܘ ܪܒܘܠܐ. ܕܠܐ
ܢܦܠ ܡܢܗܘܢ ܒܪܫܐ ܐܝܟ ܡ̈ܫܒܠܢܐ: ܕܠܐ ܟܠܒܝܢ ܗܘܘ
ܪܒܘܠܐ: ܐܠܨܝܢ ܕܐܬܬܠܠ ܒܟܘܣܐ ܒܡ ܫܪܒܠ: ܡܢ
ܒܪܘܚܢܐ ܡܥܒܪܢܐ ܕܥܕܬܐ ÷ ܡܛܠ ܪܒܘܠܐ ܡܫܝܚܐ:
ܐܠܗܝܐ ܕܗܘ ܕܬܦܝܐ ܡܠܠܘܗܝ ܕܥܕܬܐ. ܘܒܗ ܒܟܬܒܬܐ ܕܫܒܚ
ܗܘܐ ܕܢܗܐ ܗܠܝܢ: ܫܕܪ ܗܘܐ ܐܢܘܢ ܠܫ̈ܪܝܪܐ ܕܡܕܝܢܬܐ:
ܘܡܢ ܩܕܡ ܐܘܦܝܣܩ ܒܟܗܢܘܢ: ܕܢܣܒܘܢ ܗܘܘ ܠܥܕܬܐ.
ܘܢܦܩܘܢ ܠܪܘܚܢܐ ܡܢ ܥܕܬܐ. ܘܒܪܘܚܗ ܗܘܘ ܘܫܠܡܘ
ܠܐܦܣܩܘܦܝܢ ܕܠܗ ܕܕܢܐ. ܘܫܠܡܘ ܗܘܘ ܒܟܗ ܒܪܘܦܠܢܐ
ܦ̈ܠܢܐ. ܟܕ ܐܬܟܢܫܘ ܗܘܘ. ܕܐܦ ܚܕ ܡܢܗܘܢ ܒܟܗܘܢ
ܕܪܘܚܢܐ. ܡܛܠ ܕܐܦ ܚܕ ܫܠܝܚܐ ܗܘ ܒܟܘܢ: ܒܬܠܡܝܕܐ
ܕܬܠܡܝܕܗ ܗܘܐ ܠܪܒܘܠܐ. ܘܒܟܠ ܡܕܡ ܕܫܠܠ ܗܘܐ ܒܟܘܢ.
ܘܒܟܠ ܡܕܡ ܕܦܩܠ ܗܘܐ ܡܢܗ. ܘܐܬܦܠܓܘ ܗܘܐ ܠܗ:
ܘܡܢܝܬ ܗܘܐ ܫܠܦ ܡܕܡ ܕܫܦܪ ܗܘܐ ܡܢܗ. ܘܟܠܗ ܗܘܘ
ܫܪ̈ܝܪܐ ܕܡܕܝܢܬܐ. ܘܐܡܪܘ ܗܘܘ ܠܗ ܠܕܢܐ. ܕܪܘܚܢܐ
ܕܡܦܕܬ ܪܒܘܠܐ: ܗܐ ܡܢܡ ܒܠ ܬܪܒܐ ܕܒܝܬ ܕܝܢܐ
ܕܫܠܠܝܢ. ܘܪ̈ܫܝܢܐ ܡܫܝ̈ܚܐ ܕܡܕܝܢܬܐ ܕܐܬܬܠܡܕܘ ܗܘܘ
ܒܡ ܫܪܒܠ: ܗܐ ܡܢܝܢ ܠܬܘܗ ܕܪܘܚܢܐ ܘܡܟܝܢ ܕܒܠ
ܡܢܬܝܢ ܒܟܗ ܕܪܘܚܢܐ. ܕܐܢܬܘܗ, ܟܠܗܝܢ ܘܡܥܒܪܝܢ ÷ ÷

ܘܟܕ ܫܒܩ ܗܘܐ ܕܢܐ: ܗܠܝܢ ܕܐܫܟܪܘ ܗܘܘ ܠܗ ܫ̈ܪܝܪܐ
ܕܡܕܝܢܬܐ. ܦܩܕ ܗܘܐ ܠܗܘܢ ܕܢܩܒܠܘܢ ܗܘܘ. ܘܢܩܬܠܘܢ

ܫܒܩܘ. ܘܡܫܡܫܝܢ ܐܢܘܢ ܒܫܘܒܚ ܡܠܟܐ ܒܪܗ ܕܐܠܗܐ
ܗܘ ܕܐܬܝܐ ܘܥܬܝܕ. ܕܢܐܬܐ ܢܐܬܐ ܘܐܠܘ ܐܝܬ ܗܘܐ ܡ̈ܠܦܢܐ
ܐܢ̈ܫܐ ܒܪ̈ܗܘܡܝܐ ܘܒܟܠܗ̇ ܐܦܪ̈ܟܝܐ. ܐܝܟ ܗܢܘܢ ܒܟܪ̈ܝܗ ܗܘܘ
ܒܫܠܝܡܘܬܗܘܢ ܐܝܟ ܕܒܪܝܘ ܗܘܘ ܫܦܝܪܐ ܘܒܡܫܝܪܘܬܐ ܕܫ̈ܠܝܚܐ
ܕܡܬܕܒܪܐ ܗܘܬ ܒܥܕܬܐ ܕܡܫܝܚܐ ܗܘܘ ܀

ܫܠܡܬ ܗܘܦܘܡܢܣܛܝܩܐ ܕܪܒܘܠܐ ܡܗܝܡܢܐ ܀

.ܘ:ܘ. .ܘ:ܘ. .ܘ:ܘ. .ܘ:ܘ. .ܘ:ܘ. .ܘ:ܘ.

ܬܘܒ ܬܫܥܝܬܐ ܕܒܪ ܫܡܝܐ ܐܦܝܣܩܘܦܐ ܕܐܘܪܗܝ

ܡܕܝܢܬܐ ܡܒܪܟܬܐ.

ܒܫܢܬ ܐܪ̈ܒܥܝܢ ܘܐܪܒܥܡܐܐ ܕܡܠܟܘܬܐ ܕܝܘ̈ܢܝܐ:
ܘܫܢܬܗ̇ ܬܠܬ ܥܣܪܐ ܕܡܠܟܘܬܗ ܕܐܘܛܘܩܪܛܘܪ ܡܪܢ
ܛܪܝܢܘܣ ܩܣܪ. ܒܗܘܦܛܝܐ ܕܣܘܒܘܪܢܘܣ ܘܕܡܪܩܠܠܘܣ ܒܟܐܢܘܢ
ܐܚܪܝ: ܒܝܘܡ ܫܒܬܐ ܒܗ: ܟܕ ܫܪܝ ܡܠܟܐ ܕܐܒܓܪ ܗܘܐ
ܠܬܫܥ ܕܫܢܝܐ ܕܐܬܪܐ ܠܡܠܟܘܬܐ ܒܡܕܝܢܬܐ: ܟܕ ܢܦܩ ܗܘܐ ܗܘ
ܕܫܢܝܐ ܒܕܡܘܣܦܪܝܢ ܕܠܗ: ܟܠܗ ܗܘܘ ܡܕܒܪܝܢ ܫܪ̈ܟܐ
ܕܡܕܝܢܬܐ ܘܐܬܪ̈ܘܢ ܠܗ. ܕܡܫܡܫܝܢ ܗܘܘ ܪܒܘܬܟ: ܟܠ ܒܪ
ܦܘܠܚܢܐ ܡܕܒܪܢܐ ܕܗܝܟܠܐ ܕܗܘ ܦܠܚ ܗܘܐ ܟܝ ܫܪܒܝܠ
ܒܡܕܝܢܬܐ: ܟܕ ܩܐܡ ܗܘܐ ܘܡܫܡܫ ܗܘܐ ܩܕܡ ܐܠܗ̈ܐ ܡܢ̈ܝܢܐ.
ܘܫܕܪ ܗܘܐ ܘܩܪܝܗܝ ܗܘܐ ܠܘܬܗ ܒܦܐܝܘܬ: ܘܡܠܠ ܗܘܐ
ܥܡܗ ܡܢ ܟܬܒ̈ܐ: ܕܢܦܪܘܩ ܒܗܘܢ ܒܟܕܝܢܬܐ ܕܒܝܬ ܒܘܫܡܗܘܢ.
ܦܬܒܥ ܗܘܐ ܠܗ ܡܫܬܘܬܗܘܢ ܕܦܘܠܚܢܐ: ܘܐܡܪ ܗܘܐ
ܠܗ. ܕܠܐ ܙܕܩ ܠܟ ܕܬܗܦܘܟ ܠܥܠܡܐ ܩܛܝܢܐ. ܐܠܐ ܐܢ

ܐܬܢܣܒܬ ܕܡܘܗܒܬܐ. ܘܥܠ ܗܘܘ ܠܡܦܪܥܐ ܕܡܕܒܪܢܘܬܗܘܢ
ܘܐܡܪܝܢ ܠܗ. ܕܐܝܟܢܐ ܡܬܬܪܐ ܐܝܬ ܒܗ ܒܡܕܒܪܢܘܬܟ ܘܗܘܢ
ܕܥܕܡ ܟܠܗ ܘܡܗܝܡܢܐ ܕܠܥܠܡ. ܐܠܐ ܟܕ ܚܙܝܢ ܚܝ ܡܠܟ
ܕܬܟܘܢ ܢܦܫ ܡܢ ܡܕܝܢܬܐ. ܘܟܕ ܟܠܢ ܗܘܐ ܕܢܦܫܘܢ ܡܢ
ܡܕܝܢܬܐ. ܐܬܟܢܫܘ ܗܘܘ ܗܢܘܢ ܐܦܝܣܩܘܦܐ ܘܐܡܪܝܢ ܠܗ
ܠܡܦܪܥܐ ܟܕ ܚܙܝܢ ܚܝ ܡܠܟ ܡܪܝ. ܟܠܗ ܕܐܦ ܠܥܡܐ
ܕܩܝܬܐ ܒܟܠ ܢܦܫܢ. ܘܟܕ ܗܘܐ ܠܗܘܢ ܕܢܬܒܥܘܢ ܗܘܘ
ܠܥܡܝܗܘܢ ܕܩܝܬܐ ܘܢܦܫܘܢ ܘܐܬܟܢܫܘ ܗܘܘ ܟܠܗܘܢ
ܐܦܝܣܩܘܦܐ ܠܡܠܟܐ ܠܥܡܝܗܘܢ ܕܢܬܒܥܘܢ ܒܐܦܐ ܘܕܦܠܛܘ
ܩܫܝܫܐ ܘܐܡܪܝܢ ܠܗܘܢ ܟܠ ܪܘܡܝܐ ܠܐ ܡܫܟܚܝܢ ܐܢܚܢ
ܠܟܘܢ ܠܥܡܝܗܘܢ ܕܩܫܝܫܐ. ܘܐܡܪܝܢ ܠܗܘܢ ܗܢܘܢ
ܐܦܝܣܩܘܦܐ. ܕܠܟܘ ܘܝܗܘ ܕܢܬܒܥܘܢ ܕܡܬܘܪܐ ܒܐܦܐ ܡܢ
ܟܠܬ ܡܕܝܢܬܐ ܗܘ ܕܠܠܠܐ. ܘܦܠܛܘ ܫܠܝܚܐ ܡܢ ܦܪܘܣܘ ܗܘ
ܡܕܝܢܬܐ ܕܫܠܝܚܐ. ܘܟܕ ܚܙܘ ܟܠ ܪܘܡܝܐ ܕܗܘܝܢܐ ܗܘ
ܥܡܘܬܐ ܗܘܝܐ. ܐܝܟ ܗܘ ܕܟܬܝܒ ܐܝܟܢ ܘܟܕ ܦܠܛܘ ܐܝܟܢ
ܘܒܢܝܢ ܗܘܘ ܡܢ ܕܩܝܬܐ ܒܗ ܒܥܕܬܐ ܗܘܐ ܗܘܐ ܘܕܒܐ
ܪܟܐ. ܘܦܠܛܘ ܗܘܘ ܡܕܝܢܬܐ ܕܡܕܝܢܬܐ ܠܟܠܠ. ܘܦܪܢܣܐ ܗܘܬ
ܠܬܘܗܡܟܘ. ܘܟܕ ܚܙܘ ܗܘܘ ܟܠ ܪܘܡܝܐ. ܗܦܟܘ ܟܠܗ ܡܢ
ܐܦܝܣܩܘܦܐ ܕܢܦܫܘܢ ܗܘܘ ܒܡܕܝܢܬܗܘܢ ܘܕܬܫܡܫܬܗܘܢ ܗܘܘ
ܩܪܝܬܐ ܒܩܘܪܝܬܗܘܢ. ܘܟܕ ܦܠܛܘ ܗܘܘ ܩܪܝܬܐ ܕܫܠܝܚܐ
ܠܩܘܪܝܬܗܘܢ ܗܘܐ ܫܠܝܚܐ. ܘܢܦܫ ܗܘܘ ܪܘܝܐ ܘܫܠܡ ܗܘ
ܪܘܡܝܐ ܘܢܦܪܘܬ ܗܘܬ ܐܬܪ ܘܐܬܦܢܝܬ ܗܘܬ ܠܘܬ ܡܕܝܢܬܐ
ܗܝ. ܘܟܕ ܚܙܘ ܡܢܘܕܝܐ ܘܫܬܦܐ. ܦܪܢܣܘ ܘܥܠܘ ܗܘܘ ܗܢܘܢ
ܥܠ ܪܥܝܗ ܕܥܡܝܗ ܐܦܝܣܩܘܦܐ ܕܡܕܝܢܬܗܘܢ ܟܕ ܡܚܝܢ
ܗܘܘ ܡܢܘܕܝܐ ܕܡܕܝܢ ܐܝܟܢ ܒܡܥܡܝܐ ܕܢܦܫܢ ܒܪܗ ܗܘ
ܕܐܠܗܐ ܚܝܐ. ܗܘ ܕܡܠܠܗ، ܢܦܫܐ ܒܐܪܥܗܘܢ ܘܥܠ ܐܦ
ܚܝܦܐ ܘܐܡܪܝܢ ܠܗ ܕܥܦܪ ܒܪܠܗܐ ܘܥܠܝܡܐ ܕܠܟܬ ܒܗܘܢ

ܘܬܘܬܐ ܕܗ̈ܠܟܘܗܝ، ܕܡܫܟܢ ܗ̇ܘܐ ܘܒܗܘܢ ܘܕܡܐ ܕܗܘ̈ܦܟܐ
ܕ̈ܐܦܘܗܝ، ܘܕܢܟ̈ܦܘܗܝ، ܘܕܡܣܟ̈ܠܢܘܬܗ ܘܕܦܬܟ̈ܘܗܝ، ܕܐ̈ܪܐ ܗ̇ܘܐ ܘܒܝܫܬ.
ܐܬܬܘ ܗܘܘ ܡܫ̈ܡܫܐ ܕܢ̈ܓܪܐ ܘܐܪ̈ܡܠܘܗܝ، ܠܗ ܒܡܘܟܠܐ
ܕܡܢܝܢܐ. ܘܫܢܝ ܠܘܗܝ، ܒܕܡܐ ܕܟܠܗ ܗܘܘ ܓ̈ܒܪܐ ܕܒ̈ܢܝܘܗܝ،
ܡܢ ܐܬܠܝܢܐ. ܘܐܪ̈ܡܠܘ ܗ̇ܘܐ ܠܘܗܝ، ܡܫܘܪܐ ܕܦ̈ܪܢܣܐ.
ܘܡܪܝܘ ܗܘܘ ܢܘܪܝ ܠܗ. ܘܟܕ ܡܢܝܢ ܗ̇ܘܐ ܕܢܦܘܩ ܕܡܟܠܐ
ܗܘܐ ܠܗ ܡܫܘܪܐ ܟܕ ܦܘܡܗ. ܡܫ̈ܐܘܗܝ، ܗܘܘ ܒܡܘܟܐ
ܘܕܟܠܘܗܝ، ܪܫܐ ܕܝ ܪܚܡ ܗ̇ܘܐ ܒܗ ܒܕܒܝܠ ܒܡܘܟܠܐ. ܘܡܢܟܬ
ܗܘܬ ܒܟܝ ܫܬܗ ܘܦܪܗܬ ܗܘܬ ܒܐܦ̈ܘܗܝ ܘܡܟܠܬ ܗܘܬ ܠܕܡܗ.
ܘܐܡܪܬ ܠܗ ܕܬܫܠܡ ܪܘܚ ܒܟ ܪܘܚܝ. ܟܕ ܡܫܝܚܐ ܕܝ ܒܬܗ،
ܘܗܡܢܬ ܒܗ. ܘܪܗܛܐ ܗܘܘ ܒܬ̈ܪܗ ܕܡܕܝܢܬܐ. ܘܟܠܗ ܗܘܐ
ܘܐܘܕܟܗܘܢ، ܠܕܢܚܐ ܐܠܝܡ ܕܐܡܕܝ ܗܘܐ ܒܪܢܫ ܒܝܠܬܗ.
ܘܕܐܢܫ̈ܐ ܡܟܠܬ ܫܬܗ ܠܕܡܗ. ܘܟܕ ܗܘܐ ܠܗܘܢ ܕܢܚܐ
ܕܒܥܘܢ ܗܘܘ ܘܢܐܡܪܝܢ ܠܡܥܒܕܢܘܬܐ ܕܒܕܘܟܬܐ ܕܡܟܠܬ
ܠܕܡܗ ܕܐܢܫܗ ܬܡܟܠ ܐܦ ܗܝ، ܡܫܡܫ ܒܢܫܐ ܕܡܘܬܐ.
ܘܠܒܟܗ ܗܘܘ ܡܥܒܕܢܘܬܐ ܘܟܠ ܚܕ ܚܕ ܡܫܝܚܐ ܠܓܒܗ
ܡܬܚܢܝ ܗܘܐ ܒܗ. ܘܟܕ ܓܒܝܢܐ ܗܘܬ ܠܕܡܗ ܕܐܢܫܗ.
ܢܦܫܗ ܡܛܠ ܦܘܫܬ ܗܘܬ. ܘܫܠܝܢܘܗܝ، ܕܡܛܠ ܒܟ ܕܫܠܗ ܘܟܕ
ܟܠܗ ܗܘܘ ܡܥܒܕܢܘܬܐ ܠܡܫܝܚܘܬܐ. ܘܪܥܝܢ ܐܢ̈ܫܐ ܘܐܢܫܐ
ܟܠܗ̈ܝܢ. ܘܓܒܪܐ ܗܘܘ ܥܡ̈ܝܐ ܕܬܫܡܫܬܗ ܘܗܡܙܡ ܗܘܘ ܐܢܫ
ܟܕܝܫܬ ܡܕܘܪܐ ܕܐܒܘܗܝ، ܕܒܡܠܦܢܐ ܐܣܘܟܣܐ ܒܫܡܫܬܐ
ܕܐܬܠܝܠ ܒܗܡܢܐ ܕܒܪܘܟܬܐ. ܒܬܪܟ ܡܘܕܥܢܘܬܐ ܗܠܝܢ
ܒܦܪܓܡܐ ܐܢܫ ܡܪܝܢܘ ܘܐܪܓܠܘ ܐܣܘܟܣܦܪܘ. ܘܗܘܡ
ܐܢܫ ܒܒܥܬ ܐܪ̈ܒܐ ܕܡܫܝܚܘܬܐ ܐܬܪ ܕܒܪܓܡܐ ܕܬ̈ܫܠܡܐ
ܘܫܡܝܢ܀ ܗܢܐ ܕܝܢ ܒܪܘܡܝܐ ܐܣܘܟܣܐ ܬܠܡܝܕܗ ܗ̇ܘܐ
ܠܐܝܢܠ ܒܡܕܝܢܐ. ܐܬܬܘܗܝ، ܗ̇ܘܐ ܕܝܢ ܒܢ̈ܘܗܝ ܒܝܢܘܗܝ
ܐܣܘܟܣܐ ܕܪܘܡܝܐ ܗܘ ܕܒܢ̈ܘܗܝ، ܒܫܢܬ ܗܘܬ ܒܠܘܬܗ

ܕܡܪܢ ܕܢܨܚܬ ܗܕܝܢ ܢܬܚܘܠ ܪܫܗ. ܒܫܢܬܐ ܕܦܩܝܕܐ. ܘܒܗ ܒܫܢܬܐ ܢܦܠܬ ܚܪܒܬܐ ܒܡܕܝܢܬܐ ܡܢ ܥܠܝܐ. ܘܐܦܩܘܗܝ ܡܦܩܕܢܘܬܐ. ܘܒܬܪ ܟܠܗܘܢ ܕܢܦܫܗ ܡܬܪܡܣܝܢ ܡܪܗܛܝܢ ܗܘܘ ܠܗ. ܘܠܒܪ ܡܢ ܡܕܝܢܬܐ ܡܛܫܝܢ ܗܘܘ ܠܗ ܒܕ ܪܗܛܐ ܗܘܬ ܐܢܬܬܐ ܠܪܓܠܗ. ܘܡܫܪܝܐ ܗܘܬ ܘܐܡܪܐ ܗܘܬ ܕܢܫܗ ܒܥܠ ܢܦܩ ܘܬܒܥܝܢ ܗܘܘ ܕܠܐ ܢܚ ܗܘܐ ܒܐܘܠܨܢܗ. ܘܒܥܘܗܝ ܒܪ ܕܦܓܥܝܢ ܗܘܘ ܗܘܘ ܥܠ ܢܛܘܪܬܐ ܕܪܒܢܗ. ܘܒܬܪ ܡܬܠ ܗܘܘ ܡܦܩܕܢܘܬܐ ܠܕܘܟܬܐ ܗܝ ܕܡܫܡܠ ܗܘܬ ܒܗ ܡܢܗܘܢ ܒܪܢܫܐ ܕܡܕܝܢܬܐ. ܘܐܝܬ ܗܘܘ ܒܡܕܝܢܬܐ ܟܠ ܡܕܝܢܬܐ ܕܢܝܚܘ ܒܗ ܐܝܟ ܕܒܥܕ ܗܘܐ ܕܢܗܐ ܒܒܝܬܗ ܗܘܘ. ܘܕܡܫܟܚܝܢ ܡܢܗܐ ܐܡܪ ܗܘܐ ܫܪܒܠ ܒܕܝܢܐ ܗܘ ܐܝܟ ܕܢܗܘܘܢ ܗܘܘ ܠܕܝܢܐ ܕܐܬܪܐ. ܘܢܩܒ ܗܘܘ ܠܗ ܚܒܝܪܐ ܕܢܨܚܬܐ ܐܝܟ ܒܝܕܐ ܕܥܬܝܕ ܦܩܝܕܐ. ܘܡܬܚܪ ܠܗܘܢ ܕܠܐ ܬܗܪܐ ܐܢܫܐ. ܡܛܠ ܕܝܬܒܐ ܐܢܫܐ ܗܘ ܕܐܬܪܐ ܒܫܘܪܐ ܕܢܩܘܡ ܐܢܬܘܢ ܠܝ. ܘܒܫܘܒܐ ܕܡܚܒܝܢ ܐܢܬܘܢ ܥܠ ܡܕܝ. ܐܠܐ ܫܠܘ ܗܢܐ ܫܒܪܐ ܕܠܐ ܡܟܝܪ ܠܝ. ܗܒܘ ܠܝ ܩܠܝܠ ܒܕܢܐ ܕܐܙܠܐ ܒܗ ܡܢܟܘܢ ܐܢܬܘܢ. ܘܗܟ ܗܘܐ ܘܫܪ ܗܘܐ ܠܡܕܝܢܬܐ ܘܐܪܝܡ ܗܘܐ ܩܠܗ ܘܐܡܪ. ܫܒܘܩ ܠܝ ܡܫܝܚܐ ܥܠ ܕܢܦܩܬ ܠܟ ܘܥܠ ܕܐܪܓܙܬܟ ܒܕܡܝܐ ܦܓܪܐ ܕܥܒܕܬܐ ܡܢܝܬܐ. ܘܫܘܘ ܥܠ ܫܒܪ. ܘܦܓܥ ܡܢ ܕܢܐ ܕܥܬܝܕ ܘܫܘܚܕ ܐܝܟ ܕܢܚܬ ܠܓܘܫܡܐ. ܘܡܩܠܝܢ ܐܝܟ ܬܘܒܐ ܕܦܩܝܕ ܘܐܬܦܩܕ ܓܐܕܝܟ ܘܕܐܬܦܫܬ ܓܐܕܝܣܘܢ. ܘܕܒܠܬ ܒܫܕܒܘܪܐ ܫܦܝܪ ܠܒܪܢܝܟ. ܫܠܘ ܕܢܐ ܦܓܥ ܡܢ ܒܐܢܬܐ. ܒܗܬܝܟ ܕܡܛܠ ܫܠܝܐ ܗܘ ܢܫܡ ܡܠܝܠܘܬ، ܒܗܒܠܐ ܕܡܐܬܝܬܝܟ. ܘܒܕ ܗܠܝܢ ܫܒܩܒ ܗܘܘ ܫܪܝܪܐ ܕܡܕܝܢܬܐ. ܐܬܡܢܥܘ ܗܘܘ ܥܠ ܡܦܩܕܢܘܬܐ ܥܠ ܕܫܒܩܘܗܝ ܗܘܘ ܕܢܝܠܐ. ܘܒܕ ܡܝܬ ܗ̈ܘ، ܦܓܪܐ ܕܡܫܝܚ ܗ̈ܘ، ܒܝܬ ܚܝ̈ܘܗܝ ܘܡܬܢܝܚ ܗ̈ܘ، ܥ̈ܠܝܗܘܢ، ܡܢ ܒܝܬ ܦܪ̈ܘܩܐ. ܘܡܢ ܡܕܝܢܐ ܓܠ̈ܝܗܘܢ،

ܡܣ̈ܪܩܝܢ ܠܗܘܢ ܕܢܬܦܫܚܘܢ. ܘܟܠܐ ܢܚܘܫܬ ܗܘܐ ܠܗ ܒܣܪ̈ܩܐ
ܘܢܦܠܬ ܗܘܐ ܠܗ ܘܐܦ ܡܢ ܥܝ̈ܢܐ ܐܚܪ̈ܢܐ. ܒܬܪ ܗܘ̣ܐ
ܘܐܫܬܘܗܝ. ܘܟܕ ܚܙܐ ܗܘܐ ܕܢܝܚܐ ܕܐܫܬܒܩܬ ܗܘ̣ܐ ܠܗ ܘܠܐ
ܡܫܟܚ ܗܘ̣ܐ ܕܢܬܒ ܢܦܫܐ ܠܗ ܒܬܫܒܘܚܬܐ. ܐܬܡܗ ܗܘ̣ܐ
ܡܠܗ ܡܠܝܠ ܗܘ̣ ܒܐܠܗܐ ܒܗ ܢܦܫܗ.○○○ ܫܪܒܝܠ ܐܡܪ. ܒܠ
ܡܢܝܐ ܚܘܫܬ ܒܠ ܐܦ ܗܢܐ ܒܝܢܐ ܕܥܘܕܪܐ. ܘܒܫܘܠܡܗ ܡܢ
ܬܘܪܥܝܐ ܕܣܥܘܕܘܬܐ ○○○ ܗܦܟܘܢܐ ܐܡܪ. ܠܐ ܡܢܝܢ
ܣܘܬ ܒܠܝܢ ܘܐܚܡܢܬ ܡܠܝܠ. ܫܬܩܢ ܗܘ̣ ܒܪ ܫܠܝܢ ܡܠܝܠ.
ܘܐܠܘ ܡܚܐ ܗܘܬ ܠܒܪ ܡܢ ܢܦܫܐ ܕܫ̈ܠܝܐ ܡܚܝܢ ܗܘܬ
ܕܐܫܬܝܢ ܒܢ. ܐܝܟ ܕܝܬܪ ܐܬܒܝܢ ܡܚܝܢ ܓܒܪܐ ܕܠܗܘܬ
ܫ̈ܠܡܐ. ܕܫܠܡܬ ܒܪ ܠܫ̈ܠܡܐ ܫܠܡܬ. ܘܐܦ ܐܢܐ ܦܘܪܥܢܟ
ܘܐܫܬܝܢܬ ܒܢ ܗܘܝܢܐ. ܐܝܟ ܓܒܪܐ ܕܫܘܝܐ ܗܘܝܢܐ. ܘܦܩܕ
ܗܘܐ ܕܢܬܐ ܘܢܦܠܬ ܗܘܬ ܘܠܐ ܡܢ ܫܠܝܐ ܒܫ̈ܦܘܗܝ، ܒܕܝܢܐ
ܕܒܘܪܐ. ܘܐܬܬܝ ܗܘ̣ܐ. ܘܥܩ ܗܘ̣ܐ ܐܦܣܩܘܦܐ ܕܝܬܒ ܗܘ̣ܐ
ܒܠܘܗܝ، ܒܠܐܝܬ. ܘܬܘܒ ܡܢ ܫܠܝܐ ܐܬܬܦܝܫܬ ܗܘܬ ܘܠܐ.
ܘܡܚܐ ܗܘ̣ܐ ܕܢܐ ܘܐܡܪ. ܫܪܒܝܠ ܗܘܝܐ ܕܐܝܬܘܗܝ، ܗܘ̣ܐ
ܡܢ ܩܕܝܡ ܒܡܬܪܐ ܕܐ̈ܠܗܐ ܘܗܫܐ ܒܬܪ ܝܘܡܢܐ ܒܐ̈ܠܗܐ
ܘܫܒܩܐ ܕܒܪܘܦܘܣܐ ܐܢܐ. ܘܠܐ ܚܕ ܡܢ ܐ̈ܠܗܐ ܘܝܫܘ.
ܘܐܦ ܡܢ ܫ̈ܠܚܐ ܠܐ ܕܚܠ ܡܢ ܦܘܪܥܢܘܗܝ. ܘܐܡܪܬ ܠܗ
ܕܢܒܥ ܠܐ̈ܠܗܐ ܒܥܒܕܗ ܡܪܚܝܐ ܘܠܐ ܕܒܚ. ܘܝܒܪ ܐܚܘܢ
ܐܦ ܡܢ ܒܪܗ. ܫܪܬ ܘܫܚܬ ܕܒܪܐ ܕܗܠܡ ܒܒܪ ܘܐܦܠܐ
ܐܢ ܡܪܒܚ ܐܪܐ ܕܢܗܘܘܢ ܒܠܘܗܝ، ܕܡܟܐ. ܘܠܐ ܐܪܐ ܕܢܝܚܐ
ܥܡܟܐ ܕܡܪ̈ܝܘܗܝ. ܒܠ ܕܐܣܠ ܢܬܦܘܫܘܢ. ܦܩܕ ܕܐܝܟ
ܕܡܢ ܢܬܦܘܐ ܕܫ̈ܠܚܐ. ܬܦܠ ܒܪܘܬܐ ܒܦܘܡܗ ܕܡܪ̈ܒܢܐ
ܐܝܟ ܕܦܘܩ ܘܦܠܐ. ܘܢܦܘܩ ܠܒܪ ܡܢ ܡܕܝܢܬܐ ܕܫ̈ܠܚܐ
ܡܗܪܡܐܝܬ ܐܝܟ ܕܝܒܪ ܠܡܪ̈ܗ ܕܡܕܝܢܬܐ ܘܠܐ̈ܠܗܐ
ܕܫܠܝܢ ܒܠܗ. ܦܩܕ ܕܢܬܢܣܪ ܒܡܣܘܪܐ ܕܩܝܣܐ. ܘܡܚܐ

ܘܡܛܠ ܕܒܝܬܗ܆ ܐܠܗܝܢ ܦܠ̈ܚܢܐ. ܕܗܐ ܥܒܕܝܢ ܘܡܫܠܡ.
ܘܡܟܣܝܢ ܒܝܫܐ ܘܡܩܘܡܐ ܡܢ ܐܝܠܝܢ ܕܦܠܚܝܢ ܗܘܘ ܠܗܘܢ
ܡܢ ܡܕܡ ○○○ ܕܢܒܝܐ ܐܡܪ. ܐܝܟܢܐ ܒܐܠܗܐ ܟܦܪ ܐܢܬ
ܘܡܟܣܢܐ ܡܘܕܐ ܐܢܬ ܗ̇ܘ ܕܐܬܬܠܠ ܥܠ ܡܘܫܐ ○○○ ܒܪܢܫܠ
ܐܡܪ. ܫܘܒܗܪܗܘܢ ܕܟܠܐ ܕܒܪ̈ܘܦܠܓܐ ܗܘ ܘܦܠܓܗ ܕܡܟܣܢܐ.
ܕܒܗ ܗ̣ܘ ܗܘܐ ܒܦܘܠܚܢܐ ܕܫ̈ܢܐ ܠܟܠܗܘܢ ܦܓܪ̈ܘܗܝ. ܘܒܗ
ܗܘ ܡܠܘ ܚ̈ܝܠܐ ܢܡܘܣ̈ܝܬܐ. ܕܠܐ ܗܘܘ ܦܠܚܝܢ ܠܒܪ̈ܝܬܐ ܡܢ
ܒܪܘܝܐ. ○○○ ○○○

ܦܠܚܘܢܐ ܐܡܪ. ܫܘܒܗܪܗܝܢ ܕܒܪܘܩܐ ܢܬܦܪ ܟܠܗ
ܙܒܢܝܢ ܘܡܩ̈ܒܠܐ ܡܢ ܐܬܝܪ̈ܝܢ ܠܐ̈ܠܗܐ ܢܬܦܪܩܘܢ ○○○ ܒܪܢܫܠ
ܐܡܪ ܠܗ ܡܟܣܝܢ ܐܝܠܝܢ ܕܦܪܫܝܢ ܒܝܫܐ ܕܬܘܒ ܢܦܠܓܘܢ
ܘܢܟܠܘܢ ܠܬܘܒܪܐ ܒܟܪ̈ܝܐ ܕܦܠܚܘܬܐ. ܒܪܬܐ ܓܝܪ ܠܒܪܬܐ
ܠܐ ܡܟܣܢܐ ܦܓܪܐ. ܡܛܠ ܕܐܦ ܗ̣ܘ ܦܓܪܐ ܗ̣ܘ ܕܝܢ
ܕܒܪܗ ܘܕܢܫܬܠܛ ܒܗ ܒܒܪܗ ܓܒܪ̈ܐ ܗ̣ܘ ܠܒܪܗ. ܐܝܟ
ܕܡܕܡܬ ܘܐܡܪܬ ○ ܦܠܚܘܢܐ ܐܡܪ ܥܒܘܕ ܒܬܪ̈ܝܢ ܕܐܠܦܝܢ
ܡܫ̈ܢܐ. ܘܒܒܪ ܒܡܘܕܝܐ ܕܬܠܒܐ ܕܠܐ ܬܬܡܗܬ ܡܢ ܢܡܘܦܐ
ܕܬܠܒܐ. ○○○ ܘܒܪܢܫܠ ܐܡܪ ܘܡܘܕܐ ܗ̣ܘ܆ ܒܐܢܘܬܐ ܕܬܠܒܐ
ܕܫܬܪ ܐܢܬ ܒܗܘܢ ܕܝܕܥܝܢ ܢܡܘܣܐ ܕܐܠܗܐ ܘܦܠܚ
ܢܡ̈ܘܣܗܘܢ ○○○ ܦܠܚܘܢܐ ܐܡܪ ܬܢܝܢܐ ܕܬܠܬܐ ܕܡܫܝܚܬ
ܒܗܘܢ ܗܢ̇ܘܢ ܕܬܢܝܬ ܡܫܝܚܘܢ. ܗܢܘܢ ܐܘܣܛܝܢ ܒܐܦ̈ܠܝܢܐ
ܗܠܝܢ. ܐܠܐ ܓܝܪ ܦܓܘܬ ܒܦܛ̈ܟܐ ܠܐܠܗܐ ܦܠܓܐ ܗܘܐ ܐܡܪܝܢ
ܐܝܟ ܡܕܡܢܐ ܐܝܟ ܒܡܟܪܐ ܕܐܠܗܐ ○○○ ܒܪܢܫܠ ܐܡܪ
ܠܗܝܢ ܒܡܘܪܐ ܡܦܬܟܪ. ܗܠܝܢ. ܐܝܟ ܗܘ ܕܐܘܠܝܢܐ
ܐܝܢ. ܠܢܗܝܢܐ ܓܝܪ ܥܙܝܪܐ ܐܘܠܝܢܐ ܡܦܟܪܢܘܬܐ ܡܗܝܢܐ.
ܘܡܛܠܗ ܐܦ ܒܗܘܢ ܘܡܛܠ ܕܒܗܘܢܐ ܦܬܓܡܐ ܕܡܒܪܢܫܘܬܐ ○○○
ܦܠܚܘܢܐ ܐܡܪ ܬܐܠܗܘܢ܆ ܘܦܘܪܩܢܗܘܢ܆ ܒܠ ܦܘܪܩܢܗܘܢ܆ ܡܕܡ̈ܝܐ.
ܘܟܣܝܬܗ܆ ܕܕܝܢܐ ܕܠܐܬ ܡܦܩܢܘܬܐ. ܡܕܒܪܝܢ ܗܘܘ ܕܐܦ

ܕܬܬܚܫܒ ܕܒܪܐ ܐܢܬ ܗܘ ܢܟܝܐ ܕܫܠܝܚܐ ܀ ܕܝܢܐ ܐܡܪ܂
ܢܬܪܡ ܒܥܡܡܗ، ܘܒܙܒܢܐ ܕܠܐܠܗܘܬܗ. ܘܟܕܘ ܘܡܫܠܡܢܐ
ܗܘܝܐ. ܒܙܒܢܐ ܕܪܕܐ ܘܢܦܩ ܕܟܠܗ ܥܠ ܐܪܥܐ ܀ ܫܪܒܝܠ
ܐܡܪ. ܥܡܪ ܒܟܪ ܐܢܬ ܠܝ ܗܘܢܐ. ܡܛܠ ܕܐܡܝܢ ܠܝ ܕܢܫ
ܡܢ ܫܠܝܚܘ̈ܗܝ ܕܒܗܬܐ ܐܡܪ ܗܘܐ ܕܡܫܬܡܥܐ ܠܗ ܕܦܘܪ،
ܕܐܬܬܐ ܠܡܫܟܚܬܐ ܕܡܢ ܒܝܬ ܟܢ̈ܫܬܐ. ܘܐܝܟܐ ܕܟܝܢܬܐ ܗܘܝܬ
ܒܣܘܦܐ. ܗܐ ܐܘܠܨܢܝܢ ܡܟܝܠ ܠܝ ܀ ܕܝܢܐ ܐܡܪ.
ܢܬܪܡ ܒܪ̈ܫܗܘܢ، ܕܠܐ ܒܣܗܕ ܡܢ ܦܬܓܡܐ ܕܢܦܩ ܒܝܬ ܒܬܪܗܘܢ،
ܘܦܪ̈ܣܗܘܢ، ܒܒ̈ܣܗܘܢ، ܘܒܝܬ ܦܬܓܡܐ ܕܢܦܩ ܒܗܘܢ ܀ ܫܪܒܝܠ
ܐܡܪ. ܠܐ ܡܬܒܥܐ ܐܢܐ ܠܫܠܝܚܐ ܕܡܕܡ ܕܢܬܦܛܪ. ܘܬܘܒ
ܡܕܡ ܕܠܘ ܡܢ ܒܝܬ ܗܘ ܕܐܠܗܐ. ܘܠܘ ܐܠܗܐ ܗܘ ܒܒܝܬܗ
ܐܠܐ ܒܒܪܐ ܗܘ ܕܒܒܕܝܢܗ ܀ ܕܝܢܐ ܐܡܪ. ܐܝܟ ܕܢܦܪܘܡ
ܫܠܝܚܐ ܦܛܪܘ ܐܦ ܐܢܬ. ܘܐܝܟ ܕܡܫܝܚܢ ܕܢ̈ܟܐ ܣܦܪ ܐܦ
ܐܢܬ ܀

ܫܪܒܝܠ ܐܡܪ. ܘܐܢ ܐܢܐ ܡܫܬܪܐ ܐܢܐ ܠܡܕܡ ܕܒܒܪܐ
ܗܘ ܕܟܠܗ ܐܢܫܐ. ܕܠܐ ܝܕܥ ܘܠܐ ܚܙܐ ܒܒܝܬܗ. ܐܢܬ ܠܐ
ܬܫܬܪܐ ܠܐܠܗܐ ܒܒܪܐ ܕܟܠ. ܘܬܦܠܘܚ ܒܒܝܬܗ ܠܡܕܡ ܕܠܘ
ܡܢܗ ܗܘ. ܘܡܒܥܪ، ܠܒܝܬܗ ܀ ܕܝܢܐ ܐܡܪ. ܗܒܝܢܐ ܡܠܟ
ܠܟܘܢ ܘܠܦܠܚܘܢ ܗܢܐ. ܕܗܘܢܬܗܘܢ ܡܫܬܪܝܢ ܐܦ ܠܢܫܪ̈ܐ
ܕܡܚܘܪܝܢ ܠܟܠ ܦܢܝܬܐ ܕܐܪܥܐ ܀ ܫܪܒܝܠ ܐܡܪ. ܐܦܢ ܠܐ
ܬܫܬܪܐ ܠܝ ܕܢܫܬܪܐ ܐܢܐ܆ ܐܠܐ ܬܫܬܪܐ ܗܘ ܠܝ ܕܠܐ ܢܫܬܪܐ
ܠܗܘܢ ܘܠܐ ܢܦܪ ܐܢܐ܆. ܒܝܕ ܕܒܒ̈ܝܬܐ ܐܢܐ܆. ܒܗܠܝܢ ܗܘ
ܒܪ ܗܢܐ ܡܬܚܙܐ ܕܢܫܬܪܐ ܒܒܝܬܐ ܒܗ ܒܒܝܬܗ. ܘܫܪܝܐ
ܗܘ ܠܒܒܝܬܐ ܕܢܬܦܪܘܩ ܒܒܗ ܒܬܪ̈ܬܗ ܀ ܕܝܢܐ ܐܡܪ.
ܒܡܫܚܐ ܐܬܬܠ ܡܫܝܚܐ ܕܐܘܕܝܬ ܒܗ. ܘܒܡܫܚܐ ܬܬܠܐ ܐܢܐ
ܠܝ ܐܝܟ ܕܠܢܟܝ. ܘܬܬܠܐܘܗܝ، ܥܠ ܡܫܚܐ ܦܠܣܐ ܥܠܝܐ ܀
ܫܪܒܝܠ ܐܡܪ. ܡܫܝܚܐ ܕܗܘܐ ܡܚܝܠ ܐܢܬ ܒܗ. ܚܙܝ ܕܠܐ

ܐܘ ܒܗܬ ܕܢܫܬܟܚ. ܠܡܘܕܝܢܘ̱ ܕܫ̈ܠܝܚܐ... ܫܪܒܝܠ ܐܡܪ. ܥܒܪ ܐܡܪܬ ܕܠܐ ܒܗܬ ܐܢܐ. ܡܛܠ ܕܡܪܢ ܗܘ ܡܕܒܪܢ. ܘܡܠܟܐ ܗܘ، ܟܠܗ ܬܪܒܝܬ ܠܗܬܗ. ܕܐܝܠܝܬܗ ܓܝܪ ܒܪ̈ܒܘܬܐ ܕܦܬܓܡܐ. ܡܪܒܝܐ ܐܢܐ ܠܗ ܘܡܫܒܚܐ ܒܐܘܢܓܠܝܘܢ ܕܡܫܝܚܐ. ܥܒܕܐ ܗܘ ܓܝܪ ܙܒܝܢ ܝܫܘܥ: ܐܠܗܐ ܕܗܘܐ ܒܪ ܐܢܫܐ... ܕܝܢܐ ܐܡܪ. ܠܥܒܕܐ ܗܘ ܗܟܝܠ ܡܫܐܠ ܐܢܐ ܘܠܥܒܕܐ ܕܠܐ ܦܓܥܐ. ܘܒܗ ܡܠܬܐ ܕܗܘܡܟ ܗܘܐ ܡܫܐܠ ܐܢܐ... ܫܪܒܝܠ ܐܡܪ. ܐܝ̱ ܫܪܝܪܐ ܠܝ ܕܥܒܕܐ ܐܢܐ. ܠܐ ܬܗܘܒ ܬܫܐܠܢܝ. ܐܝܬ ܓܝܪ ܥܒܕܐ ܕܡܫܬܐܠ. ܘܐܘܕܝܬ ܓܝܪ ܒܡܠܬܐ ܐܢܐ ܕܗܘܝܬ ܐܝܟ ܕܐܡܪܬ... ܕܝܢܐ ܐܡܪ ܐܝܟܢܐ ܐܫܬܥܝܢ ܡܠܬܐ ܕܗܘܐ ܡܫܬ ܕܠܐ ܡܕܒܫ ܐܢܐ...

ܫܪܒܝܠ ܐܡܪ. ܐܦ ܐܢܐ ܠܐ ܝܕܥ ܐܢܐ ܐܝܟܢܐ ܐܦܢܐ ܠܝ ܦܬܓܡܐ ܕܦܪܘܫ ܡܠܬܐ. ܘܗܟܝܢ ܐܢܬ ܡܫܐܠ ܐܢܬ ܠ ܐܝܟ ܫܢܐ... ܕܝܢܐ ܐܡܪ. ܥܒܪ ܦܪܫܬܢ ܡܠܬܐ ܕܡܘܫ̱ ܬ̈ܠܝܢ ܘܠܐ ܟܠܠ ܠܝ ܘܡܫܪ̈ܝܢ ܐܩܦܝܢ ܘܐܬܝܬ ܐܢܬ. ܘܡܟܡܟܡ ܩ̈ܠܐ ܒܗܬ ܒ̈ܬܪܝܢ ܘܠܐ ܫܡܥ ܠܝ. ܘܡܬܘܚܡ ܐ̈ܠܗܝܢ ܡܢ ܒܗܬ ܗܘ̈ܡܐ ܘܡܨܒܪ ܐܢܬ ܠܫ̈ܠܝܚܐ. ܘܡܬܠܝܫ ܒܠܗ ܦܓܪܝ ܘܡܗܘܢ ܒܥܙ̈ܪܐ ܘܡܨܪܦ ܐܢܬ ܒܠ ܐ̈ܠܗܐ. ܘܡܛܠ ܕܗܘܝܬ ܦܓܪܝ ܗܐ ܐܡܪ ܐܢܬ ܒܠܗܕܡ ܕܥܒܪ ܠܝ... ܫܪܒܝܠ ܐܡܪ. ܐܘ̱ ܐܢܐ ܕܗܘܒܪܬ ܗܠܝܢ ܦܪܘܬܢ ܡܪܝܫܐ. ܐܢܬ ܕܗܘܒܪܬ ܐܢܝܢ ܝܬܝܪ ܕܗܦ ܕܬܬܗܪܐ ܡܛܠܠܐ ܒܒ̈ܬܕܝܢ ܘܡܨܕܩܢܐ ܒ̈ܬܠܝܢ... ܕܝܢܐ ܐܡܪ ܗܐ ܝܒܪܬ ܠܫ̈ܠܝܚܐ ܘܐܦ ܠܐ̈ܠܗܐ. ܘܗܐ ܘܐܦ ܠܐ ܡܨܒܪ ܐܢܬ. ܐܝܟ ܕܐܦܘܡ ܒܠܝܢ ܡܘܬܐ ܘܠܠܐܝܬ. ܫܠܘ ܗܕܐ ܕܡ ܕܫܐܪ ܐܢܬ ܡܛܠܒ ܐܢܐ ܗܘ ܕܬܗܘܒ ܫܪ̈ܪܐ ܡܪ̈ܝܪܐ ܘܩ̈ܫܝܐ ܐܫܬܝܢ ܒܝ... ܫܪܒܝܠ ܐܡܪ. ܝܕܥ ܐܢܬ ܗܘ ܕܐܡܪܬ ܠܝ ܕ̈ܒܪܬܐ ܦܬܓܡ̈ܬܐ ܕܫܠܘ ܪ̈ܡܫܐ ܕܠܘܫܟܐ ܗܘ ܒܒܕܗ ܕܠܘܫܟܐ ܗܘܝܬ ܡܫܘܐ ܝܒܪ..

ܣܗܕܘܬܐ ܕܫܪܒܝܠ

ܣܦ̈ܪܬܐ ܕܡ̈ܠܟܐ ܕܐܡܪ ܐܢܬ. ܐܠܐ ܕܡܫܬܡܥܝܢ ܠܡܠܝ
ܐܠ̈ܗܝܢ ܫܒܝܚܐ ooo ܫܪܒܝܠ ܐܡܪ. ܐܢ ܫܪܝܪܢ ܠܝ
ܚܙܐ ܡܢ ܬܫܒܚܬܗ ܕܚܕ ܡܢ ܐܠܗܝܢ. ܒܡܬܬܐ ܗܝ ܕܢܐܡܪ
ܕܐܡܕܝܢܐ ܐܢܬܘܢ. ܚܙ ܠܒܪ ܗܘܐ ܚܢܝܢ ܒܡ ܬܠܝܐ. ܡܕܡ
ܕܠܐ ܙܕܩ. ܘܐܢܫܝܐ ܚܕ ܡܢ ܒܢ̈ܝܠܬܐ ܕܐܬܟܢܫܬ ܒܐܠܗܐ.
ܐܝܟ ܕܐܡܪܬ ܬܫܒܚܬܗܘܢ ܕܒܡܬܬܐ o.o ܕܢܐ ܐܡܪ. ܗܢܐ
ܕܡܢܗܪܢܐ ܗܘܐ ܕܐܠܗܐ ܡܢ ܡܕܡ ܘܗܦܟ ܠܒܪ ܐܢܘܢ
ܦܫܐ. ܘܠܐ ܕܝܢ. ܘܐܦ ܐܦ ܒܗܕܝܐ ܕܡ̈ܠܟܐ ܘܠܐ ܙܒ.
ܐܘܟܡܘܗܝ ܒܠ ܦܪܨܘܦܐ ܒܪ ܐܢܫܐ ܒܠܘܪܐ. ܘܒܒܕܘ
ܟܦܝܪܐ ܗܒܠܐ. ܒܕܡܐ ܕܢܒܙ ܗܘܐ ܬܫܬܐ ܕܪ̈ܓܠܘܗܝ o.o
ܫܪܒܝܠ ܐܡܪ. ܘܐܦ ܒܫܪ̈ܒܝܗܘܢ ܗܝܢܐ ܘܦܪ̈ܫܐ ܕܐܠܗܝܢ
ܗܠܝܢ ܪܘܓܙܝܢ ܒܗܘܢܒܪ̈ܝܬܗܘܢ ܒܕܡܐ ܕܬܪ ܙܕܩ ܠܝ ܕܬܒܥܗܬ.
ܗܐ ܠܒܪ ܐܢ ܐܚܪ ܗܒܪ ܡܕܡ ܕܗܒܪ ܚܕ ܡܢ ܐܠܗܝܢ
ܘܡܠܝܢ ܠܗ ܡܕܡܝܢ. ܒܡܬܬܐ ܒܡܙ ܐܢܬ ܠܒܗ̈ܝ o.o ܕܢܝܐ
ܐܡܪ. ܢܡܕܝܢܐ ܬܟܒ ܐܢܐ ܡܢܝܢ ܠܒܪܦܝܢ ܕܒܠ ܐ̈ܠܗܐ
ܘܡܪܚܡܬܝܢ ܕܢܝܪܬ ܐܦ ܠܡ̈ܠܟܐ. ܘܠܐ ܡܟܪܢܐ ܐܢܐ ܡܢܝܢ
ܒܕܡܐ ܕܗܘܐ ܐܢܬ [ܠܗܘܢ ܒܩܘܒܠܐ ܒܟܢ̈ܘܫܝܐ ܩ̈ܕܡܝܐ ∴ ∴
ܫܪܒܝܠ ܐܡܪ. ܡܢܘ ܒܗܘܢ ܒܪ̈ܚܡܝܢ ܗܒܠ ܘܠܐ ܗܦܘܟ
ܦ̈ܓܥܠ. ܘܫܘܐ ܝܐܝܬ ܒܟܒܕܐ ܫܘܠܛܢܐ ܕܡ̈ܠܟܐ ܕܢܗܒ
ܠܝ. ܘܠܐ ܬܦܝܫܐ ܐܢܬ ܠܡ̈ܠܟܐ ܒܪ̈ܓܠܘܗܝ: ܘܬܬܫܒܩ ܘܐܦ
ܐܢܬ] ܒܚܝ̈ܠ ܐܘܦܣܝܢ ܕܠܝܢ o . o ܕܢܝܐ ܐܡܪ. ܠܒܪܦܝܢ ܕܒܠ
ܐ̈ܠܗܐ ܘܡܪܚܡܬܝܢ ܕܠܗܬ ܡ̈ܠܟܐ. ܐܬܝܘ ܠܡܠܝܢ ܫܪܒܐ ܗܠܝܢ
ܕܡܟܪܡ ܐܢܬ ܒܗܘܢ. ܘܐܢ ܬܗܒ ܡܫܘܦ ܐܢܬ ܒܠ
ܡܪ̈ܚܡܬܝܢ. ܬܗܒ ܡܬܬܗܦܟ ܠܠܝܢ ܐܓ̈ܠܝܢܐ. ܕܡܢ ܗܠܝܢ
ܡܪܢܝܢ o.o ܫܪܒܝܠ ܐܡܪ ܫܠܝܛ ܐܢܬ ܐܝܟ ܕܢܐܡܪ. ܒܒܙ ܡܕܡ
ܕܝܬܐ ܐܢܬ ܘܠܐ ܬܫܘܘ o . o ܕܢܝܐ ܐܡܪ. ܦܡ ܕܒܠ ܦܓܪܗ
ܠܐ ܫܘ ܕܫܘܒܪ ܒܗ ܗܠܝܢ ܫܪܒܐ. ܐܡܕܢܐ ܡܫܚܫ ܕܢܠ

ܢܚܬܡ ܠܢ ܢܟ̈ܣܐ ܕܡܪܘܡܝܐ ܘܪܘܚܢܐ: ܒܝܘܡܐ ܕܦܘܪܥܢܘܬܐ
ܕܠܥܠܡ :. ܡܫܡܠܝܐ ܐܡܝܢ. ܢܬܬܘܚܡܘܢ ܡܢܗܘܢ ܕܩܕܡܐ
ܘܬܠܝܠܐ ܒܗܬ ܢ̈ܟܣܬܐ ܕܐܒ̈ܗܘܗܝ: ܘܢܬܚܝܘܢ ܘ ܒܠܥܘܢ
ܡܢܝܐܬ. ܘܚܟܘ ܠܗ ܡܒܝܢ. ܒܝܘܡܐ ܕܢܦܩ ܗܘܐ ܕܡܟܐ
ܡܢ ܬܫܥܝܬ ܦܓܪܐ] ܕܝܬܒܘܬܗ ○○○ ܫܪܝܪ ܐܡܝܢ. ܐܦ ܠܐ
ܘܟܒܬ ܚܒܝܒ ܡܢ ܫܘܘ̈ܗܝ ܕܦܓܪܐ ܬܘܒ ܐܘܣܦ ܠܗ ܥܠ
ܫܘܘ̈ܗܝ ܡܕܡ ܕܢܟܐ ܐܝܬ ○○○ ܕܢܐ ܐܡܝܢ ܢܬܪܡ ܢ̈ܟܣܬܐ
ܕܐܒ̈ܗܘܗܝ ܘܐܬܬܟܒܘܗܝ. ܥܠ ܐܪܥܐ ܘܟܒܘܪ ܐܒ̈ܗܘܗܝ. ܥܠ
ܒܝܬ̈ܒܘܗܝ. ܘܐܟܠܘ ܡܢܐ ܬܫܥܝܬ ܒܝܬ̈ܒܘܗܝ. ܘܢܒܢܐ ܥܠ
ܦܓܪܐ ܕܐ̈ܒܗܘܗܝ. ܘܬܠܐܝܘܗܝ ܒܢ̈ܝܠܘܗܝ ܒܪ ܒܝܫܡ ܒܗܬ ܪܫܘ.
ܘܢܬܟܒ ܒܦܓܪܗ. ܘܚܟܘ ܠܗ ܡܒܝܢܐ ○○○ ܫܪܝܪ ܐܡܝܢ.
ܠܐ ܡܟܒܫܝܢ ܐܢܫ ܐܝܟ ܕܒܗ ܐܠܗܐ ܡܫܪܝܢ ܘܠܐ ܡܢܝܢ
[ܢܫܒܝܢ] ܐܝܟ ܕܐܠܗܐ ܗܘ ܬܘܒܠܝܢܘܢ. ܘܡܛܠ ܗܢܐ ܐܡܝܢ
ܐܢܐ. ܕܠܐ ܢܦܪܐ ܘܠܐ ܟܦܢܐ ܘܠܐ ܡܘܬܐ ܘܠܐ ܚܝ̈ܐ. ܘܠܐ
ܪܘܡܐ ܘܠܐ ܒܘܡܩܐ. ܡܟܒܫܝܢ ܦܪܫܝܢ ܠܗ ܠܐܢܫ ܡܢ
ܚܘܒܗ ܕܐܠܗܐ ܕܒܡܪܢ ܢܘܒ ܡܫܝܚܐ ○○○ ܕܝܢܐ ܐܡܝܢ
ܐܝܟܘ ܐܘܦܪܐ ܕܐܟܪܐ ܘܕܝܫܐ ܘܗܟܘ ܬܫܥܝܬ ܫܘܒܬܗ.
ܘܚܟܘ ܡܒܝܢܐ ܒܝܘܡܐ ܕܐܬܝ ܗܘ ܢܪܐ ܕܝܠܕܘܗܝ ○.○
ܫܪܝܪ ܐܡܝܢ ܕܒܘܪܐ ܐܝܟ ܬܒܬܝܟ ܕܝܐܝ ܡܢ ܚܝܬܝܟ
ܕܠܘܬ. ܐܝܠܐ ܚܝܬܝܟ ܗܘܘܬ ܕܒܘܪܐ ܘܬܒܬܝܟ ܗܘܘ ܢܘܪܝܡ ○.○
ܕܝܢܐ ܐܡܝܢ. ܠܐ ܫܦܝܪ ܐܝܬ ܠܝ ܒܥܠܡ ܕܐܡܝܢ ܐܝܬ. ܐܝܬ ܗܘ
ܒܪ ܐܬܪܐ ܒܪܢܫܐ. [ܕܐܬܪ ܪܘܚܐ. ܘܐܢܫܐ ܥܠ ܡܕܡ ܕܒܝܫ
ܘܦܠܐ ܘܡܢܝܢ. ܐܢܫܐ ܒܥܘܠܐ ܕܦܓܪܝܟ. ܥܠ ܕܠܐ
ܡܬܦܠܛ ܐܝܬ ܕܬܘܒ ܠܐܠܗܐ ܕܦܓܪ ܗܘܬ ܠܗܘܢ :. :. :.
ܫܪܝܪ ܐܡܝܢ. ܐܝܟ ܕܐܡܪܬ ܘܬܘܒ ܡܕܝܢܝܟ: ܠܐ ܢܕܥ ܐܝܬ
ܕܒܦܘܪܥܢܘܬܟ] ܕܬܫܒܚ ܐܢܫ. ܐܝܟܢܐ ܐܝܟ ܕܐܝܬ ܒܪܢܫ
ܘܒܪ ܐܝܬ ܕܢܕܥ ܐܝܬ ○.○ ܕܝܢܐ ܐܡܝܢ ܠܐ ܡܒܥܪܢ ܠܟ

ܐܝܬ ܒܡ̈ܠܐ ܕܐܡܪܬ ܕܝܢܐ. ܘܐܢܐ ܚܝܘܐ ܐܢܐ ܠܟ ܒܥܒܕܐ. ܕܫܠܡ ܗ̇ܘ ܕܝܢܐ ܕܒܬܪܗ. ܗܢ ܗܢܐ ܕܡܕܡ ܥ̈ܠܝܟ ܕܗܘܐ ܡܫ̇ܡ ܐܝܬ ܒܗ. ܗܘܝܬ ܝܕܥ ܘܪܢܠ. ܘܠܐ ܬܦܘܟܐ ܬܬܟܠܠ ܡܕܡܝ ܀ ܒܪܘܒܠ ܐܡܪ ܗ̇ܝ ܕܐܝܟܢܐ ܕܒܥܡ ܐܠܗܐ ܡܕܡ ܥ̈ܒܕܘܗܝ ܒܡܐܢܬ. ܗܘ ܐܠܗܐ ܗ̇ܘܐ ܡܢ ܕܚܝܠܘܗܝ. ܘܐܢܐ ܠܐ ܕܝܠ ܐܢܐ ܡܢ ܠܗ̈ܘܦܟܐ ܕܒ̈ܢܝܐ ܕܟ̇ܠܡ ܐܝܬ ܘܡܕܝܢܠ ܐܝܬ ܠܝ ܒܗܘܢ ܀ ܕܝܢܐ ܐܡܪ. ܕܢܦܪܩܟ ܡܟܝܢܐ ܕܐܘܕܝܬ ܒܗ. ܗܢ ܟܠ ܡܕܡ ܕܐܫܬܒܕܬ ܠܟ. ܘܕܒܬܪ ܐܢܐ ܬܘܒ ܕܐܫܬܒܕ ܠܟ: ܘܢܫܘܐ ܦܪܘܣܗ ܠܬܘܟ ܠܒܐܝܬ: ܘܢܦܪܘܩ ܡܢ ܐܝܕ̈ܝ ܀

ܒܪܘܒܠ ܐܡܪ. ܗܢܐ ܗܘ ܦܪܘܣܗ ܒܪܝܪܐ ܕܡܫܝܚܐ ܕܐܝܬܝܒ. ܢܦܠܐ ܒܡܫܐ ܗܢܐ ܕܢܗܘܐ ܠܝ. ܕܐܫܟܚ ܠܒܝܬ ܡܕܡ ܕܡܬܬܒܥܬ ܒܝ. ܘܟܠ ܡܕܡ ܕܡܣܒܪܐ ܒܥ̈ܝܢܝ ܕܬܘܒ ܕܐܫܬܒܕ ܒܝ. ܘܟܕ ܝܗܒ ܝܗܘܬ ܗܒܝܒ. ܠܐ ܢܦܩܬ ܕܬܬܪ ܡܠܬܝ ܀ ܕܝܢܐ ܐܡܪ. ܐܒܒܪܘܗܝ ܡܢ ܡܕܡܝ. ܘܬܬܠܐ ܒܡܫܘܐ ܒܬܪ ܪܘܫܗ ܗܦܟܐܝܬ. ܘܢܦܠܘ ܒܥ̈ܩܬܐ ܒܪ ܬܠܝܐ. ܘܒܒܪܘ ܠܗ ܡܦܝܠܣܘܦܐ ܗܟܢܝ ܒܬܪܟܐ ܕܒܝܬ ܕܝܢܐ ܀ ܀ ܀

ܘܦܩܕ ܗܝܡܢܘܬܐ ܘܐܟܠܘܗܝ ܡܕܡܘܗܝ. ܘܐܡܪ ܗܘܐ ܠܗ. ܕܢܩܘܡ ܠܐ̈ܠܗܐ ܘܒܒܪ ܥ̈ܒܕܐ ܕܡ̈ܠܟܐ. ܒܗܢܐ: ܕܦܘܐ ܐܡܬܝ ܘܢܘܩܡ ܥܒܕܐ ܫܠܡܘܗܝ ܀

ܒܪܘܒܠ ܐܡܪ. ܗܟܢܐ ܗܘܝܬ ܬܗܝܬ ܡܠܬܟ ܘܐܡܪܬ ܐܝܬ ܕܐܬܦܫܝ: ܒܬܪ ܦܝܠܣܘܦܘܬܐ ܕܡܫܝܚܐ ܗܘ ܕܠܐ ܬܘܒ ܥܒܕܝܢ ܐܢܐ. ܠܐ ܗܘܐ ܓܝܪ ܡܦܝܪܐ ܕܦܝܠܣܘܦܘܬܐ ܒܠܝ ܡܢ ܕܚ̈ܝܠܐ ܐܠܝ ܒܪܘܗܝ ܗܘ ܦܪܘܩ ܡܢ ܦܘܫܩܘܬܐ ܕܡܫܝܚܘܬܐ ܀ ܕܝܢܐ ܐܡܪ. ܢܦܠ ܒܝܫܐ ܕܦܪܐܠܐ ܐܝܟ ܦܝܠܣܘܦܐ. ܘܬܬܦܪܫ ܒܦܝܠܣܘܦ ܐܝܟ ܟܕܒ ܬܘܒܐ. ܘܒܒܪܘ ܡܦܝܠܣܘܦܐ ܗܟܢܐ. ܒܕܡܘܬܐ ܕܠܐ ܦܩܬ ܒܗ ܕܡܫܬܐ ܕܒܪܘܒܠ ܀ ܒܪܘܒܠ ܐܡܪ. ܗܠܝܢ ܬ̈ܒܐ ܕܐܫܟܚ ܐܝܬ ܒܠܝܗܘܢ ܕܡ̈ܕܡܢ. ܗܢ ܒܗ ܡܬܪܘܬܗܘܢ

ܡܕܡ ܠܒܪ ܕܒܚܝܠܗ ܗܘ ܘܒܨܒܝܢܗ ܗܘ. ܘܫܠܝܛܐ ܗܘ ܕܒܡܘܬܗ. ܘܠܐ ܗܘܐ ܫܠܝܛܐ ܗܘ ܒܡ ܒܪܘܚܗ ܐܝܟ ܕܦܪܝܢ ܐܢܬ ܀

ܗܓܡܘܢܐ ܐܡܪ. ܠܐ ܗܘܐ ܗܕܐ ܕܦܩܕܘ ܠܝ ܡܠܟܐ ܕܐܬܟܬܒ ܒܐܓܪܬܗܘܢ: ܕܐܝܟܢܐ ܕܐܝܬ ܕܚܠܬܐ ܘܬܫܒܘܚܬܐ ܒܬܪ ܡܠܟܘܬܗܘܢ ܕܡܫܝܚܝܐ. ܐܦ ܠܐ ܟܠ ܗܕܐ ܦܩܕ ܠܝ: ܕܐܢ ܗܘ ܕܡܬܬܦܝܣ ܒܡܠܬܐ ܘܐܢ ܠܐ ܡܬܬܦܝܣ. ܠܝ ܗܕܐ ܗܘ ܦܩܕܘ ܠܝ ܡܠܟܝ. ܕܟܠ ܡܢ ܕܠܐ ܡܕܒܚ ܠܐܠܗܐ ܘܣܐܡ ܠܗܘܢ ܒܣܡܐ ܒܦܓܪܐ ܘܒܣܝܦܐ ܚܪܝܦܐ ܐܬܚܝܒ ܒܪܫܗ ܀

ܥܙܐܝܠ ܐܡܪ. ܡܠܟܐ ܕܗܢܐ ܥܠܡܐ. ܒܗܢܐ ܗܘ ܥܠܡܐ ܫܠܝܛ ܙܒܢܝܐ. ܡܠܟܐ ܕܝܢ ܕܡܠܟܐ ܫܠܝܛ: ܗܘ ܠܥܠܡ ܘܒܗ, ܠܝ ܕܐܝܬ ܥܠܡܐ ܐܚܪܢܐ ܘܕܝܢܐ ܕܠܥܠܡ. ܕܒܗ ܗܘܐ ܦܘܪܥܢܐ ܥܡ ܐܝܠܝܢ ܕܫܠܡܘ ܠܐܠܗܐ: ܠܐܝܠܝܢ ܕܠܐ ܫܡܥܘܗܝ, ܘܠܐ ܐܘܕܝܘ ܒܗ. ܡܛܠ ܗܢܐ ܡܢܐ ܐܢܐ. ܕܠܐ ܬܘܒ ܡܕܒܚ ܐܢܐ ܠܦܬܟܪܐ. ܘܠܐ ܣܓܕ ܐܢܐ ܠܢܘܪܐ. ܘܠܐ ܣܓܕ ܐܢܐ ܠܣܝܕܐ ܀ ܕܝܢܐ ܐܡܪ. ܢܬܝܩܪ ܦܬܓܡܐ ܕܦܩܘܕܐ ܒܝܬ ܡܠܟܘܬܗ, ܕܡܠܟܐ: ܘܐܙܠ ܠܗܘ ܥܠܡܐ ܕܡܠܟܘܬܐ ܠܗ ܐܝܟ ܒܪܢܫܐ ܥܠܝܐ. ܘܡܒܥܕ ܠܗ ܡܫܒܚܘܬܐ ܗܢܝܐ. ܒܪ ܡܫܬܒܚܢ: ܗܘܐ ܘܠ ܢܦܫܐ ܕܦܘܩܕܐ ܕܡܠܟܘܬܗ. ܗܘ, ܒܗ ܣܓܕܬ ܀ ܥܙܐܝܠ ܐܡܪ. ܦܩܕܐ ܢܦܩܬ ܒܝܬ ܡܠܟ ܐܝܟ ܡܢܐ ܕܐܬܦܩܕ ܗܘ, ܦܩܕܐ ܒܐܒܘܗܘܢ, ܕܗܘ ܐܪܡܠܬܐ ܡܫܝܚܝܐ ܕܒܝܬܐ. ܡܛܠ ܗܢܐ ܕܝܢ ܗܘܐ ܘܐܒܠܘ ܒܢܝܐ ܠܗܘܢ ܕܒܝܬܐ ܒܗܘ ܒܝܬ. ܗܠܝܢ ܠܒܪ ܕܗܘܐ ܡܫܬܐܠ ܐܝܬ ܒܝ. ܒܟܠ ܗܘ ܕܝܢܐ ܕܒܬܪ ܠܗ ܡܕܡ ܐܚܪܝܢ. ܐܝܠܝܢ ܠܒܪ ܕܥܒܕܝܢ ܐܘܪܚܬܗܘܢ ܒܥܠܡܐ: ܡܛܠ ܕܠܝܬ ܕܝܢܗ ܕܐܠܗܐ ܡܕܡ ܒܢܝܫܘܢ. ܡܛܠ ܗܢܐ ܐܦܠܐ ܕܐܝܟܘܬܗ, ܐܠܗܐ ܦܩܕ ܡܢ. ܘܐܦܠܐ ܗܘ ܦܩܕܐ ܒܗܘܢ ܀ ܕܝܢܐ ܐܡܪ. ܐܝܬ ܐܢܬ

ܘܐܬܛܪ ܥܠ ܦܘܪܩܢܗ، ܘܡܩ̈ܕܫܐ ܘܫܠܚܐ ܘܫܠܐ ܠܬܫܒܘܚܗܘܢ
ܒܦܘܪܩܢܐ ܕܠܒ̈ܢܝܗܘܢ. ܘܐܡܪ ܠܗ ܠܐ ܬܬܕܡܪ ܒܡ̈ܠܝܗܐ ܕܡܪܝܐ
ܗܘܝܬ ܒܗܘܢ .. ܙܪܒܒܠ ܐܡܪ. ܫܡܥ ܠܝ ܬܘܒ. ܕܐܢ̈ܫܝ ܕܐܝܬ
ܐܠܗܐ ܘܡ̈ܠܐܟܐ ܘܫܠܡܐ ܘܟܝܬ ܬܠܬܐ. ܐܠܐ ܡܘܕܐ ܐܢܐ
ܟܕ ܐܠܗܐ ܕܟܠ ܫܡܝܐ ܘܐܪܥܐ ܘܡ̈ܠܟܐ ܘܟܠ ܕܐܝܬ
ܒܗܘܢ. ܘܒܪܝܐ ܕܒܝܬ ܟܠܗܐ ܡܫܝܚܐ .. ܕܢܝܐ ܐܡܪ ܠܐ
ܗܘܐ ܥܠ ܗܕܐ ܐܬܬܐܠܬ ܡܢܝ ܕܟܠܢܐ ܗܝ ܗܝܡܢܘܬܐ
ܕܦܘܪܩܢܐ ܕܐܘܕܝܬ ܒܗ. ܐܠܐ ܗܕܐ ܗܘ ܐܡܪܬ ܠܟ. ܕܠܐ
ܬܬܕܡܪ ܒܡ̈ܠܝܗܐ ܡܠܝܢ ܕܟܬܝܒ ܗܘܝܬ ܠܗܘܢ ܒܡܘܬܪܐ..

ܙܪܒܒܠ ܐܡܪ: ܐܝܟܐ ܗܘ ܡܫܝܚܟ ܘܡ̈ܠܟܐ ܕܢܬܪ ܐܢܬ
ܒܗܘܢ ܕܠܟܠ ܐܢ̈ܫܐ ܕܐܘܡܬܐ ܦܪܘܩ ܐܢܬܘܢ ܘܡܘܕܝܢ
ܐܢܬܘܢ. ܘܠܗܘܢ ܠܐܘܡ̈ܬܐ ܕܟܒܪ ܐܝܟ ܠܡܠܟܐ ܡܢ̈ܝܢ
ܐܢܬܘܢ ܒܫ̈ܠܝܐ ܘܡܫܬܥ̈ܒܕܐ ܕܐܝܬܝܢ ܐܢܬܘܢ ܒܠܚܘܕ.
ܐܘܡܬܐ ܡܐܡ ܡܢ ܡ̈ܕܝܢܬܐ ܠܐܘܪ̈ܫܠܡ ܕܠܝ. ܘܐܝܬ ܡܐܡ
ܐܝܬ ܒܝܕ ܒܢ̈ܝܐ ܕܐܘܡܬܐ ܘܡܫܝܚ ܐܝܬ ܠܗ ܘܫܠܝܛ ܐܝܬ
ܠܗ. . . . ܕܢܝܐ ܐܡܪ. ܠܐ ܗܘܐ ܬܫܒܘܚܬܐ ܐܝܬ ܕܗܠܝܢ.
ܡܬܬܒܥܐ ܕܡܢ ܡܬܬܒܥ ܐܝܬ. ܕܟܠ ܡܕܡ ܒܒܪܬ ܒܡ̈ܠܝܗܐ
ܘܠܐ ܥܒܕܐ ܐܝܬ ܕܬܫܡܫ ܠܗܘܢ ܒܫܘܒܚܐ ܐܝܟ ܒܡܕܝܢܬܐ
ܫܒ̈ܝܢ .. ܙܪܒܒܠ ܐܡܪ. ܡܛܠ ܕܗܟܢ ܗܕܐ ܫܢܐ ܐܢܘܢ
ܣܪ̈ܝܐ. ܠܐܝܠܝܢ ܕܡܘܕܝܢ ܒܡܠܟܐ ܡܫܝܚܐ ܘܐܦ ܗܘ ܡܘܕܐ
ܒܗܘܢ ܡܢܐ ܐܒܘܗܝ، ܡܫܝܚܐ .. ܕܢܝܐ ܐܡܪ. ܒܟܠ ܦܬܓܡ
ܕܢܘܪܐ ܘܢܬܒܥܘܢ ܠܫ̈ܘܦܗܘܢ، ܘܠܓܒ̈ܝܐ ܕܦܘܪܫܗܘܢ. ܘܒܥܒܕ
ܡܟܝܠ ܓܘܪܐ ܦܓܥܐ .. ܙܪܒܒܠ ܐܡܪ ܫܦܝܪ ܡܘܕܝܬ ܐܢܬ
ܠܝ ܒܢܘܪܐ ܗܕܐ ܕܐܬܦܓܥ ܡܢ ܗ، ܢܘܪܐ ܕܠܐ ܕܡܟܐ ܘܬܘܠܥܐ
ܕܠܐ ܡܝܬܐ. ܗܝ ܕܠܡܫܝܚܐ ܠܐܝܠܝܢ [ܕܦܓܪܝܢ ܠܡ̈ܟܘܢܐ
ܫܠܡ ܟܡܘܕܐ. ܠܐ ܓܝܪ ܒܥܝܬ ܠܗܘܢ ܠܦܘܪܫܢܐ: ܕܢܗܘܘܢ
ܘܢܫܬܒܩܘܢ. ܠܒܪ ܕܠܒܪ ܡܢ ܚܝܐ ܗܘ ܕܐܠܗܐ ܡܪܝܡܐ.

ܕܡܬܦܫܩܐ ܐܝܕܗ ܗܘ ܕܐܡܪ ܗܘܐ ܒܗ ܠܐ̈ܠܗܐ. ܟܠ ܕܗܘ، ܒܫܪܪܐ ܡܠܬܗ. ܘܟܕ ܬܠܐ ܗܘܐ ܒܐܝܕܗ ܫܐܠܗ، ܘܐܡܪܝܢ ܠܗ. ܡܬܦܫܩܐ ܐܝܬ ܕܬܒܥܝܢ ܠܐ̈ܠܗܐ. ܗܘ ܕܝܢ ܠܐ ܡܫܟܚ ܗܘܐ ܕܢܦܢܐ ܠܗܘܢ ܦܬܓܡܐ ܡܢ ܦܘܫܩܐ ܕܪ̈ܘܚܗ. ܘܟܕ ܗܘܐ ܕܢܐ ܘܫܪܐܘܗ، ܗܘܘ ܘܐܫܬܩܘܗ.. ܘܠܐ ܡܫܟܚ ܗܘܐ ܕܢܦܩ ܗܘܐ ܕܪܒܗ ܠܒܪܗ ܒܪܡܫܐ ܕܒܥܐܘܗ، ܗܘܘ ܡܬܦܢܝܢܐ ܘܐܡܩܡܘܗ، ܠܒܪܗ . . . .

ܕܢܐ ܐܡܪ. ܘܥܡ ܒܥ̈ܘܬܐ ܘܐܦ ܠܐܡܐ ܕܝܠܕܬܐ ܐܝܬ. ܘܠܐ ܐܝܟ ܚܙܝܐ ܠܝ ܕܬܘܒ ܛܘܒܐ ܒܥܘܬܐ. ܘܐܦ ܠܐ ܝܕܥܐ ܐܝܬ ܕܡܪܢܝܢ ܡܢ ܗܠܝܢ ܡܫܘܐ ܐܢܐ ܠܝ. . . . ܫܪܝܬ ܐܡܪ ܠܐ̈ܠܗܐ ܕܫܡܝܐ ܘܐܪܥܐ ܠܐ ܒܟܕ ܢܐܟܪܘܢ. ܡܢ ܛܘܒܬ ܫܡܝܐ ܗܠܝܢ. ܐܝܬ ܕܝܢ ܠܐ ܗܘܬ ܚܕܐ ܒܟ̈ܠܠܐ ܕܠܘܫܟܐ ܐܠܐ ܣܓܝ ܬ̈ܠܬܐ ܣܘܐ ܝܐܝ، ܒܢ̈ܝܐ ܕܠܘܫܟܐ. ܕܠܐ ܛܘܒ ܐܫܬܡܥ ܒܠܝܢ ܕܡܕܒܪ ܐܝܬ ܫܒܚܐ ܕܐ̈ܠܗܐ ܣܪܝܩܐ . . ܕܢܐ ܐܡܪ ܬܘܒܐ ܒܒܗܠܐ ܕܢܘܪܐ ܡܪܢܝܐ ܒܝܬ ܚܝܘܗܝ، ܘܒܦܩܘܗܝ.. ܘܒܪܘܗ ܡܬܦܢܝܢܐ ܡܥܠܢܐ ܒܢܣܐ ܕܚܦܪ ܙܘܥ ܒܘܢܐ ܟܠܗ ܒܝܬ ܕܒܝܐ. ܘܠܐ ܝܕܥܐ ܕܢܕܒܘܢ. ܫܪܝܬ ܐܡܪ ܫܡܥܬ ܠܝ ܡܢ ܕܐܡܪܝܬ ܠܝ ܕܠܐ ܙܒܢ ܐܝܬ ܒܦܢܝܐ ܕܦܠܓܘܬܐ ܕܢܘܪܐ ܕܡܦܢܝܢܐ ܠܐܢܠܝܢ ܕܡܕܝܢ ܒܡܬܒܪܐ ܒܢ̈ܝܐ ܐܒܗܬܟ. ܘܒܦܩܝܢ ܒܐܠܗܐ ܚܝܐ ܒܪܡܘܬܟ. . . ܕܢܐ ܐܡܪ. ܡܛܠ ܐܠܦܟ ܗܠܝܢ ܒܗܠܝܢ ܕܬܐܡܪ ܡܢ ܗܘܢܐ ܠܒܪܐ ܕܐܬܬܟ ܗܘܬ ܙܘܥܐ ܕܐ̈ܠܗܐ ܘܒܠܒܒܗ ܕܡܫܝܚܐ. ܕܗܐ ܒܟܕ ܐܝܬ ܦܢܝܬܗ. . ܫܪܝܬ ܐܡܪ. ܡܫܝܚܐ ܕܐܘܕܝܬ ܒܗ. ܗܘܘ ܐܠܦܢ ܕܐܡܪ ܗܘܢܐ. ܠܐ ܓܒܪ ܦܫܛ ܕܐܗܘܐ ܠܗ ܦܢܝܬܐ. ܙܕܩܘܗܝ، ܓܒܪ ܐܬܚܘܝ ܦܠܓܘܬܐ ܬ̈ܠܬܐ ܣܓܝ ܫܢ̈ܝܐ ܕܕܡܝܢ ܠܝ. ܘܗܢܘܢ ܡܢ ܕܢܗܘܘܢ ܣܓܝ ܒܚܝܐ ܒܡܘܡܐ ܕܗܘܝܢ ܒܗ ܒܦܘܩܕܢܐ ܠܟܠܢ. . . . ܕܢܐ ܐܡܪ ܬܘܬܠܐ

ܬܠܐܘܗܝ ܘܦܘܪܫܢܘܗܝ ܒܟܬܒ̈ܘܗܝ܆ ܘܟܕ ܡܫܬܘܬܦ ܗܘܐ ܦܟܐ
ܗܘܐ ܘܐܡܪ. ܫܠܘ ܡܫܝܚܐ ܕܐܬܝܚ ܠܡܪܗ ܒܫܠܝܐܝܬ
ܒܫܡܥܘܬܗ ܕܪܘܚܐ. ܘܟܕ ܐܡܪ ܗܟܢܐ. ܫܡܥ ܬܘܒ ܕܢܐ
ܕܫܬܦܪ ܒܥܒ̈ܕܘܗܝ܆ ܀

ܪܒܢ ܐܡܪ. ܚܙܝ ܕܬܬܚܙܐ ܒܝ ܐܝܬ ܥܠ ܕܠܐ ܡܫܡܫ
ܐܢܐ. ܘܠܐ ܕܐܬܕܡܝ ܬܘܒ ܥܠ ܕܡܫܡܫ ܗܘܝܬ ܠܗܒܝ ܐܚ̈ܝܐ
ܕܥܠ ܐܝܟܢܐ ܀ ܕܢܐ ܐܡܪ ܬܬܒܥܐ. ܘܡܘܬܗ ܠܫܬܪܗ.
ܘܬܫܦܪ ܒܪܘܐ ܒܐܝ̈ܕܘܗܝ܆ ܘܒܬܠܝܗܝ܆ ܘܟܕ ܒܥܒܕ.
ܠܫܬܪܗ ܢܬܠܥܙ ܥܠ ܒܪܫܗ. ܘܢܕܘܗܝ܆ ܗܒܢܐ ܐܝܟ ܦܘܪܢܝܗ
ܕܕܢܚܐ. ܘܟܕ ܗܘܐ ܕܢܫܡ ܗܘܐ ܠܒܝܬ ܐܘܪ̈ܚܐ ܘܢܬܕܐ
ܗܘܐ ܒܟܘܒܐ ܫܡܘܒܐ. ܘܦܠܢܘܗܝ܆ ܗܘܘ ܡܫܦܠܝ̈ܬܐ.
ܘܒܪܘܦܠܢܐ ܡܠܝܢ ܕܫܠܘ ܗܘܘ ܒܟܗ ܡܢ ܒܕܬܐ. ܡܦܠ
ܕܠܐ ܡܫܡܫ ܗܘܐ ܕܢܬܠܝܟ ܗܘܐ ܥܠ ܬܠܡܝܕܘܗܝ܆ ܡܢ ܗܘ ܕܒܦܝܫ
ܗܘܐ ܠܫܬܪܗ. ܘܗܘܐ ܒܝܬ ܢܒܘܥܐ ܕܡ̈ܝܬܐ ܦܟ̈ܝܗܐ.
ܒܬܪܐ ܕܡܢ ܒܐܠܘܠ ܒܬܠܬܐ ܒܫܒܐ. ܟܕ ܗܘܐ ܕܢܐ ܘܢܫܬ
ܗܘܐ ܠܕܡܫܦܪܝܢ ܕܠܗ ܒܠܠܝܐ. ܘܒܠܗܘܢ ܒܬܪ ܐܘܦܝܩ ܐܢܬ
ܗܘܘ ܒܟܗܘܢ. ܘܟܕ ܗܘܐ ܠܬܦܪ ܒܝܬ ܐܘܪ̈ܚܐ ܘܐܬܘܬܗܘܢ܆ ܗܘܘ
ܡܕܒܪܗܘܢ܆ ܘܐܡܪ ܠܗ ܕܢܐ. ܒܗܢܐ ܢܦܩܐ ܗܘܝܬ ܒܝܬ
ܐܘܪ̈ܚܐ. ܡܢܐ ܫܘܒܚܐ ܗܘܐ ܠܝ ܥܠ ܐܝܠܝܢ ܕܐܬܬܐܠܬ
ܗܘܝܬ ܡܕܒܪ. ܡܬܦܠܫ ܐܝܬ ܕܬܫܒܚ ܠܐܠܗܐ ܒܚܝܠܝ
ܡܕܒܪܢܐ ܐܝܟ ܦܘܪܢܝܐ ܕܬܠܡܝ̈ܕܐ ܀ ܪܒܢ ܐܡܪ ܗܢܐ
ܫܘܒܚܐ ܗܘܐ ܠܝ ܒܝܬ ܐܘܪ̈ܚܐ ܕܗܘ ܡܢܟ ܕܪܒܬ ܗܘܝܬ
ܒܗ ܡܕܒܪܝ. ܒܗ ܐܫܠܡ ܒܪܝܟܐ ܠܫܪܬܐ܆ ܘܠܐ ܐܬܟܠ
ܒܟܠܬ܆ ܠܐ ܚܙܝ ܒܥܬܪܐ ܕܒܦܪܬ ܒܗܘܢ ܬܘܒ ܡܟܝܟܐ
ܐܢܐ. ܐܦ ܠܐ ܒܚܠܒܐ ܡܫܝܚܐ ܕܐܘܕܝܬ ܒܗ ܒܦܪܢܐ ܀
ܕܢܐ ܐܡܪ ܬܠܡܝܕܘܗܝ܆ ܒܐܝܕܗ ܕܡܫܝܚܐ ܥܠ ܕܡܫܡܫ ܡܢ
ܙܒܢ̈ ܬܠܡܝܕܐ ܕܠܐ ܬܘܒ ܢܦܩ ܒܗ ܒܫܡܗܐ ܒܕܡܐ

ܕܒܫ̈ܠܡܐ. ܟܠ ܡܢܐ ܗܘܝܬ ܐܡܪܐ ܘܝܗܒܬ ܝܬܝܪܐ ܡܢܐ. ܐܦ ܟܕ ܐܢܬ ܕܠܐ ܢܦܘܩ ܡܫܠܠ ܐܢܬ. ܐܠܐ ܐܢܐ ܠܐ ܡܫܟܚ ܐܢܐ ܕܐܫܬܐܠ ܡܢ ܢܦܫܬܗܘܢ ܕܡ̈ܠܟܐ ܀ ܥܪܘܒܬܐ ܐܡܪ. ܐܝܟܢܐ ܕܐܢܬ ܚܙܐ ܐܢܬ. ܘܠܐ ܬܦܩܘܕ ܡܢ ܢܦܫܗܘܢ ܕܡ̈ܠܟܐ. ܘܐܦ ܕܡܢ ܢܦܩ ܐܢܬ. ܚܕ ܐܢܬ ܗܘ ܡܢܐ ܦܩܘܕ ܥܠܝ. ܗܟܢܐ ܐܦ ܐܢܐ ܚܙܐ ܐܢܐ ܕܠܐ ܐܘܦܬܐ ܡܢ ܢܦܫܗ ܕܗܘ ܕܐܡܪ ܕܠܐ ܬܫܟܚܘܢ ܠܡܐܠ ܝܠܕ ܘܠܥܠ ܕܟܢܐ. ܘܡܛܠ ܗܢܐ ܠܐ ܡܫܟܚ ܐܢܐ ܠܡܬܒܪܐ ܒܟܢܫܐ. ܗܦܟ ܟܕ ܘܟܠܐ ܒܟܠܐ ܕܕܟܝܬ ܠܗܘܢ ܒܗ ܠܐ ܚܕ ܗܘܝܬ ܀ ܕܢܐ ܐܡܪ. ܠܝ ܬܗܘܐ ܠܝ ܕܝܢܐ ܥܠ ܕܝܢܐ ܕܡܢܟ ܐܢܬ ܒܗ. ܗܦܟ ܠܝ ܕܐܡܪܬ ܕܠܐ ܡܫܟܚ ܐܢܐ. ܠܐ ܬܡܪܘܚ ܘܬܬܚܪ ܠܡ̈ܠܟܐ ܘܬܬܡܪܐ ܐܢܘܢ ܒܬܒܪܐ ܚ̈ܒܪܐ ܠܗܠܝܢ ܕܟܬܝܒܝܢ ܠܗܘܢ ܘܐܦ ܡ̈ܠܟܐ ܀ ܥܪܘܒܬܐ ܐܡܪ. ܘܐܦ ܫܠܘ ܡ̈ܠܟܐ ܕܪܚܡܝܢ ܘܠܐ ܡܪܚܡ ܘܠܐ ܡ̈ܢܗܝܢ ܒܐܝܠܝܢ ܕܡܗܠܟܝܢ ܒܦܘ̈ܩܕܢܘܗܝ. ܐܡܪ ܐܢܬ ܠܝ ܕܐܡܪܬ. ܫܠܘ ܒܬܒܪܐ ܕܗܘܐ ܡܢܗܘܢ ܘܡܬܚܫܝܢ ܘܠܐ ܫܪܝܢ. ܐܝܟܢܐ ܐܡܪ ܐܢܬ ܠܝ ܕܐܡܪܬ. ܘܟܡܐ ܐܘܪܚܬ ܡܢ ܟܠܗ ܐܘܦܝܘܢ ܕܠܝ. ܕܡܛܠ ܕܦܘܩܕܢܐ ܐܢܬ ܠܗܘܢ ܘܠܐ ܡܫܬܠܚܝܢ. ܗܐ ܒܟܢܫ ܐܢܬ ܗܘܐ ܟܕܪܐ ܫܠܝܚܝܗܘܢ. ܡܢܗܘܢ ܕܐܬܒܬܗܘܢ ܢܦܫܗܘܢ ܒܦ̈ܘܩܕܢܝܗܘܢ ܘܟܠ ܟܡ ܕܬܒܥܠ ܒܠܒܗܘܢ ܐܟܘܬܟܘܢ ܀ ܕܢܐ ܐܡܪ. ܠܐ ܗܘܐ ܠܡܪܐ ܐܬܡܪܬ ܡܕܡ ܕܫܠܘ ܐܡܪܐ ܕܕܝܢ ܬܘܒ ܠܡ̈ܠܟܐ. ܘܠܫ̈ܠܡܐ ܡܪܘܒ. ܘܕܟܝ ܘܚܕܘܗ ܟܠ ܢܦܫܝ ܡܛܠ ܢܦܫܗ ܀

ܥܪܘܒܬܐ ܐܡܪ ܡܢܐ ܡܬܡܟܟܝܢ ܗܘܟܢ̈ܘܬܐ ܕܬܫܐܠܬܐ. ܒܬܪ ܗܝ ܕܐܡܪܬ ܠܝ ܕܠܐ ܡܫܟܚ ܐܢܐ ܘܕܬܪܬܝܢ ܡܛܠ ܢܦܫܗ. ܐܫܬܘܐ ܕܝܢ ܡܢ ܟܠܝܘܬܗ ܗܘܐ ܗܘܐ ܠܝ ܗܢܐ ܙܒܢܐ. ܘܝܗܒܬ ܗܟܢܐ ܢܦܫܝ ܕܐܟܘܬܐ ܗܘܬ ܀ ܕܢܐ ܐܡܪ.

ܡܨܪܝܐ. ܕܠܐ ܡܨܐ. ܐܢܐ ܟܝ ܥܠ ܐܝܠܝܢ ܕܗܝܡܢܘ ܐܝܟܘܬܟ܀
ܚܝܩܪ ܐܡܪ ܡܢ ܡܠܟܐ ܕܡ̈ܠܟܐ ܕܝܠ ܐܢܐ. ܘܡܢ ܡܠܟܐ
ܕܐܬܘܪ ܠܐ ܙܥܘܪ ܐܢܐ. ܘܐܦ ܠܐ ܡܢ ܠܒܘܫܝܟ ܕܠܘܬܟ،
ܕܗܐ ܡܬܠܒܫ ܐܢܬ ܥܠ ܦܪ̈ܨܘܦܘܗܝ، ܕܡܫܝܚܐ ܕܐܬܕܝܢܬ ܒܗ
ܐܬܡܠܝ. ܘܗܐ ܡܬܕܡܐ ܐܢܐ ܡܠܠܬܗ ܘܡܫܝܚܐ. ܐܝܟ
ܕܐܬܕܡܝ ܗܘ ܡܠܟܐ ܫܡܫܐ ܕܕܡܝܢ ܠܗ܀ ܕܢܐ ܐܡܪ ܐܦ ܐܢܬ
ܠܐ ܫܡܫܐ ܐܢܬ ܥܠ ܢܗܪܝܢ ܐܠܐ ܐܢܐ ܫܡܫܐ ܐܢܐ ܗܘ
ܥܠܝܟ ܕܐܫܬܘܘ ܐܪ̈ܥܬܟ ܗܠܝܢ ܕܫܡܫܬ ܒܗܘܢ ܒܫ̈ܡܫܐ ܡܕܡ
ܫ̈ܠܡܐ. ܘܐܫܘܪ ܐܪ̈ܥܬܟ ܒܚܪ̈ܫܝܢ ܕܐܫܟܚ ܗܘ، ܐܪ̈ܥܬܗܘܢ
ܘܥܠܝܟ ܕܐܬܪܬܟ ܘܫܒܘܩ ܠܝ ܦܬܓܡ̈ܝܗܘܢ: ܒܫܡܗܘܢ ܗܘ، ܗܘܐ
ܕܝܠ ܐܢܐ ܘܫܡܫܐ ܐܢܐ ܥܠܝܟ. ܐܦ ܕܝܢ ܗܟܢܐ ܡܬܩܢܐ
ܗܢܘܢ ܫ̈ܠܡܐ ܢܗܘܘܢ ܠܝ ܦܩܘܕܐ ܕܠܐ ܫܡܫܐ ܐܢܐ ܥܠܝܟ܀
ܚܝܩܪ ܐܡܪ ܐܝܟ ܓܒܪܐ ܕܕܝܠ ܐܢܬ ܡܢ ܡ̈ܠܟܐ ܘܐܡܪ
ܐܢܬ ܡܢ ܦܬܓܡܐ ܠܐ ܬܫܘܐ ܥܠܝ. ܐܢܐ ܓܒܪ ܠܐ ܕܝܢ ܐܢܐ
ܡܠܟܐ ܐܡܪ ܐܢܬ ܡܠܠ ܗܘܐ ܐܦ ܠܐ ܙܒܢ ܐܬܬܪܝܡ
ܘܐܬܪܗܒ ܒܐܝܠܝܢ ܕܐܡܪ ܐܢܬ. ܒܪ̈ܢܫܝܢ ܓܝܪ ܦܠܚܝܢ ܡܢ
ܕܒܢܐ ܕܒܝܬܝ ܥܠ ܐܝܠܝܢ ܕܠܐ ܦܠܚܝܢ ܠܡܪܝܐ ܕܠܘ ܐܠܗܐ ܗܘ
ܒܫܡܗ܀ ܕܢܐ ܐܡܪ ܢܬܝܒ ܟܠ ܦܪܨܘܦ ܥܠ ܕܐܡܪܬ ܗܟܢܐ
ܠܡܒܢܐ ܠܝ ܦܬܓܡܐ ܘܡܢ ܠܗܘܢ ܦܘܩܕܢܐ ܕܡ̈ܠܟܐ ܘܠܐ
ܦܪܥ ܐܝܩܪܐ ܕܩܢܘܗܝ، ܫ̈ܠܡܐ: ܕܗܐ ܒܦܪ ܒܗܘܢ. ܘܐܬܚܙܝ
ܡܢ ܒܬܪܐ ܕܠܒܢܝܢ ܗܘܘ ܠܗ ܐܝܟ ܦܘܩܕܢܐ ܕܕܝܢܐ܀܀܀
ܚܝܩܪ ܐܡܪ ܠܐ ܙܒܢ ܐܢܬ ܒܝܬܒܪܐ ܕܒܐܢܘܬܐ ܕܗܘ
ܠܡܠܟܐ ܕܒܬܝܪ. ܐܢܬ ܓܝܪ ܒܬܠܬ ܘܐܦ ܕܒܢܝܟ ܒܒܢܝܢ.
ܒܐܢܘܬܐ ܕܝܢ ܠܐ ܒܒܢܐ. ܘܐܬܒܢܝܬܗ ܠܐ ܒܒܢܝ܀܀ ܕܢܐ
ܐܡܪ ܡܠܟܐ ܙܘܬ ܒܗ ܒܦܪܘܦܘܣܬܐ ܒܕܡܐ ܕܠܐ ܬܕܒ
ܡܕܡ ܡܢ ܡܬܕܡ ܐܢܬ ܘܡܢ ܡܢܘ ܡܬܬܢܐ ܐܢܬ ܡܢ ܗܢܘܢ
ܕܡܫܪܝܢ ܗܘܘ ܠܝ ܡܢ ܡܕܡ ܘܡܬܕܡ ܗܘܐ ܠܡܬܪܘܬܟ

ܢܐܕܝܢܘܗܝ ܠܐ ܒܦܪܘܫ ܒܡܕܡ ܕܫܘܚܝܢ ܒܗ. ܐܝܟ ܡܐ
ܕܒܥܪܬ ܐܢܬ. ܒܗܘ ܡܕܡ ܕܠܝܬ ܐܢܬ ܒܗ. ܐܦ ܚܪܝܢ ܠܟ
ܫ̈ܠܡܐ. ܐܡܝܢܐ ܒܥܪܬ ܒܗܘܢ ܘܡܚܝܢܐ. ܘܐܦ ܕܝܢ ܠܐ ܚܪܝܢ
ܠܟ ܐܡܝܢܐ ܕܗܟܢ ܐܢܬ ܚܠܝܡܘܢ. ܐܡܝܢܐ ܡܐܒܝܢ ܗܘܝܬ
ܠܗܘܢ ܘܗܦܟܬ ܗܘܝܬ ܠܗܘܢ. ܚܪܒܠ ܐܡܪ. ܒܪ ܘܡܚܝܢܐ ܗܘܝܬ
ܒܪܚܡ ܘܗܦܟܬ ܗܘܝܬ ܠܡܕܡ ܕܠܐ ܝܕܥ ܗܘܝܬ. ܘܡܚܝܢܐ ܕܝܢ
ܕܡܫܬ ܒܢܝܢܐ ܢܡܘܣܝܬܐ ܕܝܚܝܕܝܐ. ܠܝܬ ܠܗ ܦܘܪܫܐ ܡܛܠ
ܕܐܬܬܘܠ ܒܡܫ̈ܘܚܐ ܠܐܘܠܝܬܐ ܐܘ ܕܐܣܘܝܐ ܬܘܒ ܚܠܦ
ܬܘܠܬܐ ܠܐܚܪܢܐ. ܚܙܘܐ ܗܘ ܓܝܪ ܝܕܥܐ ܠܟܠܗ ܕܬܘܚܡ
ܚ̈ܝܘܗܝ. ܘܐܝܟ ܢܚܠ ܕܫܡܝܐ ܡܫܡܫܢܐ ܀ ܕܝܢܐ ܐܡܪ.
ܡܛܠ ܕܡܫܡܫܐ ܗܘܝܬ ܕܫ̈ܠܡܐ ܡܫܘܕܥܐ ܘܒܪ ܐܪܙܐ ܗܘܝܬ
ܕܡܠܝܠ ܕܗܦܟܝܢ ܠܗܘܢ ܫ̈ܠܡܐ ܒܬܪܝܐ. ܡܛܠ ܐܢܐ ܙܘܥ
ܒܡܟ ܕܬܦܢܐ ܠܟ ܘܠܐ ܬܫܒܘܩ ܡܢ ܬܫܡܫܬܐ ܕܫ̈ܠܡܐ.
ܘܐܦ ܕܝܢ ܠܐ ܡܬܦܢܐ ܐܢܬ ܠܝ. ܒܗܘܢ ܒܫ̈ܠܡܐ ܕܒܥܪܬ
ܒܗܘܢ ܢܚܐ ܐܢܐ. ܕܐܝܟ ܕܠܟܪܝܐ ܘܦܠܓܐ ܗܘܝܢܐ ܐܬܝܢ
ܒܟ. ܘܐܬܬܒܒ ܡܢܝܟ ܠܦܘܠܚܢܐ ܕܫ̈ܠܡܐ ܕܡܢܪܬ ܚܠܝܡܘܢ
ܘܒܥܪܬ ܒܗܘܢ. ܘܐܦ ܓܒܪܐ ܕܡܠܟܪ ܐܢܬ ܠܗܘܢ ܒܪ ܠܐ
ܚܟܡ ܐܢܐ ܟܠ ܚܝܕܝܢ ܕܠܐ ܡܬܒܥܝ ܐܢܐ ܠܟ. ܘܐܝܟ ܕܗܘܟ
ܗܘܐ ܐܡܝܪ ܡܢ ܩܕܡ. ܗܟܢܐ ܐܗܘܐ ܠܟܪܝܟ ܘܡܚܝܢܐ ܀
ܚܪܒܠ ܐܡܪ. ܘܐܦܠܐ ܐܢܐ ܡܢܚ ܐܢܐ ܕܬܗܘܪ ܒܟ ܐܝܟ
ܕܡܢ ܩܕܡ ܕܗܘܐ ܗܘܝܬ ܠܫ̈ܠܡܐ ܒܚ̈ܝܐ. ܐܠܐ ܗܘܪ ܒܟ
ܘܡܚܝܢܐ ܘܫܐܠܝܢ ܐܝܟ ܕܠܟܪܝܐ ܒܪܘܦܝܢܐ. ܒܬܪ ܒܬܫܡܫܬܐ
ܘܡܘܕܥܐ ܒܒܠܒܐ ܡܚܣܢܐ ܀ ܕܝܢܐ ܐܡܪ ܐܡܝܢܐ ܠܐ ܕܢܠ
ܐܢܬ ܡܢ ܬ̈ܠܒܐ ܘܠܐ ܒܗܘܬ ܐܢܬ ܡܢ ܐܠܝܢ ܕܡܫܡܫܝܢ ܕܝܠܝ
ܕܬܐܡܪ ܕܒܪܘܦܝܢܐ ܐܢܐ. ܐܠܐ ܐܘܕܐ ܕܡܕܝܢ ܐܢܬ
ܠܫ̈ܠܡܐ ܒܒܢܝܐ ܘܡܚܝܢܐ ܐܝܟ ܕܠܗܘܟܐ ܐܡܘܪܝܢ ܐܝܟ

ܠܘܬܗ ܕܪܘܡܢܝܐ ܒܠܠܝܐ ܗܘ ܘܥܒܪ ܚܘܬܗ. ܘܐܬܩܛܠ ܗܘܐ
ܡܢ ܟܠܗ ܥܕܬܐ. ܘܐܡܪ ܗܘܐ ܠܗܘܢ ܕܩܪܒܘ ܚܠܦ ܓܠܘܬܐ
ܘܟܗܢܘܬܐ. ܕܢܫܘܐ ܠܝ ܡܫܝܚܐ ܒܠ ܕܢܦܩܬ ܠܗ ܒܗܘܢܐ
ܟܠܗ ܢܘܟܪܝܐ ܕܫ̈ܢܝܐ. ܘܡܛܠ ܕܢܦܩܝܢ ܗܘܘ ܡܢ ܪ̈ܕܘܦܐ.
ܡܚܒ ܗܘܘ ܘܢܣܒܘ ܠܗ ܦܘܪܢܣܐ ܕܫܢܝܐ ܒܕ ܡܘܕܐ
ܗܘܐ ܒܐܒܐ ܘܒܒܪܐ ܘܒܪܘܚܐ ܕܩܘܕܫܐ: ܀
ܘܒܕ ܫܠܡܬ ܗܘܬ ܡܕܝܢܬܐ ܟܠܗ ܕܢܫܬ ܗܘܐ ܠܕܘܬܐ.
ܫܪܐ ܗܘܐ ܠܡܢܝܐ ܒܗܘܠܝܬ̈ܐ. ܘܡܚܒܐ ܗܘܘ ܘܢܣܒܘ
ܗܘܘ ܠܘܬܗ. ܘܢܦܩ ܗܘܘ ܠܗ ܕܠܒܫ ܗܘܐ ܕܡܘܬܐ
ܕܩܪܘܦܝܠܐ. ܘܐܡܪ ܠܗܘܢ. ܢܫܘܐ ܠܝ ܒܪܐ ܡܫܝܚܐ
ܒܠ ܬ̈ܘܦܣܐ ܕܢܦܩܬ ܒܗܘܢ. ܘܒܠ ܡܕܡ ܕܐܘܟܪܬܒܘܢ
ܕܐ̈ܠܗܐ ܡܚܠܠܝܢ ܚܒܝܒ ܒܪ ܠܐ ܡܚܠܠܝܢ. ܘܕܗܘܢܬ
ܠܒܘܢ ܒܠܬܐ ܦܢܝܬܐ. ܐܝܟܢܐ ܠܒܘܢ ܗܕܐ ܒܠܬܐ
ܥܢܝܬܐ. ܚܠܦ ܕܦܠܓܬܘܢ ܠܬܠܬ̈ܐ ܒܢ̈ܝܐ. ܬܦܠܓܘܢ
ܡܒܠ ܠܐܠܗܐ ܒܢ̈ܝܐ. ܘܒܪ ܥܡܒܘ ܗܘܘ ܗܠܝܢ. ܡܘܢ
ܠܗܬܗ ܒܢܥܐ ܦܠܝܐ ܕܒܪ̈ܐ ܘܕܢ̈ܥܐ. ܘܐܦ ܠܒܘ ܘܢܦܫܗ.
ܘܒܪܠܒܐ ܘܒܡܘܢܝܐ ܕ̈ܥܢܐ ܕܒܪܝܬܐ. ܐܡܪܘ ܗܘܘ ܠܗ
ܠܗܘܢ ܠܥܪܒܠ. ܕܡܒܠ ܘܐܦ ܚܢ ܒܦܪܝܢ ܐܚܝܢ ܒܡܕܡ
ܕܒܦܪܬ ܒܗ. ܘܡܘܕܝܢ ܚܢ ܒܡܠܒܐ ܡܫܝܚܐ ܕܐܘܪܬ ܒܗ. ܀
ܠܦܘܢܝܐ ܕܝܢ ܕܢܟܐ ܕܐܬܪܐ ܒܪ ܫܡܥ ܗܘܐ ܕܗܪܐ ܒܟܪ.
ܗܘܐ ܥܪܒܠ. ܫܪܪ ܗܘܐ ܠܠܝܐ ܘܢܦܩܗ ܗܘܐ ܡܢ
ܥܕܬܐ. ܘܠܒܘ ܗܘܘ ܒܥܡܗ ܒܪܘܦܝܢܐ ܦܠܝ̈ܓܐ ܘܢܬܒ ܗܘܐ
ܕܢܥܡܗ ܘܢܕܘܢܗ. ܡܕܡ ܟܠܬܐ ܕܡܩܒܠܬ ܪܒܐ ܐܢܒܐ
ܕܡܕܒܢ ܗܘܐ ܠܐ̈ܠܗܐ. ܘܐܡܪ ܠܗ. ܕܠܡܢܐ ܒܦܪܬ
ܒܐ̈ܠܗܐ ܕܦܠܓ ܗܘܝܬ ܠܗܘܢ ܘܡܕܒܢ. ܘܪܒܐ ܕܒܡܕܪܐ
ܒܢܝܢ ܗܘܝܬ ܠܗܘܢ ܘܐܢܐ ܡܕܡܝܬ ܒܡܢܝܢܐ ܕܒܕܪ
ܗܘܝܬ ܒܗ ܡܢ ܩܕܡ. ܫܘ ܓܝܪ ܕܒܪܘܦܝܢܐ ܐܘܢ ܕܐܬܠܬ

ܕܐܦ ܗ̈ܠܝܢ ܒܚܫܒܐ ܐܝܟ ܕܒܪܝܬܐ. ܐܬܦܢܝܘ ܩܕܡ ܠܗܠܝܢ ܕܐܡܪܬ ܠܟ: ܕܗܘܝܢ ܐܝܟ ܡܫܟܚܘܬܗ̇ ܕܟܝܢܐ. ܗܟܢ ܐܢܐ ܐܡܪ ܕܟܢ ܗܘ ܣܝܪܐ ܒܗܘܢ ܗܕܐ ܐܢܫܘܬܐ. ܘܣܘܪܐ ܠܐ ܕܐܢ ܡܬܦܠܓܐ ܐܝܬ ܘܐܦ ܫ̈ܘܚܠܦܐ ܡܬܦܠܓܢ ܒܟܠܗܝܢ ܀

ܐܡܪ ܠܗ ܒܪܕܝܨܢ. ܗܟܢ ܐܬܦܩܕ ܥܠ ܟ̈ܠܗܘܢ ܗܠܝܢ ܕܐܡܪܬ ܡܕܡ. ܘܐܬܦܩܕ ܥܠ ܙܘܕܐܝܬ. ܐܠܐ ܐܢܐ ܡܛܠ ܐܢܐ ܕܐܡܪ ܐܢܐ ܡܢ ܗܠܝܢ ܟܠܗܝܢ. ܘܬܘܒ ܠܝܬ ܠܟ ܐܫܘܝܘܬܐ. ܘܡܛܠ ܕܗܘܐ ܠܟ ܦܘܡ ܦܪܝܐ. ܡܢܐ ܠܐܢܫ ܒܡܢܝܢܬܐ ܦܘܠܐ ܕܠܝܬ ܦܪܝܐ ܕܢܣܒܐ ܠܡܦܬܗ. ܡܛܠ ܐܢܐ ܗܘ ܓܒܪ ܠܚܝܠܘܬܐ. ܘܗܘܘܬ ܠܐ ܡܣܬܗ ܕܟܝܢܐ ܒܟܝܢܐ ܘܒܢ̈ܦܫܐ ܕܐܦܝܬܐ ܓܒܪܘܬ ܒܠܗܘܢ ܢܦܫ̈ܬܐ ܀

ܘܟܕ ܥܒܕ ܗܘܐ ܗܠܝܢ ܒܪܘܚܐ ܐܦܘܡܦܐ. ܢܦܠ ܗܘܐ ܡܢܗ [illegible]. ܘܐܡܪ ܠܗ. ܐܝܬ ܗܘ ܡܕܝܢܐ ܠܐ̈ܘܪܚܬܐ ܘܐܝܬܘܗܝ ܠܡ̈ܠܟܝܐ. ܐܢܐ ܐܡܪ ܐܢܐ ܠܟ ܥܠ ܢ̈ܡܘܣܐ ܕܐ̈ܬܪܘܬܐ ܒܟܠܐܬܪ. ܕܗܘ ܥܒܕ ܠܟ ܥܠ ܕܢܦܠܬ ܠܗ. ܕܟܬܒܬ ܘܗܦܟܬ ܠܒܪ̈ܢܫܐ ܫܠܡܘܗܝ. ܗܘ ܓܝܪ ܫܘܠܛܢܐ ܕܟܬܝܒ ܢܦܩܗ ܥܠ ܦܘܠܚܢܐ ܕܟܘܬܐ. ܠܐ ܥܠܬܐ ܫܘܝܗ ܡܢ ܢܦܫ̈ܬܐ. ܕܡܬܦܠܓܢ ܘܡܬܚܠܦܢ ܒܟܠܗܘܢ ܦܘܠܚܢܘܗܝ. ܕܡܬܘܡ ܒܠܝܢ ܐܝܟ ܕܟܒܪ ܗܘܐ ܠܗܘܬ ܚܢܢܐ. ܡܫܟܚ ܗܘ ܕܢܟܒܪ ܢ̈ܟܝܪܝܢ ܘܐܦ ܝܘܡ ܐܠܝܢ ܕܐܡܪܬܘܢ ܐܝܟ. ܐܡܪ ܠܗ ܒܪܕܝܨܢ ܐܝܬ ܐܝܟ ܐܘܚܪܢܐ ܕܟܐܢ ܠܗ ܡܢ ܟܐܡܐ ܕܐܬܠ̈ܝܢܐ ܥܡܪ ܒܒܪܝܬ ܕܐܬܟܠܠ ܠܟ ܟܠ. ܗܟܢܐ ܕܝܢ ܡܬܦܠܓ ܕܟܐܕܐ ܗܘ ܡܟܝܢܐ ܕܟܝܢܐ ܗܘܝܐ ܕܟܠܝܢ. ܠܐ ܡܟܝܢ ܐܢܐ ܕܐܢܫܘܬ ܒܟܝܢ ܡܟܝܢܐ ܠܒܪܝܬܐ. ܐܠ ܫܘܬ ܐܝܬ ܒܐܢܫܐ ܘܠܟܢܝܢ ܟܠܠܝܐ ܫܘܬ ܐܢܐ ܢ̈ܟܝܪܝܢ. ܐܢܐ ܡܟܝܠ ܒܪܝܬ ܠܝ ܒܟ̈ܠܗܝܐ ܒܚܝܪܐ ܘܡܟܝܢܐ ܐܢܐ ܒܟܝܢܐ ܡܟܝܢܐ ܒܟܝܢܐ ܕܟܠܗܘܢ ܟ̈ܠ ܐܢܫܐ. ܘܒܬܪ ܡܟܝܢܐ ܡܢ ܗܘܐ ܒܪܕܝܨܢ ܘܢܫܬ ܗܘܐ

ܠܡܠܟܐ ܗܢܐ. ܕܒܗ ܐܠܗܐ ܐܡܪ ܠܝ ܕܐܡܪ ܠܟܘܢ ܕܡܛܠ
ܕܚܛܗܝܟܘܢ ܘܡܘܪܕܝܢܘܬܟܘܢ܆ ܥܒܕ ܐܢܐ ܫܢܝܐ ܠܡܫܪܝܬܟܘܢ ܗܢܐ.
ܘܟܠ ܐܡܪ ܥܒܕ ܐܢܐ ܗܟܢܐ ܪܒܐ ܒܐܪܥܟܘܢ. ܘܠܐ
ܦܪܫܝܢ ܗܘܘ ܕܫܡܥܝܢ ܡܢܝ ܕܡܠܟܘ ܡܠܟܐ ܐܝܬ ܒܗܘܢ.
ܡܛܠ ܕܦܘܡܐ ܐܝܬ ܠܗܘܢ ܘܠܐ ܡܡܠܠܝܢ. ܘܥܝܢܐ ܐܝܬ ܠܗܘܢ
ܘܠܐ ܚܙܝܢ ܒܗܝܢ. ܗܢܘܢ ܕܐܢܬܘܢ ܦܠܚܝܢ ܐܢܬܘܢ ܠܗܘܢ.
ܘܠܐ ܗܘܐ ܗܢܘܢ ܦܠܚܝܢ ܠܟܘܢ ܐܝܟ ܕܦܠܚܝܢ ܐܢܬܘܢ.
ܘܐܢܬܘܢ ܠܗܘܢ ܡܩܪܒܝܢ ܐܢܬܘܢ ܦܬܘܪܐ. ܘܠܐ ܗܘܐ ܗܢܘܢ
ܡܬܪܗܒܝܢ ܠܟܘܢ. ܘܗܫܐ ܐܬܦܢܝ ܠܝ ܠܡܕܡ ܕܐܡܪ ܐܢܐ ܠܟ
ܘܡܠܟ ܐܢܐ ܠܟ. ܐܘ ܢܓܕܐ ܐܝܬ ܕܡܫܬܡܥܝܢ. ܥܒܕܘ ܦܬܘܪܐ
ܪ̈ܘܝܐ ܘܣܓܕܘ ܠܐܠܗܐ ܒܟܘܕܐ ܘܠܒܪܗ ܥܡܗ ܡܫܝܚܐ.
ܠܐ ܗܘܐ ܡܛܠ ܕܠܒܫ ܦܓܪܐ ܘܗܘܐ ܒܪ ܐܢܫܐ ܘܐܬܡܫܚ
ܥܠ ܙܘܥܐ ܕܒܗܬܐ ܬܒܘܥ ܒܟܘܢ ܘܠܐ ܬܣܓܕܘܢ ܠܗ. ܗܠܝܢ
ܟܕ ܒܠܒܝܗܝܢ ܕܗܘܒܪ ܡܛܠ ܫܡܥܘܢ ܗܘ ܕܒܬܪ ܐܢܫܐ
ܘܡܛܠ ܦܪܘܣܗܘܢ ܗܘ. ܗܢܐ ܟܕ ܕܠܒܫ ܦܓܪܐ ܐܠܗܐ
ܗܘ ܒܪ ܐܠܗܐ ܒܪ ܐܝܬܘܬܗ ܕܐܒܘܗܝ. ܘܒܪ ܐܢܫܐ ܕܠܘܬܗ.
ܓܡܝܪܐ ܗܘ ܒܪ ܦܓܪܐ ܕܐܠܗܘܬܗ. ܘܐܢܫܐ ܗܘ ܥܡܝܩܐ
ܕܪܒܘܬܗ. ܘܒܗ ܐܒܘܗܝ ܐܝܬܘܗܝ، ܘܗܘܐ ܒܗ ܡܬܘܡ ܘܒܗ
ܟܠܗ. ܕܪܒܗ ܘܫܒܝܚ ܘܫܠܝܛ ܘܫܒܚܬܗ ܘܬܘܩܦܗ. ܘܪܘܚܐ
ܚܝܐ ܕܒܪܗ ܡܫܘܚܐ ܘܡܒܙܒܙܢܐ ܕܟܠܗܘܢ ܣܓܘܕܘܗܝ.
ܗܠܝܢ ܕܐܠܦ ܗܘܐ ܠܝ ܦܠܘܣ ܗܘ ܕܙܒܢܐ ܠܗ ܣܒܪܬܟ. ܘܙܕܩ
ܐܝܬ ܕܦܠܘܣ ܬܠܡܝܕܗ ܗܘܐ ܕܐܕܝ، ܫܠܝܚܐ. ܘܐܟܪܙ ܡܠܬܐ
ܕܡܫܝܚ ܡܢ ܗܢܐ ܐܬܪܐ ܕܗܢܐ ܣܓܝ. ܒܟܠܝ ܠܡܕܝܢܬܐ. ܡܛܠ ܗܟܢ
ܗܘܐ ܐܦ ܗܘ ܒܡܠܟܐ ܡܫܝܚܐ ܒܪܗ ܕܗܘ ܕܫܪܪܬ ܠܗ ܡܢܐ
ܕܒܠܒܗܘܢ ܐ̈ܠܗܐ. ܠܐ ܟܕ ܦܬܚ ܠܗܘܢ ܠܬܪܥܝܬܐ ܕܫܡܥܘ
ܠܡܕܡ ܕܒܟܬܒܐ ܗܘ. ܘܡܪܢܬܐ ܗܘ ܘܟܢܝܫ ܠܐ ܐܝܬܘܗܝ، ܐܠܗܐ.
ܐܝܟ ܡܢܐ ܕܣܦܪܝܢ ܐܢܘܢ ܠܦܬܪܐ ܟܬܝܒܐ ܕܟܠ ܐܢܫܐ. ܗܢܘܢ

ܐܝܟܢܐ ܗܘܐ ܗܘܐ ܒܡܬܚܫܢܘܬܐ ܒܝܘܡ̈ܝ ܒܬܠܬܐ ܒܫܒܐ. ܒܚܫܬ
ܒܥܠܝܗ̇ ܡܕܒܪܢܬܐ ܐܝܟ ܕܠܬܐ ܐܝܠܬܐ ܕܐܝܬ ܗܘܐ ܒܡܟܝܟܘܬܗ
ܕܪܥܝܐ ܠܗܘܢ ܟܠܗ ܚܝܠܐ. ܡܢ ܒܝܫܬ ܗܘܘ ܟܠܗܘܢ ܐ̈ܠܗܐ
ܘܡܬܟܬܫܝܢ ܘܡܬܒܥܝܢ ܒܐܣܝܪܐ. ܘܢܒܘ ܘܒܠ ܒܡ ܣܓ̈ܕܝܗܘܢ
ܘܒܘܡ̈ܝܐ ܟܠܗܘܢ ܡܬܦܪܩܝܢ ܗܘܘ ܒܫܘ̈ܝܐ ܘܢܘ̈ܪܐ ܘܪܝܚܐ
ܕܣܘܬܐ ܦܐܝܫ ܗܘܐ. ܘܒܪ̈ܝܐ ܘܬܘܪ̈ܐ ܢܬܪܥܝܢ ܗܘܘ. ܘܠܐ
ܘܚܙܐ ܘܩܛܠܐ ܒܥܠܡ ܕܝܪܐ ܡܬܬܚܒܠ ܗܘܐ. ܐܪܒܝܠ ܕܝܢ
ܙܒܢܐ ܘܒܗܘܢܐ ܕܟܠܗܘܢ ܒܡܕܝܢܬܐ ܐܬܪܘܗܝ ܗܘܐ. ܘܩܒܠ ܡܢ
ܟܠܗܘܢ ܣܓ̈ܕܘܗܝ ܘܗܘ ܡܬܝܗܒ ܗܘܐ ܘܡܢܗܪܐ ܡܨܛܒܬܐ
ܘܡܬܦܪܣܬܐ ܠܒܝܫ ܗܘܐ. ܘܣܘܪܐ ܕܡܝܢܐ ܗܘܐ ܒܡܕܝܢܬܐ
ܕܕܗܒܐ ܒܪܝܫܗ ܦܣܩ ܗܘܐ. ܘܒܪܡܐ ܕܡܠܬܗ ܥܠ ܕܟܦ̈ܐ
ܗܘܐ ܗܘܐ. ܘܐܟܪܙ ܡܠܟܐ ܒܪ ܐ̈ܠܗܐ ܒܪ ܒܝܬܐ ܦܐܝܡ
ܗܘܐ. ܘܡܬܦܪܣܝܢ ܗܘܘ ܠܗ ܠܐܪܒܝܠ. ܡܛܠ ܕܐܢܫ ܡܢ ܟܠܗܘܢ
ܣܓ̈ܕܘܗܝ ܗܘ ܡܢ ܒܝܬ ܗܘܐ ܐܝܟ ܐ̈ܠܗܐ ܟܠܗܘܢ. ܘܐܝܟ ܗܘ
ܕܒܝܬ ܝܬܒ ܗܘܐ ܡܢ ܐ̈ܠܗܐ. ܦܬܟܪܐ ܠܟܠ ܐܢܫ ܡܦܩܝܐ
ܗܘܐ. ܘܒܪ ܗܠܝܢ ܡܢ ܦܘܪܣܝܐ ܕܡܠܟܐ ܡܗܝܡܢܐ ܗܘ̈.. ○○○
ܒܪܡܫܐ ܐܦܣܩܘܦܐ ܕܒܪܣܛܝܢܐ ܦܠܛ ܗܘܐ ܐܝܟܕܗܘ،
ܕܐܪܒܝܠ ܗܘ ܘܡܬܪܕܬ ܡܫܝܚܐ ܘܢܨܠܘܬܐ ܡܫܡܫܢܐ. ܘܐܡܪ
ܗܘܐ ܠܗ ܠܐܪܒܝܠ ܒܡܕܝܢܬܐ ܪܒܬܐ. ܢܣܒ ܡܠܟܐ ܡܫܝܚܐ
ܒܐܬܪ̈ܝܢ ܗܘ ܕܘܡܝܗ ܥܡܡܐ ܘܐܪܒܥܐ: ܟܠܗܘܢ ܢܦܫ̈ܬܐ ܗܠܝܢ
ܕܢܦܠܐ ܐܝܬ ܒܗܘܢ. ܘܡܛܠܒܐ ܐܝܬ ܠܗܘܢ ܘܡܣܒܥܝܢ ܐܝܬ
ܠܗܘܢ ܡܢ ܐܝܟ ܐܠܗܐ ܕܡܨܬܐ ܘܕܥܪܪ̈ܐ. ܐܝܟ ܦܬܟܪܐ
ܒܣܝܒܐ ܘܦܠܚܐ. ܗܢܘܢ ܕܠܐ ܦܩܕܐ ܒܐܬ̈ܪܘܬܗܘܢ ܡܢ ܠܡܟܒܫ.
ܘܐܦܠܐ ܚܙܘ ܐܝܬ ܒܠ ܢܦܫܟ ܕܐܒܝܕܐ ܡܢ ܫܢܐ ܥܪ̈ܝܪܐ
ܕܐܠܗܐ. ܘܡܫܡܥ ܐܝܬ ܠܗ ܠܒܥܠܐ ܗܝܢܐ ܕܦܬܟܪܐ ܣܓ̈ܝܐ
ܡܒܠܠܝܢ ܒܟܦܝ. ܘܐܝܟ ܗܘ ܕܒܝܬ ܝܬܒ ܐܝܬ ܡܥܡܘܕ
ܡܦܪܢܒ ܐܝܬ ܐܪܕܝܟ ܐܝܟ ܣܝ ܡܥܡܘܕ. ܘܐܡܪ ܐܝܬ

ܕܦܝܠܛܘܣ. ܗܘܐ ܗ̇ܘܐ ܓܘܕܫܢܐ ܦܓܥܐܐ ܠܓܒܐ ܘܒܡܘܬܐ ܡܪܕܘܬܐ ܒܟܠܗ ܒܪܬܐ. ܐܝܟ ܕܐܬܟܠܘ ܗܘܘ ܡܢ ܚܝܘܬܐ ܕܥܠܝܡܐ. ܘܡܢ ܗܘܐ ܐܝܣܘ ܡܕܒܪܢܐ ܘܡܦܣ ܗܘܐ ܦܬ̈ܓܡܘܗܝ ܒܠܠܝܐ. ܘܡܒܪ ܗܘܐ ܐܝܠܝܢ ܒܐܝܣܪܐ ܙܒܢܐ ܘܗܘܐ ܗܘܐ ܬܡܢ ܒܝܬ ܓܘܒܐ ܠܦܓܥ̈ܐܐ. ܘܒܗ ܒܪܒܢܐ ܗܘ ܐܝܟ ܕܡܢ ܕܢܐ ܕܒܝܘܬܐ ܥܒܡ ܗܘܐ ܢܝܪܗ ܡܠܟܘܬܗ ܘܒܝܪ. ܘܗܘܐ ܥܠܝܐ ܘܠܠ ܡܢ ܙܕܘܩܝܐ ܕܐܘܣܡ ܗܘܐ ܒܠܝܗܘܢ ܢܝܪܗ ܥܘܙ. ܘܡܢ ܒܬܪ ܥܢܝܐ ܦܓܥ̈ܐܬܐ ܕܒܘܠܠܗܘܢ ܙܒܢܐ ܕܥ̈ܠܝܡܐ ܕܢܦܘ ܗܘܘ ܡܢ ܒܠܒܐ ܒܕ ܙܕܝܩܐ ܗܘܬ ܐܝܕܐ ܕܒܗܝܡܘܬܗܘܢ ܒܟܠܗ ܙܗܘܡܐ ܘܒܟܠܗ ܐܢܦܠܝܐ. ܒܕ݂ܝܢ ܕܝܢ ܘܗܘܐ ܗܘܐ ܒܒܝܐ ܙܒܢܐ ܒܙܗܘܡܐ ܡܕܝܢܬܐ.

ܫܠܡܬ ܡܫܠܡܢܘܬܗ ܕܥܒܕܗܘܢ ܒܐܦܐ.

ܗܘܦܘܡܢܡܛܐ ܕܓܒܪܝܠ. ܕܐܬܘܗܝ ܗܘܐ ܒܡܕܝܪܐ ܕܒܬܪܐ. ܘܐܬܘܗܝ ܗܘܐ ܠܡܕܒܪܢܘܬܐ ܕܐܦܝܣܩܘܦܘܬܐ ܕܟܫܟܪ..

ܒܝܘܡܝ ܡܫܡܫܢܐ ܕܐܦܛܪܘܦܘܣ ܦܛܪܘܣ ܡܪܝ. ܘܒܫܢܬ ܬܠܬ ܕܡܠܟܘܬܗ ܕܐܒܓܪ ܡܠܟܐ ܫܒܝܥܝܐ. ܕܐܬܘܗܝ ܫܢܬ ܐܪܒܥܡܐܐ ܘܐܫܬܒܥܝܢ ܕܐܠܟܣܢܕܪܘܣ ܡܠܟܐ ܕܝܘܢܝܐ. ܘܒܡܕܒܪܢܘܬܗ ܕܓܒܪܝܠ ܘܒܪܝܫܘܬܐ. ܦܓܥ ܗܘܐ ܦܪܝܘܣ ܡܪܝ ܠܦܓܥ̈ܘܢܐ ܕܐܬܪܘܬܐ ܕܡܠܦܢܘܗܝ. ܕܢܦܠܘ ܕܟܝܐ ܘܢܩܘܡܐ ܒܠܒܗܘܢ ܡ̈ܕܢܚܬܐ ܕܡܕܒܪܢܘܬܗܘܢ. ܘܐܡܠܟ ܕܠܐ ܡܕܒܫܝܢ. ܢܬܠܒܒܘܢ ܘܢܫܬܠܒܘܢ ܠܬܪܒܐ ܘܠܣܘܪܩܐ ܘܠܐܘ̈ܠܝܢܐ ܡܪܢܝܬܐ ܕܟܠ ܫܪ̈ܝܢ. ܘܒܬܪܝܢ ܢܦܠܘܢ ܡܢܗܘܢ ܒܪܫܐ ܕܦܘܫܐ. ܘܒܕ ܐܬܐ ܗܘܐ ܦܘܡܢܐ ܠܒܪܫܐ ܕܐܪܥܐ ܕܡܬܪܘܢܐ. ܒܐܪܥܐ

ܘܒܒܝܬܗ ܕܡܠܟܘܬܗ ܕܐܒܗ̈ܘܗܝ ܚܝܐ ܗܘܐ ܡܢܗܪܬܐ ܗܘ ܘܦܫ ܗܘܐ ܡܢ ܣܘܪܝܐ. ܘܚܝܐ ܠܗ ܒܥܡܐ ܘܐܬܕܒܪ. ܘܐܬܢܨܪ ܗܘܐ ܠܗ ܠܐܒܗ̈ܘܗܝ. ܕܪܕܪ ܗܘ ܡܫܝܚܐ ܕܡܕܢܪ ܐܝܬ ܠܗ ܘܡܟܐ ܦܬܓܡ̈ܐ ܘܐܡܪܝܢ. ܢܛܪܝܢ ܦܩܕ̈ܘܗܝ ܚܪܫܐ ܘܡܟܫܦܢܐ ܕܟܠ. ܦܩܕ̈ܘܗܝ ܕܝܢ ܒܡܠܟܘܬܗ ܕܗܘܦܟ ܗܘܐ ܠܗ ܟܠܗ ܕܚܝܐ ܠܡܠܬܐ ܗܘ ܕܚܝܐ. ܦܠܓ ܗܘܐ ܡܢܗܘܢ ܡܢ ܥܡܡܐ ܠܡܕܝܢܬܐ ܘܡܢ ܕܪܬܐ ܠܕܪܬܐ ܘܠܐ ܢܦܠ ܗܘܐ ܒܐܬܪ̈ܘܬܗܘܢ ܒܗܘ ܙܒܢܐ. ܡܕܝܢܬܐ ܕܝܢ ܟܠܗ ܐܚܪܬ ܗܘܬ ܠܐܒܗ̈ܘܗܝ ܒܐܝܩܪܐ ܘܡܟܠܗܘܢ، ܗܘܘ ܚܕܐܝܬ ܘܫܒܚܐܝܬ. ܒܪ ܡܢ ܐܬܬ̈ܐ ܘܕܪܕܪܬܐ ܠܐ ܓܠܐ ܠܐ ܗܘܐ ܕܢܒܒܪ ܒܥܡܗ ܕܡܫܝܚܐ. ܘܡܫܡܫܝܢ ܗܘܘ ܒܗ ܦܬܓܡ̈ܐ. ܘܡܦܪܢܣ ܕܝܢ ܐܚܡܗ، ܕܗܘ ܕܚܝܐ ܗܘܐ ܐܘܟܠܗ ܗܘܐ ܒܥܡܗ ܠܥܡ̈ܡܐ ܒܐܦܝܐ ܠܚܝܬܗ ܘܟܠܗ ܗܘܐ ܐܝܟ ܕܪܝܘ. ܒܪ ܡܗܝܡܢ ܗܘܐ ܗܘ ܘܒܢ̈ܝ ܒܝܬܗ ܟܠܗܘܢ ܒܡܫܝܚܐ ܕܒܪܗ ܗܘ ܕܐܠܗܐ ܚܝܐ. ܘܐܬܬܠܡܕܘ ܗܘܘ ܬܡܢ ܦܬܓܡ̈ܐ ܡܢ ܡܗܝܡܢܐ ܘܚܣܝܐ. ܘܟܕ ܦܠܚ ܗܘܬ ܚܕܘܬܐ ܒܡܠܟܘܬܗ ܟܠܐ ܗܘܐ ܬܡܢ ܒܕܪܬܐ ܒܪܘܚܐ ܘܒܟ̈ܕܢܘܬܐ ܕܚܕ̈ܘܗܝ ܘܒܡܘܪܐ ܟܠܗܝܢ ܕܒܢ̈ܝ ܐܦܠܢܐ ܘܥܒܕ ܗܘܐ ܬܡܢ ܕܢܟܐ ܕܡܕܒܪܢܘܬܐ ܕܡܦܩܕܐ ܒܣܘܪܝ ܘܥܒܕ ܥܬܝܪ. ܘܡܢ ܟܬܪ ܗܠܝܢ ܥܬܝܐ ܠܒܒܗ ܗܘܐ ܢܘܪܐ ܡܥܪ. ܘܚܒܫܗ ܗܘܐ ܒܝܬ ܐܣܘܪ̈ܐ. ܘܫܒܩ ܗܘܐ ܕܢܦܘܩ ܗܘܐ ܠܗ. ܘܦܩܪܐ ܗܘܐ ܠܐܚܣܢܘܣ ܡܫܡܫܢܐ ܘܒܒܪܗ ܗܘܐ ܐܦܣܩܘܦܐ ܢܠܦܘܗܝ، ܒܪܘܡܐ. ܘܗܢܝܢ ܗܠܝܢ ܐܡܪ ܗܘܐ ܗܘ ܥܡܡܐ ܘܥܪܒܐ ܬܘܒ ܐܦ ܐܚܪܢܬܐ ܕܐܝܬ ܗܘ، ܠܗ ܦܩܕܗ ܗܘܐ ܠܐܚܣܢܘܣ ܕܗܘܐ ܡܠܦ ܡܢܡ ܒܥܡܐ ܒܪ ܐܡܪ ܗܘܐ ܠܗ ܕܒܥܡ ܕܢܬܦܐ ܚܕܬܐ ܘܚܬܝܬܐ. ܠܐ ܗܘܐ ܡܬܦܪܐ ܡܢܡ ܒܥܡܐ ܡܢܡ ܐܚܪܢܐ ܕܠܐ ܙܕܩ. ܒܪ ܕܝܢ ܦܩܕ ܗܘܐ ܡܛܪ ܕܢܕܘܩ ܗܘܐ ܥܡܡ̈ܐ ܒܠܘܪ ܪܥܡ ܐܝܟ ܕܗܘ ܒܒܐܐ ܗܘܐ ܡܢ ܡܛܪ ܘܕܥܬܦܠ ܗܘܐ ܪܥܡ

ܐܢܬܘܢ ܕܗܘܝܢ ܡܫܝܚܗ. ܠܐ ܢܛܥܝܘܢ ܫܡܥܘܢ ܚܪܫܐ
ܒܬܡܗ̈ܬܐ ܕܡܚܘܐ ܠܗܘܢ. ܕܠܐ ܒܨܒ̈ܝܐ ܐܝܟ ܕܠܐܢܫܐ ܕܠܐ
ܗܘܝܢ. ܕܠܐ ܢܚܙܘܢ ܕܢܦܪܩܘܢ ܡܕܡ ܕܚܝܠ ܘܡܫܬܡܥܝܢ. ܫܪܪܘ
ܗܒܠ ܐܢܬܘܢ، ܐܝܟܐ ܕܒܥܝܐ ܥܠܝܟ ܒܬܘܠܬܟܘܢ. ܘܦܝܣܘ
ܠܗܘܢ ܐܬܪܐ ܡܕܡ ܕܢܚܙܘܢ ܡܕܝܢܬܐ. ܘܗܘ ܐܢܫܐ ܕܢܚܡ
ܐܢܬܘܢ ܕܒܥܝܢ ܠܗ ܠܗ، ܐܬܪܐ ܕܠܟܘܢ ܗܘ، ܕܬܗܡܢܘܢ ܒܗ.
ܘܒܗ ܒܥܠܬܐ. ܫܪܝ ܐܢܬܘܢ، ܗܘܘ ܠܡܫܝܚܐ ܫܪܪܐ. ܘܐܡܪܘ
ܗܘܘ ܠܗ ܐܢܫܐ ܬܪܝܢ ܐܚܝܢܐ. ܐܝܟ ܚܒܪܐ ܕܬܟܠܝܢ ܥܠܝܟ.
ܕܐܢܬ ܥܡ ܚܕܐ ܕܠܟܘܢ ܬܒܥܐ. ܚܙܘ ܐܬܪܐ ܡܕܡ ܡܕܡ
ܒܗܠܝܢ. ܘܢܣܒܐ ܗܘܐ ܥܡܗܘܢ ܟܠܢܐ ܕܡܢܪ ܠܡܫܝܚܐ. ܘܒܗ
ܡܕܢܐ ܐܡܪܝܢ ܗܘܘ ܠܗ ܐܢܬܘܢ ܕܒܬܪ ܗܘܬ ܡܕܝܢܬܐ ܚܕ
ܒܪܗ ܕܚܕ ܡܢ ܬܪܥܐ ܘܦܬܚܐ ܘܡܬܩܪܝܐ ܕܒܗܘܢ. ܘܐܡܪܘ
ܗܘܘ ܠܗ ܥܠܘܗܝ ܒܗ ܒܝܬܝܢ ܗܘܘ. ܕܐܢܫܐ ܡܢܗܘܢ ܕܡܫܝܚܐ
ܠܗ ܠܡܢܐ ܡܢܬܐ. ܗܘ ܗܘ ܚܙܪ ܘܡܗܝܡܢ ܘܡܬܡܠܠ.
ܘܟܬܒܗ ܐܘܠܝܢ ܥܠ ܒܥܠܕܒܒ ܕܐܡܪ ܠܝ. ܘܐܡܪܘ ܗܘܘ ܠܗ
ܠܫܡܥܘܢ ܚܪܫܐ ܡܠܠ ܕܐܢܬ ܗܘ ܡܕܡ ܐܢܬ ܠܫܡܥܘܢ
ܟܠܝܠܐ ܗܪܟܐ. ܘܠܝܟ ܗܘ ܢܚܝܢ ܡܕܡܟܘܢ. ܐܢܬ ܚܘܐ ܚܝܠܐ
ܕܠܘܐ ܠܟ ܡܕܡܐܢܬ. ܫܡܥܘܢ ܕܝܢ ܢܦܠܐܢܬ ܡܢܟ ܗܘܐ
ܟܪܘܙܗ، ܕܡܢܬܐ ܘܫܡܥܘܗ̇ ܗܘܘ ܠܟܪܘܙܐ ܡܕܡܗܘܢ. ܘܣܓܝ
ܗܘܐ ܠܡܚܙܝܗ ܘܠܡܫܡܥܗ. ܘܒܥܓܠܐ ܡܬܡܠܐ ܗܘܐ. ܟܕ ܐܡܪ
ܗܘܐ ܬܠܬܐ ܦܠܓܘܬܐ. ܡܗܝܡܢ ܕܝܢ ܒܡܫܝܚܐ ܐܡܪ ܗܘܐ.
ܘܡܗܝܡܢ ܒܫܡܗ ܕܠܐ ܡܫܬܐ. ܘܐܦܢ ܗܘܐ ܠܦܘܪܐ ܦܘܠܚܢܐ
ܘܡܕܡ ܠܐ ܗܘܐ ܗܘܐ ܘܠܐ ܐܫܬܟܚ. ܘܡܫܬܐ ܗܘ ܒܪܘܫܗ
ܕܡܢܐ ܗܘܐ. ܘܒܗ ܒܫܒܬܐ ܡܢܟ ܗܘܐ ܫܡܥܘܢ ܟܐܦܐ
ܬܠܡܝܕܘܗܝ ܠܘܬܗ ܕܡܫܬܐ ܗܘ. ܘܥܒܕ ܗܘܐ ܡܕܡ ܥܠܘܗܝ ܒܢܝܐ
ܕܐܡܪ ܗܘܐ ܬܗܪ. ܒܫܡܗ ܕܝܫܘܥ ܡܫܝܚܐ ܗܘ ܕܐܘܫܥ ܗܘܘ
ܡܘܕܝܢ ܒܐܘܪܫܠܡ ܘܐܢܫܝܢ ܡܗܝܡܢܝܢ ܚܝܢ ܠܗ. ܘܡܢ ܡܢ ܬܗܪ.

ܘܕܫܪܪܐ. ܗܘܘ ܕܝܢ ܩܕܡ ܠܟܠܗܝܢ ܒܪܝܬܐ. ܗܘܘ ܒܪܐ
ܕܡܫܝܚܘܬܐ ܘܦܐܪܐ ܫܒܝܚܐ ܕܝܢ ܐܒܘܗܝ، ܕܒܪܐ. ܐܠܐ ܣܝܡ
ܐܢܬܘܢ ܚܒܪܝܐ ܬܫܒܘܚܬܐ ܕܠܒܝ ܘܢܦܩܝܢ ܠܥܠܡ ܗ̇ܟܢ ܠܐ ܐܢܫ
ܢܬܠܟܘܢ ܘܒܠܐ ܗ̇ܘ ܕܒܘܪܐ ܗܐ ܡܢ ܕܢܠܡ ܠܗܘܬ ܐܒܘܗܝ،
ܘܫܢܐ ܐܝܟܢܐ ܦܪܘܩ ܘܒܪܬܗ ܒܟܠܗ ܒܪܝܬܐ ܕܒܗܕܐ ܢܬܝܕܥ
ܘܢܬܗܝܡܢ ܕܗܘܝܘ ܒܪܘܐ ܕܒܪܝܬܐ. ܘܒܪܝܬܗ ܩܕܡ ܒܪܝܬܐ.
ܘܕܢܝܚܘܢ ܫܒܝܚܐ ܕܝܫܘܥ ܗܘܐ ܒܟܘܬܗ ܐܦ ܐܢܬܘܢ
ܗܘܕܝܢ ܐܢܬܘܢ. ܐܝܟܢܐ ܕܝܢ ܕܐܬ ܗܘܐ ܒܥܠܡܐ. ܘܐܦ ܬܪܝܢܐ
ܕܐܬܓܠܝ، ܗܘܐ ܒܟܘܬܗ ܘܒܠ ܗ̇ܠܝܢ ܗܘܕ ܗܘܐ ܐܦ ܦܠܓܗܘܢ
ܡܟܗܢܐ. ܕܗܘ ܫܪܪ ܗܘܐ ܘܐܘܕܥ ܗܘܐ ܠܗܘܢ ܘܐܬܚܙܝ،
ܗ̇ܘ، ܡܢ ܟܡܐ، ܗ̇ܠܝܢ ܘܕܗܘܝܢ ܡܢ ܗܠܝܢ. ܘܩܕܡ ܪ̈ܘܚܢܝܐ
ܕܡܫܝܚܘܬܐ. ܘܡܛܠ ܗܢܐ ܪܚܡ ܗܘܐ ܩܕܡ ܟܠ ܦܠܓܗܘܢ. ܟܠ
ܕܠܐ ܒܪܘܚܐ ܐܬܓܠܝܘ ܗܘܐ ܠܡܫܝܚܐ ܘܡܛܠ ܗܢܐ ܫܪܪ
ܗܘܐ ܫܠܡܐ ܒܗܘܢ ܫܘܠܛܢܐ ܕܗܘܒ ܗܘܐ ܠܗ. ܘܗܘ، ܗܕܐ
ܐܬܓܠܝܬ ܘܐܬܝܕܥܬ ܒܟܠܗ ܐܘܪܚܐ ܕܡܫܝܚܐ. ܗ̇ܘ ܗܟܝܠ
ܡܢ ܕܚܙܐ ܗܘܐ ܦܠܓܗܘܢ ܘܐܘܕܥ ܗܘܐ ܠܗܘܢ ܘܠܡܘܕܥܢܘܬܗܘܢ
ܡܫܪܪܐ ܕܠܒܗܘܢ. ܠܗ ܗ̇ܘ ܡܕܒܪ ܐܢܐ ܘܡܫܡܠܝ ܐܢܐ ܘܒܠܒܝܫܐ
ܣܓܝܐ، ܘܡܢ ܐܢܬܘܢ ܕܠܐ ܡܬܚܙܝܢ ܗܘܐ ܦܠܓܗܘܢ ܕܒܟܘܬܗ
ܗܘܐ ܠܡܠܟܘܬܐ ܡܢ ܕܠܐ ܗܘܐ ܗܘܐ ܘܚܙܐ ܒܟܝܢܗ،
ܐܠܐ ܗ̇ܘ ܡܢ ܕܗܘܐ ܗܘܐ. ܘܐܬܗܦܟ ܒܟܝܢܗ. ܗ̇ܘ ܗ̇ܘ
ܠܟܠ ܗܘܐ ܘܐܘܕܥ. ܫܪܪܐ ܕܝܢ ܕܗ̇ܠܝܢ ܕܗ̇ܘ، ܬܘܒ ܘܢܗܪܐ
ܕܡܟܝܢ. ܗܘܘ ܐܝܟ ܫ̈ܒܝܚܐ. ܘܒܪ ܐܢܫܘܬܐ ܗܘܘ ܩܕܡ ܦܠܓܗܘܢ
ܗܢܘܢ ܢܗܘܪܐ ܐܘܕܥܘ ܗܘܘ ܡܕܡܗܘܢ، ܒܟܠܗ ܫܘܝܐ ܗ̇ܢܐ
ܗܘܘ ܠܗܘܢ ܬܪܝܢ ܒܟܠܗ ܕܡܘܪܝܐ ܐܝܟ ܕܢܐܡܪܘܢ ܗܘܘ
ܕܐܢܫܝܢ ܬܠܡܝܕܘܗܝ، ܟܠܡ ܥܠܝܗ ܕܡܫܝܚܐ. ܗܐ ܗܟܝܠ
ܫܒܚܘܢ ܡܫܒܚܬܐ. ܘܐܦ ܕܝܢ ܠܐܠܗܐ ܕܫܒܚܘܢ ܠܗ
ܢܩܝܡ ܐܢܬܘܢ ܕܬܬܠܟܘܢ. ܐܬܠܟܘܢ ܐܝܟ ܠܫܡܥܐ ܕܫܡܝܢ

ܕܐܡܝܢܐ ܗܘ، ܡܠܬܐ ܕܢܘܬܪܢ ܦܘܩܕ̈ܢܘܗܝ ܕܫ̈ܠܝܚܐ. ܒܗܝܡܢܘܬܐ
ܕܗܘܝܢ ܟ̈ܠ ܐܢܫܐ ܦܬܓܡܐ ܕܟ̈ܬܒܐ ܬܫܠܡܬܐ ܟܠܗ ܕܢܒܝܐ.
ܡܛܠ ܕܡܢ ܕܫܠܡ ܐܬܬܝܢ ܗܘܝܢ ܬ̈ܪܥܐ ܕܢܦ̈ܫܐ. ܘܠܐ ܗܘܐ ܦܩܪܐ
ܕܬܬܒܥܐ. ܡܛܠ ܗܢܐ ܗܘ ܐܡܪ ܠܝ. ܕܡܫܪܪ ܐܢܐ ܠܟܘܢ
ܕܗܘܝܐ ܦܪܘܩܝ. ܕܗܘ ܢܠܦܘܢ ܡܢܢ ܕܠܐ ܢܕܥܝܢ ܐܢܬܘܢ.
ܒܡܗܡܢܘܬܗ ܗܘ ܓܒܪ ܕܠܗ ܐܡܝܪ ܚܢܢ: ܐܝܠܝܢ ܕܡܫܝܚܝܢ
ܐܢܬܘܢ. ܘܟܕ ܬܗܘܘܢ ܡܦܪܫܝܢ ܒܫܪܪܐ ܠܒܢ̈ܝܟܝ ܘܫܠܡܐ
ܠܡܐܟ̈ܠܐ. ܕܡܢ ܢܡܘܣܐ ܕܫܠܡܘܬܗ ܘܡܢ ܒܫܪܪܐ ܕܫܠܡܗ.
ܬܗܡܝܢܘܢ ܒܡܫܝܚܐ ܕܐܬܘܗܝ، ܐܠܗܐ ܒܪܐ ܕܐܠܗܐ.
ܬܬܦܪܫܘܢ ܡܢ ܦܘܠܚܢܐ ܕܒܒܕܘܬܐ. ܘܬܬܦܩܕܘܢ ܠܗ
ܘܠܐܟܘܠܗܝ، ܘܬܫܟܚܘܢ ܠܢܘܚܐ ܕܐܠܗܘܬܗ. ܟܕ ܓܒܪ ܠܐܒܐ
ܡܫܝܚܝܢ ܚܢܢ. ܐܦ ܠܒܢ̈ܝ ܒܒܗ ܡܫܝܚܝܢ ܚܢܢ. ܘܟܕ ܠܒܪܐ ܡܘܕܝܢ
ܚܢܢ. ܐܦ ܠܐܒܐ ܒܒܗ ܡܘܕܝܢ ܚܢܢ. ܘܟܕ ܒܪܘܚܐ ܡܗܕܝܢ.
ܐܦ ܒܐܒܐ ܘܒܒܪܐ ܡܗܕܝܢ ܚܢܢ. ܡܛܠ ܕܒܫܡ ܐܒܐ ܘܒܪܐ
ܘܪܘܚܐ ܐܬܦܩܕܢܢ. ܕܢܥܡܕ ܠܐܝܠܝܢ ܕܡܗܝܡܢܝܢ ܕܢܫܘܢ ܠܟܠܗ ⁘

ܒܪܘܚ ܡܫܝܚ ܡܢ ܟܠܗ ܕܡܫܚܬܐ ܕܗܘܝܐ ܒܠܒܐ ܕܠܝܬ
ܒܗܝܢ ܡܬܪܢܝܐ. ܘܐܬܡܪܟܒ ܠܗܬ ܐܝܠܝܢ ܕܫܪܝܪܢ ܘܡܗܝܡܢܝܢ:
ܘܡܦܩܠܝܢ ܡܢ ܐܠܗܐ. ܘܢܛܪ ܐܚܪ̈ܢܝܢ ܘܡܢܝܢ ܦܘܪ̈ܫܢܝܢ.
ܘܡܟܝܠ] ܕܕܢܚ ܠܗ ܢܗܘܪܐ ܒܒܪܝܬܐ. ܘܗܢܐ ܠܗ ܟܠܡܐ ܒܒ̈ܢܝܐ
ܕܪܚܡܐ ܕܢܣܐ ܟܠ ܐܢܫ ܘܢܬܒܢܝܢ: ܕܠܐ ܙܕܩ ܕܢܫܬܓܐ.
ܒܪ̈ܝܬܐ ܚܠܦ ܒܪܘܢܐ ܐܦܠܐ ܒܡ ܒܪܘܢܐ. ܡܛܠ ܕܒܟܠ ܡܕܡ
ܕܒܪ̈ܝܬܐ ܗܘ ܡܬܒܕܪܐ ܗܘ ܕܒܟܘܕܗ. ܘܠܐ ܗܘܐ ܡܬܒܢܐ ܗܘ
ܐܝܟ ܒܪܘܗ. ܗܢܐ ܕܝܢ ܕܐܬܬܐ ܝܐܕܝܢ. ܐܠܗܐ ܗܘ ܒܪ ܐܠܗܐ
ܒܟܝܢܗ. ܐܦ ܐܠܗܘܬܗ ܫܠܝܛ ܗܘܐ ܒܢܫܘܬ ܕܠܢܫܘܬ ܢܣܒܬ
ܒܒܪܝܢܐ ܕܐܠܗܘܬܗ. ܘܡܛܠ ܗܢܐ ܙܕܩ ܗܘ ܠܝ ܕܢܫܬܡܥ ܠܗ.
ܡܛܠ ܕܡܬܒܕܪܐ ܗܘ ܒܡ ܐܒܘܗܝ. ܘܠܐ ܢܬܒܕܪ ܠܒܪ̈ܝܬܐ
ܕܐܬܒܪܝ، ܠܡܬܒܕܪܘ ܕܒܪܘܢܐ. ܗܘܘ ܓܒܪ ܐܠܗܐ ܕܗܘܝܬܐ

ܠܒܢܝ̈ ܚܐܪ̈ܐ ܕܡܬܠܡܕܝܢ ܐܬܘ ܗܘܘ ܠܐܪܘܡܝ. ܕܢܚܙܘܢܝܗܝ
ܘܢܫܡܥܘܢ ܗܘܘ ܡܠܬܗ. ܘܟܕ ܟܢܝܫܐ ܗܘܬ ܡܕܝܢܬܐ ܟܠܗ ܠܘܬܗ.
ܡܢ ܗܘܐ ܕܡܬܟܠܠ ܒܫܡܗܘܢ. ܘܫܘܐ ܠܗܘܢ ܒܪܘܚܬܐ
ܕܡܠܟܘܬܗ ܐܡܝܢܬܐ ܐܫܬܕܝ ܗܘܬ. ܘܥܕ، ܗܘܐ ܕܢܐܡܪ ܠܗܘܢ
ܗܢܐ. ܚܒܝܒ̈ܐ ܒܢܝ̈ ܪܗܘܡܝܐ ܡܫܝ̈ܚܝܐ ܕܐܬܦܠܓܬ ܒܠܗ. ܫܡܥܘ
ܡܢܝ ܕܐܡܪ ܐܢܐ ܠܟܘܢ. ܕܡܠܟܐ ܡܫܝܚܐ ܐܢܐ ܘܡܟܪܙ ܐܢܐ.
ܠܫܘܒܚ ܫܡܗ ܕܐܠܗܐ. ܕܢܚܬ ܡܢ ܫܡܝܐ ܘܗܘܐ ܒܪ ܐܢܫܐ.
ܘܗܘܐ ܒܝܢܬܢ ܐܝܟܘܬܢ ܘܣܒܠ ܚܫ̈ܐ ܨܠܝܒܘܬܗ. ܘܐܬܩܒܪ
ܘܐܬܟܪܙܬܐ ܡܬܟܪܙ ܘܩܡ ܒܬܠܬܐ ܝܘܡܝܢ ܕܐܬܐ ܒܐܪܒܥܐ
ܕܟܠܗܘܢ. ܟܕ ܐܦ ܐܢܘܢ ܫܡܥܝܢ ܗܘܘ ܢܦܠܝܢ ܗܘܘ
ܕܒܕ ܗܘܐ. ܡܛܠ ܕܐܦ ܡܢ ܐܬܘܬܐ ܐܣܘܬܐ ܐܬܝܢ ܗܘܘ
ܠܘܬܗ. ܟܠ ܛܒܐ ܕܐܣܝܘܬܗ. ܘܟܠ ܫܡܥܐ ܕܥܒܕܘܗܝ
ܦܠܓܘܬܐ. ܘܟܠ ܡܢ ܕܚܙܐ ܗܘܐ ܠܗ ܡܬܕܡܪ ܗܘܐ ܒܡܠܬܗ.
ܘܡܛܠ ܕܐܠܗܐ ܗܘܐ. ܟܕ ܐܣܘܬܗ ܐܦ ܢܦܫܐ ܥܒܕ
ܗܘܐ. ܐܣܘܬܗ ܓܝܪ ܕܠܒܐ. ܡܢ ܦܘܡܗ ܟܠ ܫܡܘܥܘܗܝ
ܗܘܐ. ܕܢܙܥ ܗܘ ܘܡܫܡܥܝܢ. ܠܗܢܐ ܓܝܪ ܫܡܥܐ ܡܬܚܙܝܢ ܗܘܘ
ܢܦܫܬܐ ܒܪ̈ܘܚܗܘܢ. ܟܕ ܡܫܬܡܥܝܢ ܗܘܘ ܕܢܚܙܘܢܝܗܝ ܘܢܫܡܥܘܢ
ܗܘܘ ܡܠܬܗ. ܕܗܘ ܕܐܝܬܘܗܝ ܗܘܐ ܥܡ ܐܒܘܗܝ ܡܢ ܩܕܡ
ܘܡܢ ܟܠܡ. ܐܠܗܐ ܕܫܘܐ ܗܘܐ ܒܪܘܚܐ ܘܐܬܚܙܝ ܒܒܣܪܢ.
ܒܪܐ ܫܒܝܚܐ ܕܡܢ ܠܥܠܡ. ܘܡܫܒܚ ܗܘܐ ܥܡ ܐܒܘܗܝ. ܘܥܡ
ܪܘܚܐ ܕܐܠܗܘܬܗ. ܘܫܘܠܛܢܐ ܕܫܡܝܐ ܕܡܪܘܬܗ. ܘܐܬܕܒܩ
ܗܘܐ ܒܪܚܡܘܗܝ ܡܢ ܐܒܐ ܕܫܠܝܚܐ. ܘܐܬܬܟܠ ܗܘܐ ܠܘܬ ܐܒܘܗܝ.
ܐܝܟ ܡܢܐ ܕܣܪܝܬ ܐܢܐ ܘܐܡܪܢ. ܘܡܛܠ ܗܘ ܕܥܒܕ ܢܫܬܐ
ܒܫܘܒܚܐ ܕܠܗ ܘܕܫܠܝܚܘܗܝ ܡܠܐܟܘܗܝ ܘܢܒܝ̈ܐ. ܐܝܟ ܡܢܐ
ܕܫܡܥܝܢ ܗܘܝܢ ܡܢܗ ܕܐܡܪ ܗܘܐ ܠܝ. ܠܐ ܓܝܪ ܡܫܡܫܝܢ
ܕܢܐܡܪ ܡܕܡ ܕܠܐ ܫܡܥ ܗܘܐ ܠܝ ܡܢܗ. ܐܦ ܠܐ ܒܟܬܒܝܢ
ܒܟܬܒܐ ܕܣܦܪܬܗ ܡܕܡ ܕܗܘ ܠܐ ܐܡܪ ܗܘܐ ܠܝ. ܡܛܠ

ܒܚܝܠ ܘܡܬܚܠܦ. ܘܐܬܬܘ̈ܬܐ ܬܘܒ ܒܥܠܡܗܘܢ ܕܡܢ ܟܠ ܓܢܣ̈ܝܢ.
ܡܢ ܐܝܟ ܒܬܪ ܫܐܪ̈ܝܐ ܬܠܡܝܕܗ ܕܐܕܝ ܫܠܝܚܐ ܀
ܫܪܒܐ ܕܝܢ ܕܡܫܝ̈ܚܝܗܘܢ ܐܘܪܚܐ ܕܫܠܝܚܐ ܐܬܘ ܗܘܘ ܠܐܬܪ̈ܘܬܐ ܡܕܢܚ̈ܝܐ ܕܒܝܬ ܐܪ̈ܡܝܐ. ܘܡܢ ܕܗܘܐ ܠܝܘܡܐ ܡܬܬܠܡܕܝܢ ܗܘܘ ܘܡܥܡܕܝܢ. ܘܬܡܢ ܫܡܫܘ ܗܘܘ ܒܥܕ̈ܬܗܘܢ. ܘܬܡܢ ܗܘܐ ܡܩܥܝܢܗܘܢ ܡܢ ܒܠܥܕ ܗܕܐ. ܒܕ ܙܒܢ ܬܠܬܝܢܗܘܢ ܒܬܪܗܘܢ ܒܫܢܐ ܠܡܫܝܚܐ. ܘܫܢܝ ܫܢܝܠܦܐ ܐܘ ܬܘܬܒܬܐ ܠܐ ܗܘܐ ܠܗܘܢ ܒܠ ܒܪ̈ܘܬܗܘܢ ܀
ܠܘܩܐ ܕܝܢ ܐܘܓܠܝܣܛܐ ܗܘܬ ܠܗ ܒܦܠܓܘܬܗ ܡܕܝܢܬܐ ܘܒܬܒ ܗܘܐ ܢܘܗܪܐ ܕܣܘܒܪ̈ܢܗܘܢ ܕܫܠܝܚܐ ܘܦܓܥܐ ܘܢܬܒܣܐ ܕܬܫܡܫܬܐ ܕܥܘܗܕܢܗܘܢ. ܘܠܐܝܕܐ ܐܝܠ ܗܘܐ ܚܕ ܚܕ ܡܢܗܘܢ. ܒܦܠܓܘܬܗ ܡܕܝܢ ܕܠܘܩܐ ܗܠܝܢ ܘܕܡܬܟܝܠܐ ܡܢ ܗܠܝܢ ܒܬܒ ܗܘܐ ܘܣܡ ܒܝܕ ܦܪ̈ܣܘܦܐ ܘܐܘܠܦ ܬܠܡܝܕܘܗܝ. ܘܠܝܬ ܗܘܐ ܠܗ ܒܕܥܐ ܠܝܘܡܐ ܕܥܘܬܗ ܐܝܟ ܕܠܐ ܗܘܐ ܠܦܠܘܣ ܦܠܣܛܘܣ ܘܐܪܣܛܘܣ ܕܡܢ ܠܘܩܪܛܐ. ܘܡܥܠܢܘܣ ܬܠܡܝܕܐ ܘܫܡܥܐ ܕܫܠܝܚܐ ܒܕܥܐ ܕܣܠܩ ܠܪܗܘܡܐ ܡܕܝܢܬܐ. ܕܡܢ ܗܘܐ ܠܡܩܒܠ ܦܪܣܠܘܣ ܪܗܛܪܐ. ܘܫܠܡ ܗܘܐ ܢܦܫܗ ܡܣܪ ܒܡܘܬܐ ܠܗ ܠܫܡܥܘܢ ܟܐܦܐ ܒܪܗܘܡܐ ܡܕܝܢܬܐ ܀

ܡܫܘܠܡܘܬܗ ܕܫܡܥܘܢ ܟܐܦܐ ܒܪܗܘܡܐ ܡܕܝܢܬܐ.

ܒܫܢܬ ܬܠܬܝܢ ܕܩܠܘܕܝܘܣ ܩܣܪ. ܢܦܩ ܗܘܐ ܫܡܥܘܢ ܟܐܦܐ ܡܢ ܐܢܛܝܘܟܝ ܕܢܐܙܠ ܠܗ ܠܪܗܘܡܐ. ܘܟܕ ܥܒܪ ܗܘܐ ܡܟܪܙ ܗܘܐ ܒܡܕ̈ܝܢܬܐ ܡܠܬܗ ܕܡܪܢ. ܘܟܕ ܩܪܒ ܗܘܐ ܕܢܥܘܠ ܗܘܐ ܠܬܡܢ: [ܫܡܥܘ ܗܘܘ ܝܗܘ̈ܕܝܐ ܘܢܦܩܘ ܠܐܘܪܥܗ. ܘܡܠܬܗ ܗܘܬ ܒܕܒܪܐ ܥܠ ܟܢܘܫܬܐ ܪܒܬܐ. ܘܡܢ ܪܘܪܒܢܐ ܕܡܕܝܢܬܐ

ܡܠܟ ܐܚܪܐ ܕܟܗܢܘܬܐ ܕܟܠܕܝܐ. ܪܗܘܡܐ ܡܕܝܢܬܐ
ܘܡܠܟ ܐܦܠܝܐ ܘܐܗܘܒܝܐ ܘܒܪܘܦܠܝܐ. ܘܟܠܗܐ ܥܡ ܫܪܟܐ
ܕܐܬܪܘܬܐ ܐܚܪ̈ܢܐ ܕܐܪ̈ܡܝܘܗܝ ܡܢ ܥܡܘܕܗ ܠܐܦܐ ܕܗܘܠ
ܗܘܐ ܡܢ ܐܬܠܘܟ ܘܗܘܐ ܗܘܐ ܬܡܢ ܦܘܪܐ ܘܡܕܒܪܢܐ
ܒܕܪܬܐ ܕܟܝܢܐ ܗܘܐ ܬܡܢ ܘܒܫܪ̈ܒܗ ܀

ܡܠܟ ܐܚܪܐ ܕܟܗܢܘܬܐ ܕܟ̈ܠܕܝܐ ܐܦܣܘܣ ܘܬܘܠܝܩܐ ܘܡܠܟ
ܐܣܝܐ ܘܐܬܪܐ ܟܠܗ ܕܦܘܪ̈ܬܝܐ ܘܕܐܟܐܝܐ ܟܠܗ ܘܫܪ̈ܒܗ. ܡܢ
ܘܡܢ ܐܘܠܘܦܛܐ ܗܘ ܕܢܦܠ ܗܘܐ ܒܠ ܫܒܚܗ ܕܡܠܟ̈ܐ. ܕܗܘ ܒܢܐ
ܗܘܐ ܒܕܪܬܐ ܬܡܢ ܘܫܠܛ ܗܘܐ ܬܡܢ ܒܡܕܒܪܢܘܬܗ ܕܬܡܢ ܀

ܡܠܟ ܐܚܪܐ ܕܟܗܢܘܬܐ ܕܟ̈ܠܕܝܐ ܢܡܘܐ ܘܢܘܡܕܝܐ ܘܡܠܟ
ܐܬܪܐ ܕܒܝܬܢܘܝܐ ܘܕܒܬܠܝܬܐ ܘܕܦܫ̈ܝܛܬܐ ܕܫܪ̈ܒܗ. ܡܢ
ܐܫܪܐܘܗ ܐܘܡܢܝ ܕܥܡܘܕܗ ܠܐܦܐ ܕܗܘ ܗܘܐ ܗܘܐ
ܡܕܒܪܢܐ ܘܦܘܪܐ ܒܕܪܬܐ ܕܟܝܢܐ ܗܘܐ ܬܡܢ ܘܒܗ ܗܘܐ
ܘܫܠܛ ܗܘܐ ܬܡܢ ܀

ܡܠܟ ܐܚܪܐ ܕܟܗܢܘܬܐ ܕܟܠܕܝܐ. ܒܘܠܦܝܐ ܘܡܠܟ ܐܬܪܐ
ܕܬܪܘܡܝܐ ܘܕܫܪ̈ܒܗ. ܒܕܡܝܐ ܠܗܪܐ ܪܒܐ ܬܫܡܫܬܐ ܕܦܪܥ
ܒܗܬ ܒܪ̈ܒܢܐ ܡܢ ܠܗܘܢ ܥܠܡܝܐ ܕܗܘ ܒܢܐ ܗܘܐ ܒܕܪܬܐ
ܬܡܢ ܘܫܠܛ ܗܘܐ ܬܡܢ ܒܟܘܪܘܬܗ ܘܒܡܕܒܪܢܘܬܗ ܕܬܡܢ ܀

ܡܠܟ ܐܚܪܐ ܕܟܗܢܘܬܐ ܕܟ̈ܠܕܝܐ ܐܪܘܪܗܝ ܘܐܬܪ̈ܘܬܐ
ܟܠܗܘܢ ܕܫܪ̈ܒܗ ܕܡܢ ܟܠ ܒܢ̈ܝܗ ܘܦܪܣܐ ܘܒܪܟ ܘܡܠܟ
ܒܪܝܟܐ ܘܒܢ̈ܝܬܐ ܕܫܪ̈ܒܗ ܘܬܫܡܫܬܐ ܘܒܗܬ ܬܫܡ̈ܫܬܐ ܟܠܗ
ܕܒܗܬ ܢܗ̈ܪܝܢ ܡܢ ܐܕܝ ܥܠܡܝܐ ܫܕ ܡܢ ܥܒܕܝܢ ܘܐܬ̈ܪܝܢ ܥܠܡ̈ܝܐ.
ܕܗܘ ܬܠܬܐ ܗܘܐ ܬܡܢ ܘܒܢܐ ܗܘܐ ܒܕܪܬܐ ܬܡܢ ܘܒܗ
ܗܘܐ ܘܫܠܛ ܗܘܐ ܬܡܢ ܒܡܕܒܪܢܘܬܗ ܕܬܡܢ ܀

ܡܠܟ ܐܚܪܐ ܕܟܗܢܘܬܐ ܕܟܠ̈ܕܝܐ ܦܪܣ ܟܠܗ ܕܐܬܘܪ̈ܝܐ
ܘܕܐܪ̈ܡܝܐ ܘܕܡ̈ܕܝܐ ܘܕܐܬܪ̈ܘܬܐ ܕܫܪ̈ܒܗ ܕܒܒܠ. ܗ̈ܘܢܝܐ
ܘܟ̈ܠܝܐ ܒܕܡܝܐ ܠܬܫܡܫܬܐ ܕܗܘܢܝܐ. ܘܒܕܡܝܐ ܠܒܢܬ

ܘܒܚܕܘܬܐ ܕܠܒܗܘܢ ܒܫܘܬܐ ܕܟܠ ܓܒܐ ܡܫܡܠܝܢ ܗܘܘ. ܘܒܐܝܕܐ ܕܟܗܢܘܬܐ ܕܩܒܠܘ ܗܘܘ ܡܢ ܡܪܢ ܗܢܘܢ ܫܠܝܚܐ ܦܪܝܫܬ ܗܒܪܬܗܘܢ ܒܐܪܒܥ ܦܢܝܬܗ ܕܥܠܡܐ ܘܠܝܠܐܝܬ. ܘܟܕ ܗܦܟܝܢ ܗܘܘ ܠܚܕ̈ܕܐ ܡܫܡܫܝܢ ܗܘܘ ܠܚܕ̈ܕܐ ܀

ܩܒܠܬ ܐܝܕܐ ܕܟܗܢܘܬܐ ܐܘܪܫܠܡ. ܘܟܠܗ ܐܬܪܐ ܕܦܠܣܛܝܢܐ ܘܒܝܬ ܫܡܪ̈ܝܐ ܘܒܝܬ ܦܠܫ̈ܬܝܐ. ܘܐܬܪܐ ܕܥܪ̈ܒܝܐ ܘܕܦܘܢܝܩܐ ܘܥ̈ܡܐ ܕܩܣܪܝܐ ܡܢ ܝܥܩܘܒ. ܗܘ ܕܗܘܐ ܗܘܐ ܦܩܘܕܐ ܘܡܕܒܪܢܐ ܒܥܕܬܐ ܕܫ̈ܠܝܚܐ ܕܐܬܒܢܝܬ ܗܘܬ ܒܨܗܝܘܢ ܀

ܩܒܠܬ ܐܝܕܐ ܕܟܗܢܘܬܐ ܕܫܠܝܚܐ ܐܠܟܣܢܕܪܝܐ ܪܒܬܐ ܘܬܒܐܝܣ ܘܟܠܗ ܡܨܪܝܢ ܓܘܝܬܐ. ܘܟܠܗ ܐܬܪܐ ܕܦܠܘܣܝܢ. ܘܥܕܡܐ ܠܬܚܘܡܐ ܕܗܢܕ̈ܘܝܐ. ܡܢ ܡܪܩܘܣ ܡܕܒܪܢܐ ܗܘ ܕܗܘܐ ܗܘܐ ܬܡܢ ܦܩܘܕܐ ܘܡܕܒܪܢܐ ܒܥܕܬܐ ܕܒܢܐ ܗܘܐ ܬܡܢ ܘܫܡܫ ܗܘܐ ܀

ܩܒܠܬ ܐܝܕܐ ܕܟܗܢܘܬܐ ܕܫ̈ܠܝܚܐ. ܗܢܕܘ ܘܟܠܗܘܢ ܐܬܪ̈ܘܬܐ ܕܠܗ ܘܕܚܕܪ̈ܝܗ. ܥܕܡܐ ܠܝܡܐ ܐܚܪܝܐ. ܡܢ ܝܗܘܕܐ ܬܐܘܡܐ ܗܘ ܕܗܘܐ ܗܘܐ ܡܕܒܪܢܐ ܘܦܩܘܕܐ ܒܥܕܬܐ ܕܒܢܐ ܗܘܐ ܬܡܢ ܘܫܡܫ ܗܘܐ ܬܡܢ ܀

ܩܒܠܬ ܐܝܕܐ ܕܟܗܢܘܬܐ ܕܫ̈ܠܝܚܐ ܐܢܛܝܘܟܝ ܘܣܘܪܝܐ ܘܩܝܠܝܩܝܐ ܘܓܠܛܝܐ ܥܕܡܐ ܠܦܢܛܘܣ ܡܢ ܫܡܥܘܢ ܟܐܦܐ ܕܗܘ ܫܡ ܗܘܐ ܫܬܐܣܬܐ ܕܥܕܬܐ ܬܡܢ. ܘܗܘ ܗܘܐ ܘܪܝܫܐ ܗܘܐ ܬܡܢ ܒܥܕܬܐ ܠܟܗܢܐ ܕܫܠܡ ܗܘܐ ܡܢ ܬܡܢ ܠܪܘܡܝܐ. ܡܛܠ ܫܘܒ̈ܚܗ ܚܣܝܐ ܕܐܬܠܒܟ ܗܘܐ ܠܗܘܢ ܠܟܠ ܪܗܘܡܝܐ ܒܫܪܟܗܘܢ ܀

ܡܢ ܕܐܬܓܠܝ ܗܘܐ ܠܗܘܢ ܫ̈ܠܝܚܐ ܘܡܠܠ ܗܘܐ ܥܡܗܘܢ
ܥܠܗ ܙܒܢܐ ܕܢܚܙܘܢ ܡܠܦܝܢ ܗܘܘ ܠܟܪ̈ܝܗܐ. ܐܦ ܗܢܘܢ
ܬܘܒ. ܒܡܘܬ̈ܗܘܢ ܐܬܓܠܝ ܗܘܐ ܘܐܫܠܡܘ ܗܘܘ ܠܬܠܡ̈ܝܕܝܗܘܢ
ܒܬܪܗܘܢ ܟܠ ܡܕܡ ܕܩܒܠܘ ܗܘܘ ܡܢ ܫ̈ܠܝܚܐ. ܐܦ ܡܕܡ ܕܟܬܒ
ܗܘܐ ܝܥܩܘܒ. ܡܢ ܐܘܪܫܠܡ. ܘܫܡܥܘܢ ܡܢ ܪܗܘܡܐ ܡܕܝܢܬܐ.
ܘܝܘܚܢܢ ܡܢ ܐܦܣܘܣ. ܘܡܪܩܘܣ ܡܢ ܐܠܟܣܢܕܪܝܐ ܪܒܬܐ.
ܘܐܢܕܪܐܘܣ ܡܢ ܦܪܘܓܝܐ. ܘܠܘܩܐ ܡܢ ܡܩܕܘܢܝܐ. ܘܝܗܘܕܐ
ܬܐܘܡܐ ܡܢ ܗܢܕܘ. ܕܐܓܪ̈ܬܗ ܕܫܠܝܚܐ ܢܬܩܒܠܢ ܘܢܬܩܪܝܢ
ܒܥ̈ܕܬܐ ܕܒܟܠ ܐܬܪ ܐܝܟ ܕܡܬܩܪܝܢ ܢܨ̈ܚܢܐ ܕܥܘܒ̈ܕܝܗܘܢ
ܗ̇ܢܘܢ ܕܟܬܒ ܗܘܐ ܠܗܘܢ ܠܘܩܐ. ܕܒܗܕܐ ܢܬܝܕܥܘܢ ܫ̈ܠܝܚܐ
ܘܢܒ̈ܝܐ ܘܕܝܬܩܐ ܥܬܝܩܬܐ. ܘܚܕܬܐ ܕܚܕ ܫܪܪܐ ܐܬܟܪܙ
ܒܟܠܗܘܢ ܕܚܕ ܪܘܚܐ ܡܠܠܬ ܒܟܠܗܘܢ ܡܢ ܚܕ ܐܠܗܐ
ܕܣܓܕܘ ܗܘܘ ܟܠܗܘܢ ܘܟܪܙܘܗܝ ܗܘܘ ܟܠܗܘܢ. ܘܩܒܠ
ܐܬܪ̈ܘܬܐ ܡܠܦܢܘܬܗܘܢ. ܟܠܡܕܡ ܗܟܝܠ ܕܐܬܡܠܠ ܡܢ
ܡܪܢ ܒܝܕ ܫ̈ܠܝܚܐ. ܘܫ̈ܠܝܚܐ ܐܫܠܡܘ ܗܘܘ ܠܬܠܡ̈ܝܕܝܗܘܢ
ܐܬܗܝܡܢ ܘܐܬܩܒܠ ܒܟܠ ܐܬܪ ܒܚܝܠܗ ܕܡܪܢ ܕܐܡܪ
ܠܗܘܢ. ܕܥܡܟܘܢ ܐܢܐ ܥܕܡܐ ܕܫܠܡ ܥܠܡܐ. ܟܕ ܕܝܢ
ܗܘܐ ܥܡ ܡܗܘܕܝܢܐ ܡܕܒܪ̈ܢܐ ܡܢ ܦܩ̈ܪܐ ܕܢܒ̈ܝܐ ܘܡܩܪܒܝܢ
ܗܘܘ ܐܦ ܥܡ ܚܬܦܐ ܠܓܒ̈ܢܐ ܒܚܝ̈ܠܐ ܕܫ̈ܠܝܐ ܕܟܕܝܢ ܗܘܘ
ܒܥܡܗ ܕܡܫܝܚܐ. ܒܫ̈ܢܝܐ ܓܝܪ ܟܠܗܘܢ ܐܦ ܗܢܘܢ ܕܡܫܒܚܝܢ
ܗܘܘ ܒܐܬܪ̈ܘܬܐ ܐܚܪ̈ܢܐ ܫܠܘ ܗܘܘ ܘܫܬܩܘ ܒܥܘܪܬܗ
ܕܡܫܝܚܐ. ܘܐܝܠܝܢ ܕܡܬܕܡܝܢ ܗܘܘ ܒܪ̈ܫܘܬܐ ܕܗܕܐ
ܙ̈ܕܩܘܬܗ ܕܡܫܡܫܢܐ ܬܗܘܐ ܗܘܐ ܠܓܪܐ ܣܠܩ ܕܗܘܝܢ
ܙ̈ܪܘܩܐ ܡܢ ܩܕܝܡ. ܐܝܟ ܗܘܐ ܠܓܪ ܡܚܝܢܘܗܝ ܕܡܚܘܬܐ ܕܗܘܦܐ
ܡܬܦܫܛ ܗܘܐ ܠܒܝܫܘܗܝ. ܘܐܝܟ ܗܘܐ ܡܚܝܢܘܗܝ ܕܡܕܡ ܕܗܘܝܢ
ܗܘܘ ܥܡܠܝܢ ܗܘܘ ܡܚܝܢܘܗܝ ܘܡܬܪܦܝܢ ܗܘܘ ܠܗܘܢ. ܘܒܟܕܡܐ
ܕܐܘܠܨܢܐ ܩܫܝܐ ܗܘܐ ܥܠܝܗܘܢ ܒܢܝ̈ܫܗܘܢ ܫܒܩܝܢ ܗܘܘ ܘܡܪܕܝܢ.

ܕܒܬܪ ܐܝܟܢܐ ܬܥܒܕܘܢ ܚܝܒܘܢ ܡܕܡ ܐܠܗܐ ܘܬܬܒܥܘܢ ܒܗ
ܐܒܗܝܟܘܢ ܕܒܗ ܕܡܫܝܚܐ ܕܡܠܟ ܒܟܠܗܘܢ. ܠܐ ܓܝܪ
ܡܡܠܠܐ ܡܕܡ ܐܠܗܐ ܕܒܗ ܐܢܬܘܢ ܒܗ ܦܓܪܘܗܝ،
ܬܐܙܠܘܢ ܘܬܬܫܠܛܘܢ ܒܗ ܡܦܩܬܐ ܕܒܪܗ ܦܓܪܐ. ܐܝܟܢܐ
ܫܪܝܪ ܐܢܬܘܢ ܕܬܬܡܠܐ ܡܫܝܚܘܬܟܘܢ ܒܗ ܥܒܪܐ. ܒܪ ܒܗ
ܕܓܠܠܐ ܐܢܬܘܢ. ܐܠܐ ܙܕܩ ܗܘ ܠܟܘܢ ܕܐܝܟ ܐܝܟܢܐ
ܕܡܫܝܚܝܢ ܒܡܫܝܚܐ ܬܘܕܘܢ ܠܟܠܐܢܫ ܒܡܫܝܚܘܬܐ
ܗܕܐ ܕܡܫܪܝܢ. ܘܒܪ ܫܒܒܐ ܗܘܘ ܗܢܝܢ ܗܠܝܢ ܡܢ ܬܠܡܝܕܐ
ܘܒܗ ܒܠܗܘܢ ܫܘܐܠܬ ܗܘܘ ܒܝܪ ܒܫܘܐܐ ܡܕܡ ܒܠܗ
ܒܡܐ ܕܥܠܝܡܐ ܕܡܫܝܚܝܐ ܕܐܘܙܠܦ ܒܡܘܕܝܢ ܘܡܫܝܚܝܢ ܫܢ
ܘܕܐܬܘܗܝ، ܡܢ ܡܬܘܡ ܒܪܐ ܕܐܠܗܐ ܡܘܕܝܢ. ܘܒܐܠܝܢ
ܕܐܡܪܝܢ ܘܡܦܩܘܗܝ، ܒܦܪܝܢ. ܐܦ ܓܝܪ ܒܫܘܒܚܗ، ܕܒܒܐ ܡܘܕܝܢ
ܐܝܟܢ ܒܡܐܢܬ ܒܡܫܝܚܐ. ܘܡܛܠ ܕܒܝܬܐ ܕܒܒܐ ܕܐܝܫܘܥ
ܠܗ. ܠܐ ܢܓܝܢ ܕܢܕܘܢ ܓܠܝܐܝܬ. ܘܦܠܓܘ ܠܗܘܢ ܕܡܬܪܢܝܐ
ܕܡܬܪܢܝܬܐ ܗܘ ܡܕܝܢܐ ܘܠܐ ܬܘܡ ܡܕܡܘܬܗ، ܢܦܫܬܐ. ܒܪ
ܕܝܢ ܫܒܒܐ ܗܘܘ ܐܒܗܝܗܘܢ ܗܢܝܢ ܗܠܝܢ ܡܢ ܒܢܝܗܘܢ ܠܫܝܚܝܢ
ܗܘܘ ܠܗܘܢ ܓܒ.. ܠܐ ܗܘܐ ܕܝܢ ܡܛܠ ܗܢ ܕܡܫܝܚܐ ܗܘܘ
ܒܡܫܝܚܐ. ܐܠܐ ܒܠ ܕܓܠܐ ܗܘܘ ܘܦܪܫܘ ܗܘܘ ܕܒܝܬܐ
ܕܐܒܗܝܗܘܢ ܡܕܡ ܒܬܪ ܒܒܗܘܢ. ܗܢܘܢ ܕܝܢ ܕܡܫܝܚܐ ܗܘܘ
ܢܦܩܘ ܗܘܘ ܠܗܘܢ ܠܬܠܡܝܕܐ ܘܡܢ ܝܐܕܥܘܢ ܠܐ ܡܫܝܚܝܢ
ܗܘܘ ܕܢܬܢ ܗܘܘ ܕܗܘ ܡܕܡ ܕܡܠܦܝܢ ܗܘܘ ܠܦܓܢܐܐ. ܗܢܘܢ
ܒܒܒܐ ܦܪܫܝܢ ܡܕܡ ܒܠ ܐܢܫ. ܘܐܡܪܘ، ܕܐܘܠܝܢܐ
ܘܕܘܦܢܐ ܡܐܡ ܗܘܐ ܒܠ ܬܠܡܝܕܐ ܫܕܝܢ ܗܘܘ ܕܬܬܐܠܝܢ ܗܘܘ
ܒܡܫܘܢ. ܘܡܫܝܚܘܬܐ ܢܓܕܐ ܦܫܝܚܝܐ ܡܡܠܠܝܢ ܗܘܘ
ܒܬܘܕܝܬܐ ܕܡܫܝܚܘܬܗܘܢ ܕܒܡܫܝܚܐ. ܘܒܠ ܢܩܝܦ ܫܢܝܗܘܢ
ܠܡܫܝܚܐ ܡܒܪܝܢ ܗܘܘ ܡܕܡ ܢܗܘܪܐ ܘܫܒܪܐ. ܘܡܢ ܒܬܪ
ܡܬܘܡܘܢ ܕܥܠܝܡܐ ܗܘܘ ܡܒܪܝܢܐ ܘܦܩܘܕܐ ܒܟܕܬܐ. ܘܗܘ

ܟܐ. ܗܟܢܐ ܗܘܘ ܬܘܒ ܫ̈ܠܝܚܐ ܕܠܝܫܟܐ ܕܩܘܪܒܢܐ ܒܢܘܡܘܣܐ
ܕܡܬܩܪܒܐ ܢܗܘܐ ܥܠ ܡܕܒܚܐ. ܘܠܐ ܥܒܪ ܡܢܬܐ ܡܕܡ
ܕܠܐ ܫܠܝܛ ܀

ܗܠܝܢ ܕܝܢ ܟܠܗܝܢ ܠܐ ܗܘܐ ܠܢܦܫܗܘܢ ܗܘܘ ܣܡܘ ܫ̈ܠܝܚܐ.
ܐܠܐ ܠܗܠܝܢ ܕܐܬܝܢ ܗܘܘ ܒܬܪܗܘܢ. ܦܩܝܕܝܢ ܗܘܘ ܓܝܪ ܕܒܬܪܝܢ
ܐܝܟ ܕܐܬܐ ܕܢܠܒܫܘܢ ܠܒܘܫܐ ܕܐܡܬܪܐ ܠܗܘܢ ܓܝܪ ܗܦܟܐ
ܗܘܬ ܪܘܚܐ ܦܘܠܓܐ ܕܒܗܘܢ. ܕܐܝܟ ܕܗܘܬ ܒܐܝܕܝܗܘܢ
ܗܠܝܢ ܢܛܘܪܐ ܬܕܒܪ ܐܝܟ ܢܡܘܣܐܝܬ. ܗܢܘܢ ܓܝܪ ܕܩܒܠܘ
ܗܘܘ ܡܢ ܡܪܢ ܚܝܠܐ ܘܫܘܠܛܢܐ. ܠܐ ܣܢܝܩܝܢ ܗܘܘ ܕܡܢ
ܐܚܪܢܐ ܢܬܬܣܝܡܘܢ ܠܗܘܢ ܢܡܘܣܐ. ܐܦ ܦܘܠܘܣ ܓܝܪ
ܘܛܝܡܬܐܘܣ ܟܕ ܡܬܟܪܟܝܢ ܗܘܘ ܒܐܬܪܘܬܐ ܕܣܘܪܝܐ
ܘܕܩܝܠܝܩܝܐ ܠܗܘܢ ܠܗܠܝܢ ܦܘܩܕܢܐ ܘܢܡܘܣܐ ܕܫ̈ܠܝܚܐ ܘܕܩܫ̈ܝܫܐ
ܠܟܠܗܘܢ ܕܐܝܬܝܗܘܢ ܗܘܘ ܬܚܝܬ ܐܝܕܐ ܕܫ̈ܠܝܚܐ ܡܫܠܡܝܢ
ܗܘܘ ܠܥܕ̈ܬܐ ܕܐܬܪ̈ܘܬܐ ܕܡܕܒܪܝܢ ܗܘܘ ܒܗܘܢ ܘܡܫܡܫܝܢ.
ܬܠܡܝܕܐ ܕܝܢ ܡܢ ܒܬܪ ܗܠܝܢ ܦܩܕܐ ܘܢܛܘܪܐ ܕܗܟܢܐ ܗܘܘ:
ܠܐ ܫܠܝܡ ܗܘܘ ܡܢ ܒܪܘܬܐ ܕܗܕܪܬܐ ܘܡܢ ܫܘܠܛܢܐ ܬܡܗܐ
ܕܗܒܪ ܗܘܐ ܡܪܢ ܒܐܝܕܝܗܘܢ. ܒܡܠܐ ܓܝܪ ܗܦܟܐ ܒܕ
ܗܘܐ ܒܠܚܘܕ ܐܝܕܝܗܘܢ ܕܡܗܝܡܢܝܢ ܗܘܘ ܒܡܫܝܚܐ ܘܡܢ
ܡܕܝܢܬܐ ܐܚܪܢܝܬܐ ܐܬܝܢ ܗܘܘ ܠܐܝܕܝܗܘܢ. ܘܡܫܡܫܝܢ ܗܘܘ
ܠܟܠܗܘܢ ܘܡܫܟܠܝܢ. ܢܚܪܝܗܘ ܕܝܢ ܘܦܛܠܝܡܘܣ ܦܪ ܒܢܘܫܬܐ
ܕܢܘܗܪܐ ܐܬܝܢ ܗܘܘ ܠܐܝܕܝܗܘܢ ܕܫ̈ܠܝܚܐ ܒܒܗܝܐ. ܟܕ ܫܠܡܝܢ
ܗܘܘ ܠܡܟܠܘܬܗܘܢ. ܗܘܕܐ ܕܝܢ ܘܠܘ ܘܦܢܪ ܘܐܗܘܦ
ܘܡܗܘܦܘ ܟܠ ܣܝܡܐ ܘܡܝܚܐ ܘܐܠܗܘܕܪܘ ܒܥܘܬܐ ܐܬܝܢ
ܗܘܘ ܐܦ ܗܢܘܢ ܠܐܝܕܝܗܘܢ ܕܫ̈ܠܝܚܐ ܒܠܠܝܐ. ܟܕ ܡܘܕܝܢ ܗܘܘ
ܒܡܫܝܚܐ ܕܒܪܗ ܗܘ ܕܐܠܗܐ ܘܡܢ ܟܠ ܥܒܕܝܗܘܢ ܕܣܠܝܢ ܗܘܘ
ܕܓܠܘ ܪܚܡܝܗܘܢ ܕܠܘܬ ܬܠܡܝܕܘܬܐ. ܘܟܠܗ ܐܝܟ ܫ̈ܠܝܚܐ
ܫܡܫܐܝܬ ܟܕ ܐܡܪܝܢ ܠܗܘܢ. ܠܐ ܡܫܟܚ ܢܦܩܐ ܘܕܠܝܬܐ

ܡܫܡܫܢܐ ܘܠܐ ܪܗܛܝܢ ܒܬܪ ܝܘܬܪܢܗ ܕܟܣܦܐ. ܗܢܘܢ ܗܘܘ
ܡܬܠܒܝܢ ܘܡܬܦܪܢܣܝܢ ܠܡܫܡܫܢܘܬܗ ܕܡܫܝܚܐ ܀

ܟܐ. ܬܘܒ ܗܘܘ ܣܡܘ ܫܠܝܚܐ. ܕܟܗܢܐ ܐܢܫܐ ܕܐܬܘܪ
ܒܪܝܫܐܘܬ ܕܠܐ ܒܝܕܥܐ ܢܩܛܠ ܡܢܗ ܒܪܢܫܐ ܒܝܕܥܐ. ܗܘ
ܕܝܢ ܕܐܬܐܡܪ ܢܫܒܘܩ ܠܟܗܢܘܬܐ ܐܝܟ ܕܡܠܦܢܘܬܐ
ܐܬܐܡܪ ܀

ܟܒ. ܬܘܒ ܗܘܘ ܣܡܘ ܫܠܝܚܐ. ܕܐܝܠܝܢ ܕܡܫܡܫܝܢ ܕܢܫܡܫܘܢ
ܕܟܢܐ ܐܦ ܐܬܦܢܝܬ ܕܢܗܘܘܢ ܬ̈ܡܝܡܐ ܘܢܗܘܘܢ ܠܓܒܝܐ ܘܕܟܝܢ
ܠܚܕܐ. ܠܐ ܬܘܒ ܢܣܒܘܢ ܕܢܫܐ ܐܚܪܢܐ. ܐܦ ܬܘܒ
ܡܫܡܫܝܢ ܪܥܝܢܐ ܕܢܦܩܘܢ ܒܐܦ̈ܝܗܘܢ ܒܥܠܡܐ ܀

ܟܓ. ܬܘܒ ܗܘܘ ܣܡܘ ܫܠܝܚܐ ܕܐܝܠܝܢ ܕܪܚܡܝܢ ܒܪ̈ܚܡܝܗܘܢ
ܘܡܫܠܡܝܢ ܒܡܬܪܘܬܐ ܕܫܘܒܗܪܘܬܐ ܠܐ ܢܬܦܪܥܘܢ
ܠܡܫܡܫܢܘܬܐ. ܡܛܠ ܗܢ ܕܟܬܝܒ ܕܪܡ ܒܗ ܒܒ̈ܢܝܢܫܐ ܩܕܡ ܐܠܗܐ
ܛܢܦ ܗܘ. ܘܒܠܚܘܕ ܐܚܪܢܐ ܐܝܟܢ ܦܘܪܫܢܐ ܒܝܢ ܐܝܠܝܢ
ܕܡܬܠܟܐܝܢ ܀

ܟܕ. ܬܘܒ ܗܘܘ ܣܡܘ ܫܠܝܚܐ ܕܢܗܘܘܢ ܦܩܘܕܐ ܒܟܠ ܡܕܝܢܐ
ܕܐܝܬ ܒܩܘܪ̈ܝܐ ܘܕܢܬܒܕܩ ܪܥܝܐ ܕܟܠܗܘܢ ܕܒܐܝܕܗ ܗܘܘ
ܡܬܬܒܥܝܢ ܟܠܗܘܢ. ܐܦ ܥܡܡܐ ܠܒܪ ܡܢܗܘܢ ܦܩܕ ܗܘܐ
ܡܢ ܕܗܘܐ ܠܪܘܚܐ ܘܟܢܫ ܗܘܐ ܀

ܟܗ. ܬܘܒ ܗܘܘ ܣܡܘ ܫܠܝܚܐ ܕܩ̈ܠܝܬܐ ܐܝܠܝܢ ܕܒܬܕܝܪ
ܕܢܫܡܫܘܢ ܒܡܫܡܫܢܐ ܗܘܐ ܢܠܦܘܢ ܠܗܘܢ ܕܢܗܘܘܢ
ܘܢܗܘܘܢ ܡܕܡ ܡܫܡܫܢܐ ܒܗ ܡܕܒܪܢܐ ܕܥܕܬܐ. ܡܛܠ
ܕܐܦ ܕܢܗܝ ܘܐܝܠܝܢ ܕܐܒܗܬܗ ܗܘܘ ܩܠܝܢ ܗܘܘ ܘܡܫܝܚܝܢ ܗܘܘ
ܡܢ ܡܫܡܫܢܐ ܀

ܟܘ. ܬܘܒ ܗܘܘ ܣܡܘ ܫܠܝܚܐ. ܕܠܐ ܐܢܫ ܢܥܒܕ ܘܢܥܒܪ
ܡܕܡ ܒܥܠܝܬܐ ܕܡܫܝܚܘܬܐ ܕܠܐ ܒܝܕܥܐ ܘܕܠܐ ܒܟܠܗܬܐ.
ܐܠܐ ܒܝܕܥܬܐ ܘܕܠܐ ܪܫܝܢܐ ܕܡܫܡܫ ܒܐܦܝܐ ܀

ܙܢܝܬܐ ܘܡܬܚܙܝܐ ܒܬܐܓܘܪܬܐ ܘܒܙܒܢܘܬܐ. ܗܢܐ ܠܐ ܬܗܘܒ
ܢܥܒܕ ܘܠܐ ܢܗܘܐ ܒܡܫܬܥܒܕܘܬܐ ܀

ܗ. ܘܐܢ ܗܘܘ ܬܗܘܒ ܝ̈ܠܝܕܐ ܕܐܝܟܢܐ ܕܟܬܝܒ ܠܗ̈ܘܕܝܐ.
ܐܝܟ ܡܬܚܙܝܢܘܬܐ ܕܙܢܝܐ ܐܢܘܢ ܐܘ ܠܚܛܝܐ ܕܡܬܒܥܝܢ ܠܒܪ̈ܬܐ
ܥܠܘ ܒܪܘܚܐ. ܠܐ ܢܦܘܠ ܒܚܝܬܗܘܢ ܘܢܥܒܕ. ܘܐܢ ܕܝܢ
ܐܢܬܘܗܝ، ܒܚܝܬܗܘܢ ܠܐ ܢܥܒܕܘܢܝܗ، ܐܠܐ ܕܢܬܦܪܫ ܡܢ
ܒܚܝܬܗܘܢ ܘܠܐ ܬܗܘܒ ܢܥܒܕ ܒܥܡܗܘܢ ܀

ܘ. ܘܐܢ ܗܘܘ ܬܗܘܒ ܝ̈ܠܝܕܐ. ܕܐܢ ܐܢܫ ܡܢ ܡ̈ܘܕܝܐ ܐܘ
ܡܢ ܫ̈ܒܒܐ ܐܬܐ ܘܡܬܬܠܠ ܒܥܡܗܘܢ ܘܐܢ ܒܗ ܕܐܬܬܠܠ
ܒܥܡܗܘܢ ܒܢܝܐ ܘܐܙܠ ܠܗ ܬܗܘܒ ܠܓܒܪܐ ܕܗܘܐ ܗܘܐ ܒܗ.
ܐܢ ܕܝܢ ܬܗܘܒ ܒܚܠܦ ܐܬܬܐ ܢܟ̈ܪܝܬܗܘܢ ܕܬܘܒܢܐ ܠܐ ܬܗܘܒ
ܢܬܩܒܠ. ܐܠܐ ܐܝܟ ܓܒܪܐ ܕܐܬܬܗܘܢ، ܗܘܐ ܒܗ ܡܢ ܡܢܝܢ.
ܘܒܢܐ ܗܘܐ ܚܙܝܢ ܒܗ ܐܠܝܢ ܕܕܒܪܝܢ ܠܗ ܀

ܙ. ܘܐܢ ܗܘܘ ܬܗܘܒ ܝ̈ܠܝܕܐ ܕܠܐ ܗܘܐ ܥܠܝܠ ܠܒܝܬ ܒ̈ܢܝܐ
ܕܒܠܒܕ ܐܠܝܢ ܕܡܥܒܕܝܢ ܒܚܡܐ ܗܘܐ ܗܘ ܦܓܪ̈ܘܬܐ
ܐܠܝܢ ܕܕܒܪܬܐ ܐܢܝܢ. ܐܠܐ ܒܓܠܓܠܐ ܕܒܠܝܬܗܘܢ ܗܘܐ ܦܩܕ
ܗܘ ܘܡܬܗܘܬܪ ܗܘ ܡܢܢ ܕܒܠܝܬܗܘܢ ܡܚܝܢ ܒܗ ܘܠܐ
ܡܚܝܢ ܀

ܚ. ܘܐܢ ܗܘܘ ܬܗܘܒ ܝ̈ܠܝܕܐ ܕܟܠ ܐܠܝܢ ܕܢܦܩܝܢ ܡܢ
ܒܠܒܐ ܗܢܐ ܒܡܗܕܢܘܬܐ ܕܦܓܪܐ ܕܡܬܚܫܒܢܘܬܗ ܕܡܢܚܫܢܐ.
ܘܒܐܘܠܨܢܐ ܕܦܓܠ ܢܦܫܗ ܗܘܐ ܒܒܪܝܢ ܠܗܘܢ ܕܗܘܒܢܐ
ܒܗܘܢܐ ܕܦܓܠܢܘܬܐ ܀

ܛ. ܘܐܢ ܗܘܘ ܬܗܘܒ ܝ̈ܠܝܕܐ ܕܒܡܫܬܥܒܕܘܬܐ ܕܐܕܒܪܬܐ ܗܘܘ
ܐܫܬܝ ܬܫܥܝܬܐ ܕܕܘܢ ܒܠܘܫ ܒܦܘܡ. ܡܦܠ ܗܢ ܕܐܬܪܝܢ
ܠܚܪ̈ܐ ܒܟܠܝܢ. ܘܒܟܠܝܢ ܬܫܥܝܬܗ ܒܦܘܡܗ. ܘܡܐܡܪܐ
ܠܝ ܘܒܠܚܘܕ ܐܢܫܐ ܘܐܡܪ ܘܐܦܝܢ ܥܠ ܡܕܝܢܐ ܀

ܝ. ܘܐܢ ܗܘܘ ܬܗܘܒ ܝ̈ܠܝܕܐ ܕܐܠܝܢ ܕܡܬܚܫܒܝܢ ܡܢ

ܗܘܘ ܐܡܪܐ ܗܢܐ ܐܬܟܢܝ ܕܗܢܘܢ ܝܗܒ ܗܘܘ ܐܦ
ܗܢܘܢ. ܘܫܡܥܝܢ ܐܘܕܝܘ.

ܚ. ܬܘܒ ܗܘܘ. ܦܩܕܘ ܫ̈ܠܝܚܐ. ܕܒܫܘܠܡܐ ܕܟܬ̈ܒܐ ܟܠܗܘܢ
ܢܬܩܪܐ ܐܘܢܓܠܝܘܢ. ܐܝܟ ܚܬܡܐ ܕܟܬ̈ܒܐ ܟܠܗܘܢ. ܘܟܕ
ܩܐܡ ܥܡܐ ܥܠ ܪ̈ܓܠܘܗܝ ܢܫܡܥܘܢܝܗܝ. ܕܣܒܪܬܐ ܗܝ
ܕܦܘܪܩܢܐ ܕܟܠܗܘܢ ܒ̈ܢܝܢܫܐ ܀

ܛ. ܬܘܒ ܗܘܘ ܦܩܕܘ ܫ̈ܠܝܚܐ ܕܒܫܘܠܡܐ ܕܚܡܫܝܢ ܝܘ̈ܡܝܢ
ܕܡܢ ܒܬܪ ܩܝܡܬܗ ܗܘܘ ܥܒܕܝܢ ܕܘܟܪܢܐ ܕܣܘܠܩܗ ܠܘܬ
ܐܒܘܗܝ ܡܫܒܚܐ ܀

ܝ. ܬܘܒ ܗܘܘ ܦܩܕܘ ܫ̈ܠܝܚܐ ܕܐܠܐ ܐܢ ܕܝܬܝܩܐ ܥܬܝܩܬܐ
ܘܢܒ̈ܝܐ ܘܐܘܢܓܠܝܘܢ ܘܦܪܟܣܝܣ ܕܢܨ̈ܚܢܝܗܘܢ ܠܐ ܗܘܘ
ܡܬܩܪܝܢ ܥܠ ܒܝܡ ܒܥܕܬܐ ܀

ܝܐ. ܬܘܒ ܗܘܘ ܦܩ̇ܕܘ ܫ̈ܠܝܚܐ. ܕܐܝܢܐ ܕܠܐ ܝܕܥ
ܗܝܡܢܘܬܗ̇ ܕܥܕܬܐ ܘܦܘ̈ܩܕܢܐ ܘܢܡ̈ܘܣܐ ܕܣܝܡܝܢ ܒܗ̇. ܠܐ
ܢܗܘܐ ܡܕܒܪܢܐ ܘܪܝܫܐ. ܘܐܝܢܐ ܕܝܕܥ ܠܗܘܢ ܘܥܒܪ
ܡܢܗܘܢ. ܠܐ ܬܘܒ ܢܫܡܫ. ܡܛܠ ܕܠܐ ܫܪܝܪ ܒܬܫܡܫܬܗ
ܕܝܠ ܀

ܝܒ. ܬܘܒ ܗܘܘ ܦܩܕܘ ܫ̈ܠܝܚܐ. ܕܐܝܢܐ ܕܝܡܐ ܐܘ ܡܕܓܠ.
ܐܘ ܣܗܕ ܣܗܕܘܬܐ ܕܫܘܩܪܐ. ܐܘ ܐܙܠ ܠܘܬ ܚܪ̈ܫܐ
ܘܩ̈ܨܡܐ ܘܟܠܕ̈ܝܐ ܘܬܟܝܠ ܠܓܕ̈ܐ ܘܠܒܝܬ ܝܠܕܐ. ܗܢܘܢ
ܕܐܚܝܕܝܢ ܐܢܘܢ ܕܠܐ ܝܕܥܝܢ ܠܐܠܗܐ. ܐܦ ܗܘ ܐܝܟ ܓܒܪܐ
ܕܠܐ ܝܕܥ ܠܐܠܗܐ ܢܫܬܕܐ ܡܢ ܬܫܡܫܬܐ ܘܠܐ ܢܫܡܫ ܀

ܝܓ. ܬܘܒ ܗܘܘ ܦܩܕܘ ܫ̈ܠܝܚܐ. ܕܐܢ ܐܢܫ ܐܢܫ ܕܪܚܡ ܥܠ
ܬܫܡܫܬܐ ܘܠܐ ܪܕܐ ܠܗ. ܗܢܐ ܬܘܒ ܠܐ ܢܫܡܫ. ܕܠܐ
ܪܕܐ ܠܗ ܒܪܫܗ ܕܬܫܡܫܬܐ. ܘܒܐܝܢܐ ܗܘ ܕܦܠܚܐ ܘܠܐ ܗܘܐ
ܒܐܠܗܐ ܗܘ ܕܠܐ ܦܩܕ ܢܬܚܘܐ ܥܠܝܗܘܢ ܀

ܝܕ. ܬܘܒ ܗܘܘ ܦܩܕܘ ܫ̈ܠܝܚܐ ܕܐܝܢܐ ܕܡܣܒ ܘܝܗܒ

ܒ. ܗܟܢܐ ܗܘܘ ܬܘܒ ܓܠܝ̈ܢܐ ܕܒܚܕ ܒܫܒܐ ܬܗܘܐ
ܬܫܒܘܚܬܐ ܘܢܘܗܪܐ ܕܥܕ̈ܬܐ ܡܪ̈ܝܐ ܘܩܘܪܒܢܐ. ܡܛܠ ܕܒܚܕ
ܒܫܒܐ ܩܡ ܗܘܐ ܡܢ ܒܝܬ ܡܝ̈ܬܐ ܡܪܢ. ܘܒܚܕ ܒܫܒܐ ܕܢܚ
ܗܘܐ ܒܥܠܡܐ. ܘܒܚܕ ܒܫܒܐ ܫܠܚ ܗܘ ܠܫܠܝܚܐ. ܘܒܚܕ
ܒܫܒܐ ܡܬܝܚܕܐ ܠܫܪܬܐ ܥܡ ܡܠܐܟ̈ܐ ܫܡܝܢܐ ܀

ܓ. ܗܟܢܐ ܗܘܘ ܬܘܒ ܓܠܝ̈ܢܐ ܕܒܐܪܒܥܐ ܒܫܒܐ
ܬܗܘܐ ܬܫܒܘܚܬܐ ܡܛܠ ܕܒܗ ܗܘ ܓܠܝܐ ܗܘܐ ܠܗܘܢ ܡܪܢ
ܥܠ ܕܝܠܗ ܘܚܫܗ ܘܨܠܝܒܘܬܗ ܘܡܝܬܘܬܗ ܘܩܝܡܬܗ. ܘܗܘܘ
ܬܠܡܝ̈ܕܐ ܒܟܪܝܘܬܐ ܗܕܐ ܀

ܕ. ܗܟܢܐ ܗܘܘ ܬܘܒ ܓܠܝ̈ܢܐ ܕܒܥܪܘܒܬܐ ܒܬܫܥ ܫ̈ܥܝܢ
ܬܗܘܐ ܬܫܒܘܚܬܐ. ܡܛܠ ܕܒܗ ܒܥܕܢܐ ܕܐܬܐܡܪ ܗܘܐ
ܒܐܪܒܥܐ ܒܫܒܐ ܥܠ ܚܫܗ ܕܦܪܘܩܢ ܒܥܪܘܒܬܐ ܐܬܓܡܪ
ܗܘܐ. ܟܕ ܒܗ ܗܘܘ ܟܠܗܝܢ ܘܒܪ̈ܝܬܐ ܘܫܡܝܐ ܗܘܘ ܠܒܝܫܝܢ
ܒܐܒܠܐ ܀

ܗ. ܗܟܢܐ ܗܘܘ ܬܘܒ ܓܠܝ̈ܢܐ ܕܢܚܘܬܗܘܢ ܗܘܘ ܡܫܝ̈ܚܐ
ܘܡܫܬ̈ܒܝܢܐ ܐܝܟ ܠܡܪܐ. ܘܡܘܦ̈ܩܢܐ ܐܝܟ ܩܢܘܡܗܘܢ ܕܐܠܗܝܢ
ܗܘܘ ܡ̈ܠܐܟܐ ܕܢܘܪܐ ܕܒܗ ܡܕܒܚܗ ܕܡܪܝܐ. ܘܕܘܡܝܐ ܕܗܘܘ
ܡܫܒ̈ܚܢܐ ܕܠܥܠ ܒܫܡܝܐ. ܐܝܟ ܐܡܪܘ ܕܫܡܝܐ ܘܐܪܥܐ
ܕܠܗܘܢ ܒܫܘܢܐ ܘܠܫܢܐ ܕܠܗ ܡܫܒܚܢܘܬܐ ܀

ܘ. ܗܟܢܐ ܗܘܘ ܬܘܒ ܓܠܝ̈ܢܐ ܕܗܘܘ ܒܟܕܡ ܫܒܬܐ ܕܕܝܢܗ
ܕܦܪܘܩܢ ܕܐܬܗܘܝ، ܕܒܐ ܕܒܐܕܡ ܕܒܪܬܐ. ܒܐܫܬܐ ܒܝܘܡ
ܐܚܪ، ܒܕܝܢܐ ܡܬܚܝܢܐ ܕܚܝ̈ܐ ܀

ܙ. ܗܟܢܐ ܗܘܘ ܬܘܒ ܓܠܝ̈ܢܐ ܕܐܪ̈ܒܥܝܢ ܝܘ̈ܡܝܢ ܡܢ ܝܘܡܐ
ܕܚܙܘ ܕܦܪܘܩܢ ܗܘܘ ܝܘܡܝܢ. ܘܗܘܕܝܢ ܒܟܕܘܢ ܠܗ ܠܝܘܡܐ
ܕܚܙܐ ܘܠܝܘܡܐ ܕܡܣܩܬܐ. ܡܛܠ ܕܐܝܟ ܗܘ ܡܪܢ ܕܗܘ
ܕܒܐܕܐ ܐܪ̈ܒܥܝܢ ܝܘ̈ܡܝܢ ܥܡ ܗܘܐ. ܘܡܫܒܚܐ ܘܐܠܗܐ ܕܠܒܝܫ

ܗܢܘܢ ܬܠܡܝ̈ܕܐ ܒܥܘܡܩܐ ܗܢܐ ܪܚܝܡ ܗܘܘ ܕܐܡܢܐ ܢܦܪܘܢ ܗܘܘ ܡܦܪܬܗ ܠܠܫ̈ܢܐ ܢܘܟܪ̈ܝܐ ܕܠܐ ܝܕܥܝܢ ܗܘܘ ܠܗܘܢ. ܘܡܘܕܥܢܐ ܐܡܪܝܢ ܗܘܘ ܚܕ ܠܚܕ. ܕܐܝܟ ܫܠܝܚܐ ܘܬܠܡܝ̈ܕܐ ܬܠܡܝܕܝܢ ܚܢܢ ܕܒܒܐ. ܗܘ ܡܫܝܚܐ ܒܐܝܕܝ ܘܡܬܕܡܪܝܢ ܢܘܟܪ̈ܝܐ ܕܠܐ ܝܕܥܝܢ ܠܥܝܢܝܗܘܢ ܐܟܠܐ ܗܢܘܢ ܡܦܩܝܢ ܠܥܠܡ. ܡܢܗ ܢܠܦܐܢܘܢ ܘܢܗܘܕܘܢ ܐܢܘܢ. ܕܒܫܡܗ ܕܡܫܝܚܐ ܕܐܬܕܒܩ ܗܘܘ ܣܓܝܐܐ ܗܠܝܢ ܘܬܠܡܝܕܘܬܐ. ܘܟܕ ܗܢܘܢ ܬܠܡܝ̈ܕܐ ܒܗܠܝܢ ܣܘ̈ܓܐܐ ܐܬܚܙܝܘ ܗܘܘ. ܡܢ ܗܘܐ ܥܡܗܘܢ ܒܐܝܟܐ ܘܐܡܪ ܠܗܘܢ. ܐܫܝܢ. ܠܐ ܕܝܠܝ ܗܝ ܗܕܐ ܕܐܡܢܘܬܐ ܢܦܪܘ ܡܢܗܘܢ ܐܠܐ ܕܡܪܢ ܗܝ ܕܗܘ ܝܗܒ ܐܡܢܘܬܐ ܡܫܝܚܐ ܢܦܪܘ ܡܢܗܘܢ ܒܟܠܗܝܢ. ܬܠܡܝ̈ܕܐ ܕܝܢ ܟܠ ܟܠܝܠܬܗ ܕܠܘܬܗ ܕܐܬܚܙܝ ܠܝ ܘܐܡܪ. ܕܡܢܐ ܕܘܠܘܬ ܠܘܬ ܐܒܐ ܡܫܕܪ ܐܢܐ ܠܟܘܢ ܪܘܚܐ ܦܪܩܠܝܛܐ ܕܗܘ ܢܠܦܟܘܢ ܟܠܡܕܡ ܕܙܕܩ ܠܟܘܢ. ܕܬܐܡܪܘܢ ܘܬܬܕܪܟܘܢ. ܘܟܕ ܗܘ ܥܡܗܘܢ ܒܐܝܟܐ ܗܠܝܢ ܠܥܠܝ̈ܬܐ ܣܓܝ̈ܐܬܐ ܐܡܪ ܗܘܐ ܘܡܚܘܐ ܗܘܐ ܠܗܘܢ. ܟܠܐ ܕܗܘܝܐ ܐܝܬܝܗ ܗܘܐ ܠܗܘܢ. ܘܐܢܫܐ ܒܗܘܒܠܐ ܕܢܘܪܐ، ܗܘܐ ܠܟܠܗܘܢ ܟܕ ܗܘܐ ܠܗܘܢ. ܘܠܫ̈ܢܐ ܕܢܘܪܐ ܒܝܬ ܥܠܐ ܠܐܢܫܐ ܢܚܬܘ ܗܘܘ ܡܢ ܫܡܝܐ ܠܬܠܡܝܕܘܬܗܘܢ. ܘܩܪܘ ܗܘܘ ܟܠ ܚܕ ܚܕ ܡܢܗܘܢ ܘܐܬܒܘ. ܘܐܝܟ ܠܫܢܐ ܕܝܗܒ ܗܘܐ ܟܠ ܚܕ ܚܕ ܡܢܗܘܢ ܗܟܢܐ ܦܫܛ ܗܘܐ ܢܦܫܗ ܕܢܐܙܠ ܠܐܬܪܐ ܕܡܬܡܠܠ ܘܡܬܬܡܟܟ ܒܗ ܠܫܢܐ ܗܘ. ܘܟܕ ܒܡܗܝܡܢܘܬܐ ܕܪܘܚܐ ܕܐܬܚܙܝܬ ܗܘܬ ܠܗܘܢ ܒܗܘ ܝܘܡܐ. ܗܟܢܐ ܗܘܘ ܦܠܓܘܗ ܘܢܬܦܣܘܗ ܐܝܟ ܕܫܠܝܚܝܢ ܗܘܘ ܠܡܟܪܙܘ ܕܟܪܘܙܘܬܗܘܢ: ܘܠܡܠܟܘܬܐ ܫܪܝܪܬܐ ܘܡܗܝܡܢܐ ܕܡܠܟܘܬܗܘܢ ○○○○

ܐ. ܘܗܟܢܐ ܗܟܝܠ ܫܠܝ̈ܚܐ ܕܠܡܕܝܢܬܐ ܗܘܘ ܡܬܟܠܝܢ. ܡܛܠ ܕܐܝܟ ܒܢܝܐ ܕܒܪܗ ܡܢ ܡܕܝܢܬܐ ܘܡܬܚܙܝܐ ܒܗܕܐ ܠܡܕܝܢܬܐ ܡܗܝܡܢܐ ܬܗܘܐ ܡܬܚܙܝܬܗ ܕܒܪܗ ܕܐܠܗܐ ܕܡܠܟܘܬܐ ܢܗܘܐ ܘܬܘܒ ܕܡܢ ܡܕܝܢܬܐ ܡܬܚܙܝܐ ܡܢ ܫܠܝܚܐ ○○

ܡܠܦܢܘܬܐ ܕܚ̈ܠܝܫܐ ܀

ܕܐܡܪܬ، ܐܬܬܠܝ ܡܣܝܢܐ ܠܘܬ ܐܒܘܗ̇، ܘܐܡܪܢܐ ܡܟܠ ܥܠܝ̈ܬܐ ܡܫܡܫܬܐ ܕܪܘܚܐ ܘܦܬܓ̈ܡܐ ܘܢܦ̈ܫܬܐ ܕܒܪܬܐ ܘܕܠܐܡܪܐ ܐܝܟ ܗ̇ܘܐ ܚܕ ܚܕ ܡܢܗܘܢ ܕܥܠܝ̈ܬܐ. ܘܡܢ ܐܡܪܐ ܡܟܠܠ ܐܚܪܐ ܕܡܫܡܠܝܘܬܐ ܐܬܪ̈ܘܬܐ ܕܒܝܬ ܙ̈ܘܡܪܐ ∘ ∘ ∘

ܒܝܬ ܬܠܬܝܢ ܘܬܫܥ ܠܡܠܟܘܬܐ ܕܝܘܢܝܐ. ܒܐܝܢܐ ܚܢܢ ܒܫܢܬ ܐܪܒܥܬܐ ܒܗ. ܕܐܬܬܘܗܝ، ܚܕ ܒܫܒܐ ܘܫܠܡܐ ܕܒܝܠܦܘܢܐ. ܒܗ ܒܫܡܫܐ ܗܘܐ ܐܬܘ ܬܠܡܝ̈ܕܐ ܡܢ ܚܪܬ ܕܓܠܝܠܐ ܡܢ ܐܢܫܐ ܕܐܝܬܘܗܝ ܒܝܬܗ ܕܡܪܝ ܠܩܘܪܝܐ ܕܡܬܘܪܐ ܕܒܝܬ ܙܟܝܐ. ܟܕ ܡܪܢ ܒܡܫܡܫ ܗܘܐ ܘܠܐ ܡܬܚܙܐ ܗܘܐ ܠܗܘܢ. ܘܟܕܒܢܐ ܕܝܗܒܐ ܙܒܢܐ ܐܝܟ ܗܘܐ ܡܪܢ ܐܬܪܘܗܝ، ܘܗܢ ܗܘܐ ܐܬܐ ܟܠ ܕܫܡܫܘ ܕܡܬܢܚܡܝܢ ܬܠܡܝ̈ܕܐ. ܘܡܫܟ ܠܗܘܢ ܡܫܡܫܬܐ ܕܫܡܫܘܬܐ. ܘܡܢ ܥܠܝܐ ܚܢܢܐ ܢܗܝܪܬܐ ܡܠܬܗ ܗܘܬ. ܘܫܐܠܘܗܝ، ܟܕ ܫܠܡ ܗܘܐ ܠܫܡܝܢܐ. ܘܐܬܐ ܗܘܐ ܡܢ ܡܫܝܚܐ ܕܐܒܘܗܝ، ܘܡܫܒܚܝܢ ܗܘܘ ܠܐܠܗܐ. ܕܫܝܘ ܗܘܠܘܗ ܐܝܟ ܕܐܡܪ ܠܗܘܢ ܘܫܡܥ ܗܘܘ ܕܡܟܠ ܗܘܘ ܡܫܝܚܐ ܕܡܫܡܫܬܐ ܕܒܝܬ ܡܘܫܐ ܘܐܬܘܪܘܗܝ. ܘܡܢ ܬܡܢ ܗܘܠܘܗ ܐܙܠܘ ܠܗܘܢ ܠܓܠܝܠܐ. ܐܝܟܐ ܕܚܙܐ ܗܘܐ ܡܪܢ ܒܫܡܫܘ ܦܪܝܫܐ. ܘܒܕܘܟܬܐ ܕܗܘܘ ܫܡ̈ܥܐܠܐ ܕܡܢܘ ܡܫܠܡ ܠܗ ܡܪܢ ܠܬܠܡܝ̈ܕܐ. ܬܡܢ ܗܘܘ ܫܡ̈ܥܐܠܐ ܐܦ ܕܐܡܪܢܐ ܢܗܘܪܘܗܝ ܗܘܘ ܗܘ ܡܫܒܚܬܗ ܒܠܡܒܐ. ܘܐܡܪܢܐ ܕܟܠܗ ܠܠܒܬܐ ܫܪ، ܗܘܐ ܐܘܪܐ ܕܦܠܚܘ ܘܕܡܒܗ ܕܡܪܢ ܕܢܬܠܝ ܗܘܐ ܒܠܡܒܐ. ܗܒܢܐ ܐܦ ܡܢ ܬܡܢ ܫܪ، ܗܘܐ ܡܠܦܢܐ ܕܒܪܘܘܬܗ ܕܢܬܠܝܬ ܗܘܐ ܒܠܡܒܐ. ܘܒܪ

ܗܘܐ ܠܥܠܡ ܘܠܡܫܠܡܢܘܬܐ ܕܟܗܢܘܬܐ ܗܢܐ ܕܡܛܠ ܫܪܪܗ ܗܘܐ
ܡܬܐܡܪܐ. ܟܕ ܫܡܥܝܢ ܘܡܩܒܠܝܢ. ܘܐܝܟ ܕܐܡܪܝܢ ܗܘܘ
ܗܕܝܐ ܫܡܥܘܗ ܗܘܘ. ܠܗܘ ܡܢ ܬܪܥܐ ܡܣܟܢܐ ܕܒܝܬܐ ܟܠܗ
ܒܪܬܐ ܠܒܢܝܐ. ܘܗܘܐ ܗܘܐ ܐܒܠܐ ܪܒܐ ܘܡܪܝܪܐ ܒܟܠܗ
ܥܕܬܐ ܘܒܟܠܗ ܡܕܝܢܬܐ. ܥܠ ܚܫܐ ܘܐܒܠܐ ܕܗܘܐ ܗܘܐ
ܒܓܘܗ. ܐܝܟ ܕܗܘܐ ܗܘܐ ܐܒܠܐ ܒܗ ܒܥܕܢ ܕܡܝܬ ܗܘ ܐܕܝ ܫܠܝܚܐ.
ܘܡܛܠ ܕܒܗ ܬܘܒܪܐ ܕܫܩܘܗܝ، ܡܝܬ ܗܘܐ ܠܗ ܪܗܝܒܐܝܬ
ܘܡܣܪܗܒܐܝܬ. ܠܐ ܐܫܟܚ ܗܘܐ ܕܢܣܝܡ ܐܝܕܐ ܥܠ ܦܠܘܛ.
ܐܙܠ ܗܘܐ ܗܘ ܦܠܘܛ ܠܐܢܛܝܘܟܝ ܘܩܒܠ ܗܘܐ ܐܝܕܐ
ܕܟܗܢܘܬܐ ܡܢ ܣܪܦܝܘܢ ܐܦܝܣܩܘܦܐ ܕܐܢܛܝܘܟܝ. ܗܘ ܕܐܦ
ܗܘ ܣܪܦܝܘܢ ܡܩܒܠܐ ܗܘܬ ܠܗ ܐܝܕܐ ܡܢ ܙܦܘܪܝܢܘܣ
ܐܦܝܣܩܘܦܐ. ܕܪܗܘܡܐ ܡܕܝܢܬܐ ܡܢ ܝܘܒܠܐ ܕܐܝܕܐ
ܕܟܗܢܘܬܐ ܕܫܡܥܘܢ ܟܐܦܐ. ܗܘ ܕܩܒܠ ܗܘܐ ܡܢ ܡܪܢ
ܘܗܘܐ ܗܘܐ ܐܦܝܣܩܘܦܐ ܬܡܢ ܒܪܗܘܡܐ ܥܣܪܝܢ ܘܚܡܫ
ܫܢܝܢ. ܒܝܘܡܝ ܩܣܪ ܗܘ ܕܐܡܠܟ ܗܘܐ ܬܡܢ ܬܠܬܥܣܪܐ
ܫܢܝܢ.. ܘܐܝܟܢܐ ܕܐܝܬ ܥܝܕܐ ܒܡܠܟܘܬܗ ܕܐܒܓܪ ܡܠܟܐ
ܘܒܟܠ ܡ̈ܠܟܘܬܐ ܕܟܠܡܕܡ ܕܦܩܕ ܡܠܟܐ ܘܟܠ ܡܕܡ ܕܡܬܐܡܪ
ܩܕܡܘܗܝ، ܡܬܟܬܒ ܘܡܬܬܣܝܡ ܒܝܬ ܥܗܕܪܢܐ ܗܟܢܐ ܐܦ
ܠܒܘܒܢܐ ܒܪ ܣܢܩ ܒܪ ܐܒܫܕܪ ܣܦܪܐ ܕܡܠܟܐ ܟܬܒ ܗܘܐ
ܗܠܝܢ ܕܐܕܝ ܫܠܝܚܐ ܡܢ ܫܘܪܝܐ ܠܫܘܠܡܐ. ܟܕ ܚܢܢ
ܗܘܐ ܐܝܕܐ ܕܣܗܕܘܬܐ. ܐܦ ܣܡ ܐܢܘܢ ܒܝܬ ܫܪܪܐ ܕܡ̈ܠܟܐ.
ܘܣܡ ܗܘܐ ܒܝܬ ܟܬܒܘܢܝܐ ܕܡ̈ܠܟܐ ܐܝܟܐ ܕܦܘܩܕܢܐ ܘܢܡܘܣܐ
ܣܝܡܝܢ ܘܕܒܝܪܝܢ ܗܘܘ ܟܠ ܒܢܝ ܒܝܬ ܡܠܟܘܬܐ ܕܠܐ
ܒܫܘܠܐ ܡܕܡ.

ܫܠܡܬ ܡܫܠܡܢܘܬܗ ܕܐܕܝ ܫܠܝܚܐ ܕܐܟܪܙ ܒܐܘܪܗܝ، ܡܕܝܢܬܐ
ܡܗܝܡܢܬܐ ܕܐܒܓܪ ܡܠܟܐ ܡܗܝܡܢܐ.

ܒܡܘܟܪ̈ܝܗܘܢ ܕܠܘܬ ܟܪ̈ܝܗܐ. ܡܠܟܘܬܗܘܢ ܓܝܪ ܫܘܟܢܐ ܡܠܟܢ
ܗܘ̈ܝ ܡܢ ܫ̈ܡܝܐ. ܘܕܘܟܪ̈ܢܗܘܢ ܬܫܒܘܚܬܐ. ܠܚܕܡܢ ܗܘܘ ܡܢ
ܢܘܟ̈ܪܝܐ. ܐܝܟܢܐ ܕܐܦ ܒܡܕܒܪܐ ܕܥܒܕ ܢܒܘ ܘܟܒܫ ܐܬܪܐ
ܠܗܘܢ ܦܠܓܝܢ ܗܘܘ. ܒܠܒܕ ܒܢܝܬܗܘܢ ܡܢܬܐ. ܒܡܠܬܗܘܢ
ܥܝܪ̈ܬܐ. ܒܦܪܗܣܝܐ ܕܐܝܬ ܗܘܐ ܒܐܝܪܘܬܗܘܢ. ܕܒܢܝܢܘܬܐ
ܠܐ ܒܪܝܢܐ ܗܘܬ. ܘܬܚܝܬ ܒܕܠܝܐ ܠܐ ܡܚܝܢܐ ܗܘܬ. ܠܝܬ
ܗܘܐ ܓܝܪ ܕܣܓܐ ܐܢܘܢ ܕܠܐ ܪܕܦ ܗܘܐ ܠܐܘܪܚܗܘܢ ܕܫܐܠ
ܗܘܐ ܫܠܡܗܘܢ ܒܢܝܪܐܝܬ. ܡܛܠ ܕܐܦ ܗܝ ܚܝܬܗܘܢ
ܫܠܡܐ ܦܪܝܫܐ ܗܘܬ ܠܟܠ ܚܢ̈ܝܐ. ܒܕܡܘܬ ܡܚܝܕܬܐ ܓܝܪ
ܦܪܫܘܢ ܗܘ̈ܝ ܡܠܝܗܘܢ ܕܫܝܢܐ ܠܟܠ ܡܕܝ̈ܢܬܐ. ܟܕ ܒܐܠܝܢ ܗܘܘ
ܠܟܘ ܡܢ ܦܠܓܐ ܕܡܫܝܚܬܐ ܘܕܪ̈ܘܪܐ. ܠܝܬ ܗܘܐ ܓܝܪ ܕܣܓܐ
ܗܘܐ ܠܗܘܢ ܘܟܘܠ ܡܢܗܘܢ ܒܕܠܐ ܦܠܓܝܢ ܗܘܘ ܡܕܡ
ܕܕܠܐ ܒܕܘܟܐ ܘܕܠܐ ܒܠܒܬܐ. ܘܟܕ ܗܠܝܢ ܟܠܗܝܢ ܗܘ̈ܝ
ܐܩܝܡܘ ܒܪܘܚܢܘܬܐ ܕܡܠܦܢܘܬܗܘܢ ܝܘܡ ܟܠܗ. ܗܘ ܓܝܪ
ܡܕܡ ܕܐܡܪܝܢ ܗܘܘ ܠܐܚܪ̈ܢܐ ܘܡܪܬܝܢ ܠܗܘܢ ܗܢܘܢ
ܒܒܕܐ ܡܚܣܢ ܗܘܘ ܠܗ ܒܢܦܫܗܘܢ ܘܫܩܠܒܐ ܕܣܝܡ
ܗܘܘ ܕܒܡ ܡ̈ܠܝܗܘܢ ܒܥ̈ܕܝܗܘܢ. ܕܠܐ ܦܢܝܐ ܫܓܝܐ
ܡܬܠܡܕܝܢ ܗܘܘ ܠܗܘܢ ܘܡܠܟܐ ܡܚܣܢܐ ܡܕܝܢ ܗܘܘ ܟܕ
ܡܚܣܢܝܢ ܗܘܘ ܠܐܠܗܐ ܕܐܦܝ ܐܢܘܢ ܠܘܬܗ ... ...

ܘܡܢ ܒܬܪ ܫ̈ܢܝܐ ܕܡܘܬܗ ܕܐܒܘܢ ܡܠܟܐ. ܡܢ ܗܘܐ ܚܕ ܡܢ
ܒܢܘ̈ܗܝ ܡܪ̈ܕܝܐ ܕܠܐ ܡܬܦܠܣ ܗܘܐ ܠܚܝܐ. ܘܫܐܠ ܠܗ
ܠܐܒܐ ܟܕ ܝܬܒ ܗܘܐ ܒܒܕܬܐ ܕܒܒ ܠܝ ܚܘܕܐ ܕܕܗܒܐ.
ܐܡܝܢ ܡܢܐ ܕܒܥܐ ܗܘܝܬ ܠܐܚܝ̈ܟ ܡܢ ܡܕܡ. ܫܐܠ ܠܗ ܐܒܐ.
ܕܠܐ ܡܪܦܐ ܐܢܐ ܬܫܒܘܚܬܗ ܕܡܫܝܚܐ ܕܐܬܟܠܒܬ ܠܝ ܡܢ
ܬܠܡܝܕܘ ܕܡܫܝܚܐ ܘܒܥܐ ܐܢܐ ܚܘܕܐ ܕܒܡܫܬܐ. ܘܟܕ ܫܡܥ
ܗܘܐ ܕܠܐ ܐܬܦܠܣ ܠܗ. ܫܕܪ ܗܘܐ ܬܒܪ ܗܘܐ ܫܩܘܗܝ
ܟܕ ܝܬܒ ܗܘܐ ܒܒܕܬܐ ܘܡܬܪܓܡ. ܘܟܕ ܡܛܐܬ ܗܘܐ. ܐܘܕܥ

ܟܠܢܫ ܡܫܡܥ ܗܘܐ ܠܟܠܗܘܢ. ܐܠܐ ܐܦ ܚ̈ܓܝܪܐ ܘܟ̈ܦܝܦܐ
ܕܐܝܬ ܗܘܐ ܒܗ ܒܒܪܢܫܐ ܗܢܐ. ܐܒܓܪ ܕܝܢ ܡܠܟܐ ܬܗܪ ܡܢ
ܟܠܝܢ ܡܚܡ ܗܘܐ ܠܟܠܗܘܢ، ܗܘ ܘܪ̈ܘܪܒܢܐ ܕܡܠܟܘܬܗ. ܘܡܒܪܘܬܐ
ܕܢܦܫܗ ܥܠ ܗܘܐ ܘܥܒܕܗ ܠܐܣܘܬܐ ܕܡܠܟܘܬܗ ܒܗܘ ܝܘܡܐ.
ܘܪ̈ܘܪܒܢܐ ܫܒ̈ܝܚܬܐ ܚܙܐ ܗܘܐ ܠܗ ܒܗ ܒܠܚܘܕ. ܘܡܕܡܐ ܟܠܗ
ܕܡܕܝܢܬܐ ܕܚܙܐ ܗܘܐ ܠܗ ܡܬܕܡܪ ܗܘܐ ܒܗ ܕܡܕܡܐ ܚܙܐ
ܗܘܐ ܠܟܠܗܘܢ. ܘܟܐܣܘܪܐ ܪܒܐ ܘܡܬܐ ܐܝܬ ܗܘܐ. ܘܡܢܗ
ܐܝܟ ܚܕ ܡܢ ܪ̈ܘܪܒܢܐ ܡܢܐ ܕܡܠܟܘܬ ܗܘܐ. ܘܦܩܕܗ ܗܘܐ
ܒܡܕܝܢܐ ܪܒܐ ܕܟܠܗ ܕܡ̈ܬܝܠܐ. ܗܘ ܐܒܓܪ ܕܦܫܝܩܝܢ ܗܘܘ ܒܗ
ܕܒܠܬ ܐܝܕܐ ܐܡ̈ܕܢܐ ܕܐܬ̈ܘܗܝ، ܕܐܒܓܪ ܡܠܟܐ. ܛܒ ܦܩܕܗ
ܗܘܐ ܫܡܥܐܝܬ ܒܪܝܘܬܐ ܘܟܗܢܘܬܐ ܪܒܬܐ. ܘܡܕܡܐ ܒܟܠܗ
ܕܒܬܪܐ. ܐܙܠ ܗܘܐ ܡܢ ܒܝܬܐ ܠܒܝܬܐ. ܘܡܠܟܐ ܗܘܐ ܛܒ
ܫܦܝܪܐܝܬ. ܘܕܘܒܪܐ ܕܡܫܝܚܐ ܒܟܢ̈ܫܐ ܗܘܘ ܡܢ ܚܕܐ ܠܚܕܐ.
ܐܝܟ ܦܘܩܕܢܐ ܘܡܠܦܢܘܬܐ ܕܡܩܒܠ ܗܘܐ ܠܗܘܢ ܡܢܗ ܐܕܝ
ܫܠܝܚܐ. ܘܐܝܟ ܡܠܬܗ ܕܐܠܗܐ ܕܗܘ ܗܘܐ ܡܕܒܪܢܐ ܘܦܩܘܕܐ
ܘܪܬܐ ܕܒܣܪܗ ܡܢ ܒܬܪܗ. ܟܐܝܢܐ ܕܒܝܘܬܐ ܕܩܒܠ ܗܘܐ
ܡܢܗ ܘܡܢ ܟܠܢ. ܐܦ ܗܘ ܒܗ ܒܐܝܢܐ ܕܩܒܠ ܗܘܐ ܡܢܗ ܒܒܕ
ܗܘܐ ܒܫܡܝܐ ܘܡܕܒܪ̈ܢܐ ܒܟܠܗ ܐܬܪܐ ܗܢܐ ܕܒܝܬ ܢܗܪܝܢ.
ܐܦ ܗܢܘܢ ܓܝܪ ܐܟܘܬܗ ܕܐܕܝ ܫܠܝܚܐ. ܗܟܢܐ ܐܚܝܕܝܢ ܗܘܘ
ܡܠܬܗ ܘܥܒܕܝܢ ܗܘܘ ܘܡܫܡܠܝܢ ܐܝܟ ܢ̈ܬܐ ܠܓܒ̈ܐ ܘܡܗܝܡܢܐ
ܕܫܠܝܚܘܬܐ ܕܡܫܝܚܐ ܦܓܪܐ. ܒܣܦܐ ܕܝܢ ܘܕܗܒܐ ܡܢ ܐܢܫ ܠܐ
ܢܣܒ ܗܘܐ. ܘܡܘܗ̈ܒܬܐ ܕܪ̈ܘܪܒܢܐ ܠܐ ܩܒܠ ܗܘ، ܐܝܟ ܕܦܩܕܗ
ܫܠܘ ܟܠܢ ܕܗܟܢܐ ܘܐܦ ܐܢܬܘܢ. ܒܦܬܟ̈ܬܐ ܕܡܫܝܚܝܐ ܡܬܒܪ
ܗܘܐ ܠܗ ܠܕܒܬܗ ܕܡܫܝܚܐ. ܣܓܝܐܐ ܕܝܢ ܟܠܗ ܕܓܒܪ̈ܐ ܘܕܢܫ̈ܐ.
ܢܟܦܝܢ ܗܘܘ ܘܩܕܝܫܝܢ ܗܘܘ ܘܕܟܝܢ. ܕܐܢܝܫܐܝܬ
ܘܡܛܟܣܐܝܬ ܒܡܕܝܢܬܐ ܗܘܘ ܕܠܐ ܦܘܠܓܐ. ܒܒܪ̈ܝܬܐ
ܕܬܫܡܫܬܐ ܘܐܝܟܢܐ ܒܫܡܠ ܦܠܚܝܢ ܕܠܘܬ ܡ̈ܫܝܚܐ

ܘܡܬܒܠܐ ܒܐܪܥܐ ܒܚܒܠܐ. ܒܬܪ ܫܥ̈ܝܐ ܙܥܘܪ̈ܐ ܘܡܬܦܢܐ ܠܦܢܝܐ. ܡܢ ܗܠܝܢ ܗܘ ܟܕ ܬܪ̈ܝܢ ܓܒ̈ܝܢ ܐܝܬ ܠܗܘܢ ܡܨ̈ܥܝܢ ܕܬܫܡܫܘܢ ܥܙܪܐ ܕܡܫܒܚܘܬܐ ܕܐܫܬܕܝܢ ܐܢܬܘܢ ܘܟܕ ܥܠܝܢ ܐܢܬܘܢ ܫܪܝܬܘܢ ܒܫܒܚܘܬܐ ܘܡܫܪܝܬܐ ܬܗܘܐ ܒܡܥܪܒܐ ܫܠܝܚܘܢ ܒܗ ܚܠܘܢ ܕܦܝܫ ܡܘܬܒܐ ܘܢܘܚܡ ܠܥܘܕܪܐ. ܠܐ ܬܗܘܘܢ ܡܡܟܝܢ ܠܡܘ̈ܗܒܬܐ ܡܢ ܒܬܪܐ. ܗܦܟ ܠܗܘܢ ܓܝܪ ܓܒܪܐ ܒܢܝܐ ܡܫܡܠܝܘܬܗܘܢ. ܠܐ ܬܬܓܠܒܘܢ ܒܫܘܒܚܐ ܗܢܝܐ ܕܗܦܟܐ ܠܐ ܬܗܘܘܢ ܒܬܓܠܝܐ ܡܢ ܡܫܡܠܝܘܬܐ ܕܠܒܝܫܝܢ ܐܢܬܘܢ܀

* * * * *

* * * * *

ܘܡܢ ܫܥ̈ܝܐ ܙܥܘܪ̈ܐ ܠܐ ܡܬܗܠܟܝܢ. ܘܫܪܪܬܐ ܗܕܐ ܕܡܒܠܝܢ ܚܝܝܢ ܠܐ ܡܬܦܣܝܢ. ܘܒܗ ܗܘ ܢܦܩܝܢ ܡܢ ܥܠܡܐ ܗܢܐ ܘܒܥܘܡܪܗ ܕܡܪܢ. ܡܛܠ ܒܢܝ ܕܕܡܝܐ ܕܒܐܝܘܬܐ. ܬܡܢ ܢܩܒܐ ܠܟ ܫܪܬܘܬܐ ܗܕܐ ܐܝܟ ܕܐܡܪܬ ܠܟ. ܘܟܕ ܐܬܐܡܪ ܗܘ̈ ܗܢܝܢ ܗܠܝܢ. ܡܢ ܗܘܐ ܐܒܓܪ ܡܠܟܐ ܗܘ ܘܪܘܪ̈ܒܢܘܗܝ ܘܐܚ̈ܪܢܘܗܝ ܘܐܙܠ ܗܘܐ ܠܐܦܝܣܐ ܕܠܗ ܟܕ ܡܟܡܢ ܗܘܘ ܒܠܒܗ, ܒܠܒܗܘܢ ܕܟܐܒܬ ܗܘܐ. ܘܫܕܪ ܗܘܐ ܠܗ ܠܒܘ̈ܫܐ ܡܝܩܪ̈ܐ ܘܪ̈ܫܝܐ ܕܢܬܟܪܟ ܗܘܐ ܒܗܘܢ܀ ܘܟܕ ܚܙܐ ܐܢܘܢ ܐܕܝ, ܫܠܚ ܠܗ ܕܠܐ ܒܥܬܕ ܥܢܕܢܗ ܡܬܒܥܐ ܡܕܡ ܐܦܠܐ ܗܘܐ ܒܡܘܬܗ, ܥܒܕ ܐܢܐ ܡܬܒܥܐ ܡܕܡ ܘܠܐ ܡܩܒܠ ܐܢܐ ܒܗ ܡܠܬܗ ܕܡܫܝܚܐ ܕܐܡܪ ܠܝ ܕܠܐ ܬܣܒܘܢ ܡܢ ܐܢܫ ܡܕܡ ܘܠܐ ܬܩܢܘܢ ܡܕܡ ܒܥܠܡܐ ܗܢܐ ...

ܘܡܢ ܒܬܪ ܬܠܬܐ ܝܘܡ̈ܝܢ ܐܚܪ̈ܢܐ ܕܐܬܐܡܪ ܗܘ̈, ܗܢܝܢ ܗܠܝܢ ܡܢ ܐܕܝ, ܫܠܝܚܐ ܘܫܡܥܢ ܗܘܐ ܘܩܒܠ ܣܗܕܘܬܐ ܕܡܠܦܢܘܬܐ ܕܪܘܚܘܬܗܘܢ ܡܢ ܟܠ ܬܫܡܫܬܗ ܡܢ ܫܦܝܪܐ ܒܫܠܡܗܘܢ ܢܦܩ ܗܘܐ ܡܢ ܥܠܡܐ ܗܢܐ. ܘܐܬܢܝܚ, ܗܘܐ ܝܘܡܐ ܗܘ ܫܦܝܪܐ ܒܚܡܫܐ ܒܐܪܒܥܐ ܒܐܝܪܚ ܐܝܪ. ܘܒܐܒܠܐ ܪܒܐ ܘܚܫܐ ܡܪܝܪܐ ܗܘܬ ܟܠܗ, ܟܠܗ ܡܕܝܢܬܐ. ܠܐ ܗܘܐ ܕܝܢ ܒܢ̈ܦܫܐ

ܢ̈ܦܫܐ ܚܕ̈ܬܐ. ܗܟܢܐ ܐܦ ܐܢܬܘܢ ܠܐ ܬܒܥܘܢ ܡܢܗܘܢ ܘܠܐ
ܬܒܣܪܘܢ ܡܢܗܘܢ ܡܕܡ. ܐܝܟܢܐ ܕܐܦ ܐܢܐ ܒܗܘܢ ܗܘ
ܡܬܕܒܪ ܐܢܐ ܒܝܬܟܘܢ ܘܠܐ ܥܒܕܬ ܡܢܗܘܢ ܠܡܣܟܢܐ ܐܘ
ܠܣܡܝܐ ܕܠܐ ܐܬܒܪܝܐ ܗܘܬ ܠܒܢ̈ܝ ܥ̈ܠܡܐ ܕܢܦܩܝܢ ܠܥܠܡ
ܕܥܠܡ ܡܬܕܒܪܝܢ. ܐܙܕܗܪܘ ܗܟܝܠ ܒܬܫܡܫܬܐ ܗܕܐ ܕܐܚ̈ܝܢ
ܐܢܬܘܢ ܘܒܕܝܠܬܐ ܘܒܪ̈ܬܬܐ ܗܘܝܬܘܢ. ܡܢܟܝܢ ܐܢܬܘܢ ܒܗ̇
ܘܡܫܬܡܫܝܢ ܠܒܘܟ. ܠܐ ܗܘܝܬܘܢ ܡܫܬܡܫܝܢ ܒܗ̇ ܒܚܕ̈ܝܐ ܒܩ̈ܠܐ
ܐܠܐ ܒܦܘܪ̈ܫܢܐ ܕܫܡܫܘܬܐ. ܘܬܫ̈ܡܫܬܗ ܕܡܫܝܚܐ ܡܢ
ܦܘܩܕܢܗ ܠܐ ܢܒܛܠ. ܘܡܫܝܢܘܬܐ ܒܝܠܕܘܬܐ ܕܫ̈ܡܝܐ
ܠܬܘܒܟܘܢ ܠܐ ܬܬܚܪܒ. ܐܙܕܗܪܘ ܒܫܪܪܐ ܕܐܚ̈ܝܢ ܐܢܬܘܢ
ܘܒܫܘܠܡܐ ܕܦܘܩܕܢܐ ܕܡܠܟܘܬܗ. ܘܒܝܪܬܘܬܐ ܕܚ̈ܝܐ ܕܡܫܬܠ
ܐܢܐ ܠܟܘܢ. ܡܛܠ ܕܗܘ ܒܝܢ ܕܡܫܝܚܐ ܡܬܬܟܠܝܢ ܐܢܬܘܢ
ܠܗ. ܗܢܐ ܕܟܠ ܡܫܬܒܚܐ ܡܢ ܐ̈ܒܗܬܐ ܘܢܒ̈ܝܐ. ܘܗܟܢܐ
ܕܢܗܘܐ ܒܦܘܡܗ ܡܢ ܬܫܒ̈ܚܬܐ ܒܪܝܫܝܬܐ ܕܢܗܝܪ̈ܐ ܒܪ ܡܠܟܐ ܗܘ
ܒܢ ܘܐܦ ܕܢܗܘܐ ܡܠܟܘܬܐ ܘܢܗܘܝ ܘܢܐܬܐ ܘܢܚܒܫ
ܢܗܘܐ ܠܟܠܗܘܢ ܬܡ̈ܢ ܐܡܝܢܐ. ܘܗܕܝܢ ܢܬܒ ܥܠ ܟܘܪܣܝܐ
ܕܡܠܟܘܬܐ ܘܕܢ̈ܐ ܫ̈ܒܛܐ ܘܫܡܝܐ ܐܝܟ ܕܐܡܪ ܠܝ. ܚܝܠܐ ܒܥܘܬܐ
ܕܬܚܝ̈ܒܘܢ ܡܢ ܪܘܚܐ ܠܐ ܬܬܟܒܫܘܢ ܕܠܐ ܢܥܒܝܢ ܬܘܩܠܬܗܘܢ
ܒܐܘܪܚܐ ܕܠܝܬ ܒܗ̇ ܬܘܩܠܬܐ. ܐܠܐ ܬܗܘܐ ܦܫܝܩܐ ܒܫܒ̈ܝܠܝܗ
ܗܘܝܬܘܢ ܒܟܝܢ ܐܢܬܘܢ ܐܒ̈ܗܬܐ ܘܦܩܝܕܝܢ ܐܢܬܘܢ ܕܐܠܦܝܢ
ܘܚܝܢ ܐܢܬܘܢ ܒܡܫܝ̈ܚܘܬܐ ܗܘܝܬܘܢ. ܒܝܢܝܢ ܬܟܒ̈ܪܬܐ ܘܬܠܦܝܢ
ܐܢܬܘܢ ܥܒ̈ܕܬܐ. ܡܛܠ ܕܒܐܬ̈ܪܘܬܟܘܢ ܡܬܬܟܠܝܢ ܢܦܫܬܗ
ܕܡܫܝܚܐ. ܠܐ ܗܘܝܬܘܢ ܚܪ̈ܝܢ ܐܢܬܘܢ ܠܐܘܪܚܐ ܒܟܘܪܐ.
ܙܒܢܐ ܓܝܪ ܕܝܗܒ ܕܢܬܦܪܫ ܡܢ ܡܕܝܢܬܗ. ܒܗ ܒܗ ܡܢܝܢܐ ܡܢܗ
ܡܕܝܢܬܗ. ܬܗܘܐ ܡܫܝܚܐ ܒܫܠܡܘܬܟܘܢ ܥܠ ܐܬܪܐ ܥܒܪܐ
ܕܡܠܟܬ̈ܗܘܢ ܣܝܡ ܦܪܨܘܦܗ ܕܐܒܐ. ܕܠܐ ܡܬܚܙܐ. ܘܠܐ
ܬܗܘܘܢ ܟܐ̈ܦܐ ܕܬܘܩܠܬܐ ܩܕܡ ܒܘܪ̈ܐ. ܐܠܐ ܢܥܠ ܐܘܪܚܐ

ܠܒܪ ܕܩܒܪ، ܕܫܪܒܬܗ ܦܩܝܕܬܐ ܕܐܦ ܐܝܟܢܐ. ܩܒܪ ܠܒܪܗ
ܗܘܐ. ܘܐܫܬܡܥ ܗܘܐ ܐܦ ܗܘ ܐܝܟ ܦܘܩܕܢܗ ܡܢ ܠܒܪܗ
ܥܠ ܫܠܝܐ ܕܥܒܕ ܗܘܐ ܐܕܝ، ܡܢ ܐܒܓܪ ܡܠܟܐ. ܘܡܢ ܕܗܘܐ
ܗܘܐ ܠܗ ܫܠܝܐ ܡܢ ܡܪܕܐ. ܒܬܪ ܡܛܠ ܗܘܐ ܡܢ ܩܕܡܐ
ܕܗܝܡܢܘܬܐ ܕܐܝܬ ܗܘܐ ܒܡܠܦܢܘܬܐ. ܘܟܕ ܫܡܥ ܗܘܐ ܐܒܓܪ
ܡܠܟܐ ܗܢܐ، ܗܘܐ ܒܗܕܐ ܦܓܪ. ܕܩܒܠ ܗܘܘ ܫ̈ܘܕܥܐ ܡܢ
ܒܝܬܐ ܐܝܟ ܕܐܕܝ ○ ○ ○ ○ ○

ܘܡܢ ܒܬܪ ܫܢܝܐ ܕܒܗܝܐ ܗܘܐ ܐܕܝ، ܫܠܝܚܐ ܒܡܕܝܢܬܐ ܒܐܘܪܗܝ،
ܘܐܬܘܣܦܬ ܗܘܐ ܒܟܘܠ ܥܕܡܐ ܕܐܕܝ ܗܘܐ ܠܗ ܘܬܠܡܝܕ ܗܘܐ
ܠܦܘܠܛܐ ܕܐܝܬܝܗܘܬܐ ܕܐܝܬ ܗܘܐ ܒܟܘܪ̈ܐ ܐܚܪ̈ܢܝܬܐ
ܕܫܡܥ ܘܥܒܕ ܒܗܐ ܗܘܐ ܒܪ̈ܬܐ ܘܟܠܠ ܘܐܬܬܘܚ ܘܥܒܕܝܢܐ
ܘܡܫܝܚܐ ܐܝܟ ܗܘܐ ܒܗܝܢ ܘܗܝܡܢ ܗܘܘ ܒܬܪܗ ܐܠܐ ܗܘܐ
ܒܗܝܢ ܘܦܠܘܛܐ ܘܬܠܡܝܕܘܬܐ ܠܒܪ ܘܠܝܗ ܐܠܐ ܗܘܐ. ܒܬܪ
ܗܠܝܢ ܒܠܝܢ ܐܬܒܪܗ ܗܘܐ ܒܡܘܬܐ. ܘܐܦ ܗܘܐ ܒܗ ܡܢ
ܒܠܒܐ ܗܢܐ. ܘܡܪܐ ܗܘܐ ܠܐܓܝ ܡܢ ܒܠܗ ܒܢܝܐ ܕܒܝܬܐ
ܘܦܪܟܗ ܗܘܐ ܘܥܒܕܗ ܗܘܐ ܡܕܒܪܢܐ ܘܦܩܘܕܐ ܒܕܘܟܬܗ.
ܘܠܟܠܗܘܢ ܕܡܫܡܫܢܐ ܗܘܘ ܥܒܕܗ ܗܘܐ ܩܫܝܫܐ. ܘܠܡܫܡܫܢܐ
ܕܦܩܪܐ ܗܘܐ ܥܒܕܗ ܗܘܐ ܡܫܡܫܢܐ. ܘܟܕ ܒܢܝܢ ܗܘܘ
ܘܡܝܬ ܠܗܘܢ ܫܢܝܐ ܘܬܘܒܐ ܒܝ ܒܠܟܐ ܒܝ ܕܓܠ ܘܡܪܢܝܗܒ
ܒܝ ܒܝܬܡܪ. ܘܗܘ ܒܝ ܒܗܕܐ ܘܐܝܠܘ ܒܝ ܦܠܝܛ ܒܢ ܫܪܒܐ
ܕܡܫܪ̈ܝܗܘܢ ܐܡܪ ܠܗܘܢ ܐܕܝ، ܫܠܝܚܐ. ܕܒܝܢ ܐܢܬܘܢ ܘܗܘܝܬܘܢ
ܒܠܒܗܘܢ ܕܡܫܡܫܝܢ ܠܝ ܕܒܠܒܢܝܢ ܕܥܒܕܬ ܗܘܝܬ ܠܟܘܢ ܘܡܢܠܦ
ܗܘܝܬ ܠܟܘܢ ܘܡܫܡܫܝܢ ܗܘܝܬܘܢ ܡܢ ܗܘܢܐ ܐܬܒܪܬ
ܒܡܠܬܗܘܢ ܘܒܪܘܚܘܢ ܐܦ ܒܡܠܘܐ. ܡܛܠ ܕܗܘܢܐ ܗܘܐ ܠܝ
ܡܢ. ܕܗܘ ܡܢ ܕܡܒܪܝ ܚܕ ܒܥܠܡܐ ܡܢ ܒܗܝܐ ܒܒܝܬܐ
ܗܘܝܢ ܘܒܪܝܢ ܠܗ ܡܢ ܒܠܒܢ. ܘܐܝܟ ܦܩܕܘܗܝ ܘܡܫܡܫܐ
ܕܗܝܡܢ ܠܬܠܡܝܕܐ ܒܐܘܪܫܠܡ ܘܡܬܕܒܪܝܢ ܗܘܘ ܒܗܘܢ ܐܦ

ܐܪܥܐ. ܘܪܒܠ ܗܘ̣، ܘܪܒ ܟܠܗܘܢ ܒܪ̈ܝܬܐ. ܘܐܝܟ ܕܥܡ ܐܢܫ̈ܝܗܘܢ ܒܗܢܐ ܗܘܦܟܐ ܐܬܗܦܟܬ ܗܘܬ ܠܗ̇ ܟܠܗ̇ ܒܪ̈ܝܬܐ ܘܒܡܗܘܪ̈ܗ ܕܒܪ̈ܝܬܐ. ܘܡܛܠ ܡܠܟܘܬܟ ܝܕܥܐ ܡܕܡ ܕܘܠܐ ܕܬܦܩܘܕ ܥܠ ܥܡܐ ܕܝܗܘ̈ܕܝܐ ܕܗܠܝܢ ܥܒܕܘ ܀

ܘܟܬܒ ܗܘ̣ܐ ܦܛܪܘܢܘܣ ܣܦܪ ܘܥܒܪ ܗܘܐ ܠܐܓܪܬ ܡܠܟܐ ܘܗܟܢܐ ܟܬܒ ܠܗ.

ܕܐܓܪܬܐ ܕܪܚܡܘܬܟ ܕܠܘܬܝ، ܩܒܠܬ ܘܐܬܩܪܝܬ ܩܕܡܝ. ܥܠ ܡ̇ܕܡ ܕܥܒܕܘ ܗܘܘ ܝܗܘ̈ܕܝܐ ܒܨܠܝܒܐ. ܐܦ ܦܝܠܛܘܣ ܗܓܡܘܢܐ ܟܬܒ ܗܘܐ ܘܐܘܕܥܗ ܠܐܘܠܝܢܘܣ ܗܦܪܟܐ ܕܝܠܝ ܥܠ ܟܠܗܝܢ ܕܠܗܝܢ ܕܗܠܝܢ ܕܟܬܒܬ ܠܝ. ܡܛܠ ܕܝܢ ܕܡܪܕܐ ܕܒܢ̈ܝ ܐܣܦܢܝܐ ܕܡܪܕܘ ܥܠ ܡܐܡ ܒܗܢܐ ܙܒܢܐ. ܡܛܠ ܗܢܐ ܠܐ ܐܫܟܚܬ ܕܐܬܒܥܐ ܠܒܘܠܐ ܗܕܐ. ܡܛܝܒ. ܐܢܐ ܕܝܢ ܕܒܥܐ ܕܗܘ̣ܐ ܠܝ ܢܝܚܐ. ܐܦܩܘܕ ܟܠܗܘܢ ܢܬܦܪܥܘܢ ܥܠ ܝܗܘ̈ܕܝܐ ܕܠܐ ܦܪܝܣ ܢܡܘܣܐܝܬ. ܘܡܛܠ ܗܢܐ ܐܦ ܦܝܠܛܘܣ ܕܡܕܒܪ ܗܘܐ ܠܗ ܬܡܢ ܗܓܡܘܢܐ. ܫܕܪܬ ܘܫܩܠܬܗ؛ ܐܚܪܢܐ ܘܥܒܕܬܗ ܠܗ ܒܕܘܟܬܗ ܥܠ ܕܢܦܩ ܡܢ ܢܡܘܣܐ. ܘܥܒܕ ܗܘܐ ܨܒܝܢܐ ܠܝܗܘ̈ܕܝܐ ܘܪܦܐ ܗܘܐ ܠܡܨܒܝܢܗ ܠܢܝܚܘܬܗܘܢ ܕܝܗܘ̈ܕܝܐ. ܗܘ̇ ܕܐܝܟ ܕܐܡܪܬ. ܐܢܐ ܟܠܗܘܢ، ܕܠܐ ܘܦܩܐ ܕܥܒܕܘܬܐ. ܕܠܡܐ ܗܘܐ ܘܫܬܠܡ ܒܝܕܗܘܢ ܘܙܩܦ ܗܘܐ. ܫܘܪܝܐ ܕܝܢ ܕܒܨܠܝܒܘܬܗ ܚܙܝܢ ܗܘܘ ܥܠ ܡܕܡ ܕܥܒܕ ܗܘܐ. ܐܢܬ ܕܝܢ ܐܝܟ ܫܪܝܪܘܬܟ ܕܠܘܬܝ، ܘܡܗܝܡܢܐ ܫܪܝܪܐ ܕܠܟܝ ܘܕܐܒܗܝܟ. ܫܦܝܪ ܒܥܒܪܬ ܕܟܬܒܬ ܠܝ ܗܟܢܐ.

ܘܡܟܠ ܗܘ̣ܐ ܐܒܓܪ ܡܠܟܐ ܠܐܪܛܚܫܫܬ ܕܐܬܘܪ ܗܘ̣ܐ ܡܢ ܦܛܪܘܢܘܣ ܣܦܪ ܐܓܪܬܗ، ܘܗܟܢܐ ܗܘ̣ܐ ܟܬܝܒ ܒܗ̇ ܒܡܠ̈ܐ ܕܐܝܣܪ̈ܐ ܕܐܬܒܢܝ ܠܗܘܢ ܡܢ ܕܟܬܒܬ ܗܘ̣ܐ ܠܗܘܢ. ܘܡܢ ܐܚܪܢ، ܐܝܠ ܗܘܐ ܠܬܫܡܫܬܐ ܐܝܟܢܐ ܕܐܬܝܗܘܢ، ܗܘ̣ܐ ܘܡܠܟܘܬ ܦܪ̈ܣܝܐ ܕܡܠܟܐ. ܘܡܢ ܬܡܢ ܬܘܒ ܐܝܠ ܗܘܐ ܠܐܪܛܚܫܫܬ ܕܬܡܢ ܗܘ̣ܐ

ܢܚ̈ܝ. ܒܪ̈ܘܚܐ ܘܫܠܝܚܘܬܐ ܐܝܟ ܒܠܚܘܕܝܗ ܕܐܕܝ ܢܐܕܕܝܢܗܘܢ.
ܘܒܢ̈ܝܕܗ ܕܡܕܝܢܬܐ ܚܙܬܐ ܡܬܚܙܝܢ ܗܘ̈ܝ، ܘܐܝܟܢܐ ܕܒܫܘܬܐ
ܡܫܬܠܡ ܗܘܘ ܡܢܗ ܦ̈ܓܪܐ. ܗܟܢܐ ܕܐܦ ܡܕܝܢ̈ܬܐ ܕܒܫܘܬܐ
ܕܬܚܝܪܐ ܠܚܕܐ ܬ̈ܗܘܡܝܬܐ ܡܕܝܢ ܗܘܘ ܕܫܡܥܘ ܗܘܘ ܐܬ̈ܘܬܐ
ܕܥܒܕ ܗܘܐ ܗܘ ܐܕܝ. ܘܐܝܠܝܢ ܕܡܬܬܠܡܕܝܢ ܗܘܘ ܡܫܬܠܡܝܢ
ܗܘܘ ܡܢܗ ܐܝܟܢܐ ܕܒܫܘܬܐ ܘܒܐܬܪܐ ܕܝܠܗܘܢ ܕܐܬܘܪ̈ܝܐ
ܠܟܠ ܒܢܝ̈ܗܘܢ ܡܬܬܠܡܕܝܢ ܗܘܘ ܘܡܫܬܐ ܕܝܠܦ̈ܬܐ ܬܘܒ ܒܒܥܝܐ
ܒܒܝܢ ܗܘܘ ܡܢ ܡܠܦܢܐ ܕܩ̈ܕܡܝ، ܠܠܘܝܐ ܘܡܫܡܫ، ܠܩܛܝܢܐ ..
ܢܦܫ، ܕܝܢ ܡܠܟܐ ܕܐܬܘܪ̈ܝܐ. ܟܕ ܥܒܕ ܗܘܐ ܗܢܝܢ ܗܠܝܢ
ܕܒܟܠ ܗܘܐ ܐܕܝ ܫܠܝܚܐ. ܫܠܚ ܗܘܐ ܠܗ ܠܐܒܓܪ ܡܠܟܐ.
ܕܐܘ ܫܕܪ ܠܝ ܠܐܒܓܪܐ ܗܘ ܕܥܠܝܢ ܐܬ̈ܘܬܐ ܒܒܝܬ ܢܐܕܕܝܢ
ܕܐܚܙܝܘܗܝ، ܘܐܫܡܥ ܡܠܬܗ ܐܘ ܫܠܘܚ ܠܝ ܟܠ ܕܚܙܝܬ ܕܥܒܕ
ܗܘܐ ܒܡܕܝܢܬܐ ܕܝܠܟ. ܘܟܬܒ ܗܘܐ ܐܒܓܪ ܠܢܪܣܝ، ܘܐܘܕܥܗ
ܗܘܐ ܟܠܗ ܬܫܥܝܬܐ ܕܥܒܕܘܗܝ ܕܐܕܝ، ܡܢ ܫܘܪܝܐ ܠܫܘܠܡܐ.
ܘܠܐ ܫܒܩ ܗܘܐ ܡܕܡ ܕܠܐ ܟܬܒ ܗܘܐ ܠܗ. ܟܕ ܕܝܢ ܫܡܥ
ܗܘܐ ܢܪܣܝ، ܐܝܠܝܢ ܕܐܬܟܬܒ ܗܘ̈ܝ ܠܗ. ܬܡܗ ܗܘܐ ܘܐܬܕܡܪ ..
ܐܒܓܪ ܕܝܢ ܡܠܟܐ ܡܛܠ ܕܠܐ ܐܫܟܚ ܗܘܐ ܕܢܥܒܪ ܠܚܕܐ
ܬ̈ܗܘܡܝܬܐ ܘܢܐܙܠ ܗܘܐ ܠܦܠܣܛܝܢܐ ܘܢܚܙܐ ܗܘܐ ܠܡܫܝܚܐ
ܟܠ ܕܥܒܕܘ، ܠܡܫܝܚܐ. ܟܬܒ ܐܓܪܬܐ ܘܫܕܪ ܗܘܐ ܠܘܬ
ܛܝܒܪܝܘܣ ܩܣܪ. ܟܕ ܟܬܒ ܒܗ ܗܟܢܐ.

ܐܒܓܪ ܡܠܟܐ ܠܡܪܝ ܛܝܒܪܝܘܣ ܩܣܪ. ܟܕ ܝܕܥ ܐܢܐ ܕܡܕܡ ܡܢ
ܡܠܟܘܬܟ ܠܐ ܡܬܟܣܝܐ. ܟܬܒ ܐܢܐ ܘܡܘܕܥ ܐܢܐ ܠܫܘܠܛܢܟ
ܕܝܗܘܕ̈ܝܐ ܕܬܚܝܬ ܐܝܕܝܟ ܕܥܡܪܝܢ ܒܐܬܪܐ
ܕܦܠܣܛܝܢܐ ܐܬܟܢܫܘ ܘܨܠܒܘ ܗܘܘ ܠܡܫܝܚܐ ܕܠܐ ܚܛܗܬܐ
ܕܡܘܬܐ. ܟܕ ܒܬܪ ܗܘܐ ܕܥܒܕ ܐܬ̈ܘܬܐ ܘܬܕܡܪ̈ܬܐ ܘܚܝܠܐ
ܗܘܐ ܠܗܘܢ ܘܚܝ̈ܐ ܡܝ̈ܬܐ. ܗܟܢܐ ܕܐܦ ܡ̈ܝܬܐ ܐܚܝ ܠܗܘܢ.
ܘܒܥܕܢܐ ܕܨܠܒܘܗܝ، ܗܘܘ ܚܫܟ ܗܘܐ ܫܡܫܐ ܘܐܬܙܝܥܬ ܗܘܬ ܐܦ

ܘܒܫܘܒܚܝܗܘܢ ܕܚ̈ܠܝܫܐ ܥܠܝܗܘܢ ܒܗܘܢ ܡܬܗܦܟܝܢ ܗܘܘ ܒܗ.
ܡܫܡܫ ܗܘܐ ܠܗܘܢ ܘܗܡܝܢܐܝܬ ܕܗܘܘ ܕܒܝܢ ܦܓܪ̈ܝܗܘܢ ܘܡܫܡܫܝܢ
ܠܡܫ̈ܡܫܢܘܗܝ. ܐܝܟ ܕܙܕܩ ܠܐܢܫܐ ܕܡܫܡܫ ܡܪܗ ܡܫܒܚܐ
ܕܐܠܗܐ. ܘܗܘܝܬܘܢ ܠܟ ܙܗܝܪܝܢ ܡܢ ܡܫܡ̈ܫܬܐ ܕܠܐ ܬܠܬܐ ܘܡܢ
ܡܠܟܐ ܕܙܘܥܐ. ܘܡܢ ܗܘܦܟܐ ܕܥܘܬܪܐ ܕܒܘܠܪܐ ܕܬܒܐ.
ܘܡܢ ܚܪܝܢܐ ܕܠܘܬ ܚܒܪ̈ܝܗܘܢ ܢܘܚܐ. ܘܡܢ ܢܫܒܐ ܘܡܩ̈ܪܒܐ
ܘܒܘܪ̈ܐ. ܘܡܢ ܚܠܡܐ ܘܟܒܬ ܠܐܚܐ ܕܡܫܬܟܚܝܢ ܒܗܘܢ ܛ̈ܠܝܐ
ܠܟ̈ܠܐ. ܘܡܢ ܒܘܟ̈ܪܐ ܘܡ̈ܠܘܫܐ ܕܡܫܬܝܢ ܒܠܝܗܘܢ ܬ̈ܢܝܢܐ.
ܘܐܢܫܘ ܡܢܒܘܢ ܡܫܘܒ ܒܐܦ̈ܐ ܕܒܘܠܐ. ܘܒܘܚܕܐ
ܘܟܘܪ̈ܟܐ ܕܡܬܚܫܒܝܢ ܒܗܘܢ ܙܟ̈ܝܐ. ܘܒܟ ܗܕܐ ܬܫܒܘܚܬܐ
ܕܐܬܦܪܫܬܘܢ ܠܝ ܠܐ ܬܒܥܘܢ ܢܗܘܐ ܠܟܘܢ ܦܘܠܚܢܐ ܐܚܪܢܐ
ܡܢܗ ܗܘ ܓܝܪ ܦܘܠܚܢܐ ܕܬܫܒܘܚܬܗܘܢ ܥܠ ܗ̈ܕܝ ܢܝ̈ܚܘܢ.
ܘܗܘܝܬܘܢ ܢܛܝܪܝܢ ܠܟܠ ܪ̈ܥܝܢܐ ܕܡܫ̈ܡܫܢܘܬܐ. ܘܠܐ
ܗܘܝܬܘܢ ܪܚܝܡܝܢ ܠܡܬܪ̈ܝܢܘܬܗ ܕܥܠܡܐ ܗܢܐ. ܘܗܘܝܬܘܢ
ܥܒܝܕܝܢ ܐܝܬܝܟܘܢ ܕܝܢܐ ܒܟܐܢܘܬܐ ܘܒܦܫܝܛܘܬܐ. ܘܠܐ ܬܗܘܘܢ
ܬܘܠܡܬܐ ܠܟܘܪܐ. ܕܕܠܟܐ ܢܬܓܪܫ ܒܗܘܢ ܥܡܗ ܕܗܘ
ܕܥܬܝܕ ܗܘܐ ܠܟܘܪܐ ܐܝܟ ܡܢܐ ܕܝܕܥܝܢ. ܟܠ ܡܢ ܗܟܝܠ ܕܝܕܥ
ܠܟܘܢ ܢܬܟܫܦ ܕܥܠܝܟܝܢ ܐܢܬܘܢ ܗܘ ܠܥܠܡܝܢ ܕܡܒܪܝܢ
ܐܢܬܘܢ ܘܡܠܦܝܢ ܐܢܬܘܢ. ܘܡܫܬܥܝܢ ܗܘܘ ܥܒܕܗ ܒܒܪܬܐ
ܕܒܢܝܐ ܗܘܐ ܗܘ ܐܒܐ.. ܡܢ ܡܠܬܗ ܘܦܘܩܕܢܗ ܕܐܒܘܢ ܡܠܦܢܐ
ܒܗ. ܡܬܦܪܫܝܢ ܗܘܘ ܡܢ ܕܡܠܟܐ ܘܡܢ ܕܐܢܫܝ̈ܘܗܝ. ܡܛܠܗܘܢ
ܠܒܝܬܐ ܕܐܠܗܐ ܘܡܛܠܗܘܢ ܠܦܘܪܫܢܐ ܕܒ̈ܥܘܬܐ. ܒܗܕܐ ܕܝܢ
ܦܬܟܪ̈ܐ ܥܠܝܗܘܢ ܒܗܘܢ ܒܒܝܬܐ ܘܐܬܘܢ ܠܡܠܟܘܬܐ ܕܡܫܒܚܘܬܐ.
ܘܠܡܬܘܬܐ ܒܥܘܬܐ ܘܩܪܝܬܐ ܕܪܒܘܬܢܘܬܐ ܘܒܝܫܬ ܬ̈ܒܥܬܐ
ܡܫܡܫܝܢ ܗܘܘ ܘܠܒܝ̈ܕܝܢܘܢ ܒܡܕܝܢܬܐ ܕܐܝܢܡܚܐ ܡܢܗܝܢ ܗܘܘ.
ܘܟܐܪ̈ܐ ܕܒܝܬܐ ܒܝܬܝܗܘܢ ܒܟܝܢ ܗܘܘ. ܘܥܠܝܗܘܢ ܒܫܘܪܐ
ܕܒܝܬܐ ܐܡܝܢܝܢ ܗܘܘ. ܘܫܘܒܚܐ ܕܝܘܩܪܬܐ ܡܫܝܢ ܗܘܘ

ܚ̈ܫܝܫܘܗܝ. ܘܥܠ ܟܠ ܡܐ ܕܥܒܕ ܗܘ̣ ܐܪ̈ܚܡܘܗܝ ܡܢܗ.
ܘܠܡܥܒܕ ܕܐܡܪܢ ܗܘܘ ܟܠܗܘܢ. ܢܫ̈ܐ ܐܦܠܐ ܗܘܐ ܡܙ̈ܡܢܘܗܝ
ܘܡܫܡܠܝܢ ܗܘܘ ܟ̈ܠܗܘܢ. ܒܗܝܡܢܘܬܐ ܘܡܗܝܡܢܘܬܐ ܘܠܝܬ ܗܘܐ
ܐܢܫ ܕܩܐܡ ܗܘܐ ܠܩܘܒܠܗ. ܠܐ ܓܝܪ ܥܒܕܝܢ ܗܘܘ ܢܟܠܐ
ܕܒܥܐ ܗܘܐ ܕܢܩܘܡ ܐܢܫ ܠܩܘܒܠܗ. ܥܘܕܪܐ ܕܝܢ ܘܒܥܒܕܝܗ
ܛ̈ܒܐ ܕܗܝܡܢܘܬܐ ܕܫܪܪܐ ܗܘܬ ܒܗ ܦܪܨܘܦ ܘܕܘܡܐ ܫܒ̈ܝܚܘܗܝ
ܟܕ ܚܙܘ ܗܘܘ ܐܢ̈ܬܬܐ ܕܟܬܒ ܗܘܐ ܪܡܠܐ ܗܘܘ ܘܡܟܪܘ
ܗܘܘ ܒܠ̈ܬܐ ܕܟ̈ܠܗܘܢ ܡܕܒܚܝܢ ܗܘܘ ܩܕܡ ܢܒܘ ܘܒܠ
ܐܠ̈ܗܝܗܘܢ ܠܒܪ ܡܢ ܒܠܬܐ ܪܒܬܐ ܕܡܪܝܡܬ ܒܪܒܐ ܘܩܒܝܢ ܗܘܘ
ܘܐܡܪܝܢ. ܕܒܪܢܐܝܬ ܕܗܢܐ ܬܠܡܝܕܐ ܕܗܘ ܪܒܐ ܡܗܝܪܐ
ܘܥܒ̈ܝܕܬܐ ܕܥܒܕܝܢ ܗܘܘ ܟܠ ܕܥܒܕ ܗܘܐ ܒܐܬܪܐ ܕܦܠܣܛܝܢܐ.
ܘܥܠ ܐܝܠܝܢ ܕܡܗܝܡܢܝܢ ܗܘܘ ܒܡܫܝܚܐ ܡܩܒܠ ܗܘܐ ܠܗܘܢ
ܐܕܝ. ܘܡܥܡܕ ܗܘܐ ܠܗܘܢ ܒܫܡ ܐܒܐ ܘܒܪܐ ܘܪܘܚܐ
ܕܩܘܕܫܐ. ܘܐܝܠܝܢ ܕܠܟ̈ܢܫܐ ܘܠܫ̈ܘܩܐ ܡܟܢܫܝܢ ܗܘܘ ܠܗܘܢ
ܟ̈ܠܗܘܢ ܡܬܝܢ ܗܘܘ. ܘܡܬܒܢܝܢ ܡܢ ܒܗܝܡܢܘܬܐ ܕܫܪܪܐ
ܕܫܒܘܚܬܐ. ܐܦ ܡܫܘܕܥܐ ܕܪ̈ܒܐ ܢܒܘܗܐ ܘܒܢ̈ܝܢܐ ܐܝܠܝܢ
ܕܪ̈ܕܝܦܐ ܡܪܕܝܢ ܗܘܘ ܐܦ ܗܢܘܢ ܐܬܦܢܝܘ ܗܘܘ
ܘܐܬܬܠܡܕܘ ܘܐܬܥܕܝܘ ܗܘܘ ܒܡܫܝܚܐ ܕܒܪܗ ܗܘ ܕܐܠܗܐ ܚܝܐ.
ܠܐ ܕܝܢ ܐܒܓܪ ܡܠܟܐ ܐܦ ܠܐ ܐܕܝ ܫܠܝܚܐ. ܟܝܐ ܗܘܐ
ܠܐܢܫ ܕܡܦܪܢܣܘܬܐ ܢܣܒ ܗܘܐ ܡܢ ܡܗܝܡܢܐ. ܡܛܠ ܕܕܠܐ
ܡܦܪܢܣܐ ܕܐܢܫ ܡܦܪܢܣ ܕܐܬ̈ܬܐ ܟܝܐ ܗܘܐ ܠܦܪ̈ܢܣܐ
ܕܢܡܫܝܢܘܢ ܗܘܘ ܒܗ. ܘܚܘܒܐ ܡܫܡܠܝܢ ܗܘܘ ܡܠܦܢܘܬܗ
ܟܠܗ ܐܬܪܐ ܗܢܐ ܕܒܝܬ ܢܗܪܝܢ ܘܡܕ̈ܝܢܬܐ ܟܠܗܝܢ ܕܚܕܪ̈ܝܗ. ...
ܐܟܢ ܕܝܢ ܒܟܪ. ܚܐܪ̈ܐ ܘܫ̈ܘܕܐ ܕܡܠܟܐ ܘܟܠܗܝܢ ܘܒܪ̈ܫܠܟܐ
ܘܒܪܘܫܡܐ ܒܗ ܥܪܒܐ ܕܐܣܝܪܐ ܚܒ̈ܝܫܘܗܝ ܢܦܩܘܗܝ ܗܘܘ
ܠܐܕܝ ܫܠܝܚܐ. ܘܥܠ ܐܝܟ ܘܫܬܦ ܐܝܟ ܒܝܬ ܟܢܫܬܐ
ܟܕ ܩܪܝܢ ܗܘܘ ܒܕܝܬܩܐ ܥܬܝܩܬܐ ܘܚܕܬܐ. ܘܒܢ̈ܝܢܐ

ܐܚܪܢܐ ܕܗܘܢ ܒܟܪܟܗ ܗܠܝܢ ܐܬܩܢܬܐ ܘܐܬܕܒܪܬܐ. ܐܠܐ
ܒܫܠܡܗ ܕܡܫܝܚܐ ܕܡܥܕܪ ܐܝܬ ܠܗ ܒܦܘܫܬܐ ܘܒܫܪܪܐ.
ܘܡܚܝܠ ܠܗ ܗܘ ܦܩܕ. ܐܝܟ ܐܝܟ ܘܡܚܘܐ ܒܪ، ܘܐܦܣܩܘܦܝܢ
ܘܫܠܝܚ ܡܠܟܬܐ. ܘܡܚܝܠ ܥܠ ܐܝܟܐ ܕܒܝܬ ܒܝ ܒܪܬܐ
ܒܝܬ ܓܘܒܐ ܕܐܝܠܝܢ ܕܗܡܝܢܘ ܘܡܗܡܢܝܢ ܒܡܠܝܟ، ܘܐܝܟ
ܡܐ ܕܦܩܕ ܠܟ ܡܢ ܡܪܟ ܗܘܝܬ ܡܫܡܫ ܐܝܬ ܒܒܪܝܐ
ܬܒܠܐܝܬ. ܘܐܝܠܝܢ ܕܗܘܘ ܒܒܝܟ ܡܠܦܢܐ ܕܦܪܘܬܐ ܗܕܐ
ܕܫܢܐ ܙܘܪܒܐ ܡܠܝܒܝ ܐܝܟ ܕܐܬܠ ܠܗܘܢ ܕܡܕܡ ܒܡ
ܬܫܡܫܬܐ ܠܐ ܢܗܘܐ ܠܗܘܢ ܒܒܕܐ ܐܚܪܢܐ ܘܡܠܒܕܡ
ܕܡܬܒܥܐ ܠܟ ܠܢܦܫܬܗ ܕܒܠܬܐ ܐܝܟ ܢܗܒ ܐܝܟ ܠܟ ܕܠܐ
ܫܘܒ ܒܪ ܗܘܐ ܡܠܬܟ ܥܠܝܬܐ ܘܡܩܠܒܐ ܒܙܪܒܐ ܗܢܐ.
ܘܕܠܐ ܐܝܟ ܐܚܪܢܐ ܗܘܝܬ ܥܠܬ ܓܐܕ، ܡܥܠܝܐܝܬ ܠܐܦܕܢܐ
ܕܐܝܣܪܘܢ ܕܡܠܒܘܬ، ܘ. ܘ ܘܒܕ ܢܚܬ ܗܘܐ ܐܒܓܪ ܠܐܦܕܢܐ
ܕܡܠܒܘܬܗ. ܚܕܐ ܗܘܐ ܗܘ ܘܪܘܒܢܘܗ، ܒܒܡܗ. ܒܒܕܘ ܒܪ
ܒܒܕܘ ܦܓܪܗ. ܘܫܡܥܓܪܡ ܘܐܒܗܒ ܘܡܗܪܕܬ. ܒܡ ܙܪܒܐ
ܕܫܒܪܝܢܘܗܝ ܒܡܠܒܕܡ ܕܚܝ، ܗܘ، ܒܢܝܢܘܗܝ ܘܫܡܒ ܗܘ، ܘܐܦ
ܐܕܪܝܢܘܗܝ ܘܒܫܕܘܬܐ ܕܠܒܗܘܢ ܡܫܒܚܝܢ ܗܘܘ ܐܦ ܗܢܘܢ
ܠܐܠܗܐ ܕܐܒܕ ܗܘܐ ܦܪܝܫܘܗܝ ܠܗܬܗ. ܒܪ ܒܦܪܝܢ ܗܘܘ
ܒܫܦܘܬܐ ܕܦܫܩܝܢ ܗܘܘ ܒܗ. ܘܡܒܕܝܢ ܗܘܘ ܒܫܒܪܬܐ
ܕܡܫܝܚܐ. ܘܒܕ ܒܢܐ ܗܘܐ ܐܕ، ܒܪܬܐ ܡܦܪܒܝܢ ܗܘܘ ܒܗ
ܢܕܪܐ ܘܩܘܪܒܢܐ ܗܢܘܢ ܘܢܫܘܬܐ ܕܡܕܢܚܬܐ. ܘܬܡܢ ܡܫܒܚܝܢ
ܗܘܘ ܥܠ ܛܘܒ ܚܝܘܗܝ. ܘܦܪܒ ܗܘܘ ܠܬܗ ܕܐܒܐ، ܒܗܢܕܐ
ܘܒܪܟܒܐ ܐܝܠܝܢ ܕܕܫܐ ܗܘܘ ܘܦܩܘܕܐ ܘܠܟܠ ܚܘܕܐ ܕܡܬܠܒܐ
ܘܡܫܬܐܠܝܢ ܗܘܘ ܠܗ ܥܠ ܫܪܒܗ ܕܡܫܝܚܐ ܕܢܐܡܪ ܠܗܘܢ
ܕܐܝܟܢܐ ܒܪ ܐܠܗܐ ܗܘܐ ܡܬܚܙܐ ܗܘܐ ܠܗܘܢ ܐܝܟ ܒܪܢܫܐ
ܘܐܝܟܢܐ ܠܡ ܡܫܒܚܝܢ ܗܘܝܬܘܢ ܚܢܢ ܗܘܝܬܘܢ ܒܗ.
ܘܠܒܠܗܘܢ ܡܚܝܕ ܗܘܐ ܠܗܘܢ ܒܠ ܗܕܐ ܒܠ ܒܠ ܕܝܢ، ܗܘ،

ܡܛܠ ܗܢܐ ܚܠܦ ܚܠܐ ܕܕ̈ܚܠܝܢ ܕܐܬܬܐܡܪ ܠܝ ܕܢܦܩ ܥܠ ܒܪܝܐ ܕܠܐ ܡܫܡܠ ܬ̈ܠܝܢ. ܗܐ ܢܦܩܬ ܢܦܫܐ ܥܠ ܐ̈ܝܕܝܐ ܕܐ̈ܚܝܟܘܢ ܦܬ̈ܓܡܐ ܕܡܦ̈ܩܬ، ܕܟܠܗܘܢ ܝܕܥܝܢ ܡܐܬܝܬܗ ܕܡܫܝܚܐ ܕܗܘܬ ܐܦ ܕܒܬܪܟ ܕܬܗܘܐ. ܘܡܥܒܕܢܘܬܐ ܘܢܘܡܘܣܐ ܕܟܠܗܘܢ ܒܢ̈ܝܢܫܐ. ܘܦܘܪܫܢܐ ܕܗܘܐ ܒܝܬ ܡܗܝ̈ܡܢܐ ܠܦܓܪ̈ܐ. ܘܡܟܝܠ ܒܪ̈ܢܫܐ ܒܢܫܐ ܕܢܦܠܢ ܠܐܠܗܐ ܕܠܐ ܝܕܥܝܢ ܠܐܠܗܐ ܘܡܘܠܕܢܐ ܒܪ̈ܢܫܐ ܕܢܣܒܘܬܐ ܕܒܬܪܟ ܕܢܣܒܠܘܢ ܐܝܟ ܕܡܫܝܚܘ ܒܗ ܒܡܫܝܚܐ ܘܫܪܪܘ ܠܗ ܘܠܐܒܘܗܝ، ܐܒܪܗܐ. ܘܐܘܕܝܘ ܒܗ ܘܒܪܘܫܐ ܕܐܠܗܘܬܗ. ܘܡܟܝܠ ܕܕܘ ܠܝ ܕܢܫܠܡ ܡܠܬܗ ܕܗܘܝܐ. ܘܐܝܠܝܢ ܕܩܒܠܘ ܡܠܬܗ ܕܡܫܝܚܐ. ܢܗܘܘܢ ܙܗܝܪܝܢ. ܘܐܦ ܐܝܠܝܢ ܕܙܒܢܝܢ ܕܢܬܬܘܣܦܘܢ ܒܗܘܢ ܒܝܠܘܬܐ ܘܡܢ ܢܗܝܪܘܢ ܠܒܬ̈ܝܗܘܢ ܘܥܕ، ܗܟܢܐ ܒܗܕܐ. ܗܘ ܐܕܝ، ܫܠܝܚܐ ܕܫܕܪ ܗܘܐ ܠܘܬ ܐܒܓܪܐ ܕܐܬܩܘܬܐ ܕܡܕܝܢܬܐ ܦܩܕ ܠܗ ܠܗܘܢ. ܘܕܠܐ̈ܢܫܐ ܗܘܘ ܐܝܠܝܢ ܕܠܐ ܡܘܬܘ ܗܘܘ ܒܗܘ ܒܝܘܡܐ ܒܪ ܐܦ ܗܢܘܢ ܕܠܐ̈ܢܫܐ ܒܬܪ ܢܦܫ̈ܬܐ ܡܠܝܠ ܡܛܠ ܗܘܐ ܠܒ̈ܢܝܗܘܢ. ܘܡܫܒܚܝܢ ܗܘܘ ܒܡܫܪܬܐ ܕܒܪܘܢܬܗ ܕܡܫܝܚܐ. ܘܒܬܪ ܐܒܓܪ ܗܘܐ ܡܠܟܐ ܐܕܝ، ܫܠܝܚܐ ܡܪܝ ܠܡ ܒܪܝܐ ܕܐܘܪܗܝ. ܘܫܪܐ ܗܘܐ ܐܒܓܪ ܡܠܟܐ ܕܠܡ̈ܐ ܡܕܝܢܬܐ ܫܕܪ ܗܘܬ ܒܡܠܦܢܘܬܗ ܠܒܝܬܐ ܘܒܫܢܐ ܫܘܐܝܬ ܘܐܡܪܝܢ ܠܗ ܕܫܕܪ ܗܘ ܘܡܫܡܫܝܢ ܡܫܝܚܐ ܕܒܕܪܟ ܠܘܬܟ ܐܦ ܗܘ ܚܕ، ܗܘܐ ܦܠ ܒܗܘܐ ܒܪ ܡܫܝܚ ܗܘܐ ܠܐܠܗܐ. ܕܐܝܟ ܡܢܐ ܕܫܒܩ ܗܘܐ ܡܢ ܚܝ ܦܠܘܛܐ ܕܠܗ ܥܠ ܡܫܝܚܐ ܡܠܟܐ ܚܝܐ ܗܘܐ ܚܝ̈ܠܐ ܬܫܒܘܚܬܐ ܕܒܪܟ ܗܘܐ ܗܘ ܐܕܝ، ܫܠܝܚܐ ܒܫܡܗ ܕܡܫܝܚܐ. ܘܐܡܪ ܠܗ ܐܦ ܗܘ ܐܒܓܪ ܡܠܟܐ ܕܐܝܟ ܡܢܐ ܕܫܠܝܚܘ ܠܗ ܠܡܫܝܚܐ ܒܐܓܪܬ، ܕܠܘܬܗ. ܘܐܝܟ ܡܢܐ ܕܫܠܚ ܠܝ ܐܦ ܗܘ ܡܠܬܗ ܘܐܦ ܡܢܝ ܕܠܝ ܢܦܩܘܢܐ ܡܢܐ ܡܦܢܝܢ ܐܢܐ ܥܠ ܢܦܫ̈ܝ ܚ̈ܝܝ. ܘܒܗܘܢ ܒܫܠܝܢ ܡܦܘܐ ܐܢܐ ܒܪ ܡܫܬܡܗܪ ܐܢܐ ܡܛܠ ܕܐܦ ܚܕ ܐܢܐ ܕܠܗ ܚܝܠܐ

ܐܚܝܕ ܘܡܕܒܪܢܘܢ ܐܝܟ ܕܡܩܒܠ ܡܢ ܡܫܡܫܢܘܬܗ ܕܡܪܢ. ܐܡܪܝܢ
ܚܕ ܘܡܠܟܝܢ ܚܕ ܘܡܫܘܕܝܢ ܚܕ ܕܬܗܘܘܢ ܫܝ̈ܢܝܢ ܘܠܐ ܬܬܦܠܓܘܢ
ܕܘ̈ܬܟܘܢ ܒܠܒܘܢ ܕܫܦܝܘܬܐ. ܡܛܠ ܕܕܚܠ ܠܗ ܢܗܘܪܐ ܫܡܫܐ
ܒܪܝܬܐ. ܘܗܘܘ ܕܙܒܢܐ ܗܘܐ ܠܐܠܗܘܬܐ ܡܕܒ̈ܚܐ ܘܠܟܐܪ̈ܐ
ܘܠܐܝ̈ܠܢܐ. ܘܡܛܠ ܗܘܐ ܒܗܘܢ ܒܟܠܝܢܐ ܕܪܘܚܐ ܕܫܐܕܐ.
ܗܘܘ ܓܝܪ ܐܠܗܐ ܕܒܗܘܪܐ ܕܙܘܩܘܗܝ، ܘܫܘ̈ܩܐ ܢܟܠܐ ܠܗ ܗܘ
ܦܬܓܡ ܐܦ. ܟܕ ܠܐ ܝܕܥܝܢ ܡܛܠ ܕܠܝܬ ܐܠܗܐ ܐܚܪܢܐ ܒܫܡܝܐ
ܘܒܐܪܥܐ ܗܘܐ ܦܠܚܐ. ܠܗ ܬܘܕܝܬܐ ܡܢ ܐܪܒܥ ܦܢܝ̈ܬܗ
ܕܒܪܝܬܐ. ܗܐ ܗܫܐ ܫܡܥ. ܐܕܢ̈ܝܟܘܢ ܡܕܡ ܕܠܐ ܫܡܥܘ.
ܗܘܐ ܠܟܘܢ. ܘܗܐ ܬܘܒ ܚܙܝ ܥܝܢ̈ܝܟܘܢ ܡܕܡ ܕܠܐ ܡܬܚܙܝܢ
ܚܙܐ ܗܘܬ ܠܟܘܢ. ܠܐ ܡܟܝܠ ܬܗܘܘܢ ܦܠܚ̈ܝܐ ܠܒܪ̈ܝܬܐ
ܕܫܝܛܘܢ ܘܡܫܬܥܒܕܘܢ. ܐܦܢܘ ܗܟܝܠ ܦܢ̈ܝܟܘܢ ܡܕܘܪܐ
ܕܐܠܗܘܬܟܘܢ. ܘܦܪܘ ܢܦܫܟܘܢ ܡܢ ܚܛܐ ܕܚܛܝܬܐ ܕܡܢܚܠܐ
ܠܟܠܟܘܢ ܒܢܘܗܝ ܘܒܪܝܚܐ ܕܒܕܡ ܬܠܝܐ. ܘܢܬܡܛܠ ܠܟܘܢ
ܥܠ ܫܢܝ̈ܟܘܢ ܐܚܪܢܐ ܘܟܠ ܡܕܡ ܕܒܥܘܢ ܒܟܠܝܠܐ. ܘܗܘܐ
ܙܒܢܐ ܚܕܬܐ ܗܘ ܕܗܘܐ ܠܟܘܡܪ̈ܐ ܘܠܐ ܠܟܘܡܪ̈ܐ. ܗܘ ܕܢܦܠ
ܒܗ ܝܠܕܐ ܕܒܬܘܠܬܐ ܘܕܫܪܪܐ ܕܐܒܐ ܘܕܒܪܐ ܘܕܪܘܚܐ
ܕܩܘܕܫܐ ܟܕ ܬܗܡܢܘܢ ܘܬܬܒܪܘܢ ܒܥܒܕ̈ܝܗܐ ܬܠܝܬܝܐ
ܘܡܥܡܘܕܝܬܐ. ܗܕܐ ܗܝ ܓܝܪ ܡܠܦܢܘܬܢ ܘܒܪܘܪܘܬܢ. ܠܐ ܗܘܐ
ܓܝܪ ܒܦܩܕܢܘܬܐ ܡܬܗܝܡܢ ܫܪܪܗ ܕܡܫܝܚܐ. ܘܐܝܠܝܢ ܕܝܕܥܝܢ
ܕܢܬܦܠܚܘܢ ܠܡܫܝܚܐ. ܝܕܥܝܢ ܐܢܘܢ ܕܒܢܝܢܐ ܦܩܕ̈ܢܬܐ
ܬܠܝܬ ܟܠ ܡܕܡ̈ܝܢ ܕܬܬܐܠܦܘܢ ܘܬܬܒܝܢܘܢ ܒܡܕܡ ܕܥܒܕܝܢ
ܐܢܬܘܢ. ܘܐܚܝܕ ܚܕܐ ܒܗܕܐ ܐܝܟ ܐܒܪܐ ܕܚܕܐ ܒܫܘܠܡܗ
ܟܝܢܬܐ ܘܐܠܗܐ ܢܬܒܥ ܒܬܫܡܫܬܟܘܢ ܕܠܘܬܗ. ܟܕ ܐܢܬܘܢ
ܚܝܝܢ ܐܢܬܘܢ ܒܗܕܐ. ܐܦ ܐܚܝܕ ܕܡܠܟܝܢ ܚܕ ܠܟܘܢ ܗܕܐ.
ܠܐ ܡܬܦܠܓܝܢ ܐܦܢܐ ܟܝܢܬܐ ܕܗܕܐ. ܘܡܛܠ ܕܬܦܠ ܐܢܫܐ
ܕܗܘܝܬܘܢ ܐܚܪܢܐ ܟܝܢܬܐ ܐܝܟ ܒܢܝܢܗ ܕܡܪܢܐ ܡܫܝܚܐ.

ܫܘܠܛܢܐ ܕܟܗܢܘܬܐ ܡܢ ܪܗܘܡܐ. ܘܠܐ ܗܘܐ ܒܒܝܕ ܐܢܫܐ
ܐܓܠܪ، ܗܘܐ ܐܦ ܛܘܟܣܐ ܕܗܝܟܠܐ ܕܫܘܕܥܐ ܡܢ ܙܒܢ ܠܙܒܢ.
ܐܠܐ ܒܗܘ ܕܐܡܪ ܗܘܐ ܠܗܘܢ ܕܗܐ ܥܒܝܕ ܒܟܬܒܗܘܢ ܢܒܝܐ.
ܗܐ ܓܝܪ ܐܦ ܠܐ ܢܕܥܘ ܗܢܘܢ ܕܘܟܝܗ، ܕܟܝܢܗ ܗܘܐ ܕܐܠܗܐ
ܠܐ ܚܘܪܒܐ ܕܡܕܝܢܬܗܘܢ ܡܚܪܒ ܗܘܘ. ܐܦܠܐ ܗܘܐ ܐܟܠ
ܢܦܫܗܘܢ ܘܗܐ ܡܦܠܓܝܢ ܗܘܘ. ܐܦܠܐ ܓܝܪ ܐܠܘ ܝܕܥܘ ܗܘܘ
ܕܢܗܦܟܘܢ ܡܢ ܗܕܐ ܬܘܕܝܬܐ: ܢܣܒܘ ܗܘܘ ܠܗܘܢ ܓܘܢܚܐ
ܕܫܢ̈ܝܐ ܕܗܘܘ ܒܗܘ ܒܙܢܐ. ܗܐ ܓܝܪ ܐܦ ܡܢ ܒܢ̈ܝܗܘܢ
ܕܩ̈ܘܦܐ ܒܒܢܝܢ ܢܘܡܒܠܐ ܒܪ̈ܘܪܐ ܘܡܗܡ̈ܢܐ ܒܡ ܒ̈ܠܝܫܐ
ܫܒ̈ܪ، ܒܟܠܗ ܐܪܥܐ ܕܦܠܣܛܝܢܐ. ܘܟܢܫ ܥܒܪ̈ܝܐ ܘܟܠܗ
ܐܬܪܐ ܕܦܠܫ̈ܬܝܐ. ܘܫܦܠܝܢ ܦܬܓ̈ܡܐ ܕܣܢܘܬܐ. ܘܡܬܢܘܪ
ܘܡܟܝܢ ܕܡܥܝܢܐ. ܘܡܥܕܝܢ ܒܫ̈ܡܥܐ ܘܒܪ̈ܝܬܐ ܒܐܠܗܐ.
ܕܗܘܐ ܒܪ ܐܢܫܐ.. ܐܦ ܚܝܬ ܒܕ ܐܬܘܗܝ، ܗܘܐ ܒܐܪܬܐ
ܢܦܩ ܡܢ ܗܝܡܢܘܬܗܘܢ ܗܢܘܢ ܒܗ ܕܟܝܢܗ ܗܘ ܕܐܠܗܐ
ܘܥܒܕ ܕܬܥܒܕܘܢ ܗܝܡܢܘܬܗܘܢ ܡܠܬܐ ܕܒܪܘܝܗ ܐܘܕܝܘ ܒܗ
ܕܐܠܗܐ ܗܘ. ܗܟܢܐ ܕܦܠܘ ܠܘܬ ܐܟܡܐ، ܘܚܙܝܬܘܢ ܐܬܘ̈ܬܐ.
ܘܬܕܡܪ̈ܬܐ ܕܗܘܝ ܒܫܡܗ. ܘܡܠܬܐ ܕܟܪܘܙܘܬܗ ܫܡܥܬܘܢ
ܒܐܕܢ̈ܝܗܘܢ ܠܐ ܐܝܟ ܡܕܡ ܢܦܠܛ ܒܪܝܫܗ ܐܝܟ ܕܢܦܘܩ
ܠܬܘܟܠܢܗܘܢ ܥܘܕܪܢܐ ܕܟܒܪܬܗ ܕܫܠܝܚ ܠܗܘܢ. ܕܐܦܩܘܗ̈ܝ
ܕܗܝܡܢܘܬܗܘܢ ܒܝ ܒܪ ܠܐ ܫܬܦܘܢ. ܘܡܛܠ ܕܗܒܢܐ ܗܝܡܢܘܬܗܘܢ
ܟܕ ܚܙܒܐ ܕܒܡܪܝܡ ܐܢܬܘܢ ܒܗ ܢܗܘܐ ܒܪܝܟ ܘܡܠܒܒܢܐ
ܠܐ ܢܬܦܠܓ ܒܗ ܠܒܟܘܢ. ܠܐ ܗܘܝܬ ܬܦܫܘܢ ܡܢ ܗܝܡܢܘܬܗ
ܕܗܐ ܥܡܕܬܘܢ ܘܚܬܡܬܘܢ ܐܝܟ ܦܘܩܕܢܗ ܠܗܝܡܢܘܬܗ ܕܒܪܐ
ܗܘ ܦܓܪܐ ܘܐܠܗܐ ܗܘ ܡܫܝܚܐ. ܘܡܠܟܐ ܗܘ ܕܒܪܐ ܘܫܠܝܐ
ܗܘ ܬܘܡܟܐ. ܘܒܡܫܝܚܘܬܗ ܗܘ ܡܫܡܫ ܐܝܟ ܦܢܐ ܒܢ̈ܝܐ
ܕܪܚܡܝܢ ܫܪܪܐ ܘܡܬܒܥܝܢ ܕܟܠ ܦܡ ܕܡܠܟ ܠܒܪ̈ܝܬܐ ܪܘܓܙܐ
ܕܟܐܢܘܬܐ ܡܕܝܢ ܠܗ ○○○○ ܫܠܡܬ ܓܝܪ ܕܐܡܪܝܢ

ܗܘ ܕܒܪܢܫܘܬܐ ܗܘܐ ܢܘܗܪܐ ܠܟܠܗܘܢ ܒܢܝܢܫܐ. ܘܒܗܘ ܒܢܝܢܐ ܡܬܚܝܢܝܢ ܕܒܪܢܫܘܗܝ ܒܫܘܠܡܗܘܢ. ܘܗܘܝܢ ܦܬܓܡܘܗܝ ܡܬܠܐ ܠܬܠܡܝܕܘܬܐ ܕܟܐܢܘܬܐ ܘܠܝܬ ܬܡܢ ܕܠܐ ܢܕܥ ܫܦܝܪܐ. ܡܛܠ ܕܟܠܢ ܒܬܫܒܚܬܐ ܕܫܘܦܪܗ ܗܘܐ ܡܪܐ * * *

* * * * *

* * * * *

ܐܢܬܘܢ ܕܐܡܪܬ ܠܟܘܢ܆ ܒܝܢܐ ܒܗܘ ܕܠܐ ܡܬܚܝܒܝܢ ܐܢܬܘܢ ܗܘܝܬܘܢ ܠܟܘܢ ܐܦ. ܐܢܬܘܢ ܐܟܘܬܗܘܢ ܕܠܐ ܚܙܝܢ ܘܠܐ ܫܡܥܝܢ ܘܐܝܟܢܐ ܗܘ ܬܫܡܫܝܢ ܘܠܗܘܢ ܣܓܕܝܢ ܠܐܒܕܢܐ ܢܦܫܬܐ. ܒܪ ܗܘܢ ܠܐ ܒܪܫܝܢ ܒܗܘ ܕܠܐ ܫܡܥܝܢ ܡܛܠ ܕܒܝܢܐ ܐܢܘܢ ܢܦܫܐ ܘܥܬܝܕܐ ܒܥܠܝܐ ܕܝܢ ܕܦܪܫܬܐ ܒܗ ܒܐܝܢܘܬܐ ܕܠܟܘܢ ܗܘ ܕܠܐ ܝܕܥܝܢ ܐܢܬܘܢ ܕܬܬܚܝܒܘܢ. ܐܝܟܢܐ ܒܗܢܐ ܥܕܡ ܕܣܝܡ ܐܢܬܘܢ. ܠܐ ܓܝܪ ܫܒܩܐ ܠܟܘܢ ܒܪܥܠܐ ܕܬܦܩܘܢ ܕܡܪܒܝܐ ܥܠ ܐܪܥܟܘܢ ܕܬܫܡܥܘܢ ܢܗܘܪܐ ܫܡܝܢܝܐ ܕܐܠܗܘܬܗ، ܒܗܢܐ ܕܐܬܚܙܝ. ܒܪܘܚܐ ܡܛܠ ܗܢܝܢ ܒܫ̈ܢܝܐ ܘܒ̈ܪܢܫܐ ܐܝܟ ܕܐܬܚܙܝ ܠܟܘܢ ܕܒܥܠܡܐ ܗܘ ܒܠܝܠܘܢ ܡܬܚܙܝܢ ܐܠܗ̈ܐ ܒܪ ܠܗ ܐ̈ܠܗܐ ܐܢܘܢ ܒܫܝܢܘܗܝ ܘܐܬܒܪܝܘ ܠܝܬ ܗܘܝܐ ܕܒܢܝܢܗ ܐܠܗܐ ܐܢܬܘܢ، ܗܘܐ. ܡܢ ܡܬܘܡ ܘܡܢ ܟܠܡ. ܘܠܐ ܗܘܐ ܒܪܢܐ ܗܘ ܐܝܟ ܦܬܟܪ̈ܝܗܘܢ ܘܐܦ ܠܐ ܒܪܢܫܬܐ ܗܘ ܘܬܘܡܢܐ. ܐܝܟ ܨܠܡ̈ܐ ܗܠܝܢ ܕܡܬܚܫܒܝܢ ܐܢܬܘܢ ܒܗܘܢ. ܡܛܠ ܕܐܦ ܠܒܪ ܦܓܪܐ ܗܢܐ ܐܠܗܐ ܐܢܬܘܢ، ܒܪ ܐܟܘܬܗܘܢ. ܒܪ̈ܢܫܐ ܓܝܪ ܕܐܬܒܢܝ ܗܘ، ܒܡܠܠܗ ܘܐܬܬܪܝܨ ܗܘ، ܒܚܫܐ ܕܒܚܘܬܗ. ܗܢܝܢ ܦܘܢ̈ܝ ܕܗܘܘ ܐܠܗܐ ܒܪܘܚܐ. ܠܐ ܗܘܐ ܓܝܪ ܚܠܦ ܒܪܢܫܐ ܕܡܢ ܐܪܥܐ. ܐܠܐ ܚܠܦ ܗܘ ܕܢܦܠ ܗܘܐ ܐܪܥܐ ܥܠ ܡܢ̈ܝܐ ܘܠܐ ܗܘܐ ܚܠܦ ܒܪܢܫܐ ܚܫܝܟ ܗܘܐ ܫܒܝܥܐ ܒܥܒܕܐ. ܐܠܐ ܚܠܦ ܗܘ ܕܚܒܒ ܗܘܐ ܢܗܘܪܐ ܙܘܥܐ ܘܠܐ ܗܘܐ ܒܒܪ ܐܢܫܐ ܐܬܚܫܒܘ ܗܘܘ ܒܐܬܪ̈ܐ ܘܕܝ̈ܢܐ. ܐܠܐ ܒܗܘ ܕܝܕܥ. ܗܘܐ

ܠܫܘܠܡܢܐ ܕܡܫܘܬܗܘܢ܂ ܐܦ ܟܕ ܠܐ ܡܪܝܡ ܗܘܘܬܘܢ
ܒܒܝܬܐ ܕܢܫܡܗ ܕܡܫܝܚܢܐ ܐܠܐ ܒܫܒܥܐ ܕܢܫܦܩ ܗܘܐ
ܘܢܫܬܘܢ ܠܗܘܢ ܘܐܬܒܝܐܘ ܥܠ ܦܠܘܛܐ ܐܝܟ ܕܗܘܐ ܒܗܘܢ
ܟܝܢܐ ܕܐܦܣܩܘܦܘܬܗ ܕܗܘ ܕܢܣܒ ܗܘܐ ܦܪܝܬܗ ܒܒܝܠܗ ܐܪ̈ܟܐ
ܒܐܬܪ̈ܬܐ ܕܒܒܝܢ ܠܛܝܡܘܬܐܘܣ܂ ܘܚܙܝܢ ܒܒܝܠܗ ܐܪ̈ܟܐ.
ܘܐܠܝܢ ܕܒܒܪܬܐ ܗܘܘ ܘܠܫܒܐ ܗܘ ܕܒܒܪ̈ܬܐ ܕܠܒܝܢ ܗܘܘ ܒܗ
ܕܒܝܢ ܗܘܘ ܒܠܫܗ ܗܐ ܫܡܝܢܐ ܡܫܠܠܝܢ ܒܟܠ ܠܒ̈ܢܝܢ ܕܫܡܝܢܘ
ܐܘܫܥܐ ܘܫܡܝܢܘ ܐܝܟ ܡܪ̈ܝܢܐ ܕܗܘܘ ܒܠܒܠ ܠܒ̈ܢܐ ܕܒ̈ܝܢܐ
ܒܫܘܬܐ ܗܕܐ ܕܡܕܝܢ܂ ܘܗܘܘ ܡܠܦ ܒܐܢܕ ܫܡܝܢܐ
ܡܫܝܚܘܬܐ ܕܦܘܠܘܛܐ ܘܕܙܘ̈ܐ ܒܣܝܢ̈ܪܐ ܘܪ̈ܘܐ ܕܡܢ ܠܠܠܐ
ܕܦܠܘܦܝܢܐ. ܐܦ ܐܢܐ ܟܕ ܕܫܡܥܬ ܠܝ ܡܢ ܦܪܐܘܣ ܐܢܬ،
ܡܢ ܐܬܪ ܕܢܦܩ ܢܛܪܝܢ ܢܘܪܐ ܘܐܬܛܠܩܬ ܒܗ ܣܒܪ̈ ܕܐܘܗܝ
ܒܪܘܪܐ * * * * *

* * * * *

* * * * *

ܐܢܐ ܟܕ ܐܝܟ ܕܦܩܕ ܠܝ ܡܪܝ ܗܐ ܡܫܕܪ ܐܢܐ ܘܡܫܕܪ ܐܢܐ
ܘܫܡܫܘ ܟܠ ܦܬܓܡܐ ܗܢܐ ܐܢܐ ܠܒܘܒܢܐ. ܘܐܙܠܐ
ܕܡܠܟܘܬܗ ܘܪܒ ܐܢܐ ܒܐܪ̈ܟܐ ܕܡܠܟܐ ܘܐܟܠܝ ܕܝܒܝܢ ܕܢܡܠܠ
ܕܠܗܘܢ ܗܘ ܦܘܪܥܢܐ ܠܟܠܐ ܕܒܪܘܟܬܐ. ܘܐܟܠܝ ܕܠܐ
ܡܬܦܫܩܝܢ ܠܗ ܕܬܟܠ ܥܠܝ ܐܢܐ ܟܠܗܘܢ ܐܝܟ ܕܐܦܩܪ ܠܝ.
ܬܘܒ ܡܫܠ ܡܬܒܪ ܡܢ ܐܘܪܫܬܐ ܒܢܗ̈ܝܪܐ ܘܡܢ ܒܒ̈ܪܐ ܩ̈ܕܝܫܐ.
ܘܐܬܒܝܐܘ ܠܗܬܗ ܒܝܬܝܐ ܠܟܠܐ ܘܥܡܪܐ. ܐܝܟ ܕܐܬܒܝܢ ܗܘ
ܠܬܒܢܘܢ ܒܫܝܢܐ ܕܢܫܡܘܗܝ ܒܬܪܐ. ܘܠܐ ܬܗܘܘܢ ܐܝܟ
ܕܪܐ ܡܕ̈ܝܢܐ ܕܒܪܘ. ܕܡܠܠ ܕܡܫܘ ܗܘܘ ܙܒܢܗܘܢ ܡܢ
ܕܫܠܡܗ ܕܐܠܗܐ ܡܟܠܘ ܗܘܘ ܡܫܡܫ ܒܪ̈ܝܐ ܠܥܠܡܬ. ܕܗܢܘܢ
ܬܐܪ̈ܘܢ ܗܘܘ. ܘܐܟܠܝ ܕܐܬܝܢ ܒܬܪ̈ܘܢ ܢܘܚܒܘܢ ܘܢܫܠܡܘܢ.
ܟܠܗ ܟܕ ܕܐܬܐ ܡܪܢ ܠܥܠܡܐ. ܕܠܗ ܘܣܗܕܝܢ ܕܒܥܠܡܐ

ܕܟܠܗ ܒܝܪܚܐ ܐܝܪ ܗܘܬ ܘܫܢܬ ܒܬܫܡܫܬܗ ܕܡܘܬ
ܚܠܦ. ܠܦܘܪܩܢܐ ܕܟܠܗܘܢ ܒ̈ܢܝ ܐܢܫܐ. ܘܐܫܬܟܚ ܗܘܐ ܡܕܡ
ܐܒܓܪ ܡܠܟܐ ܘܡܕܡ ܪܘܪ̈ܒܢܘܗܝ ܘܫܐܪ̈ܘܗܝ. ܘܡܕܡ ܐܓܠܘܦܣ
ܐܚܘܗ ܕܐܒܓܪ. ܘܡܕܡ ܫܠܡܬ ܒܪܬ ܡܗܪܕܬ ܐܢܬܬܗ ܕܐܒܓܪ.
ܐܬ̈ܘܬܗ ܕܡܪܢ ܘܬܕܡܪ̈ܬܗ ܘܚܝ̈ܠܐ ܫܒܝܚܐ ܕܥܒܕ ܗܘܐ.
ܘܚ̈ܝܘܗܝ ܐܠܗܝ̈ܐ. ܘܫܘܠܡܗ ܕܠܘܬ ܐܒܘܗܝ. ܘܕܐܝܟܢܐ ܡܚܠ
ܗܘܘ ܚܝܠܐ ܘܫܘܠܛܢܐ. ܘܒܝܕܝܐ ܗ̇ܘ ܕܐܬܚܙܝ ܗܘܐ. ܕܒܗ
ܗܘ ܒܗ̇ܘ ܚܝܠܐ ܐܣܝܗ ܗܘܐ ܠܐܒܓܪ. ܘܠܥܒܕܘ ܒܪ ܥܒܕܘ
ܬܪܝܢܐ ܕܡܠܟܘܬܗ. ܘܐܝܟܢܐ ܐܘܕܥ ܐܢܘܢ ܕܡܬܟܠܐ ܠܫܪܪܐ
ܕܒ̈ܢܝܐ. ܘܡܫܠܡܢܐ ܕܒܪ̈ܝܬܐ ܟܠܗܝܢ. ܘܠܫܘܒܚܐ ܘܡܘܕܝܬܐ
ܕܡܬܝܗܒܐ ܕܬܗܘܐ ܠܟܠܗܘܢ ܒ̈ܢܝ ܐܢܫܐ. ܘܦܘܪܫܢܐ ܕܗܘܐ ܒܝܬ
ܐܡ̈ܪܐ ܠܕ̈ܝܒܐ. ܘܒܝܬ ܡܣܟ̈ܢܐ ܠܥܬܝܪ̈ܐ. ܘܐܡܪ ܗܘܐ
ܠܗܘܢ: ܕܡܛܠ ܕܬܪܥܐ ܕܚ̈ܝܐ ܦܬܝܚܐ ܗܘ. ܘܐܘܪܚܐ ܕܫܪܪܐ
ܐܠܝܨܐ ܗܝ. ܡܛܠ ܗܢܐ ܕܠܬܠܐ ܐܢܘܢ ܡܗܝܡ̈ܢܐ ܕܡܫܬܘܬܐ.
ܘܟܕ ܕܡܥܘܪܐ ܢܣܒ ܗܘ ܕܘܦܠܢܐ. ܡܛܠ ܗܢܐ ܦܬ̈ܚܝܢ
ܐܢܘܢ ܬܪ̈ܥܐ ܕܡܦܬܚܝܢ ܠܫܪܪܐ. ܐܠܐ ܠܐ ܓܝܪ ܡܛܠ ܕܐܝܬ
ܫܪܪܐ ܦܬܚܐ ܠܐܢܫܐ ܡܗܝܡܢܐ. ܠܐ ܢܦܩܬ ܗܘܐ ܡܢܗ ܡܢ
ܥܩܒܝܐ. ܘܐܬܐ ܗܘܐ ܠܠܒܐ ܘܠܫܝܢܐ ܕܡܗܝܡܢܐ. ܘܐܬܐ ܗܘܐ.
ܘܠܐ ܕܠܐ ܡܥܕܪ ܗܘܐ.

* * *

* * * * *

---

* * * * *

ܕܡܫܝܚܘܬܐ ܕܡܟܪܙܢܘܢ ܕܐܠܗܐ ܐܕܝܘܣ * * * ܫܠܡܘ
ܒ̈ܢܝ ܐܢܫܐ. ܘܗܘ ܐܝܬ ܐܠܗܝܢ ܕܠܐ ܝܕܥܝܢ ܕܢܬܦܠܚܘܢ
ܠܟܠܝܢ ܗܠܝܢ. ܢܦܪܫܘܢ ܝܐܝܕܝܢ ܘܢܚܠܘܢ ܠܗ ܡܢܗ ܕܒܝܫܘܢ.
ܕܐܒܘܬܗ ܕܒܪܘܢܐ * ܬܪܥܝܬܗܘܢ ܢܦܪܫ ܫܡܥܐ ܡܫܐܘܠܐ

ܘܐܘܦܝܗ ܗܘܐ. ܘܬܘܒ ܠܐ ܗܘܬ ܠܗ ܦܠܓܘܬܐ. ܘܐܦ
ܒܡܕܝܢܬܐ ܟܠܗ̇ ܐܬ̈ܘܬܐ ܪܘܪ̈ܒܬܐ ܡܬܚܙܝܐ ܗܘܐ. ܘܣܓܝ̈ܐܐ
ܬܟܝ̈ܠܐ ܒܢܦܫܐ ܗܘܘ ܒܗ̇. ܐܡܪ ܠܗ ܐܒܘܢ ܗܟܢܐ ܕܐܦ
ܥܠ ܐܝܟ ܕܒܚܝܠܗ ܕܡܫܝܚܐ ܡܥܒܕܢܐ ܗܠܝܢ ܬܕܡܪ̈ܬܐ ܥܒܕ ܐܢܬ.
ܘܗܘܐ ܬܡܝܗܝܢ ܐܢܫܝܢ ܒܥܒ̈ܕܝܟ. ܒܚܝܠܐ ܗܘܝܠ ܡܢܟ.
ܕܬܬܥܒܕܢ ܠܝ ܥܠ ܡܛܠܬܗ ܕܡܫܝܚܐ. ܐܝܟܢܐ ܗܘܬ. ܘܥܠ
ܚܝܠܗ ܕܡܫܝܚܐ. ܘܥܠ ܬܕܡܪ̈ܬܐ ܕܢܬܥܒܕ ܗܘܐ ܠܝ ܕܐܒܕ ܗܘܐ.
ܐܝܠܝܢ ܕܐܝܬ ܠܘܬ ܐܢܝ: ܒܡܬܠܬܒܪܐ ܕܚܙܝܢ. ܐܡܪ ܠܗ ܐܒ̈ܐ܆
ܡܢ ܗܕܐ ܠܐ ܬܕܘܩ ܐܢܬ. ܕܐܡܪ. ܡܛܠ ܗܢܐ ܗܘ ܠܒܪ
ܐܬܬܪܝܪܬ ܠܗܪܟܐ. ܕܐܡܪ ܘܐܙܠ ܠܟܠ ܡܢ ܕܓܒܐ ܕܢܦܫܟ
ܐܡܘܬܟ. ܠܡܦܪܫ ܒܝܢ ܠܝ ܒܡܠܝ̈ ܒܪܘܚܢܬܐ. ܘܐܙܪܘܒ ܒܗ̇
ܡܠܬܐ ܕܚܝ̈ܐ. ܒܪܘܪܘܬܐ ܕܡܟܝܪ: ܐܝܟ ܐ ܕܥܡܗ̈ܘܢ: ܥܠ
ܡܬܬܗܘܐ ܕܡܫܝܚܐ. ܐܝܟܢܐ ܗܘܬ. ܘܥܠ ܥܠܝܗ ܕܐܠܗܐ
ܘܐܝܟܢܐ ܥܠܝܗ ܗܘܐ. ܘܥܠ ܚܝܠܗ ܘܒܥܘܕܪܗ ܬܡܝܗܐ. ܘܥܠ
ܐܙܠܐ ܥܕܡܐ ܕܡܬܬܗܘܐ. ܐܝܠܝܢ ܕܝܠܠ ܗܘܐ ܒܠܠܒܐ. ܘܥܠ
ܫܘܬܦܘܬܐ ܕܪܘܚܘܬܗ. ܘܐܝܟܢܐ ܘܡܛܠ ܡܢܐ ܐܙܪ ܗܘܐ
ܢܦܫܗ. ܘܐܡܪܢ ܗܘܐ ܐܠܗܘܬܗ ܡܪܝܡܬܐ. ܒܐܝܢܘܬܐ ܕܥܠ
ܗܘܐ. ܘܐܙܕܗܦ ܗܘܐ ܘܢܦܩ ܗܘܐ ܠܒܪ ܡܢܬܐ. ܘܬܪܒ ܗܘܐ
ܦܓܪܐ. ܗܘ ܕܡܢ ܡܬܘܡ ܠܐ ܐܬܬܪܒ ܗܘܐ. ܘܐܝܟ ܗܘܐ
ܬܢܬܐ ܒܦܓܠܗ. ܘܢܦܩ ܗܘܐ ܠܥܘܕܪܗ. ܘܦܠܓ ܗܘܐ ܒܡ
ܦܓܪܐ ܠܘܬ ܐܒܗܘܗܝ ܡܫܝܚܐ. ܗܘ ܕܒܗ ܐܝܬܘܗܝ ܗܘܐ
ܡܢ ܡܬܘܡ ܒܚܕܐ ܐܠܗܘܬܐ ܡܪܝܡܬܐ. ܘܟܕ ܗܘܐ ܐܒܘܢ
ܕܢܬܠܘܢ ܠܐܒ̈ܐ܆ ܒܥܘܢܐ ܘܕܡܘܟܐ. ܐܡܪ ܠܗ ܐܒ̈ܐ܆ ܐܝܟܢܐ
ܡܫܟܚܝܢ ܐܢܫܝܢ ܢܣܒܝܢ ܐܢܫܝܢ ܡܕܡ ܕܠܐ ܕܝܠܗ ܗܘ. ܕܗܐ ܡܕܡ
ܕܕܝܠܝ ܗܘܐ ܫܒܩܬܘܗܝ. ܐܝܟ ܕܐܬܦܩܕܬ ܡܢ ܡܪܢ. ܕܕܝܠܟ
ܒܥܩܐ ܘܕܠܐ ܬܬܒܥܐ. ܒܪ ܕܚܝܠ ܐܢܫܝܢ ܕܡܣܒܐ ܥܠ
ܡܬܦ̈ܬܐ. ܐܬܦܩܕܢ ܕܢܬܪ ܦܪܘܬܗ ܒܟܠܗ̇ ܒܪܝܬܐ. ܗܘ

ܚܝܠܗ ܘܬܫ̈ܒܚܬܗ. ܘܥܠ ܐܘ̈ܪܚܐ ܕܗܠܟ ܒܗܠܟܘܬܗ. ܘܒܐܝܕܐ ܚܝܠܐ ܗܠܝܢ ܥܒܕ ܗܘܐ. ܘܥܠ ܒܝܘܬܗ ܢܗܪܬܐ ܘܥܠ ܕܘܪܫܬܗ ܘܡܠܟܘܬܗ. ܘܕܐܝܟܢܐ ܡܢܝܢ ܘܩܪܘ ܘܐܘܟܪ ܢܦܫܗ ܘܐܫܬܠܒ ܘܢܦܫܗ ܠܚܒܠ. ܘܩܪ̈ܒܐ ܗܕܝܐ ܕܡܢ ܟܠܗ ܠܐ ܐܬܩܪ̈ܒ ܘܐܘܣܦ ܡܬܒܪܬܐ. ܘܢܚܬ ܠܫܝܘܠ. ܘܣܠܩ ܒܥܢܢܐ ܫܡܝܢܐ ܠܘܬ ܐܒܘܗܝ ⁘ ⁘

ܒܬܪ ܗܠܝܢ ܐܡܪ ܕܢܦܩܘܢ ܬܠܡܝ̈ܕܘܗܝ ܟܠܗܘܢ ܒ̈ܢܝ ܡܕܝܢܬܗ. ܘܢܫܡܥܘܢ ܒܪܘܟܬܗ ܕܐܕܝ. ܘܟܕ ܗܘܢ ܒܬܪ ܕܢܦܩܘ ܠܗ ܕܡܘܬܐ ܘܗܘܐ ܗܘ. ܘܗܘ ܕܝܢ ܠܐ ܩܒܠ. ܘܐܡܪ. ܐܢܫܘ ܕܕܠܗ ܥܒܕܝܢ ܐܚܪܢܐ ܢܣܒ ܕܐܢܫܝ̈ܢܐ ⁘ ܐܬܗܘܕܥ ܗܠܝܢ ܒܫܢܬ ܬܠܬܝܢ ܘܐܪܒܥ. ܕܠܐ ܕܝܢ ܗܘܐ ܒܝܘܡܐ ܢܝܫ ܗܠܝܢ ܒܟܠ ܡܬܠܒܢܐ ܡܢ ܐܪܥܐ. ܒܝܘܡܗܘܢ ܐܬܬܗܘܡ ܗܘܐ ⁘ ⁘ ⁘

ܫܠܡ ܗܦܟܐ ܘܕܡܐ

ܡܠܦܢܘܬܐ ܕܐܕܝ ܫܠܝܚܐ

* * * * *

* * * * *

ܠܗ ܐܕܝ. ܡܛܠ ܕܗܘܐ ܗܘܐ ܡܫܝܚܐ ܐܝܟ ܕܐܡܪ ܐܕܝ ܠܒܝܬ.
ܒܫܢܬ ܕܗܘ(ܬ) ܕܗܘܬ ܡܬܚܙܝܐ ܒܗ(ܡܫܝܚܐ) ܘܒܗ ܒܫܢܬܐ ܕܗܝ ܗܘܐ Phil.
ܐܝܟ ܕܠܗܘܢ. ܐܬܐܘܗܝ، ܡܢ ܢܘܗܪܐ ܕܫܡܝܐ ܕܐܝܬ ܗܘܐ ܠܗ
ܢܛܪܐ. ܘܬܡܢ ܗܘܐ ܐܟܪܙ ܘܐܬܬܕܒܪ. ܕܐܝܟܢܐ ܕܥܒܕ
ܗܘܐ ܠܗ. ܟܠ ܚܘܒܐ ܕܟܪܙ ܗܘܐ ܘܡܫܠܡܢܘܬܐ. ܗܟܢܐ ܘܐܦ
ܗܘ ܐܕܝ ܕܠܐ ܗܡܢܐ ܕܟܕܪ ܡܫܠܡܢܘܬܐ ܗܘܐ. ܒܫܢܬܗ ܕܫܢܬ.
ܘܐܦ ܠܒܝܬܐ ܒܪ ܒܝܬܐ ܦܠܛܪܐ ܐܬܬ ܗܘܐ ܠܗ ܒܪܓܠܗܘܢ.
ܘܐܦ ܗܘ ܡܪܝ ܗܘܐ ܠܗ ܪ̈ܓܠܘܗܝ. ܘܗܘ ܗܘܐ ܐܝܕܐ ܒܠܚܘܕ

ܘܢܬܠ ܠܝ ܚܝܠܐ. ܘܬܘܒ ܚܟܝܡܐ ܘܐܡܪ. ܡܛܠ ܕܙܘܪܒܐܝܬ
ܡܒܟܝܬ ܒܗ ܒܗܘ ܕܚܠܝܠ. ܡܛܠ ܗܢܐ ܐܙܕܠܚܬ ܠܗܬܝ.
ܘܬܘܒ ܐܦ ܬܗܘܝܢ ܒܗ ܢܗܘܐ ܠܝ ܫܐܠܬܗ ܕܠܒܝ. ܘܗܘ
ܐܡܪ ܐܡܪ ܠܗ. ܕܗܢܐ ܠܟ ܡܫܬܒܩ ܒܗ. ܐܝܟܢܐ ܕܐܦ
ܠܬܘܕܝܐ ܫܘܝܐ ܕܢܠܒܘܗܝ ܒܢܝܬ ܕܐܝܟܢ ܚܝܠܐ ܘܐܚܪܘܒ
ܐܘܝ. ܐܠܐ ܠܐ ܕܐܬܚܢܢܬ ܡܛܠ ܡܠܟܘܬܐ ܕܫܘܡܠܝܐ.
ܘܬܘܒ ܐܡܪ. ܡܢ ܝܕܥܬ ܕܐܒܘܗܝ ܫܡܠܐ. ܘܒܕ ܫܡܠ
ܐܬܒܠ ܠܘܬ ܐܒܘܗܝ. ܐܡܪ ܠܗ ܐܒܘܢ. ܐܦ ܐܢܐ ܡܫܬܒܩܬ
ܒܗ ܘܒܐܒܘܗܝ. ܘܬܘܒ ܐܡܪ. ܡܛܠܡܢܐ ܫܐܠ ܐܢܐ ܠܠܒܝ
ܐܝܟ ܒܝܫܐ. ܘܒܕ ܒܥܕ ܗܕܐ. ܡܣܝܒܐ ܐܬܐܘ، ܡܢ ܒܘܪܗܢ
ܘܡܢ ܒܐܒܝܐ ܕܐܝܬ ܗܘܐ ܠܗ. ܘܐܬܕܟܪ ܐܒܘܢ. ܕܐܝܟ
ܕܫܒܝܒ ܗܘܐ ܠܗ ܒܠ ܢܦܫ ܡܒܝܐ ܚܝܐ ܒܒܝܬܐ ܒܝܬ ܗܕܐ،
ܬܠܡܝܕܘܗܝ. ܕܕܠܐ ܡܫܒܚܢܐ ܘܡܘܪܝܐ ܐܘܫܝ. ܠܐ ܕܝܢ ܠܗ
ܒܠܚܘܕ. ܐܠܐ ܐܦ ܠܟܠܗܘܢ ܒܢ ܒܝܬܗ ܕܐܝܬ ܗܘܐ ܠܗ
ܦܘܪܩܢܐ. ܕܐܦ ܗܘ ܓܠ ܘܢܦܠ ܒܠ ܬܠܡܝܕܘܗܝ. ܘܒܕ ܓܠ
ܠܠܗܘܢ، ܐܬܐܘ. ܘܠܐܚܪܢܐ ܦܠܚܐ ܒܬ ܡܕܝܢܬܗܘܢ
ܐܘܝ. ܘܒܬܪ ܗܘܐ ܕܘܪܒܬܐ ܘܡܒܕܪ ܡܠܬܐ ܕܐܠܗܐ ܀ ܒܬܪ
ܗܠܝܢ ܐܡܪ ܠܗ ܐܒܘܢ. ܐܢܬ ܗܕܝܢ. ܚܝܠܐ ܕܐܠܗܐ ܗܠܝܢ
ܒܬܪ ܐܢܬ. ܐܦ ܚܢܢ ܐܬܕܟܪܢ ܒܗܠܝܢ. ܐܠܐ ܒܟ ܗܠܝܢ
ܠܗܘܢ ܒܒܢܝܐ ܡܢܝܢ. ܕܬܫܬܒܚ ܠܟ ܒܠ ܡܐܬܝܬܗ ܕܡܫܝܚܐ.
ܘܕܐܝܟܢܐ ܗܘܬ ܘܒܠ ܚܝܠܗ. ܘܕܒܐܝܢܐ ܚܝܠܐ ܗܠܝܢ ܕܫܡܥܬ
ܦܬܪ ܗܘܐ ܀ ܀

ܘܬܘܒ ܐܡܪ. ܗܫܐ ܫܡܥ ܐܢܐ. ܡܛܠ ܕܝܢ ܕܠܒܪܝܘ
ܡܠܬܐ ܕܐܠܗܐ ܐܫܬܠܡܬ. ܡܫܪ ܒܢܫ ܠܝ ܠܒܝ ܡܕܝܢܬܝ
ܒܗܠܝܢ. ܘܡܕܡܫܘܢ ܡܒܕܪ ܐܢܐ ܘܙܪܥ ܐܢܐ ܒܗܘܢ
ܡܠܬܐ ܕܚܝܐ. ܘܒܠ ܡܐܬܝܬܗ ܕܡܫܝܚܐ ܕܐܝܟܢܐ ܗܘܬ܆
ܘܒܠ ܫܠܝܚܘܬܗ ܕܗܠܝܢ ܐܝܟܐ ܐܫܬܠܡ ܡܢ ܐܒܘܗܝ. ܘܒܠ

ܕܐܫܬܠܡܬ ܗܪܟܐ ܥܠ ܗܕܐ ܕܫܠܡܘܬܗ ܐܫܬܕܪܬ. ܘܡܐ ܕܣܠܩܬ
ܕܡܫܬܠܡܐ ܐܢܐ ܗܕܝܢ ܐܬܦܢܐ ܠܘܬ ܡܢ ܕܫܠܚܢܝ. ܘܡܐ
ܕܐܬܦܢܝܬ ܡܫܕܪ ܐܢܐ ܠܟ ܚܕ ܡܢ ܬܠܡܝܕܝ، ܕܟܐܒܟ ܢܐܣܐ.
ܐܦ ܚܝܐ ܢܬܠ ܠܟ ܘܠܐܝܠܝܢ ܕܐܝܬ ܥܡܟ. ܠܗܢ ܕܝܢ ܠܗܠܝܢ
ܐܓܪ̈ܬܐ ܐܦ ܗܠܝܢ ܢܦܩ ܠܗܘܢ ܒܠܥܕܐ ܐܪ̈ܡܝܐ. ܕܒܗ ܒܬܪ
ܕܐܣܬܠܩ ܝܫܘܥ. ܫܕܪ ܠܗ ܝܗܘܕܐ ܬܐܘܡܐ ܠܐܕܝ، ܫܠܝܚܐ
ܚܕ ܡܢ ܫܒܥܝܢ. ܘܟܕ ܐܬܐ ܫܪܐ ܗܘܐ ܠܘܬ ܛܘܒܝܐ ܒܪ
ܛܘܒܝܐ. ܟܕ ܕܝܢ ܐܫܬܡܥܬ ܥܠܘܗܝ ܫܡܥܬܗ، ܐܬܐܡܪ ܠܐܒܓܪ: ܕܐܬܐ
ܫܠܝܚܐ ܕܝܫܘܥ ܠܗܪܟܐ ܐܝܟ ܕܫܠܚ ܠܟ. ܫܪܝ ܗܘܐ ܕܝܢ ܗܘ
ܐܕܝ، ܕܢܐܣܐ ܥܠ ܟܠ ܟܐܒ ܘܟܘܪܗܢ ܒܚܝܠܐ ܕܐܠܗܐ ܐܝܟܢܐ
ܕܟܠ ܐܢܫ ܢܬܕܡܪ ܀ ܟܕ ܕܝܢ ܫܡܥ ܐܒܓܪ ܕܪ̈ܘܪܒܬܐ ܘܬܕܡܪ̈ܬܐ
ܕܥܒܕ ܗܘܐ ܘܡܐܣܐ ܗܘܐ. ܣܒܪ ܕܗܘܝܘ ܗܘ ܕܫܠܚ ܠܗ ܝܫܘܥ
ܘܐܡܪ ܠܗ. ܕܡܐ ܕܐܬܦܢܝܬ ܡܫܕܪ ܐܢܐ ܠܟ ܚܕ ܡܢ
ܬܠܡܝܕܝ، ܕܗܘ ܢܐܣܐ ܟܐܒܟ. ܘܫܕܪ ܩܪܐ ܠܛܘܒܝܐ ܗܘ
ܕܠܘܬܗ ܫܪܐ ܗܘܐ ܘܐܡܪ ܠܗ. ܫܡܥܬ ܕܓܒܪܐ ܚܝܠܬܢܐ ܐܬܐ
ܘܓܠ ܫܪܐ ܒܒܝܬܟ. ܐܣܩܝܗܝ، ܗܟܝܠ ܠܘܬܝ. ܟܕ ܐܬܐ ܕܝܢ
ܛܘܒܝܐ ܠܘܬ ܐܕܝ، ܐܡܪ ܠܗ. ܐܒܓܪ ܡܠܟܐ ܫܕܪ ܩܪܢܝ ܘܐܡܪ
ܠܝ ܕܐܣܩܟ ܠܘܬܗ ܕܬܐܣܝܘܗܝ. ܘܗܘ ܐܕܝ، ܐܡܪ ܣܠܩ ܐܢܐ.
ܡܛܠ ܕܒܚܝܠܐ ܠܘܬܗ ܗܘ ܐܫܬܕܪܬ. ܩܕܡ ܗܒܠ ܛܘܒܝܐ
ܠܕܪܬܗ ܕܡܠܟܐ ܘܕܒܪ ܠܐܕܝ، ܘܐܝܬܝܗ ܠܘܬ ܐܒܓܪ. ܟܕ ܕܝܢ ܣܠܩ
ܐܫܬܘܪܝܘ ܩܝܡܝܢ ܬܡܢ ܪ̈ܘܪܒܢܘܗܝ. ܘܡܢ ܚܙܐ ܟܕ ܥܐܠ ܗܘܐ.
ܚܙܘܐ ܪܒܐ ܐܬܚܙܝ ܠܐܒܓܪ ܒܦܪ̈ܨܘܦܗ ܕܐܕܝ، ܫܠܝܚܐ. ܘܟܕ
ܚܙܐ، ܐܒܓܪ ܠܐܕܝ، ܣܓܕ ܠܗ. ܘܐܬܕܡܪܘ ܗܘܘ ܟܠܗܘܢ ܕܩܝܡܝܢ
ܗܘܘ ܬܡܢ. ܡܛܠ ܕܠܐ ܚܙܐܘܗܝ، ܠܗܘ ܚܙܘܐ. ܗܘ ܕܠܗ
ܠܐܒܓܪ ܒܠܚܘܕܘܗܝ، ܐܬܚܙܝ. ܘܗܘ ܡܫܐܠ ܗܘܐ ܠܗ ܠܐܕܝ،.
ܕܐܢ ܒܫܪܪܐ ܐܢܬ ܬܠܡܝܕܗ ܕܝܫܘܥ ܒܪܗ ܕܐܠܗܐ. ܗܘ
ܕܐܡܪ ܠܝ ܕܡܫܕܪ ܐܢܐ ܠܟ ܚܕ ܡܢ ܬܠܡܝܕܝ، ܕܗܘ ܢܐܣܝܟ

ܗܦܟ ܒܟܘܪ̈ܗܢܐ ܕܐܝܬ ܗܘܐ ܒܐܘܪܗܝ. ܕܗܘܝܢ ܒܪܒܝܬ ܦܘܠܚܢܐ
ܗܘܬ ܠܟܠܗܘܢ. ܒܕܪܩܘܦܣܐ ܗܟܝܠ ܕܐܝܬ ܗܘܐ ܬܡܢ: ܕܐܝܬ
ܗܘܐ ܒܗܘܢ. ܡܢܕܡ ܕܐܬܗܦܟ ܡܢ ܦܘ̈ܠܚܢܐ ܒܝܫܐ ܠܐܒܓܪ.
ܐܦ ܗܠܝܢ ܒܪܫܐ ܠܗܫܐ ܡܫܬܒܚܝܢ ܕܠܒܪ̈ܝ ܬܡܢ. ܠܝܬ ܕܝܢ
ܡܠܬܐ ܕܢܫܬܒܚ ܐܝܟ ܐܦ ܠܐܠܗܘܬܐ ܕܫܡܥܬ ܠܝ ܡܢ ܒܝܬ
ܐܘܓܢ. ܕܐܝܬ ܠܗܘܢ ܠܦܘܩܕܢܐ ܕܗܠܝܢ ܡ̈ܠܐ: ܕܡܦܩܝܢ ܡܢ
ܐܘܪܚܐ ܠܗܘܢܐ. ܀

ܦܫܩܐ ܕܐܓܪܬܐ ܕܟܬܝܒܐ ܡܢ ܐܒܓܪ ܡܠܟܐ ܠܝܫܘܥ.
ܘܐܫܬܕܪܬ ܠܗ ܒܝܕ ܚܢܢ ܛܒܠܪܐ ܠܐܘܪܫܠܡ ܀ ܐܒܓܪ
ܐܘܟܡܐ ܪܫ ܐܬܪܐ. ܠܝܫܘܥ ܐܣܝܐ ܛܒܐ ܕܐܬܚܙܝ
ܒܐܬܪܐ ܕܐܘܪܫܠܡ ܫܠܡ ܀ ܫܡܥܬ ܠܝ ܥܠܝܟ ܘܥܠ ܐܣܝܘܬܐ
ܕܗܘܝܐ ܒܐܝܕܝܟ ܕܠܐ ܣܡ̈ܡܢܐ ܘܥܩܪ̈ܐ. ܐܝܟ ܕܡܬܐܡܪ
ܓܝܪ. ܥܒܕ ܐܢܬ ܠܣ̈ܡܝܐ ܕܢܚܙܘܢ. ܘܠܚܓܝܪ̈ܐ ܕܢܗܠܟܘܢ.
ܘܠܓܪ̈ܒܐ ܡܕܟܐ ܐܢܬ. ܘܪ̈ܘܚܐ ܛܢ̈ܦܬܐ ܘܫܐܕ̈ܐ ܡܦܩ
ܐܢܬ. ܘܠܐܝܠܝܢ ܕܡܫܬܢܩܝܢ ܒܟܘܪ̈ܗܢܐ ܢܓܝܪ̈ܐ ܡܐܣܐ ܐܢܬ؛
ܘܡܝ̈ܬܐ ܡܩܝܡ ܐܢܬ. ܘܟܕ ܫܡܥܬ ܥܠܝܟ ܗܠܝܢ ܟܠܗܝܢ.
ܣܡܬ ܒܪܥܝܢܝ ܚܕܐ ܡܢ ܬܪ̈ܬܝܢ. ܐܘ ܕܐܢܬ ܗܘ ܐܠܗܐ ܕܢܚܬܬ
ܡܢ ܫܡܝܐ ܘܥܒܕ ܐܢܬ ܗܠܝܢ. ܐܘ ܕܒܪܗ ܐܢܬ ܕܐܠܗܐ
ܘܗܠܝܢ ܥܒܕ ܐܢܬ. ܡܛܠܗܢܐ ܗܟܝܠ ܟܬܒܬ ܒܥܝܬ ܡܢܟ
ܕܬܫܬܡܠܐ ܘܬܐܬܐ ܠܘܬܝ. ܘܗܢܐ ܟܐܒܐ ܕܐܝܬ
ܠܝ. ܐܦ ܫܡܥܬ ܓܝܪ ܕܝܗܘ̈ܕܝܐ ܪ̈ܛܢܝܢ ܥܠܝܟ ܘܪ̈ܕܦܝܢ
ܕܢܒܐܫܘܢ ܠܟ. ܡܕܝܢܬܐ ܕܝܢ ܙܥܘܪܬܐ ܘܫܦܝܪܬܐ ܐܝܬ ܠܝ
ܕܣܦܩܐ ܠܬܪ̈ܝܢ. ܀ ܦܫܩܐ ܕܐܝܠܝܢ ܕܐܬܟܬܒ ܡܢ ܝܫܘܥ. ܒܝܕ
ܚܢܢ ܛܒܠܪܐ ܠܐܒܓܪ ܪܫ ܐܬܪܐ. ܀ ܛܘܒܘܗܝ ܠܐܢܫܐ
ܕܗܝܡܢ ܒܝ ܟܕ ܠܐ ܚܙܢܝ. ܟܬܝܒ ܓܝܪ ܥܠܝ ܕܐܝܠܝܢ ܕܚܙܝܢ
ܠܝ ܠܐ ܢܗܝܡܢܘܢ ܒܝ. ܘܐܝܠܝܢ ܕܠܐ ܚܙܘܢܝ ܗܢܘܢ ܢܗܝܡܢܘܢ
ܘܢܚܘܢ. ܥܠ ܗܝ ܕܝܢ ܕܟܬܒܬ ܠܝ ܕܐܬܐ ܠܘܬܟ. ܘܠܐ ܗܘ

ܡܢ ܬܫܥܝܬܐ ܕܥܕܬܐ

ܕܬܠܬܥܣܪ ܬܫܥܝܬܐ ܥܠ ܡܠܟܐ ܕܐܘܪܗܝ.

ܬܫܥܝܬܐ ܕܝܢ ܕܗܘܬ ܡܛܠ ܗ̇ܕܐ، ܕܐܝܟ ܗܢܐ ܗܘܐ ܛܘܦܣܐ.
ܟܕ ܡܬܟܪܙܐ ܗܘܬ ܐܠܗܘܬܗ ܕܦܪܘܩܢ ܘܡܪܢ ܝܫܘܥ ܡܫܝܚܐ
ܠܘܬ ܟܠܗܘܢ ܒܢܝ̈ ܐܢܫܐ. ܡܛܠ ܚܝܠܐ ܬܡܝܗܐ ܕܥܒܕ ܗܘܐ.
ܣ̈ܓܝܐܬܐ ܕܝܢ ܐܦ ܡܢ ܐܬܪ̈ܘܬܐ ܕܪ̈ܚܝܩܢ ܡܢ ܐܪܥܐ ܕܝܗܘܕ
ܕܐܬܢܣܝܘ ܗܘܘ ܒܣܘ̈ܥܪܢܐ ܘܒܟܐ̈ܒܐ ܕܟܠ ܓܢܣ. ܥܠ
ܣܒܪܐ ܕܐܣܝܘܬܐ ܐܬܝܢ ܗܘܘ ܠܘܬܗ. ܐܦ ܐܒܓܪ ܡܠܟܐ:
ܕܥܡ̈ܡܐ ܕܠܥܒܪ ܦܪܬ ܡܫܬܡܗ ܗܘܐ ܒܓܢܒܪܘܬܐ.
ܐܬܟܪܗ ܗܘܐ ܦܓܪܗ ܒܟܐܒܐ ܩܫܝܐ. ܕܐܝܟ ܕܒܢܝ̈ ܐܢܫܐ
ܠܝܬ ܠܗ ܐܣܝܘܬܐ. ܘܟܕ ܫܡܥ ܘܝܠܦ ܫܡܗ ܕܝܫܘܥ ܘܥܠ
ܚܝܠܐ ܕܥܒܕ ܗܘܐ: ܕܫܘܐܝܬ ܟܠܢܫ ܡܣܗܕ ܗܘܐ ܥܠܘܗܝ.
ܫܕܪ ܐܓܪܬܐ ܕܒܥܘܬܐ ܒܝܕ ܓܒܪܐ ܕܝܠܗ ܘܡܒܥܐ ܗܘܐ ܠܗ
ܕܢܐܬܐ ܢܐܣܝܘܗܝ ܡܢ ܟܘܪܗܢܗ. ܗܘ ܕܝܢ ܦܪܘܩܢ ܒܗ̇ܘ ܙܒܢܐ
ܕܩܪܝܗ، ܠܐ ܐܬܛܦܝܣ ܠܗ. ܠܐܓܪܬܐ ܕܝܢ ܐܫܕܪܗ. ܐܫܬܘܕܝ،
ܠܗ ܕܢܫܕܪ ܠܘܬܗ ܡܢ ܬܠܡܝ̈ܕܘܗܝ، ܘܢܐܣܐ ܟܘܪ̈ܗܢܘܗܝ. ܘܢܬܠ
ܠܗ ܚܝ̈ܐ ܘܠܟܠܗܘܢ ܩܪ̈ܝܒܘܗܝ. ܠܐ ܕܝܢ ܐܫܬܘܚܪ ܕܢܫܠܡ ܠܗ
ܫܘܘܕܝܗ. ܡܢ ܒܬܪ ܕܝܢ ܕܣܠܩ ܡܢ ܒܝܬ ܡܝ̈ܬܐ ܘܐܬܥܠܝ
ܠܫܡܝܐ. ܬܐܘܡܐ ܫܠܝܚܐ ܚܕ ܡܢ ܬܪ̈ܥܣܪ ܠܐܕܝ، ܗ̇ܘ ܕܬܠܡܝܕܐ
ܗܘܐ ܐܦ ܗ̣ܘ ܡܢ ܫܒܥܝܢ ܬܠܡܝ̈ܕܘܗܝ ܕܡܫܝܚܐ. ܐܝܟ ܕܡܢ
ܡܥܒܕܢܘܬܐ ܕܐܠܗܐ ܫܕܪܗ ܠܐܘܪܗܝ، ܕܢܗܘܐ ܟܪܘܙܐ
ܘܡܣܒܪܢܐ ܕܣܘܠܦܢܐ ܕܡܫܝܚܐ. ܘܫܘܘܕܝܐ ܕܦܪܘܩܢ ܒܐܝܕܗ
ܐܬܡܠܝ. ܐܝܬ ܠܢ ܒܡܟܬܒ̈ܢܘܬܐ ܣܗܕܘܬܐ ܕܗܠܝܢ ܕܐܫܬܟܚ ܡܢ